CCH BUSINESS OWNER'S TOOLKIT

START RUN & GROW

A SUCCESSFUL SMALL BUSINESS

Third Edition

A *CCH Business Owner's Toolkit* Publication

Susan M. Jacksack

CCH INCORPORATED
Chicago

© 2000, **CCH** INCORPORATED

Published by **CCH** INCORPORATED

Small Office Home Office Group
CCH INCORPORATED
2700 Lake Cook Road
Riverwoods, Illinois 60015

This publication is designed to provide accurate and authoritative information in regard to the subject matter covered. It is sold with the understanding that the publisher is not engaged in rendering legal, accounting, or other professional service, and that the authors are not offering such advice in this publication. If legal advice or other expert assistance is required, the services of a competent professional should be sought.

Cover designed by Tim Kaage, Laurel Graphx, Inc.

Books may be purchased at quantity discounts for educational, business or sales promotion use. For more information please contact:

Small Office Home Office Group
CCH INCORPORATED
2700 Lake Cook Road
Riverwoods, Illinois 60015

ISBN 0-8080-0413-1

Printed in the United States of America

THE CCH BUSINESS OWNER'S TOOLKIT TEAM

Susan M. Jacksack is frequently quoted as a small business expert in national publications including *The Wall Street Journal, The New York Times, Money,* and *Worth,* and has made several guest appearances to discuss small business issues on CNBC. She has over 13 years of experience advising and writing for small business owners and consumers on tax, personal finance and other legal topics, and has conducted seminars for new and prospective entrepreneurs on tax issues, business planning, and employment law. Susan is an attorney and a graduate of the University of Illinois, Urbana-Champaign.

Alice Magos has over 35 years of experience running the operations of numerous small businesses. She is the author of the *CCH Business Owner's Toolkit*™ online advice column "Ask Alice." Alice is a popular instructor at small business seminars on accounting, financial planning, and using the Internet; is an accountant and a Certified Financial Planner; and holds degrees from Washington University in St. Louis and Northwestern University.

Joel Handelsman has 20 years of experience writing about business, tax, and financial topics. He has experience with multiple new product and business ventures in the publishing industry, and has held a variety of management positions. Joel is an attorney and holds degrees from Northwestern University and DePaul University.

John L. Duoba has more than 12 years of small business experience in book and magazine publishing, fulfilling various roles in editorial and production management. He has been involved in the publication of scores of titles, with multiple editions and issues raising the total well into the hundreds. John is a professional journalist and holds a degree from Northwestern University's Medill School of Journalism.

Martin Bush has over 15 years of experience providing legal, financial and tax advice to small and large businesses in various industries. He is a frequently quoted small business expert and has appeared on CNBC and National Public Radio. Martin is an attorney and a CPA, and holds degrees from Indiana University, DePaul University, and Northwestern University.

We would also like to acknowledge the significant efforts of others who contributed to this book: Bob Barnett, Tom Blazek, Jim Fortmann, Catherine Gordon, Ron Hirasawa, Janet McCabe, Kathleen Larrison, Richard Larson, Tom Lauletta, Todd Mata, Erich Schuttauf, John Siegel and Richard Yamamoto.

In addition, we would like to thank LaVerne Dellinger and Drew Snider for their contributions in the production of this book.

PREFACE

Congratulations! As an owner (or soon-to-be owner) of a small business you are a member of one of the fastest growing sectors of the U.S. economy. People like you start two to three million small businesses every year. And the Bureau of Labor Statistics predicts that by the year 2005, the number of self-employed individuals will be almost 12 million.

While the number of entrepreneurs seeking the American dream of "being their own boss" is growing, the reality is that about 50 percent of small businesses fail within five years. Why? Most experts agree that there are three primary reasons: lack of adequate research and planning, mismanagement, and lack of financial resources.

So how can you improve your odds of being on the better side of this success or failure equation? Use this book!

Written by a special team of small business experts, accountants, and attorneys, *Start, Run & Grow a Successful Small Business* will help you get the most from your business. With coverage of topics like business planning, how to get financing, managing your finances, and handling your employees, this complete resource will help you make more informed management decisions. And well-thought-out decisions will keep your business on a path to success.

Now in its third edition, this updated guide reflects the latest small business trends and the changes in those laws that affect you most, on both the state and federal level.

Why should you turn to us? **CCH** INCORPORATED is a leading provider of information and software to the business and professional community. More than four generations of business advisors have trusted our products, and now you can too.

A caution and an invitation — the discussions of the laws contained in this book are current as of the date of publication. But remember, things change. To keep abreast of the latest news affecting your business, visit *CCH Business Owner's Toolkit* on the Internet (www.toolkit.cch.com) or on America Online (keyword: CCH). Take a look at the interactive information and tools we offer to assist you in running your business. You can also ask follow-up questions of our team of small business experts. We welcome and look forward to your questions and comments.

Martin Bush

Publisher, Small Office Home Office Group

Table of Contents

PART IV: MARKETING YOUR PRODUCT

PART V: YOUR OFFICE AND EQUIPMENT

PART VI: PEOPLE WHO WORK FOR YOU

Part I

Getting Started

Many of us hear the Siren song of small business. Complete freedom. Unlimited opportunity. Dreams realized. But of those who answer it, most don't succeed. Why? What separates those who succeed from those who fail?

In the U.S., it's estimated that only about 50 percent of all startups are still in business after five years. The better you prepare yourself and understand the challenges ahead of you, the more likely it is that you'll be one of the success stories.

Knowledge of the business, sufficient capital, good experience, and a unique idea at the right time are just some of the characteristics of a successful business owner. Although there isn't any way that you can guarantee that you'll be successful, you can greatly improve your odds by becoming well-prepared for the task.

The key point to remember is that you shouldn't start the company before you've done all your homework and you're convinced that you're ready for the challenges, the responsibility, and the time commitment that go into starting your own business.

That's where we come in. In Part I, our small business experts will take you through the process of starting a new business, from thinking up new business ideas, to evaluating the profit potential of a business concept, to actually taking the first steps toward operation.

Chapter 1: Are You Ready To Be an Entrepreneur? is a look at what it means to own your own business, from the sacrifices you'll have to make to the skills you'll need if you're to succeed.

Chapter 2: The Right Small Business for You explains an effective method for thinking up new business ideas, and explores the pros and cons of buying an existing business or a franchise.

Chapter 3: Evaluating Your Chance for Success is a "look before you leap" examination of what it will really cost you to start a new business. In addition, it gives you some help in evaluating the marketing, legal, and financing issues associated with startups and in finding more information about your specific industry.

Chapter 4: Setting Up the Business tells you what you need to do to turn your small business idea into a reality, including hiring professionals to assist you, deciding on the organizational form of your business, registering your name, and legally protecting your ideas.

Chapter 1

Are You Ready To Be an Entrepreneur?

Starting a small business takes a lot of courage. But, as they say, courage doesn't pay the bills. To be successful — to stay in business — you need more than courage. You need a combination of hard work, skill, perseverance, and good old-fashioned luck. You need to know what you can expect from a small business, as well as what a small business will expect from you.

To evaluate your own aptitude for small business ownership, you need to understand the responsibilities of ownership: what's involved in running a small business, and what are some of the roles you'll have to play if you own one.

You also need to have a good understanding of what you want to get out of your business. Simply knowing that you want to "succeed" isn't enough, because everyone has a different definition of success.

Finally, you need to evaluate your skills and determine whether you have all the important ones you'll need, or whether you can develop them or hire someone who already has them.

RESPONSIBILITIES OF OWNERSHIP

Probably the two most common reasons that a business doesn't succeed are that (1) the owner lacks the necessary skills to manage the business well and (2) the owner underestimates how much money it will take to start the business (known as "under-capitalization"). In this chapter, we'll look at the first cause and try to help you get a good sense of the skills a small business owner must have. In Chapter 3, we'll look at the second issue.

Pros and Cons of Owning a Business

Owning a small business is not just another job. It's a totally different lifestyle. You have to ask yourself whether you're ready for a complete commitment to the success of your business. Just as importantly, you have to ask your partner, if you're in a relationship, whether he or she is completely committed.

As a small business owner, you may have less time for your personal life and if you need a loan, you may be using much of what you own as collateral. If you are willing to make those sacrifices, then let's move on to some of the advantages and disadvantages of owning your own business.

Pros:

- *You have the chance to make a lot more money.*

- *You'll be your own boss and make all the crucial business decisions.*

- *You may be the boss of other people.*

- *You'll have job security — no one can fire you.*

- *You'll have the chance to put your ideas into practice.*

- *You'll learn more about every aspect of a business and gain experience in a variety of disciplines.*

- *You'll have the chance to work directly with your customers.*

- *You'll be able to benefit the local economy, such as by hiring other people.*

- *You'll have the personal satisfaction of creating and running a successful business.*

- *You'll be able to work in a field or area that you really enjoy.*

- *You'll have the chance to build real retirement value (for example, by selling the business when you retire).*

- *You'll have the chance to put down roots in a community and to provide a sense of belonging and stability for your family.*

Cons:

- *You may have to take a large financial risk.*

- *You may have to work long hours and have little chance of taking a vacation.*

- *You may end up spending a lot of your time attending to the details of running a business and less time on those things you really enjoy.*

- *You may find that your income is not steady and that there are times when you don't have much income at all.*

- *You may have to undertake tasks you find unpleasant, such as firing someone or refusing to hire a friend or relative.*

- *You may have to learn many new disciplines, such as filing and bookkeeping, inventory control, production planning, advertising and promotion, market research, and general management.*

Special pros and cons of the home-based business:

- *Your startup costs will be lower.*

- *Your operating costs will be lower than if you were renting space and paying utilities.*

- *Your commute will be shorter.*

- *If your location is unimportant to your business, you can theoretically live anywhere and still operate your business.*

- *You may have a more flexible schedule if your business can be conducted at your convenience or outside "normal" weekday business hours.*

- *On the other hand, you're much more vulnerable to interruptions from family members, neighbors, and door-to-door salespeople.*

- *You may have an image problem, although with the growing popularity of home businesses, that's less common.*

- *You may run out of space at home if your business grows.*

The Many Roles of the Small Business Owner

We've all heard of the beleaguered executive who moans that he's overworked because he has to wear two or three hats at his company. Well, most small business owners would give anything if they had to wear *only* two or three hats. Here's a look at some of the roles you can expect to play if you own your own business:

- **Tax collector** — if you sell goods at the retail level, you're responsible for collecting sales tax for various government entities. If you have employees, you're responsible for collecting payroll taxes from them.

- **Manager/boss** — if you have employees, you'll be responsible for all of the human resources-related functions, including recruiting, hiring, firing, and keeping track of all the benefits information. You'll be the one filling out all the insurance forms, answering employee questions and complaints, and making the decisions about whether you should change the benefits package you offer your employees.

- **Sales/marketing/advertising executive** — in addition to having to plan your marketing or advertising campaign, you'll have to carry it out. You may write advertising copy, do some preliminary market research, visit potential customers, and make sure existing customers stay happy. Depending upon the type of business you own, you may have to join business groups, attend various functions, and just generally network with anyone who could help your business prosper.

- **Accountant** — even if you have an accountant, you'll have to know a lot about accounting, since you'll have to know which records to keep and how to keep them. If you don't have an accountant, you'll also have to prepare all of your tax forms, and you'll have to know how to prepare and interpret all of your own financial statements.

- **Lawyer** — even if you have a lawyer, you'll have to know a lot about the law. If you don't have a lawyer, you'll have to prepare all of your own contracts and other documents, and know what to do if a potential lawsuit arises.

- **Business planner** — as time passes, you'll inevitably want to make changes, perhaps to expand the business or add a new product line. If you want to make a change, you'll have to plan it and execute the plan.

- **Bill collector** — when customers don't pay, it'll be up to you to collect from them. You'll have to know what you can and can't do and when to give up.

- **Market researcher** — before you start your business, you'll have to find out who your customers are and where they're located. You may also have to conduct market research at various times during the life of your business, such as when you are considering the introduction of a new product.

- **Technology expert** — as a small business owner, you will probably come to depend upon your computer. You'll have to fix it when it breaks, install upgrades, and load software; you'll also have to keep up with the new products.

- **Clerk/receptionist/typist/secretary** — even if you have clerical help, you'll inevitably do some of your filing, some of your typing, some of your mailing, and some of your telephone answering. If you hire someone, you'll have to teach them what to do.

DO YOU HAVE THE RIGHT STUFF?

If asked whether they had the "right stuff" to run a small business, most people who are interested in starting a new business would answer with a resounding "yes." But the purpose of this section is not to arrive at a yes or no answer; it's really just to help you evaluate your strengths and weaknesses so that you'll be in a better position to decide whether you need to improve your skills or take on a partner, hire a manager, bookkeeper, marketing consultant, etc.

Successful small business owners know their own strengths and weaknesses. They build their businesses around their strengths and they compensate for areas where their skills are not so strong.

As you evaluate yourself, be honest, and don't panic if you discover that you have weaknesses, since everyone does. The key to success is not so much having every skill (although that would help) as it is finding ways to compensate for the weaknesses.

Strengths and Weaknesses Checklist

The chart below will help you identify your strengths and weaknesses and will give you a better idea of whether you're ready to become a small business owner. Rate your skills in each area by circling the appropriate number, using a scale of 1-5, with 1 as low and 5 as high.

Skills	Rating (circle one)				
Sales sales planning, negotiating, direct selling to buyers, customer service follow-up, managing other sales reps, tracking competitors	1	2	3	④	5
Marketing advertising/promotion/public relations, annual marketing planning, media planning and buying, advertising copy writing, strategic marketing, distribution channel planning, pricing, packaging	1	②	3	4	5
Financial planning cash flow planning, budgeting, managing credit lines and bank relationships	1	2	3	4	⑤
Accounting bookkeeping, billing, payables, monthly profit and loss statements/balance sheets, quarterly/annual tax preparation	1	2	3	4	⑤

Skills	Rating (circle one)				
Administrative scheduling, payroll handling, benefits administration	1	2	3	4	(5)
Personnel management hiring employees, firing employees, motivating employees, general management skills	1	2	3	4	(5)
Personal business oral presentation skills, written communication skills, computer skills, word processing skills, e-mail experience, organizational skills	1	2	3	(4)	5
Intangibles ability to work long and hard, ability to manage risk and stress, family support, ability to deal with setbacks, ability to work alone, ability to work with and manage others	1	2	3	4	(5)
Total					

After you've rated yourself in each area, total up the numbers.   Then apply the following rating scale:

- *If your total is less than 20 points, consider putting off the opening of your business for six months to a year while you do more research and gain more skills or experience.*

- *If your total is between 20 and 25, you're on the verge of being ready, but you may be wise to spend some time strengthening some of your weaker areas.*

- *If your total is above 25, you're mentally ready to start a new business now.*

Essential Qualities for Owners

You can still be successful even if you don't possess every skill needed to run a small business. There are, however, certain qualities that you should possess if you're to be successful. Let's take a look at them:

- **Willingness to sacrifice** — you must be willing to accept the fact that, as a small business owner, you are the last one to be paid, after your vendors, the bank, and your employees. You must also be willing to sacrifice much of your free time, and may find it hard to take a vacation, at least at first.

- **Strong interpersonal skills** — if you thought that getting along with your boss was tough, wait until you have to deal with suppliers, customers, employees, lawyers, accountants, government officials, and everybody in between. Successful owners are able to work with all personality types, and they're able to find out from their customers what they like and don't like.

- **Strong leadership skills** — successful owners understand that others may be looking to them to be led to the promised land. Others will be constantly looking to *you* for the answers.

- **Strong organizational skills** — successful owners are able to keep track of everything that's going on in their business, and they're able to set priorities and get things done.

- **Intelligence** — we're talking about street smarts and common sense. Successful owners are able to anticipate problems before they arise and to take preemptive steps to avoid them, and they know how to solve crises if they occur.

- **Management ability** — small business is all about managing relationships, with your customers or clients, with your employees, with your suppliers, with your accountant and lawyer, with your banker, and with your family.

- **Business experience** — without some solid business experience, you're probably not going to be able to borrow any money. If you lack experience in your type of business, go get it any way you can: volunteer at an existing business or try to get a part-time or weekend job in the field.

- **Optimism** — how will you react when business isn't going as well as you expected? A pessimist may fold the tent, but an optimist will keep going. Successful owners are optimists who are able to weather the rough spots.

Compensating for Undeveloped Skills

Once you've looked at your own strengths and weaknesses, and compared them with the traits you'll need to have if you're to be successful, the next step is to figure out what to do if you don't yet possess all of those traits.

First of all, don't despair. Your options include hiring someone who can handle tasks you may not be good at, partnering with someone who has the traits you lack, or developing traits or skills yourself.

For example, if you don't like to sell, you can hire a salesman or if you don't like to do accounting work, you can hire an accountant. Down the road, as you get farther along in setting up your new business, you may determine that the convenience of paying someone else to do the work is outweighed by the costs. But for now, all you have to do is identify whether someone else *could* do the work for you.

If your list of things you don't like to do includes items that you *can't* hire someone else to do, such as working with others, the solution is not so easy. Your best bet may be to partner up with someone whose skill set complements yours.

Learning New Skills

The third possibility is to develop the traits and skills yourself. There are at least three ways to do this. The first is by trial and error — also known as learning from your mistakes. The downside to this approach is that most small businesses won't give you much time or allow you to make many mistakes. If you benefit from trial and error, it'll usually be with the third or fourth new business you start.

The second method is to take business classes at a college or university. Your local community college may offer courses at a reasonable price, and we know of several entrepreneurs who used a class on starting a business as a stepping stone to success. However, the quality of instruction varies widely.

The third method is to locate your business in a small business incubator. Incubators are programs that provide you with office space and access to office equipment and services in a nurturing environment, and frequently with personalized advice from the incubator operator as well. Most are run by government-sponsored economic development agencies, but there are also some privately operated incubators. For more information and the location of the incubator nearest you, call the National Business Incubator Association at 740-593-4331 or the Small Business Administration at 800-827-5722.

Chapter 2

The Right Small Business for You

Most of the books you can read on the subject of finding a small business will tell you that the best place to start is with a matching of your skills, interests, and experiences to some business that requires those skills. For example, if you love to cook, they'll suggest you open a catering business or a restaurant.

Investigating a business based on your interests is a good place to start, but your idea has to be further analyzed by examining the market potential, competition, resources required to enter the market, consumer/buyer demand, and uniqueness of the idea.

In many cases, you can save time and money by buying an existing business or franchise, rather than starting from the ground up.

RESEARCHING NEW BUSINESS IDEAS

If money were not an issue, you could contact a market research firm and have it analyze your community and find out for you where small business opportunities exist. But if, as for most of us, money *is* an issue for you, you'll have to gather the information yourself.

A good place to start looking for new business ideas is with the mainstream press: your local newspaper, *The New York Times*, *The Wall Street Journal*, *Time*, *U.S. News and World Report*, and *Newsweek*. You should also look at the business press: *Fortune*, *Forbes*, *Business Week*, and other business periodicals. Look for trends that may be emerging, not just in business but in our culture at large, that are creating needs for new products or services you could provide.

In addition to reading newspapers and magazines, talk to friends, relatives, business associates, and other small business owners about their ideas and their frustrations with existing products and services. And, last but not least, don't forget the often most-overlooked resource — yourself. You're a consumer. If you've wished that a particular service were available, chances are that others have too.

Work Smart

When you think about market opportunities, one possibility is to think about how you can improve upon a product or service that is already being provided. But be aware that there are at least two potential stumbling blocks here.

The first is the tendency to believe too readily that you can improve upon an existing product or service. This is just old-fashioned overconfidence. Be sure that you've thought through the specific things you can do to improve what's already out there.

The second is the fact that your being able to improve upon a product or service is no guarantee of its success. You need to assess the brand loyalty customers feel towards your competitors, the costs of breaking that loyalty, and your ability to keep the transferring customers for the long haul, once they've switched over to you.

Niche Marketing

An approach that can be more effective than tackling brand-new business ideas head-on is to look for ways that you can perform a service or provide a product that fulfills the special needs of a smaller subset of the customer population. By specializing, you may be able to meet these customers' needs much better than larger competitors.

Example

Betsy Mirkin was an accountant in a large accounting firm that occasionally did work for film companies that came to town for a shoot. Betsy did a little research and found that there weren't any other accountants who specifically served the film market. She also found out that there were enough film companies that came to town each year for her to make a nice living serving only them.

Betsy quit the accounting firm, and started her own home-based business, specializing in accounting for the film industry.

To develop a niche, you should be looking for anomalies in the market. An anomaly, in marketing terms, is an unmet need whose time has come to be filled. To support a profitable business, the need must be fairly widespread or growing rapidly.

Example

Although people wanted to be able to send letters and packages overnight anywhere in the country, they didn't think it was possible. Enter Federal Express and — presto — a $500 million startup business serving an anomaly.

Where are today's anomalies? Perhaps one lies hidden in the social and business trends now underway. For example, a lot of working couples would like hot, delivered, home-cooked meals that vary each night. But no one believes that it's possible . . .

Matching Your Skills with New Business Ideas

After you've identified some needs in the market that aren't being met, or that you can meet better than the competition, you're ready to match your skills with those unmet needs. The following chart is designed to help you choose the business that's right for you.

To fill it out, follow these steps: In the far left-hand column, list the business ideas you're considering. In the top left-hand blank space, put the idea you think you're most interested in. Underneath it put the next idea and so forth until you've listed all of your possible ideas down the left side of the chart.

Now take each idea and rate it on a scale of 0-3 in each of the areas listed. Use the following rating system: 0—none, 1—below average, 2—average, and 3—above average.

Business Idea	Knowledge	Experience	Skills	Ease of Entry	Uniqueness	Total
1. *Entertainment*	0	0	2	1	3	6
2. *Consulting*	1	3	2	1	0	6
3. *Child care*	1	0	0	3	0	4

Here's a look at each of the categories and some of the things you should consider when rating them:

Your knowledge of the business. *How much do you know about the type of business you're considering? Will you have to spend extra time and money teaching yourself the business? Will you have to take on a partner because you don't know the business well enough? Rating: 0—no knowledge of the business; 1—some indirect knowledge of the business; 2—limited knowledge; 3—working knowledge.*

Your experience in the field. *In some cases, you may have a lot of knowledge about the subject, but not much experience. Have you ever owned or worked in this type of business before? To what extent is hands-on experience crucial to the business?* Rating: *0—no experience; 1—indirect experience; 2—limited experience; 3—familiar with the business.*

Your skills. *Ignore, for now, those skills that might be common to each of your ideas, and try to concentrate on skills that are unique to that business. To what extent do you possess those skills? If you lack them, how difficult will it be to acquire them?* Rating: *0—none; 1—limited skills; 2—some skills; 3—extensive skills.*

Ease of entry. *Think of the costs of entering the business in both money and time. For example, a service business that you can run from home might be relatively inexpensive to start, whereas a manufacturing plant would be much more expensive.* Rating: *0—very difficult or expensive to enter; 1—limited entry available; 2—relatively easy and inexpensive; 3—you've already got everything you need to start.*

Uniqueness. *Uniqueness does not necessarily mean that literally no one else is providing the same product or service; it can mean that no one else is providing the product or service in the same way you intend to provide it, or it can mean that no one else is providing that product or service in your area. You're looking for some way to distinguish your product or service from others who are already in business. Consider also how hard it would be for others to duplicate your offering.* Rating: *0—your product or service widely available; 1—a few to several others offering your product or service; 2—only one or two others; 3—no others providing your product or service.*

Now total up the numbers. Here are some tips for making sense of the numbers and for narrowing your list of business possibilities:

- *Eliminate any of your ideas that scored less than a total of 10.*

- *Eliminate any idea that did not score at least a 2 in every category.*

- *Eliminate any idea that did not score at least a 3 in the uniqueness category.*

How many ideas are left? If the answer is "none," then you can use the list to identify where you need to improve. If the answer is "more than one," you have a pleasant dilemma: a choice of which business to start. If the answer is "one," you may have just found the business that's perfect for you.

Here are some more tips and suggestions for choosing a new business:

- Eliminate any business that you don't believe you'll *really* enjoy owning. As a small business owner, you'll be living, sleeping, and breathing your new business — you'd better enjoy that type of work!

- On the other hand, be wary of relying too heavily on your list of interests when making your choice. Don't forget that much of a small business owner's time is spent on tasks such as dealing with customers, haggling with suppliers, bookkeeping, etc.

- If you don't have a lot of money to start with, look for a business where you get paid up front and you don't have a lot of startup costs, to avoid cash flow problems.

- Look for businesses where you will have a lot of repeat customers or where people will need to keep buying supplies from you. It's much easier to keep selling to the same customers than it is to continually be developing new customers.

- Seasonal businesses add an extra level of complexity to planning — avoid them if possible.

- Avoid competing with discounters, especially very large, well-established ones, since it will be nearly impossible to compete with their prices. You'll have to compete with better service.

START FROM SCRATCH, OR BUY A BUSINESS?

If you think that starting a business from scratch is too difficult but still want to have your own small business, you have choices. You should consider either buying an existing business, perhaps from an owner who wants to retire, or buying a franchise.

Advantages of Buying an Existing Business

- *Immediate operation* — someone else has gotten the company started, and once you take over, you can usually continue the status quo.

- *Quick cash flow* — existing inventory and receivables can generate income from the first day.

- *Existing customers* — customers and suppliers have already been located, and relationships with them have been established.

- *Easier financing* — financing is easier to obtain because the business has a track record.

- *Less competition* — buying a business may eliminate a competitor that you would have had if you had started from scratch.

Disadvantages of Buying an Existing Business

- *Cost* — buying a business is sometimes more costly than starting one from scratch.

- **Problems** — there may be inherent problems in the business, some of which may not be apparent until after the sale. Be sure to find out why the owner is selling.

- **Personality conflicts** — you may clash with existing managers and employees.

- **Obsolete goods** — inventories and equipment may be obsolete.

- **Uncollectable receivables** — receivables listed on the balance sheet may be stale and uncollectable.

The steps involved in purchasing a business are similar to those you need to take whenever you make any major purchase. You need to locate some good businesses to buy, and then research your first choice thoroughly before deciding to go ahead with the deal.

Caution should be exercised throughout the whole process, not only because it will help you to find the business that is right for you, but it will also help you to avoid being taken advantage of by unscrupulous sellers. Your attorney and your accountant should be actively involved in your search (and they may know of good companies for sale, too). You may also want to read our detailed description of selling a business in Part X to get the seller's point of view.

Finding a Good Business To Buy

If you know what type of business you are looking for, trade publications and associations for that industry may be a good place to start your search. Some other places to look are:

- **Newspapers** — most newspapers, and specialized magazines like *Entrepreneur* and *Home Office Computing*, have a classified ad section in which businesses are listed for sale. Some, such as *The Wall Street Journal*, even have a specific classified section for business opportunities. Be careful. Publications don't screen their advertisers, and there are scam artists out there.

- **Internet** — there are many Internet sites that list businesses for sale and there are more appearing all the time. You can do a general search for sites that offer businesses for sale, or you can do a specific search for the particular type of business you're interested in.

- **Business brokers** — one of the benefits of using a broker is that the broker, at least a good one, will screen businesses that are for sale to determine if there are major problems and to make certain that the business being sold exists. The broker will also guide you through the process of selling, and help you deal with snags that may develop along the way. However, the broker's fee will probably result in a higher sales price, even if the seller nominally pays the commission.

Work Smart

You don't have to limit your search to businesses that have been listed for sale. If you find a business that you would like to own, tell the owner you'd like to buy it and make an offer (subject to your attorney's approval of the contract, of course). The worst that can happen is that the owner will say "no."

Researching the Target Business

After finding a business that is for sale and that seems a likely prospect for you to run successfully, you should spend at least a month investigating the business. You should definitely get your lawyer and accountant involved in this process, as well.

By thoroughly investigating the business (using "due diligence"), you increase the chances of catching any major problems that may exist. The time spent investigating the business, the industry, and the market will make you confident that your decision to buy (or not to buy) was the right one.

In many cases, the seller will not give you any sensitive information about the business unless you have signed a letter of intent that essentially makes a non-binding offer for the business, and unless you have also signed a confidentiality agreement promising that you'll use the information only to make a decision about buying.

Keep in mind that if a business is for sale, *there must be a reason why.* That reason may be a problem you can solve, such as bad management, or a problem that you can't, such as an obsolete product or a poor local economy. A thorough investigation should reveal the existing problems and enable you to weigh those problems in your purchasing decision.

Following is a checklist of documents you should obtain from any business you are thinking about buying.

Due Diligence Checklist

Before you purchase an existing business, try to get your hands on as many of the following as apply to your situation:

❑ *asset list including real estate, equipment, and intangible assets like patents, trademarks, and licenses*

❑ real and personal property documents (e.g., deeds, leases, appraisals, mortgages, loans, insurance policies)

❑ bank account list

❑ financial statements (balance sheet, income statement, cash flow budget) for the last three to five years

❑ tax returns for as many years as possible

❑ customer list

❑ sales records

❑ supplier/purchaser list

❑ contracts that the business is a party to

❑ advertisements, sales brochures, product packaging and enclosures, and any other marketing materials

❑ inventory receipts (also take a look at the inventory itself, to check the amount and condition)

❑ organizational charts and resumes of key employees

❑ payroll, benefits, and employee pension or profit-sharing plan information

❑ certificates issued by federal, state, or local agencies (e.g., certificate of existence, certificate of authority to transact business, liquor license)

❑ certificates, registration articles, and any amendments filed with any federal, state, or local agency (e.g., articles of incorporation for a corporation; assumed name papers)

❑ organizational documents (e.g., corporate bylaws, partnership agreements, operating agreements for limited liability companies)

❑ list of owners, if more than one (e.g. all shareholders if a corporation, all partners if a partnership, all members if a limited liability company)

CONSIDERING A FRANCHISE

First of all, let's define what we mean by some key terms.

"Franchising" refers to an arrangement in which a party, the franchisee, buys the right to sell a product or service from a seller, the franchisor. The right to sell a product or service is the franchise.

There are basically two types of franchises: (1) product and trade-name franchises and (2) business-format franchises. A product and trade-name franchise generally involves the distribution of a product through dealers. Common examples are auto dealerships and some gas stations.

Business format franchises provide the product, trade names, operating procedures, quality assurance standards, management consulting support, facility design, and generally everything necessary to start and operate the business in one package. Many familiar fast food outlets and convenience stores are business format franchises.

Advantages of Franchising

- **Risk minimized** — *a well-established franchise is a proven business method.*

- **Name recognition** — *a well-known name can bring customers into the business and provide a competitive advantage for the franchisee.*

- **Training** — *a franchisor can provide a regimented training program to teach the franchisee about the business operation and industry even if the franchisee has no prior experience.*

- **Support** — *a franchisor can provide managerial support and problem-solving capabilities for its franchisees.*

- **Economies of scale** — *cost savings on inventory items can be passed on to the franchisee from bulk purchase orders made by the franchisor.*

- **Advertising** — *cooperative advertising programs can provide national exposure at an affordable price.*

- **Financing** — *a franchisor will generally assist the franchisee in obtaining financing for the franchise. In many instances, the franchisor will be the source of financing. Lenders are more inclined to provide financing to franchises because they are less risky than businesses started from scratch.*

- **Site selection** — *most franchisors will assist the franchisee in selecting a site for the new franchise location.*

Disadvantages of Franchising

- **Franchise fees** — *franchise fees are required to be paid to the franchisor at the inception of the franchise agreement. These fees can range from a few thousand dollars to hundreds of thousands of dollars, depending on the franchise.*

- **Royalties** — *the cost of many franchises includes a monthly royalty (fee) based on a percentage of the franchisee's income or sales, and you pay even if the business is not profitable.*

- **_Loss of control_** — *franchise agreements usually dictate how the franchise operates. The franchisee must adhere to the standards in the franchise agreement, which thereby leaves the franchisee with little control over the operation.*

- **_Required purchases_** — *the franchisor may require the franchisee to purchase certain materials for the purpose of producing uniform franchise products.*

- **_Termination clause_** — *the franchisor may require that it retain the right to terminate the franchise agreement if certain conditions are not met. The franchisor may then terminate the agreement and offer the franchise location to another.*

Buying a Franchise vs. an Independent Business

In deciding whether to buy a franchise or to start an independent business, perhaps the best place to begin is to ask yourself why you want to own a business. The answer you give may provide some insight into which path you should choose.

You want to be your own boss. If your answer is that you want to own a business because of the freedom it will bring you, you probably shouldn't buy a franchise. If you buy a franchise, the franchisor will dictate much of what you have to do, when you do it, and how you do it. You'll have far more control if you start your own business.

You have a business idea that you believe has a lot of promise. If you want to nurture an idea you have into full bloom, you probably shouldn't buy a franchise. You won't have much control or be given much of an opportunity to pursue your ideas (try telling McDonald's that they need to provide waiters and real silverware).

You want to make lots of money. If you want to own your own business because of the financial opportunities it presents, you should look long and hard at a franchise. Franchises don't necessarily make more money than other types of businesses, but they do have higher success rates. Of course, you'll be paying for the higher success rate in the fees you'll be paying to the franchisor. In many cases, you need to own several franchises to become really wealthy.

You have money but you're looking for something to keep you busy. If you have startup funds in hand, a franchise may be ideal for you, particularly if you lack hands-on experience. You'll get help with everything you need to set up your business: site selection, inventories, management counseling, hiring practices, and every other necessary function for the operation of your business.

A lot of people in the franchising field will tell you that franchises have a failure rate of about 5 percent within five years, compared to the 50 percent failure rate of independent entrepreneurs in the same time frame.

You should be aware, however, of studies that question the 5 percent rate. For example, a 1995 study by Dr. Timothy Bates, a professor at Wayne State University in Detroit, found that the franchise failure rate actually exceeded 30 percent and that franchises made lower profits than independent entrepreneurs. Dr. Bates' study also found that the average capital investment of franchisees was $500,000, compared to $100,000 for independent entrepreneurs.

Finding the Right Franchise

If you're not sure which franchise you're most interested in, a good place to look is at annual franchising trade shows. These trade shows provide an opportunity to talk to many franchisors and industry experts in one location. Often, the shows will have seminars to educate potential franchisees on what they can expect and the advantages and disadvantages of being a franchisee. Details of trade shows can be obtained on the Internet at Trade Show Central (http://www.tscentral.com).

If you have a pretty good idea of which franchise you want to own, the most obvious place to start is by contacting the franchisor. The franchisor can give you all the information you'll need about the availability, cost, and other details about their franchises.

An alternative that isn't so obvious but that can achieve the same result, and possibly at a savings, is to contact existing franchisees who are looking to sell their franchises. You might save some money because you may be able to avoid some of the initial franchise fees.

Investigate the Franchise Before Buying

Buying a franchise, like buying an existing business, should involve a thorough investigation. The time spent investigating the franchise, the industry, and the market will make you confident that your decision to buy (or not to buy) was on the money. Making the wrong decision can cost you tens of thousands of dollars or more, not to mention the loss of time and energy on your part, so don't give short shrift to this very important step.

Before you buy, you should be convinced that the prospective franchise has an established reputation, sufficient capital, high-quality products or services, and satisfied franchisees.

A reference list of current and former franchisees should be available from the franchisor. (If a reference list isn't available, be *very* cautious!) Talk to as many of these people as you can – they are the ones who can give you the inside story about the business.

Getting Information from the Franchisor

Every franchisor must provide "offering documents" to prospective franchisees. According to federal law, the offering documents must be given to the prospective franchisee no later than 10 days before the franchise agreement is signed or before any cash is paid.

The federal government, as well as most state governments, have rules and regulations regarding the content of the offering documents. For one thing, offering documents must be written in "plain English." Offering documents should include the following information: the history of the franchise and its owners, procedures for terminating and renewing the franchise relationship, quality controls, fee structures, and financial statements.

Franchise Agreements

A franchise agreement is a contract between the franchisor and the franchisee. The agreement should balance the interests of the parties. However, in reality, if the franchise is a well-known organization like McDonald's, the agreement is going to be very favorable to the franchisor, and you may have to "take it or leave it." Nevertheless, have your attorney try to negotiate the best terms you can get.

Checklist of Basic Franchising Agreement Terms

The checklist should be used either before you see the franchise agreement, in order to get an idea of what should be in it, or after you have a copy of the agreement, in order to review its terms. In any event, don't sign any agreements until you've discussed your options with your attorney.

Issues Pertaining to the Franchise Cost

❑ *What does the initial franchise fee purchase?*

❑ *Does it include an opening inventory of products and supplies?*

❑ *What are the payment terms: amount, time of payment, lump sum or installment, financing arrangements, etc.?*

❑ *Does the franchisor offer any financing, or offer help in finding financing?*

❑ *Is any part or all of the initial fee refundable?*

❑ *Does the contract clearly distinguish between "total cost" and "initial fee," "initial cash required," or "initial costs," etc.?*

❑ *Are there periodic royalties? If so, how much are they and how are they determined?*

❑ *If royalty payments are in whole or part payment for services by the franchisor, what services will be provided?*

❑ *Are accounting/bookkeeping services included or available?*

❑ *How are advertising and promotion costs divided or allocated?*

❑ *Is a specified amount of working capital required of the franchisee to cover operating costs until profits can be made?*

❑ *Must premises be purchased or rented, and are there further conditions on either of these (from franchisor, selected site, etc.)?*

❑ *How and by whom will the building be financed, if purchased?*

❑ *Does the franchisee have to make a down payment for construction and/or equipment?*

Issues Pertaining to the Franchise Location

❑ *Does the franchise apply to a specific geographical area? If so, are the boundaries clearly defined?*

❑ *Who has the right to select the site?*

❑ *Will other franchisees be permitted to compete in the same area, now or later?*

❑ *Does the franchisee have a first refusal option as to any additional franchises in the original territory if it is not exclusive?*

❑ *Does the franchisee have a contractual right to the franchisor's latest products or innovations? If so, at what cost?*

❑ *Will the franchisee have the right to use currently owned property and/or buildings? If not, will the franchisor sell or lease his property to the franchisee?*

❑ *Who is responsible for obtaining zoning variances, if required?*

Issues Pertaining to the Buildings, Equipment, and Supplies

❑ *Are plans and specifications of the building determined by the franchisor? If so, does this control extend to selection of contractor and supervision of construction?*

❑ Are there any restrictions on remodeling or redecorating?

❑ Must equipment or supplies be purchased from the franchisor or an approved supplier?

❑ When the franchisee must buy from the franchisor, are sales considered on consignment? Or will they be financed and, if so, under what terms?

❑ Does the agreement provide for continuing supply and payment of inventory (by whom, under what terms, etc.)?

❑ Does the franchise agreement bind the franchisee to a minimum purchase quota?

❑ What controls are spelled out concerning facility appearance, equipment, fixture and furnishings, and maintenance or replacement of the same? Is there any limitation on expenditures involved in any of these?

❑ Does the franchisor have a group insurance plan? If not, what coverage will be required, at what limits and costs? Does the franchisor require that it be named as an insured party in the franchisee liability coverage?

Issues Pertaining to the Operating Practices

❑ Must the franchisee participate personally in conducting the business? If so, to what extent and under what specific conditions?

❑ What degree of control does the franchisor have over franchise operations, particularly in maintaining franchise identity and product quality?

❑ What continuing management aid, training, and assistance will be provided by the franchisor, and are these covered by the service or royalty fee?

❑ Will advertising be local or national and what will be the cost-sharing arrangement, if any, in either case?

❑ If local advertising is left to the franchisee, does the franchisor exercise any control over such campaigns or share any costs?

❑ Does the franchisor provide various promotional materials (point-of-purchase, mail programs, etc.) and at what cost?

❑ What are the bookkeeping, accounting, and reporting requirements, and who pays for what?

❑ Are sales or service quotas established? Are there penalties for not meeting them?

❑ Are operating hours and days set forth in the franchise contract?

❑ Are there any limits as to what is or can be sold?

❑ Does the franchisor arrange for mass purchasing, and is it mandatory for the franchisee to be a participant buyer?

❑ Who establishes hiring procedures initially and through the franchise term?

Issues Pertaining to Termination and Renewal

❑ Does the franchisor have the absolute privilege of terminating the franchise agreement if certain conditions have not been met, either during the term or at the end?

❑ Does the franchise agreement spell out the terms under which the franchisor may repurchase the business?

❑ Does the franchisor have an option or duty to buy any or all of the franchisee's equipment, furnishings, inventory, or other assets in the event the franchise is terminated for good cause by either party?

❑ If the preceding situation occurs, how are purchase terms determined?

❑ Is there provision for independent appraisal? Is any weight given to good will or franchisee equity in the business?

❑ Does the original agreement include a clause that the repurchase price paid by the franchisor should not exceed the original franchise fee? If so, this eliminates any compensation for good will or equity.

❑ Under what conditions (illness, etc.) can the franchisee terminate the franchise? In such cases, do termination obligations differ?

❑ Is the franchisee restricted from engaging in a similar business after termination? If so, for how many years?

❑ If there is a lease, does it coincide with the franchise term?

❑ Does the contract provide sufficient time for amortization of capital payments?

❑ Has the franchisor, as required, provided for return of trademarks, trade names, and other identification symbols and for the removal of all signs bearing the franchisor's name and trademarks?

Other Points To Consider

❑ Can the franchisee sell the business and assign the franchise agreement to the buyer?

❑ Is the franchise assignable to heirs, or may it be sold by the franchisee's estate on death or disability?

❑ Does the lease permit assignment by the franchisee?

❑ *How long has the franchisor conducted business in its industry, and how long has it granted franchises?*

❑ *How many franchises and company-owned outlets are claimed, and can they be verified?*

❑ *If there is a trade name of a well-known person involved in the franchise, is this person active, and what kind of a financial interest does the person have?*

❑ *Are all trademarks, trade names, or other marks fully identifiable and distinct, and are they clear of any possible interference or cancellation owing to any pending litigation?*

❑ *What is the duration of any patent or copyright material to the franchise? If time is limited, does the franchisor intend to renew, and is this spelled out in the franchise agreement?*

❑ *Has the franchisor met all state law requirements (registration, escrow or bonding requirements, etc.), if applicable?*

❑ *Are there state laws governing franchisor/franchisee relationships, including contract provisions, financing arrangements, and terminations? If so, does the contract meet all requirements?*

Chapter 3

Evaluating Your Chance for Success

After you've decided that you have the right stuff to be an entrepreneur, you're ready to determine if your business idea also has the right stuff. Before you pump your life savings into a small business, you want to know if it has a chance to succeed.

ASSESSING THE MARKET

One of the first steps in examining your business idea is to get to know more about your market. If you have an idea for a business but you're not sure whether a market for it exists or is big enough to support your business, you're getting ahead of yourself.

But even if you are reasonably sure that a market exists, you need to know a good deal about the size and shape of the market in order to forecast your chances for success. The smaller your business, the more important this may be. If Procter & Gamble puts out a product that doesn't sell, it moves on to the next idea. If you put out a product that doesn't sell, you may be out of business.

When you conduct research, you'll want to find out the following information:

- Who are your likely customers? Will their identity affect where you need to be? For example, if students are your customers, you may need to be near schools.

- How much will they pay for your product or service? Are there improvements you can add to increase the price?

- How can you reach your customers? Which marketing options will reach the most customers at the lowest cost?

- Who are your direct competitors? Have you also considered those who aren't direct competitors but who might nevertheless compete against you? For example, if you sell an online magazine, you're competing not just against other online magazines but against other products that occupy someone's leisure time.

Researching Your Industry

Where can you go to find out more specific information about the costs and risks associated with starting a particular type of business? The following are some of our favorite sources.

Small Business Administration

The federal government's main conduit to help the new business person is the Small Business Administration (SBA). While many people have heard about the existence of SBA loans (discussed in Chapter 10), you may not know that the SBA is also the federal government's main provider of information and counseling to the small and new business person. Below is a list of some of the types of information that the SBA provides:

- **Business initiatives, education, and training** — the SBA provides a wide range of publications and audio-visual materials. This material is geared toward management of a small business and technical assistance.

- **International trade** — the SBA is available to provide guidance to a business in the export trade area, in particular to those wishing to take advantage of the new world markets in Mexico, the Pacific Rim, Canada, and Europe.

- **Veterans' affairs** — the SBA provides training conferences specifically for veterans who are prospective or established business owners.

- **Women's business ownership** — the SBA also provides training conferences specifically for women who are prospective or established business owners.

Contact your nearest SBA office by looking in the telephone directory under U.S. Government or try their Internet home page at http://www.sba.gov.

Bureau of the Census

The Bureau of the Census information is a general term used for a wide variety of information. Most people think of the Census Bureau as just counting people living in each city. Actually, this is done only every 10 years. The rest of the time, the Bureau is preparing other types of statistics and publications that could be useful to you in researching your new business, including:

- **Catalog of United States census publications** — this is published monthly with quarterly and annual compiling. This catalog contains a list of all publications with appropriate descriptions.

- **Census of retail trade** — this publication lists statistics for more than 100 different types of retail establishments by state, metro area, county, and community (population over 2,500). This includes information on the number of outlets, total sales, employment and payroll. Similar information exists for wholesale trade.

- **Census of service industries** — this publication is similar to the census of retail trade for retail service organizations, such as auto repair centers and hotels.

- **Census of manufacturers** — this publication lists statistics for 450 different classes of manufacturing industries. The statistics are compiled by industry and include information on capital expenditures, number of establishments, employment data, material costs, assets, rent, and inventories.

- **Statistical abstract of the United States** — this annual publication is a source for finding current and historical statistics about various aspects of American life. The publication includes statistics on income, prices, education, population, law enforcement, environmental conditions, local government, labor force, manufacturing, and many other topics.

- **State and metropolitan area data book** — this is a supplement to the statistical abstract listed above. It provides statistics on states and metropolitan areas in the United States and on subjects such as housing, income, manufacturers, population, retail trade, and wholesale trade.

SCORE — Free Business Counseling

SCORE, the Service Corps of Retired Executives, is a national organization sponsored by the SBA. This organization has over 12,000 member volunteers.

SCORE provides free counseling to new and existing small businesses. It also provides workshops that can give you a general overview of what it takes to start a new business.

SCORE also provides one-on-one counseling and training to existing businesses. The volunteers can help you identify management problems, determine the causes, and propose solutions to the problems. To contact SCORE, look in the telephone directory under U.S. Government or call the SBA, which is also listed under U.S. Government. You can opt for SCORE counseling via e-mail at www.score.org.

Customized Economic Research

Customized economic research covers a wide range of activity. The research can range from sitting in your car and counting the number of people who walk by a specific location, to hiring a professional research firm to do your market research and analysis for you.

Generally the do-it-yourself economic research approach will provide you with the necessary information to evaluate your new business.

Case Study — Researching a Fast Food Business

 Assume that you plan to open a submarine sandwich shop in a strip mall that has a vacancy. Some of the questions that should be addressed are as follows:

Was there a store in this location before? *If two other restaurants have already tried it and failed, do you want this location? The best and easiest way to find out this information is to ask business people in the same strip mall or the mall management. Be careful that they are not just "telling you what you want to hear" to avoid having an empty storefront in their vicinity.*

Are there competing or complementing stores in the same area? *If three restaurants are already there and all appear to be extremely busy, then maybe your research may be almost done for you. This may be a location that has a high need for more restaurants. But, if two of the restaurants are also sub shops, why will somebody come to yours instead of the other ones?*

What time of the day will your sub shop make money? *Is this a strip mall that is a destination for the lunch crowd or is it busiest in the evening after work? The most effective way to answer these questions may be to sit in your car and watch the traffic patterns. If you note that over the lunch period the parking lot is packed and most of the people are there for lunch, this may be the place where you want to open your restaurant. If you notice that in the evening hours very little traffic comes to this strip mall and the other restaurants have very few customers, then you will know that you probably will not be able to depend on the evening hours to make any money.*

Talk to shoppers that are in the area. *Ask them questions on why they shop or eat in this location. Be careful how you phrase your questions or they may tell you the answer you want to hear instead of their true beliefs.*

What is in the future for this location? *Will major road construction or store closings affect your new business location? Is the population of the area growing?*

To answer the questions on population, market size, etc., look at available government information sources in your local public library. This will provide you with a road map on more specific economic research.

State and Local Government Help

Most states and local governments have some type of economic development program. These programs will range from providing economic information to giving low interest loans and even forgivable grants.

To find out what is available in your state, contact your state department of economic development for eligibility requirements. The city and county governments are also a source of assistance. Look in the local government section in the telephone book, under "economic development."

Work Smart

Loan officers at your bank may also be a valuable resource in identifying state, local, and agency assistance to the new business person. They may have gone through the steps with other new businesses in your area.

Another suggestion is to call the regional or federal HUD office. HUD (the federal Department of Housing & Urban Development) provides job and other grants to startups and small businesses for job creation (e.g., $10,000 per job created) in the form of low interest loans, often in conjunction with the SBA. HUD will be able to provide the names and phone numbers of local city, county, and state organizations in your area that represent HUD for development of targeted geographic urban areas.

For more information on conducting research on your industry, see *Chapter 11, Analyzing the Market Environment.*

ASSESSING YOUR POTENTIAL PROFITABILITY

One of the most common reasons small businesses fail is that the owners seriously underestimate how much money they will need to start the business. You need to be extremely careful when determining how much money you need to start. Don't fall into the "rosy forecast" trap in which the new owner over-optimistically predicts robust sales in the first year and, as a result, doesn't have enough money on hand when the cash flow slows down a bit.

For a complete picture of what it will cost you to start a new business, you need to look very carefully at three key areas:

- **Your living expenses** — you need to know the fixed and variable living expenses your family will face during the startup period. Ideally, you'd have this money in the bank before you even get started, or you'd have another source of income (such as a spouse's wages, or investment income) to cover the bare-bones costs.

- **Costs of setting up the business** — next, you should add up the costs of everything you need to do before opening your doors or making your first sale.

- **Costs of running the business** — finally, you need to look at the costs of operating the business for the first 90 days.

Once you have a handle on these three types of costs, you should look at the revenue side, and attempt to forecast your sales for the first 90 days. When you have good, solid estimates of both revenues and sales for the initial period of operation, you'll be in a position to evaluate the profitability of your business.

Budgeting for Personal Living Expenses

Before you start planning for the cash needs of your new business, you must determine how much money you and your family will need to survive for at least the first six to 12 months of your business's operation. It would be nice to think that your business will support you from the first day you open the doors, but that's not realistic.

The best way to start is to prepare a family budget schedule that shows where you spent your money in the last 12 months. Be sure to look over the entire 12-month period because expenses often fluctuate greatly from month to month. When preparing the schedule, be on the watch for expenses that could be reduced or eliminated if necessary.

On the next page you'll find a form that you can copy and use to create your own family budget. For an interactive version of the budget, visit our Website at http://www.toolkit.cch.com.

Work Smart

Ideally, you should have access to enough cash to cover your living expenses for at least the first six months, without assuming you'll get any income from your business. If not, consider waiting until you can raise more money or getting a part-time job to bring in some cash until your business gets on its feet.

Family Monthly Budget Schedule

	JAN	FEB	MAR	APR	MAY	JUN	JUL	AUG	SEP	OCT	NOV	DEC	TOTAL
Income Description:													
Wages (take-home) - partner 1													
Wages (take-home) - partner 2													
Interest and dividends													
Other													
Total Income													
Expense Description:													
Auto expense													
Auto insurance													
Auto payment													
Beauty shop and barber													
Cable TV													
Charity													
Child care													
Clothing													
Credit card payments													
Dues and subscriptions													
Entertainment and recreation													
Gifts													
Groceries and outside meals													
Health insurance													
Home repairs													
Household													
Income tax (additional)													
Laundry and drycleaning													
Life insurance													
Medical and dental													
Mortgage payment or rent													
Other debt payments													
Telephone bill													
Tuition													
Utilities													
Vacations													
Other													
Total Expenses													
Cash (Shortfall) Extra													

Costs of Setting Up the Business

The first time you go through the costs to start up your new business, you do not need to be particularly precise. You can just "ball park" the amount to get a rough idea of your expected startup costs.

As you refine your business idea and shop around for the various items you need to make it happen, you will be continually narrowing down your estimates, and eventually you'll arrive at the actual dollar figures.

Work Smart

As you work through these expenses, don't forget that your accountant can be a great source of information for helping you make startup cost estimates. If the accountant has small business experience, he or she should be able to tell you whether your estimates are on target.

Here are the most common kinds of startup expenses that most small businesses face:

Common Startup Expenses

- ***Advertising and marketing promotion expenses*** — *you'll want to prime the pump by scheduling some advertising to appear before you officially open, and you may want to plan for a "grand opening" promotion as well.*

- ***Beginning inventory*** — *for retailers, this is the amount of inventory that you will need to have in place on the first day you open the doors for business. This could be your most significant start-up cost, so make sure you get an accurate estimate. Your suppliers, if you know who they will be, should be able to provide you with some help on required inventory levels for your type of business.*

- ***Cash*** — *include in this the amount of cash you'll need to run the cash register.*

- ***Decorating*** — *this will include cosmetic improvements to the new business facility. Usually it is possible to get bids and ideas from interior decorators, which will give you a cost estimate even if you ultimately do the decorating yourself.*

- ***Deposits*** — *include all amounts required by utilities and telephone companies. The utilities will be able to provide you with an estimate based on the type of business.*

- ***Fixtures and equipment*** — *include all fixtures and equipment needed for your new business. Finance this amount on a long-term basis if possible.*

- **Hiring employees** — *although most employees won't start until you actually open, you may want to hire a key employee earlier to help with the initial tasks.*

- **Installing fixtures and equipment** — *this should be the amount necessary to make all the fixtures and equipment ready for use.*

- **Insurance payments** — *ordinarily the first premium is due when you purchase the policy. You will need liability and property insurance to protect yourself and any business assets. Depending on your business, you may also need some or all of the following: workers' compensation, health, life, disability, key person, business interruption, product liability, and professional malpractice.*

- **Lease payments** — *include amounts that must be paid for equipment and facility leases before opening. Expect to pay several months' worth of lease payments before you open the doors.*

- **Licenses and permits** — *this amount will include all fees charged by local, state, and federal agencies. If your new business is in a highly regulated industry, expect these charges to be somewhat high. For example, an elder-care facility or a company that handles toxic substances will have higher fees than a clothing store.*

- **Professional fees** — *if you form a partnership, limited liability company, or corporation, you'll probably need the assistance of an attorney in drawing up the proper documents and filing them with the state. You may also want to pay an accountant to set up your books.*

- **Remodeling** — *if your new business location will require any remodeling, include it here. Contractors will usually provide free bids after you have the plans drawn up.*

- **Signs** — *signage costs can be substantial. Obtain bids from sign companies. Finance this amount through long-term borrowing, if possible, or it will hurt your short-term cash flow.*

- **Supplies** — *include all office, cleaning, and employee supplies in this amount.*

- **Unanticipated expenses** — *a good rule of thumb is to compute the unanticipated expenses as 10 percent of the total cost of your startup dollars.*

Costs of Running the Business: The First 90 Days

Many new business owners plan only for their cash flow needs up to the day they open for business. But you also need to take a close look at the costs for the first 90 days of operation, since most businesses will take at least that long to build up a reliable stream of revenue.

The amount you need to keep the business running, called working capital, will vary by the type of business you own. If your new business is a one-employee consulting firm, you will have a much smaller working capital requirement than a retail establishment that has a large inventory.

Example

Assume your new business is a retail establishment that is selling furniture and, as a promotion, you plan to give buyers 90 days to pay. Your working capital needs could be enormous.

First, you have to buy your inventory; then, after it sells, you must pay for the replacement inventory. This could mean that you will not receive one dollar to pay bills for at least 90 days after you open the doors. If you do not plan for this working capital need in advance, you may not even stay in business for 90 days.

A good rule of thumb is to have access to enough working capital to pay all of your bills, except inventory purchases, for the first three months of operations. Inventory purchases will follow the special rules noted below.

Listed below are the most common cash requirements needed to keep the business open for the first 90 days.

Common Cash Requirements — The First 90 Days

- *Advertising* — *how much to spend on advertising depends on the type of business and the amount of competition. If you will be opening a retail establishment and plan to get your competitor's customers, your advertising budget will have to take that into account. You may be able to glean the approximate amount that should be spent on advertising from trade publications. Your advertising may be any combination of coupons, direct-mail, newspaper, radio, or television. See* Part IV, Marketing Your Product, *for more information on new business advertising.*

- *Bank service charges* — *these usually aren't a significant amount, but your bank should be able to give you an idea of how much to budget per month for these charges. Some banks will charge you for every check you deposit and every check you write on your business account.*

- *Credit card fees* — *these fees are usually based upon card usage. Normally the costs are about 3 to 5 percent of the total charges. If you intend to allow your customers to buy your product or services by credit card, and you expect your business to have high credit card usage, allow for charges of 3 percent of sales. A chief benefit of credit card sales is the immediate business bank account deposit made electronically at the end of each day, making same-day payment a reality for any business doing credit card sales. This is especially advantageous if 30-day or longer payment terms can be arranged for inventory suppliers and other vendors.*

- **Delivery charges** — these charges are for the cost of having inventory delivered to you. When you arrange for your inventory purchasing, ask about delivery charges.

- **Dues and travel expenses** — these expenses will vary by type of business. If you are in a regulated or professional industry, the expenses will be higher. For most retailers, trade association dues are nominal, but travel expenses may be substantial for the many regional and national trade shows.

- **Interest** — if you will be financing your new business with loans, compute the expected interest payments in your working capital needs.

- **Inventory** — when planning your working capital needs, include the additions to inventory for which you will not receive cash immediately. If inventory purchases are to replace inventories from cash sales, do not include them in your working capital budget.

- **Lease payments** — include the amount that will be paid for equipment and facility leases in the first 90 days of your new business.

- **Loan payments** — this is the principal amount related to interest, above.

- **Miscellaneous** — use this category as a catch-all for unanticipated costs and miscellaneous items that you will incur during the first 90 days.

- **Office expenses** — these are various types of costs associated with running your business. They include paper, postage, photocopy expenses, etc.

- **Payroll other than owner** — compute the amount that you will incur in the first 90 days of your business, by multiplying the number of employees that will be required for each hour, by the expected hourly rate, times the number of hours.

- **Payroll taxes** — these include Social Security and Medicare tax, and the federal and state unemployment tax. Generally, the total employer's share of Social Security and Medicare tax is 7.65 percent of payroll unless you will be paying people over the $75,000 range; at that point, a different set of rules will come into play. Unemployment rates vary on a state-by-state basis. See Part VIII: Controlling Your Taxes for specifics on computing the various employment taxes.

- **Professional fees** — in many cases, the largest professional fees will be incurred before you open the doors. In this category, include fees for accounting, consulting, or payroll services that you may need.

- **Repairs and maintenance** — in the first 90 days of your new business, this amount should be minimal, particularly if you are using new equipment.

- **Salary of owner or manager** — remember to include 90 days' worth of your own salary, if you intend to draw a salary, as well as 90 days' worth of a manager's salary, if you intend to hire a manager.

- **Sales tax** — *sales tax varies on a state-by-state basis. The customer normally pays all sales taxes; however, you will have to pay sales tax on supplies, equipment, and other items your business uses in its operations.*

- **Supplies** — *include the amount you intend to spend on supplies in the first 90 days of your new business.*

- **Telephone charges** — *check with your local phone company for the business rates. If your business will consist of high telephone usage, get bids from several different carriers.*

- **Utilities** — *include all utilities that your business will require, such as electricity, gas, water, sewer, and refuse collection. These amounts can be estimated by the applicable carriers.*

Startup Costs Worksheets

On the next two pages, you'll find worksheets that can help you to compute your initial cash requirements for the new business. They list the things you need to consider when figuring out your startup costs, and include both the one-time initial costs needed to open your doors, and the ongoing costs you'll face each month for the first 90 days.

Forecasting Sales

To get an accurate read on how much money you'll need to keep your business running in the first 90 days, you can't just look at the costs. You'll also need to figure out how much revenue your business will produce in those 90 days.

In an ideal world, your business revenues would take care of all your expenses (and then some), and you wouldn't have to figure out how much more you'll have to pay out of your pocket to keep the business going. It might happen, but probably not within the first few months of operation.

Estimating your sales will be an inexact science. Don't count too heavily on your projections and, if you're going to err, err on the conservative side in predicting how much business you'll do in your first 90 days.

If you have significant experience in the type of business and are familiar with the local economic conditions, your prior knowledge may give you the best estimate but you may still want to back up your knowledge with outside verification.

Initial Cash Requirements for the New Business
One-Time Startup Expenses

Startup Expenses	Amount	Description
Advertising	_____	Promotion for opening the business.
Beginning inventory	_____	The amount of inventory needed to open.
Building construction	_____	The amount per contractor bid and other.
Cash	_____	Requirements for the cash register.
Decorating	_____	Estimate based on bid if appropriate.
Deposits	_____	Check with the utility companies.
Fixtures and equipment	_____	Use actual bids.
Installing fixtures and equipment	_____	Use actual bids.
Insurance	_____	Bid from insurance agent.
Lease payment	_____	Amount to be paid before opening.
Licenses and permits	_____	Check with city or state offices.
Miscellaneous	_____	All other.
Professional fees	_____	Include CPA, attorney, engineer, etc.
Remodeling	_____	Use contractor bids.
Rent	_____	Amount to be paid before opening.
Services	_____	Cleaning, accounting, etc.
Signs	_____	Use contractor bids.
Supplies	_____	Office, cleaning, etc. supplies.
Unanticipated expenses	_____	Include an amount for the unexpected.
Other	_____	
Other	_____	
Other	_____	
Other	_____	
Total Startup Dollars		Total amount of costs before opening.

Initial Cash Requirements for the New Business
Repeating Monthly Expenses[1]

Expenses	Amount	Description
Advertising	_____	
Bank service charges	_____	
Credit card fees	_____	
Delivery charges	_____	
Dues and subscriptions	_____	
Health insurance	_____	Exclude the amount shown on preceding page.
Insurance	_____	Exclude the amount shown on preceding page.
Interest	_____	
Inventory	_____	See note 2, below.
Lease payments	_____	Exclude the amount shown on preceding page.
Loan payments	_____	Principal and interest payments.
Miscellaneous	_____	
Office expense	_____	
Payroll other than owner	_____	
Payroll taxes	_____	
Professional fees	_____	
Rent	_____	Exclude the amount shown on preceding page.
Repairs and maintenance	_____	
Salary of owner or manager	_____	Only if applicable during the first three months.
Sales tax	_____	
Supplies	_____	
Telephone	_____	
Utilities	_____	
Other	_____	
Total Repeating Expenses	_____	
Total Startup Expenses from preceding page	_____	
Total Cash Needed	_____	

[1] Include the first three months' cash needs unless otherwise noted.

[2] Include the amount needed for inventory expansion. If inventory is to be replaced from cash sales, do not include here. Assume that sales will generate sufficient cash for the replacements.

Most libraries have a wide range of information available for specific types of enterprises. The trade publications and trade associations are good sources of overall sales information for your specific industry. These publications will generally break out sales by geographic region and by business type. The publications may also provide key financial ratios that will be useful in your cash flow planning.

Product vendors may be an excellent source of sales data. If your new business is one that will have high inventory levels, product or warehouse facilities may be a potential source of sales data.

For example, assume you plan to open a grocery store. You would purchase the majority of your product from a primary grocery distributor. Usually a distributor of any significant size will have access to other grocery stores' sales in your trade area. This could be your starting point for your sales potential.

Warning

Be careful when asking product vendors about your new business's sales potential. Some may just tell you what you want to hear in order to get your business. Back up their forecasts with estimates from other sources.

Cash Flow Forecasting

Simply put, cash flow forecasting is a method of comparing your revenues for any given time period with the out-of-pocket expenses you expect to have over the same time period. The difference between revenues and expenses is your "cash flow" for the period. Hopefully the number is positive, meaning that you have more money coming in than going out; however, for the first few months (or even years), it's more likely that you'll experience a negative cash flow.

All new businesses should prepare a monthly cash flow forecast for the first year and an annual forecast for the first five years of the business. Cash flow forecasting is critical because while your revenues may exceed your expenses *for the year*, they may greatly lag behind your revenues during any given month. You'll need to know the size and duration of the potential gaps, so that you can find other ways to cover them. For more information, see *Chapter 24: Managing Your Cash Flow.*

ASSESSING YOUR FINANCING OPTIONS

Finding the money needed to start a new business is almost always one of the most difficult hurdles new owners face. At this point in the process of analyzing your business idea, you should have examined the costs of starting a business and your sales forecast, with the result that you have a good idea of how much you should budget for expenses and how much you should be able to earn.

Assuming that the startup costs (including the one-time setup costs, the recurring monthly expenses for the first 90 days, and any family living expenses that aren't covered by other sources of income) are more than you have on hand and more than you'll be able to earn right out of the gate, the next step is to figure out whether you can raise the difference.

It's important to recognize that most small businesses won't be able to get a bank loan for their initial startup costs. Banks tend to be very conservative lenders, and want to see a track record before they invest in you. You may have heard that the SBA lends money to small businesses, but this is not strictly true — the SBA merely guarantees loans; they still have to be approved by the bank.

Your initial costs will most likely have to be funded by personal savings, loans from family and friends, home equity loans, or even credit card loans. You might also consider partnering up with someone who has money to invest, or searching for other business owners who'd like to invest in another small company. In some cases, local governments or community agencies may make small loans available to businesses based on nothing more than the owner's business plan and good credit, but this is relatively rare.

Once you have established a track record for your business, you may be able to convince a bank to invest in you. One possibility is to start your business part-time, while maintaining another job. If you're successful at this for a couple of years, you'll have a compelling story to tell at the bank.

If you're interested in a detailed explanation of financing options, see *Part III: Getting Financing for Your Business.*

ASSESSING YOUR LEGAL LIABILITY

In making a legal assessment of your business idea, you need to determine the extent to which the operation of your business might expose you to legal liability.

Save Money

 If all you want is an overview of the types of liabilities your business may be exposed to, ask your insurance agent rather than your lawyer. Your insurance agent will have a good idea of the overall picture — and, unlike the visit to the lawyer, the agent's advice is free.

Of course, this tip applies only to an overview of your potential liabilities. If you need legal advice (for example, if you need an assessment of the odds that a suit will be filed against you in a given situation), you should consult your lawyer.

Once you determine the risks, there are, of course, steps that you can take to protect yourself. One way is by purchasing insurance.

Another way to protect yourself is by incorporating your business so that the risks would be borne by the company and not by you. But corporations may not be for everyone because they can be expensive to create ($400-$500 if you do it yourself vs. $1,000-$5,000 if a lawyer does it for you) and a lot of trouble to maintain.

LIMITING YOUR RISKS

Perhaps your analysis of the available market, your potential profitability, your financing options, or your legal liability has left you with questions as to whether your business idea is really viable. You may not want to jump in with both feet, when you don't know how deep (or how hot) the water is!

Following are some suggestions for hedging your bets on the success of your new venture.

Get Advice from Other Owners

Talk to others who operate the same or similar businesses. You may be surprised at how many small business owners will be willing to share their insights with you. Provided that you're not asking for trade secrets — and especially if you'll be competing in a different geographic area — you may pick up some valuable information. The local chamber of commerce or other business association meetings may provide access to business owners that you can talk to.

If you don't make much headway by attending such meetings or by directly approaching business owners, you may wish to offer a business owner a consulting fee. If you can find out what you need to know about the day-to-day operation of your prospective business, this one-time expense will probably be money well spent.

Work for Someone Else

A time-honored way of learning a business is to work in a similar business as an employee. Not only will you be getting on-the-job training, but you'll be getting a paycheck, and will be avoiding overhead expenses. If you don't already have experience in your chosen type of business, look for one that is successful and well run. Although there may be a few different ways to do any job successfully, there are probably a thousand ways to mess it up! You need not learn all of these "don'ts" in order to figure out the "do's."

Start by Moonlighting

For those who are unsure about whether they can make a go of a new business, starting out on a part-time basis is probably the best alternative. A part-time business will reduce your financial risk significantly while you gain the experience you need, assuming that you maintain your regular job elsewhere.

Going into a part-time new business will also enable you to get the kinks worked out of your new business before operating on a full-time basis. Remember that a part-time business will usually not generate a large profit. In some instances, a person may be able to live off of a part-time business, but this is not usually the case.

Warning

 You may be surprised at how much time a "part-time" business will take, even if you have only one client or customer. If you decide to work part-time, be prepared to work long hours.

Also, even though you consider your new business part-time, many of the costs of doing business will not necessarily go down. For example, suppose you're planning to open a home-based business. The office may require a complete separate set of office equipment. A desk and chair cost the same, whether you sit in it for 10 hours a day or two.

As a variation on the part-time business theme, you could decide to operate your business "full-time," while maintaining a part-time job elsewhere. This can be a way to make sure you can pay the rent and keep food on the table while your new venture is in its red-ink period.

Use a Home Office

If a home office makes sense for your type of business and your home situation, this option will significantly reduce the risks of starting a new business in many cases, since you can save on rent and other costs associated with opening a business outside the home. In some instances, home office startup costs will be next to nothing.

If your new business is not a success, the shut-down costs should also be minimal. For more information on working at home, see page 224.

Hire Family Members

The majority of new small businesses involve the owner's family in some way. This involvement may range from having the spouse do the bookkeeping to having the children work part time after school.

Getting help from family members can be a great, not to mention inexpensive, way to help you get through the startup phase of your new business. Family members can also help alleviate the additional time and frustration aspects of your new business.

Do consider how hiring family members might affect family relations. If your spouse works with you on a full-time basis in the business, how will that affect your relationship? Are you capable of firing a family member if necessary? Another consideration is how it will affect nonfamily employees, if you have any. When it is time to promote an employee, will it automatically be the family member?

On the positive side, you'll be able to keep more of your business profits in the family, and a family member may be more flexible in the amount and type of work they're willing to do. There are certain tax advantages to hiring family members — see page 536.

Hire a Professional Manager

If you're uncertain about your ability to run a small business, one good way to offset that concern is to hire someone to run the business for you. This accomplishes two things. First, the manager can bring instant experience to the new business. Second, if you have another job, you'll be able to continue with your current employment, and you'll have something to fall back on if your new business fails.

But a few words of caution: First, if you by chance hire a bad manager, your new business may never recover from it. Second, hiring a new manager can be expensive, especially if you want one with experience in the field. Third, even if you hire a competent manager, you'll be amazed at how much time your small business will demand of you.

Chapter 4

Setting Up the Business

Once you've decided that you have what it takes to start a business of your own, determined the kind of business you want, and evaluated your chances of success, you have to begin the process of actually setting it up.

To get started, on the next page we provide a checklist of the steps most small businesses will have to complete before opening their doors.

HIRING PROFESSIONALS

Among the professionals you may need to work with are a lawyer, an accountant, and, in some cases, a marketing or business consultant.

You'll probably also need to develop a relationship with a banker and an insurance agent. You might as well think of them as being part of your business family because they'll play an extremely important role in your success or failure.

The general rule for determining whether you should hire professionals is if (1) they have expertise you need but personally lack or (2) you have the expertise, but they can do what they do cheaper than you can do it.

Example

Suppose you know how to prepare your own financial statements and tax forms. If, however, you lose business because you're too busy doing your own accounting work, you'll have to weigh the lost business against the cost of hiring an accountant.

Owner's Checklist for Starting a New Business

Background Work

- ❑ Assess your strengths and weaknesses.
- ❑ Establish business and personal goals.
- ❑ Assess your financial resources.
- ❑ Identify the financial risks.
- ❑ Determine the startup costs.

- ❑ Decide on your business location.
- ❑ Do market research.
- ❑ Identify your customers.
- ❑ Identify your competitors.
- ❑ Develop a marketing plan.

Business Transactions

- ❑ Select a lawyer.
- ❑ Choose a form of organization.
- ❑ Register your name.
- ❑ Select an accountant.
- ❑ Prepare a business plan.
- ❑ Select a banker.

- ❑ Set up a business checking account.
- ❑ Apply for business loans.
- ❑ Establish a line of credit.
- ❑ Select an insurance agent.
- ❑ Obtain business insurance.

First Steps

- ❑ Get business cards.
- ❑ Review local building codes.
- ❑ Obtain a business license or permit (if applicable).
- ❑ Obtain a lease.
- ❑ Line up suppliers (if applicable).
- ❑ Get furniture and equipment.
- ❑ Get federal and state employer identification numbers (if applicable).
- ❑ Send for federal and state tax forms.
- ❑ Set a starting date.

Let's take a quick look at the tasks that your "team" of professionals can perform for you:

- **Accountant** — can set up your bookkeeping; can set up your system for handling the cash you receive; can do your taxes and advise you on how to operate your business to reduce your taxes; can provide financial planning advice.

- **Lawyer** — can help you choose the form of business you need and can help you prepare the necessary paperwork; can help you make sure you've complied with all local laws; can help you draft contracts and leases; can provide legal advice for many of your business decisions; can defend you if you get sued and can advise you if you are considering legal action against someone else.

- **Banker** — helps you get financing; helps you establish credit card accounts; works, in many cases, as your silent partner, providing you with business operation advice.

- **Insurance agent** — evaluates your insurance needs; provides you with advice on which types of coverage you need.

- **Management and marketing consultant** — provides basic business operation advice; provides pricing and inventory advice; provides sales and advertising advice.

Warning

Be careful about using relatives or close friends as professional advisors. Sometimes they may not be as brutally honest as you need them to be because they don't want to upset you. This doesn't mean that you shouldn't hire a relative or friend; it just means that you should be careful.

If you have an accountant, lawyer, insurance agent, or other professional who handles your personal matters, chances are they will be happy to handle your business matters, or at least provide a reference to someone who will. Otherwise, ask for referrals from friends, relatives, and other small business owners that you're acquainted with.

You can also find a professional as follows:

Accountant — contact the American Institute of Certified Public Accountants (AICPA) at 1211 Avenue of the Americas, New York, New York 10036-8775; (212) 596-6200. You can also get more information from state or local CPA societies, or from your local chamber of commerce. When all else fails, look in the Yellow Pages.

Be sure you shop around and compare rates. Negotiate the fees in advance.

Attorney — many state or local bar associations offer referral services, or contact the American Bar Association at 750 North Lake Shore Drive, Chicago, IL 60611; (312) 988-5522. Again, you may be able to get more information from a trade association, or look in the Yellow Pages. Initial consultations are often free, but make sure that's true before you make an appointment.

Work Smart

 Don't be scared off by a lawyer who wants a retainer, which is a lump sum of several hundred to several thousand dollars that you pay up front, and then draw against every time the lawyer advises you. This is a growing practice. In some ways, it's a good method for budgeting your legal costs since you'll know early on how much you'll be spending.

Bankers — start with the bank where you have your personal accounts. If that doesn't work out, ask business associates and other small business owners. Or contact the SBA at 1-800-827-5722. They keep track of which banks in your area have the best small business-lending records.

CHOOSING A FORM OF ORGANIZATION

Whether you've purchased an existing business or started one from scratch, you must decide which form of organization (sometimes referred to as "business entity") is best for your company. The decision can be difficult to make. You can choose to set up a sole proprietorship, partnership, corporation, S corporation, or limited liability company, and each has its advantages and disadvantages. Make sure that you consult with your attorney or accountant before making a final decision.

Remember, the form that you choose does not have to be permanent. If the circumstances of your business change, you can always change the form of your business. For example, you may start your business as a sole proprietorship, but, as your business grows, you may decide to incorporate or to take on a partner and become a partnership.

Sole Proprietorships

The easiest and least expensive way to begin operating a business is as a sole proprietorship. There are no documents or forms needed to become a sole proprietor, unless the business will operate under a name other than the owner's name.

Advantages of a Sole Proprietorship

- **Control** — the owner has complete control over the business.

- **Simplicity** — a sole proprietorship is easy to start and operate.

- **Inexpensive** — startup organization expenses are minimal since few, if any, legal documents need to be created to begin the enterprise, and there are no ongoing state filing fees as there are with corporations or LLCs.

- **No double taxation** — the business is not treated as a separate taxable entity. The business income is reported on the owner's individual tax return and is therefore taxed only once. The owner may be subject to Social Security and Medicare taxes on all profits.

Disadvantages of a Sole Proprietorship

- **Liability** — the owner is personally liable for any obligations of the business. Business creditors can go after your personal assets, if you can't pay your bills.

- **Limited ownership** — a sole proprietorship by definition is limited to one person. Thus, if the owner wants to admit another owner, such as a spouse, family member, or friend, the sole proprietorship would have to end. A new business arrangement, such as a partnership, would be created either by default or by intent.

Partnerships

There are basically two types of partnerships: general partnerships, which consist of general partners who share the management of the entity, and are personally responsible for the partnership's obligations and each other's actions; and limited partnerships, which consist of two classes of partners: general partners who run the business, and limited partners who are essentially investors.

General Partnerships

If a business is going to be owned by more than one owner, the simplest business form to create and operate is a general partnership. In fact, if two or more people go into business together without incorporating, the law will presume they are a partnership even if they do nothing to set one up.

Forming a partnership entails an agreement between two or more prospective partners. The agreement can be oral, but we never recommend that you rely on an oral agreement. The partnership agreement should be written up and signed by all partners to avoid conflicts later. Your lawyer can help you make sure that your agreement covers all the bases and is enforceable in your state.

Virtually anyone can be a partner. A partner can be an individual, a partnership, a limited liability company, a corporation, or a trust.

The flexibility of a partnership allows the business to operate in a manner that best suits the business needs at the time the business starts and later when the business has matured. For example, when the business is just beginning, one partner may have skills that are valuable to the business, but little capital. Another partner may have money, but few relevant skills. The partner with skills can contribute services to the partnership while the other partner contributes capital.

When a partner contributes capital to a partnership, the partner receives an ownership interest in all assets of the partnership, not just in the property contributed. A partnership interest is a capital asset that can be bought or sold (with permission of the other partners), and that can increase or decrease in value over time.

Advantages of a General Partnership

- **Multiple owners** — *a partnership may have more than one owner, unlike a sole proprietorship.*

- **Simplicity** — *a partnership is relatively easy to form and operate.*

- **Flexibility** — *the partnership is the most flexible form of business. Partners don't have to own equal shares; the partnership agreement can divide up rights and duties unequally, as long as a sufficient business purpose is shown.*

- **Favorable tax treatment** — *partnerships themselves don't pay federal income taxes. Instead, all the profits, losses, credits, and certain other tax items flow through the partnership to the individual partners, and are taxed on the partners' returns. Partners may have to pay Social Security and Medicare taxes on all profits.*

Disadvantages of a General Partnership

- **Unlimited liability** — *each partner is jointly and severally liable for all obligations of the partnership, meaning each individual can become liable for the entire obligation.*

- **Ease of dissolution** — *a partnership dissolves upon the death or withdrawal of a partner unless safeguards are in place.*

- **Each partner is an agent of the partnership** — *any partner can sign contracts, take out loans, and make other business decisions that will be binding on the entire partnership and for which the other partners can be personally liable.*

Protective measures. A partnership of two or more individuals may require the efforts of all the partners to succeed, especially in the early life of the business. If one of the partners withdraws or dies, the existence of the partnership may be threatened. To protect the partnership and the remaining partners, you should consider setting up buy/sell agreements and "key man" life insurance policies on the partners.

A buy/sell agreement specifies how the value of a partner's interest will be determined if a partner wants to leave the partnership. Having a buy/sell agreement in place minimizes disputes over value and smoothes out the purchase of the withdrawing partner's interest by the partnership or other partners.

Key man life insurance is a life insurance policy on the life of key members of an organization to provide cash in the event of death. The beneficiaries of a key man policy are the organization or the organization's members. In a partnership, key man life insurance can be purchased for all partners or on some designated class of partners, such as senior partners. The life insurance proceeds can be used by the partnership to keep the business going in the absence of the key partner. The proceeds can also be used to buy out the deceased partner's interest pursuant to a buy/sell agreement.

What's in the Partnership Agreement?

The partnership agreement is a complicated document that should be drafted by an attorney. At a minimum, it must address the following subjects:

- *__Contributions__ — the amount and time of contributions (in money or in labor) to be made by each partner should be specified.*

- *__Management and control__ — identify whether some or all partners will manage and control the day-to-day operations of the partnership. In most states, all partners must be allowed some participation in the most basic management decisions.*

- *__Profit and loss__ — specify how the profits and losses will be allocated to the partners. One of the beauties of the partnership form is that division of profits and losses need not be the same — for example, one partner might receive 60 percent of any losses, but only 40 percent of any profits — as long as a valid business purpose can be shown for the division.*

- *__Distributions__ — indicate when distributions of cash or property will be made.*

- *__Partner's responsibilities and duties__ — describe each partner's responsibilities and duties.*

- *__Withdrawal__ — identify how a partner's interest will be valued if the partner withdraws from the partnership.*

- **Death of a partner** — *identify how a partner's interest will be valued if the partner dies.*

Additional topics to be included in a partnership agreement, if applicable:

- **Admission of new partners** — *indicate the process for admitting new partners into the partnership.*

- **Right of first refusal** — *specify that the partnership or individual partners will have the right to purchase a withdrawing partner's interest before the partner can offer to sell the interest to someone outside the partnership.*

- **Duration of the partnership** — *indicate the life of the partnership along with any events that may cause the partnership to dissolve prematurely.*

- **Continuation of the partnership** — *identify the criteria to enable the partners to continue the partnership if an event that would otherwise causing the dissolution of the partnership occurs.*

Limited Partnerships

A limited partnership is a partnership with two classes of partners: general partners and limited partners. The general partners operate the business and are personally liable for all obligations of the partnership. The limited partners don't have any control over the business, other than to determine who will manage it. Limited partners share in the profits of the partnership but their potential losses are limited to the amount of their contributions.

Formation. A limited partnership is a creature of state law. As such, a limited partnership does not exist until the requirements specified in the state law are met. Generally, a certificate of limited partnership is required to be signed and filed with the secretary of state's office, and in some instances a limited partnership agreement is also required to be filed. If the requirements are not met, the business will be treated as a general partnership or an association taxable as a corporation.

A certificate of limited partnership contains information about the limited partnership such as its name, address, purpose, who the general partners are, and their business addresses, etc. Consult your lawyer about the rules that apply in your state.

A limited partnership agreement contains the same basic information as a general partnership agreement, but addresses some additional provisions pertaining to limited partners.

Limited partnerships are generally not the best choice of entity for a new business because of the required filings and administrative complexities. For a new business with two or more working partners, a general partnership would be much easier to form. If many passive investors will be needed, a corporation generally offers more flexibility.

Limited Liability Companies

A limited liability company (LLC) is a hybrid entity that combines the advantageous tax flow-through aspects of a partnership with the liability protection of a corporation or a limited partnership. What's more, unlike a limited partner, a member of an LLC is not prohibited from getting involved in managing the business.

Although the limited liability company form generally results in limited liability for its members, lenders usually require some or all members of a limited liability company to personally guarantee corporate loans.

The LLC is a relatively new type of entity that has only recently become available in all 50 states. Since it is so new, the laws among the various states differ somewhat in their definitions and treatment of LLCs. As a result, transactions outside the state of formation by the LLC may be treated differently from transactions within the state of formation.

Work Smart

One key area where state laws differ is in whether they permit single-owner LLCs. In some states, you must have at least two owners to form an LLC, but this is not universally true. However, at the federal level, an LLC is required to have two members in order to qualify for taxation as a partnership. A single-member LLC will be taxed as a sole proprietorship. If you intend to be the only owner of your business, you may want to consider forming an S corporation instead of an LLC.

Tax Issues

An LLC is generally treated as a partnership for both federal and state income tax purposes. Under regulations that were in effect prior to 1997, there was a chance that an LLC could be taxed as a corporation under federal law if the LLC possessed more than two of the four characteristics that generally pertain to corporations. (The four corporate characteristics are: continuity of life, centralization of management, limited liability, and free transferability of interests.) Now, however, the regulations permit business owners to elect whether they wish to be taxed as a partnership or as a corporation, and if no election is made, the IRS will presume that a non-publicly-traded, multiple-owner business should be taxed as a partnership.

Since the individual members are treated as partners, they may be subject to Social Security and Medicare taxes on their profits.

Forming an LLC

To form an LLC, articles of organization must be filed with the secretary of state's office. Some jurisdictions also require that an operating agreement be filed. The articles of organization contain information about the LLC, such as its name, address, purpose, who organized it, who the registered agent is, etc. The operating agreement is similar to a partnership agreement. Its purpose is to guide the conduct of the business. If the operating agreement is not required to be filed with the articles of organization, it can generally be in written or oral form. As a precautionary measure, the operating agreement should be written to limit future conflicts regarding the terms of the operating agreement.

Advantages of a Limited Liability Company

- *Limited liability* — members are shielded from being personally liable for acts of the LLC and its members.

- *Flexible membership* — members can be individuals, partnerships, trusts, or corporations.

- *Management* — members can manage the LLC or elect a management group to do so.

- *Flow-through tax treatment* — under federal law, LLCs are identical to partnerships: income, losses, deductions, and tax credits are not taxed at the business entity level, but flow through the LLC to be taxed to the individual members. Some states tax LLCs as corporations, however.

Disadvantages of a Limited Liability Company

- *Limitations on one-member LLCs* — some jurisdictions do not allow LLCs to have only one member.

- *Free transferability of interests* — transferability of interests is usually restricted.

- ***Nontraditional entity*** *— an LLC is a new entity type for which there is little legal precedent available. For example, the protections that most states provide for minority shareholders are not necessarily available to LLC members.*

- ***Cost*** *— an LLC usually costs more to form and maintain than a sole proprietorship or a general partnership. States may also charge an initial formation fee and an annual fee; check with your state's secretary of state's office.*

Limited Liability Partnerships

Limited liability partnerships are similar to limited liability companies in terms of the tax advantages, and a general partnership can usually be transformed into a LLP by filing a simple registration with state officials. Interest in this form of ownership is growing, and all states now permit LLPs, although a handful of states limit their availability to professionals, such as doctors or lawyers.

Corporations

One of the best-known and most widely used business entity forms is the corporation. For small businesses, the main advantage of a corporation is the liability protection it provides its owners or shareholders.

Liability is limited because the corporation is a legal entity that is separate from its shareholder owners. It can buy and sell assets, take out loans, create contracts, hire employees, and do many other things that a person can do. As a separate legal entity, the corporation has a perpetual life. Also, as a separate legal entity, the corporation is liable for its own debts and can be held liable only to the extent of the corporation's assets.

Warning

Although the corporate form generally results in limited liability, lenders usually require the shareholders of small, closely held corporations to personally guarantee corporate loans. If you personally guarantee the loans, you will have to pay the lender if the corporation is unable to pay.

Formation of Corporations

Forming a corporation is more complicated and more expensive than forming a sole proprietorship or a simple partnership. To form a corporation, articles of incorporation must be filed with the secretary of state's office in the state in which the corporation is being organized. If the secretary of state's office accepts the articles of incorporation, it will send a certificate of incorporation. Many states require that a copy of the certificate of incorporation be recorded in the local recorder's office where the corporation resides.

A corporation need not be organized in the state in which it is going to do business. Many corporations organize in states like Delaware to take advantage of favorable corporate laws (however, you'll probably have to apply for permission and pay fees to any state in which your corporation will do business). As a practical matter, we generally advise that you incorporate in your home state.

Operation of Corporations

A corporation is owned by its shareholders. The shareholders don't have any direct control over the daily operations of the business, but are responsible for electing the directors of the corporation.

The directors oversee the operation of the business and make major corporate decisions, such as appointing the officers. The directors meet at least annually to assess the past performance of the corporation and to plan for the future. The officers of the corporation are responsible for the day-to-day operations of the company.

Once the directors are elected and the corporate officers are appointed, the corporation can begin to operate. However, to preserve limited liability status, it is important that the corporation observe all the formalities of being a corporation. The formalities include, among other things, issuing stock certificates to the shareholders, holding annual meetings, recording the minutes of the meetings in the corporate register, and electing directors or ratifying the status of existing directors. The corporation's assets must be properly titled (owned) in its name, separate bank accounts must be maintained for the corporation, and the owner must not treat the corporation like his or her own back pocket.

Advantages of a Corporation

- ***Limited liability*** — *corporate shareholders are generally not responsible for the debts and obligations of the corporation.*

- ***Better fringe benefits for owner-employees*** — *corporations are the only entities that can provide fully deductible health insurance to the business owner, and have more options as to pension plans.*

- ***There may be several classes of stock*** *(preferred, nonvoting etc.) that give different attributes of ownership to different stockholders. Certain limitations apply to S corporations.*

- **Multiple ownership is easy** — there may be dozens or even hundreds of shareholders, or just one.

- **Earnings can be retained** — the corporation can retain some of its profits for future investment, without the owners' having to pay tax on them (this does not apply to S corporations — see the discussion below).

Disadvantages of a Corporation

- **Formalities required** — a corporation must follow certain formalities dictated by law to begin its existence and to maintain its corporate status. This can mean ongoing franchise taxes and legal fees to ensure that the proper steps are being followed.

- **Administration** — the administration of a corporation is complicated since certain federal and state tax procedures are necessary and certain accounting methods may not be available.

- **Cost** — incorporating even a simple business can cost more than $500. Also, the administrative costs of accounting and tax preparation may be expensive due to the complexity of complying with corporate laws.

Close Corporations

Many states allow a type of corporation called a close corporation, which may appeal to small business owners. A close corporation is one that is managed by its shareholders. Directors do not have to be elected and officers do not have to be appointed. In addition to these formalities being eliminated, the laws usually streamline some of the other meeting and voting requirements. The intent is to relieve some of the administrative burdens to the small corporation owner. If a close corporation appeals to you, consult an attorney in the state in which you are incorporating to determine if the option exists there.

Protective Measures

A corporation with two or more shareholders may require the efforts of all of the shareholders to succeed, especially in the early life of the business. If one shareholder withdraws or dies, the existence of the corporation may be threatened. To protect the corporation and the remaining shareholders, consider buy/sell agreements and key man life insurance policies on the shareholders, as discussed above under "Partnerships."

Tax Issues for Corporations

In general, corporations are separate taxable entities that are subject to federal and state income taxation. Corporate income is taxed at the corporate level. When that income is passed on to the shareholders as a distribution or dividend, it is taxed again on the shareholder's individual tax return. Double taxation may be partially or completely avoided in a small service business by paying a salary to the employee-shareholders. However, the tax laws governing this area are complex and should be discussed with your accountant or your attorney.

Also, be aware of the tax consequences upon dissolution of a corporation. With all forms of business entity except a regular corporation (a so-called "C corporation"), dissolution and distribution of the business's assets to the owners is, at worst, a single taxable event. In a C corporation, a double tax may be due: the corporation may owe a capital gains tax when the assets are sold, and the individual shareholders also must recognize a gain upon liquidation of the corporation. Consequently, dissolving a C corporation can have serious tax ramifications, so think carefully about incorporating in this form if you anticipate a short-term business opportunity.

Save Money

 If limited liability is not a concern for your business, one strategy you can implement is to begin the business in an unincorporated form, such as a sole proprietorship or partnership, so that business losses in the early years of the business can shelter your other income. These "passed through" losses can be used to offset other income you may have. When the business becomes profitable, you can incorporate.

S Corporations

For most purposes, an S corporation operates in the same manner as a regular corporation, as discussed above. It must have directors, officers, and shareholders who function in the same manner as their regular corporation counterparts.

The difference between an S corporation and a regular corporation is that the S corporation has elected to be taxed similar to a partnership for federal tax purposes.

After making the S election, the income, losses, tax credits, and other tax items of the corporation flow through the corporation to the shareholders. Thus, income is only taxed once, at the shareholder level.

Advantages of an S Corporation

- **Cash method of accounting** — *corporations must use the accrual method of accounting unless they are considered to be small corporations (a small corporation has gross receipts of $5,000,000 or less). S corporations, however, usually don't have to use the accrual method unless they have inventory.*

- **No double taxation** — *the S corporation pays no tax at the business entity level; all profits, losses, and other tax items flow through to the shareholders and are taxed on their individual income tax returns.*

- **Favorable capital gains treatment** — *in an S corporation, capital gains are passed through to the shareholders without having the character of the gain changed. Thus, shareholders can take advantage of the lower maximum tax rate on capital gains (20 percent, or 10 percent for those otherwise in the 15 percent bracket). Corporations that do not elect S corporation status pass the capital gains to their shareholders as dividends, which are treated as ordinary income. Dividends treated as ordinary income can be taxed at a rate of up to 39.6 percent.*

- **One-person S corporations are permitted** — *in states where single-owner LLCs aren't permitted, the S corporation is generally the only business structure that allows a single-owner business to obtain both limited liability and favorable flow-through tax treatment.*

Disadvantages of an S Corporation

- **Limit on number of shareholders** — *for many years, S corporations were limited to 35 shareholders; however beginning in 1997, S corporations may have up to 75 shareholders.*

- **One class of stock** — *an S corporation can only have one class of stock, which can impair the corporation's ability to raise capital. Nonvoting stock is not considered a "separate class" for this purpose, however.*

- **Taxable fringe benefits** — *some fringe benefits provided by the S corporation are taxable as compensation to employee-shareholders who own more than 2 percent of the corporation.*

NAMING YOUR BUSINESS

When selecting a name for your business, try to make it short, easy to remember, descriptive of the business, and capable of drawing attention. While this advice seems elementary, in practice it can be very hard to do. You may want to gather a group of friends and spend several hours or even days brainstorming to find possible names for the company. Be sure to rule out those that have negative attributes or that are very similar to names of existing businesses.

Once you decide on the name, you may have to register and/or receive approval from the local or state government that your business is formed in.

The name of your business must not be misleading or in any way imply something that the business is not. For example, you can't imply that your business is a licensed plumbing contractor if you haven't received a plumbing license. Likewise, you cannot imply that you are a professional and are providing professional services if you don't have professional credentials.

If the business will operate under a name that's different from the owner's full, legal name, most jurisdictions require that a fictitious owner affidavit be filed. A fictitious owner affidavit informs the local government and the public that the business is operating under an assumed name and indicates who the owner is. The fictitious owner affidavit usually has to be filed with the office of the county recorder of deeds rather than the secretary of state's office.

Work Smart

 If you are going to use a name other than your own for your business, contact the office of the recorder of deeds for the county that your business will be operating in, to get specific information and any necessary forms.

If you operate under a fictitious name, make sure that you file an affidavit in each county where you do business. If you do business across state lines, it gets a little trickier because the rules can vary among the states. In that event, you should discuss your options with your attorney.

Choosing a name for a limited partnership, corporation, or limited liability company involves more formalities than choosing a sole proprietorship or partnership name. In each case, the name has to be reserved with the secretary of state's office, and cannot duplicate the name of any other business in the state.

Also, the type of business organization must be included in the name. For example, the name of a corporation must include the words corporation, incorporated, limited, company or chartered, the letters Inc. or Corp., or some other phrase indicating that the entity is a corporation.

GETTING LICENSES AND PERMITS

Most state and local governments require businesses operating in their area to obtain licenses or permits. In some instances, the federal government may also require you to obtain a license or permit.

There are essentially two types of licenses, general and special. A general business license is issued annually for the privilege of operating a business in the jurisdiction. A special license is one that is issued to a business that will provide products or services that require specific regulation. Special licenses are issued to professionals, such as doctors, lawyers, barbers, and others who have met a certain level of training or education, or engage in certain occupations.

State and local governments regulate the safety, structure, and appearance of the community through the use of local laws, called ordinances. Zoning ordinances, which regulate how property can be used, are a common type of ordinance. Once the jurisdiction determines that you have complied with such ordinances, it will issue a permit that will enable you to operate your business.

If, for some reason, your business is unable or unwilling to comply with an ordinance, you can petition the jurisdiction for a special permit, called a variance, that would allow you, in effect, to violate the ordinance. If you're interested in a variance, talk to your lawyer. Variances are not routinely granted and they can be expensive (in terms of legal fees) to obtain, so make sure you really need the variance before you request it.

Work Smart

You can find out which licenses and permits are required for your business by calling the state and local government offices in the area in which you are going to operate. Ask them to send you information and any forms that may be required.

If you decide to start a home-based business, one of your first steps should be to find out what your local zoning ordinances allow. For more information, see the discussion of zoning in Chapter 15.

PROTECTING YOUR IDEAS

Patents, trademarks, copyrights, and trade secrets are collectively known as intellectual property and generally refer to the rights associated with intangible knowledge or concepts.

Intellectual property may be a concern if your business is developing (or has developed) a product, process, or concept that you are going to market, or has developed any special information that you want to keep away from your competitors.

Intellectual property may also be a concern if your business is using a process that was created by someone else, whether you know about it or not. For example, if you start selling a product that someone else has patented, you could be sued for infringement.

The laws surrounding intellectual property are quite complicated. If you believe that your business has any intellectual property concerns, you should ask your attorney what to do. If some legal work needs to be done, your attorney will probably recommend you to another attorney who specializes in this area.

The Four Types of Intellectual Property

Patents. *A patent is a grant of a right to the inventor by the U. S. government. The right embodied in a patent allows the inventor (or the patent holder, if the patent has been assigned) to exclude others from making or using the invention for a period of time, usually seventeen years. This right prevents anyone, even someone who came up with a similar product independently of the patent owner, from using the patented item or process during the protected time period.*

Patent searches can be conducted to find out if someone else already has a patent on a product, process, or concept that you're planning to build or market.

Trademarks. *A trademark is the right to a name, word, phrase, symbol, logo, color, design, or combination of these elements to identify your products. Like a patent, a trademark right allows the owner to exclude others from using the trademark or from using a mark that is similar enough to cause confusion in others. If you have a name or some other item that you plan on using as a symbol of your business, you may want to have a trademark search conducted to make certain that your name or other item isn't already being used by someone else. If no one else is using it, you should register the trademark with the federal government so that you can prevent anyone else from using it.*

Copyrights. *A copyright is the right to reproduce a certain work if the work is in fixed form. A copyright is created automatically when the work is created and is identified by the symbol ©. However, to be enforceable, the copyright should be recorded with the federal government. A copyright term is for the life of the creator plus 50 years. Copyright infringement can be avoided by showing that the work in question was created independently of the copyrighted work; unlike patent protection, a copyright does not prevent others who create similar works from selling them during the protection period.*

Trade secrets. *An alternative to patent or copyright protection is offered by the state laws on trade secrets. One of the disadvantages of patents and copyrights is that they expire after a fixed time period. In contrast, a trade secret can last forever, so long as the information is kept "secret." Trade secrets do not have to be registered with the government to be enforced; furthermore, things which are not novel enough to be patented (i.e., a method of operation or a customer list) can still be protected by trade secret law. If you feel your business has trade secrets, you must take all reasonable steps to protect their confidentiality; then, if someone steals your secret, you can sue them for misappropriation.*

Part II

Your Business Plan

If you've ever considered or even dreamed of going into business for yourself, you've already engaged in some degree of business planning. Most likely your planning involved a lot of thinking about the personal issues that go with a decision to start your own business.

In its most general sense, business planning is all about taking your entrepreneurial dream and turning it into reality. A business plan is the document you create when you take an idea for a commercial endeavor and work through all the factors that will have an impact on the successful startup, operation, and management of the business or project.

Smart entrepreneurs plan, not because accountants or business advisors tell them to, but because they understand that it increases their chances for success. Sure, there are successful businesses whose owners never create a written plan. But they succeeded *despite* the lack of a formal plan, not *because* of it. How much better might they have done, had their good ideas been coupled with some solid planning?

A business plan can be the vehicle that carries your new idea from the conceptual and planning phase down the road to the building and operational phases.

Or, it may help to establish your business's credentials for purposes of obtaining bank financing or investment by future partners.

A plan for an existing business may deal with just a single aspect of your business, such as a new product introduction and its impact on financial management and other ongoing operational issues.

Once you've created the plan, you can use it to track your progress and to make changes if it appears that you won't be able to hit your targets. We recommend that you revisit your plan at least once a year, to ensure that you spend some time considering long-range plans for your company.

In the next two chapters we'll address your questions about business plans, including:

Chapter 5: Creating Your Business Plan — what can a business plan do for you? What are the key elements of the plan, and what kinds of information should be included? How can you use the plan, once it's committed to paper?

Chapter 6: A Sample Business Plan — what should a business plan look like? We provide a sample of a manufacturer's plan for business expansion, to be financed with a bank loan. You can use this as a model to create your own plan.

Chapter 5

Creating
Your Business Plan

Many busy entrepreneurs think that the only reason to develop a business plan is to convince potential lenders or investors to provide financial backing. This view is a little short-sighted, however. A well-developed plan can serve as one of your most important management tools. A good plan will provide a blueprint and step-by-step instructions on how to translate your idea into a profitably marketed service or product.

In this chapter, we'll explain the parts of the business plan, paying attention to the types of documents that should be included and why they are important. We'll also provide some ideas on how you can use your plan after it's completed. But first, let's look at some of the reasons why creating a business plan can be a very valuable exercise.

WHAT CAN A BUSINESS PLAN DO FOR YOU?

Everyone who opens his or her own business has a plan, however informal. Many small business owners feel that they can keep track of everything without needing to write it down. However, the structure a written plan provides can make it more likely that you will consider all relevant factors and that nothing important will slip through the cracks.

Example

The camera store clerk who decides to open a photographic studio may not have a formal, written plan. Hopefully, however, at some level she organized the relevant information and decided that she can make a living by starting out on her own.

Perhaps she has been moonlighting by taking pictures at weddings and other special occasions, and the demand for her services seems sufficient to support her without the camera store job.

What steps did she take to reach that decision? Hopefully, at a minimum, she sat down and tried to compile a list of what it would mean to leave a salaried position and take on a freelance career. At the top of the list would be a comparison of the net income from freelancing to the net salary from her current job. That would involve estimating the number of jobs she could reasonably expect, the cost to provide the required services, and the prices she could charge. The irregular timing of payments versus a steady income might present personal cash flow problems. The availability and cost of benefits would also rank high. So would all the intangible factors that differentiate self-employment from employee status.

However, even if our hypothetical camera store clerk had a well-thought-out plan entirely in her head, at some point she may need to communicate it to others, such as suppliers, professional advisors, and perhaps a banker from whom she wants to obtain a line of credit. Having a written plan is an essential communication tool, since it's not practical to explain your operations in person each time someone needs to know who you are. Moreover, the odds are that our budding entrepreneur has not thought out every significant aspect of her future business. Going through the process of creating a written plan can help her to be sure she hasn't missed any significant factors that can cause her fledgling business to do a quick nose-dive.

What justifies the additional time and energy you'll spend creating a written plan that presents a blueprint of your business idea? There are a number of good reasons, but they all boil down to this one: *an increased chance for success.*

The Business Plan as a Reality Check

The primary reason that most small business owners need to spend the time writing up a business plan is that the planning process is an excellent way of evaluating your idea before you commit to pursuing it. The plan can also assist in determining if the return on your business idea is greater than the risks you assume. The process of creating the plan is likely to reveal factors that you might otherwise not consider. And that can save you big money, and a lot of time.

Case Study — What Poor Planning Can Do

Some years back, before there were a dozen gourmet coffee shops in every town, most people bought coffee in the grocery store. There were a few specialty stores that roasted and sold their own beans, and a couple of mail order firms that sold rather expensive whole bean coffee.

An entrepreneur saw an opportunity to bridge the gap between the specialty shops, which purchased the beans green and roasted them, and the supermarkets, which mostly carried canned coffee.

He took a chance, borrowed some money, and opened a coffee store. He found a mail order source that would sell to him cheaply enough so that he could compete against the few local specialty shops that existed. As time went on, he found a local roaster that didn't operate a competing retail outlet, and he was able to reduce his cost while maintaining or increasing the quality of the product.

Even though sales volume slowly increased and his profit margin rose as he reduced costs, it seemed that he could never make ends meet. He restocked coffee only as his bins were depleted, added teas, spices, and brewing equipment, but never really hit it big as he had hoped. Sales growth slowly declined as more competitors arrived on the scene. When the bigger chains entered his midwestern market, the game was over. He couldn't hope to compete with Gloria Jean's or Starbuck's. The business slowly ground to a halt, superseded by the larger mass marketers.

What went wrong? It would be easy to say that he failed because of the unanticipated entry of new competitors into the market. But that was really just a symptom of the failure to plan. When he opened his first store, he knew what coffee cost, he knew what his fixed expenses were, and he set prices that let him cover expenses and generate a small living wage. But he didn't go any further. He had no plan that tied advertising to specific sales targets. When business was slow, his creditors and suppliers were paid late. And the big chains were already swiftly expanding across the country, even though they hadn't reached his market yet.

In retrospect, this entrepreneur often bemoaned the fact that he could have positioned the business in such a way that the big chains, rather than ignoring him, would have bought him out. Perhaps he could have. Had he kept closer tabs on trends in the industry, he would have realized that the competition wasn't just selling beans anymore. They were opening early to offer commuters fresh morning coffee and bakery goods.

Moral of the story: if he had taken the time to create a formal business plan, he would have had the opportunity to more closely examine some of the assumptions he made when he started out.

Your Business's Resume

Just as a person seeking a job prepares a resume that outlines qualifications, experience, and other relevant information, a business will have a variety of uses for a "resume" of its own.

Probably the most common reason for writing a business plan is that when you apply for a bank loan, you'll usually be asked to provide a business plan as part of your loan application package. It's unlikely that you'll qualify for financing if you don't have a plan that clearly demonstrates how your business will thrive and prosper (and thus, how it will be able to pay back the loan).

Portions of the plan can also be used to introduce prospective employees to your business. Particularly if you intend to hire long-time or high-level employees, you'll want to present a fair picture of what your business does and what the employee can expect regarding income and growth opportunities based on the plan's projections.

A Timetable for Operations

A business plan identifies the essential events that must occur and actions that must be taken in the correct order, and it sets forth a clear timetable for accomplishing them.

It can also provide the foundation for a tracking system that lets you evaluate your business's progress. Deviations between actual and planned results provide clues that you need to make changes to reduce costs, increase revenues, or change other aspects of operations.

Example

If your plan projects that the business will be the successful bidder on five jobs in the first quarter of the year, and on April 1 you've only gotten two jobs, you can take steps to adjust. But you need to know that there is a need to adjust. That's why a good business plan has definitive targets associated with a timetable for achievement. It's a lot easier to know how you're doing if you started out with solid performance expectations.

Planning for the Future

Preparing for the future is what a business plan is all about. So why is it listed here as a separate reason for having a business plan? Simply because a business plan positions you to *continue* your planning habit beyond the period covered by your first plan. You've already paid the upfront cost in time and effort to assemble a plan. Refining it, revising it, and extending your projections beyond the original planning window will consume far less of your time.

Events Triggering the Need for a Plan

- *You want to open a new business.*

- *Your business has grown.*

- *You want to introduce a new product or enter a new market.*

- *You want to acquire a new business or a franchise.*

Preparing To Write Your Business Plan

Putting a business plan together requires you to translate your thoughts about how you're going to run your business (and how it will perform) into a format that is dictated, in large part, by the business you're in and the expectations of your audience.

There are a few key issues you need to examine before you can actually start to write your plan.

Who Are Your Audiences?

As you're developing your business plan, you'll need to keep in mind who will be reading it and what they will expect to learn from it. One way to categorize the people who will make up your audience is to divide them into two groups: the internal audience, namely, you and any key employees or co-owners; and the external audience, including your banker or potential investors.

If you're creating a business plan primarily for the purpose of evaluating the viability of a new business, or an expansion or other change to an existing business, the primary audience is you. In that case, the process of considering a lot of details and contingencies is the most important aspect of the plan (for example, what will you do if sales are 5 percent, or 20 percent, lower than you expect.)

If you have partners, co-owners, or a board of directors, they should see the plan after its completion. They may also have significant input into the plan as it's being developed. Give some consideration to the level of detail that your internal audience will need or want. In many cases, you may want to share parts of the plan with your key employees — most likely your executive summary which contains your top-line goals for the year.

If the plan is destined to be shown to a lender, you will want to emphasize the financial side of your business, including detailed historical and projected cash-flow budgets. You will also have to do a certain amount of "selling" or explaining why you and your business are such worthy investments.

If the plan is being created for venture capitalists or outside investors, they will want all the financial information that a banker would need, plus all the marketing, operational, and personnel information they can get their hands on. These investors view themselves as owners, so they want a lot of detail. They also need to get a strong sense of your vision, experience, and commitment to the company. You may want to hire a consultant to help you polish up your plan or even write it for you.

How Far Out Can You Plan?

By its nature, a business plan requires you to project how events will turn out in the future. If the assumptions on which you base your planning are sound, the results of your operations may be very close to what you predicted. Over time, however, small deviations add up, and a plan that accurately predicted how your first few months would turn out will become increasingly inaccurate. So, how far out do you plan?

As a general rule, for an "average" business, a three-to-five-year plan is a reasonable starting point. The level of detail will drop as your plan covers periods further into the future. The cash flows that are tracked weekly or monthly during the first year of operation may be projected by quarter in the second year, and annually in the third through fifth years.

WRITING YOUR BUSINESS PLAN

After you've considered the purpose of your plan and done some background preparation, it's time to consider the actual elements that you'll include in the written document.

A business plan customarily has certain elements or sections. The following pages identify and describe each of the elements that will make up your plan. They are presented in the order in which they *usually* appear in the plan. But don't feel constrained to follow this exact format if another way makes more sense because of the nature of your business.

In any event, it pays to at least mention all the major issues listed below, even the ones that are relatively less significant to your particular business. Someone who's reading your plan will be more confident about your assessment of the situation if you identify such issues and resolve them, however quickly.

Common Components of a Business Plan

Cover page — identifies you and your business, and dates the plan.

Table of contents — makes it easy for readers to find particular documents.

Executive summary — this is arguably the most important single part of your document. It provides a high-level overview of the entire plan that emphasizes the factors that you believe will lead to success.

Business background — provides company-specific information, describing the business organization, history, and the product or service the business will provide.

Marketing plan — *presents an analysis of the market conditions that the business faces, sets forth the marketing strategy that the business will follow, and provides a detailed schedule of marketing activities to support sales.*

Action plans — *shows how operational and management issues will be resolved, including contingency planning.*

Financial projections — *your projections (and historical financial information, if you have it) demonstrate how the business can be expected to do financially if the business plan's assumptions are sound.*

Appendix — *presents supporting documents, statistical analysis, product marketing materials, resumes of key employees, etc.*

Format and Presentation Issues

You want your plan to look professional and be a useful tool. There are a number of things to do to ensure that is the case:

- Print the plan on a high-quality paper. Print on one side of the paper only.

- Use a typeface that is easy to read, and a font size that is large enough to prevent eyestrain. This may require financial projections to be spread over several pages in order to maintain readability.

- If those in your business or industry use specialized language or acronyms, use them sparingly and be sure to define any terms that someone outside your area of expertise wouldn't readily know.

- Keep the plan fairly short and concise. For most businesses, 15-30 pages will be sufficient. You can always provide additional detail in an appendix, if required.

- Include samples of ads, marketing material, and any other information that aids in the presentation of your plan.

- Be certain to carefully edit the document. Spelling and grammar errors do not make a good impression.

- Bind the plan so that it lies flat when opened. But don't go overboard on expensive binders, embossing, etc. Elevating the form of the plan over its substance can raise doubts among those reading the plan.

The Cover Page and Table of Contents

If you have spent any time and effort at all on a company logo, slogan, or other identifying graphic or text, the cover page is the place to highlight it.

In addition, the cover sheet contains identification information about the business, including business address, telephone numbers, facsimile numbers, etc. The cover sheet should state the date that the plan was prepared, and the period it covers. It should identify the person to contact regarding any questions about the plan (generally, you).

Work Smart

If you have prepared multiple copies of your business plan, you might also put a copy number on the cover page to help you ensure that none of them go astray.

The table of contents should fit on one page, and accurately lead a reader to each of the documents in the plan. If the plan is lengthy, consider dividing it up into separately numbered sections to make it easier for readers to find specific documents.

The Executive Summary

The executive summary must be concise, specific, and well-written. It summarizes the highlights of the plan, for those who won't read any further.

So, it should provide a brief snapshot of the plan, with sales, spending, and profit summary figures. The summary emphasizes those factors that will make the business a success. It must contain the key facts about market size, trends, company goals, spending, return on investment, capital expenditures, and funding required.

Work Smart

For new businesses or businesses seeking funding, credibility and excitement are key elements of the executive summary. Venture capitalists receive hundreds of plans each month, and read just a few from cover to cover. The decision not to invest in your business can be based on nothing more than a 20-second scan of the executive summary.

Business Background

The business background section of your business plan generally consists of two to four sections that present information that is specific to your business. You may have gathered substantial information about competitors and the industry in general in the course of considering your business plans. This is *not* the place for that information. Instead, concentrate solely on your own business.

The Business Organization

This portion of the plan sets forth the current status of operations, the management structure of the organization, and the identification of key personnel. If the plan is being created for an existing business, historical information is also included. By reading this section, the reader can determine:

- the type of business (e.g., wholesale, retail, manufacturing, service, etc.)

- the type of legal entity (e.g., corporation, partnership, sole proprietorship, etc.), and who are the major owners or shareholders

- when the business was established, and under what conditions

- where it is located

- the type of facilities, if any (e.g., retail store, manufacturing plant, etc.), although you may need to devote a separate section to this subject if your facilities are very important to your business

- the number and type of employees, if any

- the organizational structure, including a chart showing who is responsible for what, if appropriate

- operational information, such as a schedule of the hours that the business is open

- identity of key employees, if any, including a description of their abilities that make them vital to the success of the business (you may decide to include resumes of key employees in the appendix).

The information you provide should go beyond a simple statement of facts. For example, if you chose to incorporate rather than to operate as a sole proprietor, what factors influenced your decision? Explaining why a particular decision was made goes a long way in helping the reader understand your decision-making process.

The business background is also the place to identify the goals and objectives of the business by explaining in general terms what business you are in or want to be in.

Product or Service Description

The starting point for this section is a clear and simple statement of what the product is or what service your business will provide.

Avoid the temptation to compare your offering to similar services or products offered by others. Reserve that analysis for the marketing plan, where you will discuss competitors and potential competitors.

Instead, focus on those factors that make your offering unique and preferable to customers. Explain what it does, how it works, how long it lasts, what options are available, etc.

A useful way to present product or service information is to create a features/benefits chart. A feature is a specific product attribute or characteristic. A benefit is the advantage a customer or user will derive from the product feature.

Consider the following table, which illustrates this type of analysis for a theoretical high-tech wristwatch:

Auto-Watch Features and Benefits Analysis	
Feature	**Benefit**
Battery has an indefinite life — recharges whenever watch is exposed to light.	Consumer doesn't have to deal with time, inconvenience, and expense of periodic battery replacement.
Time signal from National Institute of Standards and Technology updates time automatically by radio.	Consumer never has to set the time and can rely on near absolute accuracy.
Dial lights up at night.	Consumer doesn't have to use two hands to see time in dark.
Receives global positioning satellite signals and uses them to determine time zone.	Consumer doesn't have to adjust watch while traveling.

Business Facility Assessment

The first question to address here is why you need a business facility, and what kind you require. At one extreme, a consultant may perform most services in space provided by clients, and may maintain a small home office to store reference materials and business records. At the other extreme, a manufacturing business may require access to rail transport, room for manufacturing operations and storage, parking facilities for a lot of employees, etc.

Once you have assessed and explained your facility requirements, you'll want to look at the cost. Your business plan should also describe the basic aspects of your facility (age, size, general location) as well as the important aspects of any equipment that you may need.

Planning for People

A business plan can help to organize the roles and responsibilities of all the people involved in your business. Even if it's just for your own benefit, a checklist of all the different tasks performed by individuals (or classes of individuals, if you have many employees) may be useful.

In writing your plan, it's a good idea to show that you've considered options other than full-time employees. In many cases, a startup business or a business taking on a new product, service, or market will experience a short-term need for a lot of help. How you fill that short-term need will be dictated in large part by your expectations regarding business direction and performance.

It can be difficult to predict how many people your business is going to need, particularly if you're just starting out. As you consider each important area, you'll develop a picture of all the activities that go into running your business. Also consider the "key person" concept. Is there anyone whose presence in the business is vital (other than you)? If so, it makes sense to consider what your business would do in the event that a key player is lost.

Marketing Plan

A business plan is the blueprint for taking your idea for a product or service and turning it into a commercially viable reality. The marketing portion of a business plan normally includes a market analysis and a description of your marketing strategy. It may include a detailed timetable of planned marketing and sales events.

Market Analysis

This section presents your conclusions regarding external market factors that will affect your business. It examines the totality of the business environment in which you will compete. Topics addressed in the market analysis include the existence and type of competitors, the characteristics of your target customers, market size, distribution costs, trends in your industry and in the market in general, etc.

The market analysis sets the stage for presenting your marketing strategy. That strategy sets forth your plan for successfully competing in your selected market.

Marketing Strategy

The marketing strategy portion of your business plan presents your approach in providing products or services to your customers. It explains, at a high level, what you've determined to do to get your customers to buy in the desired quantities. Someone who reads your marketing strategy should come away with a "big picture" view of how your business will present itself to the market segment in which you will compete.

In the marketing strategy section of your plan, you'll address issues such as:

- identification of your target buyers

- the market segment in which you'll compete

- the reasons why the product or service you offer is unique

- your pricing philosophy

- plans for further market research

- ongoing product or service development plans

You'll find it useful to keep in mind the 4 Ps of marketing as you define the scope of your marketing strategy.

The "Four Ps" of Marketing

- **Product** — *what is the good or service that your business will offer? How is that product better than those against which it will compete? Why will people buy it?*

- **Price** — *how much can you charge? How do you balance between sales volume and price to maximize income?*

- **Promotion** — *how will your product or service be positioned in the marketplace? Will your product carry a premium image with a price to match? Will it be an inexpensive, no-frills alternative to similar offerings from other businesses? What kinds of advertising and packaging will you use?*

- **Place** — *which sales channels will you use? Will you sell by telephone or will your product be carried in retail outlets? Which channel will economically reach your market?*

Marketing and Sales Plan

Your marketing and sales plan provides the details on how you plan to reach your targeted customers and how you will effectively market your product or service to those customers. For example, the marketing plan specifies the types of advertising that you will use and the timing of those advertisements. In essence, the marketing plan takes the marketing strategy that you developed to a practical, action-oriented level. It sets forth the specific steps you will take to sell your product or service and provides a timetable for those actions to occur.

The marketing and sales plan usually includes a calendar that ties marketing and sales activities to specific operational events. For example, an advertising campaign may begin some months before a new product is ready to be sold. As the date of the new product introduction approaches, the ad campaign would be stepped up. Once the new product hits the market, additional advertising is used to support specific sales objectives.

Action Plans

Action plans are what we call the portion of the business plan that explains how you will operate and manage your business, in areas not covered in the marketing plan. It can include activities such as:

- employee hiring and management

- obtaining and working with vendors for needed materials and supplies

- ensuring that production takes place as planned

- order fulfillment

- collections

- providing customer service and support after the sale

- dealing with unexpected occurrences or changing conditions

These types of issues can be conveniently grouped into three categories for purposes of dealing with them in your plan. The categories are the operations plan, the management plan, and contingency plans. For a new business, you should cover all of these areas. If you're expanding an existing business, it may be sufficient to concentrate on those areas that will change because of the expansion.

Planning Your Business Operations

Your operations plan summarizes how you will create and deliver your product or service. You may find it useful to look at your business as if it were a linear process that starts with raw materials and ends with a delivery to a satisfied customer.

You'll probably be surprised at how many steps there are and how critical the timing and duration of each step is.

While it's easy to relate to production issues in a manufacturing or other process where goods are fabricated, grown, or otherwise produced, the concept is also applicable to other types of businesses.

Example

As a consultant you are engaged to help a company convert from a paper-based billing system to a computer-based system. The end "product" that you will deliver is assistance in selecting the appropriate software and hardware, training on that new equipment, and supervision of the process by which the data is converted to electronic format. You can do a great job without "producing" anything tangible beyond, perhaps, documentation of the process.

This doesn't mean that you can ignore "production." Consider all the work that you would have to do. First, a working knowledge of the client's existing system has to be acquired. Then, software and hardware combinations are evaluated in light of the client's needs and budget. A conversion process has to be developed so that those portions of the existing data that carry over to the new system are available in the new format. Documentation must be prepared to train the client's employees in using the new system. Whether you thought of them that way or not, each of these activities would be part of your production process.

Another production issue you may have to consider in drafting a plan is that there may be situations in which completing the job requires work outside your areas of expertise.

Example

A self-employed plumber deals primarily in pipes, faucets, and fixtures. Those pipes have a nasty habit of being inside walls, and when the plumbing goes bad, the walls frequently stand between the plumber and the pipe. A good plumber knows that the production process goes beyond his or her primary area of expertise and will plan for the time and costs associated with the non-plumbing activities, such as plastering, required to satisfy customers.

Planning Management Activities

Small business owners have to orchestrate all of the different activities that are needed to make a business work. These activities include managing any employees you have, as well as performing the back office or administrative duties required to keep the business running.

It's easy to overlook management as a major drain on your time and resources, but even a very small business can present some complex logistical issues. Almost every business relies to some extent on outsiders to contribute to the success of the business. Keeping everything on schedule requires you to monitor all of the diverse activities and actively intervene when things aren't going according to plan. If you operate an existing business, you know just how many balls you have to keep in the air at once. If you are just starting out, don't underestimate the demands of managing.

Planning for Contingencies

No matter how carefully you plan, the likelihood of everything going exactly as you anticipate is small.

Whenever you make assumptions regarding the market and the capabilities of your business, you know that many of those assumptions aren't very precise. While your assumptions may realistically account for reasonably foreseeable events, that doesn't ensure their accuracy.

For example, if your business is dependent on borrowed funds and you plan to obtain and use a line of credit, you have to make some assumptions about interest rates. It's a good idea to look at a range of rates, rather than a single number, to test the impact of changes. Making alternate assumptions and planning around them is the best way to deal with events that are out of your control.

Example

Let's say that your business plans to obtain a line of credit, and you negotiate an interest rate of prime plus 2 percent. You estimate that the rate you'll pay is 9 percent, but you can live with a rate as high as 12 percent.

Obviously, anything below 9 percent makes it that much easier to meet your planned goals. But what happens if the rate goes to 14 percent or even 20 percent? It happened in the early 1980s, and the change happened over a relatively short period of time. What would you do?

A contingency plan is an effort to avoid having your business disrupted when market or economic conditions change beyond what you're prepared to handle without major adjustments to your business.

It's a good idea to think about the kinds of changes that would have the greatest impact on your business. For example, if a major external threat is a direct competitor opening up near your location, you can plan for that eventuality. Perhaps you'll lower your prices, stay open longer hours, or institute a frequent customer bonus plan.

Contingency plans can be included in your business plan in a number of ways. For example, your financial statements can incorporate a footnote explaining that the projected interest rate can go up by as much as 3 percent before your profit margin is seriously affected. Or your discussion of how many employees you'll need can state that an additional production person will be hired when sales of $X are achieved.

Interestingly, contingencies don't always involve things going worse than expected.

Example

Assume that your initial marketing plan calls for a mass mailing to 1,000 prospective customers. Assume further that a primary selling point is the immediacy of the need for the customers to act. You expect to get perhaps 10 to 20 paying customers out of the mailing.

Instead, you get 243. What do you do? You've sold the market on the need to act quickly, but your business isn't prepared to handle that many customers in the time frame required. If you have a contingency plan, you're ready to act. In this example, it may involve bringing in temporary help, outsourcing certain tasks, or even asking competitors to do the work on a contract basis.

Ultimately, you can only go so far in contingency planning. What's important is that you've identified those areas in which your plan is vulnerable to variable factors that can affect your business. If you have already considered possible responses to changes in the market, you can react more quickly than if you've never even thought of the consequences. Thus, whether things go better or worse than expected, you have already identified the likely causes and considered your responses.

Financial Statements and Projections

Unless you are thinking of starting a religious or charitable organization, the main reason you want to own a business is because you think you can make money at it. The drive to be your own boss might have caused you to quit being an employee and *start* your business, but the quest for income is what keeps it going. When you develop a business plan, financial projections and cash flow analysis are among the most critical elements.

The type of financial information that you're going to need to prepare this analysis will depend on whether your business is an established enterprise or is just starting out.

If you're writing a plan for a new business, you'll need to survey your personal assets and borrowing ability. However, since your business probably has few assets and no prior financial history, you're going to have to rely almost entirely on financial projections; that is, *prospective* financial statements based upon assumptions that you've made regarding how your business is going to perform in the future.

You plan to open a business that builds custom furniture. You used your projected cash flow statement to study the effect of changes in the cost of materials and supplies. It reveals that, if those costs rise by more than 20 percent from their present levels, your monthly receipts might not be enough to pay your suppliers and employees. Your contingency plans might include raising your sales price or securing a line of credit until costs return to expected levels.

You have a close personal interest in the financial performance of your business. So does everyone else who might be looking at your business plan. Not surprisingly, the portions of your plan dealing with the projected financial performance of your plan will come under the closest scrutiny. A potential lender will want to know what you'll be doing with the money it lends you and how you plan to generate the necessary income to pay the money back.

Fortunately, the financial projections are the most formalistic and stylized documents that you will have to prepare. There are certain accounting conventions that you are expected to follow. The point is to project, in a mathematically correct fashion, the anticipated monetary results of your business operations.

Items To Include in the Financial Portion of the Business Plan

- *projected profit and loss statements*

- *projected cash flow budgets*

- *current and historical financial information, or startup business financial information*

In some cases, you may need to prepare the financial portions of your plan in conformance with generally accepted accounting principles (GAAP). This will usually occur when you're preparing a plan in an effort to obtain a loan or line of credit, and the bank or potential investor you're dealing with requests it.

In that case, it's likely you'll need to get an accountant involved in preparing that portion of the plan. If the financial material was created in conformity with GAAP, that fact should be noted in the plan. The same is true if the financial statements have been audited.

Projected Profit and Loss Statements

A projected profit and loss statement is a financial document that reflects the amount of profit or loss you expect your business to generate in future periods.

More specifically, it lists revenues (from sales or services provided), your cost for goods or services provided, operating expenses (such as wages, rent, advertising), and net income or loss. You should include projections for at least three years, including the current year. See the projected statements in our sample business plan in the next chapter.

Save Time

Depending on whether you are preparing a projected profit and loss statement for an existing business or a startup enterprise, you may have some difficulty coming up with reliable estimates. Financial information services like Dun & Bradstreet can provide information regarding average industry expenditures for cost of goods sold and general and administrative expenses.

You'll also want to talk to your prospective vendors and suppliers. These businesses are not only a good source of market information, but they can also provide you with fairly accurate estimates of what your startup expenses may include.

Projected Cash Flow Statements

Your projected cash flow is very important to most lenders because it provides an indication of whether you will have enough cash to pay your suppliers, vendors, and other creditors on time (not to mention the lender itself). This information also functions as a planning tool for you. If your cash flow estimates show that you will occasionally not have enough money to pay your bills, you can arrange in advance for other sources of funds to get you through cash flow crunches.

You determine your cash flow by taking your inflows of cash (cash you're receiving) and subtracting your outflows of cash (cash you're paying out). We recommend that you use the format of the cash flow budget worksheet provided in our sample business plan. You'll generally need to include three years' worth of projected statements.

Historical Financial Information

An existing business can bolster the credibility of its business plan by documenting the results of its ongoing operations. A proven track record is very persuasive evidence of your chances for continued success. Hopefully, you've been creating and maintaining financial records since the inception of your business. If so, most of your work is done.

The following list describes the types of information that you would ordinarily include in a business plan. As always, the relative importance of each type of document will vary with the characteristics of your particular business.

What To Include for an Existing Business

If you're assembling a business plan for an existing business, you're going to want to make sure that you include the following historical financial information for the last three to five years (or from the inception of the business if less than three years old):

- *A balance sheet,* which lists the type and value of your business's assets, liabilities, and ownership interest.

- *An income statement,* which lists the revenues, expenses, and net income of your business for a stated period of time, usually a year.

- *Your business's tax returns* for the three most recent years.

- *A cash flow budget,* which lists by month the cash you took in, the cash you spent, and the cash surplus or deficit you had at the end of a month.

Startup Business Financial Information

If you're just starting out, you face a special challenge because you don't have an established track record on which to rely. There is no history of operations, profitable or otherwise. Instead, you must rely heavily on your ability to sell yourself as a potentially successful business owner.

Therefore, your plan should include personal financial information that will identify the amount and source of funding that you have available to invest in the business. It should provide specific details regarding any personal assets that you plan to use in running your business. Other documents that may be required, particularly if you're trying to obtain outside financing, are your personal income tax returns for the last few years.

As with an established business, you're also going to need to provide projected profit and loss statements and projected cash flow budget worksheets. These documents quantify the results you expect to achieve through your operations. Be sure to include any startup costs that you'll incur prior to opening your business when you develop these estimated financial statements.

Business Plan Appendix

The appendix is the repository for those items that aren't part of the plan itself but that are helpful or useful to someone reading the plan. It contains the material that supports and explains the conclusions and assumptions contained within the plan. If you think it's likely that a reader will seek further information regarding some portion of the plan, include the appropriate material in the appendix.

The appendix might include sample marketing material, such as copies of ads you plan to run or brochures to be distributed to potential customers. If you are just starting out, consider including your resume or resumes of key employees.

KEEPING YOUR PLAN CURRENT

In order to continue benefiting from your plan, you must keep it current. You preserve your time invested in the plan by periodically making changes that reflect actual business results, assumptions, and the market. Remember, it's almost always easier to edit an existing document than to create a new one from scratch.

Many people think of "planning" as an annual process. Thousands of companies publish an annual plan each year, outlining their expectations about operating results for the coming 12 months.

Many factors that affect your business will be tied to some annual cycle. For example, income taxes are due yearly, and federal safety rules require posting annual summaries of information. If you don't engage in some planning at least once a year, you can get some unpleasant surprises when, for example, you prepare your income tax return. This and other factors make annual planning a reasonable starting point, though your circumstances may require a different planning interval.

In between the scheduled planning windows, you can use the plan to track actual performance against projected performance. Many large businesses routinely schedule a mid-year or quarterly review of the plan to ensure that there's an opportunity to make mid-course corrections when things aren't going as planned.

Chapter 6

A Sample Business Plan

To see how the parts of the business plan described in the last chapter can fit together, take a look at the sample plan that follows.

While we've described the documents that should be included in a typical business plan, keep in mind that the presentation of the information is, to a large extent, dependent on the purpose for which the plan is written and the business it describes. Moreover, every business plan should capture the unique characteristics of the business and the people who will run it.

Our sample plan is one that's designed to be presented to the bank, in an effort to obtain financing for a manufacturing firm's business expansion. As a result, it emphasizes those elements of the business's operations that will change if the financing is obtained, and presents a substantial amount of historical financial information.

If your business is new and you're creating a business plan as a way of determining the viability of your enterprise, your plan will contain more comprehensive explanations of anticipated operations, but fewer financial documents. See *Chapter 5: Creating Your Business Plan,* for more information on what should go into a plan for a new business.

Note: to conserve space, the cover page and table of contents has been omitted, as have all graphics, such as company logos. These elements should be included in any business plan that you prepare.

Breakaway Bicycle Company — Business Plan

Breakway Bicycle Company is a small manufacturer of high-end bicycle frames. It builds both mountain bike and racing bike frames for sale primarily to professional bicycle racers. In the 1990s, increased interest in mountain biking as a competitive sport and the exposure that bike racing received as a result of Olympic and Tour de France events provided BBC with an opportunity to expand its business. Up to that time, a small number of BBC's frames were sold to non-professional riders who nevertheless want the very best equipment available, regardless of price.

In order to better serve this emerging market, BBC proposed to add additional workstations and designer-builders to increase its capacity for custom frames. The BBC business plan envisions making better use of existing leased space and leasing additional space to meet its needs. In addition, the frame-building equipment necessary to create three more workstations had to be acquired. The company's owners prepared this business plan in 2000 to present to bankers with the goal of obtaining expansion financing.

Executive Summary

Breakaway Bicycle Company designs and builds custom bicycle frames to the exact specifications of the finest road and mountain bike racing professionals in the world. Breakaway has earned this right because its founder and master builder, Mike Giro, handcrafts road and mountain frames that satisfy the one common specification of all competitive cyclists — they help them to win races.

Since 1990, Breakaway has designed and built bike frames for racing professionals and those biking enthusiasts who take their riding seriously and want to own the best equipment. As more and more of the population gains an interest in competitive cycling, the demand for custom built bicycles has also increased. Many individuals, particularly those interested in mountain biking, have found that there is a tremendous interest in competitive mountain biking, which includes grueling cross-country races and gravity-defying events such as the "in your face" downhill racing. Based on marketing figures, this interest increased following the 1996 Summer Olympics in Atlanta where mountain bike racing made its Olympic medal debut.

To meet the expected demand for custom built bike frames that can handle this type of riding, as well as road racing, Breakaway is seeking the financing necessary to add new workstations and hire additional designer-builders. The cost to purchase and install the additional workstations is $60,000. The additional salary expense is projected to increase labor expenses by $6,250 per month. If this investment is made, marketing projections and written commitments from several mountain bike racing teams in the U.S. and Europe reflect a 25% increase in bike frame sales. This increase translates into sales revenue of $1,390,800 for 2000 and $1,619,600 for 2001.

Business Overview

Breakaway Bicycle Company was started by Mike Giro in 1990 and began building high quality hand-crafted bicycle frames. Because these bike frames were popular with serious bicycle enthusiasts, Breakaway moved from a workshop behind Mr. Giro's house to a larger shop located on LeTour Street in Boulder, Colorado in 1993. The company now employs 10 people, including Mr. Giro, who design, build, and test each new bicycle frame. The great majority of customers that Breakaway builds bikes for are serious cyclists who require their road bikes and mountain bikes to be light, stiff, responsive, and race worthy.

Business Structure

Breakaway Bicycle Company is a closely held Colorado corporation created in 1990. For federal income tax purposes, Breakaway is classified as a subchapter S corporation. There are three shareholder directors, each of whom is an officer working for the company.

Organization

Mike Giro	Managing Director of Operations
Steve Brown	Director of Marketing and Sales
Jane Giro	Chief Financial Officer and Treasurer

Management Profiles

Mike Giro has 20 years of experience designing and building high performance bicycle frames and components. Mr. Giro became involved with designing frames as a teenager when he assisted a local frame builder in designing the bike frames for the U.S. Junior National Bicycle Team. As a member of this team, Mr. Giro was able to address the technical aspects of design with the practical insight developed from personally experiencing the shortcomings of various bike frames.

Over the next 10 years, Mr. Giro worked for various frame builders and experimented with different metal alloys and carbon composite designs to find a feather-light frame that would meet the heavy demands of a professional racer. As a result of his success in this research, he became an integral member of the production team that changed the face of cycling by designing a large part of the aerodynamic frames and components that provided the decisive advantage in several racing victories, not the least of which was the 1989 Tour De France.

In 1990, Mr. Giro started his own custom frame building company. Almost immediately, he obtained contracts to build racing bicycles for two of the top professional teams in the United States. As a result of this exposure and a number of very favorable articles in industry periodicals, the demand for Breakaway bike frames continued to increase. To meet this demand, Mr. Giro hired six designers-framebuilders and moved to a larger facility near downtown Boulder in 1992. Since 1992, Mr. Giro has gained recognition for the custom-made mountain bicycle frames he has designed for two professional downhill racing teams. Currently, Mr. Giro is paid a salary of $100,000.

Steve Brown has been involved in bicycling almost as long as Mike Giro, but from a different perspective. Steve Brown was a professional racer on the European circuit for 12 years prior to coming to work for Breakaway. As a member of several European teams, Mr. Brown developed relationships with several Director Sportifs (Racing Team Managers), which he has utilized to gain access to those individuals who make the decisions regarding team frame builders. To date, Mr. Brown has obtained contracts to build bicycle frames for four racing teams in Europe.

Currently, Mr. Brown has made great inroads in the European mountain bike racing sport by providing frames to a number of mountain bike teams. He has also had success in gaining corporate sponsorship for mountain bike racing events in France and Germany. Currently, Mr. Brown is paid a salary of $60,000 plus bonuses.

The financial management experience that Jane Giro brings to Breakaway has been a key component in its continued financial stability. Ms. Giro, a certified public accountant, developed substantial experience during her nine years at a public accounting firm that specialized in consulting with small and midsize corporations. Using this experience, she was able to plan many of Breakaway's expenditures for plant and equipment as well as marketing and advertising so that they coincided with Breakaway's period of cash flow surpluses. By prudently managing Breakaway, the company was able to avert the financial disaster that many bicycle companies experienced in the early 1990s when demand for bikes temporarily contracted. Currently, Ms. Giro has been closely monitoring the market expansion in Europe and reviewing the contracts and initial startup costs related to this expansion. Ms. Giro is paid a salary of $45,000.

Marketing Plan

Market Analysis

According to a study done by the Department of Transportation, approximately 25 million bicycles are purchased every year. The vast majority of these bicycles (96%) are built on an assembly line and sell for an average price of $200. The remaining 4% of the market are high-end custom built bicycles that cost an average of $1,500. Accordingly, the custom built bicycle market generates revenues of $1.5 billion on sales of one million frames. Because the Summer Olympic Games are scheduled for 2000, projected sales are expected to be significantly higher. An industry study assembled in 1997 reflected that the sale of all types of bicycles and accessories increased 30% following the 1996 Summer Olympics.

A survey taken by The Bike Tour, a monthly bicycling periodical, shows that the type of individual that purchases a custom built bicycle typically is a serious bicycling enthusiast. This person rides over three thousand miles a year and is interested in using the equipment that is best suited to handle this much riding. Accordingly, this individual may spend several thousand dollars a year to purchase equipment that will improve the performance and enjoyment of a bike ride. It is these bicycle enthusiasts that are the target market in which Breakaway Bicycle Company is hoping to increase its market share.

A large number of individuals who purchase custom built bike frames live in the Western, Southwestern, and Pacific Northwestern sections of the U.S. They are between the ages of 24 and 45, have some college education, and have a median income of $45,000. In the past, the target market was predominately male, but the efforts made by bike companies, like Breakaway, to market high end bikes to women in recent years has had a significant impact. Sales figures for 1997 show that 25% of all custom made frames were sold to women, an 80% jump over 1992 sales figures.

There are currently two general categories of bicycle riders — mountain bike riders and road bike riders. The popularity of mountain bikes is so great that most, if not all, custom built frame companies have added at least one, if not several, mountain bike frames to their sales catalogue.

In fact, in almost all cases, mountain bike sales have far outpaced road bike sales every year for the last five years. Based on an industry survey of all bike makers included in the Bike Tour article, the sale of mountain bikes is expected to increase by 20% every year for the next five years. This projection is based on the fact that serious road bike enthusiasts are finally being converted to mountain bikes and the second-ever Olympic mountain biking event in 2000 should generate even more interest in mountain bike racing.

Currently, there are five large custom bike frame companies in the U.S. that split up a large share (75%) of this market. Breakaway is not currently among this group of five. However, if the company can expand production to meet current demand, projected sales indicate that Breakaway will also experience an increase in mountain bike sales within the next three years (see Revenue Projections). This increase in sales is attributable to the increasing popularity of mountain bike racing in the U.S. and Europe and the name recognition that Breakaway is building for the quality of their road and mountain bikes.

Strengths, Weaknesses, Opportunities, and Threats Analysis

Strengths. The strengths that Breakaway brings to the marketplace are considerable. Breakaway has built a very good reputation with professional road and mountain bike racers in the United States. With the work Mr. Brown is doing in Europe, Breakaway is continuing to take market share even from those frame builders who have been around since the 1920s. But the greatest strength that Breakaway possesses is the innovative approach it has taken to designing and building frames. Being a smaller company, Breakaway has greater flexibility than its larger competitors to try different materials, geometries, and welding methods since it does not have to consult with 20 engineers to see whose idea is best. This means that the latest breakthrough in design will be implemented and tested before it is even off the drawing board at other companies.

Weaknesses. Because of its relative small size, Breakaway is not a common name among non-professional cyclists. If Breakaway had the resources to produce more custom designed bikes, it would be possible to increase sales revenues in the lucrative market that is made up of non-professional riders who, nevertheless, are serious about their cycling and want the best equipment in the market. Currently, five of the larger custom design framebuilders in the U.S. and Europe are dominating this market that research has shown generates total sales of $800 million worldwide.

Breakaway also has a substantial amount of work to do in order to obtain a large portion of the European market. Breakaway is currently competing with frame builders who have been designing and building frames for professionals since the 1920s and whose names are now almost synonymous with cycling. Furthermore, with European cyclists, national loyalty often is a factor in choosing a framebuilder.

Opportunities. If Breakaway can obtain the necessary resources, the opportunities are almost limitless. Under the marketing efforts of Mr. Brown, Breakaway has made steady inroads in establishing a presence in the European road racing circuit. Furthermore, several professional riders have test ridden Breakaway frames and have found them to be far more technically innovative then many European custom built frames. Clearly, the market for Breakaway frames would increase if the company had the manpower, machinery, and facility space to custom build a greater number of frames. Based on the Bike Tour survey, the demand for custom road frames can be expected to increase by 20 percent in the year following the Olympics, and then experience 2 to 3 percent annual growth for the next four years. Accordingly, Breakaway anticipates experiencing at least a 15 percent increase in road bike sales in 2000 and then 3 percent every year after that for the next four years.

The mountain biking rage also has a firm grasp on the European market. While there was initial resistance to mountain bikes from some of the cycling traditionalists in Europe, this is quickly crumbling as the new generation of bike racers find mountain biking to be an excellent form of off-season training as well as just plain fun. Because Breakaway has been active in sponsoring and organizing mountain biking competitions, the company has developed name recognition in the U.S. and Europe. This name recognition has resulted in a large share of the custom mountain bike frame market in Europe and a healthy market share in the U.S. If Breakaway can obtain the necessary financing to expand its operations, it anticipates a steady 15 percent growth rate based on current sales figures and market conditions.

Threats. During the early nineties, a great number of bicycle frame builders who had not foreseen the tremendous popularity of mountain bikes experienced financial difficulties when the demand for assembly line-produced road bikes fell. As a result of these difficulties, many companies either merged with other bike companies or simply went out of business. For companies like Breakaway, whose revenues were not as dependent on purchases by recreational users, the effect was not as great. However, this industry downturn did have a negative impact on most companies' plans for future expansion and development. Until recently, in fact, Breakaway was one of the few American bike companies to aggressively pursue a share of the European market road and mountain bike market. Now, a number of the high-end bike companies have retooled their facilities to take advantage of the sustained demand for mountain bikes and have been aggressively pursuing market share in the U.S. and abroad.

While Breakaway has a significant presence in European mountain biking, this is changing as other international competitors move into this market. European bike companies have recently begun entering the mountain bike market. While they still have considerable ground to cover to match the quality of American frame builders like Breakaway bikes, name recognition with Europe's serious cyclists is opening the market to them. Accordingly, to maintain a significant presence in the high end market of American and European mountain biking, Breakaway is going to have to step up production of its custom bikes to meet the demand of its potential customers. If it does not, there is an increasing number of competitors in Europe and America willing to fill this demand.

Marketing Strategy

Breakaway currently sells all of its bicycles through catalogue sales and mail order sales. While this is an effective way of reaching cycling enthusiasts, Mr. Giro has been working on developing a home page on the Internet that will describe the company, its philosophy, and the specifications of its various bike frames. An electronic order form will also be developed that will allow the customer to order the bicycle after designating the customer's measurements, color preference, and other specifications. Mr. Giro is working with a computer consultant from Computing Development Strategies to add graphics that include color pictures of the various frames and samples of the available colors. The cost of this development has been estimated to be $5,000. However, based on discussions with various bicycle component distributors, the Internet is a particularly effective means of advertising to Breakaway's target market. In fact, based on a recent survey in a popular computer magazine, the typical Internet user is very similar to the target market Breakaway is hoping to reach. Consequently, Breakaway is projecting that Internet advertising will generate an additional 5 percent in sales and revenues.

Breakaway has advertised, and will continue to advertise, in various bicycling magazines in the U.S. The average monthly cost of this type of advertising is $3,125 per month. Breakaway has received very favorable ratings from these magazines for its innovative frame designs and quality of workmanship. These reviews will be included in the magazine ads.

Breakaway will continue sponsoring mountain bike racing events in the U.S. and in Europe. Based on previous experience, this is an excellent way to generate exposure for Breakaway and it fortifies Breakaway's reputation as a mountain bike frame builder. In 2000, Breakaway anticipates sponsoring three races at a cost of $25,000 per race. In 2000, Breakaway has tentatively committed to sponsoring five races at $40,000 per race.

Business Expansion Plan

Unit Price. Breakaway currently builds road and mountain bike frames. The price of a road frame is $1,800 and the price of a mountain frame is $1,600. The prices of these bikes are not expected to increase during the three-year period included in the financial projections.

Unit Cost. The following breakdown lists the material and labor expenses incurred in building a bike frame:

Computer Design and drawing (5 hours of labor)	$ 50
Pouring the cast iron mold for the frame (2.5 hours of labor and $25 for materials)	$ 50
Pouring the graphite composite material (2.5 hours of labor and $100 for materials)	$125
Shaping and finishing the frame (6 hours of labor and $15 for materials)	$ 75
Painting and buffing the frame (5 hours of labor and $10 for material)	$ 85
Packing and shipping the frame to the customer	$ 80
Total cost to produce and ship one bike frame	$465

Inventory Costs. The fact that Breakaway custom builds bike frames to each individual's specifications means that there is no inventory of frames in stock. The company does maintain the necessary inventory of graphite composite building material necessary to build and ship one week's worth of orders (approximately 18 bikes). The cost of 200 pounds of the graphite material is $8,000. The cost of maintaining this perpetual inventory is $200 a month for space at a nearby storage facility.

Labor Costs. Breakaway has 10 employees, which include the officers and owners of the company. The seven designer-builders that Breakaway has hired are paid an average salary of $35,000 per year. If Breakaway obtains the necessary financing, then three additional designer-builders will be hired at an individual annual salary of $25,000. Based on previous years,

Breakaway has generally given 7% or greater salary increases to non-owner employees every year. The corporation will continue giving a like percentage for the next three years.

Capital Equipment Purchases and Maintenance Costs. The machinery used to design and build Breakaway bicycles is sufficient for its current production level. However, if demand increases to its projected level, then three additional workstations will be needed for three new designer-builders. The cost for the machinery and computer equipment for each workstation is $20,000. If Breakaway obtains the necessary financing ($100,000), this equipment will be ordered and placed into service within two months.

Additional Facility Space. The new equipment that will be purchased will obviously require additional floor space. To meet this requirement, Breakaway management considered:

- leasing additional space in a unit adjacent to the present workshop

- moving the whole workshop to a larger facility

- moving the administrative offices out of the current workshop and leasing office space for the management and administrative staff two rental units away from the present workshop

Leasing the unit that is adjacent to the present workshop is a favorable option because it will be relatively easy to shuttle designer-builders and materials between workstations in both units since they are right next to each other. However, the adjacent unit is 1,500 square feet and Breakaway has calculated the required additional floor space to be only 600 square feet. This means that Breakaway would be paying $2 per square foot for 900 square feet that it does not need. Moving all the graphite inventory from the storage facility to this adjacent workshop was considered as a cost saving way to utilize the additional space. However, this would save Breakaway only $200 per month.

The second alternative was quickly dismissed because the indirect costs of the move far outweighed the benefit of having all the workstations in one building. It was estimated that the move would take approximately one month and hinder the building of 80 bicycles. The related lost revenue would be approximately $128,000. Furthermore, this did not take into account the cost of printing new ads, brochures, and mailings that would have to be distributed to reflect the change of address.

Accordingly, the best option open to Breakaway was to move the administrative offices down the block. This was considered the best alternative because it would not disrupt the builder-designers' workflow, the square foot price of the new office space was actually cheaper than the present workshop, and the new workstations could be easily accommodated in the space currently occupied by the administrative offices. The new office space is approximately 800 square feet. The terms of the new lease are $1,200 per month for 36 months.

Financial Statements are attached. (Note: Historical statements and tax returns have been omitted. Normally statements from the last three years would be included in the plan.)

Breakaway Bicycle Company, Inc.
Balance Sheet - December 31, 1999

Assets				Liabilities and Capital		
Current Assets:				**Current Liabilities:**		
Cash		$50,000		Accounts Payable	$4,200	
Accounts Receivable	$20,000			Sales Taxes Payable	2,000	
Less: Bad Debt Reserve	5,000	15,000		Payroll Taxes Payable	1,523	
Merchandise Inventory		5,000		Accrued Wages Payable	4,125	
Prepaid Expenses		500		Unearned Revenues	20,000	
Notes Receivable		0		**Total Current Liabilities**		$31,848
Total Current Assets			$70,500			
Fixed Assets:				**Long-Term Liabilities:**		
Vehicles	15,000			Long-Term Notes Payable	0	
Less: Accum. Depreciation	15,000	0		Mortgage Payable	0	
Furniture and Fixtures	15,000			**Total Long-Term Liabilities**		0
Less: Accum. Depreciation	5,000	10,000				
Equipment	100,000			**Total Liabilities**		31,848
Less: Accum. Depreciation	48,000	52,000				
Total Fixed Assets			62,000	**Capital:**		
Other Assets:				Paid-in Capital	100,652	
Goodwill		0		**Total Capital**		100,652
Total Other Assets			0			
Total Assets			$132,500	**Total Liabilities and Capital**		$132,500

Breakaway Bicycle Company, Inc. Cash Flow Worksheet - 1999						
	JAN	FEB	MAR	APR	MAY	JUN
Beginning Cash Balance		$3,600	$21,801	$51,143	$68,343	$89,211
Cash Inflows (Income):						
Accounts Receivable Collections	$8,500	$8,000	$7,000	$7,850	$7,952	$6,210
Sales & Receipts	$65,000	$75,000	$85,996	$86,000	$84,520	$85,115
Total Cash Inflows	$73,500	$83,000	$92,996	$93,850	$92,472	$91,325
Available Cash Balance	$73,500	$86,600	$114,797	$144,993	$160,815	$180,536
Cash Outflows (Expenses):						
Advertising	$1,500	$2,500	$1,000	$3,000	$1,500	$4,500
Bank Service Charges	$300	$300	$300	$300	$300	$300
Credit Card Fees	$200	$200	$200	$200	$200	$200
Delivery	$4,500	$4,500	$4,500	$4,500	$4,500	$4,500
Health Insurance	$1,200	$1,200	$1,200	$1,200	$1,200	$1,200
Insurance	$600	$600	$600	$600	$600	$600
Inventory Purchases	$13,050	$14,550	$7,804	$18,800	$16,654	$14,445
Miscellaneous	$15,000	$7,899	$12,500	$15,000	$8,500	$6,520
Office	$200	$200	$200	$200	$200	$200
Payroll	$28,000	$28,000	$28,000	$28,000	$28,000	$28,000
Payroll Taxes	$2,800	$2,800	$2,800	$2,800	$2,800	$2,800
Rent or Lease	$1,200	$1,200	$1,200	$1,200	$1,200	$1,200
Subscriptions & Dues	$50	$50	$50	$50	$50	$50
Supplies	$200	$200	$200	$200	$200	$200
Taxes & Licenses	$100	$100	$100	$100	$100	$100
Utilities & Telephone	$500	$500	$500	$500	$500	$500
Subtotal	$69,400	$64,799	$61,154	$76,650	$66,504	$65,315
Other Cash Out Flows:						
Owner's Draw	$500		$2,500		$5,100	
Subtotal	$500	$0	$2,500	$0	$5,100	$0
Total Cash Outflows	$69,900	$64,799	$63,654	$76,650	$71,604	$65,315
Ending Cash Balance	$3,600	$21,801	$51,143	$68,343	$89,211	$115,221

Breakaway Bicycle Company, Inc.
Cash Flow Worksheet - 1999

JUL	AUG	SEP	OCT	NOV	DEC	TOTAL
$115,221	$137,331	$167,270	$177,785	$183,947	$180,315	
$5,260	$9,850	$9,852	$7,888	$9,520	$7,550	$95,432
$88,500	$83,339	$70,520	$62,500	$55,000	$81,000	$922,490
$93,760	$93,189	$80,372	$70,388	$64,520	$88,550	$1,017,922
$208,981	$230,520	$247,642	$248,173	$248,467	$268,865	
$1,500	$2,500	$1,000	$3,000	$1,500	$4,500	$28,000
$300	$300	$300	$300	$300	$300	$3,600
$200	$200	$200	$200	$200	$200	$2,400
$4,500	$4,500	$4,500	$4,500	$4,500	$4,500	$54,000
$1,200	$1,200	$1,200	$1,200	$1,200	$1,200	$14,400
$600	$600	$600	$600	$600	$600	$7,200
$14,800	$13,200	$11,587	$12,589	$12,300	$11,899	$161,678
$5,500	$7,700	$5,420	$8,787	$6,002	$6,000	$104,828
$200	$200	$200	$200	$200	$200	$2,400
$28,000	$28,000	$28,000	$28,000	$28,000	$28,000	$336,000
$2,800	$2,800	$2,800	$2,800	$2,800	$2,800	$33,600
$1,200	$1,200	$1,200	$1,200	$1,200	$1,200	$14,400
$50	$50	$50	$50	$50	$50	$600
$200	$200	$200	$200	$200	$200	$2,400
$100	$100	$100	$100	$100	$100	$1,200
$500	$500	$500	$500	$500	$500	$6,000
$61,650	$63,250	$57,857	$64,226	$59,652	$62,249	$772,706
$10,000		$12,000		$8,500	$18,750	$57,350
$10,000	$0	$12,000	$0	$8,500	$18,750	$57,350
$71,650	$63,250	$69,857	$64,226	$68,152	$80,999	$830,056
$137,331	$167,270	$177,785	$183,947	$180,315	$187,866	

Breakaway Bicycle Company, Inc.
Income Statement - December 31, 1999

Revenue:

Gross Sales		$1,057,008
Less: Sales Returns and Allowances		$22,890
Net Sales		$1,034,118

Cost of Goods Sold:

Beginning Inventory	$15,000	
Add: Purchases	$124,500	
Freight-in	$2,500	
Direct Labor	$241,000	
Indirect Expenses	$0	
	$383,000	
Less: Ending Inventory	$16,500	
Cost of Goods Sold		$366,500
Gross Profit (Loss)		$667,618

Expenses:

Advertising	$47,000	
Amortization	$0	
Bad Debts	$42,280	
Bank Charges	$3,600	
Charitable Contributions	$2,500	
Commissions	$0	
Contract Labor	$0	
Credit Card Fees	$2,400	
Delivery Expenses	$65,760	
Depreciation	$10,000	
Dues and Subscriptions	$600	
Insurance	$7,200	
Interest	$0	
Maintenance	$2,400	
Office Expenses	$2,400	
Operating Supplies	$2,400	
Payroll Taxes	$42,500	
Permits and Licenses	$1,200	
Postage	$2,400	
Professional Fees	$2,400	
Property Taxes	$0	
Rent	$24,000	
Repairs	$0	
Telephone	$5,200	
Travel	$9,000	
Utilities	$6,000	
Vehicle Expenses	$2,510	
Wages	$205,000	
Total Expenses		$488,750
Net Operating Income		$178,868

Other Income:

Gain (Loss) on Sale of Assets	$0	
Interest Income	$0	
Total Other Income		$0
Net Income (Loss)		$178,868

Breakaway Bicycle Company, Inc.
Revenue Projections

2000 Q1, Q2

	JAN	FEB	MAR	APR	MAY	JUN
NUMBER OF:						
Road Frames	30	26	30	34	36	34
Mountain Frames	40	38	38	41	43	41
INCOME GENERATED FROM:						
European Sales - Road ($1,800/frame)	$10,800	$9,360	$10,800	$12,240	$12,960	$12,240
U.S. Sales - Road ($1,800/frame)	$43,200	$37,440	$43,200	$48,960	$51,840	$48,960
European Sales - Mountain ($1,600/frame)	$32,000	$30,400	$30,400	$32,800	$34,400	$32,800
U.S. Sales - Mountain ($1,600/frame)	$32,000	$30,400	$30,400	$32,800	$34,400	$32,800
	$118,000	$107,600	$114,800	$126,800	$133,600	$126,800

2000 Q3, Q4

	JUL	AUG	SEP	OCT	NOV	DEC	TOTAL
NUMBER OF:							
Road Frames	34	32	29	26	22	44	377
Mountain Frames	40	36	32	29	19	48	445
INCOME GENERATED FROM:							
European Sales - Road	$12,240	$11,520	$10,440	$9,360	$7,920	$15,840	
U.S. Sales - Road	$48,960	$46,080	$41,760	$37,440	$31,680	$63,360	
European Sales - Mountain	$32,000	$28,800	$25,600	$23,200	$15,200	$38,400	
U.S. Sales - Mountain	$32,000	$28,800	$25,600	$23,200	$15,200	$38,400	
	$125,200	$115,200	$103,400	$93,200	$70,000	$156,000	$1,390,600

2001 Q1, Q2

	JAN	FEB	MAR	APR	MAY	JUN
NUMBER OF:						
Road Frames	40	35	36	38	42	40
Mountain Frames	44	42	41	46	48	45
INCOME GENERATED FROM:						
European Sales - Road ($1,800/frame)	$14,400	$12,600	$12,960	$13,680	$15,120	$14,400
U.S. Sales - Road ($1,800/frame)	$57,600	$50,400	$51,840	$54,720	$60,480	$57,600
European Sales - Mountain ($1,600/frame)	$35,200	$33,600	$32,800	$36,800	$38,400	$36,000
U.S. Sales - Mountain ($1,600/frame)	$35,200	$33,600	$32,800	$36,800	$38,400	$36,000
	$142,400	$130,200	$130,400	$142,000	$152,400	$144,000

2001 Q3, Q4

	JUL	AUG	SEP	OCT	NOV	DEC	TOTAL
NUMBER OF:							
Road Frames	38	35	32	29	25	60	450
Mountain Frames	44	38	35	32	26	65	506
INCOME GENERATED FROM:							
European Sales - Road	$13,680	$12,600	$11,520	$10,440	$9,000	$21,600	
U.S. Sales - Road	$54,720	$50,400	$46,080	$41,760	$36,000	$86,400	
European Sales - Mountain	$35,200	$30,400	$28,000	$25,600	$20,800	$52,000	
U.S. Sales - Mountain	$35,200	$30,400	$28,000	$25,600	$20,800	$52,000	
	$138,800	$123,800	$113,600	$103,400	$86,600	$212,000	$1,619,600

Breakaway Bicycle Company, Inc. Projected Profit and Loss Statement - 2000						
	JAN	**FEB**	**MAR**	**APR**	**MAY**	**JUN**
Revenue:						
Gross Sales	$118,000	$107,600	$114,800	$126,800	$133,800	$126,800
Less: Sales Returns	$5,900	$5,380	$5,740	$6,340	$6,690	$6,340
Net Sales	$112,100	$102,220	$109,060	$120,460	$127,110	$120,460
Cost of Goods Sold:						
Materials	$14,160	$12,912	$13,776	$15,216	$16,056	$15,216
Labor	$14,160	$12,912	$13,776	$15,216	$16,056	$15,216
Other Direct Expenses	$5,310	$4,842	$5,166	$5,706	$6,021	$5,706
Indirect Expenses	$1,770	$1,614	$1,722	$1,902	$2,007	$1,902
Total Cost of Goods Sold	$35,400	$32,280	$34,440	$38,040	$40,140	$38,040
Gross Profit (Loss)	$76,700	$69,940	$74,620	$82,420	$86,970	$82,420
Expenses:						
Advertising	$2,500	$2,500	$3,000	$5,000	$3,000	$3,000
Bad Debts	$5,605	$5,111	$5,453	$6,023	$6,356	$6,023
Bank Charges	$300	$300	$300	$300	$300	$300
Charitable Contributions	$100	$100	$100	$100	$100	$100
Credit Card Fees	$0	$0	$0	$0	$0	$0
Delivery Expenses	$200	$200	$200	$200	$200	$200
Depreciation	$5,480	$5,480	$5,480	$5,480	$5,480	$5,480
Dues and Subscriptions	$888	$888	$888	$888	$888	$888
Insurance	$50	$50	$50	$50	$50	$50
Interest	$600	$600	$600	$600	$600	$600
Maintenance	$401	$401	$401	$401	$401	$401
Miscellaneous	$200	$200	$200	$200	$200	$200
Office Expenses	$500	$500	$500	$500	$500	$500
Operating Supplies	$200	$200	$200	$200	$200	$200
Payroll Taxes	$200	$200	$200	$200	$200	$200
Permits and Licenses	$3,792	$3,792	$3,792	$3,792	$3,792	$3,792
Postage	$100	$100	$100	$100	$100	$100
Rent	$200	$200	$200	$200	$200	$200
Telephone	$3,200	$3,200	$3,200	$3,200	$3,200	$3,200
Travel	$400	$400	$400	$400	$400	$400
Utilities	$200	$1,000	$1,000	$1,000	$1,000	$1,000
Wages	$24,257	$25,505	$38,417	$23,201	$22,361	$23,201
Total Expenses	$49,373	$50,927	$64,681	$52,035	$49,528	$50,035
Net Operating Income	$27,327	$19,013	$9,939	$30,385	$37,443	$32,385
Other Income:						
Gain (Loss) on Asset Sales	$0	$0	$0	$0	$0	$0
Interest Income	$0	$0	$0	$0	$0	$0
Total Other Income	$0	$0	$0	$0	$0	$0
Net Income (Loss)	$27,327	$19,013	$9,939	$30,385	$37,443	$32,385
Cumulative Net Income (Loss)	$27,327	$46,340	$56,279	$86,664	$124,107	$156,492

Breakaway Bicycle Company, Inc.
Projected Profit and Loss Statement - 2000

JUL	AUG	SEP	OCT	NOV	DEC	TOTAL
$125,200	$115,200	$103,400	$93,200	$70,000	$156,000	$1,390,800
$6,260	$5,760	$5,170	$4,660	$3,500	$7,800	$69,540
$118,940	$109,440	$98,230	$88,540	$66,500	$148,200	$1,321,260
$15,024	$13,824	$12,408	$11,184	$8,400	$18,720	$166,896
$15,024	$13,824	$12,408	$11,184	$8,400	$18,720	$166,896
$5,634	$5,184	$4,653	$4,194	$3,150	$7,020	$62,586
$1,878	$1,728	$1,551	$1,398	$1,050	$2,340	$20,862
$37,560	$34,560	$31,020	$27,960	$21,000	$46,800	$417,240
$81,380	$74,880	$67,210	$60,580	$45,500	$101,400	$904,020
$2,500	$2,000	$2,000	$3,000	$4,000	$5,000	$37,500
$5,947	$5,472	$4,912	$4,427	$3,325	$7,410	$66,064
$300	$300	$300	$300	$300	$300	$3,600
$100	$100	$100	$100	$100	$100	$1,200
$0	$0	$0	$0	$0	$0	$0
$200	$200	$200	$200	$200	$200	$2,400
$5,480	$5,480	$5,480	$5,480	$5,480	$5,480	$65,760
$888	$888	$888	$888	$888	$888	$10,656
$50	$50	$50	$50	$50	$50	$600
$600	$600	$600	$600	$600	$600	$7,200
$401	$401	$401	$401	$401	$401	$4,812
$200	$200	$200	$200	$200	$200	$2,400
$500	$500	$500	$500	$500	$500	$6,000
$200	$200	$200	$200	$200	$200	$2,400
$200	$200	$200	$200	$200	$200	$2,400
$3,792	$3,792	$3,792	$3,792	$3,792	$3,792	$45,504
$100	$100	$100	$100	$100	$100	$1,200
$200	$200	$200	$200	$200	$200	$2,400
$3,200	$3,200	$3,200	$3,200	$3,200	$3,200	$38,400
$400	$400	$400	$400	$400	$400	$4,800
$1,000	$1,000	$1,000	$1,000	$1,000	$1,000	$11,200
$23,393	$24,593	$26,009	$27,233	$30,017	$19,197	$307,884
$49,651	$49,876	$50,932	$52,671	$55,353	$50,118	$625,179
$31,729	$25,004	$16,279	$7,909	($9,853)	$51,282	$278,842
$0	$0	$0	$0	$0	$0	$0
$0	$0	$0	$0	$0	$0	$0
$0	$0	$0	$0	$0	$0	$0
$31,729	$25,004	$16,279	$7,909	($9,853)	$51,282	$278,842
$188,221	$213,225	$229,504	$237,413	$227,560	$278,842	

Breakaway Bicycle Company, Inc.						
Projected Profit and Loss Statement - 2001						
	JAN	**FEB**	**MAR**	**APR**	**MAY**	**JUN**
Revenue:						
Gross Sales	$142,400	$130,200	$130,400	$142,000	$152,400	$144,000
Less: Sales Returns	$7,120	$6,510	$6,520	$7,100	$7,620	$7,200
Net Sales	$135,280	$123,690	$123,880	$134,900	$144,780	$136,800
Cost of Goods Sold:						
Materials	$17,088	$15,624	$15,648	$17,040	$18,288	$15,624
Labor	$17,088	$15,624	$15,648	$17,040	$18,288	$15,624
Other Direct Expenses	$6,408	$5,859	$5,868	$6,390	$6,858	$5,859
Indirect Expenses	$2,136	$1,953	$1,956	$2,130	$2,286	$1,953
Cost of Goods Sold	$42,720	$39,060	$39,120	$42,600	$45,720	$39,060
Gross Profit (Loss)	$92,560	$84,630	$84,760	$92,300	$99,060	$97,740
Expenses:						
Advertising	$2,700	$2,700	$3,100	$5,200	$3,100	$3,100
Bad Debts	$6,764	$6,185	$6,194	$6,745	$7,239	$6,840
Bank Charges	$300	$300	$300	$300	$300	$300
Charitable Contributions	$100	$100	$100	$100	$100	$100
Credit Card Fees	$200	$200	$200	$200	$200	$200
Delivery Expenses	$6,000	$6,000	$6,000	$6,000	$6,000	$6,000
Depreciation	$888	$888	$888	$888	$888	$888
Dues and Subscriptions	$50	$50	$50	$50	$50	$50
Insurance	$600	$600	$600	$600	$600	$600
Interest	$401	$401	$401	$401	$401	$401
Maintenance	$200	$200	$200	$200	$200	$200
Miscellaneous	$500	$500	$500	$500	$500	$500
Office Expenses	$200	$200	$200	$200	$200	$200
Operating Supplies	$200	$200	$200	$200	$200	$200
Payroll Taxes	$2,750	$2,923	$2,894	$2,754	$2,630	$2,896
Permits and Licenses	$100	$100	$100	$100	$100	$100
Postage	$400	$400	$400	$400	$400	$400
Rent	$3,200	$3,200	$3,200	$3,200	$3,200	$3,200
Telephone	$400	$400	$400	$400	$400	$400
Travel	$1,000	$1,000	$1,000	$1,000	$1,000	$1,000
Utilities	$500	$500	$500	$500	$500	$500
Wages	$27,495	$29,229	$28,935	$27,543	$26,295	$28,959
Total Expenses	$54,948	$56,276	$56,362	$57,481	$54,503	$57,034
Net Operating Income	$37,613	$28,354	$28,399	$34,819	$44,558	$40,706
Other Income:						
Gain (Loss) on Sale of Assets	$0	$0	$0	$0	$0	$0
Interest Income	$0	$0	$0	$0	$0	$0
Total Other Income	$0	$0	$0	$0	$0	$0
Net Income (Loss)	$37,613	$28,354	$28,399	$34,819	$44,558	$40,706
Cumulative Net Income (Loss)	$37,613	$65,967	$94,366	$129,185	$173,743	$214,449

Breakaway Bicycle Company, Inc.						
Projected Profit and Loss Statement - 2001						
JUL	**AUG**	**SEP**	**OCT**	**NOV**	**DEC**	**TOTAL**
$138,800	$123,800	$113,600	$103,400	$86,600	$212,000	$1,619,600
$6,940	$6,190	$5,680	$5,170	$4,330	$10,600	$80,980
$131,860	$117,610	$107,920	$98,230	$82,270	$201,400	$1,538,620
$15,648	$17,040	$18,288	$15,624	$15,648	$17,040	$198,600
$15,648	$17,040	$18,288	$15,624	$15,648	$17,040	$198,600
$5,868	$6,390	$6,858	$5,859	$5,868	$6,390	$74,475
$1,956	$2,130	$2,286	$1,953	$1,956	$2,130	$24,825
$39,120	$42,600	$45,720	$39,060	$39,120	$42,600	$496,500
$92,740	$75,010	$62,200	$59,170	$43,150	$158,800	$1,042,120
$2,700	$2,100	$2,100	$3,100	$4,200	$5,500	$39,600
$6,593	$5,881	$5,396	$4,912	$4,114	$10,070	$76,933
$300	$300	$300	$300	$300	$300	$3,600
$100	$100	$100	$100	$100	$100	$1,200
$200	$200	$200	$200	$200	$200	$2,400
$6,000	$6,000	$6,000	$6,000	$6,000	$6,000	$72,000
$888	$888	$888	$888	$888	$888	$10,656
$50	$50	$50	$50	$50	$50	$600
$600	$600	$600	$600	$600	$600	$7,200
$401	$401	$401	$401	$401	$401	$4,812
$200	$200	$200	$200	$200	$200	$2,400
$500	$500	$500	$500	$500	$500	$6,000
$200	$200	$200	$200	$200	$200	$2,400
$200	$200	$200	$200	$200	$200	$2,400
$2,894	$2,754	$2,630	$2,896	$2,894	$2,754	$33,669
$100	$100	$100	$100	$100	$100	$1,200
$400	$400	$400	$400	$400	$400	$4,800
$3,200	$3,200	$3,200	$3,200	$3,200	$3,200	$38,400
$400	$400	$400	$400	$400	$400	$4,800
$1,000	$1,000	$500	$500	$500	$200	$9,700
$500	$500	$500	$500	$500	$500	$6,000
$28,935	$27,543	$26,295	$28,959	$28,935	$27,543	$336,666
$56,361	$53,517	$51,160	$54,605	$54,882	$60,306	$667,436
$36,380	$21,493	$11,041	$4,565	($11,732)	$98,494	$374,689
$0	$0	$0	$0	$0	$0	$0
$0	$0	$0	$0	$0	$0	$0
$0	$0	$0	$0	$0	$0	$0
$36,380	$21,493	$11,041	$4,564	($11,732)	$98,494	$374,689
$250,829	$272,322	$283,363	$287,927	$276,195	$374,689	

Breakaway Bicycle Company, Inc. Cash Flow Budget Worksheet - 2000						
	JAN	**FEB**	**MAR**	**APR**	**MAY**	**JUN**
Beginning Cash Balance		$63,642	$84,601	$109,750	$141,881	$181,622
Cash Inflows (Income):						
Accounts Receivable Collections	$0	$5,605	$5,111	$5,453	$6,023	$6,356
Loan Proceeds	$100,000					
Sales & Receipts	$106,200	$96,840	$103,320	$114,120	$120,420	$114,120
Other:						
Total Cash Inflows	$206,200	$102,445	$108,431	$119,573	$126,443	$120,476
Available Cash Balance	$206,200	$166,087	$193,032	$229,323	$268,324	$302,098
Cash Outflows (Expenses):						
Advertising	$2,500	$2,500	$3,000	$5,000	$3,000	$3,000
Bank Service Charges	$300	$300	$300	$300	$300	$300
Credit Card Fees	$200	$200	$200	$200	$200	$200
Delivery	$5,480	$5,480	$5,480	$5,480	$5,480	$5,480
Health Insurance	$3,000	$3,000	$3,000	$3,000	$3,000	$3,000
Insurance	$600	$600	$600	$600	$600	$600
Interest	$401	$401	$401	$401	$401	$401
Inventory Purchases	$14,160	$12,912	$13,776	$15,216	$16,056	$15,216
Miscellaneous	$7,580	$6,956	$7,388	$8,108	$8,528	$8,108
Office	$200	$200	$200	$200	$200	$200
Payroll	$37,917	$37,917	$37,917	$37,917	$37,917	$37,917
Payroll Taxes	$3,792	$3,792	$3,792	$3,792	$3,792	$3,792
Professional Fees	$0	$0	$0	$0	$0	$0
Rent or Lease	$2,000	$2,000	$2,000	$2,000	$2,000	$2,000
Subscriptions & Dues	$50	$50	$50	$50	$50	$50
Supplies	$200	$200	$200	$200	$200	$200
Taxes & Licenses	$100	$100	$100	$100	$100	$100
Utilities & Telephone	$900	$900	$900	$900	$900	$900
Other:						
Travel	$200	$1,000	$1,000	$1,000	$1,000	$1,000
Maintenance	$200	$200	$200	$200	$200	$200
Subtotal	$79,780	$78,708	$80,504	$84,664	$83,924	$82,664
Other Cash Out Flows:						
Capital Purchases	$60,000					
Loan Principal	$2,778	$2,778	$2,778	$2,778	$2,778	$2,778
Owner's Draw						
Other:						
Subtotal	$62,778	$2,778	$2,778	$2,778	$2,778	$2,778
Total Cash Outflows	$142,558	$81,486	$83,282	$87,442	$86,702	$85,442
Ending Cash Balance	$63,642	$84,601	$109,750	$141,881	$181,622	$216,656

Breakaway Bicycle Company, Inc.
Cash Flow Budget Worksheet - 2000

JUL	AUG	SEP	OCT	NOV	DEC	TOTAL
$216,656	$250,705	$272,794	$291,096	$300,494	$291,703	
$6,023	$5,947	$5,472	$4,912	$4,427	$3,325	$58,654
						$100,000
$112,680	$98,496	$93,060	$83,880	$63,000	$140,400	$1,246,536
						$0
$118,703	$104,443	$98,532	$88,792	$67,427	$143,725	$1,405,190
$335,359	$355,148	$371,326	$379,888	$367,921	$435,428	
$2,500	$2,000	$2,000	$3,000	$4,000	$5,000	$37,500
$300	$300	$300	$300	$300	$300	$3,600
$200	$200	$200	$200	$200	$200	$2,400
$5,480	$5,480	$5,480	$5,480	$5,480	$5,480	$65,760
$3,000	$3,000	$3,000	$3,000	$3,000	$3,000	$36,000
$600	$600	$600	$600	$600	$600	$7,200
$401	$401	$401	$401	$401	$401	$4,812
$15,024	$13,824	$12,408	$11,184	$8,400	$18,720	$166,896
$8,012	$7,412	$6,704	$6,092	$4,700	$9,860	$89,448
$200	$200	$200	$200	$200	$200	$2,400
$37,917	$37,917	$37,917	$37,917	$37,917	$37,917	$455,004
$3,792	$3,792	$3,792	$3,792	$3,792	$3,792	$45,504
$0	$0	$0	$0	$0	$0	$0
$2,000	$2,000	$2,000	$2,000	$2,000	$2,000	$24,000
$50	$50	$50	$50	$50	$50	$600
$200	$200	$200	$200	$200	$200	$2,400
$100	$100	$100	$100	$100	$100	$1,200
$900	$900	$900	$900	$900	$900	$10,800
						$0
$1,000	$1,000	$1,000	$1,000	$1,000	$200	$10,400
$200	$200	$200	$200	$200	$200	$2,400
$81,876	$79,576	$77,452	$76,616	$73,440	$89,120	$968,324
						$60,000
$2,778	$2,778	$2,778	$2,778	$2,778	$2,778	$33,336
						$0
						$0
$2,778	$2,778	$2,778	$2,778	$2,778	$2,778	$93,336
$84,654	$82,354	$80,230	$79,394	$76,218	$91,898	$1,061,660
$250,705	$272,794	$291,096	$300,494	$291,703	$343,530	

Note 1.   Breakaway hopes to secure a three-year, 9% loan for $100,000 loan to purchase and install three new workstations to handle the expected order increase. The additional $40,000 would provide working capital during the expansion period.

Breakaway Bicycle Company, Inc. Cash Flow Budget Worksheet - 2001						
	JAN	**FEB**	**MAR**	**APR**	**MAY**	**JUN**
Beginning Cash Balance		$32,058	$60,937	$89,066	$123,789	$168,670
Cash Inflows (Income):						
Accounts Receivable Collections	$0	$5,605	$5,111	$5,453	$6,023	$6,356
Loan Proceeds						
Sales & Receipts	$128,160	$117,180	$117,360	$127,800	$137,160	$129,600
Other:						
Total Cash Inflows	$128,160	$122,785	$122,471	$133,253	$143,183	$135,956
Available Cash Balance	$128,160	$154,843	$183,408	$222,319	$266,972	$304,626
Cash Outflows (Expenses):						
Advertising	$2,700	$2,700	$3,100	$5,200	$3,100	$3,100
Bank Service Charges	$300	$300	$300	$300	$300	$300
Credit Card Fees	$200	$200	$200	$200	$200	$200
Delivery	$6,000	$6,000	$6,000	$6,000	$6,000	$6,000
Health Insurance	$3,000	$3,000	$3,000	$3,000	$3,000	$3,000
Insurance	$600	$600	$600	$600	$600	$600
Interest	$401	$401	$401	$401	$401	$401
Inventory Purchases	$17,088	$15,624	$15,648	$17,040	$18,288	$15,624
Miscellaneous	$9,044	$8,312	$8,324	$9,020	$9,644	$8,312
Office	$200	$200	$200	$200	$200	$200
Payroll	$44,583	$44,583	$44,583	$44,583	$44,583	$44,583
Payroll Taxes	$4,458	$4,458	$4,458	$4,458	$4,458	$4,458
Professional Fees	$0	$0	$0	$0	$0	$0
Rent or Lease	$2,100	$2,100	$2,100	$2,100	$2,100	$2,100
Subscriptions & Dues	$50	$50	$50	$50	$50	$50
Supplies	$400	$400	$400	$400	$400	$400
Taxes & Licenses	$100	$100	$100	$100	$100	$100
Utilities & Telephone	$900	$900	$900	$900	$900	$900
Other:						
Travel	$1,000	$1,000	$1,000	$1,000	$1,000	$1,000
Maintenance	$200	$200	$200	$200	$200	$200
Subtotal	$93,324	$91,128	$91,564	$95,752	$95,524	$91,528
Other Cash Out Flows:						
Capital Purchases						
Loan Principal	$2,778	$2,778	$2,778	$2,778	$2,778	$2,778
Owner's Draw						
Other:						
Subtotal	$2,778	$2,778	$2,778	$2,778	$2,778	$2,778
Total Cash Outflows	$96,102	$93,906	$94,342	$98,530	$98,302	$94,306
Ending Cash Balance	$32,058	$60,937	$89,066	$123,789	$168,670	$210,320

Breakaway Bicycle Company, Inc.
Cash Flow Budget Worksheet - 2001

JUL	AUG	SEP	OCT	NOV	DEC	TOTAL
$210,320	$247,321	$269,258	$280,168	$284,334	$271,759	
$6,023	$5,947	$5,472	$4,912	$4,427	$3,325	$58,654
						$0
$124,920	$111,420	$102,240	$93,060	$77,940	$190,800	$1,457,640
						$0
$130,943	$117,367	$107,712	$97,972	$82,367	$194,125	$1,516,294
$341,263	$364,688	$376,970	$378,140	$366,701	$465,884	
$2,700	$2,100	$2,100	$3,100	$4,200	$5,500	$39,600
$300	$300	$300	$300	$300	$300	$3,600
$200	$200	$200	$200	$200	$200	$2,400
$6,000	$6,000	$6,000	$6,000	$6,000	$6,000	$72,000
$3,000	$3,000	$3,000	$3,000	$3,000	$3,000	$36,000
$600	$600	$600	$600	$600	$600	$7,200
$401	$401	$401	$401	$401	$401	$4,812
$15,648	$17,040	$18,288	$15,624	$15,648	$17,040	$198,600
$8,324	$9,020	$9,644	$8,312	$8,324	$9,020	$105,300
$200	$200	$200	$200	$200	$200	$2,400
$44,583	$44,583	$44,583	$44,583	$44,583	$44,583	$534,996
$4,458	$4,458	$4,458	$4,458	$4,458	$4,458	$53,496
$0	$0	$0	$0	$0	$0	$0
$2,100	$2,100	$2,100	$2,100	$2,100	$2,100	$25,200
$50	$50	$50	$50	$50	$50	$600
$400	$400	$400	$400	$400	$400	$4,800
$100	$100	$100	$100	$100	$100	$1,200
$900	$900	$900	$900	$900	$900	$10,800
						$0
$1,000	$1,000	$500	$500	$500	$200	$9,700
$200	$200	$200	$200	$200	$200	$2,400
$91,164	$92,652	$94,024	$91,028	$92,164	$95,252	$1,115,104
						$0
$2,778	$2,778	$2,778	$2,778	$2,778	$2,778	$33,336
						$0
						$0
$2,778	$2,778	$2,778	$2,778	$2,778	$2,778	$33,336
$93,942	$95,430	$96,802	$93,806	$94,942	$98,030	$1,148,440
$247,321	$269,258	$280,168	$284,334	$271,759	$367,854	

Note 1.   Breakaway hopes to secure a three-year, 9% loan for $100,000 to purchase and install three new workstations in year 1 to handle the expected increase in bicycle orders. The additional $40,000 would provide working capital during the expansion period.

Breakaway Bicycle Company, Inc.					
Pro Forma Balance Sheet - December 31, 2000					
Assets			**Liabilities and Capital**		
Current Assets:			**Current Liabilities:**		
Cash		$452,578	Accounts Payable		$5,500
Accounts Receivable	$74,520		Sales Taxes Payable		400
Less: Reserve for Bad Debts 7,452		67,068	Payroll Taxes Payable		16,000
Merchandise Inventory		21,000	Accrued Wages Payable		55,880
Prepaid Expenses		5,000	Unearned Revenues		15,060
Notes Receivable		0	Short-Term Notes Payable 0		
Total Current Assets		$545,646	Short-Term Bank Loan Payable 0		
Fixed Assets:			**Total Current Liabilities**		92,840
Vehicles	0				
Less: Accumulated Dep.	0	0	**Long-Term Liabilities**:		
Furniture and Fixtures	25,000		Long-Term Notes Payable	75,000	
Less: Accumulated Dep.	7,000	18,000	Mortgage Payable		0
Equipment	160,000		**Total Long-Term Liabilities**		75,000
Less: Accumulated Dep.	54,000	106,000			
Buildings	0		**Total Liabilities**		167,840
Less: Accumulated Dep.	0	0			
Land		0	**Capital:**		
Total Fixed Assets		124,000	Paid-in Capital	501,806	
Other Assets:			Additional Capital	0	0
Goodwill		0	**Total Capital**		501,806
Total Other Assets		0			
Total Assets		$669,646	**Total Liabilities and Capital**		$669,646

Breakaway Bicycle Company, Inc.
Pro Forma Balance Sheet - December 31, 2001

Assets			Liabilities and Capital		
Current Assets:			**Current Liabilities:**		
Cash		$815,840	Accounts Payable	$7,500	
Accounts Receivable	$22,000		Sales Taxes Payable	800	
Less: Reserve for Bad Debts	1,980	20,020	Payroll Taxes Payable	17,500	
Merchandise Inventory		15,000	Accrued Wages Payable	60,000	
Prepaid Expenses		5,200	Unearned Revenues	78,000	
Notes Receivable		0	Short-Term Notes Payable	0	
Total Current Assets		$856,060	Short-Term Bank Loan Payable	0	
Fixed Assets:			**Total Current Liabilities**		$163,800
Vehicles	0				
Less: Accumulated Dep.	0	0	**Long-Term Liabilities:**		
Furniture and Fixtures	25,000		Long-Term Notes Payable 50,000		
Less: Accumulated Dep.	9,000	16,000	Mortgage Payable	0	
Equipment	160,000		**Total Long-Term Liabilities**		50,000
Less: Accumulated Dep.	60,000	100,000			
Buildings	0		**Total Liabilities**		213,800
Less: Accumulated Dep.	0	0			
Land	0		**Capital:**		
Total Fixed Assets		116,000	Paid-in Capital	758,260	
Other Assets:			Additional Capital	0	0
Goodwill		0	**Total Capital**		758,260
Total Other Assets		0			
Total Assets		$972,060	**Total Liabilities and Capital**		$972,060

Part **III**

Getting Financing For Your Business

The perception that many small business owners have is that financing means taking whatever money you can get, and the faster and easier you can get it, the better. Unfortunately, this approach doesn't take into account the fact that getting money for your business involves a variety of tradeoffs, financial and nonfinancial, good and bad.

Finding "smart" money. Small businesses usually need more than just cash: they need "smart" money. By that we mean the financier should provide not only capital, but support and expertise to your business. Smart money could be an SBA guaranteed loan that allows you to keep your ownership interest intact until your business reaches the stage at which you want to sell shares of the business. On the other hand, money that comes from letting your brother, Stanley, become a partner because you need his $10,000 before the end of the week might be far more costly than you ever imagined.

The problem in locating "smart" money is that the capital market for small businesses is imperfect and consists of a great variety of underpublicized and poorly organized financing sources.

Whether you are trying to locate a bank that is willing to lend you money or whether you are looking for a business "angel" who will contribute needed equity capital, your quest for financing will require that you devote the same attention to obtaining it as you give to decisions involving the business's basic product or service.

The discussion in Part III is designed to help you identify relevant traits about your business's financing profile and understand the various financing sources that may be available to you, with an emphasis on practical information about selecting the most suitable sources of funding for your business.

Chapter 7: Your Business's Financing Profile presents basic definitions of debt and equity financing, and explains how the organization of your business and your position in the business life cycle influence your financing options. It also points out ways in which you can find money in your own back yard by tapping friends, family, and personal assets.

Chapter 8: Equity Financing explains the advantages and disadvantages of using venture capital, "angels," sales of securities, franchising, and employee stock ownership plans to raise capital.

Chapter 9: Debt Financing discusses where and how to get a business loan, and the types of loans available. We include a sample commercial loan application and explain how banks evaluate such applications.

Chapter 10: Government Financing Programs describes the many ways that the federal Small Business Administration can help to finance your small business, and describes other government financing assistance.

Chapter 7

Your Business's Financing Profile

The process for selecting an appropriate financing approach for your business is more of an art than a science. You need to consider many factors and evaluate them in the context of your own specific business and its needs. However, some general guidelines to assess the whole range of financing options can be helpful. It is the goal of this chapter to provide you with such a framework.

We recommend that you start by answering the following questions:

- How much money does my business really need?

- What are the differences between debt and equity financing?

- What is the right balance of financing for my business?

- At what stage of the "business life cycle" is my business?

- What effect does the organization of my business have on my financing options?

- How attractive is my business to lenders or other investors?

- Are my business's financing needs long or short term?

- What financing sources are available based on my business circumstances?

This exercise will not only help you to narrow your options, but enhance your chances for a favorable outcome.

ESTIMATING THE MONEY YOU NEED

Whether you want capital for startup costs, short-term operating costs, or long-term strategic development, your first step must be to accurately estimate the amount of money you need. Preparing a realistic projection of the necessary funding will not only force you to consider the wide variety of costs associated with your plans, but also help convince a lender or investor that you understand your business and the relevant market realities.

Warning

 Although some government and local community agencies are working on developing sources of smaller loans, it is still difficult to get a bank interested in making a loan of less than $50,000. Their paperwork and monitoring costs are usually too high to make smaller loans profitable for them.

That doesn't mean that you should automatically ask for more than $50,000, since you will generally need to put up collateral equal to the entire amount of the loan. Moreover, your projected financial statements must prove that your business will be able to generate the revenue needed to pay back the larger loan amount. It does mean that greater persistence and creativity may be needed to locate a source of financing for small loans, and you may have to resort to patchwork financing from several different sources.

DEBT AND EQUITY FINANCING

Business financing is commonly categorized into two fundamental types: debt financing and equity financing.

"Debt financing" means borrowing money that is to be repaid over a period of time, usually with interest. Debt financing can be either short-term (due in less than one year) or long-term (due over more than one year). Debt financing is attractive because the lender does not gain an ownership interest in your business. Your obligations are limited to repaying the loan, and perhaps meeting some very general business performance goals. This means that the financing cost is a relatively fixed expense. In addition, the interest on the loan is tax deductible.

"Equity financing" describes an exchange of money for a share of business ownership, the classic example being the sale of stock in your company. This form of financing allows you to obtain funds without having to repay a specific amount of money at any particular time. The major disadvantage to obtaining equity financing (from anyone other than yourself) is the dilution of your ownership interest and possible loss of management control.

Finding the Right Balance

It's important to maintain a balance between debt and equity financing in your business.

Excessive debt financing may impair your credit rating and your ability to raise more money in the future. In addition, you may be unable to weather unanticipated business downturns, credit shortages, or an interest rate increase if your loan's interest rate floats.

Conversely, too much equity financing can indicate that you are not making the most productive use of your capital, because the capital is not being used advantageously as leverage. Too little equity may suggest the owners are not committed to their own business.

Generally speaking, a local community bank will consider an acceptable debt-to-equity ratio to be between 1:2 and 1:1. For startup businesses in particular, the owners need to guard against cash flow shortages that can force the business to take on excess debt, thereby impairing the business's ability to subsequently obtain needed capital for growth.

Warning

Be cautious when making equity contributions of personal assets (cash or property) to your business. Usually your rights to that contribution become secondary to the rights of business creditors if the business goes bad.

As an alternative, you may be able to protect your assets by incorporating and then making secured loans or "straw man" transactions; i.e., you loan money to a third-party relative or friend who then loans the funds to the corporation. The insider then takes a secured interest in the property. Talk to your attorney if you think this strategy is one you might want to pursue.

THE BUSINESS LIFE CYCLE

Where your business is in its financial life cycle — from startup to mature — will often dictate the available financing alternatives.

Startups

New small businesses have trouble securing conventional financing because they present a tremendous risk to lenders and investors. The result is that nearly three-quarters of startup businesses are funded through the owner's own resources, such as personal savings, residential mortgages, or consumer loans. Family members, friends, and investments by private contacts or "angels" provide most of the remaining seed funds for new small businesses. Perseverance and a willingness to investigate all sources of financing — from personal contacts to government loan programs — are invaluable at this stage.

Growing or Mature Businesses

A growing or mature business usually has sufficient stability in its operations so that cash flow problems are not a constant crisis. If the business is successful, internally generated funds from sales and investments can fund many of the business's needs.

Typically, growing and mature businesses have more financing options available to them because of their operating history, established value, credit history, and availability of inventory and accounts receivable financing. In addition, the advantages of having established customers and suppliers, efficient internal operating procedures, more sophisticated marketing and advertising, realistic long-term business plans, and the company's emerging goodwill help improve the business's creditworthiness and investor appeal.

If the business has been profitable, debt financing is generally the preferred way to raise new capital for an existing business. Nonetheless, a growing business may be stifled by inadequate capital for expansion that stems from the reluctance of an entrepreneur to dilute his or her ownership through equity financing.

Acquired Businesses

In many respects, the financing options available when you purchase an existing business are similar to the options for raising capital in a growing business that you already own. Debt and equity vehicles are typically more available to you than if you were starting a similar business from scratch, because the target business has a credit history, existing assets, an established operating cycle and business goodwill.

Acquiring a business offers the opportunity for seller-financing. Entrepreneurs looking to sell their small businesses usually realize that the sale may not go through unless they finance part of the purchase price, and they may be willing to negotiate a very favorable debt or equity arrangement with you.

Advantages of Seller Financing

- *You may get a reasonable interest rate and a less demanding credit review.*

- *The existing assets of the business are often the exclusive collateral for the financing. In contrast to the common practice of conventional lenders, buyers rarely need to pledge additional or personal assets on a seller-financed loan.*

- *Personal guarantees are less likely to be required of you.*

- *A seller may be willing to take a subordinate (secondary) security interest, so that you can also obtain a conventional bank loan for part of the purchase price. The incentive for the seller is that the more money you can obtain from other sources, the more money the seller gets upfront.*

FORMS OF BUSINESS ORGANIZATION

The specific types of financing available to you are likely to be affected by the organizational form of your small business; that is, whether it's a sole proprietorship, partnership, corporation, etc.

Unincorporated Businesses

Fewer and fewer new businesses are finding it necessary to incorporate these days, since the limited liability formerly available only to corporations is now achievable in other business forms which have the added benefit of avoiding the corporate income tax. However, you should be aware that it's somewhat more difficult to raise money for an unincorporated business.

While simple to form and maintain, the sole proprietorship is the most restrictive form of organization for financing because its total capital is limited to whatever personal funds you are willing to contribute, and whatever you can borrow against personal assets.

Financing for partnerships is somewhat easier, because the partners can raise equity funds through their own capital contributions or by adding a new partner. Debt financing for general partnerships is similar to financing for sole proprietorships, because the individual creditworthiness of the owners largely determines the business's creditworthiness.

Warning

Remember that in a general partnership, each partner has unlimited, joint-and-several personal liability for business debts and liabilities. That means that you can be personally liable for the entire amount of any loan the partnership takes out, not just your share.

In a limited partnership, there must be at least one general partner who is required to assume personal liability for the business. There will also be other partners (limited partners) who do not incur personal liability, and who are essentially investors who supply capital but are prohibited from involvement in the day-to-day management of the business. In some situations, a limited partnership can provide a vehicle for attracting investment by outsiders.

Warning

A sale of ownership interests in a limited partnership may be treated as a sale of securities, and state and federal securities laws must be consulted before taking this action.

The limited liability company (LLC) is a hybrid between a corporation and a partnership that offers the best of both worlds for some businesses. There's no limit on the number of members, and all members enjoy limited personal liability for the company's debts.

For financing purposes, LLCs are attractive to investors who might balk at investing in a risky general partnership. Yet unlike a limited partnership, the members of an LLC can be (but don't have to be) actively involved in management. If your business will need more than one investor to operate successfully, you should at least consider using this form of organization.

Corporations

For many small businesses, incorporation provides the easiest method for raising capital from multiple investors, particularly those investors who are not necessarily interested in actively participating in the business. It's often easier to persuade 15 people to invest $5,000 than to convince one person to contribute $75,000, and a corporation permits this kind of widespread ownership.

Stock comes in a variety of different types and a small business can limit the extent of ownership control being sold by limiting the number of shares for sale and/or the rights associated with each class of stock. Nonvoting shares, preferred shares, redeemable shares, and a variety of hybrid shares are possible.

Example

The sale of nonvoting shares or a minority percentage of voting shares in a small company might be an acceptable investment to a family member who doesn't want to be actively involved in the company and who trusts the judgment of the company's active managers.

INVESTOR APPEAL: NOTHING SELLS LIKE SUCCESS

Every small business owner is convinced that the enterprise will be successful. However, to obtain financing, you will need to provide objective evidence that your business will succeed.

On the most basic level, every potential lender or investor evaluates a business by looking at how the injection of cash will be used and how the money will either be repaid or result in a profitable return. Many of these questions may be answered by data contained in your business's financial statements and projections; however, lenders and investors also make more subjective evaluations of you and your company. These assessments may affect your financing requests even more than the objective numbers.

Keep in mind that most lenders and investors are followers, not leaders, and the best evidence of a good investment will be your prior success in raising capital. A financier wants to spread risk as much as possible, and a certain comfort level may be reached if other investors have a significant vested economic interest in your business.

Warning

As a rough rule of thumb, most lenders will expect owners to have an equity investment of at least 25 percent of the total cost of establishing the business.

Your past business experiences, your expertise, and your managerial skills likewise play a crucial factor in determining the appeal of your business. If you can establish a personal relationship with a particular financier, such as a local community banker, your past successes and business experience are more apt to be considered in determining the likely future success of your business. Use your personal resume, as well as letters of reference from community professionals and business persons, to help project yourself as a reputable, reliable, and creative business person.

Work Smart

Additional evidence of future success for your business can sometimes take the form of contract commitments from existing or prospective customers, expert or professional opinions, and market research, even if the "research" is mostly informal testimonials.

In your business plan or loan application, make sure to note advantageous market trends, consumer appeal, retention of skilled employees, and availability of any special resources, e.g., a valuable patent. Identifying a lender whose strategic approach or special industry focus matches your business will also improve your chance of success.

PERSONAL FINANCING

Most small startup business are initially funded by the personal assets of the entrepreneur. Some funding for your small business is likely to come from your direct contributions of personal savings or assets to the business (e.g., an early retirement incentive payout). Additional personal funds are often contributed by borrowing money through a personal consumer loan, and then contributing that money as an equity investment into the business.

Save Time

The majority of business or consumer loans will require that you secure the loan with collateral: that is, an equity (ownership) interest in an asset that exceeds the amount of the loan. Unless you have an extremely solid personal credit history with a lender, the institution is unlikely to grant an unsecured loan to a startup business.

There's a great variety of personal assets that you can use as collateral to obtain cash from a lender, but the most common one is a personal residence. You can obtain a first or second mortgage, refinance an existing mortgage, or take out a home equity loan or line of credit. The major disadvantage to using your house as collateral is that if you default on the loan, you can lose your home.

For second mortgages or lines of credit, lenders will usually allow a maximum total mortgage debt, including preexisting mortgages, of approximately 70 to 85 percent of the current market value of your residence. Some lenders will allow a maximum debt that exceeds 100% of current market value, but the rate on the loan is likely to be steep, and these loans are very risky for the borrower.

Example

If your property is currently valued at $180,000 and you have an existing mortgage of $80,000, your equity value in the house is $100,000. If the lender's maximum loan-to-value percentage is 80 percent, your maximum second mortgage would be for $64,000. The reason is that you must continue to maintain at least 20 percent equity in the home ($36,000), leaving $144,000 available to be financed. $144,000 - $80,000 (your existing mortgage) = $64,000.

Other than your residence, commonly used collateral for secured loans include other real estate, life insurance policies, any existing machinery or business equipment, and stock.

Work Smart

If you can qualify for a consumer or home equity loan, you might be better off not trumpeting the fact that the proceeds of your loan will be used to start a new business. Conservative lenders may be more skeptical of making a consumer loan if they know that the money will be invested in a startup.

INSIDER FINANCING

After considering their personal resources, the next place most entrepreneurs look for financing is to family, friends, or associates.

Borrowing from insiders is attractive because it's private, easier to qualify for, usually unsecured, and often includes favorable terms, and because legal default proceedings are seldom invoked.

However, financing from family and friends is often a double-edged sword. You may be setting yourself up for misunderstandings, personal conflicts, and other problems that can arise from a lack of business formality or economic success. These dangers can seriously damage both the business and the long-term personal relationship between the parties.

Gifts vs. Loans

If a friend or relative is contributing capital as a gift, they should give you a "gift letter" stating the facts. Otherwise, on future loan applications, a bank may be concerned that you'll need to repay the "gift" and your cash flow may not support an additional loan.

Work Smart

The federal government allows each individual to make an annual tax-free gift of up to $10,000 per recipient. For example, if your parents wanted to give you a tax-free gift, they could each give you $10,000 per year (total gift of $20,000 annually). They could also give your spouse a total of $20,000 annually.

If the transfer of funds is *not* intended to be a gift, an enforceable agreement such as a promissory note should be drafted that reflects the nature and terms of the exchange. On the next page we've reproduced a basic promissory note form that you can use to document your loan agreement and make it legally binding.

The absence of interest charges, or below-market rates, may be a red flag for the IRS to question whether an insider transaction is really a gift, rather than a loan. If the IRS accepts your treatment as a loan, but finds that little or no interest is being charged, it may "impute" interest and tax the lender on the interest that he or she "should" have received.

Installment Note

$_____   _____, 20_____

    FOR VALUE RECEIVED, the undersigned promise(s) to pay to

_____ the principal sum of

_____ DOLLARS

($ _____) and interest on the balance of principal remaining from time to

time unpaid at the rate of _____ per cent per annum, such principal sum

and interest to be payable in installments as follows: _____

DOLLARS ($ _____) on the _____ day of _____, 20 _____ ,

and _____DOLLARS ($ _____) on the

_____ day of each and every month thereafter until this Note is fully paid, except

that the final payment of principal and interest, if not sooner paid, shall be due on

the _____ day of _____ , 20 _____.   All such payments on account of the

indebtedness evidenced by this Note shall be applied first to accrued and unpaid

interest on the unpaid principal balance and the remainder to principal.

    Payments are to be made at _____, or at such other

place as the legal holder of this Note may from time to time in writing appoint.

    And to secure the payment of said amount, the undersigned hereby authorizes,
irrevocably, any attorney of any Court of Record to appear for the
undersigned in such Court, in term time or vacation, at any time after maturity, and
confess a judgment, without process, in favor of the holder of this Note, for such
amount as may appear to be unpaid thereon, together with reasonable costs
of collection, including reasonable attorney's fees and to waive and release all errors
which may intervene in any such proceedings, and consent to immediate execution
upon such judgment, hereby ratifying and confirming all that said attorney may
do by virtue hereof.

    At the option of the legal holder hereof and without notice, the principal sum
remaining unpaid hereon, together with accrued interest thereon, shall become at
once due and payable at the place of payment aforesaid in case default shall occur in
the payment, when due, of any installment of principal or interest in accordance
with the terms hereof.

    All parties hereto severally waive presentment for payment, notice of
dishonor, protest and notice of protest.

                           (signed)_____

                           _____

INSTALLMENT NOTE	Received on the within Note the following sums				
_____	Date	Interest		Principal		Remarks
	20	Dollars	Cts.	Dollars	Cts.	

INSTALLMENT NOTE

_____

TO

_____

_____

Date _____
20 _____

Amount $ _____

Monthly $_____

Last payment due:

MM-DD-YY

Date 20	Interest Dollars	Cts.	Principal Dollars	Cts.	Remarks

Equity Financing by Insiders

If you want the insider to become an owner of your business in exchange for financing, documentation of the arrangement is again important, but the paperwork will vary according to the type of ownership interest you are transferring.

For example, if the business is incorporated, a sale of stock to family or friends can be fairly simple. Make sure that the price they pay fairly represents the value of the ownership interest being sold; otherwise gift tax and director liability issues may arise.

If the business is not incorporated, equity financing should include a drafting or redrafting of the partnership, limited partnership, or limited liability company operating agreement, or joint venture arrangement. The rights, liabilities, and responsibilities of the new participants should be defined clearly to avoid later confusion, disagreements, or unanticipated liabilities.

Bootstrapping: Internal Sources of Funds

Bootstrapping is a buzzword that basically means generating needed funds by deftly managing your cash inflows and outflows. Improving cash flow should be a daily task, like housekeeping.

Monitoring, forecasting, and analyzing cash flows are essential to liquidity and profitability, even for the Fortune 500 crowd. A basic list of areas of concentration would include:

- **Collection of accounts receivable** — Can credit terms or collection procedures be improved? How about billing cycles and/or cash discount incentives?

- **Inventory management** — Do you really need all that inventory? It ties up cash, takes up expensive space, ups insurance costs, and often "shrinks," so if you don't absolutely need it for immediate shipping or manufacturing purposes, keep it lean and mean.

- **Accounts payable cycle** — Vendors make good financiers. If they offer 30 days to pay, take 30 days and think about asking for 45. Set up a system to take advantage of early payment discounts too.

- **Expense control** — Make every dollar count. Do you really need to rent that expensive postage meter or can you just buy self-stick stamps for awhile? Does your company van need to be washed at the fancy place down the block or can you spare a little time to do it yourself on the weekend? Thrift applies to fixed assets, too. Will a used computer do the job you were going to buy that Pentium III for?

A little frugality and sensible use of available resources will pay big dividends in the long run. The old cliché "watch the pennies and the dollars will take care of themselves" is the bootstrapper's fight song.

Quick Pick Chart: Financing Sources

Our "quick pick" chart of suggested financing options, found on the next page, is loosely arranged according to the age of the business and whether the financing is for long-term or short-term needs. For each type of financing, checkmarks in the columns marked "P" indicate primary or commonly used sources of funding, and checkmarks in the columns marked "S" indicate secondary or less-commonly used sources. Each type of financing is described in more detail in the next three chapters.

As you read the chart, keep in mind that our arrangement of financing options merely reflects how each option is *often* used, not how the option is *always* used. Most types of financing may be used, under certain circumstances and in certain businesses, throughout the life cycle of a business.

One of the most important points to remember is that there is no cookbook recipe to follow for obtaining small business financing. Our chart can give you some general guidance, but attempting to slot your business into a rigid financing profile can limit your own creative thinking as well as the impression you give to financiers.

With small businesses, the risk to investors and creditors is so high that each financial trait is exaggerated, and any shortcomings must be balanced by a compensating advantage. You need to be flexible in considering how the strengths and weaknesses of your business can be presented so that you can have access to as many different sources of financing as possible.

Quick Pick Chart for Financing Sources

Type of Business ⇒	Startup				Growing/Maturing			
Length of Financing ⇒	Short-Term		Long-Term		Short-Term		Long-Term	
	P	S	P	S	P	S	P	S
Angels			√					√
Asset-based financing				√	√			
Bank lending — lines of credit, short-term commercial loans	√				√			
Bank lending — secured and unsecured longer term loans							√	
Business alliances				√			√	
Commercial finance companies		√			√			√
Credit cards	√							
Equity financing			√				√	
ESOPs								√
Factoring					√			
Franchising				√				√
Initial public offerings								√
Insider (family/friends) financing	√		√					
Leasing			√				√	
Limited private offerings							√	
Personal financing	√		√					
SBA CAPlines		√				√		
SBA Export Working Capital Loan Guarantee Program						√		
SBA International Loan Program								√
SBA LowDoc	√		√					
SBA microloans	√							
SBA regular 7(a) program				√			√	
SBA Section 504 — Community Development Companies								√
SBICs				√			√	
State and local public financing		√		√	√			
Trade credit	√				√			
Venture capital				√			√	

Chapter 8

Equity Financing

Equity financing requires that you sell an ownership interest in the business in exchange for capital. Obviously, the most basic hurdle to equity financing is finding investors besides yourself who are willing to buy into your business.

BUSINESS COMBINATIONS

The business climate of the '90s has encouraged the use of joint ventures and alliances between businesses as a means of reducing costs without incurring debt or trading away any equity. Most of these arrangements are for a limited time period and a specific purpose, and are governed by a detailed contract.

For small businesses, strategic alliances often consist of simple bartering with customers, suppliers, and even competitors. For example, if you own a manufacturing business, you might be able to get a better price for component parts if you will agree to put a label on your final product that includes the supplier's trademark. Your networking ability plays a major role in locating and investigating strategic partnering opportunities.

Warning

When choosing a business partner or alliance, make sure to research the operating and credit history of the potential candidate. Several credit reporting agencies offer business financial reports on other businesses. These reports may include not only prior credit experiences, but also financial information from the potential partner's bank (e.g., account balance amounts) and personal background information regarding the principals of that business (e.g., education, relevant work experience, etc.).

PRIVATE INVESTORS/BUSINESS ANGELS

A less-formal source for external equity financing is through private investors, called silent partners or "angels," who are seeking new business investments for a variety of economic and personal reasons.

Angels are often individuals or groups of local professionals or businesspersons who are interested in assisting new companies that will enhance the immediate community. They are generally not interested in controlling the business, although they may require you to meet certain business goals or follow certain practices.

Most entrepreneurs already recognize that potential angel investors might be just about anywhere. Networking within your community and your business circles can often provide a good starting point. Potential financing contacts can arise through your business associates, affiliations with relevant trade associations, inquiries through your local banker, accountant or attorney, local chambers of commerce, and through other small business entrepreneurs.

Most commonly, angels will want an equity interest in the business and some guaranteed exit provisions, such as a mandatory buyout, a "put" option requiring the business to repurchase the stock at the investor's option, or a public offering of stock. In a five-year period, angels might expect a return on investment of three to five times their initial investment.

Work Smart

When looking for "angel" investors, do your best to shop for "smart money;" in other words, try to get more from an angel than just financing. Many angels will serve as advisors, to offer the value of their experience and strategic advice on operating the enterprise. In addition, the angels will frequently use their own connections to assist the business in finding additional financing, growth opportunities, favorable suppliers, new customers, etc.

Angel Networks

In addition to your own efforts at finding interested investors in your community, you can take advantage of a growing cottage industry of "angel network" firms that will, for a subscription fee, try to match up prospective investors with small businesses.

A number of these firms exist, including the Technology Capital Network at the Massachusetts Institute of Technology, 617-253-7163, and the Capital Network in Austin, TX, 512-305-0826. The U.S. Small Business Administration provides an angel network on the Internet called ACE-Net, at http://www.sba.gov.

VENTURE CAPITAL

Venture capital ("VC") firms supply funding from private sources for companies that have high, rapid growth potential and a need for large amounts of capital. The firms typically invest for periods of three to seven years and expect at least a 20 percent to 40 percent *annual* return on their investment.

When dealing with venture capital firms, keep in mind that they are under great pressure to identify and exploit fast growth opportunities before more conventional financing alternatives become available to the target companies. Venture capital firms have a reputation for negotiating tough financing terms. Three bottom-line suggestions:

- *Make sure to read the fine print.*

- *Watch for delay maneuvers (they may be waiting for your financial position to weaken).*

- *Guard your trade secrets and other proprietary information zealously.*

Venture capital financing will not be a good choice of financing (or even available) for most small businesses. Usually, venture capital firms favor businesses that have been operating for several years. Their financing of startups is limited to situations where the high risk is tempered by special circumstances, such as a company with extremely experienced management and a very marketable, high-tech product or service. The target companies often have revenues in excess of two million dollars and a preexisting capital investment of at least $1 million. Due to the amount of money that they spend in examining businesses before they invest, VCs will usually want to invest at least a quarter of a million dollars to justify their costs.

Demands by the VC for an ownership interest of 30 to 50 percent of the target company are not uncommon, and financing for a startup or higher risk venture could require transfer of a majority interest. The investing company will usually want at least one seat on the target company's board of directors and involvement, for better or worse, in the major decisions affecting the direction of the company.

Venture capital firms are located nationwide, and a directory is available for $40 through the National Venture Capital Association, 1655 N. Fort Meyer Dr., Arlington, VA 22209, (703) 524-2549. In addition, other sources for venture capital can be found through bankers, insurance companies, and business associations.

SMALL BUSINESS INVESTMENT COMPANIES

The federal government sponsors its own *public* venture capital organization through the Small Business Investment Company (SBIC) program.

An SBIC is a privately owned and operated company that partners with the federal government to provide venture capital to small business. Using a combination of private funds and funds borrowed from the federal government, the SBICs provide equity capital, long-term loans (up to 20 years, with a possible 10-year extension), and management assistance to eligible small businesses.

Like a VC firm, an SBIC is most commonly a source of financing for a fast-growing, existing business (rather than a startup) that needs a substantial amount of capital to keep up with its rapid expansion. An SBIC may offer more flexible terms than a venture capital firm, and is not permitted to control any small business permanently.

Currently there are about 200 active SBICs. You can locate the nearest ones by calling your local SBA office — consult the telephone directory under "U.S. Government," call the Small Business Answer Desk at 1-800-8ASK-SBA, or visit online at http://www.sba.com/inv.

In 1971, Congress created a second category of small business investment companies, the Specialized Small Business Investment Company (SSBIC). They operate in the same manner as SBICs, but can obtain additional government financial assistance by investing in small businesses owned by socially or economically disadvantaged minorities.

INITIAL PUBLIC OFFERINGS

It seems that every week, some small company becomes an overnight success story by deciding to "go public" through an initial public offering (IPO) of its stock. Going public simply means that a company that was previously owned by a limited number of private investors has elected, for the first time, to sell ownership shares of the business to the general public.

Despite the IPO hype, most small companies are not going to go public. IPOs largely remain a financing option for rapidly growing businesses that generate over a million dollars in net annual income.

The use of IPOs is limited primarily because:

- There is a very high cost and much complexity in complying with federal and state laws governing the sale of securities (the cost for a small business can run from $50,000 to $500,000).

- Offering your business's ownership for public sale does little good unless your company has sufficient investor awareness and appeal to make the IPO worthwhile.

- Management must be ready to handle the administrative and legal demands of widespread public ownership, dilution of the existing shareholders' interests, and the possibility of takeovers or adjustments in management control.

ALTERNATIVES TO GOING PUBLIC

Under federal law, a "security" is broadly defined and includes stocks, notes, bonds, and most ownership interests.

While many small businesses sell interests in their companies that are technically securities, the transactions are often exempt from registration regulations because the offerings are sufficiently small in dollar amount, and they are restricted to a limited number or type of investors. These exempt offers are called "limited private offerings" and they can avoid much of the cost and delay of a public offering.

Unfortunately, to avoid registration, you must fit the criteria for exemption from *both* federal and state security laws, so you'll still need expert legal advice before selling any stock in your company.

Federal Exemptions

At the federal level, the most popular exemption from registration requirements for small businesses is Rule 504, commonly known as "Regulation D." Under this provision, *private* companies that are selling less than $1 million worth of securities to any number of investors within a 12-month period are exempt from federal registration requirements. Most startups and smaller businesses would fall within this exemption.

Warning

Even if a securities offer is exempt from the registration requirements of federal or state law, the anti-fraud provisions of those laws still apply. Therefore, you must take care to prevent misrepresentations or omissions in the offering that create an overly optimistic picture of the investment.

Another exemption is available to private or publicly held companies that sell less than $5 million within a 12-month period, if the sales are made only to no more than 35 *"accredited investors."* Accredited investors include banks, brokers and dealers, insurance companies, company officers and directors, and wealthy investors having an annual income over $200,000 or a net worth of over $1 million. Finally, there's an exemption for private offerings of stock sold only to people living in the state where the company is incorporated and does significant business.

State Exemptions

Because each state also has securities regulations, the local exemptions must also be checked. Just because a sale may be exempt from federal registration does not mean that state registration is not required.

As of this writing, 45 states currently have relaxed their securities regulations for small business by offering a Small Company Offering Registration (SCOR) procedure. Even if your business is not based in one of these states, you may still register and sell your securities in the states which have adopted SCOR. For a current list of eligible states, contact the North American Securities Administrators Association at 202-737-0900, or http://www.nasaa.org.

FINANCING THROUGH FRANCHISING

In Chapter 2, we discussed the major pros and cons of buying a franchise. But there's another side to franchising that some small business owners might want to explore.

For *franchisors,* franchising is a means of equity financing in which the franchisor sells off expansion rights in the business. In return, the franchisor typically receives an initial franchise fee, service fees, equipment sale or lease fees, and royalties from each franchisee. In this way the franchisor can achieve much faster growth in a wider geographic market. Disadvantages of franchising are the unique development and overhead costs associated with franchising, the heightened legal risks from vicarious liability for the acts of franchisee operations, increased regulatory costs, and a dilution of ownership.

Work Smart

If you think that your business is a good prototype for similar businesses in other locations, we recommend that you establish at least a couple of other sites yourself. If the expansion is successful for at least a year, talk to a good franchise attorney about testing the waters by selling one or two franchises.

EMPLOYEE STOCK OWNERSHIP PLANS

An employee stock ownership plan (ESOP) is a qualified retirement plan in which the major investment is made in the employer's stock. In an ESOP, employees can purchase shares of stock in the company by paying cash or by agreeing to reductions from salary or benefits.

In addition, the company contributes to the ESOP either by making an annual cash contribution to the plan for the purchase of company securities or by directly contributing stock to the plan. Either way, the company's contribution results in the cash price of the stock being returned to the company, as the employees purchase the stock over time. The company gets a tax deduction for the ESOP contribution while effectively retaining the cash.

Because an ESOP requires that you have employees and because implementing an ESOP can be expensive and time-consuming, this financing tool may not be sensible for many startup and existing small businesses. ESOPs are, however, commonly used by business owners seeking to retire because the ESOP provides a ready-made buyer for their stock. For more information, contact the ESOP Association, 1726 M Street NW, Suite 501, Washington, DC 20036, or see their Internet site at http://www.the-esop-emplowner.org.

Chapter 9

Debt Financing

There are a number of types of institutions that offer loan products useful to small businesses. Each type of lender and loan product may be better suited to different lending situations. In this chapter we'll discuss your major debt financing options, as well as what lenders are looking for when they make a loan decision.

SELECTING A BANK OR OTHER LENDER

Banks are generally the first place small business owners think of when they need a loan, and, in fact, SBA statistics show that 60% of measurable small business lending is obtained from commercial banks. Banks are highly regulated in order to minimize the government's risks from insuring the accounts of depositors. As a consequence, bank lending policies toward small businesses tend to be very conservative.

Many large banks are making efforts to compete for small business borrowers by creating small business departments that actively solicit local business.

However, the target customer for these banks is still more likely to be a "big" small business, with a proven track record and significant available collateral.

In short, aside from secured loans and mortgage financing, larger banks are still not a major participant in small business finance. You may want to give a big bank a try, but small, community banks often offer your best option.

These institutions tend to be less rigid or formulaic in assessing loan applications and are more willing to consider individual factors in their decision-making.

Work Smart

You should attempt to establish an ongoing working relationship with a specific bank even before setting up shop, or as soon as possible thereafter. Establishing a small line of credit with a bank, even if your business does not immediately need funds, is often a good way of getting to know your banker. The more knowledgeable and familiar the lender is with you, the more likely the lender is to understand and accommodate the individual needs of your business. And if you apply for a line of credit and then don't need to use it, you'll build up a very favorable impression with your banker.

Commercial Finance Companies

Commercial financing companies are subject to less regulation than banks, and can assume more risk. As a result they are less conservative than a traditional bank in making small business loans, and offer more flexible lending terms. Typically they will make only highly collateralized loans to established businesses. Loans must be secured by readily marketable assets, such as equipment, inventory, or accounts receivable.

Because their loans may be riskier, commercial finance companies usually charge higher rates of interest than banks. They may also insist on significant prepayment penalties to deter a borrower from refinancing with a conventional bank if the borrower improves his or her creditworthiness.

Less-standard loans allow for flexibility, but also require you to review very carefully the terms of the loan, including interest computation and payment method, prepayment rights, and default terms.

COMMON TYPES OF LOANS

The length of time over which you want to borrow money, and the amount and type of collateral you can put up as security for the loan, will generally determine the type of loan and lender that are right for you.

Working Capital Lines of Credit

A line of credit sets a maximum amount of funds available from the bank, to be used when needed, for the ongoing working capital or other day-to-day cash needs of a business.

The lines are typically offered for renewable periods that range from 90 days to several years, although extended periods are usually subject to annual reviews by the lender. The maximum amounts vary greatly; interest rates usually float and you pay interest only on the outstanding balance. Money is typically used for daily operations, such as inventory purchases, and to cover periodic or cyclical business fluctuations. Collateral for the loan is often accounts receivable or inventory.

From a lender's perspective, the adequacy of the borrower's cash flow is the most critical consideration in making this type of loan. A commitment fee may be assessed by the bank for making a line of credit available to the borrower, even if the full amount is never used. An established business with a sound credit history may be able to obtain an unsecured revolving line of credit.

Warning

A commercial line of credit can, for better or worse, become an "evergreen" never-ending debt to a small business.

Frequently, a small business will open a working capital line of credit of, for example, $40,000. Because of the immediate cash needs of the business, the credit line is quickly topped out. The borrower's continuing cash shortage forces it to pay only interest on the loan and the principal is not reduced.

Commonly, working capital lines of credit are reviewed annually by the lender and they can either be renewed or called due. However, while lenders typically want the line of credit to carry a zero balance at some time during the annual period, the competitive banking environment may lead a bank to continually renew a maximized line of credit as long as the institution is receiving timely interest on the loan. Evergreen lines of credit become, in effect, indefinite term loans with a balloon payment of principal that poses risks to both the lender and the borrower.

Credit Cards

The competitive banking environment has forced many institutions to seek new sources of income and develop new financial products. One of the less publicized developments has been the growth of the small business credit card.

As a source for working capital, revolving credit cards offer a hassle-free, quick source for limited funds. However, their convenience is costly. The cards typically offer an interest rate slightly lower than the rate on individual consumer cards and have lending limits that average just over $15,000.

Short-Term Commercial Loans

Although short-term commercial loans are sometimes used to finance the same type of operating costs as a working capital line of credit, they differ from lines of credit in that a fixed amount of money is borrowed for a set time with interest paid on the lump sum. Most short-term commercial loans are taken out for a specific expenditure (e.g., to purchase a specific piece of equipment).

For nearly all startup businesses, and most existing businesses, a short-term commercial loan from a bank will have to be secured by adequate collateral, such as accounts receivable or inventory, or fixed assets such as equipment or real estate. Cash flow and a regular sales history will also be very important to the lender. A fixed interest rate may be available because the duration of the loan, and therefore the risk of rising rates, is limited. While some short-term loans have terms as brief as 90-120 days, the loans may extend one to three years for certain purposes.

Long-Term Commercial Loans

Long-term commercial loans (those repaid over more than one to three years) are typically more difficult to obtain for smaller businesses because the longer the term of the loan, the greater the risk to the lender. With small businesses, a lender may not be willing to assume the risk that the company will be solvent for, say, 10 years. Occasionally, exceptions for a longer term may be negotiated. Also, loans secured by real estate can carry an extended term.

The purposes for long-term commercial loans vary greatly, from purchases of major equipment and plant facilities to business expansion or acquisition costs. These loans are usually secured by the asset being acquired, and financial loan covenants such as limitations on future financing are usually required.

Work Smart

Some small business advisors discourage the use of debt financing for fixed assets, particularly long-term assets such as equipment, office space, or fixtures. They suggest that the cash flow problems of small businesses require that borrowed money be directed to generating immediate revenue through spending on inventory and marketing activities. Buying a new expensive piece of machinery may take many years to pay for itself. Instead, you should do whatever you can to minimize the costs of fixed assets by leasing, buying used equipment, sharing equipment, etc.

Letters of Credit

Letters of credit are not the most common means of small business financing, but they are an important financing tool for companies that engage in international trade.

A letter of credit (LC) is simply a guarantee of payment upon proof that contract terms between a buyer and seller have been completed. LCs are just fancy, two-way IOUs often used to facilitate international credit purchases.

You, the buyer, go to your bank and request a letter of credit, which it will grant you only if you have an adequate line of credit established with it. On your behalf (and for a fee), your bank promises (via the LC) to pay the purchase price to a seller (or his or her appointed bank) if stipulated and highly detailed conditions are met.

These conditions might include any or all of the following:

- complete, on-board, ocean bills of lading

- commercial invoice, original, six copies

- packing slip, original, six copies

- insurance certificates

- inspection certificates

- strict date limitations

- precise name, and address of the beneficiary (seller)

- references to mode of transport and

- dozens of other conditions covered by the "Rules."

The "Rules" were drafted by the International Chamber of Commerce (ICC) in 1933 and revised as recently as 1993. They govern a standard letter of credit format accepted internationally and are known as the "Uniform Customs and Practice for Commercial Documentary Credits (UCP)."

The buyer's bank works as a kind of transfer agent, usually with the seller's bank, to exchange the purchase price for title or claim to goods. The parties thereby use their banks as intermediaries or middlemen to limit the risks of doing business with foreign trading partners. These risks include foreign currency exchange rate fluctuations as well as frequent shipping delays and the multitude of perils inherent in international trade.

Letters of credit are available in a variety of forms — confirmed irrevocable letters of credit, confirmed letters of credit, acceptance letters of credit, or back-to-back letters of credit with differing degrees of bank commitment. Generally you will only be dealing with irrevocable LCs.

If you are the importer, for example, you need to be assured that the proper goods will be delivered to you intact, on a date certain, in good condition and at the agreed upon cost. The sellers (exporters) need to know that when they comply with all the terms you've set forth in the letter of credit, they'll be paid the amount due in a timely manner. And everything must be thoroughly documented at both ends

Asset-Based Financing

To generate working capital or to meet specific short-term cash needs, small businesses may use certain short-term assets as collateral or inventory for commercial loans.

Accounts Receivable Financing

This form of financing is a type of secured loan in which accounts receivable are pledged as collateral, and the loan is repaid within a specified short-term period as the receivables are collected.

Accounts receivable financing is most often used by businesses facing short-term cash flow problems. The major sources are commercial finance companies, although banks will also consider receivables as security for a business loan.

Accounts receivable are typically "aged" by the borrower before a value is assigned to them. The older the account, the less value it has. For example, financiers often lend approximately 75 percent of the face value of accounts less than 30 days old. Some lenders don't pay attention to the age of the accounts until they are outstanding for over 90 days, and then they may refuse to finance them. Other lenders apply a graduated scale to value the accounts so that, for instance, accounts that are from 31-60 days old may have a loan-to-value ratio of only 60 percent, and accounts from 61-90 days old will have a ratio of only 30 percent. Delinquencies in the accounts and the overall creditworthiness of the account debtors may also affect the loan-to-value ratio.

A monthly interest rate on accounts receivable is calculated by applying a daily percentage rate to the receivables outstanding each day (the less the outstanding receivables, the lower the interest charge). Some states require notice to the business's debtors that their debt has been pledged as loan security. In states that do not have this requirement, some businesses do not notify their customers because customers might perceive this method of financing as a sign of financial instability.

Inventory Financing

Inventory financing is similar to accounts receivable financing, except the business's current inventory is used as collateral for the secured loan. Automobile dealers are among those who use this technique.

You can anticipate a very conservative valuation of your inventory and a maximum loan amount that is somewhat less than 100 percent of the lender's valuation figure. Average lender discounting would allow lending of no more than 60 to 80 percent of the value of your ready-to-go retail inventory. A manufacturer's inventory, consisting of component parts and other unfinished materials, might qualify for a loan of only 30 percent of its value. The key factor is the merchantability of the inventory — how quickly and for how much money could the inventory be sold.

Factoring

Factoring is the *sale* of accounts receivable, as opposed to *borrowing* against them as described above. The factor company that purchases the receivables then collects them when they are due, assuming responsibility for all of the costs, as well as the hard work and hassle, that comes with customer debt collection.

Commercial finance companies, some banks, and a variety of specialized factor companies will purchase receivables. If you have small monthly amounts of receivables (e.g., less than $10,000), it may require some effort to locate a factor company willing to purchase them. Your local telephone book may list factoring brokers that can assist you in locating suitable factor companies.

The downside to factoring is that it's not cheap; the cash price of the accounts receivable is discounted by the factor company, which then charges interest on the amount advanced. Your final cost will nearly always exceed the amount you would pay on a short-term commercial loan for an equal amount. Factoring is generally a last ditch method of raising cash, although it's commonly used in the garment industry.

Leasing

Leasing companies, as well as banks and some suppliers and vendors, will rent equipment and almost any other business asset. Leasing assets, rather than purchasing them, is a form of financing because it avoids the large downpayment frequently required for asset purchases and it frees up funds for other business expenditures.

However, you should be aware that leasing from conventional lenders may be difficult for startup businesses because traditional lenders require an operating history from prospective lessees. For more information on leasing, see Chapter 16.

THE REAL COST OF BORROWING MONEY

The final cost of borrowing money often involves much more than just the interest rate. A variety of other monetary and nonmonetary costs should be considered in determining the real cost of borrowing. For example, a loan that requires you to maintain certain financial ratios may be unrealistic for your particular business. The following pages describe the main features to think about and compare.

Interest Rates

Any interest rate that exceeds the bank's prime rate should be considered negotiable. The negotiable range is likely to be very small, but even an eighth of a point in interest can be meaningful. As a small borrower, you should expect to pay a point or two over the bank's prime lending rate. Generally, the longer the term of the loan, the higher the interest rate.

Variable interest rates. Banks often prefer floating interest rates (that is, interest rates that fluctuate over time in response to changing economic conditions) in making small commercial loans, to minimize the already significant risks of lending to a small business. As a borrower you should try to negotiate a rate cap on any variable rate loan, so that you have some idea of your maximum exposure.

Fixed interest rates. In some instances, you might also consider "buying" a fixed rate from the lender. Many banks will give you a fixed interest rate for a rate slightly higher than the current floating rate, e.g., an additional ½ percent.

Save Money

Competition among banks makes shopping around for the best rates worthwhile. Occasionally, a local bank may decide that it needs to increase its small business lending by aggressively discounting its rates for a limited time period to new borrowers. Unfortunately, these banks often don't do a good job of advertising their programs and you might not discover an attractive rate unless you actively investigate.

Points or Fees

Points are one-time charges computed as a percentage of the total loan amount, and allow the bank to get some interest on the loan immediately. If you pay points, you should get a lower overall rate.

On lines of credit, some institutions may charge a commitment fee for keeping credit available to you. This fee typically runs approximately half a point or less on the *unused* portion of the credit line. Upfront bank charges for a loan can also be assessed for reviewing and preparing documents, performing credit checks, and simply agreeing to give you a loan.

If a borrower prepays any of the principal on a loan, the bank does not get all the interest it expected to receive on that amount. Some institutions will charge a fee for prepayment of certain loans (usually long-term) to discourage such prepayments.

Compensating Balances

Some banks will require a short-term borrower to establish and maintain a specified balance in an account at the institution as a condition of the loan. For example, the bank may require you to keep at least 10 percent of the outstanding loan balance in a low-interest-bearing account. This "compensating balance," in effect, allows the bank to reduce the principal amount of the loan and increase the real rate of interest.

A compensating balance is negotiable and some banks simply request an informal "depositor relationship" with the borrower. This relationship requires only that the borrower use the bank for some other type of business, e.g., to maintain a credit card or open some type of traditional savings account.

Periodic Reporting

Lenders will typically require periodic reports on the status of your business. Local community banks will probably require only quarterly and annual financial statements (balance sheets and income statements) and annual personal financial statements and income tax returns. However, if the loan is secured by accounts receivable (or sometimes inventory), monthly reporting and aging statements on these items will be required. In some cases, the bank will insist that statements be prepared by a CPA, which adds to the cost of the loan.

Work Smart

Don't be overly concerned about reporting requirements. Some smaller, local banks rarely confirm the accuracy of these financial statements by any type of independent audit, and as long as a quick review reveals no significant problems, the reporting requirements are usually considered technicalities. As one banker noted, "In 15 years, I've only had five loans where the bank became significantly concerned due to unfavorable financial reporting requirements, and all of the situations were resolved after conference with the borrower."

Financial Covenants

Conventional lenders typically include a variety of covenants and restrictions in the loan agreement. Some banks may place restrictions on the use of loan funds, require proper maintenance of business facilities (e.g., insurance coverage), require maintenance of key financial ratios such as a certain debt to equity ratio, current ratio, and coverage of fixed charges ratio, as well as minimum working capital balances, restrictions on the amounts of dividend payments and salaries, mergers and acquisitions, and limits on secondary or further pledges of assets.

A subordination agreement is a special type of loan covenant that stipulates that all corporate obligations such as rights of shareholders, officers, and directors are subordinated (made lower in priority) to the bank loan. Default on these terms can mean foreclosure on the secured assets. Nearly all small business commercial loans allow the bank to "call" the loan due if the bank feels that repayment is seriously threatened.

Personal Guarantees

A personal guarantee is a pledge, by someone other than the named borrower, that he or she will pay any deficiencies on a specific loan. Guarantees are often required from all owners and their spouses.

Most guarantee forms require joint and several liability, meaning that each individual who signs a guarantee can be held responsible for the whole amount of the loan. Consequently, even if someone is only a 10 percent owner in the business, that person is personally liable for 100 percent of the amount being guaranteed. In effect, when you sign a personal guarantee, you become personally liable for the loan, even if your business is incorporated.

Work Smart

Now, with some lenders, the name of the game is "take it or leave it" and everyone must sign a guarantee or there's no deal. However, depending upon collateral and the credit-worthiness of the business, you may have some room for negotiation, particularly when dealing with smaller, community banks. Naturally, the banker is unlikely to tell you this. You won't know until you try to negotiate this point.

Always try to emphasize, if applicable, that your business has sufficient collateral to secure the loan and that a pledge of personal assets is excessive security. As your business matures and establishes a credit history, the lender's need for personal guarantees should correspondingly decline and you should continue to negotiate the issue of personal guarantees whenever the business seeks borrowed funds.

If giving a personal guarantee cannot be avoided (and for most younger businesses, it can't be), try negotiating the terms of the agreement. Offer a limited personal guarantee, for instance, of 25 percent of the loan.

Finally, if your personal portfolio contains sufficient assets to cover the loan, and your spouse independently owns other significant assets, be prepared to present a case for why at least your spouse's personal guarantee is unnecessary.

WHAT BANKS LOOK FOR

Whether you are applying to a bank for a line of home equity credit, a line of credit for business working capital, a commercial short-term loan, real estate financing, or some other type of commercial or consumer loan, a prospective lender will examine four fundamental characteristics.

The Four "Cs"

- **credit history** of the borrower

- **collateral** that is available to secure the loan

- **cash flow** history and projections for the business

- **character** of the borrower

Credit History

Lenders will want to review both the credit history of your business (if the business is not a startup) and, because a personal guarantee is often required for a small business loan, your personal credit history.

It's often wise to obtain a credit report on yourself and your business before you apply for credit. If you discover any inaccuracies or problems, you can correct them before any damage to your loan application has occurred.

Save Time

Try to find out which credit reporting company your prospective lender uses and request a report from that company. The three major consumer credit reporting companies are TransUnion (800-916-8800), Experian (TRW) (800-682-7654), and Equifax (800-685-1111). Dun & Bradstreet (800-234-3867) is the largest business credit reporting agency.

Collateral

Collateral may be defined as property that secures a loan or other debt, so that the property may be seized by the lender if the borrower fails to make proper payments on the loan.

In order to ensure that the particular collateral provides appropriate security, the lender will want to match the type of collateral with the loan being made. For example, the useful life of the collateral will typically have to exceed, or at least meet, the term of the loan; otherwise the lender's secured interest would be jeopardized. Consequently, short-term assets such as receivables and inventory will not be acceptable as security for a long-term loan, but they are appropriate for short-term financing such as a line of credit.

In addition, many lenders will require that their claim to the collateral be a "first secured interest," meaning that no prior or superior liens exist, or may be subsequently created, against the collateral. By being a priority lien holder, the lender ensures its share of any foreclosure proceeds before any other claimant is entitled to any money.

Loan-to-Value Ratio

To further limit their risks, lenders usually discount the value of the collateral so that they are not extending 100 percent of the collateral's highest market value. This relationship between the amount of money the bank lends to the value of the collateral is called the loan-to-value ratio.

The type of collateral used to secure the loan will affect the bank's acceptable loan-to-value ratio. These ratios can vary between lenders and the ratio may also be influenced by other lending criteria; e.g., a healthy cash flow may allow for more leeway in the ratio.

Example

A representative listing of loan-to-value ratios for collateral used by a community bank is:

- **Real estate** — *if the real estate is occupied, the lender might provide up to 75 percent of the appraised value. If the property is improved, but not occupied (e.g., a planned new residential subdivision with sewer and water, but no homes yet), up to 50 percent. For vacant and unimproved property, 30 percent.*

- **Accounts receivable** — *you may get up to 75 percent on accounts that are less than 30 days old, and as little as 30 percent on accounts that are 61-90 days old.*

- **Securities** — *marketable stocks and bonds can be used as collateral to obtain up to 75 percent of their market value.*

- **Inventory** — *a lender may advance from 60 to 80 percent of value for ready-to-go retail inventory. A manufacturer's inventory, consisting of component parts and other unfinished materials, might be only 30 percent.*

- **Equipment** — *if the equipment is new, the bank might agree to lend 75 percent of the purchase price; if the equipment is used, then a lesser percentage of the appraised liquidation value might be advanced. However, some lenders apply a reverse approach to discounting of equipment: they assume that new equipment is significantly devalued as soon as it goes out the seller's door (e.g., a new car is worth much less after it's driven off the lot). These lenders would use a higher percentage loan-to-value ratio for used goods because a recent appraisal value would give a relatively accurate assessment of the current market value of that property.*

Cash Flow from Operations

The cash flow from your business's operations — the cycle of cash from the purchase of inventory through the collection of accounts receivable — is the most important factor for obtaining short-term debt financing. A lender's primary concern is whether your daily operations will generate enough cash to repay the loan. In addition, cash flow shows how your major cash expenditures relate to your major cash sources. This information may give a lender insight into your business's market demand, management competence, business cycles, and any significant changes in the business over time.

While a variety of factors may affect cash flow and a particular lender's evaluation of your business's cash flow numbers, a small community bank might consider an acceptable working cash flow ratio — the amount of available cash at any one time in relationship to debt payments — to be at least 1.15:1. Lenders will typically require both historic and projected cash flow statements as part of the loan application package.

Character

The weight given to a lender's assessment of a borrower's character can vary tremendously between lending institutions and between individual lending officers. Many small businesses have found more success selling their reputation and good character to smaller community banks who may be more directly affected by the economic health of the surrounding community.

The following traits are typically cited as important to a bank's consideration of your character: successful prior business experience, an existing or past relationship with the lender (e.g., prior credit or depositor relationship), referrals by respected community members, references from professionals (accountants, lawyers, business advisors) who have reviewed your proposals, and your own community involvement. In addition, evidence of a borrower's care and effort in the business planning process suggests that the borrower is committed and confident about the new business proposal.

One additional factor that many banks consider as evidence of a borrower's "character" is the amount of investment that the owners themselves are committing to the business. Many commercial lenders want the owner to finance between 25 percent to 50 percent of the projected cost of a startup business or new project. An insignificant investment by an owner may suggest a lack of both owner confidence and dedication to the business.

Warning

 One banker noted to us that he often relies upon reaching a personal "comfort level" with a borrower before making a loan. This comfort level is based upon the degree of trust or confidence that the banker has in the accuracy of the information and documentation being presented to him.

He observed that in their zeal to "sell" him on the profitability of their business, small business borrowers sometimes talk him out of this comfort level by disclosing that their tax returns underreport income and overstate expenses. Such disclosures cast doubt upon the credibility of the loan applicant, and impair any sort of trust or confidence between the banker and the prospective borrower.

Bank Loan Documentation

The process of applying for a loan involves the collection and submission of a large amount of documentation about your business and yourself. The documents required usually depend upon the purpose of the loan, and whether your business is a startup or an already-existing company.

Documentation for Startups

- *a personal financial statement (usually lender's own form) and personal federal income tax returns for the last one to three years*

- *projected startup cost estimates (see the discussion on page 34)*

- *projected balance sheets and income statements for at least two years*

- *projected cash flow statement for at least the first 12 months*

- *evidence of ownership interests in assets (e.g., leases, contracts) and collateral*

- *a business plan that includes a narrative explaining the specific use for the requested funds, and how the borrowed funds will be repaid*

- *A personal resume, or at least a written explanation of your relevant past business experience*

Documentation for Existing Businesses

- *income statements and business balance sheets for the past three years*

- *projected balance sheets and income statements for two years*

- *projected cash flow statements for at least the next 12 months*

- *personal and business tax returns for the last three years*

- *a business plan; depending upon the credit history of your business and the purpose for the loan, a business plan for a loan to an existing business may be unnecessary, and a brief narrative of your intentions may suffice*

How Banks Judge Your Application

Traditionally, banks focused more upon collateral than any other factor in making loans; however, bankers now claim that lending competition has forced them to focus more on a business's ability to repay the debt as it comes due. Nevertheless, banks still place considerable emphasis upon collateral, especially when the projected cash flow of the debtor is as fragile as it often seems to be in a small business.

Work Smart

Some banks will require that your financial statements be prepared or reviewed by an accountant. If no such requirement is stated, you may be able to do much of this financial planning yourself; however, local lenders may find your proposals more credible if a reputable local CPA or attorney — whom the lender already knows — has participated in reviewing or preparing your financial statements.

Lenders will sometimes contact accountants and financial advisors directly to discuss a business plan or a financial statement. These conversations can have a powerful influence on the outcome of a loan application.

Some lenders rely heavily upon certain financial ratios, such as debt-to-equity, quick ratio, current ratio, etc., in assessing the creditworthiness of a prospective borrower. With many small businesses, however, these ratios may misrepresent the overall value of the enterprise. The most important assets of a small business are often the experience of the owners, the potential value of prospective customers, and other non-balance sheet items.

In addition, because of tax or strategic business purposes, some entrepreneurs may choose *not* to list assets on personal statements or they may list important assets on the financial statements of different businesses that they own. In these situations, your financial ratios may understate your true financial condition. It's up to you to convince the lender of this, however!

Work Smart

 If your loan application is denied, find out as much as you can about the review of your loan, which factors hurt you the most, how you can improve your chances for obtaining a loan in the future, and whether the bank would consider being a secondary financier if a primary lender were obtained.

To give you an idea of what banks specifically focus on when reviewing a loan request, on the next page we reproduce a sample business loan application that is typical of the kind of documentation you'll need to complete as part of your loan application package.

TRADE CREDIT

"Trade credit" is the generic term for a buyer's purchase of supplies or goods from a seller (supplier) who finances the purchase by delaying the date at which the price is due, or allowing installment payments. Vendors and suppliers are often willing to sell on credit, and this source of working capital financing is very common for both startup and growing businesses.

The major advantages of trade credit are that it is often readily available; it allows you to spread your payments over several months or years; and minimal, or no, downpayment or interest charges are assessed.

Suppliers know that small businesses typically represent relatively small order risks; as long as the supplier keeps a tight rein on credit terms and receivables, most small businesses are a worthwhile gamble for future business.

BUSINESS LOAN APPLICATION

Date: _____

New Relationship ____
Existing Relationship ____

Branch: _____

Officer: _____

BUSINESS INFORMATION

Business Name	
Address	
Telephone ( )	Tax I.D.
Individual Name(s)	
Address	
Telephone ( ) Social Security #	Date of Birth:

Proprietorship _____   Partnership _____   Sub-Chapter S ____   Corporation _____

Non-Profit _____   Individual _____   LLC _____

Ownership Distribution: (List stockholders, partners, owner names)
Note: Attach separate sheet if additional space needed.

Name	Title	# of Years	%	SS#
Name	Title	# of Years	%	SS#
Name	Title	# of Years	%	SS#

Nature of Business	Year Established	Number of Employees
Years at Present Location	[ ] Own	[ ] Lease
Accountant	Telephone ( )	
Insurance Agent	Telephone ( )	
Attorney	Telephone ( )	

FINANCIAL INFORMATION

Bank of Account   **Account Number**

Credit Relationships: Please provide details of your business credit relationships below:

Name of Creditor	Purpose of Loan	Original Loan Amount	Amount Presently Owing	Repayment Terms	Maturity Date
		$	$		
		$	$		
		$	$		

LOAN REQUEST

Amount of Loan Requested

_____

_____

Requested Term of Loan _____

Type of loan

[   ] Line of Credit

[   ] Term Loan

[   ] Business Home Equity

[   ] Commercial Real Estate

Specific Loan Purpose (Check all that apply)

[   ] Working Capital

[   ] Finance Purchase of Inventory

[   ] Finance Purchase of Equipment

[   ] Finance Purchase of Real Estate

[   ] Finance Purchase of Business

[   ] Refinance Existing Loan or Debts

[   ] Other (Loan type required and purpose)

_____

_____

_____

_____

_____

Collateral Available* (Check all that apply)

[   ] All Assets (accounts receivable, inventory, machinery and equipment)

[   ] Specific Equipment (Please attach equipment list, including serial numbers or description of equipment, and invoices for new equipment.)

[   ] Real Estate (Please attach property address, legal description and a copy of most recent tax bill.)   Square Feet _____   Acres _____

[   ] Cash on Deposit at <u>(name of bank)</u>   Branch _____   Account # _____

[   ] Personal Assets (As described in Personal Financial Statement.)

*Collateral: Loans are secured by collateral, which is property in which a security interest is granted to secure repayment of the loan. The loan collateral may include business assets, stocks, bonds, certificates of deposits, or personal assets. Consider (1) the value of the loan collateral must be equal to or greater than the amount of the loan, (2) expected economic life of collateral will be considered by the Bank in evaluating the collateral offered for the loan, (3) formal collateral appraisals may be required, and (4) a pledge of personal assets may be required as additional collateral for the business loan requested.

[   ] **Guarantors**** (Please list)

Name	Social Security #
Address	
Name	Social Security #
Address	

**Guarantors: For incorporated borrowers, guarantee of owner(s) is usually required, unless secured by Bank deposits or marketable collateral. If personal assets are in joint names, a sole proprietorship, and/or partnership, the Bank may require all parties to pledge collateral.

152

BUSINESS BACKGROUND INFORMATION

Please provide a brief history of your business, future plans and projections, and describe your products and/or services and competition.

_____

_____

_____

_____

PERSONAL BUSINESS EXPERIENCE

If you have been in your present business for under five years, please describe your previous business experience. (Include business background, management experience, and training, or include a resume.)

_____

_____

_____

_____

MISCELLANEOUS INFORMATION

Are tax liabilities current? [ ] Yes [ ] No   Settled through _____

Is the business an endorser, guarantor, or co-maker for any obligation not listed in the financial statements?   [ ] Yes [ ] No

    If yes, what is the contingent liability? _____

Has the business or principal owner ever declared bankruptcy?   [ ] Yes [ ] No

    If yes, provide details on a separate sheet.

Is the business a defendant in any lawsuit?   [ ] Yes [ ] No

    If yes, provide details on a separate sheet.

Are any of the business assets encumbered by liens or attachments of any type? [ ] Yes [ ] No

What	By whom	Amount $
What	By whom	Amount $
What	By whom	Amount $

Does the business have a pension fund?[ ] Yes [ ] No profit-sharing plan?   [ ] Yes [ ] No

If so, does the plan have any unfunded pension liabilities? [ ] Yes [ ] No

    Amount $_____

CERTIFICATION

The undersigned certifies that, to the best of his or her knowledge and belief, all information contained in this loan application and in the accompanying statements and documents is true, complete, and correct. The undersigned agrees to notify the Bank immediately of any material changes in this information. It is further agreed that, whether or not the loan herein applied for is approved, the undersigned will pay or reimburse the bank for the costs, if any, of surveys, title or mortgage examinations, appraisals, etc., performed by non-Bank personnel with the consent of the applicant. The undersigned authorizes the Bank to contact any bank and trade creditors it deems necessary without further notice, including, but not limited to, Dun & Bradstreet reports or information from Experian Credit Data.

Business Name (print):

Applicant Signature: _____ Date: _____

Applicant Title: _____

Guarantor(s) Signature: _____ Date: _____

Guarantor(s) Signature: _____ Date: _____

BUSINESS LOAN APPLICATION CHECKLIST

Please be sure all of the following documentation has been included in order for your business loan application to be processed.

[ ] Business Loan Application

[ ] Accountant-Prepared Business Financial Statements (Profit and Loss, Balance Sheet) for the past three fiscal years

[ ] Business Federal Tax Returns for past three fiscal years

[ ] Interim Financial Statements (if available)

[ ] Most Recent Federal Tax Returns for each principal owner listed in the first   section of the Business Loan Application

[ ] Personal Financial Statement

[ ] Organizational Papers (Articles, dba papers, etc.)

[ ] OTHER: _____

Chapter 10

Government Financing Programs

For many small businesses, government assistance can make the difference in getting the money that's vitally needed to start, continue, or expand operations.

The SBA offers a number of financing and operations assistance programs to small businesses. The programs include loan guarantees, educational programs, advisory services, publications, financial programs, and contract assistance.

While the SBA is the primary source, state and local governments also offer an array of financing assistance.

SBA LOAN GUARANTEES

The SBA does not make direct loans to small businesses. Instead, it offers banks and other private lenders a guarantee on loans that they make to qualified small businesses.

What does that mean? It means that, to get an "SBA loan," you must apply to a bank. If the bank would normally turn down your loan, but thinks that it might be acceptable with a government guarantee, it will let you know that additional paperwork is required to submit the loan to the SBA for approval.

The government guarantee encourages lenders to grant credit that otherwise would not be available on reasonable terms and conditions. Most often, an SBA guarantee is sought when a conventional lender feels that the prospective borrower has insufficient collateral to support the small business loan request.

A Limited Guarantee

There is no maximum cap on *loans* that can qualify for an SBA guarantee; instead, the agency limits the *guaranteed portion* of the loan to the lesser of $750,000 or 75 percent of the loan amount. For loans of $100,000 or less, the SBA will guarantee 80 percent of the loan; for certain loans to women or minority-owned businesses the guarantee is 90 percent.

Adequate Security for the Loan

The SBA states that a guarantee will not be denied merely because of inadequate collateral; however, in most instances, the private lender will still demand collateral, and the SBA's guarantee of an under-collateralized loan will be extended only if the business shows other favorable factors (e.g., solid cash flow) to support the credit-worthiness of the borrower.

The most important consideration for the SBA is whether the loan is collateralized *to the maximum capability of the individual business owner.* An owner who has valuable personal assets may be requested to pledge those assets as security on the business loan before the SBA agrees to guarantee the loan.

Required Owner's Equity and Guarantee

The SBA prefers an owner's equity investment to be at least 25 percent of the total cost of the project. While no fixed legal requirement actually exists, the SBA (and the lender) want proof that you won't walk away from your business at the first sign of trouble.

Nonetheless, a lesser percentage of ownership equity can be negotiated. The stated bases for granting an SBA loan guarantee are the borrower's character, credit, experience, and proof of a sufficient commitment to the business. Weakness in one area may be balanced by strength in another.

Unlike some of the other requirements, a personal guarantee by all owners having at least a 20 percent interest in the company is usually nonnegotiable.

Sometimes a Higher Loan Cost

A private lender can charge a slightly higher interest rate for an SBA-guaranteed loan than for a similar conventional loan.

The SBA continues to put a maximum cap on the interest rate and prohibits extraneous fees. On loans for less than seven years, the rate cannot exceed 2.25 percent above the New York bank prime rate. For loans with maturities of seven years or longer, the rate cannot be more than 2.75 percent above New York prime.

To encourage banks to make relatively small loans to small businesses, an extra interest point (up to 3.75 percent over prime) can be charged for loans between $25,000 and $50,000, and an extra two points (up to 4.75 percent over prime) can be assessed for loans under $25,000. Floating rates can be used, if the spread will not increase.

The SBA charges a guarantee fee based on the following schedule, which can be passed on to the borrower.

Amount of SBA Loan Guarantee		Guarantee Fee
Over	But not over	
$0	$80,000	2% of the amount
80,000	250,000	$1,600 + 3% of the amount over $80,000
250,000	500,000	$6,700 + 3.5% of the amount over $250,000
500,000	750,000	$15,450 + 3.875% of the amount over $500,000

Warning

To avoid multiple applications by borrowers trying to avoid the higher guarantee fees on large, single loans, all loans made to the same borrower within 90 days will be treated as a single loan for purposes of calculating the guarantee fee.

While these additional costs may sometimes make an SBA-guaranteed loan more expensive than a conventional loan, SBA loans prohibit any points from being assessed in addition to the guarantee fee. Without the guarantee, the lender might charge additional points because of the higher risk (if it approved the loan at all).

Longer Loan Terms

One of the significant benefits of an SBA loan guarantee is that the government's backing will often support a longer-term loan. Instead of three- to five-year maximums on conventional bank loans for a small business, the SBA guarantee commonly covers loans up to 10 years, and some real estate loans have maturities up to 25 years.

Eligibility for SBA Loan Guarantees

To be eligible for an SBA loan guarantee, a business must meet all of the following criteria:

- be small enough to fit SBA's criteria

- be a type of business acceptable to the SBA

- be independently owned and operated

- not be dominant in its industry

- have applied for, and been denied, a conventional loan by a private lender

Warning

 If at least two conventional lenders have denied your loan application, you may want to rethink, or rework, your business plans. Try to assess whether the denials are based upon factors that you can realistically overcome if your business gets going or whether adjustments in your plans are necessary.

How Small Is a "Small Business?"

The general rule is that a business is small enough to qualify for SBA assistance if it has fewer than 500 employees. However, this general rule is subject to industry-by-industry variations. Below is a summary of the industry standards that the SBA uses to define a business as "small." Under these standards, 99 percent of U.S. businesses can qualify for an SBA guarantee.

Type of Concern	Standards
Manufacturing	The maximum number of employees may range from 500 to 1,500 depending upon the type of product.
Wholesaling	The total number of employees may not exceed 100.
Providers of services	Annual receipts may not exceed $3.5M to $13.5M, depending upon the industry.
Retailing	Annual receipts may not exceed $3.5M to $13.5M, depending upon the industry.
Construction	Annual receipts may not exceed $7M to $17M.
Special trade construction	Annual receipts may not exceed $7M.
Agricultural	Annual receipts may not exceed $0.5M to $3.5M, depending upon the industry.

Ineligible Businesses

Certain types of businesses are ineligible to apply for or receive loans guaranteed by the SBA: nonprofit organizations other than sheltered workshops; certain cooperatives; businesses dealing in the creation or distribution of ideas, values, thoughts or opinions; cable TV systems; academic schools; automobile floor planning concerns; gambling concerns; concerns involved in speculation, lending, or investment; pyramid sales distribution plans; illegal activities. Loans may not be made that would encourage a monopoly.

SBA "LowDoc" Loan Guarantee Program

Currently, the most popular form of financial assistance from the SBA is the agency's Low Documentation ("LowDoc") Program. LowDoc expedites the procedures for obtaining SBA guarantees on commercial loans under $150,000. Processing time for a LowDoc application is usually about one week.

In addition to meeting the general eligibility criteria discussed above for an SBA loan guarantee, qualification for the LowDoc program requires that both of the following be true:

- The average annual sales of your business for the preceding three fiscal years were less than $5,000,000.

- You do not employ more than 100 individuals, including the owner, partners, or principals.

To encourage lenders to make small loans, the SBA allows lenders making loans of $50,000 or less with maturities greater than 12 months to retain half of the guarantee fee that is normally paid to the SBA. (Loans under $50,000 can carry higher interest rates so that private lenders have more of an incentive to make such small loans.)

LowDoc Still Isn't NoDoc

Although the LowDoc program requires less documentation than the SBA previously required, you must still submit certain paperwork and comply with the private lender's ordinary loan application procedures. An application for an SBA loan guarantee is submitted through a participating lender and the lender typically uses its regular processing procedures. For a guarantee on a loan of $50,000 or less, the SBA requires:

- *proof that the borrower was denied a loan from a conventional lender*

- *a completed LowDoc one-page application*

- *a personal financial statement*

- *a personal guarantee from anyone owning 20 percent or more of the business*

For loan requests of $50,000 to $150,000, the borrower must submit the same documents listed above, plus:

- *copies of the applicant's tax returns for the prior two years*

- *if the loan is for an existing business, year-end statements from the last two years*

- *a cash flow projection*

To get your copies of the proper SBA forms, visit the SBA online at http://www.sba.gov/library/forms.html.

SBA Regular 7(a) Loan Guarantees

For loans in excess of $150,000, the SBA continues to administer its traditional Section 7(a) guarantee program. Currently, this program allows the SBA to guarantee up to $750,000 or 75 percent of the loan amount, whichever is less.

Unfortunately, because the amount of the loan is greater than in the LowDoc program, the amount of paperwork to obtain this type of guarantee is also greater. Turnaround time can range from weeks to months.

While most entrepreneurs can complete a LowDoc application with limited assistance from the private lender, a Section 7(a) loan guarantee application is considerably more complicated. Average time for completing a successful loan guarantee package is about 25 hours.

Save Money

 To get assistance in completing the paperwork, check with any local municipal, county, or state economic development agencies in your area. Some of these groups will provide no-cost or low-cost assistance in preparing the application.

Otherwise, consider engaging one of the various services or professionals that prepare loan packages. For a listing of these services, check your phone book under "Loans" or request a referral from your lender.

The price range for loan packaging is approximately $1,200 - $5,000. To avoid unnecessary expenses, make sure that you have spoken with your banker and obtained at least an informal bank commitment prior to engaging a loan guarantee packaging service.

To make an informal commitment, the bank will need only about one-half of the material and information that is necessary to meet the SBA requirements.

Maximum loan maturity varies according to the estimated economic life of the assets being financed and the applicant's ability to repay.

Purpose	Loan Life
Working capital	Maturity up to 7-10 years
Machinery and equipment	Maturity up to 10-25 years
Building purchase/construction	Maturity up to 25 years

When loan proceeds will be used for a combination of purposes, the maximum maturity can be a weighted average of those maturities, which allows for regular, equal payments. Or it can be the sum of equal monthly installments on the allowable maturities for each purpose, which results in unequal payments.

The interest rate for guaranteed loans reflects prevailing market rates and can either be fixed over the life of the loan or can fluctuate with the market.

Regular 7(a) guarantees prohibit a balloon payment (a large, final lump sum payment due after a set time period) or a prepayment penalty by the lender.

Special 7(a) Programs

In an effort to expedite processing of larger loan applications under Section 7(a), the SBA has two special lender programs: the Certified Lender Program and the Preferred Lender Program. Neither of these lender programs applies to LowDoc loans.

Certified Lenders Program (CLP). Certified lenders receive a partial delegation of authority, and their loan guarantee applications are given a three-day turnaround by the local SBA office. This loan process accounts for about 30 percent of all business loan guarantees. There are approximately 660 certified lenders across the nation.

Preferred Lenders Program (PLP). Preferred lenders can decide unilaterally on SBA participation in eligible business loans. These lenders can determine eligibility, creditworthiness, loan structuring, loan monitoring, loan collection/servicing, and loan liquidation actions, and make necessary decisions at each stage of the procedure without, in most instances, SBA's prior review or consent. Preferred loans have a maximum SBA guarantee of 70 percent.

Save Time

There are over 150 preferred lenders across the nation. To locate the nearest local Certified or Preferred Lender, call your nearest SBA office, which should have an up-to-date directory.

SBAExpress (formerly called the FA$TRAK program). To further accelerate the 7(a) program, the SBA is experimenting with a pilot program called SBA Express.

Under the program, selected lenders are authorized to make, service, and liquidate loans in amounts up to $150,000 using their own application and disbursement documents and processes. Lenders are given the authority to attach an SBA guarantee to an approved loan without having to submit the loan application to an SBA field office for a credit analysis or review.

In exchange for this convenience, lenders agree to limit the loan amount to $150,000, and to accept a maximum SBA guarantee of 50 percent.

Women's Pre-Qualification Pilot Loan Program. The Women's Pre-Qualification Pilot program allows SBA to work with intermediaries such as community service agencies, which will assist female small business owners in creating their loan application package, and will then review and pre-qualify the loans prior to their submission to a participating lender.

The SBA pre-qualification letter assures the lender that SBA has seen the loan application and has determined that, if the lender agrees to make the loan, an SBA guarantee will be available.

Minorities' Pre-Qualification Pilot Loan Program. The SBA also has a similar program for minorities, whereby third-party agencies will assist in working with the small business owner to apply and qualify for the loan. Once the loan package is assembled, it is submitted to the SBA for expedited consideration; a decision usually is made within three days.

The maximum amount for loans under the women's program is $250,000; under the minority program, it is generally the same, although some districts set other limits. With both, the SBA will guarantee up to 90 percent of the loan. The intermediary then helps the borrower locate a lender offering the most competitive rates.

CAPlines: Short-Term Financing

The CAPline program provides SBA loan guarantees on working capital loans and lines of credit, in contrast to the more conventional 7(a) term loans.

Repayment of a CAPline loan is tied to the business's cash cycle, rather than an arbitrary time schedule.

The following chart describes the major CAPline programs.

CAPline Program	Who Is Eligible	Major Characteristics and Requirements
Small Asset-Based Lines of Credit	Businesses meeting the general SBA eligibility criteria.	Revolving lines of credit of up to $200,000, for up to five years. Banks may charge loan servicing fee of 2 percent. Secured by accounts receivable or inventory.
Standard Asset-Based Lines of Credit	Businesses meeting the general SBA eligibility criteria.	Revolving lines of credit of $200,000 or more, for up to five years. Secured by accounts receivable or inventory.
Seasonal Lines of Credit	Businesses meeting the general SBA eligibility criteria, who have operated continuously for one year and have established a pattern of seasonal activity.	Short-term lines of credit for up to 12 months. Only one loan may be outstanding at any time; each must be followed by a debt-free period of 30 days.
Contract Lines of Credit	Businesses meeting the general SBA eligibility criteria, who have operated continuously for one year and who provide a product or service under an assignable contract.	Line of credit for up to 5 years. Proceeds may be used only to finance labor and materials needed under the contract.
Builder's Lines of Credit	Construction contractors and home builders meeting the SBA's general requirements, and who have demonstrated ability to complete projects, and who submit certification from a mortgage lender, a real estate broker, and an architect or appraiser.	Loan for each project may be up to 36 months plus a reasonable estimate of the construction period. Interest is paid at least twice a year; principal payment is due when the project is sold.

SBA MICROLOANS

Small businesses needing small-scale financing and technical assistance for startup or expansion may be able to obtain up to $25,000 through short-term loans of public money called "microloans." These loans are administered through responsible nonprofit groups, such as local economic development organizations or state finance authorities, that are selected and approved by the SBA. The SBA loans the money to the nonprofit organization which then pools the funds with local money and administers direct loans to small businesses.

These loans are administered much like a line of credit and are intended for the purchase of machinery and equipment, furniture and fixtures, inventory, supplies, and working capital.

The funds are intended to be disbursed with close monitoring of the recipient, and a self-employment training program may accompany the loan. The maximum maturity for a microloan is six years. The loan cannot be used to pay existing debts.

Work Smart

Money allocated to this program is limited. Checking with local sources prior to your actual need for the money may be the best plan for staking a claim to these funds.

Section 504 Loan Program (CDCs)

The SBA 504 Loan Program provides long-term, fixed rate financing for investment in fixed assets. The loans were intended to help small and medium-sized businesses avoid large downpayment and floating interest rates that are typically associated with the purchases of "bricks and mortar" fixed assets. The program is also aimed at aiding local economies by increasing employment opportunities and the loans are tied to certain job creation mandates. Typically a borrower is required to either create or retain one job for every $37,500 of total project cost.

Section 504 loans are extended through SBA-approved companies called Certified Development Companies (CDCs). A CDC is a private nonprofit corporation set up to contribute to the economic development of its community or region. Typical CDC-financed projects range in size from $500,000 to $2 million, with an average cost of $1 million. The total size of projects using CDC financing is unlimited, but, as with SBA loan guarantees, the maximum amount of CDC participation in any individual project is $750,000 (or $1 million for some public projects).

CDC loans typically require that 50 percent of the funding come from a bank or other private lender, 40 percent from an SBA loan instrument, and 10 percent from the business owner (but 20 to 30 percent will be required from a startup business).

SBA FINANCING FOR EXPORTING

For those small businesses considering exporting outside the U.S., the SBA and several other government agencies offer special financing programs.

Export Working Capital Program

This program provides short-term financing guarantees on loans for specific export needs. The loans can be structured as revolving lines of credit or term loans, or be tied to a specific contract or cash cycle. The interest rate of these loans is not regulated by the SBA.

The EWCP is available only to small businesses that have been in business, although not necessary exporting, for at least one year. The loans can be used for pre-export costs of labor and materials, financing receivables from sales, or standby letters of credit used as performance bonds or payment guarantees to international buyers. As with other SBA loan guarantees, the maximum government repayment is limited to $750,000 or 75 percent of the loan amount, whichever is less.

International Trade Loan Program

The International Trade Loan Program provides long-term loans to small businesses that are engaged or are preparing to engage in international trade, as well as small businesses adversely affected by competition from imports. In addition to the general eligibility criteria for an SBA loan guarantee, a small business applicant for the International Trade Loan Program must establish either of the following:

- The loan proceeds will significantly expand existing export markets or develop new export markets. The applicant must submit a business plan, including sufficient information to reasonably support the likelihood of expanded export sales.

- The applicant is adversely affected by import competition.

The SBA can guarantee up to $1.25 million, less the amount of SBA's guaranteed portion of other loans outstanding to the borrower under the SBA's regular lending program. Only $750,000 can be for working capital needs; consequently, the maximum guarantee amount is available only if used for a combination of working capital and facilities/equipment. The working capital portion of the loan may be made according to the provisions of the SBA's Export Working Capital Program (EWCP).

STATE AND LOCAL PUBLIC FUNDING

In an effort to improve their local economies, most states, and many municipalities and counties, sponsor a variety of public funding sources for small business concerns. At the state level, nearly all states have some form of economic development agency or finance authority that makes loans or loan guarantees to small businesses. State commerce departments often have direct or participating loan programs that may be even more attractive than SBA-guaranteed loan programs.

Although state programs and funding options vary, a popular form of program is a participating loan arrangement in which the state pools its public funds with money from a conventional lender to meet the needs of a small business borrower.

Example

In Illinois, the state will loan up to 25 percent of the total cost of a small business project, with a maximum loan of $750,000. So, for example, if you needed a $100,000 loan, but a bank would lend only $75,000, the state "participates" in the loan by contributing public funding of $25,000 to the total loan package. The bank then processes the total loan of $100,000. The state is spared the administrative expenses of loan processing and the bank receives a priority lien on collateral.

States also receive federal money through federal Housing and Urban Development (HUD) block grants that can be used for a variety of local improvements, including small business financing programs.

While the criteria for a small business to obtain a loan of grant money vary between states, the state will typically expect evidence that a clear economic or social benefit to the local community will result from the funding. The amount of money made available at the local level will usually depend upon the perceived need for job creation in the area and the relative income level of that community.

In addition to state money, local county or municipal governments often loan small amounts of capital to local businesses. These local, "microloan" programs may be characterized by minimal (and sporadic) funding, so the timing of your request can be critical. Try to contact any local agencies as soon as possible, even if you don't need the money immediately, to determine the available funds at that time and when the program is expected to receive any additional money. Local programs can loan small amounts of money, e.g., under $10,000, for working capital, equipment or inventory purchasing, or property improvements.

Part IV

Marketing Your Product

For most small businesses, highly effective marketing is a make-or-break necessity. It's really impossible for you to be successful without good marketing and sales techniques — that's what brings the dollars in the door. You've got to let people know about all the wonderful things your business can provide to them, which means that your business must first provide wonderful things that people are willing to pay for. And that, in turn, means knowing who your customers are and getting so close to them that you can virtually anticipate their needs and desires.

To many time-starved business owners, marketing means two things: advertising and selling. However, we think that ultimately you'll be more successful if, every so often, you try to look at the "big picture" by taking the time to thoughtfully analyze your products or services and your business as a whole in relation to your competition, to your customers, and to trends and conditions in society as a whole.

We might say that the key to successful marketing is answering the following question for your business: *How will you communicate a meaningful difference about your business idea (product or service) to the people who might be most interested in buying it?*

Our discussion here is intended to introduce you to some of the concepts and strategies that professional marketing experts in large companies use, and show you how they can be adapted to help your small business thrive.

Chapter 11: Analyzing the Market Environment discusses the competitive environment and cultural trends you need to examine in order to assess your business's place in the market. It also describes market research techniques, with an emphasis on those that will be more useful and affordable for smaller businesses.

Chapter 12: Developing and Refining Your Product emphasizes the importance of providing unique products or services that meet customers' needs, even before the first sale, and presents a process you can use to develop new products for your business.

Chapter 13: Distribution Methods, Packaging, and Pricing is a look at the impact of presentation and price on your product's success, and describes some of your options in getting your product or service to your customers.

Chapter 14: Promotion, Advertising, and P.R. presents the primary methods of communicating your message to your target customers, and includes numerous tips on promoting your business on a shoestring budget.

Chapter 11

Analyzing The Market Environment

Conceptually, all of marketing is based on the idea that you must thoroughly know the environment in which your business operates in order to successfully promote and sell your product or service.

Ultimately, your business idea must fulfill a need for your buyers and must do so in a way that's somehow superior to the competition, however you define it. If you want to be sure that your idea will do these two crucial things, you need to know as much as you can about the following:

- why your business idea is unique

- who your closest competitors are

- who your target buyers are

- how the current business and marketing environment may affect your company

WHAT'S YOUR UNIQUE BUSINESS IDEA?

Intuitively, or better yet, based on sound research, you believe your business will succeed because you are doing something *different* from some or all of your competitors. The first test of any business, small or large, is its uniqueness when compared to its competitors.

Now, that doesn't mean you can't borrow a good idea from some other company and build a successful business around it. For example, every town needs a certain number of dry cleaning operations, and most of them look very much alike.

However, if you examine the more successful dry cleaners in your area, you'll notice that each one tends to emphasize and promote something special. It may be lower prices, faster service, better cleaning, a drive-up window, or more frequent coupons in the local shopping news. Some of these business owners undoubtedly borrowed their ideas from other companies they've dealt with, or promotions they may have noticed when traveling in other cities. The point is, successful businesses find ways to make their products or services stand out from the crowd, or at least the crowd in their immediate geographic area.

There are two main issues to consider here:

- **How is your business different?** Can you express it in terms of a concise statement, known as a "unique selling proposition" or USP, that will form the basis for all your advertising, promotions, sales communications, and other marketing activities?

- **Is this a difference that customers appreciate,** so that they'll prefer or even seek out your business's offerings rather than those of your competitors?

Your Unique Selling Proposition

The best way to focus on what's special about your business is to try to express this uniqueness in a single statement.

Rosser Reeves was the author of the phrase, "unique selling proposition," which is a unique message about itself versus the competition that each business or brand should develop and use consistently in its advertising and promotion. By USP we don't necessarily mean a slogan or a phrase that will appear in your advertising, although that's one possible use for it. However, at this point we're focusing on its usefulness as a tool to help *you* focus on what your business is all about.

If you cannot concisely describe the uniqueness of your idea (and create some excitement in potential users), you may not have the basis for a successful business. There are several questions to ask about your business to determine a USP:

1. What is unique about your business or brand vs. direct competitors? You'll probably find a whole list of things that set you apart; the next questions will help you decide which of these to focus on.

2. Which of these factors are most important to the buyers and end users of your business or brand?

3. Which of these factors are not easily imitated by competitors?

4. Which of these factors can be easily communicated and understood by buyers or end users?

For examples of USPs, think about different brands of products you've seen advertised on TV. What's the main message underlying the ad?

Do Customers Value Your Uniqueness?

One of the quickest ways to go out of business is to market a product or service that hardly anyone wants, needs, or understands.

Ideally, you should always research and test your idea against the realities of the marketplace. Many business owners have tested their ideas by working as employees in their industry for a number of years and have seen firsthand what works and what doesn't. But even well-seasoned industry experts can benefit from analyzing the market environment in a way that will help to evaluate the potential of an idea.

In order to be able to accurately determine whether your business idea has enough appeal to a sufficient number of customers, you'll have to become very aware of who your target buyers are.

WHO ARE YOUR TARGET BUYERS?

Do you know precisely who your customers are, or will be? If you've been in business for a while, you may know many of them by name, but do you really know what type of people or businesses they are?

For example, if you sell to consumers, do you have demographic information (e.g., what are their average income ranges, education, typical occupations, geographic location, family makeup, etc.) that identifies your target buyers? What about lifestyle information (e.g., hobbies, interests, recreational/entertainment activities, political beliefs, cultural practices, etc.) on your target buyers? You can find out all this and more by doing some basic market research, as described later on in this chapter.

Once obtained, this type of information can help you in two very important ways. It can help you develop or make changes to your product or service itself, to better match with what your customers are likely to want. It can also tell you how to reach your customers through advertising, promotions, etc.

Example

A company that sells athletic shoes may know that its typical customer is also a sports fan. Thus, if it can build shoes good enough to be worn by professional athletes, it will have a convincing story about quality to tell. It can also benefit by using well-known athletes as spokespersons in its advertising, and by placing advertisements in sports magazines where its customers are likely to see them.

Niche Marketing

Most marketers know that "20 percent of buyers consume 80 percent of product volume." If you could identify that key 20 percent and find others like them, you could sell much more product with much less effort.

The heavy users of your product can be thought of as a market "niche" that you should attempt to dominate. The driving force behind niche marketing is the need to satisfy and retain those consumers who really love your products or services, and to find more who are just like them. It is much more efficient to continue selling to the same customers than it is to continually go out and find new ones.

It is also important to be able to estimate the size of your target market, particularly if you're thinking about a new venture, so that you can tell if the customer base is large enough to support your business or new product idea. Remember that it's not enough that people like your business concept. There must be enough target buyers on a frequent-enough basis to sustain your company sales, spending, and profits from year to year. The advantage that small businesses have here is that they can often be profitable serving a relatively small niche — one that, say, a Fortune 500 company would consider too small to pursue.

Influences on Consumer Behavior

If your customers are primarily the ultimate consumers or end users of your product or service, identification is generally done in terms of demographic and lifestyle factors.

Demographics are tangible, measurable facts that distinguish one group of people from another, whereas lifestyle analysis is more concerned with the intangibles.

Demographic Factors

- ethnic background
- age
- income
- education
- sex

- location
- occupation
- number of people in family
- children's ages

Lifestyle Factors

- cultural background
- religious beliefs
- political beliefs
- value systems
- recreation and hobbies
- social interaction patterns

- music preferences
- literature preferences
- food or menu preferences
- entertainment preferences
- travel preferences
- media habits

For example, heavy coffee, liquor, and tobacco users are not easily identified with demographic information. They may be found in any age group or socio-economic category. However, lifestyle analysis shows high correlation with certain characteristics, including media habits, recreational pursuits, social interaction patterns, music, and other attributes. If you can identify these, you can make your promotions or advertising more appealing to these target buyers.

When Buyers Are Channel Buyers

If you sell to other businesses, who turn around and resell your products and services, your buyers are predominantly channel buyers. Examples of channel buyers from the grocery and drug industry are:

- national master distributors
- local/regional distributors
- chain store wholesaler buyers
- individual retail store buyers

Influences on channel buyers may include attributes such as the item's margin and profitability, discounts, free goods, cash fees, and personal relationships — things that have little to do with what you consider the key benefits of your products.

Influences on Channel Buyer Decisions

- **Profitability of the item** — *the higher the margin and dollar profit per item vs. competitive category products, the more likely the trade will accept it, regardless of product quality.*

- **Availability of discount deals** — *they can increase margin, volume, and velocity of the item. For example, 10 percent to 25 percent off invoice each quarter for all purchases during the period are typical discounts for grocery and drug retailers.*

- **Advertising and promotion support programs** — *multi-media TV, radio, print and PR support, plus heavy consumer couponing, sweepstakes, and contests are typical consumer packaged goods programs that may be run one to four times a year.*

- **Other cash deals** — *for example, new item "slotting fees" are the subject of controversy and frustration for many manufacturers supplying grocery, drug, and mass merchandiser retailers. Slotting fees are cash payments and/or free goods that are not refundable, even if the products are dropped after six months by the retailer. Slotting fees range from a few hundred dollars to over $25,000 per item in some chains.*

- **Availability of free goods** — *for example, one free case per store is common for new grocery item distribution.*

- **Personal buyer/seller relationships** — *there will always be personal relationships influencing buying decisions as long as there are people selling to people. That's why you hire good salespeople!*

- **Sales incentive programs** — *these programs may spur salespeople on to greater productivity and sales of a particular item or offering.*

WHO ARE YOUR COMPETITORS?

Once you've identified what's unique about your business and who your target buyers are, you need to take a good, long look at your competition.

Identifying your direct competitors is important before you finalize your decision about which business category and market segment to compete in. It is vital to the success of a new or existing business because it reduces risk, time, required resources, and expense.

Example

A new salty snack chip product may have a unique taste, texture, appearance, and health benefits. But effectively competing with every salty snack (both direct competitors like salty chips and indirect competitors like popcorn, salty nuts, etc.) in a $14 billion product category is difficult, even for a large, successful snack food company like Frito-Lay. If the competition is too strong, it's going to be extremely difficult for a newcomer to break in.

Direct and Indirect Competition

It may help to think of your competitors as a series of concentric circles, like a bulls-eye target. In the center are your most direct competitors, and moving outward from the center the competition grows progressively less direct.

- **First ring, center of target** — the specific businesses in your geographic area that offer a product or service that's interchangeable with yours in the eyes of the consumer (although of course you hope you hold the advantage with better quality, more convenient distribution, or other features). For example, if you operate a local garden center, you may compete against the other garden centers within a 10-mile radius.

- **Second ring** — competitors who offer similar products in a different business category or who are more geographically remote. Using the example of the garden center, a discount chain that sells garden supplies and plants in season is also your competitor, as is a landscaping contractor who will provide and install the plants, and a mail-order house who sells garden tools and plants in seed or bulb form. None of these competitors provides exactly the same mix of products and services as you, but they may be picking off the most lucrative parts of your business.

- **Third ring** — competitors who compete for the "same-occasion" dollars. Inasmuch as gardening is a hobby, third-level competitors might be companies that provide other types of entertainment or hobby equipment; inasmuch as gardening is a type of home improvement, competitors might be providers of other home improvement supplies and services.

The point of this analysis is to consider carefully, from the buyer's point of view, all the alternatives that there are to purchasing from you. Knowing that, you can attempt to make sure that your business provides advantages over your competitors, beginning with those who are most similar to you. In fact, you can even borrow ideas from second- or third-level competitors in order to compete more effectively against your first-tier competitors.

Competitors' Strengths and Weaknesses

It's to your advantage to know as much as you reasonably can about the details of your competitor's businesses. Study their ads, brochures, and promotional materials. Drive past their location (and if it's a retail business, make some purchases there, incognito if necessary). Talk to their customers and examine their pricing. What are they doing well that you can copy, and what are they doing poorly that you can capitalize on?

Secondary data, as well as information from your sales force or other contacts among your suppliers and customers, can provide rich information about competitors' strengths and weaknesses. Basic information every company should know about their competitors includes:

- each competitor's market share, as compared to your own

- how target buyers perceive or judge your competitors' products and services

- your competitors' financial strength, which affects their ability to spend money on advertising and promotions, among other things

- each competitor's ability and speed of innovation for new products and services

There may be a wealth of other facts that you need to know, depending on the type of business you have. For example, if you're in catalog sales, you'll want to know how fast your competitors can fulfill a typical customer's order, what they charge for shipping and handling, etc.

What Will Your Competitors Do Next?

Once you know the identity of your most direct competitors and have a good idea as to your second- and third-tier competitors as well, you should give some thought to which actions they are likely to take in the next year or so. Estimates of competitors' future activity depend on your knowing and understanding their objectives, strength in the marketplace, and resources. This important intelligence is key to your company's:

- annual forecast of sales, spending, and profits

- promotion and advertising programs

- introduction, support, and success of new products and services

- market, product, or service category, and sub-category trends

- direction for future growth

Gathering competitive intelligence can be the difference between realizing your company's annual plan and losing business that may never be recouped.

THE GENERAL BUSINESS ENVIRONMENT

Today's marketing environment is influenced by the global marketplace and the explosion of the information age to a degree unprecedented in history. To be fully prepared, a company must recognize and understand:

- cultural influences

- governmental and political influences

- demographic and lifestyle trends

- local, national, and world economic trends

- the strengths of multi-national competitors

- the influence of technology on physical distribution

Local, state, and federal trade organizations are often the best source of information on the trends that are likely to influence your business. Local and national general interest and business publications are also good sources of this type of information. Get in the habit of constantly asking yourself how events in the news could affect your business.

MARKET RESEARCH

How can you find the answers to the questions and issues we've raised in the first part of this chapter? Through market research, of course.

While you probably won't be able to afford a separate marketing research department to gather and monitor all the information that could possibly help you, all successful business owners must know their markets, competitors, customer wants and needs, and what it takes to be competitive. You should expect to budget at least a minimal amount of time and money for research, especially if you are starting a new business or branching out into a new direction.

Determine Your Research Needs and Objectives

The first step in doing market research is to decide what you really need to find out. The kind of information you are seeking should determine the type of research you will do, although of course budgetary constraints will play a part in your decision.

Do you need to obtain a general feel for how key target buyers think about your product category and its various types of items, brands, and buying occasions? If so, interviewing groups of target buyers in focus groups may be the way to go, even though this type of research indicates only directional trends and may not be statistically reliable. Or is the confirmation of general trends in your industry sufficient? In that case, reading information from outside information services, industry trade associations, and industry experts may be all that you need to do.

You may wish to conduct blind tests of different formulas before finalizing recipes for a new product. In that case, you can do "laboratory" tests, where brands, packages, and names of products are not revealed to the test subjects, and achieve statistically reliable results at the 90 percent to 95 percent confidence level of predictability. Or perhaps you have completed extensive product development and testing and are now ready for a field test of your prototype products.

Conceptually, market research breaks down into the following categories:

- **Primary research** — involves the actual data-gathering about the specific usage patterns, product feature likes and dislikes, etc., of target buyers or current users of your products.

- **Secondary research** — with this type of research, someone else has done the actual data-gathering in the field and has written it up in a form that's easier for you to use. Secondary research is generally much less time-consuming and cheaper than primary research.

Secondary Market Research

Secondary research is something every student has completed at one time or another, usually by doing library research with books and periodicals. It may be less useful and reliable than primary research because the information you obtain was not developed with your particular problem or situation in mind.

Nevertheless, for some types of information (for example, questions about your competitor's market share, or the absolute numbers of potential customers for a new product), secondary market research is the only kind available. Secondary research can be divided into two categories: external and internal.

External Secondary Market Research

You can often obtain key information about the total size of your market, the major competitors, and the characteristics of your target buyer/users, free of charge, from the following sources:

- trade associations

- industry publications and databases

- government databases (e.g., Census Bureau, state commerce departments)

Even for new businesses, company data from competitors may be available by interviewing competitor company executives, attending industry trade shows, and asking the right questions of industry experts. They may be unaffordable as consultants but willing to direct you to free databases that you would not ordinarily know of or have access to. And don't overlook your competitor's suppliers. They can be excellent sources of information to aid your research.

Internal Secondary Market Research

Secondary research involving the study of information generated by your own company is "internal" research. Here we're talking about information that was gathered for purposes other than marketing — for example, it may have been gathered for financial or management purposes. The most commonly available internal company information includes:

- daily, weekly, monthly, and annual sales reports, broken down by geographical area, by product line, or even by product

- accounting information (e.g., spending and profitability)

- competitive information gathered by the sales force

If you're in retailing or wholesaling, you'll have a wealth of information at your disposal if you keep detailed information about your sales, by product. You may be able to determine not only the types of products that sell best at various times of the year, but even the colors and sizes that your customers prefer. There are a number of inventory tracking software products on the market that can help you keep track of all this information, not only for financial and tax purposes, but for marketing purposes as well.

Primary Market Research

Primary research is *original* research; that is, data collected directly from the source. The advantage of doing primary research is that you can get information on the specific question or problem you need answered, not information that merely applies to your industry or type of business in general.

Although there are many types of primary research, there are three types that are most useful for small businesses: field studies, qualitative research, and quantitative research.

Field Studies

Field studies are real-world tests of a new product or service in a limited area or even a single store. Such a test can provide significant useful feedback, although the results may not always be translatable to other geographic areas.

Larger national and multi-national companies often spend hundreds of thousands of dollars in market research prior to launching a test market for a single product. A large company may spend over $1 million in a single test market for the first six months. While you probably don't have the desire or the resources to do such extensive testing, the fact that large companies are willing to invest so much money in this type of research should convince you that a small field test of your business idea is worth the effort, before you commit all your funds to the project.

Example

 A single-person car-detailing company conducted a test of the business with a local car repair shop. This entrepreneur spent weekends at the repair shop offering customers on-the-premise cleaning and home pickup of their cars for cleaning, washing, waxing, and other car-detailing services. He refined his "bundle" of services and prices prior to conducting his business full-time and eventually offered his services as a sub-contractor to many other auto repair shops in the city.

Qualitative Research

This research is primarily concerned with getting a subjective "feel" for the research topic, *not* a numerical, statistically predictable measure.

Traditionally, qualitative research consists of focus groups and individual interviews. Focus groups can be thought of as "group interviews," where a manageable number of target buyers are brought together, presented with an idea or a prototype product, and asked to discuss their opinions with a moderator and with each other.

You can hire a market research company to locate the focus group members according to criteria you specify, and to conduct the session using a professional moderator, while you watch from behind a one-way mirror. Or you can do it the economical way by conducting the sessions yourself, using target buyers you've located via the phone book.

Save Money

Focus group participants generally expect to be paid for their time. Rates might range from $30 to $100 or more per participant for a two-hour session, though you might be able to get away with providing a free meal instead. Generally, groups that are discussing business products or services are paid more than groups discussing consumer products.

You can also conduct your own individual interviews with potential target buyers or with people who already purchase a competitive product.

The problem with qualitative research is that your confidence level that the results are indicative of the general population or key target group trends will be somewhat low. At this statistically low level of predictability, you should be looking for broad general indicators or trends to guide the next steps.

Quantitative Research

Quantitative research is distinguished from qualitative research primarily by the large numbers of people who are questioned and the type of questions asked. Generally, results that are 95 percent reliable as representing the entire market of buyers can be obtained if you question at least 100 people and questions are of the simple "yes/no" variety. To increase the accuracy to 97 percent, the sample sizes would have to increase to 400 to 2,000 or more, depending upon the subject matter and complexity of questioning.

To do good quantitative research, you need the following two elements:

- a well-designed questionnaire

- a sample that is randomly selected, and sufficiently large.

Quantitative questionnaires usually gather information that can be numerically tabulated. Questions may be posed in writing, by fax, or over the phone, but generally phone interviews have a better response rate. If you use the phone, you will want the telemarketer to use a script, to be sure that each respondent is answering the same questions.

For example, a questionnaire could include:

- demographic information (age, sex, occupation, home locale, income range, etc.)

- confirmation that the respondent uses the product or service you're testing

- which brands are used or purchased

- how often brands are purchased

- why the respondent likes different brands

- what is disliked about brands

- importance of different brand images

- ranking of brands by preference

- whether price makes a difference to the frequency of purchasing different brands

- evaluation of different product attributes

- ranking of product attribute importance for buyers

- evaluation of brand positioning and advertising

- purchase intent on a five-point scale (definitely, maybe, indifferent, maybe not, definitely not)

- brands that would be replaced by the new product prototype

Sample selection. When doing quantitative market research, you'll get more accurate results by using randomly selected samples. "Randomly selected" means that each test respondent sampled has an equal chance of being selected for testing.

Also keep in mind that the larger the sample size, the more accurate the results, not only for predictions of total population behavior, but also for the degree of variation in that behavior.

Customer Satisfaction Survey Tool

Small companies often provide simple questionnaires to customers when they come into the store or purchase products and services. They may use the questionnaires to obtain a qualitative "pulse," or check, mainly to verify that nothing is going terribly wrong in their day-to-day operations. Or they may use the questionnaires to measure the effectiveness of local advertising media in generating store traffic. Customer database-building is another possible objective.

Over time, you may obtain results that are almost as good as quantitative test results, particularly if you ask simple "yes/no" questions (on customer satisfaction, for example). Here is a simple customer satisfaction survey that you can distribute to your customers to obtain feedback on your business.

Sample Customer Satisfaction Survey

We are constantly looking for ways to improve the quality of our products and services. To do that, we need to know what you think. We'd really appreciate it if you would take just a few minutes to respond to the questions below. Please return this survey [describe how you want the survey returned]. Please circle "Outstanding" or "Needs Improvement" and comment:

Products: **Outstanding**   **Needs Improvement**

_____

_____

_____

Services and Support: **Outstanding**   **Needs Improvement**

_____

_____

_____

Delivery: **Outstanding**   **Needs Improvement**

_____

_____

_____

Employees: **Outstanding**   **Needs Improvement**

_____

_____

_____

Chapter 12

Developing and Refining Your Product

Today's accelerated rate of change and information growth means that your company will inevitably face increased competition in your market niches. The majority of new consumer products are not patentable and thus are easily duplicated by other competitors. And many small companies do not have the resources to spend heavily to protect a new product idea from copycats.

Small businesses need to embrace and seek out change, rather than avoid it or wait until change is forced upon them by competitors. One way to do this is to constantly be on the lookout for ways to expand your business by offering new products or services to your customers, or by combining products or services in innovative ways.

Sadly, new product development is often a hit or miss program in many smaller companies. Frequently, new products are introduced only as a reaction to meet competitive challenges or because of a fortuitous development of proprietary technology or patents.

You can greatly increase your odds for success by budgeting a specific period of time each week to consider new products, and by adapting the new product development path used in large companies:

1. Determine your overall company mission.

2. Generate a large number of new product ideas.

3. Screen the ideas for potential profitability and fit with company goals, and choose the most promising ones for further development.

4. Develop and refine prototype products.

5. Develop packaging, pricing, and distribution strategies.

6. Develop advertising, promotion, and public relations strategies.

7. After introducing the product, measure its success and look for ways to improve it.

DEVELOPING A COMPANY MISSION STATEMENT

A company mission statement can be a powerful force to clearly define your company's purpose for existence, and to determine the direction that new product development should take.

In Chapter 11, we encouraged you to develop a unique selling proposition, or USP. The USP expresses what your business provides to customers, right now, and can become the foundation for your promotional communications to customers. A company mission statement differs from a USP in that it focuses on the future and often expresses a more expansive view of your company than a USP.

The most successful company missions are measurable, definable, and actionable project statements with emotional appeal that everyone knows and can act upon. For example, a mission to "be the best health-care provider in the world" for a multi-national HMO organization sounds good. But a simple mission statement from Honda — "beat GM!" — is better because it's a project statement that can be measured every day by every employee.

Case Study — Creating a Company Mission Statement

 As an example of how a company mission statement can serve as a focus for improvement in your business's performance, consider the case of Fred's Grocery, a small one-store business, which suffered sales declines when a large chain supermarket opened in the neighborhood.

Fred initially considered lowering prices and adding many new items to compete, at great expense and lower margins. However, a family discussion about the "mission" of Fred's Grocery caused Fred to respond in a less direct, less costly, less risky manner.

Fred and his family realized that their mission was to serve the convenience needs of local, upscale neighborhood shoppers for specialty items and "fill-in" grocery items that they needed. The majority of Fred's shoppers spent an average of only $12 ($5-$25 per visit), considerably less than at the larger chain store. Fred and his family decided they would offer more services and specialty items than the larger chain store. Their array of specialty goods, prices, and services also separated them from convenience store chains like 7-11.

Fred's carried all groceries to the shoppers' cars and apartments and delivered gift baskets/flowers, at no extra charge within a five-block radius of the store.

They also added specialty items to their store, putting in an espresso coffee bar, wine kiosk, and food/flower gift assortments. They upgraded and limited the amount of fruits and fresh vegetable selections and added fresh, warm breads and cookies.

After one year, Fred's Grocery realized its best year ever and increased both shopper traffic and average sale by 100 percent to an average of over $25 per shopper. Fred felt the new chain store was the best thing that ever happened to his business, thanks to the time he took to discuss and refine his mission statement!

GENERATING NEW PRODUCT IDEAS

Once you've created your company mission statement (or have explicitly recognized the mission you've been pursuing), you can begin considering how to accomplish that mission by developing and refining your product or service offerings. New product development can be categorized into:

- **Products that create a new market or niche segment** — paper disposable diapers are a good example of an entirely new-to-the-world product that, when introduced, created an entirely new and explosively large growth segment for infant care.

- **Additions or line extensions to existing products** — new flavors and new sizes of existing products are examples of line extensions. For example, new Life Savers™ flavors continue to proliferate (over 50 to date), continually refreshing a brand name and product line over several decades.

- **Product improvements** — cars are a good example of products where continuous improvements are made each year, with increased safety, road handling, driver/rider comfort, entertainment feature improvements, etc., that competitors strive to quickly copy.

- **Repositioned products** — Tums™ (the anti-acid stomach product) has successfully repositioned itself to feature its high calcium content as a benefit primarily for women's health needs, along with its original antacid claims.

There are many approaches that can be used to generate new ideas, including examining your current products, examining your competitors' products, investigating consumers' needs, and generating new ideas through brainstorming.

Screening Your Current Products

Are there any opportunities for your company's products to be refreshed in the marketplace by being repositioned, improved, or brought out in a new size, flavor, or package? Identifying these opportunities is often the easiest way to keep the new product pipeline full.

At a minimum, small companies should compare the competitive strengths of their products against those of their direct and indirect competitors' products at least once a year. In addition to new product opportunities, you may also discover some old products that should no longer be offered.

Preliminary Product Screening for Small Companies

Here are some ways that you can re-evaluate your existing products, without spending more time and money than you can afford:

1. *Try out your products with an "expert panel" of internal company personnel (or your family and friends, if you have no employees) plus external product users. Use a written evaluation form to keep track of results from year to year.*

2. *Add competitors' products to the evaluation with your expert panel of users.*

3. *Compare evaluations between your company's products and competitors' products, paying particular attention to:*

   - *differentiation of your products' features and positioning compared to competitive products*

   - *ability of the competition to develop similar, stronger products*

   - *cost of pioneering a new product compared to a less-expensive "me-too" introduction*

   - *your ability to introduce products in the marketplace compare to a competitor's ability to defend markets*

4. *Decide if your company needs to make improvements. Key question: will your competitor's improvements in products affect your sales?*

5. *Screen existing products against pre-established company criteria:*

   - *your company's mission, ethics and philosophy, and strategies*

   - *business goals and product categories*

   - *customer and buyer profiles*

- *sales volume, share, and profitability objectives*

- *your company's operational expertise and distribution methods*

- *your company's ability to invest in new technology or marketing spending*

Improving a Competitor's Product

Part of examining your existing products or services is comparing them with similar ones offered by your competitors, as discussed above. But it's likely that your competitors offer some products that you don't, and you should take a look at those as well. Sometimes the fastest, cheapest, and least risky way to introduce new products is to copy or improve upon a competitor's new product introduction.

Many companies, large and small, consciously adapt a strategy to "follow the leader" when it comes to new product introduction, pricing, and other business changes. It saves scarce funds for expensive R&D and for educating the target buyers.

However, companies that successfully adapt this new product strategy have to:

- be able to move quickly to commit company resources to capitalize on a competitor's new products

- compete in product categories where innovation does not necessarily depend upon proprietary technology, large capital improvements, and pre-emptive patents to protect new ideas

- often settle for less sales potential than the innovator

For example, an independent, local car repair shop could institute a 20-minute "quick lube" oil change service at a slightly lower price than national chain shops.

Examining Users' Needs

Another approach to new product development is to start with the target buyers — either your current buyers, or those who inhabit a niche you feel is attractive — and try to uncover those buyers' unsatisfied needs and wants.

Sometimes uncovering new product ideas is as easy as:

- **Staying close to your customers** — for example, how often do you ask them what they want/need that they are not getting from anyone?

- **Staying close to the ultimate product user** — how often do you talk with the end users of your product, if they are not the same people who actually buy your product?

- **Staying close to your sales force,** if you have one — when was the last time you asked anyone in sales if they have seen anything that is better or that they like better?

- **Staying close to your suppliers** — suppliers are often the closest to the latest technology, materials, ingredients, international advances, and competitive improvements.

Brainstorming for New Ideas

Good ideas can come from anywhere! But can one consciously foster creativity and new ideas on demand? Certain successful companies and creative experts suggest that it is not as hard as most people think. *Everyone* can be more creative with technique, practice, and motivation.

Brainstorming is a way of generating a lot of new ideas, quickly. Once you have a long list of possibilities to work from, you can begin to evaluate each idea from a more practical standpoint. Brainstorming techniques include:

- a small group of six to 10 people

- a moderator who also functions as a "policeman" for the session

- one-hour sessions

- revised group behavior rules

Rules for Brainstorming

- *Criticism is not permitted in any verbal or non-verbal form.*

- *Bits and pieces of ideas are encouraged. No idea is rejected at this point.*

- *A large quantity of ideas is encouraged.*

- *Combining and using pieces of other ideas from the group are encouraged.*

- *All ideas are recorded as they are stated, in short phrases or words.*

The moderator acts as official encourager, policeman against improper group or individual behavior, and recorder of all ideas on large sheets of paper or a whiteboard visible to the group.

Ideas are edited *later* by the primary user of the creative information, which will usually be you. Unusable ideas or incomplete ideas are discarded. In longer sessions, group participants may break into smaller groups and be asked to provide a shorter list of ideas (or combined ideas) that they unanimously recommend.

A small company of even one person can gather a group to practice informal brainstorming. All that is needed is an easel or two (or even a large memo pad) to record ideas. Seven individuals alone will seldom, if ever, produce the volume or creative range of ideas of a group of seven people together, practicing brainstorming techniques.

SCREENING NEW PRODUCT IDEAS

Once you've come up with a quantity of possible new product ideas, you need to narrow them down and prioritize the "winners."

Small companies cannot afford to incur costly product development failures as part of the normal course of business. Even one product failure in a small company may threaten its survival if a large amount of time, scarce resources, and personnel are committed to it.

The risks of product development failure can be reduced with careful screening of new ideas:

1. **Screen new products against company sales and profitability minimums.** A new product must have the potential to generate minimum sales to cover the costs of producing the product itself, to cover some portion of your company's overhead, and to meet your company's profitability goals.

2. **Screen your new product concept with key customers and buyers.** An important step that's often overlooked is obtaining input and evaluation of new product ideas at an early stage with key customers (e.g., key account buyers and their management) and end user buyers. Business owners may become so committed to a favorite new product development concept that they proceed to full development of a product prototype before outside input is obtained.

Qualitative and quantitative consumer studies can be invaluable in this stage.

NEW PRODUCT PROTOTYPES

The fastest way to go out of business is to introduce a great idea, but to never completely deliver the features or benefits that were promised. People who initially buy and then reject a new product are almost impossible to interest in trying the same brand again, no matter how much you improve it. It's worth the time to test the execution of your ideas by building prototypes, testing them with customers, and making any adjustments necessary before releasing the item to the general public.

Many low- and high-tech products lend themselves to testing to see how well the product really works and to "benchmarking" against current competitor's products already in the marketplace. You may find that the qualities you thought would "sell" your product are not so important to consumers, after all.

Example

Folger's Coffee spent years, a small fortune, and three tries at bringing out a freeze-dried coffee that "tasted, smelled, and looked like fresh-brewed coffee." Each time, consumers voted thumbs down, saying, "It just doesn't taste enough like fresh-brewed coffee."

Finally, the third (and last) product development project and market testing was completed with improved, state-of-the-art, freeze-dried coffee crystals that looked and tasted like fresh-brewed coffee, and even real coffee aroma captured in the jar. It was discovered that the key target consumer group, freeze-dried coffee users, were accustomed to their instant coffee and really didn't know or like actual fresh-brewed coffee!

MEASURING THE SUCCESS OF NEW PRODUCTS

Once you've introduced a new product or service or developed significant improvements to existing ones, you'll naturally want to do some follow-up to measure the success of the project. Whether the introduction is ultimately successful or not, you need to be able to learn from the process to achieve more success down the line.

Two simple ways to measure your success are to talk to buyers and consumers about their product satisfaction, and examine weekly company sales receipts for new account sales, compared to receipts for reorders. This is an indirect, but free, way to measure initial purchase vs. reorder sales.

Chapter 13

Distribution Methods, Packaging, and Pricing

Packaging, pricing, and distribution methods are three very nuts-and-bolts issues that you'll have to resolve before you can advertise and promote your product. But they also represent very good ways to persuasively communicate with your target buyers.

Distribution methods refers to the ways your products will be sold and delivered to customers; e.g., through retail outlets, personal sales to end users, direct mail or telemarketing, or even through the Internet. The methods you choose will significantly affect both your costs and your revenues.

Package design will be strongly affected by your distribution method. However, packaging is more than just the design and look of the physical wrapper or outer container that a product comes in.

For service businesses, packaging can be the way in which services are bundled together for an intermediate buyer or end user. For products, the package label or wrapper may represent the product's entire business positioning, list of features and benefits, advertising, and promotion.

Pricing must reflect not only your costs to produce the product or service, package it, and distribute it to customers at the expected volume, but also the value your customers place on what you offer.

What's more, price can be an important way to differentiate your business from others, especially in the consumer market.

CHOOSING DISTRIBUTION METHODS

It's fairly easy to change many of your marketing tactics and strategies on a periodic basis; pricing, packaging, and product mix are among these flexible choices. However, distribution and sales decisions, once made, are much more difficult to change. And distribution affects the selection and utilization of all your other marketing tools. There is a wide variety of possible distribution channels, including:

- **retail outlets** owned by your company or by an independent merchant or chain

- **wholesale outlets** of your own or those of independent distributors or brokers

- **sales force** compensated by salary, commission, or both

- **direct mail** via your own catalog or flyers

- **telemarketing** on your own or through a contract firm

- **cybermarketing**, surfing the newest frontier

- **TV and cable** direct marketing and home shopping channels

Distribution choices for a service business follow the same lines as those for a physical product. For example, financial planning services may be offered through printed material such as books or newsletters, sold at retail by consultants, delivered electronically by computer, or relayed by phone, fax or mail.

To select the optimum distribution options, you must:

1. Identify how your direct competitors' products are sold.

2. Examine the costs of your channel and sales force options.

3. Determine which distribution options best match your overall marketing strategy.

How Are Competitors' Products Sold?

As a starting point, make a list of any competitors that could compete *directly* with you for the same customers. Then divide these competitors into categories based on the distribution channels they currently use.

The result will be a picture of which channels are being successfully used in your type of business and location.

Example

A local one-man architect business, Life Designs, provides residential home design and competes indirectly with all architectural design firms and home building suppliers.

These include large firms that do both industrial and residential designs and suppliers of home-building kits (e.g., log houses and A-frames). However, Life Designs' direct competition is a small group of similar firms that specialize only in local area home designs and remodeling. A list of competitors broken down by the different local distribution channels they use includes:

- *competitors who advertise in local city and county magazines, newspapers, and real-estate flyers, subdivided by home-design only firms and home-design and industrial-design firms*

- *competitors who work with contractors and developers in the local county*

- *the local university's architectural design department*

Costs of Distribution Channels

Obviously, financial resources and cost-effectiveness are important in considering distribution and sales force options. What can you afford, and what will give you the most bang for your buck?

Example

Continuing with the example above, Life Designs looks at the costs of using each channel:

Media sales *— Life Designs can place ads in local city and county magazines, newspapers, and real-estate flyers.*

Contractors and developers *— Life Designs can pursue referrals from contractors and developers who receive a commission from home owners and buyers. The contractors and developers are the "sales" personnel, who expect some "wining and dining."*

University design department *— this is a closed distribution channel for architectural students and professors only, and not available to Life Designs.*

Life Designs knows from talking with media suppliers, competitors, and contractors that the least expensive distribution channel is sales from contractors and developers. However, the frequency of sales referrals and volume of business are unpredictable. Life Designs decides to work with both distribution channels concurrently. The contractor/developer channel requires personal time and some minor entertainment expenses. Media spending will provide a good alternative when the architect is busy with a project.

Matching Distribution to Your Goals

A small company must work harder at focusing its limited resources of time and money, especially with distribution and sales force options. Key factors to prioritize your choice of channels include the costs and time involved in entering the channels, your experience with the channels, and which channels best reflect the product positioning that you believe is crucial to your success.

Case Study — Matching Distribution Options to Goals

A company selling gourmet cooking equipment found that it had many options for distribution and sales force representation, including:

- *company retail stores, with company sales personnel*

- *specialty food stores, with sales brokers*

- *department stores, with sales brokers*

- *hardware stores, with sales brokers*

- *specialty chains (e.g., Williams-Sonoma, Crate & Barrel), with sales brokers*

- *direct mail, with company personnel*

- *distributors, with company sales managers, brokers, distributor sales reps*

The company's products are positioned as the highest-quality cookware, used by celebrity chefs and guaranteed for the life of the end user/buyer. Target end users/buyers are upscale, well-educated, urban consumers who read upscale food magazines (e.g., Gourmet, Food & Wine), dine out at gourmet restaurants, drink wine, travel, drive expensive cars, and spend heavily on luxury purchases. Ideally, the company wants their products distributed through every upscale channel that caters to this exclusive target group.

The company believed that hardware stores and direct mail were not consistent with the image and reputation that they were trying to establish with their positioning. Company retail stores, while desirable, were financially risky and too expensive at the early stage of development. Distributors were also eliminated because of the belief that distributors could not be encouraged to learn enough or devote enough time to the product line. In addition, the estimated 35 percent to 40 percent discount with shipping expense to distributors was financially unattractive.

The company decided the best distribution channels were direct sales to specialty stores and upscale department stores such as Marshall Field's, Bloomingdale's, and Nieman-Marcus. Their sales force consisted of three regional managers with professional cooking experience, who also did demos in stores with the cookware. In addition, the company had the extra margin available to afford this highly trained and motivated sales force since distributors were not utilized.

PACKAGE DESIGN

To a large extent, your packaging decisions will flow from your distribution channel decisions. For example, if you're going to sell software that will be downloaded over the Internet, you won't need to design a box to sit on the shelf at the local computer retailer.

Packaging must, at a minimum, be functional. When designing a new product, you should test the packaging under real-life conditions for things like:

- storage under varying temperature, lighting, and humidity conditions

- shipping through all distribution channels, assuming that rough handling may occur

- shelf life studies for age deterioration (for some products, the size should not be larger than a quantity that can be used by the average consumer before "going bad")

For service businesses, "packaging" represents the way the firm communicates its sources of uniqueness to buyers and end users. Packaging for service companies can be a collection of logo identifications on clothing, uniforms, tools, stationery, forms, hang tags, and other paraphernalia. Packaging can also be the unique style in which a company provides its services. For example, certain elite hotels are distinguished by their concierge services as much as by their guest rooms and physical amenities.

Package Designs for Positioning

Packaging designs should communicate the business's positioning or unique set of values.

Example

Marshall Field's department stores are positioned as upscale and fashionable, but a good value for high-income shoppers. Clothing boxes are more expensive white, glossy stock on both sides, imprinted with the Marshall Field's logo in dark green.

This contrasts with specialty clothing stores (e.g., Kohl's in the Midwest), who do not carry a full line of clothing, and who target middle-income shoppers. Clothing boxes, available mostly during the Christmas season, are unbleached brown stock on both sides, with a red printed logo. It would be a disadvantage for these stores to have the same package box as Marshall Field's for their price-conscious middle-income shoppers.

Designing for Graphic Identity

Walk through any store and look at packages on the shelves. Decide which ones catch your eye in any given section, and why. Chances are the majority of packages that stand out have what's called "graphic identity."

Graphic identity is defined as a unique two- or three-dimensional graphic symbol that may be recognized by target buyers as being associated with a particular brand or business. Sometimes this graphic identity takes the simple form of a unique brand logo or name with unusual letter shapes.

Example

Exxon is an artificial computer-derived name without prior meaning. However, the unusual double XX in the name provides a unique graphic identity that makes this name recognizable even at distances where normal words are unreadable.

Packaging To Reflect Buyers' Values

A precise definition of your target buyer's demographics, lifestyle, activities, and interests is key to designing a package that reflects your buyers' values and will attract buyers to it on the shelf, or wherever else your products or services are available.

Case Study — Package Design That Reflects Values

An energy snack bar could target buyers with the following profile information:

Demographics: *middle to upscale income ($30,000 - $60,000), high-school educated consumers, age 18-49, located primarily in western states, mostly married with one or two children, living in smaller cities near outdoor recreation areas.*

Activities: *are outdoor sports enthusiasts, shop in natural health food and outdoor equipment stores, maintain active life styles every week (e.g., bike to work), seek non-traditional work environments (e.g., no coats or ties).*

Interests: *family-oriented; not fashion-conscious; interested in outdoor gear, clothing, and equipment; try to eat a healthy, nutritionally sound diet; view little TV.*

Package name and communications points: *the name of the energy bar would attempt to relate to this carefully defined target buyer, perhaps with a derived reference to the environment or natural foods:*

- *MOUNTAIN GOLD*

- *PURE & NATURAL*

- *NATURE'S TREAT*

Colors of the package may reflect the natural colors of the outdoors in various seasons: yellow, orange, and green for spring and summer; brown, gold, and orange for fall; white and silver for winter. Product features communicated on the package may include: 100 percent all-natural ingredients, no preservatives or additives, biodegradable wrapper. Product benefits communicated on the package may include: safe energy for the whole family; environmentally compatible.

PRICING YOUR PRODUCT

From the buyer's standpoint, the right price is a function of product purchase value and other competitive choices in the marketplace. From the seller's viewpoint, the basic concern is to price products to maximize both sales and profits, while providing enough margin to take care of applicable marketing and overhead expenses.

The following steps are recommended for determination of product pricing for any size business:

1. Analyze the size and composition of your target market.

2. Research price elasticity for your product, and estimate your sales volume at different prices.

3. Evaluate your product's uniqueness and perceived value in relation to your competitors.

4. Analyze your costs and overhead, and make sure your pricing makes hitting your breakeven point likely.

5. Consider any secondary pricing strategies.

6. Select final pricing levels, while recognizing that changing conditions may require adjustments.

Analyzing Size and Composition of Market

In setting prices for your product or service, one of the first calculations you must do is to estimate approximately how large your potential sales volume could be, based on a reasonable assessment of your potential market share in the product category, at different price levels. Knowing the size of the existing market is critical to determining if there are enough customers to establish and grow your business.

Researching Product Price Elasticity

If demand for your type of product or service changes significantly with slight changes in price, the product category is considered to be *elastic* with respect to price. If no significant volume changes occur, even with significant price changes, the category is *inelastic.*

Example

Grocery store items are often very price sensitive, with a 10 percent price increase or decrease resulting in significant share and volume changes per brand. On the other hand, gourmet food categories are often inelastic. It may require a price increase or decrease of 50 percent to create any perceptible changes in consumers' behavior.

The greater the price elasticity, the closer you should price your products to similar competitive products. While your product may have some special features, consumers will not pay much more for it if there are similar choices at lower prices.

To find out more about price elasticity in your industry, you might study secondary data sources (e.g., A.C. Nielsen Company; Informational Resources, Inc.) for share and volume results correlated with brand pricing reductions. Talk to trade and association experts to obtain a feel for pricing elasticity.

At this point, you can combine your research on price with your research on the total available market for your product or service and the strength of the existing competition, to arrive at some estimates of your sales volume and revenues at various price points.

Evaluating Your Product's Uniqueness

If you have a premium-quality product, with premium packaging, graphics, and unique features and benefits, perhaps a premium price is necessary to reinforce the premium brand image. Higher margins than normal may be one benefit. High prices confirm perceptions of high value in consumer minds.

On the other hand, the more closely your product resembles competitive products, the smaller the price differences that buyers will tolerate. And the fewer differences between brands, the greater the probability that the category is price-elastic, and that brand-switching will occur when products go on sale.

Product uniqueness does not guarantee a significant price premium over a competitive product, if the product differences aren't recognizable and meaningful to consumers. And depending upon the category, even recognizable and meaningful product differences may not be enough to get buyers to switch to the new product, even at parity pricing, let alone at a premium price over the competition.

Analyzing Your Costs

The most common errors in pricing are pricing products or services based *only* on the cost to produce them, and pricing products based *only* on competitors' prices. Both factors must be balanced.

In terms of covering costs, your pricing must do all of the following:

1. Cover the cost of producing the goods or services.

2. Cover marketing and overhead expenses.

3. Afford distribution margin discounts, if these are a factor in your distribution channel.

4. Afford sales commissions, if appropriate to your channels.

5. Meet profit objectives.

Breakeven Analysis

Breakeven analysis is a commonly used method that focuses on the volume of sales you need to achieve before your total revenues will equal total costs.

The idea is to set the unit price of product or service at a level where it will, at a minimum, cover all its own variable costs (material, labor, commissions, etc.) plus its portion of the fixed costs of the company (overhead). At the point where enough units have been sold to cover all fixed and variable costs, breakeven is achieved. After that point, the sales price of a unit sold minus the variable (direct) cost to produce it equals pure profit.

Example

Let's assume that a case of tea beverages in 12-ounce ready-to-drink bottles has a cost of goods of $3.82 per case of 12. Factory price to distributors is $6.54/case. Gross margin (price minus cost of goods) is $2.72/case. If the company's fixed costs (e.g., overhead, factory expenses, etc.) are estimated at $75,000 per year, then the breakeven point would be 27,573.5 cases of tea ($75,000 divided by $2.72/case).

Keystone Pricing

Many small businesses such as restaurants, retail establishments, and consulting services operate on the "keystone" pricing principle:

- The cost of goods is limited to 33 percent of retail prices.

- Labor and overhead is limited to another 33 percent.

- Gross profits are a minimum of 33 percent of retail prices.

Wholesaling and Retailing Markups

Retailers and wholesalers need to consider the issue of markups in their pricing structure, and manufacturers or other product producers need to be aware of the average markup in their industry. If you sell a large number of different types of products, it may be most efficient to determine an average markup you'll apply to all items, and then adjust this average for individual items as necessary.

Be aware that there are two different ways to calculate markup — as a percentage of the cost to you, or as a percentage of the selling price to your customer. In retailing, the industry standard is to compute markup as a percentage of selling price.

Example

 Let's say Joel received a shipment of clocks that he will sell in his gift store. He paid $12.00 for each clock and plans to make $4.00 on each one. The selling price is then $16.00.

The markup percentage on cost is equal to the dollar markup (4.00) divided by cost (12.00) or ***33%***.

However, the markup percentage on selling price is equal to the dollar markup (4.00) divided by selling price (16.00) or ***25%***.

As a product wends its way through a distribution channel, each step along the journey adds a markup, as the table shows:

Level	Category	$	%
Producer	Cost	20.00	80.0
	Markup	5.00	20.0
	Selling Price	25.00	100.0
Wholesale Outlet	Cost	25.00	71.5
	Markup	10.00	28.5
	Selling Price	35.00	100.0
Retailer	Cost	35.00	70.0
	Markup	15.00	30.0
	Selling Price	50.00	100.0

Considering Other Pricing Strategies

In addition to the primary goal of making money, a company can have many different pricing objectives and strategies. Larger companies may utilize product pricing in a predatory or defensive fashion, to attack or defend against a competitor.

Example

Maxwell House introduced a second, low-priced brand into its own dominant eastern United States markets during the 1970s to slow and confuse the introduction of Folger's Coffee into the market. This new product was packaged and designed to resemble Folger's familiar red can, with pricing set below Folger's Coffee. The new temporary product clogged grocer shelves and made it more difficult and expensive for Folger's to introduce its coffee into new eastern markets.

Selecting Final Pricing Levels

The pricing levels you finally select for your products should have flexibility for both increases and discounts to customers. Price increases may be inevitable because of increases in materials, wages, or other items. The market may or may not absorb price increases without decreasing volume effects.

If in doubt, price on the high side. It's always easier to discount prices than to raise them.

TYING IT ALL TOGETHER

This case study shows how distribution, packaging, and pricing are all interrelated and can change over time as a business grows.

Case Study — Alice's Dressings

Alice's is a small, one-store family restaurant known for its delicious, unique, homemade salad dressings (e.g., Pomegranate Vinaigrette, Rum-Raisin-Orange Ranch, Blue Cheese Catalina). Initially, the dressings were only available to customers eating at Alice's. Then customers began requesting bottles to buy. Initially, the product was packaged in a 32-ounce canning jar with a handmade label.

New distribution channels cause packaging and pricing changes. *Then Alice's Dressings were sold to a local grocery store at a discounted wholesale price, 28 percent less per ounce than the retail restaurant price, packaged in a smaller, 26-ounce bottle. As local demand grew, Alice decided to have the dressings made in an independent packing facility and sold to other stores in the area, which raised the cost of making the dressings.*

Alice's husband, brothers, and a sister-in-law divided up initial sales responsibilities to call on local and regional stores in their spare time.

The popularity of Alice's Dressings caused Alice to consider the possibility of selling large pallet quantities to distributors in other states. The distributors needed another 25 percent discount from wholesale price, along with free shipping. Sales brokers were also needed, at 5 percent commission on net distributor sales, since the family could no longer call on everyone. Marketing the dressings would require full-time management.

Distribution channels are key to pricing and packaging decisions. *In this case, a separate business, new distribution channels, and sales representation grew out of Alice's initial one-store restaurant. Alice's restaurant was initially able to sell the salad dressings at $5.00 per 32-ounce jar (15.6 cents per ounce) directly to customers. However, once a decision was made to sell Alice's Dressings as a shelf-stable item in grocery stores, the bottles changed to a standard 26-ounce size to compete with other dressings sold in this size.*

Alice was concerned that grocery consumers, unfamiliar with the restaurant, would not pay over $3.99 retail per 26-ounce bottle when competing brands ranged from $1.29 to $2.69 for the same 26-ounce size. Wholesale prices were 28 percent less than retail, at $2.89 per bottle. However, the cost of ingredients was substantially more than competing brands, at $1.00 per bottle, and packaging and processing costs added another $0.50 per bottle. Profits were reduced from restaurant sales per bottle, but still acceptable (i.e., from $3.50 a bottle, or 11 cents per ounce, to $1.39 per bottle, or five cents per ounce), since the total amount of sales and profits were expected to be substantially greater through grocery sales.

Further research with marketing experts in the industry and sales brokers indicated a further 40 percent reduction in delivered distributor price (including brokerage commissions and shipping costs). Alice would net $1.73 per bottle at delivered distributor price with brokerage commissions of 5 percent, leaving an unacceptable gross margin of only 23 cents per bottle (13 percent), even at the higher retail price of $3.99 per bottle.

Alice finally decided to upgrade the bottle and label to a unique, tall, triangular, Italian glass bottle and cork, with gold and black labels and recipe hang-tags by a local design studio. She sold the dressings directly to upscale specialty and grocery stores. Distributors would not be used. Specialty brokers were hired to aid in selling directly, at a 10 percent commission on net sales. The premium pricing was also retained in this non-elastic market segment, with the new bottles retailing at $4.99 each. Final net factory sales per bottle were $2.69 after deducting 10 percent brokerage commissions, with net factory profits of $1.10/bottle. Specialty food stores took a 40 percent gross margin, but paid for shipping.

Chapter 14

Promotion, Advertising, and P.R.

There is never enough money to do everything desirable to build the business. Often a budget permits a little promotion, advertising, or PR, but not all three at the same time. Start by constructing a positioning statement for your business, which expresses the key points you'll include in all promotion, advertising, and PR programs. Then set your marketing budget, and make choices among your marketing options.

POSITIONING YOUR BUSINESS

"Differentiation" is the collection of differences in features and benefits versus competitive products. The key is to determine how important these collective differences are to the buyer.

"Positioning" is adding brand value to this collection of differences in the mind of the buyer. In other words, you must solve the problem of how to communicate a meaningful difference about your business idea to the people who are most interested in buying it.

In some cases, there may actually be little or no difference between your product or service and that of your competitors. Or the differences may be very difficult to communicate (think of the difference between Coke and Pepsi). In that case, it's up to you to create some differences through your positioning.

Positioning Strategy Statement

A small business positioning strategy statement acts as a guideline to measure the consistency of all marketing programs.

Example

Joe's Redhots *will sell premium-quality hot dogs and other ready-to-eat luncheon products to upscale business people in high-traffic urban locations.* Joe's Redhots *will be positioned versus other luncheon street vendors as the "best place to have a quick lunch." Reasons why are that* Joe's Redhots *have the cleanest carts, the most hygienic servers, the purest, freshest, products, and the best values. Prices will be at a slight premium to reflect this superior vending service.* Joe's Redhots *will also be known for its fun and promotional personality, offering consumers something special every week.*

The following example illustrates how a positioning statement can be used in advertising, promotions, and other marketing activities.

Example

A small local gas company (in Fargo, ND) with one or two local service stations could differentiate itself from its competition by positioning itself as "the fastest gas in the West," advertising with on-premise signs, handouts, premiums, T-shirts, local tie-ins, and other reminders. The gas tank pumping islands could be maintained at maximum pressures and speed of filling at all times, with the most powerful gasoline pumps available.

Premiums, given away with every 25 and 100 gallons, credited on a frequent filler card, could reinforce this positioning: handiwipe cloths imprinted with the company slogan, baseball caps, and model cars, boats, motorcycles, etc.

If the station's target consumer is primarily male and 16-49, then local celebrity speeders (e.g., dragsters, racing cars, motorcycles, etc.) could exhibit their vehicles at the station. Logos and slogans on the vehicles could also promote the station's market positioning.

SETTING A MARKETING BUDGET

Spending on marketing support ranges from less than 1 percent of net sales for industrial business-to-business operations, to 10 percent or more for companies marketing consumer packaged goods.

Small businesses often estimate their sales revenue, cost-of-goods, overhead, and salaries, and estimated gross profit. Anything left is considered available funds for marketing support. A more rational approach is to estimate what your direct competitors spend in marketing support and then try to at least match that amount.

If you are the new competitor in the marketplace, you will have to spend more aggressively to establish your market share objective.

Case Study — Marketing Budgets

Joe's Redhots, *a hotdog cart selling to office workers, wanted to use popular media such as TV, radio, and newspapers to advertise, along with promotional free product samples and coupons. Joe learned from his suppliers that his competitors in the downtown office area were spending little or no money to promote and advertise their cart luncheon business. He estimated that the most successful hot dog cart spent 5 percent of net sales revenue for promotion and advertising. Joe decided to spend at least 10 percent of his net sales during the first year.*

Joe ranked all his possibilities in order of probable effectiveness, with estimated costs:

Advertising	Promotion
TV ($500/30-second ad/station)	Free samples ($25/day @$0.25 each)
Radio ($50-100/60-second ad/station)	Coupons ($5/day @$.025 each)
Newspaper ads ($500/ad)	Frequent purchase book ($15/day)
Cart signage ($100)	Soft drink premiums (supplied by drink companies.)
Flyers ($100 @$0.10 each)	

Joe found that any broadcast ad required additional production costs that were at least as much as the cost of a single ad. In addition, he needed to run at least four or five ads per station to be effective. Breakeven cost coverage would be exorbitant, with over a year's estimated sales needed just to pay for a small TV and radio campaign. And it's difficult to advertise with available media just to his target group of office workers within a radius of six city blocks.

Joe decided to have his cart painted ($100) with a clever message (see our example of Joe's unique selling proposition and slogan, above), hand out 1,000 flyers ($100) over three months to offices, do the soft drink premium program (collect can tabs for free gifts provided by local soft drink distributors), and try to get a free PR article mention in local newspapers and downtown TV and radio stations by sending free samples to editorial staff before lunch. He figured he could afford to hand out flyers and samples all year long and stay within his 10 percent budget limit.

PROMOTION IDEAS

Once a small business has determined both its business positioning strategy and the size of the marketing budget, specific promotional activities can be selected.

"Promotion" programs provide direct purchase incentives, in contrast to "advertising," which provides reasons to buy your product instead of the competing brand.

Promotion Ideas on a Budget

Games and contests can be conducted on a small, local scale. For example, many restaurants ask customers to leave a business card in a bowl. Drawings are held periodically and winners are awarded a free meal or other prize. The restaurant owners can collect information from the cards and use the list to solicit parties, meetings, etc.

Whatever games you devise, play fair with your customers. Don't charge them to enter, and be sure to state how and when the winners will be selected, say that the offer is void after a certain date, and that any taxes are the responsibility of the winner.

Premiums and gifts, sometimes called "ad specialties," have been around a long time. Their main purpose is to enhance name awareness: magnets, calendars, luggage tags, T-shirts, pens, pencils, or coffee mugs carry your name, logo, and perhaps phone number or Internet address. Anything that lasts and will be used by your prospective buyer can be effective. You may give these tokens out directly or have a buyer send in the proverbial "box top" and receive the valuable merchandise ... with your name all over it!

Coupons are a favorite way to entice new customers to buy from you. They generally entitle the bearer to some benefit, such as a price reduction on a particular item. Others reward frequent customers for their loyalty. For example, a coffee shop may give each of its customers a card that is punched when a pound of coffee is purchased. When the card is completely punched (perhaps after 10 or 12 pounds), the customer gets a free pound.

Product demonstrations are often more expensive per individual reached than advertising, but are many times more effective than single advertising ad exposures in any media. Demonstrations should be conducted at point-of-purchase whenever possible to maximize the opportunity for a buyer or end user to purchase immediately. And free trial services are sensational ways to introduce your expertise to a customer.

ADVERTISING IDEAS

To be effective, advertising must be interruptive — that is, it must make you stop thumbing through the newspaper or thinking about your day long enough to read or hear the ad. Advertising must also be credible, unique, and memorable in order to work. And finally, enough money must be spent to provide a media schedule for *ad frequency*, the most important element for *ad memorability*.

Advertising Checklist

❑ *Communicate a simple, single message.* People have trouble remembering someone's name, let alone a complicated ad message. For print ads, the simpler the headline, the better. And every ad element should support the headline message, whether that message is "price," "selection," "quality," or any other concept.

❑ ***Stick with a likable style.*** *Ads have personality and style. Find a likable style and personality and stay with it for at least a year, to avoid confusing buyers.*

❑ ***Be credible.*** *If you say your quality or value is the "best" and it clearly is not, advertising will speed your demise, not increase your business. Identifying and denigrating the competition should also be avoided. It is potentially confusing and distracting and may backfire on you by making buyers more loyal to competitors.*

❑ ***Ask for the sale.*** *Provide easily visible information in the ad for potential customers to buy: location, telephone number, store hours, charge cards accepted.*

❑ ***Make sure the ad looks professional.*** *If you have the time and talent, computer graphics and desktop publishing software can provide professional-looking templates to create good-looking print ads. Consider obtaining writing, artistic, and graphics help from local agencies or art studios who have experienced professionals on staff, with expensive and creative computer software in-house. Electronic ads (e.g., TV, radio, Internet) and outdoor ads are best left to professionals to produce.*

❑ ***Be truthful.*** *Whatever advertising medium you select, make sure your message is ethical and truthful. There are stringent laws regarding deceptive practices and false advertising.*

There's an old adage that holds that at least 50 percent of all advertising is a waste of money. It's probably true — and if you can figure out which half of your ad budget is useless, you'll save a bundle. But until you achieve this wisdom (which has so far eluded most marketers), you'd be wise to continue advertising full tilt and not take a chance on eliminating something that just might work.

Low- and No-Cost Advertising

- *Print attractive and informative business cards that include your logo and hand them out everywhere, consistently! If you use letterhead stationery in your business, have it match your business card. Keep your identity as consistent as possible.*

- *Print up some gift certificates. These let your customers introduce you to new customers. Since you get paid up front for the product or service, they are good for your cash flow.*

- *Brochures let you provide a lot of detail about your product or service. Simple three-fold brochure stock may be purchased from mail order suppliers such as Paper Direct (800-272-7377) in small quantities.*

- *Flyers can be created very inexpensively on your computer, or by a local print shop. You can use as much color as you like, with a color printer or old-fashioned colored paper stock. They can be used as bag stuffers or inserts to include with billings.*

- *Doorhangers are very effective and widely used by fast food and home delivery and service businesses. If you choose this medium, use heavy stock so it won't blow off doorknobs and litter the neighborhood.*

- *Inserted ads include mailbox inserts and free-standing inserts. The science behind the mass distribution of inserts is beyond the scope of our discussion here. If you think that inserts could successfully reach your market, call one of the big distributors and learn how much it would cost you to try this kind of program. The industry leaders are ADVO (call 860-520-3200, and they'll give you the local contact) and Val-Pak which is so big that you can find it under "V" in most local phone books.*

- *Paper or plastic bags and packaging make economical billboards. Print your name, logo, and message on anything you can, on all sides. Mailing labels are another perfect medium. Everyone who handles your mail will see your ad at no cost to you.*

Telephone Directories and 800 Numbers

Advertising in telephone directories is, for some businesses, critically important. But it's definitely not cheap! Check out all the alternative books in your region, get all their prices and pick their reps' brains for information and advice on how to make your ad stand out. Be very careful making your listing category choice. Do you want to position yourself as "pizza" or "restaurant" or "carry-out?"

800 numbers. The cost of your own 800 number may be less than you may think, because of competition among the major carriers. The calls can be forwarded to any line you choose. This might just be the most bang for your advertising buck — to be able to publish an 800 number in your print ads.

Local Print Ads

Classified ads and small display ads in local newspapers or magazines are a good way to reach your buyers. Get media kits from all your local publications (and any regional or national publications you may want to use as a model). The media kit will give you the demographic and geographic reach of the publication as well as rate information.

Remember that the lowly classifieds are perused by a huge number of people, especially on weekends. If you slip a classified ad into the right category and keep it running consistently, you'll probably get a response strong enough to at least pay the cost of the ad.

Another good way to reach customers is through your own newsletter, which can be a blend of advertising and informational text that refreshes your logo and identity and keeps you in touch with customers.

Signs and Displays

Cars and trucks are great traveling billboards. You can readily find a magnetic sign supplier that can fashion a flexible, detachable rubberized sign for your company truck or your personal car.

Interior and exterior signs should be lighted to take advantage of every opportunity to be seen. Reader boards, those signs using individual letters so you can change the message at will, are very useful if well-positioned, lighted, and maintained. Changing the message often will enhance their effect. Zoning ordinances often limit the use of reader boards.

Point-of-purchase displays. Impulse buying accounts for a huge amount of product sales. POP can take the form of danglers, signs, posters, banners, custom display racks, special lighting, or video monitors with promotional loops playing all day long. Bounceback and register tape coupons (printed on the back of the cash register receipt) are good to give at a POP location to stimulate customer's return to your business in the future.

Higher-Cost Advertising Alternatives

If you get big enough to contemplate advertising in major newspapers or magazines or on radio or television, form your own in-house ad agency and save the usual 15 percent commission. This is standard procedure for medium-sized businesses that handle their own ad buys and is as easy to do as printing up some letterhead with a name like XYZ Advertising Agency.

Of course, if you can afford it, you can hire a professional ad agency and learn the ropes before plunging in on your own. Sometimes the money they save you in good media buys may make up for their commission.

Electronic Marketing

For a small business, the best use of telemarketing might be to call people you've been referred to by current clients or networking contacts. Look at telephone contact as a way of giving out information or keeping in touch, not a way to close a sale.

Cybermarketing is a new frontier. Although it's considered poor "netiquette" to do any selling via e-mail, there are increasingly more opportunities via home pages and bulletin boards (BBS) to reach people or make it easy for them to reach you.

Direct Mail and Catalogs

Whether you use direct mail promotions or develop your own catalog, the demographics of your mailing list is the key to success.

You also have to maintain a flawless 800-number service with customer-centered operators, and make sure your delivery services are prompt, your warehouse well-stocked, your order pickers mistake-free, and your merchandise return policies correct. To start with, you may want to consider using a fulfillment house that can take calls, handle the customer credit process, and even ship products.

PUBLIC RELATIONS

Public relations (PR) efforts, like advertising, can help to build business and product awareness among target buyers and end users, often at a fraction of the cost of advertising. PR can be an effective way to generate valuable word-of-mouth advertising, sometimes due to the greater credibility and availability of information provided in editorial articles and interviews with your company personnel.

Public Relations Ideas

Press releases, if you make them newsworthy, can lead not only to great free publicity but to valuable reprints you can use in your ad efforts. For example, a simple story (and perhaps product samples) about the company's background, founders, and products can be written and sent to editors of local newspapers, magazines, TV, and radio stations. If the subject is of sufficient interest to editors, they may call to interview and run a free editorial story reaching thousands or millions of people.

Public service activities are a super way to good public relations and free publicity of the best kind. Participate in service clubs such as Rotary or Lions and the Chamber of Commerce. Offer to be a speaker at schools or senior centers. Donate your goods or services to local schools or churches, to be given away as raffle or silent auction prizes.

Grand openings (or re-openings) are always attention-getters as are anniversary sales and seasonal promotions. A small business can host open house events and invite key target buyers to explain and demonstrate products and services.

Part V

Your Office And Equipment

One of the most exciting, and important, aspects of planning your business is deciding on the facility in which you will conduct it. For those who are starting a new business, signing a lease for a business location can mark the turning point from planning the business on paper, to actually making those plans real.

Of course, once you have a place to operate your business, you're probably going to need some equipment and possibly a car or truck to effectively do your work. You're also going to need to insure your workplace and equipment, and to be concerned about security and safety issues.

Chapter 15: Your Business Facility explores the choices you must make in planning your business's location. Should you purchase or lease a facility? How do you select the right property? What kind of facility do you need? If you choose to establish a home business, you'll find practical tips on setting up the home office and complying with zoning restrictions.

Chapter 16: Business Equipment discusses the equipment you'll need to operate your business, how to acquire that equipment, and how to obtain the maximum use from your equipment once you get it.

Chapter 17: Protecting Your Business helps you prepare for, and prevent, many of the unfortunate things that can happen to your business's property. Obtaining insurance, taking security measures, and complying with safety regulations under OSHA are among the topics discussed.

Your Business Facility

However you envision your ideal facility, as a business owner your vital concern is to see that it contributes to your profitability, rather than detracting from it. In this chapter, we'll help you analyze your business facility needs, give you some tips on looking for a site, and help you decide whether you should rent or buy the facility.

For many young businesses, home is the right place to set up shop. Towards the end of this chapter, we address some of the unique issues faced by businesses located in the owner's home.

DETERMINING FACILITY NEEDS

Your search for the ideal facility will go much more smoothly — and will more likely be successful — if you are armed with a firm, fairly detailed list of your facility requirements.

To create this list, you need to answer questions like: What are the essential operating steps you must do to bring your product or service to your customers? In what logical order should these steps be done? How many employees will you need? Will they be using specialized machinery? Don't forget about functions such as marketing, billing, collection, payroll, facility maintenance, and security that are necessary to support the essential steps. Once you have identified the steps, you can translate them into facility needs.

Proximity to Customers, Employees, and Suppliers

When looking for any kind of real estate, it's best to start with the general geographic region and community in which you'd like to locate, and then narrow your search to specific properties in that general area. You can change many things about a building's layout and appearance, but you can't change its location once you move in!

In selecting a community, the primary consideration is usually whether there's ready access to enough potential customers to support your type of business. What constitutes "ready access" varies tremendously based on the type of business.

Work Smart

If your business depends in large part on drive-in or walk-in customers, even the side of the street you are on can make a difference. If you are on a street where most of the commuter traffic goes one way in the morning and the other way in the late afternoon, you'll probably do better with a location that's on the return-home side of the street. (Unless a large part of your business involves the sale of items to be consumed at, or on the way to, work — such as coffee and donuts.)

For many small businesses, the ability to attract and retain qualified employees can be critical to success. Because of this, you should carefully consider the availability of qualified employment prospects within a half-hour drive of your location.

It's likely that you also depend on suppliers (distributors, wholesalers, manufacturers, etc.) to provide you with the items you need to create and market your product. From the point of view of timely delivery and cost, it's usually best to be close to your important suppliers.

Character of the Community

The community's zoning laws and other rules relating to businesses (such as licensing fees, "head" taxes, and rules restricting time or manner of business operation), can indicate the community's attitude towards businesses like yours. By looking into these zoning rules and business taxes, you can estimate some of the economic costs of locating within that community, and get an idea about how likely it is that the zoning authorities will give you a variance (special exemption from the rules), if needed. You should also pay attention to the quality of police and fire departments in the area.

Nearby Businesses and Competitors

By deciding where to locate your business, you may be able to "piggy-back" on a neighbor's ability to draw customers to the area. Many small businesses may benefit by being close to a "magnet" store, that is, a large store that attracts a large number of customers.

In certain instances, competitors may "cluster" in close proximity for the betterment of all. For example, several stores selling unique, but similar, items such as art, antiques, or sporting equipment might cluster so as to draw more customers than any one store could hope to attract.

Most retail and service businesses, however, would find the absence of nearby competitors to be a great advantage. But before you are tempted to rush into a facility based on the fact that there are no nearby competitors, consider these points:

- The location may not support the kind of business that you wish to operate there.

- Competitors who are not located in the area may do business there by phone, mail, or a sales force.

Building Size, Layout, Appearance

The physical structure and layout of your facility should function as a tool that helps you to efficiently do all the things necessary to bring your business's products or services to its customers.

Retail and service businesses. Retail and service businesses that depend on customers coming into the store must make sure that the exterior and interior design, decorating, and maintenance all entice customers into the business. Depending on your type of business, the interior of the facility may be primarily set up to "get them in, get them out." Or the facility could be set up to encourage customers to browse through the store, hopefully finding something to buy in addition to what they came for. Don't forget to consider your need for on-site inventory or supply storage.

Wholesalers and manufacturers. Wholesale businesses often require large, open facilities that put a premium on efficient material handling. They often need wide aisles and storage racks that allow the use of lift trucks, large shipping and receiving docks, and a location that has good access to transportation facilities.

The facilities of manufacturers may need to be highly specialized to accommodate heavy machinery and assembly lines, materials and product storage areas, and shipping areas.

Building modifications. You may find a facility that is well located, and that generally meets your requirements, but may require a few changes before you can use it. Before you jump into acquiring this *almost perfect* facility, you should consider these factors:

- **How much would it cost?** If the work will be costly and vital to the operation of your business, you may want to press for price or rent concessions from the seller or landlord. You should also consider getting actual bids on the work.

- **Would the change be allowed?** You'll need to investigate what permits (if any) you would need from local authorities to do the work, and whether you would need a zoning or building code variance for the modification.

- **How long would it take?** If the modification to the building would take months or weeks to complete, can you afford to wait?

Adequate parking. No matter who visits your business, adequate parking is a major concern. In some cases, businesses can strike deals with other businesses, or with local governmental bodies, to meet their parking needs at a reasonable cost.

Example

We know of a business that was able to solve a critical employee parking problem by entering an agreement with a local park district. Under the agreement, the business's employees could park their cars in a nearby parking lot owned by the park district, which had adjoining softball fields and tennis courts. In exchange for this, the business, at its own expense, paved and maintained the lot, which would continue to be open for public use. Since the business's parking needs were generally limited to weekday business hours, while the park district patrons normally used the parking facilities after work or on weekends, this joint use agreement benefited both parties, while disadvantaging neither.

Environmental Issues

Federal law frequently requires the owners of property that is polluted with hazardous wastes to bear the cost of cleaning them up. Although you would not be without defenses to such a government claim, merely proving that you were not the cause of the pollution is not enough. You must have had no knowledge of the condition, and you must have made a good faith effort to uncover any hazardous condition. Thus, it is vitally important that you avoid facility sites that may have been environmentally damaged by hazardous wastes.

At a minimum, before you sign a rental or sales contract for the property, your attorney should require the seller or landlord to disclose whether there were prior uses that may have had an environmental impact and any federal and state environmental notices or investigations relating to the site. Your attorney can also tell you whether you need an environmental inspection of the site.

If your own business uses, generates, or receives toxic wastes or other environmentally damaging materials (such as used petroleum products), don't agree to move into any facility until you know that you can obtain, and legally use, adequate refuse disposal equipment.

Security Issues

Crimes against people or property can significantly add to your cost of doing business. Shoplifting, employee theft of inventory (sometimes called "shrinkage"), and theft of business property are all too common and costly. Crimes against business owners, employees, customers, and others who enter the premises are less common, but can be more tragic and traumatic when they occur.

If you locate in a high-crime area, you'll likely need to invest in more facility security features than if you locate in a low-crime area. However, remember that higher-crime areas are usually significantly cheaper in terms of rent, and if you can save 60% in rent you can buy a very nice security system and still come out ahead.

Allowing for Future Growth

All things being equal, a business facility that can accommodate potential future growth would be more attractive than one that does not. Realistically, though, if one facility offers more room, you can expect to pay for it somehow, usually in price, location, or other terms or features. If this is true, does it make sense to pay *now* for the benefit of easy expansion *later*? It may, but only if you reasonably believe (not just hope) that you will need the extra space in the not-too-distant future and that any costs that go along with this extra space will not be an undue drag on *current* business growth.

Accomplishing Goals Economically

There is one more important attribute of the "ideal" facility: It should fulfill your space needs economically.

Save Money

Share space with others. *Certain start-up businesses — particularly service providers, such as lawyers and accountants — are able to keep down their overhead expenses by sharing space, telephone, and secretarial services with like businesses.*

Locate within a business incubator. *Business incubators are groups (run either as private, for-profit organizations, or as not-for-profit groups) that are designed to help small businesses survive and succeed through the startup phase of their existence. Besides shared space and office services, they also provide management and financial assistance. Although incubators may greatly improve a startup business's chances of success, not all types of businesses benefit equally from incubators. Because incubators are usually located in low-rent, often out-of-the-way facilities, they tend to work best when your business does not need to draw in-store customers.*

FINDING THE RIGHT FACILITY

If you know the areas where you are looking like the back of your hand, know how to ferret out commercial properties for sale, can invest a good bit of time in the search, and are knowledgeable about local commercial real estate practices, you may be able to locate an acceptable property by yourself, or with the help of real estate agents representing sellers. If not, you may want to employ your own real estate agent (that is, a "buyer's agent").

Commercial properties are generally *not* listed on the multiple listing service that serves all real estate agents in the area. This means that if you don't have a buyer's agent working for you, you'll probably have to contact a large group of sellers' agents to get a good idea of available properties.

Commissions for commercial real estate agents are often the subject of negotiation between the buyer and the seller, with the buyer often paying at least part of the commissions. The total percentage of sales price paid out as commissions may also be larger for commercial properties than that customarily charged on residential sales.

SHOULD YOU LEASE OR BUY YOUR FACILITY?

New business owners have a tendency to concentrate on the short-term consequences of leasing or buying, such as the first-year cash flow projections that would result for each of the alternatives. This is probably altogether necessary: if things don't go well in the first couple of years, your business may not be around to see how a particular decision would have benefited you 10 years down the road.

However, it's a good idea to consider some of the long-term implications, as well. In some cases, buying the facility will be much better for you in the long run, and if you can't afford to buy now, at least you can make it one of your long-term goals.

The main advantage of *leasing* a business facility is that your initial outlay of cash to gain the use of an asset is generally less for leasing than it is for purchasing. However, perhaps the main advantage of purchasing is that your facility costs are fixed, and you'll probably end up paying out less in the long term than you would have paid if you leased the facility. Moreover, if you purchase, you get the benefit of any appreciation in the value of the property.

How do you weigh these factors? You can do a mathematical analysis of your net cash flows that would result from leasing and compare those that would result from purchasing. For an example, see the case study on page 232.

When Buying Makes Sense

Aside from the economic issues, the following factors may indicate that you should purchase, rather than lease, your business facility.

- **You want control of the property** — maybe you intend to make substantial additions or renovations to the property. If you own the property, you have much more freedom to make whatever modifications are needed, provided you observe the local zoning laws and building codes.

- **You want to stay at the same location** — for some businesses, such as certain retail and service businesses, location is all important. If you have established a winning business location, you don't want to lose it because of a rent escalation or because the landlord wants the property for another use.

- **You are in an area of appreciating land values** — if you think land values will continue to increase, it would be better to own the property (and thereby get the benefit of this appreciation if you ever sell) rather than to rent it.

When Leasing Makes Sense

The following factors may indicate that you should lease, rather than purchase, your business facility.

- **You don't want maintenance duties** — many leases place the duty of maintaining the property on the landlord. In that case, you won't have to worry about things like roof repairs, tuckpointing, maintenance of heating and cooling equipment, plumbing, snow removal, and even ordinary housekeeping.

- **You want to retain your mobility** — maybe you're not sure that the facility that you will select now will serve your needs several years in the future.

- **Your company's credit rating may not support a mortgage** — if your business is rather new, or has experienced some financial difficulties, lenders may not be willing to extend it sufficient credit for a mortgage on the facility.

- **The facility is in an area of declining real estate values** — you may find a facility that meets your needs, but be concerned that the real estate values in the area are stagnant, or may actually drop in value.

Basic Leasing Terminology

There is no real legal distinction between a "lease" and a "rental." In practice, however, rentals generally are considered short-term arrangements (a day, a week, a month), while leases extend for longer periods (a year or more).

Common Lease Provisions

If you have decided that you would rather lease your business facility than purchase it, you should familiarize yourself with the following types of leases and terms that are commonly found in commercial leases:

- ***Gross lease*** — *this is the most traditional type of lease: the tenant pays rent; the landlord pays taxes, insurance, and maintenance expenses relating to the property.*

- ***Net lease*** — *a net lease transfers some or all of the expenses that the landlord is traditionally responsible for to the tenant. With a single net lease, the tenant pays rent plus taxes relating to the tenant's portion of the property. Under a double net lease, the tenant also pays its proportional part of insurance premiums. Finally, with a triple net lease (which is often favored by larger businesses), the tenant pays all charges payable under a double net lease, plus maintenance expenses.*

- ***Fixed lease*** — *a fixed lease provides for a fixed amount of rent over a fixed rental period (term). These types of leases usually seem the least threatening for the small business owner tenant, since you don't obligate yourself today for rent increases in the future.*

- ***Step lease*** — *a step lease provides for set rent increases to take effect at stated times. This will provide you with the peace of mind of knowing what your rental amounts will be for a longer time period, while giving the landlord some protection against rising costs.*

- ***Percentage lease*** — *with a percentage lease, your landlord shares in your good (or bad) fortune. The lease provides for a fixed amount of rent, plus an additional amount that is set as a percentage of your gross receipts or sales. This may be advantageous for businesses whose income fluctuates a great deal from month to month, but may also involve opening up your business records to your landlord.*

- ***Lease term*** — *identifies how long the lease will be in effect. If you suspect that you will want to stay at this same business location beyond the initial term, try negotiating the inclusion in the agreement of a renewal option that entitles you to renew the lease for a specified period and a specified rent.*

- ***Rental rate*** — *tells how much the rent is and when it must be paid, and whether additional charges are due if you fail to pay the rent on time or within a specified grace period. If your business experiences seasonal or irregular sales activity, try negotiating a flexible rental rate that corresponds to the changes in your cash flow.*

- **Escalation clause** — this clause provides for increases in rent over a specified time period. The escalations can be fixed, or determined with reference to an outside factor, such as increases in the landlord's operating costs, increases in a cost index (such as the consumer price index), or increases in the tenant's gross receipts or sales.

- **Maintenance** — specifies who is required to maintain which portions of the building and land. If you are responsible for maintenance, the lease should say whether you can contract with anyone of your choosing to provide these services, or whether the service providers have to be approved by the landlord.

- **Competition** — in a lease of retail space, such as a store in a shopping mall, there may be restrictions placed on the landlord's right to lease nearby space to businesses similar to your business. (If there are not, you should consider pushing for such a provision.)

- **Subletting** — spells out whether, and under what conditions, you are entitled to sublease the premises to another. Remember, if you sublet the property, you normally will still be liable for paying the rent if the subletting tenant does not pay.

- **Improvements and modifications** — identifies whether you have the right to make improvements or modifications to the facility so that it better suits your needs.

- **Taxes** — specifies who is responsible for the real property taxes.

- **Insurance and liability** — fixes who is responsible for casualty and liability insurance and how much coverage must be carried.

- **Renewal option** — specifies whether you have the option to renew the lease when it expires, and if so, specifies the amount of rent to be paid (or how the rental amount is to be determined) in the future. A renewal option can protect you against an unreasonably large rent increase when your first lease term expires.

- **Purchase option** — tells whether you'll have the right to purchase the facility at the end of the lease term, and if so, at what price.

- **Destruction or condemnation** — states whether the landlord is required to rebuild if the property is destroyed. Specifies whether rent will be abated, and whether you can terminate your lease obligations if the facility is totally or partially destroyed.

- **Landlord's solvency** — spells out your rights as a tenant if your landlord's mortgage company forecloses on the leased premises.

- **Tenant "going dark" rights** — a fear of many small tenants in a shopping center is that a major tenant will go out of business or not renew its lease ("going dark"). One approach to this problem would be for you to negotiate a clause that gives you the right to close your store or get a large rent reduction if a major tenant or several other tenants go dark.

WORKING AT HOME

If you're thinking of starting a home-based business, you have a special set of issues to consider, along with all the usual issues that must be faced by anyone who is starting a business.

While working at home can provide you with a freedom from structure not possible in a traditional work setting, it can also result in loneliness and lack of concentration. However, if you make a conscious effort, these common pitfalls can be overcome.

Work Smart

Here are some steps you can take to avoid feeling isolated and to make and maintain new business contacts:

- *Join professional groups such as industry organizations or associations.*

- *Join professional groups for people working at home or people in small business.*

- *Take classes in areas that are pertinent to your business and interest you.*

- *Participate in and plan events that involve people in the business community.*

- *Keep an eye open for business contacts and interaction wherever you are. Don't overlook the health club, the supermarket, the bookstore, or the neighborhood block party as places where those with interests similar to yours will be found.*

Working at home can also make it difficult to focus on your work. There are many distractions that don't exist in a traditional workplace such as chores and errands that need to be done, and guilty pleasures such as watching television or going to the park may be very tempting.

We have a few suggestions for staying focused:

- Set up a routine to get yourself on task immediately. For example, upon entering the work area, you could close the door and fire up your computer as a mental cue to begin work.

- It's also a good idea to have a daily list of goals, or at least one task, to attack as soon as you enter the work area.

- Despite all plans to the contrary, recognize that distractions are inevitable when you work at home. Even a traditional work setting has its own distractions. To deal with the inevitable distractions, work them into your schedule where you can.

Jason starts work in his home office each day at 10:00 a.m. Every day, his mail is delivered at 12:30 p.m. The mail carrier usually has packages and certified letters that must be signed for, and Jason finds it hard to get right back to work after this daily interruption. To avoid this problem, Jason takes his lunch break every day at 12:30.

Setting Up the Home Office

The area of your home where you operate your business — your workplace — will have an impact on the success of your business venture. To make sure that this impact is positive, organize it so that it becomes an efficient tool of your business. Your workplace should encourage productivity when you deal with customers or clients, suppliers, family, friends and neighbors, and yourself!

Defining Your Work Area

The two main goals in creating a work space are functionality and low cost. Your home office work area should allow you to perform all necessary duties of your business without unduly disrupting the functioning of the rest of your household, and should do so at a cost that doesn't put your new business too deeply in the hole.

Most people working out of their homes find it helpful to have the work area somewhat isolated from the "personal" areas of the home, particularly if clients and customers will be coming into the work area. If feasible, a separate entrance (or even a detached building on your property) for the work area might be best. A traditional work setting contains natural boundaries for the people in your personal life. However, when you work at home, you will need to create these boundaries so that your business, as well as your personal life, can run smoothly and successfully.

When people try to interrupt you while you're working, whether it's in person or on the telephone, tactfully let them know that you can't be disturbed because you're working on something, you're on a business call, you're with an employee, or you're in a meeting. Then let them know when you will be available and make sure it's outside your regular business hours. It may take some time, but your neighbors, friends, and family will learn to take your home business as seriously as you do!

Watch the Cost!

Possibly you have decided where to put your work area, and are thinking that physical changes should be made to enhance its efficiency (new walls, wood paneling, soundproofing, carpeting, etc.).

All of these may be good ideas — and possibly some or all of these changes should be made — but the question is, when? If you are just starting your home business, economy and efficiency should be your watchwords.

You can always upgrade your work area when the profits roll in. You might even include your desire for a better work area as a business goal: "When my weekly sales reach $X, then I'll carpet the office."

If you are able to qualify, Uncle Sam may partially subsidize your home office in the form of income tax write-offs. See our discussion of business deductions in Chapter 26.

Equipping Your Home Office

In planning your home office, keep in mind that some people have the preconceived notion that home businesses are not as committed or as efficient as other businesses. So, if you bring customers or other people into your home work area, you should consider whether your desk, furnishings, and other equipment convey the right impression.

Although these items usually don't have to be expensive or elegant, they may detract from your business image if they are battered or appear unbusinesslike. Your office equipment should convey the impression that you are serious (but not stodgy!) about your business, and you are able and willing to provide your customers with superior products or services.

Home Office Safety

Your business visitors may not think to look for hazards that are a part of the home, but are not usually encountered in the workplace. If possible, try to keep your visitors out of the personal areas of the house where the belongings of family members may create hazards (such as the skateboard at the bottom of the steps). Likewise, aggressive dogs or other animals should be kept away from visitors.

Regardless of how hard you try to keep your business area safe for visitors, you should always have adequate liability insurance. See the discussion of insurance in Chapter 17.

Zoning Restrictions on Home Offices

You may think that your home is your castle, but the government will beg to differ with you! Zoning rules are often used by local governments to bar or limit the types of businesses that can be operated in a residence.

The main rationale behind these prohibitive or restrictive zoning laws is to maintain the residential character of a neighborhood. On the flip side, it is often illegal to live in some commercially zoned areas where you are running a business.

Some localities restrict the right of property owners to build separate structures. There may also be restrictions on how much of your home can be used exclusively for your home office or business. For example, in Chicago you may not use more than 10% of the home exclusively for business. Local zoning laws can limit the number of employees you are allowed to have, or may not allow you to have any employees working in your home (other than domestics).

Zoning ordinances may also affect your ability to post signs outside your home advertising the business, or to allow business visitors to park on the street. Noise, smoke and odor, certain types of equipment, or disposal of certain chemicals can all be subject to zoning rules.

Getting Zoning Information

Every public library should contain a copy of the local ordinances, including zoning rules. You can pore over these at your leisure, without alerting any government officials about your plans for a home-based business.

Perhaps an easier, although less anonymous, way to get zoning information is to contact your local planning department or zoning board. These are usually accessible through your county offices if you live outside city limits or through city hall if you live within city limits. Also, if you live in an apartment building, we suggest you contact the manager or board responsible for setting up rules for activities in the building, and make sure your lease doesn't prohibit home businesses.

If you live in a condominium or co-op, check the lease or ownership agreement to find out if running a business out of your home is prohibited. Similarly, if your neighborhood has a homeowner's association, check its policy on businesses run out of the home.

Depending on your local laws, you may need a home-occupation permit or a business license to have a home office or business. The cost is usually a flat fee or a percentage of your annual receipts.

Consequences of Zoning Violations

While home offices or businesses have been shut down for violating zoning rules, the rules are often enforced only if neighbors complain about disturbances resulting from the operation of a home-based business. That's why arguably the most crucial step in operating a home business free and clear of zoning problems is getting your neighbors' approval. Their approval need not be explicit — although being upfront with them about what you are doing may work best.

If, according to your judgment and personal history with your neighbors, you don't feel comfortable approaching them directly, you can get their implicit approval of your home business. You can do this by keeping increased traffic, noise, and any other undesirable traits for residential neighborhoods to a minimum, so that they barely notice your business is there.

If, despite your efforts to the contrary, you run into zoning problems, you can apply to the zoning or planning board for a variance. Keep in mind that avoiding this step is extremely desirable because variances are not easily granted. The following criteria are often used to determine whether variances should be granted:

- Applying the zoning ordinance would deprive you of your livelihood.

- The business use of your home would not harm the neighborhood.

- The requested business use of your home is similar to one currently allowed in the area.

Chapter 16

Business Equipment

The type of business you operate will in large part dictate what equipment and other fixed assets you'll require to properly run your business. We can't say exactly what you should acquire without first knowing what you'll be doing. However, we will provide some general points you should consider before you acquire any business equipment, as well as advice on using equipment productively and on disposing of equipment you no longer need.

Save Money

By their nature, fixed assets represent relatively long-term investments of capital. In most cases, it will take several years to recover the money you spend in acquiring the asset, even if everything goes well. Accordingly, unless you have unlimited financial resources, you should avoid acquiring any asset that you can't reasonably expect to bring a significant increase in your profits, efficiency, or productivity over the course of the asset's useful life in your business. Be especially careful about tying up capital in fixed assets in response to short-term needs.

ACQUIRING THE EQUIPMENT YOU NEED

So you've concluded that your business really does need a particular item of equipment or other fixed asset. Before you rush out and spend some of your valuable capital, invest a little time considering how you can best meet that need. There are basically three alternatives: leasing, purchasing, or using assets you already own.

Using Personal Assets for Business

Putting items you already own, such as cars, office furnishings, and computer equipment, to work in your business can free up many dollars that you would have otherwise spent on acquisition costs. This may seem obvious, but you'd be amazed at how many people spend more money furnishing their office than they could possibly hope to earn in the first year.

If you're conducting business as a sole proprietorship, there's really no trick to converting your personal assets. All it takes is to start using them in your business. Perhaps your only real concern will be confirming whether you'll lose insurance coverage for the converted items under your homeowners policy. If so, you'll want to be sure to have the items covered by your business policy. (Regarding the tax treatment of converted property, see page 464.)

Saving with Used Equipment

If there's equipment that you need but don't already own, be sure to investigate the used equipment market. Depending on the item, you may be able to purchase used equipment for a small fraction of what you would have paid if the equipment were new, and without any loss of functionality.

This is especially true for restaurant equipment, store counters and fixtures, office furnishings and, perhaps surprisingly, computers. The equipment is usually generic enough to be adaptable to many different types of businesses, perhaps with some modifications, upgrades, or cosmetic improvements.

Where can you find high-quality used equipment? Start by checking the Yellow Pages for listings of thrift stores and secondhand dealers. The classified sections of your local newspaper and trade publications are another good place to look. Be especially watchful for ads mentioning sales related to an office remodeling or business liquidation. And as more people get into — and sometimes out of — home businesses, yard and estate sales may also provide bargains to those with the time and patience to seek them out.

Leasing Your Equipment

Nowadays, you should view leasing companies as potential suppliers for virtually all of your equipment and other tangible business assets. You should have little trouble finding companies willing to lease or rent motor vehicles, office furniture, store fixtures, computers, communications devices, manufacturing equipment, and other items you may need. The trick, of course, is determining when you would be better off leasing an asset instead of purchasing it.

The main advantage of leasing is that you can generally gain the use of an asset with less initial cash than you'd need to buy it. Equipment leases rarely require down payments. In other words, leasing may effectively provide the benefit of up to 100-percent financing (although a refundable security deposit may be required in some instances). In contrast, purchase loans frequently require down payments of up to 25 percent or more.

If yours is a start-up business that is strapped for cash or if you are finding it difficult to secure the credit necessary to finance your purchases, leasing may be your only real option to obtain needed business assets. Before you sign a lease agreement, you should know some basic facts.

True Leases and Financial Leases

The two main types of equipment leases you'll encounter are "true" leases and "financial" leases. You also may hear about "sales and leaseback" leases, which in reality are sophisticated financing transactions.

True leases. If the lessee acquires no rights to the property other than its use, then the lease is commonly referred to as a "true" (or "straight") lease. Under a true lease, the lessor is treated as the owner of the leased property for both tax and non-tax purposes, and the lessee's rental payments do not establish any equity in the property. A true lease usually gives the lessee the option to prematurely end the lease, subject to conditions that are spelled out in the agreement.

If the lessor remains responsible for maintaining the property, then a true lease also may be referred to as an "operating" (or "maintenance") lease.

Financial leases. A lease that is used to effectively finance the purchase of assets is commonly referred to as a "financial" lease. The distinguishing characteristics of financial leases are that (1) the term of the lease generally coincides with the functional or economic life of the property, (2) the lease may not be canceled, and (3) the lessee is responsible for maintaining the property.

Frequently, a financial lease will be structured so that the lessee's only practical choice at the end of the lease is to purchase the asset, for a specified price. For accounting and tax purposes, a financial lease is generally treated as a sale.

Comparing Leasing and Purchasing

How can you determine whether a lease or a purchase of a given piece of equipment is better for your business? One way is to do a mathematical analysis of your net cash outflows that would result from leasing and from purchasing.

A cash flow analysis provides an estimate of how much cash you would need to set aside today to cover the after-tax costs of each acquisition alternative. The analysis takes into account the "time value of money," which basically is the concept that you don't need to have $50 today to pay a $50 expense at some point in the future, due to the fact that you can earn interest on your money.

Case Study — Leasing vs. Purchasing

Let's assume you're faced with the following lease-or-buy decision. You can purchase a $50,000 piece of equipment by putting 25 percent down and paying off the balance at 10 percent interest with four annual installments of $11,830. The equipment will be used in your business for eight years, after which it can be sold for scrap for $2,500. The alternative is that you can lease the same equipment for eight years at an annual rent of $8,500, the first payment of which is due on delivery. You'll be responsible for the equipment's maintenance costs during the lease.

You expect that your combined federal and state income tax rate will be 40 percent for the entire period at issue. You further assume that your cost of capital is 6 percent (the 10-percent financing rate adjusted by your tax rate).

The following tables demonstrate how you can use a cash flow analysis to assist you with a lease-or-buy decision. In this case, if cost were the sole criterion for the decision, you would be inclined to purchase the asset because in current dollars, the cost of purchasing is $32,204, while the cost of leasing is $34,838. Even if cost isn't your sole criterion, a cash flow analysis is useful because it can show you how much you're paying for non-cost factors that may dictate your decision to lease.

Cash flow analysis of purchase. *Assume that all payments are made on the first day of the year. Interest is deemed to accrue on the outstanding balance of the loan at the end of each year, and is computed as follows (the last column shows the portion of each annual payment that goes to principal and that reduces the outstanding loan):*

Year End	Outstanding Loan	Interest	Principal
1	37,500	3,750	8,080
2	29,420	2,942	8,888
3	20,532	2,053	9,777
4	10,755	1,075	10,755

Depreciation is computed on the basis of the 200-percent declining balance method.

(A) Year	(B) Cash Pmts.	(C) Prior Year's Interest	(D) Prior Year's Dep.	(E) Tax Savings [40% x (C+D)]	(F) Net Cash Flow [B - E]	(G) Discount Factor (6%)	(H) Present Value [F x G]
1	$12,500	$0	$0	$0	$12,500	1.0000	$12,500
2	11,830	0	10,000	4,000	7,830	0.9434	7,387
3	11,830	3,750	16,000	7,900	3,930	0.8900	3,498
4	11,830	2,942	9,600	5,017	6,813	0.8396	5,720
5	11,830	2,053	5,760	3,125	8,705	0.7921	6,895
6		1,075	5,760	2,734	(2,734)	0.7473	(2,043)
7			2,880	1,152	(1,152)	0.7050	(812)
8							
9	(2,500)			(1,000)	(1,500)	0.6274	(941)
Net Cash Flow							$32,204

Cash flow analysis of leasing. *Assume that the first lease payment is due on delivery and the following payments are due on the first day of each subsequent year. The business is assumed to have a combined federal and state income tax rate of 40 percent (tax benefits are computed as of the first day of year following the year for which the rental deduction was claimed) and a 6 percent cost of capital.*

(A) Year	(B) Lease Payment	(C) Prior Year's Tax Savings [40% x B]	(D) Net Cash Flow [B - C]	(E) Discount Factor (6% Cost of Capital)	(F) Present Value [D x E]
1	$8,500		$8,500	1.0000	$8,500
2	8,500	3,400	5,100	0.9434	4,811
3	8,500	3,400	5,100	0.8900	4,539
4	8,500	3,400	5,100	0.8396	4,282
5	8,500	3,400	5,100	0.7921	4,040
6	8,500	3,400	5,100	0.7473	3,811
7	8,500	3,400	5,100	0.7050	3,596
8	8,500	3,400	5,100	0.6651	3,392
9		3,400	(3,400)	0.6274	(2,133)
Net Cash Flow					$34,838

USING YOUR EQUIPMENT PRODUCTIVELY

There is no right or wrong way to design and equip a workspace. What works for someone else may not work for you. However, we suggest that you keep in mind the following priorities:

- **Productive** offices are organized so that equipment, records management, and communications systems not only work, but work together.

- **Efficient** offices should be both cost-effective and time-effective. If your office is set up right, it allows you to do more, with less money, in less time.

- **Comfortable** offices help you to do your work with minimal stress and strain on your body.

Tips for Setting Up a Workspace

The following tips apply specifically to office-type settings, but can be adapted to almost any workspace.

- ***Power availability*** — *consider the effect of supplemental heating and air conditioning units on power availability when the weather starts changing. Some equipment may also distort radio transmissions or cause static on a cordless phone.*

- ***Temperature discrepancies*** — *be wary of placing equipment that generates heat (for example, a photocopier) or magnetic fields too close to computer disks and other sensitive equipment.*

- ***Lighting conditions*** — *many people working on computer terminals like the room to be darker to minimize screen glare. The same darkness causes problems for solar powered devices, and your eyes, if you're trying to read. Arrange lights so that you can turn some off when you are working on-screen and turn others on when you are working at your desk.*

- ***Infrared system failures*** — *there's much talk today about the wireless office. Some systems send data over the airwaves to a printer or fax machine in the corner. Will putting two of these machines in the same room cause a problem? Will such a machine interfere with a burglar alarm system? Plan accordingly.*

- ***Noisy equipment*** — *it can render the dictation tape you prepared for your transcriptionist — or worse, the phone message you left for an important client — unintelligible. Try to keep noisy equipment away from your primary workspace.*

- ***Built-in desks and other furniture*** — *avoid if possible. Movable equipment can be rearranged as your workflow changes. Similarly, use adjustable shelving.*

- ***Filing systems*** — *should be organized so that you will handle a piece of paper only once before it goes where it belongs.*

- ***Windows*** — *put equipment where you can take advantage of natural lighting. This may enable you to use fewer lights at lower wattage.*

- ***Environmental hazards*** — *don't place your equipment where it will be subjected to extreme heat and cold. Heavy dust (and spilled coffee!) can also cause extreme damage to delicate equipment like computers. This is especially important to think about if you work out of a home office in a garage, attic, or cellar.*

Remember that your time is worth money. Any system that helps you to work faster saves money if it frees you to work on other matters that help to generate profits.

Disposing of Unproductive Equipment

Every item of equipment that you acquire for your business represents an investment of your business capital. Taken a step further, an item that is not currently being used represents capital on which the current return is zero or even negative (if property taxes and insurance costs attributable to the item are taken into account).

Adopt a practice of taking regular inventories of all of your equipment to confirm each item's current level of use. If you come across an item that you're currently not using, try to determine whether you have a definite future use for the item that justifies the continuing cost of holding it. Otherwise, consider selling or disposing of the item.

If you're unable to sell an unproductive item of equipment, or to use it as a trade-in on the purchase of an item you need, you may be able to generate a tax deduction by donating the item to charity or by simply abandoning (junking) it.

Chapter 17

Protecting Your Business

Floods, hurricanes, earthquakes. Robbery, forgery, computer piracy. It is a fact of life, and business, that Mother Nature sometimes strikes, accidents happen, and some people steal things. Just as you take steps to ensure the safety of your home and family, so too must you take steps to minimize the risks to your business. To do this, you need to be concerned about insurance and security precautions. You also need to be concerned about safety in the workplace, particularly if you have employees.

INSURING YOUR OFFICE AND EQUIPMENT

If you have recently gone into business, your view of insurance may be that it is a luxury that big, thriving companies can afford to purchase but something you can't worry about right now. After all, you have tight cash flows, you have employees (or at least yourself) to pay, and you need to market your product. So you may be thinking, "If I get robbed or my old truck gets stolen, I'll deal with it then. I'd rather spend money dealing with what I know will happen, rather than what could happen."

But we'd like to get you out of the mode of thinking of insurance as only protection against casualties. In fact, the most important reason you may need insurance is for protection from legal hazards.

Generally speaking, if you run a business as a sole proprietorship or partnership, you will be personally liable for any debts or legal judgments that your business owes. The amount that you can be required to pay is not limited to the income you make from the business, or its value.

If you run the business as a corporation (including an S corporation) or as a limited liability company, you have what is called "limited liability." In theory, this means that your legal liability for the debts and acts of your business will be limited to the amount of your investment in the company. However, there are exceptions to limited liability. You may lose your limited liability if:

- You fail to respect the corporate structure by actions such as treating corporate property or money as your own personal property.

- Your corporation is undercapitalized; that is, the corporation does not have anything near the amount of assets that it may need to meet its liabilities.

- You voluntarily waive limited liability, such as by agreeing to guarantee, as an individual, the debts of your corporation.

And when a significant amount of money is at stake in a lawsuit, attorneys will work hard to exploit those exceptions so that they can collect legal judgments against you personally.

As a business owner, you're going to have to weigh the cost of insuring against a variety of risks against the economic impact of an uninsured loss. How do you obtain the right coverage at the right price without spending a lot of time and money on research? We suggest the following process:

1. Learn about the different types of business insurance.

2. Determine which types of insurance and how much coverage you need.

3. Explore alternatives to insurance.

Types of Insurance You May Need

To avoid spending money on coverage you don't need, consider carefully the various types of insurance customarily available to small businesses, before you talk to your insurance agent:

Homeowner's Insurance

Even if you have incorporated your business or formed an LLC, you and your business are joined economically. Any economic disaster that hits your personal assets will make it hard for you to give your business the time and monetary support that it needs. A homeowner's policy can help ensure that a non-business casualty or liability will not drag down your business.

And those of you with home-based businesses will be especially concerned about shielding your residence from possible losses.

What's covered by a homeowner's policy? There are several different types of policy in terms of the types of risks that are covered. The most common type of homeowner's policy in use today (known as "comprehensive coverage" or "HO-3" in the insurance industry) covers things like: damage to home and personal property caused by fire, lightning, wind, or storm; medical payments for occupants for injuries caused by fire, lightning, wind, or storm damage; medical and legal liabilities to persons injured by accident while in the home; and loss or theft of personal property, even if not in your home, with some restrictions on things like jewelry or laptop computers.

What's not covered by a homeowner's policy? For our purposes, the major risk that your comprehensive policy normally does not cover is any claim arising from a business use of the premises. The claim could arise from your conduct of business in the home (such as a business visitor who trips and falls on your carpet) or simple storage of business property (such as a theft of your business computer).

You should be upfront with your insurance agent about your home business, or business property kept at home. If your business does not involve the coming and going of customers or employees, or the storage of hazardous materials or large quantities of valuable inventory in your home, you may be able to add an inexpensive rider covering the business. Otherwise, check out other insurance companies, or purchase a business owner's policy as discussed below.

Automobile Insurance

Auto insurance has two main components: liability insurance and insurance for property damage. Liability insurance is the most important. It provides compensation to persons who would be able to sue you for personal injuries, medical payments, loss of earnings, or damage to their property arising out of an auto accident.

Property damage coverage includes such collision and comprehensive coverage, which compensate you for damage to your car, and assorted damage to it caused by such things as fire, theft, and vandalism.

Do you need auto insurance? In most states, all motorists are required to have a specified amount of liability insurance, although it's usually not enough to protect you or your business. If your auto is financed through a bank or other commercial lender, the lender will require you to carry both collision and comprehensive coverage. Otherwise, you don't have to carry this coverage.

Impact on your business. If your policy does not cover business travel, you usually can get coverage by way of a policy add-on (known as a "rider") for a reasonable additional amount.

If you have employees who drive your car on business, you should have what is known as "non-owned" coverage. This coverage pays for injury to people and property damage caused by the employee.

Work Smart

 If you are wondering how much auto insurance is likely to cost you, or you would like more information on how to lower your auto insurance premiums, you could start on the Internet with the Insurance News Network's web page at http://www.insure.com/auto/index.html. In addition to a discussion of some basics, you'll find valuable links to the crash safety, theft, and state data that drive most insurance rates. For example, you can determine how likely it is that someone would steal your vehicle based on its model and year.

Business Owner's Policies

Like a comprehensive homeowner's policy, a business owner's policy protects against economic losses caused by damage to the owner's property and by legal liability to others for bodily injury and property damage involving the business.

Usually, the policy primarily applies to your business facility, not your home. But if you operate a business out of your home and can't get your business covered by way of a rider to a homeowner's policy, you'll need to purchase business owner's insurance.

Damage to business owner's property. A business owner's policy covers the same kind of perils that the typical homeowner's policy does, but it does so for business property.

Look for a policy that's written on an "all-risks" basis as opposed to on a "named-peril" basis. An all-risk policy generally provides coverage for all risks or perils, excepting only those that the policy specifically identifies. In contrast, a named-peril policy covers only the specific risks and perils that the policy identifies. For this reason, an all-risk policy reduces the chance that you'll have gaps in coverage or duplication of coverage.

We also suggest that you carefully consider whether it's worth the extra premiums to secure a policy that provides replacement value coverage. Under this type of policy, you'll be covered for the cost of replacing your stolen or damaged equipment (subject to your policy's limit) rather than only for what you initially paid for the equipment. In addition to this coverage, you can also purchase coverage, at extra cost, for income lost as a result of a loss to the business's property.

Bodily injury and property damage liability. This is probably the most important part of the business owner's policy — certainly so if you have business visitors in your workplace. It will cover injuries to your visitors, whether they were injured in your business facility, or in your home if you maintain an office there.

Product liability insurance. This is another type of coverage that you can add to a business owner's policy for extra cost. If your business includes the selling of a product, you may be sued if someone is injured using the product, even if you had nothing to do with its design or manufacture. Depending on how potentially dangerous the product is, who the user will be, and in what part of the country it will likely be sold or used, the cost for this additional coverage could be reasonable or extremely expensive.

Commercial Policies

A business owner's policy is often the most economical way to protect against a broad range of risks that may befall your business. This type of policy is available for many specified types of lower-risk small businesses (such as retail shops and professional offices). If your business does not qualify for a business owner's policy, such as if you operate a restaurant or manufacturing business, you'll need what is known as a commercial policy.

A commercial policy is usually more expensive than a business owner's policy, but is more flexible. It's also more difficult to understand, since it must be tailored to your particular business and its risks. Thus, your selection of an insurance agent or broker becomes much more important. It is vital that your agent or broker be familiar with the operation of your type of business, as well as the commercial policies that he or she offers.

Work Smart

Each insurance company has its own rules for what types of businesses will qualify for their business owner's policies (which will usually be significantly cheaper when compared to identical coverage under a commercial policy). So if one insurer won't cover your business under a business owner's policy, ask your agent or broker to check whether it could be obtained through another company.

Professional Malpractice Insurance

If you provide advice or services to the public where significant liability could result if something went wrong, you may be required to carry professional malpractice insurance or errors and omissions coverage.

Even if not required, some policies will provide you with low cost legal representation in the event you are sued. Remember, even if your work is flawless, a customer could still claim that you did something wrong. A good professional insurance policy would help you defray the costs of *any* lawsuit, regardless of whether the underlying claim has merit.

The following occupational groups are among those who should consider malpractice insurance: accountants, attorneys, advertising agencies, computer analysts, consultants, data processors, dentists, doctors, financial planners, notaries, occupational therapists, real estate agents, and reporters and writers.

How Much Insurance Do You Need?

Too little insurance leaves you vulnerable. On the other hand, paying $500 a year for theft insurance on a vehicle with a book value of only $1,000 will bleed cash from your business and get you very little protection in return.

Determining Insurance Coverage Needs

Use the following process to help you buy enough insurance without overdoing it:

1. *Ask yourself if the insurance in question is designed to protect you if your property is damaged, or if it insulates you from the liability associated with hurting other people and their property. In most policies, these components have separate limits. As a small business owner, it's probably better to be a little overprotected on the liability side, versus the property side, of the insurance equation.*

2. *If you're dealing with property insurance:*

   - *Know your lender's limits. If a bank or other commercial lender has given you a loan on the piece of property that you're about to insure, you will usually be required to maintain a certain level of insurance.*

   - *Know the value of your property. There are really two "values" to a piece of property. The first is what you paid for it. The second value is what it would cost to replace the property if it was lost to fire, theft, or other unfortunate circumstances. If your business could not do without the property in question, you probably need to insure the property for its replacement value.*

3. *If you're dealing with liability insurance:*

   - *Know the legal minimums. Ask your agent, or state insurance commissioner, whether there are any minimum insurance levels set by law. Also check to see whether these limits are higher for certain type of businesses, or if you must have greater coverage to do business with the state.*

- *Know your business. If your business is incorporated and you obey all the rules of running your business as a corporation, you can probably get away with buying insurance with lower limits. On the other hand, if you are a sole proprietorship or partnership, you generally need more liability insurance because you can be held personally responsible for judgments against your business. Knowing your business also means accurately assessing how likely it is that someone, or someone's property, could be hurt in the routine course of your business.*

- *Know your people — both your employees and yourself. Is your business staffed with highly skilled professionals with years of experience in their field, or high school kids? Are you, or any of your employees, accident-prone? If you're prone to having trouble, plan for trouble.*

Exploring Alternatives to Insurance

These days, when everyone seems to be suing everyone else, insurance premiums continue to soar. Yet some insurance companies, fearing that the possibility of such lawsuits is too great, actually refuse to make certain types of insurance available to businesses. So in most cases you have insurance you can barely afford, and in some cases you can't even get insurance. What's a small business owner to do?

One solution is to explore some alternatives to traditional insurance. But please remember that some insurance is required as a matter of law (auto liability, for example), or may be so important given your line of work (general liability insurance or malpractice insurance) that if you can't afford it or can't get it, you simply don't belong in that business.

Self insurance. With self insurance you simply set aside money — some businesses choose to set aside what they would be paying in premiums if they had purchased insurance — and use that money when an unfortunate event occurs. For a small business, the best place to think about self insuring is with property, rather than liability, insurance because the risks are more manageable.

Example

Suppose you are paying for auto theft, fire, and collision (that is, the kind of insurance that replaces your car if it's in an accident, not someone else's) protection on your vehicle. If you dropped this coverage and put your savings in premiums into a bank, eventually you would save enough money to replace a vehicle from these funds.

Reducing risk. You may be able to get by with less insurance if you have a solid risk reduction plan that you and your employees follow very carefully. For example, you can buy less burglary and theft protection if you take steps to assure the security of your workplace as discussed below. You can also set up a safety program that will serve to significantly reduce your risks of accidents in the workplace.

SECURITY IN YOUR WORKPLACE

The security of your workplace, your property, and to a lesser degree the security of your employees' property, are responsibilities you cannot afford to overlook. The costs, both in dollars and peace of mind, can be staggering when you find that you've been "ripped off."

Preventing Burglary and Other Crimes

Protecting your office and equipment — and your employees' property — from vandals and thieves should be an important part of your safety program. There are a variety of steps that you can take to safeguard your business. These include locks and key control, lighting, and alarm systems.

Locks and Key Control

Use of dead bolt locks, where appropriate, and the use of double cylinder dead locks requiring that a key be used to open the door from either side, can go a long way in discouraging burglary. Additionally, you can get some discounts from your insurer when you are adequately locked-up.

But locks don't help if you don't remember to use them. Get into the habit of checking all the doors and windows before you lock up and leave for the night. Don't assume that because a door was locked yesterday — and because you didn't see anyone use the door — that it is still locked. Be safe rather than sorry.

To make sure keys don't fall into the wrong hands:

- Issue as few keys as possible.

- Establish specific rules regarding the "loaning-out" of keys by those to whom they are issued.

- Take a periodic inventory of keys.

- Get keys that say "do not duplicate."

Remember, too, that locks aren't just for doors and windows. There are desk locks, file cabinet locks, and even computer hard drive locks. Make sure you have keys and key control for all of them.

Good Lighting and Alarms

Lighting, both indoor and outdoor, can be of great assistance in burglary prevention. Darkness hides burglars and makes their work easy. If you are trying to decide whether to light an area, compare the expense of lighting it with what you'll lose if you are vandalized.

Work Smart

Consider timers that turn lights on at certain intervals to keep thieves guessing as to whether or not anyone is in your place of business. You may also want to have motion-sensitive lighting installed near doors and windows. It serves a dual purpose: When thieves approach your building, lights may surprise and deter them, and when you or employees approach in the dark, it lights your way and makes your entry safer.

Burglar alarms, either silent or with a siren or bell, should also be used as part of any burglary prevention program. Since there are numerous types of alarm systems on the market today, do your homework before buying a system and evaluate several systems' benefits and drawbacks.

Preventing Embezzlement

Embezzlement has been defined as "the fraudulent appropriation of property by a person to whom it has been entrusted."

The best ways to combat embezzlement are to recognize the warning signs, establish internal audit controls, and have your employees bonded.

Warning Signs of Embezzlement

- *A large increase in overall sales returns might represent a concealment of accounts receivable payments.*

- *Unusual bad-debt write-offs could be covering up a fraudulent scheme; a decline or unusually small increase in cash or credit sales could mean that some sales are not being recorded.*

- *Bounced business checks could indicate that funds are being siphoned out of your bank account.*

- *Inventory shortages could indicate fictitious purchases, unrecorded sales, or employee pilferage.*

- *Profit declines and increases in expenses could be a sign that cash is being siphoned off.*

- *Slow collections can be a device to mask embezzlement.*

Establishing Internal Controls

If you have employees or co-owners, there are several basic things that you can do to implement an internal system of controls:

- Screen job applicants very carefully before they are hired.

- Open all the mail yourself.

- Periodically examine bank statement reconciliations to see if there is anything unusual.

- Take precautions in preparing payroll: Have more than one person prepare it, have several different people prepare it, or oversee it yourself. Personally sign all paychecks.

- Have two people sign off on checks, preferably in front of each other. Ideally, it would be better to sign all checks yourself.

- Make sure the employee ordering materials and supplies is not the same person who receives them or pays for them.

- Backup all computer files daily.

Dividing financial responsibilities and functions is not enough, though. Take an inventory of your merchandise at least annually, and have an outside public accountant audit your cash and accounts receivable annually.

Bonding Your Employees

Even if you have an internal auditing system that makes embezzlement difficult, dangers still exist. Consequently, some companies protect themselves from employee dishonesty by bonding their employees, which basically means buying an insurance policy that repays you for the loss of money or other property sustained through dishonest acts of the "bonded" employees.

Bonding can cover many types of acts, including larceny, theft, embezzlement, forgery, misappropriation, willful misapplication of funds, or other fraudulent or dishonest acts committed by an employee, alone or in collusion with others. There is a great deal of choice in features and coverage as well as cost differences in bonding coverage. Discuss them with your agent to determine which type is best for your business.

SAFETY IN YOUR WORKPLACE

Why worry about safety? Simply because workplace accidents can literally destroy your business.

Besides the incalculable cost of pain and grief, there are high monetary costs attached to workplace accidents. These costs can include the inability to meet your obligations to customers, wages paid to sick and disabled workers, wages paid to substitute employees, damaged equipment repair costs, insurance claims, workers' compensation, and administrative and recordkeeping costs.

In addition, the monetary penalties for failing to comply with federally mandated safety requirements alone could destroy your business. In recent years, the Occupational Safety and Health Administration's minimum penalty for willful violations of safety rules that could result in death or serious physical harm increased to $5,000, with a maximum of $70,000. (OSHA is the federal agency that enforces federal safety requirements.)

Absent an accident, a small business owner isn't likely to be visited by federal health and safety inspectors very often, if at all. Unfortunately, if an accident does occur and you're found to be in violation of applicable safety rules, you may have to pay government fines and other costs. So, it's worthwhile to have a general understanding of the legal underpinning of the safety standards that apply to almost every employer.

Are You Subject to OSHA?

If you have employees, you are probably subject to OSHA. If you have none, you generally aren't covered, although in some cases businesses who use nonemployee workers such as independent contractors are still subject to OSHA.

As a practical matter, small employers (10 employees or less) are exempt from regularly scheduled inspections and from injury and illness reporting. This doesn't mean that you are free from other OSHA requirements, however.

A worker will be considered your employee under OSHA if you:

- are responsible for controlling the actions of the employee

- have the power to control the employee's actions

- are able to fire the employee or to modify the employment conditions.

State Safety Regulation

Although your safety obligations originate at the federal level, states have the right to substitute their own standards under a federally approved state plan. The standards under a state plan may differ from federal OSHA regulations, but must be at least as strict as the federal standards.

State Safety Plans

The states listed below have established and administer their own state plans for workplace safety. You can get more specific information about the rules in your state by contacting your state department of labor. If your state is not listed, you must comply with OSHA.

• *Alaska*	• *Michigan*	• *South Carolina*
• *Arizona*	• *Minnesota*	• *Tennessee*
• *California*	• *Nevada*	• *Utah*
• *Hawaii*	• *New Mexico*	• *Vermont*
• *Indiana*	• *North Carolina*	• *Virginia*
• *Iowa*	• *Oregon*	• *Washington*
• *Kentucky*	• *Puerto Rico*	• *Wyoming*
• *Maryland*		

Complying with OSHA Requirements

The heart of OSHA compliance is becoming aware of its published standards, which address specific workplace hazards. The standards are divided into four major categories (general industry, construction, maritime, and agriculture) based on the type of work being performed.

Every business must comply with the general industry standards, which cover things like walking/working surfaces, means of egress, ventilation, hazardous materials, personal protective equipment, sanitation, medical and first aid, and fire protection.

There is also a general duty under OSHA to maintain a safe workplace, which covers all situations for which there are no published standards. Thus, you aren't off the hook merely because you complied with all the specific written standards that apply to you — you also have to be aware of safety hazards that come with new technology or unusual situations the government might not have thought of.

Work Smart

If you need financial help in complying with the standards, OSHA authorizes loans (either directly or in cooperation with banks or other lending institutions) to assist any small business in making additions to or alteration in the equipment, facilities or methods of operation of such business, in order to comply with OSHA standards or those adopted by a state pursuant to an approved state plan.

OSHA Recordkeeping Requirements

OSHA requires every covered employer to comply with certain posting and recordkeeping requirements.

- All employers must display a poster notifying employees of their OSHA rights. You can get a copy of this poster from your nearest OSHA office. You must also make available to employees any Material Safety Data Sheets you get from makers or distributors of chemicals used in the workplace.

- Accident reporting requirements apply to all employers. If a workplace accident involves a fatality or the hospitalization of three or more employees, you must report it within eight hours to the nearest OSHA office, or by calling OSHA at 1-800-321-OSHA.

- Businesses that have 10 or more employees, full- or part-time, and that are not exempt as "low hazard" businesses must maintain certain illness and injury records for each serious incident. These records are not filed with the government, but must be kept for five years following the year in which the incident occurred, and must be available to inspectors or employees. Low-hazard businesses exempt from this requirement are those in retail trade, finance, insurance, real estate, or services; however, building materials and garden suppliers, general merchandise and food stores, hotels and lodging places, auto and miscellaneous repair services, amusement and recreation services, and medical services are not exempt.

OSHA Inspections and Penalties

OSHA enforces occupational safety and health regulations by inspecting workplaces, issuing citations, and imposing monetary penalties for violations of OSHA safety and health standards. What can trigger an inspection of your business? The government's priorities for scheduling OSHA inspections are as follows:

1. investigation of imminent dangers

2. fatality and catastrophe investigations

3. investigations of complaints, such as complaints made by employees

4. Programmed (regularly scheduled) inspections in "high hazard" industries. Businesses with 10 or fewer employees are exempt from these, so long as they have an occupational injury/lost workday rate lower than the national average, as published by the Bureau of Labor Statistics.

Inspections are conducted by compliance officers, usually without advance notice and during normal work hours.

When an OSHA compliance officer arrives for an inspection, you have the right to deny entry and to demand that OSHA obtain a warrant to inspect the premises. Your failure to object to the inspection or ask for a warrant constitutes voluntary consent.

Representatives of the employer and employees are entitled to accompany the OSHA inspector on the "walk around" tour of the workplace. The compliance officer may interview employees privately during the course of the inspection.

Citations

If a workplace inspection reveals violations of safety and health regulations or of your general duty to provide a safe and healthful workplace, OSHA will issue you a citation. The citation will charge you with a particular violation, set a time for abatement or correction of the condition, notify you of proposed penalties, and inform you of the procedure for contesting the charges before the Review Commission, should you choose to do so.

If you receive a citation, you have the choice of correcting the violations and paying the penalties, negotiating with OSHA to have the citation or penalties amended or withdrawn, or contesting the citation before the Review Commission. OSHA policy is to attempt to settle most cases, reserving litigation for the most significant cases. Only in the most egregious cases will OSHA interfere with the operation of your business by shutting it down.

The minimum penalty for a serious willful violation of OSHA is $5,000, and the maximum penalty is $70,000. The penalty amount depends on such things as the gravity of the violation, the employer's good faith, the business's size and financial condition, and any history of prior violations.

If you cannot correct the condition, you can apply for a variance.

Work Smart

You should apply for a variance as soon as you know that there's a hazard in your workplace that will take some time to fix, before OSHA gets involved, since the agency may decline to consider a variance application when a hearing is pending on a citation.

You may defend against a citation and penalties by showing that:

- You lacked knowledge of the violation.

- No employees were exposed to a hazard.

- The violation was caused by an unanticipated employee violation of your work rule.

- Compliance with the standard would have created a greater hazard to employees.

- Compliance with the standard was impossible or not feasible.

Work Smart

Employers have been penalized even when employees deliberately violated safety rules, because the employer did not consistently enforce discipline for safety violations or provided inadequate training.

Employers are responsible for the acts of supervisors even though they have no knowledge or may not approve after the fact of a supervisor's actions. Thus a supervisor who fails to prohibit unsafe practices is condoning the unsafe practice and the company is responsible.

Getting Help from OSHA

The Occupational Safety and Health Administration can provide helpful information and resources for you, designed to help you comply with OSHA requirements and create a safety program for your business.

In each state, there's an officially recognized agency that is part of the national consultation program funded by OSHA. Services carried out by these agencies include on-site consultation visits, as well as training of supervisors and employees and other assistance in developing safety and health programs. To locate the agency in your state, call your nearest OSHA office or your state department of labor. There are also private consultants who specialize in helping small businesses design safety programs that will ensure you're in compliance with OSHA. Your attorney may be able to direct you to one in your area.

Part VI

People Who Work for You

Chances are that if your business becomes successful, it will grow and, at some point, you'll need some help on a temporary or permanent basis.

Good employees can be a business's biggest asset, but the paperwork and concerns that come with them can almost make it seem that having them is more trouble than it's worth.

Most employers find that their major legal and financial questions about employees tend to arise at three key points: at the very beginning of the relationship, when they first hire someone; when they're figuring out how much to pay and what to include in their compensation package; and when they have a problem employee who must be dealt with, or even fired. Our discussion will help you navigate around these major pitfalls successfully and legally.

Chapter 18: Recruiting and Hiring assists you in figuring out what you need done, deciding whether to hire someone or use an independent contractor, and advertising for, interviewing, screening, and hiring an employee.

Chapter 19: Pay and Benefits guides you through the ins and outs of paying your employees, following minimum wage and overtime laws, and understanding the pros and cons of various benefit plans.

Chapter 20: Managing Your Employees shows you how to detect and fend off problems with morale, turnover, productivity, and employee loyalty. It also aids you in one of the toughest parts of being a boss — setting and enforcing workplace rules — by giving you tools to help you coach a wayward employee and document any disciplinary actions.

Chapter 21: Firing and Termination navigates you through the unpleasant tasks of having to let a worker go, from planning the termination meeting to dealing with unemployment claims.

Chapter 18

Recruiting and Hiring

When most people think of recruiting a new employee, they tend to think only of classified ads and interviews. But there's much more to successful hiring than that.

In this chapter we'll discuss the legal responsibilities of employers; the pros and cons of different staffing options, including independent contractors; how to publicize job openings; and how to interview candidates, check references, and make the hire.

SHOULD YOU HIRE SOMEONE?

When the work gets to be too much, you may find yourself toying with the idea of adding staff to help out. But first, ask yourself if you need to hire someone, or just be better organized. If you're having trouble getting organized, try local libraries, community centers, or colleges for time management courses.

If you're still sold on the idea of getting someone to take over part of your work, there are a number of staffing options to choose from: full-time or part-time employees, temporary help, leased workers, independent contractors, or even your own children.

Full-Time Employees

There are several advantages to hiring full-time staff. Because most people work only one full-time job, you are more likely to have control over the employee's time and to get increased employee loyalty from a full-time worker. You may have the peace of mind that there will be someone around to "mind the store" in your absence. You may also be looking ahead to the day when you want to sell your business, and full-time employees who already know the ropes make excellent buyers.

On the other hand, full-time employees are covered by numerous labor laws, and may expect benefits such as health insurance and paid vacation. Will you have to provide these types of benefits to be competitive?

Part-Time Employees

Using part-time employees allows you to have control over the employees' work, but generally at a lower cost. As a rule, part-timers don't get as many benefits as full-time employees, and they are often willing to adjust their schedules according to the amount of work you happen to have.

Of course, part-time employees may have full-time jobs elsewhere, so employee loyalty may be sacrificed. They may also tend to leave your business if an offer of full-time employment comes along, so you may end up with an employee turnover problem. Remember, part-time employees are still counted as employees for purposes of determining liability under antidiscrimination laws.

Temporary Help

Traditionally, temporary help firms have been useful when you need a replacement for a full-time employee who is away from work for vacation, leave of absence, or illness. But temporary help may be just what you need to fill longer-term needs.

By using temporary workers obtained through an agency, you may save on payroll administration and fringe benefits, since you'll only have to cut one check to the agency each period. The agency will do the recruiting and send you people with the qualifications you specify, thus saving you time.

There's no long-term commitment between you and the temporary worker, which can be a problem if the position you want to fill takes a good deal of training or experience to do well. You may tire of training a series of workers who leave at unpredictable times. On the upside, you may be able to convince a good temp to work for you permanently, avoiding the risks of a probationary period.

If you use a temporary help agency, you must realize that you're going to pay more for the convenience of having someone else do the legwork. For example, for a worker who gets $8.00 per hour in pay, you may actually pay $12.00 or $15.00 per hour to the agency. Nevertheless, for short-term projects or situations where the worker will need a lot of supervision (for example, receptionists, secretaries, telemarketers), temp agencies are a great alternative.

Leased Employees

"Leasing employees" generally refers to a situation where another business "employs" your staff — which includes doing the payroll, administering benefits, etc. — and you pay them a fee plus expenses to do it. In many cases, the leasing agency (sometimes called a Professional Employer Organization or PEO) simply takes over your existing staff of permanent employees, and there's little change in the actual makeup of your workforce.

Because PEOs aggregate the employees of many companies in negotiating for health insurance, pensions, etc., you can sometimes provide more benefits at a much lower cost. Also, the leasing company can achieve economies of scale in hiring, doing the payroll, and keeping records on all these workers, so their fees for performing these services might be lower than what you'd pay to do it yourself.

Work Smart

If you're going to use an employee leasing firm, be careful in how you communicate the new arrangement to your existing employees. They may find it unsettling if they don't understand that the leasing arrangement is mainly "on paper" and they aren't really losing their jobs. One way to overcome this fear is to have your employees meet with current employees of the leasing company who have successfully made the transition.

Independent Contractors

By using independent contractors, it's possible to have personnel to work on (or off) your premises without becoming subject to payroll taxes or to many state and federal employment laws. Independent contractors are particularly useful when you need a specific skill or technical knowledge for a special project that's expected to last a relatively short length of time.

Independent contractors control the performance of the work based on their experience, a special license, or special education or training required for the job. In most cases, you tell them the outlines of the project that needs to be done and the due date, and they determine how to accomplish it, on their own schedule. They are generally paid based on results (i.e., a flat rate per job, or a per-unit-completed rate) rather than by the hour.

Definition of independent contractor for tax and benefits purposes. For tax purposes, the main issue is the degree of control you have over the worker. A worker will be treated as an employee if you as the business owner have the right to determine not just *what* the employee does, but *when, where, or how* the worker does it.

The IRS has a 20-factor test that it uses to determine whether an employee is an independent contractor or an employee in disguise (for a list of these factors, see *Chapter 28, Doing the Payroll*). Traditionally, the IRS has frowned on the use of independent contractors, and in borderline situations is likely to rule that the workers are really employees.

Independent contractors under labor law. Under the Fair Labor Standards Act (FLSA), independent contractors are not entitled to minimum wage and overtime protections. Unfortunately, the FLSA definition of independent contractor is slightly different from the IRS's definition. In order to be truly sure that you're safe in treating workers as independent, you must meet *both* definitions.

For FLSA purposes, there are six factors for determining whether a worker is an "employee," as opposed to an independent contractor:

- the extent of the company's right to control the manner in which the work is performed

- the worker's opportunity for profit or loss depending on managerial skill

- the worker's investment in equipment or materials required for the work

- whether the service rendered requires special skills

- the degree of permanence of the working relationship

- whether the service rendered by the worker is an integral part of the alleged employer's business

No single factor is more important than the others in determining independent contractor status. When the issue comes up in courts, the judge must consider whether, as a matter of economic reality, a worker is dependent on the business to which a service is rendered for continued work. If so, he or she is more likely to be an employee.

Whenever you use an independent contractor, it's best to put your agreement in writing, using a document like the one that follows. However, be aware that signing a contract, by itself, won't transform an employee into an independent contractor. It is the nature of the entire working relationship that determines the worker's status.

INDEPENDENT CONTRACTOR AGREEMENT

This Agreement is entered into as of the [   ] day of [   ], 20[ ], between [   ] ("the Company") and [   ] ("the Contractor").

Independent Contractor. Subject to the terms and conditions of this Agreement, the Company hereby engages the Contractor as an independent contractor to perform the services set forth herein, and the Contractor hereby accepts such engagement.

Duties, Term, and Compensation. The Contractor's duties, term of engagement, compensation, and provisions for payment thereof shall be as set forth in the estimate previously provided to the Company by the Contractor and which is attached as Exhibit A, which may be amended in writing from time to time, or supplemented with subsequent estimates for services to be rendered by the Contractor and agreed to by the Company, and which collectively are hereby incorporated by reference.

Expenses. During the term of this Agreement, the Contractor shall bill and the Company shall reimburse [him or her] for all reasonable and approved out-of-pocket expenses which are incurred in connection with the performance of the duties hereunder. Notwithstanding the foregoing, expenses for the time spend by Consultant in traveling to and from Company facilities shall not be reimbursable.

Written Reports. The Company may request that project plans, progress reports, and a final results report be provided by Consultant on a monthly basis. A final results report shall be due at the conclusion of the project and shall be submitted to the Company in a confidential written report at such time. The results report shall be in such form and setting forth such information and data as is reasonably requested by the Company.

Inventions. Any and all inventions, discoveries, developments, and innovations conceived by the Contractor during this engagement relative to the duties under this Agreement shall be the exclusive property of the Company; and the Contractor hereby assigns all right, title, and interest in the same to the Company. Any and all inventions, discoveries, developments, and innovations conceived by the Contractor prior to the term of this Agreement and utilized by [him or her] in rendering duties to the Company are hereby licensed to the Company for use in its operations and for an infinite duration. This license is non-exclusive, and may be assigned without the Contractor's prior written approval by the Company to a wholly-owned subsidiary of the Company.

Confidentiality. The Contractor acknowledges that during the engagement [he or she] will have access to and become acquainted with various trade secrets, inventions, innovations, processes, information, records, and specifications owned or licensed by the Company and/or used by the Company in connection with the operation of its business including, without limitation, the Company's business and product processes, methods, customer lists, accounts, and procedures. The Contractor agrees that [he or she] will not disclose any of the aforesaid, directly or indirectly, or use any of them in any manner, either during the term of this Agreement or at any time thereafter, except as required in the course of this engagement with the Company. All files, records, documents, blueprints, specifications, information, letters, notes, media lists, original artwork/creative, notebooks, and similar items relating to the business of the Company, whether prepared by the Contractor or otherwise coming into [his or her] possession, shall remain the exclusive property of the Company. The Contractor shall not retain any copies of the foregoing without the Company's prior written permission. Upon the expiration or earlier termination of this Agreement, or whenever requested by the Company, the Contractor shall immediately deliver to the Company all such files, records, documents, specifications, information, and other items in [his or her] possession or under [his or her] control. The Contractor further agrees that [he or she] will not disclose [his or her] retention as an independent contractor or the terms of this Agreement to any person without the prior written consent of the Company and shall at all times preserve the confidential nature of the relationship to the Company and the services hereunder.

Conflicts of Interest; Non-hire Provision. The Contractor represents that [he or she] is free to enter into this Agreement, and that this engagement does not violate the terms of any agreement between the Contractor and any third party. Further, the Contractor, in rendering [his or her] duties shall not utilize any invention, discovery, development, improvement, innovation, or trade secret in which [he or she] does not have a proprietary interest. During the term of this agreement, the Contractor shall devote as much of [his or her] productive time, energy, and abilities to the performance of [his or her] duties hereunder as is necessary to perform the required duties in a timely and productive manner. The Contractor is expressly free to perform services for other parties while performing services for the Company. For a period of six months following any termination, the Contractor shall not, directly or indirectly, hire, solicit, or encourage to leave the Company's employment, any employee, consultant, or contractor of the Company or hire any such employee, consultant, or contractor who has left the Company's employment or contractual engagement within one year of such employment or engagement.

Right to Injunction. The parties hereto acknowledge that the services to be rendered by the Contractor under this Agreement and the rights and privileges granted to the Company under the Agreement are of a special, unique, unusual, and extraordinary character which gives them a peculiar value, the loss of which cannot be reasonably or adequately compensated by damages in any action at law, and the breach by the Contractor of any of the provisions of this Agreement will cause the Company irreparable injury and damage. The Contractor expressly agrees that the Company shall be entitled to injunctive and other equitable relief in the event of, or to prevent, a breach of any provision of this Agreement by the Contractor. Resort to such equitable relief, however, shall not be construed to be a waiver of any other rights or remedies that the Company may have for damages or otherwise. The various rights and remedies of the Company under this Agreement or otherwise shall be construed to be cumulative, and no one of them shall be exclusive of any other or of any right or remedy allowed by law.

Merger. This Agreement shall not be terminated by the merger of consolidation of the Company into or with any other entity.

Termination. The Company may terminate this Agreement at any time by 10 working days' written notice to the Contractor. In addition, if the Contractor is convicted of any crime or offense, fails or refuses to comply with the written policies or reasonable directive of the Company, is guilty of serious misconduct in connection with performance hereunder, or materially breaches provisions of this Agreement, the Company at any time may terminate the engagement of the Contractor immediately and without prior written notice to the Contractor.

Independent Contractor. *This Agreement shall not render the Contractor an employee, partner, agent of, or joint venturer with the Company for any purpose. The Contractor is and will remain an independent contractor in [his or her] relationship to the Company. The Company shall not be responsible for withholding taxes with respect to the Contractor's compensation hereunder. The Contractor shall have no claim against the Company hereunder or otherwise for vacation pay, sick leave, retirement benefits, social security, worker's compensation, health or disability benefits, unemployment insurance benefits, or employee benefits of any kind.*

Insurance. *The Contractor will carry liability insurance (including malpractice insurance, if warranted) relative to any service that [he or she] performs for the Company.*

Successors and Assigns. *All of the provisions of this Agreement shall be binding upon and inure to the benefit of the parties hereto and their respective heirs, if any, successors, and assigns.*

Choice of Law. *The laws of the state of [   ] shall govern the validity of this Agreement, the construction of its terms and the interpretation of the rights and duties of the parties hereto.*

Arbitration. *Any controversies arising out of the terms of this Agreement or its interpretation shall be settled in [   ] in accordance with the rules of the American Arbitration Association, and the judgment upon award may be entered in any court having jurisdiction thereof.*

Headings. *Section headings are not to be considered a part of this Agreement and are not intended to be a full and accurate description of the contents hereof.*

Waiver. *Waiver by one party hereto of breach of any provision of this Agreement by the other shall not operate or be construed as a continuing waiver.*

Assignment. *The Contractor shall not assign any of [his or her] rights under this Agreement, or delegate the performance of any of [his or her] duties hereunder, without the prior written consent of the Company.*

Notices. *Any and all notices, demands, or other communications required or desired to be given hereunder by any party shall be in writing and shall be validly given or made to another party if personally served, or if deposited in the United States mail, certified or registered, postage prepaid, return receipt requested. If such notice or demand is served personally, notice shall be deemed constructively made at the time of such personal service. If such notice, demand, or other communication is given by mail, such notice shall be conclusively deemed given five days after deposit thereof in the United States mail addressed to the party to whom such notice, demand, or other communication is to be given as follows:*

If to the Contractor:	[name]	If to the Company:	[name]
	[street address]		[street address]
	[city, state, zip]		[city, state, zip]

Any party hereto may change its address for purposes of this paragraph by written notice given in the manner provided above.

Modification or Amendment. *No amendment, change, or modification of this Agreement shall be valid unless in writing signed by the parties hereto.*

Entire Understanding. *This document and any exhibit attached constitute the entire understanding and agreement of the parties, and any and all prior agreements, understandings, and representations are hereby terminated and canceled in their entirety and are of no further force and effect.*

Unenforceability of Provisions. *If any provision of this Agreement, or any portion thereof, is held to be invalid and unenforceable, then the remainder of this Agreement shall nevertheless remain in full force and effect.*

IN WITNESS WHEREOF the undersigned have executed this Agreement as of the day and year first written above.

[company name]   *[contractor's name]*

*By:*_____   *By:*_____

Its: [title or position]   *Its: [title or position]*

SCHEDULE A: DUTIES, TERM, AND COMPENSATION

Duties: *The Contractor will [describe here the work or service to be performed].*

[He or she] will report directly to [name] and to any other party designated by [name] in connection with the performance of the duties under this Agreement and shall fulfill any other duties reasonably requested by the Company and agreed to by the Contractor.

Term: *This engagement shall commence upon execution of this Agreement and shall continue in full force and effect through [date] or earlier upon completion of the Contractor's duties under this Agreement. The Agreement may only be extended thereafter by mutual agreement, unless terminated earlier by operation of and in accordance with this Agreement.*

Compensation: *(Choose A or B)*

A. As full compensation for the services rendered pursuant to this Agreement, the Company shall pay the Contractor at the hourly rate of [dollar amount] per hour, with total payment not to exceed [dollar amount] without prior written approval by an authorized representative of the Company. Such compensation shall be payable within 30 days of receipt of Contractor's monthly invoice for services rendered supported by reasonable documentation.

B. As full compensation for the services rendered pursuant to this Agreement, the Company shall pay the Contractor the sum of [dollar amount], to be paid [time and conditions of payment.]

Hiring Your Children

If you hire your children to work in your business, you could be eligible for special tax breaks. One such break is an exemption from the requirement to withhold FICA (Social Security and Medicare) from your child's paychecks. Normally, a business pays 7.65 percent of each employee's salary in Social Security and Medicare taxes and withholds another 7.65 percent from the employee for the employee's share of those taxes. By not paying or withholding FICA from your child's paycheck, the two of you save 15.3 percent.

Hiring Teenagers

Hiring teenagers can be a good, inexpensive solution when your workflow is increasing, particularly if you need help for just a few hours per week. However, if you hire workers under 18, you'll have to be aware of child labor laws that place restrictions on what kind of work children can do, when they can do it, and how old they have to be to do it.

You are not subject to child labor requirements if you hire your own child; if the child will be working as a theatrical, television, or radio performer; or if the child will be working on a farm and is over the age of 12.

Restrictions on Employees Under 18

Federal law does not limit the hours that minors 16 and 17 years of age may work when the next day is a school day, but some states do. Generally, where such a rule exists, minors who are 16 and 17 may work after 6 a.m. and before 10 or 11:30 p.m. on school nights.

The FLSA specifically prohibits minors under the age of 18 from working in certain hazardous occupations including mining, logging, occupations involving many types of power machinery, demolition, excavation, and roofing.

In some hazardous occupations, minors under 18 can work if certain conditions are met. Most notably, they may be used for the operation of motor vehicles on roads and grounds so long as they remain in vehicle cabs, only occasionally drive vehicles not exceeding 6,000 pounds of gross vehicle weight, or drive school buses.

Restrictions on Employees Under 16

Federal law limits work by 14- and 15-year olds to the following:

- must be outside of school hours

- may not be more than 18 hours per week when school is in session, or more than 40 hours per week when school is not in session

- may not be more than three hours per day when school is in session, or more than eight hours per day when school is not in session

- must be between 7 a.m. and 7 p.m. except during the summer (June 1 through Labor Day), when the evening limit is 9 p.m.

In addition to the time restrictions, there is a list of specific types of jobs that minors under 16 can hold, including: office and clerical work; cashiering or selling; modeling; art work and work in advertising departments; window trimming; price marking and tagging; assembling orders; packing and shelving; bagging and carrying out customers' orders; errand and delivery work; cleanup or grounds maintenance work not involving power-driven mowers or cutters; kitchen work and other work involved in preparing and serving food and beverages; and attending gas stations or car washes.

State Child Labor Laws

All states have some laws restricting the employment of minors. Generally, there are restrictions in two areas: (1) the type of occupation and (2) the hours of employment. In addition, many states provide for the issuance of employment certificates or work permits as a prerequisite to employment.

If you should decide to hire a minor, check with your state labor agency or your attorney for your state's requirements.

EMPLOYERS' LEGAL RESPONSIBILITIES

If you decide to hire employees, it's extremely important that you become aware of all the federal and state laws that can affect your relationship.

Whether or not a business is subject to specific employment laws depends on how many employees that business has and for how long. There's a large array of federal and state laws and it takes only one employee to make you subject to several of them.

The following table provides a broad overview of the major federal laws that apply to most employers. Normally, the effect of these laws starts with the hiring process and continues through the termination of the employment relationship. In most cases, civil rights laws will be interpreted as applying to leased workers, sometimes temporary workers, but not independent contractors.

Federal Law	What It Does	Who's Subject to the Law
Fair Labor Standards Act (FLSA)	Requires you to pay minimum wage and overtime pay to nonexempt workers.	All employers of employees engaged in interstate commerce.
Occupational Safety and Health Act (OSHA)	Requires you to maintain a safe workplace and comply with specific safety standards and recordkeeping rules.	All employers, except that in states where a federally certified plan has been adopted, the state plan governs.
Federal Insurance Contributions Act (FICA)	Requires you to pay Social Security and Medicare taxes, and withhold such taxes from workers' pay.	All employers.
Federal Unemployment Tax Act (FUTA)	Requires you to pay federal unemployment payroll taxes.	All employers.
Equal Pay Act	Requires you to pay men and women equally if they do the same work.	All employers.
National Labor Relations Act	Prevents discrimination against employees who engage in or who refuse to engage in union activity. Also protects nonunion employees who act together to improve or protest working conditions that affect them on the job.	Employers whose business has a significant impact on interstate commerce.
Employee Retirement Income Security Act (ERISA)	Prevents employees from being discharged solely to prevent them from vesting or qualifying for benefits under qualified pension plans.	Employers who maintain qualified pension plans for their employees' benefit.
Immigration Reform and Control Act	Prevents discrimination against employees on the basis of national origin or citizenship status.	Employers having at least four employees.
Americans with Disabilities Act (ADA)	Prevents discrimination against disabled employees.	Employers having at least 15 employees.
Civil Rights Act, Title VII	Prevents discrimination against employees on the basis of race, color, religion, sex, or national origin.	Employers having at least 15 employees.
Age Discrimination in Employment Act (ADEA)	Prevents discrimination on the basis of age against employees who are over 40 years old.	Employers having at least 20 employees.
Family and Medical Leave Act (FMLA)	Requires employers to grant unpaid leave of up to 12 weeks per year for new births or adoptions, or certain medical conditions of the worker or a family member.	Employers having at least 50 employees.

Your State Liability

While you must have 15 or more employees to become subject to the most complex and comprehensive federal antidiscrimination laws, similar state laws sometimes apply to employers with only one employee. State laws can also be broader in scope, so that protection is provided to additional groups beyond those covered by federal law.

The chart below presents the high points of each state's law.

State	Number of Employees That Will Cause an Employer To be Covered	Prohibited Types of Discrimination
Alabama	20 or more	Age (40 and over).
Alaska	One or more	Race, religion, color, national origin, age, physical or mental disability, marital status, change in marital status, sex, pregnancy, or parenthood.
Arizona	15 or more; one or more for sexual harassment	Race, color, religion, sex, age (40 and over), handicap, genetic testing, or national origin.
Arkansas	Nine or more	Race, religion, color, ancestry or national origin, gender, or sensory, mental, or physical disability.
California	Five or more, except that for purposes of the prohibition against discrimination on the basis of mental disability, the threshold is 15 or more.	Race, religion, color, national origin, ancestry, physical disability, mental disability, medical condition, marital status or sex (sex includes pregnancy, childbirth and related medical conditions, age (over 40), sexual orientation, participation in politics, or becoming a candidate for public office.
Colorado	One or more.	Disability, race, creed, color, sex, age, national origin, ancestry, or lawful activities during nonworking hours.
Connecticut	One or more	Race, color, religious creed, age, sex, marital status, national origin, ancestry; present or past history or mental disorder, mental retardation, learning disability, blindness, or physical disability; sexual orientation; genetic information; or smoking outside the job.
Delaware	Four or more, except that for disability discrimination, the threshold is 15 or more.	Race, marital status, color, age (includes only persons between the ages of 40 and 70), religion, sex, national origin, genetic information, or disability.
District of Columbia	One or more	Race (of the employee or job applicant and that of anyone with whom they employee or applicant has a relationship), color, religion, national origin, sex (include pregnancy, childbirth, and related conditions), age (between 18 and 65), marital status, personal appearance, sexual orientation, family responsibilities, physical handicap, matriculation in a college, school, or adult educational program, use of tobacco products, or political affiliation.
Florida	15 or more	Race, color, religion, sex, national origin, age, handicap or marital status, HIV/AIDS, or sickle cell trait.

Georgia	One or more for age discrimination; 10 or more for the prohibition against unequal pay for equal work based on sex; 15 or more for discrimination against people with disabilities.	Sex, age (between the ages of 40 and 70 years), and disability.
Hawaii	One or more	Race, sex (including pregnancy, childbirth, and related conditions), sexual orientation, age, religion, color, ancestry, disability, marital status, arrest and court records, and assignment of income for child support.
Idaho	Five or more; one or more for gov't contractors.	Race, color, religion, sex, national origin, age (40 and over), or disability.
Illinois	15 or more, except that for sexual harassment and disability discrimination, the threshold is one or more, and for gov't contractors, the threshold is one or more for all purposes.	Race, color, religion, sex, national origin, citizenship, ancestry, age, marital status, physical or mental handicap, military status or unfavorable discharge from military service, or use of legal substances outside of working hours.
Indiana	Six or more, except that for age discrimination, the threshold is one or more.	Race, religion, color, sex, disability, national origin or ancestry, age (40 to 70), or smoking outside the course of employment.
Iowa	Four or more	Age, race, creed, color, sex (including pregnancy, childbirth, and related conditions), national origin, religion, disability, or AIDS.
Kansas	Four or more	Race, religion, color, sex (including pregnancy and childbirth), disability, national origin, or ancestry, age (18 or more).
Kentucky	Eight or more , except that for unequal pay based on sex, the threshold is two or more, and for disability, the threshold is 15 or more.	Race, color, religion, national origin, sex (including pregnancy, childbirth, and related conditions), age (40 and over), disability, or smoking preference outside the workplace.
Louisiana	15 or more, except that for age discrimination the threshold is 20 or more, for pregnancy and childbirth it is 25 or more, and for sickle cell it is one or more.	Race, color, religion, sex, disability, national origin, age (over 40), sickle cell trait, worker's compensation claims, pregnancy and childbirth, or smoking outside the course of employment.
Maine	One or more	Race, color, sex (including pregnancy and related medical conditions), physical or mental disability, religion, age, ancestry or national origin, or use of tobacco outside the course of employment.
Maryland	15 or more	Race, color, religion, sex, age, national origin, marital status, or physical or mental disability.
Massachusetts	Six or more	Race, color, religious creed, national origin, sex, sexual orientation (except pedophiles), ancestry, age, disability, or failure to furnish an arrest record that is 5 or more years old.

Michigan	One or more	Disability, religion, race, color, national origin, age, sex (including pregnancy, childbirth, or related conditions), height, weight, marital status, or refusal to provide arrest records.
Minnesota	One or more	Race, color, creed, religion, national origin, sex, marital status, status with regard to public assistance, membership in a local commission, disability, sexual orientation, age (under 70), or use of lawful substances outside the course of employment.
Mississippi	One or more	Smoking outside the course of employment. Any employer supported in whole or in part by public funds is prohibited from discriminating against individuals with disabilities.
Missouri	Six or more, except that for discrimination based on an individual's refusal to participate in an abortion, the threshold is two or more.	Race, color, religion, national origin, sex, ancestry, age (40 to 70), disability, refusal to participate in an abortion, genetic testing, or use of lawful products outside the course of employment.
Montana	One or more	Race, creed, religion, color, national origin, age, physical or mental disability, marital status, sex (including pregnancy), or use of lawful products outside the course of employment.
Nebraska	15 or more; 25 or more for age discrimination	Age, race, color, religion, sex (including pregnancy, childbirth and related conditions), disability, marital status, national origin, or AIDS.
Nevada	15 or more	Race, color, religion, sex, age, disability, national origin, sexual orientation, genetic information, or use of lawful products outside the course of employment.
New Hampshire	Six or more	Age, sex, race, color, marital status, physical or mental disability, religious creed, national origin, sexual orientation, or use of tobacco outside the course of employment.
New Jersey	One or more	Race, creed, color, national origin, ancestry, age (up to 70), marital status, affectional or sexual orientation, sex, disability or atypical hereditary cellular or blood trait, military service, or use of tobacco products.
New Mexico	Four or more	Race, age, religion, color, national origin, ancestry, sex, physical or mental disability, medical condition (including AIDS), or smoking preference.
New York	Four or more	Age, race, creed, color, national origin, sex, disability, marital status, genetic condition, or legal use of consumable products outside the course of employment.
North Carolina	15 or more, except that for discrimination against use of a legal product, the threshold is three or more.	Race, religion, color, national origin, age (40 and over), sex, disability, sickle cell or hemoglobin C trait, use of lawful products, military service, or AIDS.
North Dakota	one or more	Race, color, religion, sex (including pregnancy, childbirth or related disabilities), national origin, age (40 and over), mental or physical disability, marital status, receipt of public assistance, or participation in lawful activity outside the course of employment.

Ohio	Four or more	Race, color, religion, sex (including pregnancy, childbirth, and related medical conditions), national origin, disability, age (40 and over), ancestry, or treatment for mental illness.
Oklahoma	15 or more; one or more for state contractors	Race, color, religion, sex, national origin, age (40 and over), disability, or smoking preference.
Oregon	One or more; for purposes of the disability discrimination law, six or more	Race, religion, color, sex, marital status, pregnancy, childbirth, sexual orientation, AIDS, national origin, age (18 and over), juvenile records that have been expunged, genetic information, disability, or use of tobacco outside the job.
Pennsylvania	Four or more	Race, color, religious creed, ancestry, age (40 and over), sex, national origin, or disability.
Puerto Rico	One or more	Age, race, color, sex, origin or social position, political affiliations, disability, or religious beliefs.
Rhode Island	Four or more	Race, color, religion, sex (including pregnancy, childbirth, and related conditions), disability, age (between 40 and 70), national origin, AIDS, use of tobacco outside the job, domestic abuse protective orders, or sexual orientation.
South Carolina	15 or more	Race, religion, color, sex (including pregnancy childbirth, and related conditions), age (40 and over), disability, national origin, or use of tobacco outside the job.
South Dakota	One or more	Race, color, creed, religion, sex, ancestry, disability, national origin, use of tobacco outside the job, or refusal to participate in an abortion.
Tennessee	Eight or more	Race, creed, color, religion, sex, age (over 40), national origin, disability, or use of legal products outside the course of employment.
Texas	15 or more	Race, color, disability, religion, sex (including pregnancy, childbirth, or related medical conditions), national origin, age (40 or older), or participation or genetic information.
Utah	15 or more	Race, color, sex, pregnancy, childbirth, pregnancy-related condition, age (40 and over), religion, national origin, or disability.
Vermont	One or more	Race, color, religion, ancestry, national origin, sex, sexual orientation, place of birth, age, or disability.
Virginia	One or more	Race, color, religion, national origin, sex, age, marital status, or disability.
Washington	Eight or more	Age (40 or older), sex, marital status, race, creed, color, national origin, disability, or job applicants thought or known to have AIDS.
West Virginia	12 or more	Race, religion, color, national origin, ancestry, sex, age, blindness or other disability, or use of tobacco outside the course of employment.
Wisconsin	One or more	Age, race, creed, color, disability, marital status, sex (including pregnancy, childbirth, or related medical conditions), sexual orientation, national origin, ancestry, arrest record, conviction record, military service, genetic testing, honesty testing, or the use of lawful products outside the job.
Wyoming	Two or more	Age (between 40 and 70), sex, race, creed, color, national origin, ancestry, disability, or smoking preference outside the course of employment, or refusal to participate in an abortion.

DEFINING THE JOB YOU NEED DONE

Once you decide that you need to hire someone, you must determine exactly what you want the person to do for your business. Particularly if you are hiring that first employee, try to narrow it down into a list of specific tasks before you decide what job qualifications you'll be looking for. Later on, you can use your list of necessary tasks to write your job description and, ultimately, to train your new employee.

One approach is to think about the things you do that could easily be taught to a new employee. Another approach is to think about the skills you and your existing employees are lacking, and try to fill those needs.

If you're replacing an employee, you will have more information. You can talk with the employee who is leaving and, if you have other employees doing the same type of work, you can also get input from them.

Defining Job Qualifications

After you've done some investigation into what the job should entail, the skills and areas of knowledge required should be translated into your job qualifications. Qualifications include such things as experience, education, ability, language skills, and physical strength or agility. You'll want to keep these qualifications in mind as you review applications and interview people for the job.

Remember that federal and state laws place restrictions on using job qualifications that could result in discrimination.

Ability and Experience

While ability to do the job is most important, judging a candidate's ability is difficult. Sometimes it is an innate, personal trait, and other times it is a by-product of education or experience. In many cases you'll have to judge the candidate's ability by asking for information about past job experiences, or by administering an achievement test as discussed below.

In most cases, the ideal candidate will have at least some exposure and experience in the areas that the job entails. The important thing, from a legal standpoint, is not to define your experience baseline so strictly that you disqualify people who could do the job.

If you need an administrative assistant who can type, answer phones, and file, chances are you'll need someone with good organizational skills. Instead of requiring one year of clerical duties, you might find a person who does not have clerical experience, per se, but who was, for example, an assistant manager at a department store or a server in a restaurant and who might have some of the same set of skills and abilities.

Education

Most employers require at least a high school degree or an equivalency certificate for most jobs they fill. Some jobs require more advanced thought and responsibilities and, therefore, may require more advanced education.

For employers of 15 or more, the Equal Employment Opportunity Commission requires only that employers can't set educational requirements so high that they tend to restrict certain protected groups of people from getting hired or promoted. If you do require a degree or level of educational attainment, be prepared to justify why the degree itself is a necessary requirement, as opposed to an ability to do certain types of work.

English Language Fluency

As with all skills and abilities, to avoid problems with civil rights laws, language fluency must be related to the performance of the job in order to be required. This doesn't mean that it is desirable to have proficiency in the language; it must be an *important* part of the job. For instance, refusing to hire computer programmers with "poor grammar" was found to be unlawful bias by one court, since grammar skills were not an important part of the job.

Physical Effort or Strength

Some jobs may require certain physical abilities or strengths. To avoid problems with workers' compensation and safety, these requirements should definitely be a part of your defined job qualifications.

If you are an employer of 15 or more employees, and are therefore subject to the Americans with Disabilities Act (ADA), the basic tenets of the law are that if an employee can do the *essential functions* of a job with *reasonable accommodation*, then the employee should not be discriminated against in the hiring process. Reasonable accommodation is a rather technical concept. If you suspect you may face this issue, check with your professional legal advisor.

Creating Job Descriptions

Once you've determined exactly what tasks your employee must perform and what your job qualifications are, you're ready to combine the two into a written job description.

Case Study — Simple Job Description

Mr. McCay runs an automobile repair business. Business is brisk and he has more customers than he can accommodate on his own. He needs to hire his first employee to help out. Here is a list of some of the things that Mr. McCay wants his employee to do: answer the phone, greet customers, write up repair orders, perform minor repairs, and pick up shop supplies.

Mr. McCay writes down all the points above and starts to notice patterns from the list. Just from using his list, Mr. McCay figures out that he needs someone who has:

- *a professional phone manner, for dealing well with customers*

- *strong writing and speaking skills, for communicating with customers and suppliers*

- *basic automotive repair knowledge, for minor repair duties*

- *organizational skills, to balance all these tasks at once*

PUBLICIZING YOUR JOB OPENING

There are several good ways to let the world know about your job opening, including advertising, personal recruiting, and using outside employment agencies.

Newspaper Advertising

A classified ad taken out in a newspaper is the most common way to advertise a job opening. Traditionally, people looking for work check out the Sunday paper, and these ads are relatively low-cost considering the number of people they reach.

As an alternative to a classified ad, you can buy a larger block of space on the classified pages or other sections of the paper and run an attractive display ad.

Blind ads. A blind ad does not identify the name of the company seeking employees, but instead lists an anonymous post office box to which job seekers can send their resumes.

Blind ads are popular with employers because they can avoid having to deal with those candidates who are rejected, and they can maintain a lower profile if they want to replace an existing employee or if they are not contemplating promoting a current employee into a position. Be aware, though, that some jobseekers avoid answering blind ads.

Trade Journals

Professional and trade journals are good places to advertise when you are looking for a professional or technical employee with special skills or backgrounds.

The cost per reader for advertising in these journals is relatively high, but the major drawback is that many journals are published monthly and it may take longer for your ad to reach its intended audience.

Electronic Posting

Many companies advertise their jobs on the Internet. In fact, many print newspapers automatically post classifieds on the Internet, for no additional cost.

Online advertising can reach people in a broader geographic area than newspapers, which may or may not be a plus. You can often achieve a quicker response time, because many people will send you resumes through electronic mail.

Currently, electronic posting is most useful for positions requiring advanced computer-related skills because many people with those skills are frequently online. As use of the Internet and commercial online services become more common, you can expect that any job posting there will reach more people than possibly any other medium you use.

Tips for Writing a Job Advertisement

Once you've chosen a medium for your advertising, you're ready to draft an ad. If you have written a job description, you can use main points in your ad and save yourself some time. Use common sense and follow these guidelines to make sure that your ad is effective. The same rules apply regardless of the media.

- *Give the job title along with a brief description of duties, especially if the job title is ambiguous.*

- *List the minimum education, experience, and skill levels that you will consider. Point out any special criteria such as extensive travel or relocation that would immediately weed out applicants unwilling to take on those aspects of the job.*

- *Avoid using abbreviations and acronyms.*

- *Be specific about the type of equipment, software programs, etc., that applicants should know how to use or operate.*

- *Tell the applicants how to respond. Generally, you'll want people to call you rather than showing up at your place of business. If you anticipate a large number of responses, you may prefer to have resumes sent to you by mail or fax.*

Federal antidiscrimination laws dictate what you can and cannot say in a job advertisement. Some state laws apply to even smaller employers. In addition, many newspapers make it a policy not to accept ads that are discriminatory, regardless of how small your company is.

Personal Recruiting

Everybody knows someone who needs a job. Referrals can come from colleagues, current employees, and friends. You can also call people you know and ask them if they are aware of anyone meeting your qualifications. Referrals can bring in quality recruits and can create a pleasant work environment where employees support one another and work harder.

School recruiting. Most large colleges and universities have a placement office or career counseling function that interacts with employers to place graduates. Often the office will put up a posting of your job and even set up an interview schedule for you.

High schools and trade schools may simply provide a bulletin board that lists part-time, temporary, and full-time job listings for students. Once you get permission from the school, you may be able to post jobs on that bulletin board, at no cost to you.

Using Outside Recruiting Companies

Some business owners opt to outsource recruiting functions, either in part or completely, instead of doing it themselves. While doing it this way can save time, the costs can add up. On the other hand, outsourcing relieves you of some of the more tedious functions of finding the right employee but leaves the ultimate decision — whom to hire — to you.

Some employment services deal solely with placing temporary help, while others specialize in placing managerial candidates within a specific industry.

All employment agencies engage in some method of screening and referring applicants to the employer. The agencies may interview applicants, determine their employment interests and qualifications, administer job skills and knowledge tests such as word processing, and run background checks. You'll have to provide a precise job description for the job you need filled, as well as feedback about candidates that have been rejected.

Although agency fees are occasionally paid by the job seeker, most reputable agencies work only with employer-paid fees. Sometimes the fees are a flat rate, but more commonly they are a percentage of the job's annual salary, which can run as high as 30 percent of the first year's salary. The agency normally guarantees that the applicant will perform satisfactorily for a minimum period or the fee will be refunded to you.

To find a helpful and reputable agency, check with others in your industry or with your employer association for recommendations, and be sure to screen your referrals with the Better Business Bureau.

SCREENING JOB APPLICANTS

Once the word is out that you have a job opening, expect to get phone calls, in-person visits, and resumes in the mail. But what will you do once the calls, letters, and people start coming in? You need to make a few decisions about the kind of information you'll require before considering individuals for employment.

Warning

Federal antidiscrimination laws require that you keep records of all "applicants" for at least one year to ensure that you aren't excluding people in protected groups (i.e., groups defined by race, color, ethnicity, national origin, religion, gender, age over 40, disability, or veteran status).

If this law applies because you have at least 15 employees, you'll need to define exactly who is an applicant. For example, you might decide that to be an "applicant," the person must fill out your business's application form, thus ruling out those who merely inquire over the phone or send unsolicited resumes.

Using Job Applications

Applications are standardized forms that serve as an easy way to gather the specific information you need about people that apply for jobs with your business. On the next page you'll find a sample application form that you can use as a guide. You can customize this document to suit your needs by adding or subtracting parts of it, but don't ask anything that does not relate to a business necessity.

Application for Employment

PERSONAL INFORMATION

LAST NAME	FIRST NAME	MIDDLE INITIAL	SOCIAL SECURITY NUMBER

STREET ADDRESS	CITY	STATE	ZIP	HOW LONG?

PRIOR ADDRESS	CITY	STATE	ZIP	HOW LONG?

HOME PHONE	BUSINESS PHONE

MILITARY SERVICE

BRANCH   DATES OF SERVICE

YES ❑   NO ❑

JOB-RELATED MILITARY EXPERIENCE

EDUCATION

HIGH SCHOOL NAME AND MAILING ADDRESS	DID YOU GRADUATE? YES ❑ NO ❑

STUDIES PURSUED

UNIVERSITY, COLLEGE, TRADE SCHOOL NAME AND MAILING ADDRESS	YEARS COMPLETED 1 2 3 4 5

MAJOR	MINOR	DEGREE

GRADUATE SCHOOL NAME AND MAILING ADDRESS	YEAR COMPLETED 1 2 3 4 5

MAJOR	MINOR	DEGREE

OTHER EDUCATION OR TRAINING

EMPLOYMENT HISTORY (LIST MOST RECENT JOB FIRST)

EMPLOYER'S NAME AND ADDRESS

STILL EMPLOYED?

YES ❑   NO ❑

NAME AND TITLE OF IMMEDIATE SUPERVISOR

MAY WE CONTACT?

YES ❑   NO ❑

DUTIES AND RESPONSIBILITIES

RATE OF PAY

REASONS FOR LEAVING

EMPLOYER'S NAME AND ADDRESS

NAME AND TITLE OF IMMEDIATE SUPERVISOR

MAY WE CONTACT?

YES ❑   NO ❑

DUTIES AND RESPONSIBILITIES

RATE OF PAY

REASONS FOR LEAVING

PROFESSIONAL REFERENCES

NAME   RELATIONSHIP   PHONE

NAME   RELATIONSHIP   PHONE

ANY RESTRICTIONS ON YOUR AVAILABILITY TO WORK?

BY SIGNING, I GRANT THE COMPANY THE RIGHT TO CHECK THE REFERENCES AND INFORMATION PROVIDED HEREIN. I ALSO ACKNOWLEDGE THAT, IF HIRED, MY EMPLOYMENT WILL BE "AT-WILL," AND SUBJECT TO TERMINATION BY ME OR THE EMPLOYER WITH OR WITHOUT CAUSE OR NOTICE.

SIGNATURE   **DATE**

What Not To Ask on Job Applications

For everything you can ask someone on an application, there's at least one that you can't legally ask. Here are some danger areas to avoid.

- **Marital status** — *don't have applicants "circle one: Mr. Mrs. Ms. or Miss" or in any way divulge their marital status.*

- **Age** — *generally, ask only whether the applicant is 18 years of age or older. Ask for the applicant's age only if you are certain that there is a legally recognized business justification for it (e.g., you need to be sure the worker is old enough to serve liquor).*

- **Birthplace** — *generally, don't ask because of the possibility of national origin or immigration issues.*

- **Residence** — *"do you rent? own? board?" Once a common question, it supposedly was a measure of stability. It may discriminate against minorities and others who tend to rent rather than own.*

- **Relationship of person to be notified in an emergency** — *don't require that the person be a relative. Better yet, don't ask the question at all until the applicant becomes an employee.*

- **Arrest and/or conviction records** — *generally, don't ask about arrest records on a job application. You may ask about conviction records in order to protect yourself from negligent hiring claims so long as you place a statement nearby to the effect that a conviction in and of itself would not prevent hiring. Another possibility is to simply state that you intend to make a criminal records check (assuming you do).*

- **Type of discharge from military service** — *some states make it unlawful to discriminate on this basis.*

- **Disability, health** — *avoid medical questions. Don't refer to medical or physical examinations until an offer of employment has been made.*

- **Workers' compensation history** — *regulations under the Americans with Disabilities Act (for employers with 15 employees or more) prohibit this type of questioning. Information that is necessary to collect under a state workers' compensation program for second injury funds can be gathered after an offer of employment has been made.*

- **Citizenship** — *discrimination based on citizenship is unlawful under the Immigration Reform and Control Act of 1986. Don't ask "Are you a U.S. citizen," or "Do you have a work visa?" (You can ask the latter question after the hire.)*

Other Items To Include in Your Application

There are certain statements and information that you may want to include on a job application, and have the applicant sign.

Release of information form. To protect yourself, ask the applicant to sign an information release form that gives you permission to check references. If you will be doing criminal record checks, be sure to mention that here. If you will be doing credit checks, a separate notice must be provided (see page 285).

Employment-at-will statement. Application forms frequently include the assertion that the applicant, if hired, will be subject to "employment-at-will;" that is, the employee may quit at any time and the employer may terminate the employee at any time, whether for cause or not.

False information statement. A statement that an employee may be terminated if false information was provided on the application gives applicants incentive to fill out the form correctly.

Work rules. Some companies choose to use the application to provide applicants with information about work rules. The application statement also provides an opportunity to have the applicant agree to abide by all work rules, if hired.

Example

"I understand that Your Company, Inc., has a drug and alcohol policy that provides for preemployment testing as well as testing after employment. I understand that consent to and compliance with the policy is a condition of my employment and that continued employment is based on the successful passing of testing under the policy."

Accepting Resumes and Other Application Materials

Often, you can assess a person's communication and writing abilities by looking at their resume and cover letter. The downside of using resumes is that their variable format and the creative license that some applicants take can make it difficult to ascertain exactly what they did in past jobs.

Some employers prefer to use *both* a resume and an application, so they can gather all the information they need on the application in a standard format, and also get a good sense of the individual's personality from the resume and cover letter.

It's a good idea to ask for other application materials, if pertinent to the job. For example, if the job involves artistic talent, it's routine to ask the applicants to send copies of work from their portfolio. If the job involves writing for the public, you will want to ask for previous clips and writing samples.

TESTING JOB APPLICANTS

There are many types of tests that you can administer to job applicants, in the hopes of screening out those who will be unable to perform the work you need done. Some employers swear by personality tests or written honesty tests, while others view them as a waste of time. On the next few pages, we'll describe two of the most useful types of tests, and alert you to some legal problems that can arise with other types.

If you have 15 or more employees, you must be prepared to prove that your test accurately measures skills or abilities needed to perform the essential duties of the job. Before testing, check with your attorney.

Achievement Tests

If you can find a good achievement test that approximates tasks your new employee must be able to do, this type of test is usually the most reliable and valid at predicting job performance.

Some achievement tests are actually performances — for example, an applicant is given a letter to be typed or a forklift to be driven. Typing, knowledge of a word processing program, and other clerical tests are, in fact, the most widely used employment tests because they are demonstrably job-related.

Another type of achievement test might be one that puts the applicants in a hypothetical situation to gauge their responses.

Example

If you want to hire someone to handle customer service inquiries, you might ask the applicant to get on a phone in an office, and then call him or her from a phone in the next room and pretend to be an angry customer to see how the person reacts.

Physical Ability/Agility Tests

Physical ability and agility tests assess an applicant's endurance, strength, or overall physical fitness needed to perform actual or simulated job-related tasks. If the job you're filling demands physical strength or stamina, we suggest that you find out beforehand whether a job applicant can actually perform the necessary tasks.

Physical ability and agility tests *are not considered medical tests* and are not prohibited before a job offer is made, even for employers who are covered by the Americans with Disabilities Act, so long as you don't test biomedical responses such as blood pressure, heart rate, etc.

Lie Detector Tests

Under federal law and the laws in many states, most private employers are prohibited from requiring or even suggesting that job applicants or employees take polygraph tests as a condition of employment. Since the federal law was enacted, polygraph testing of job applicants has been virtually eliminated by private employers.

Limited exceptions exist for certain job *applicants* of security service firms, and certain *employees* of pharmaceutical manufacturers, distributors and dispensers.

Drug Testing

Many businesses realize that substance-abusing employees cost them money, and they want to reduce those costs by aggressively screening out alcohol or drug abusers before they become employees.

Giving applicants an alcohol or drug test can help to protect your company from negligent hiring claims that can arise from violence or safety violations. It is also true that drug abusers tend to avoid firms that test, thus saving you the trouble and expense of dealing with them later.

Drug and alcohol testing of applicants is required where mandated by federal or state law based on the demands of certain occupations. For example, railroad and other public transportation employees must be tested for drug and alcohol use periodically.

If you have 15 or more employees and therefore are covered by the Americans with Disabilities Act, you should test only those people who have been given a conditional job offer. Why? Because as part of the test, the examinee is asked about prescription drugs or other conditions that could account for a false positive reading. If you asked for this information *before* a preliminary job offer was made, it might appear that you were trying to screen out medical disabilities.

State Laws on Drug and Alcohol Testing

The following states have enacted laws regulating the use of drug and/or alcohol testing. If your state's name is listed, check with your attorney before requesting such a test.

- Alabama
- Alaska
- Arizona
- Arkansas
- Connecticut
- Delaware
- Florida
- Georgia
- Hawaii
- Idaho
- Illinois
- Indiana
- Iowa
- Louisiana
- Maine
- Maryland
- Minnesota
- Mississippi
- Missouri
- Montana
- Nebraska
- North Carolina
- North Dakota
- Ohio
- Oklahoma
- Oregon
- Rhode Island
- South Carolina
- South Dakota
- Tennessee
- Utah
- Vermont
- Virginia
- Washington

Medical Exams

The most obvious instance when a medical exam would be useful is if the position requires a tremendous amount of physical activity and exertion. If a person's medical condition would not prevent that person from doing a job, information about that condition is not considered legally "relevant" to you or your business.

If you have 15 or more employees, proceed carefully. The basic requirement under the ADA is that medical tests can be requested only after a conditional job offer has been made, as a "final check" on the candidate's suitability.

INTERVIEWING JOB APPLICANTS

Assessing applicants' qualifications by talking to them is a highly subjective method of choosing employees. But used in partnership with other screening methods, such as applications and background checking, it can be an extremely useful selection tool. After all, one of the most important qualifications a person must have for any job is the right personality to work well with you and any co-workers, and you can't get that information from a resume or application.

Planning for the Interview

Preparing beforehand is the key to a successful interview. Here are some steps to take:

- For most jobs, you should interview three to six candidates.

- Decide where you will hold the interviews. If you have an office, it's often best to hold interviews there so the candidate can see the working environment. If you work at home, hold the initial interview over the phone or in a neutral, public place like a restaurant.

- Formulate some questions to ask the candidate after reviewing the application, resume, and any supplementary materials.

- Be sure to allot plenty of time for the meeting. It can take anywhere from 15 minutes to two hours or more.

Conducting the Interview

There are distinct parts to an interview, and each of them is important. Use this outline as a guide:

- **Establish rapport.** Greet the applicant and attempt to put him or her at ease with a casual statement or two.

- **Gather information.** Verify specific information from the resume or application. Be certain to use open-ended questions (how, what, when, etc.), and always follow up a yes or no answer with an open-ended question.

- **Give information about the job and your business, and even "sell" the position.** Be sure to do this *after* you've let the applicants answer your interview questions. If you tell the applicants exactly what you're looking for first, they can adapt their answers to fit what they perceive as your needs.

- **Close the interview.** Thank the candidate for his or her attention and interest. Indicate what the next step will be and the time frame within which it will occur.

DOING A BACKGROUND CHECK

Because so many people misrepresent their background and credentials, it is important to do at least a little checking. The applicant may be unqualified for the job, or have some personality trait or past experience that causes problems for you later. Moreover, if your applicant will have contact with other employees or with the public, an important reason to do that checking is to avoid negligent hiring claims. If you have an employee who turns violent and harms either a customer or another employee, you could be slapped with a lawsuit if reference checking would have kept you from hiring that person.

Guidelines for Reference Checking

- *Tell applicants that no employment offer will be made until satisfactory reference checks are made.*

- *Phone conversations generally reap more information than letters, although many employers are reluctant to disclose much about a former employee because they are afraid of being sued. You can always offer to fax a copy of the job applicant's signed release permitting disclosure of the information you want.*

- *Keep records of all information that you receive. Also document unsuccessful tries at gathering information, to protect yourself from negligent hiring claims.*

- *If you can't get the requested information from references, ask the job applicant for more information or to clear the way for you with the references he or she gave.*

Checking Employment References

Former employers are in the best position to tell you about an applicant's work history, including employment dates, job titles, rates of pay, nature of the tasks performed, and work habits — including conscientiousness, level of expertise, sense of responsibility, and ability to work with others.

Work Smart

If an applicant tells you not to contact the current employer, but you feel strongly that you need to make sure (a) that the worker is indeed employed in the position listed on the resumé, or (b) that there is no major problem with the worker's job performance, you can ask the applicant if there are any co-workers or former supervisors who are familiar with his or her work and can provide a reference. If you merely want to verify that the worker is employed at a certain level of pay, you can ask to see his or her last pay stub.

Sometimes, the employer won't tell you anything more than "name, rank, and serial number" information for fear that the employee may sue them. If you run into this, remind the employer that most states consider the information "qualifiedly privileged." That means that the employer is protected from liability unless the employer knows that the information is false, or shows reckless disregard for the truth (e.g., reports unsubstantiated stories).

A number of states *require* former employers to provide a job reference letter or some information about people who worked for them. See the discussion in *Chapter 21: Firing and Termination.*

Checking Education Records

Education is very frequently misrepresented on resumes and job applications. Common problems are the applicants' saying that they graduated from a particular school when they may have only attended it for a short time, or saying that they have a degree in one field when they really have a degree in another field.

Most colleges or universities will verify a job applicant's degree or attendance, and many will do it over the phone. In many cases, you can also obtain a transcript if you follow the school's guidelines.

Checking Credit Reports

If an applicant is going to be handling large sums of money or exercising financial discretion, you may want to run a credit check. Some businesses routinely run credit checks on all job applicants, under the theory that a good credit report shows a high degree of responsibility.

Hiring is a permissible reason to do a credit check under federal law, but you must keep the results confidential and must not put the results of the check in the person's personnel file. However, the federal Bankruptcy Act states that bankruptcy is not a valid reason to deny employment.

Before doing the credit check you must give the applicant a separate document stating that a consumer credit report will be requested; the applicant must sign the document and thus give written permission to run the check. Your credit agency can furnish forms that can be used for this purpose and that comply with all the federal legal requirements. Make sure to keep a copy in your files.

If you do deny employment because of something on the credit report, you must inform the applicant, and give him or her a copy of the report along with a summary of a consumer's rights to correct inaccurate or outdated information. Again, the credit agency will supply you with properly worded forms to use for this purpose.

Checking Driving Records

If your job opening requires any driving on company business, the applicant's driving record should be checked to be sure the applicant's license hasn't expired or been suspended.

Driving record information is available from a state's department of motor vehicles. Generally, they keep records of all traffic violations, driving-related offenses, and identifying information contained on the license. The cost for checking these records can range from nothing to $10 or more per record.

Checking Criminal Records

You should protect your business from liability by doing criminal checks on applicants who will:

- be bonded because of access to money or valuables

- carry a weapon

- have a great deal of contact with the public, especially patients, children, or the elderly

- drive a company vehicle

- have access to master keys, controlled drugs, or explosives

- be filling a position that requires a criminal record check under your state law

In general, checking for criminal *convictions* is permitted, but checking for *arrests* is not. The easiest way to check conviction records is to have a private detective agency do it for you.

State Laws on Criminal Records Checks

The following states currently have laws on the books restricting checks of criminal records.

• California	• Massachusetts	• Pennsylvania
• Colorado	• Michigan	• Rhode Island
• Connecticut	• Minnesota	• Vermont
• District of Columbia	• New York	• Virginia
• Illinois	• Ohio	• Wisconsin
• Maryland		

On the other hand, the following states require *that criminal checks be done on applicants for certain types of jobs with private employers, such as childcare or eldercare work:*

• Alabama	• Kentucky	• Ohio
• Alaska	• Louisiana	• Oklahoma
• Arizona	• Maine	• Oregon
• Arkansas	• Massachusetts	• Puerto Rico

- California
- Colorado
- Connecticut
- Delaware
- Florida
- Georgia
- Hawaii
- Idaho
- Illinois
- Indiana
- Kansas

- Maryland
- Michigan
- Minnesota
- Mississippi
- Missouri
- Nebraska
- Nevada
- New Hampshire
- New Jersey
- New Mexico
- North Carolina

- Rhode Island
- South Carolina
- South Dakota
- Tennessee
- Texas
- Utah
- Vermont
- Virginia
- Washington
- Wyoming

MAKING THE HIRE

After you've interviewed your top candidates for a job and checked their backgrounds, you must decide which one you want to hire, and make a job offer to that individual.

We recommend that you make your job offer over the phone, so you can get a quick answer to the offer and so that your chosen applicant doesn't get snapped up by someone else while your written offer is still in the mail.

No matter what form the job offer takes, the principle is the same. *Do not make promises, or statements that can be construed as promises, that you cannot or do not intend to keep.* Those statements can sometimes lead to expensive litigation if you later decide to terminate the employee.

Example

Statements that designate employees as "permanent" in contrast to those designating employees as "probationary" were found to constitute a contract for long-term employment.

"You will have a long, rewarding and satisfying career ahead of you" and "we will pay one-half your moving expenses now and the balance after one year" were statements construed as meaning that the employment relationship was intended to be at least one year long.

When a job offer is extended, it should include the position offered, salary and benefits (although sometimes these must be negotiated before the applicant will accept), starting date, any papers or information that should be brought on the first day of work, and a deadline by which the applicant must respond to your job offer.

Completing Required Paperwork

One of the first things you should do when your new employee shows up for work is to have the employee complete some important pieces of documentation:

- IRS Form W-4 (for payroll withholding, tax, and state new-hire reporting purposes)

- Immigration and Naturalization Service Form I-9

- any necessary enrollment forms for employee benefit plans

The Form W-4 must be completed so that you know how much federal income tax to withhold from your new employee's wages. See the discussion of payroll withholding in Chapter 28.

Most states require that you also send a copy of the W-4 to the state unemployment agency (or some other agency) within 20 days of hiring a new employee. Some states have developed their own forms, and some have shorter reporting windows — contact your state labor department for more information and the address to which forms must be sent. Federal law requires that all states establish new-hire reporting programs, primarily to facilitate collection of child support payments.

The I-9 form is used to fulfill your obligation to verify the identity and the eligibility to work in the United States of all employees you hire. The form should be completed within three days of hire. Once completed, the form is not sent to the government, but you must keep it in your files in case an INS inspector ever wants to see it.

To complete the form, the worker must show you certain official documents. The most common documents that employees will present are:

- **A passport** — if an employee presents a U.S. passport, expired or not, that's the only document needed.

- **A driver's license and a social security card** — the driver's license verifies the identity and the SSN card verifies the right to work in the US. The worker should have both documents; the driver's license alone is not sufficient.

If a new employee is unable to produce the required documents within three business days of hiring, the employee must present a receipt for the application of replacement documents within the three business days, and then present the documents themselves within 90 days of the hire.

Chapter 19

Pay and Benefits

The compensation package that you offer your employees is important not only because it costs you money, but because, let's face it, it's the primary reason employees work for you. Compensation packages with good pay and benefits can help you attract and retain the best employees.

Meeting the payroll from week to week is the best some businesses can hope for. However, if you find your business in a more secure position, you may want to offer some benefits to your employees (and to yourself). In fact, one of the many reasons that small businesses are so attractive is the opportunity to obtain tax-deductible benefits for the owner and his or her family.

In this chapter we'll discuss employee compensation issues, including how much to pay, how to comply with minimum wage and overtime laws, and the basics of employee benefits.

DECIDING HOW MUCH TO PAY

When you hire a new employee, deciding how much to pay will probably be a major concern. You want to pay your employees enough to recruit and keep the good ones, but not so much that your business's cash flow is jeopardized.

The quickest and easiest way to find out the going rate for a particular kind of work is to see what others are offering. Check the classified ads in your local newspapers, to see if you can find ads for positions that entail the same kinds of work. If you find that not enough of the ads include a pay range, you can always call the number listed in some of them and ask!

In addition to using the classified ads for salary data, you can ask other small business owners, employment agencies, or temporary help agencies, or local chapters of trade groups in your industry. You can even try calling your competitors, especially if they happen to have job openings.

Public Sources for Salary Data

The federal Bureau of Labor Statistics has Occupational Compensation Surveys (OCS) for most geographical areas in the United States. The information is broken down by the type of occupation as well as by various levels within that occupation. The government also has information about benefits and other statistical information related to employment.

You can access these reports on the Internet at http://stats.bls.gov:80, and also from the Bureau of Labor Statistics' regional offices. For price information or to order by phone, call the General Printing Office at (412) 395-5021.

GIVING EMPLOYEES RAISES

Besides deciding how much to pay new hires, the other major concern of employers related to paying employees is how much of a raise to give an existing employee. There are probably as many ways of deciding this as there are managers!

However, there are two basic approaches to giving raises:

- Give everybody the same percentage or dollar amount raise, every year or two.

- Give employees different raises based on the quality of each individual's performance, also known as a merit system.

Giving everyone the same raises, either in terms of equal dollar amounts or equal percentages of their current salary, has this advantage: you won't be accused of favoritism towards, or discrimination against, any employee. This may be your best course of action in a small office where pay envy can cause problems.

On the other hand, some business owners have the philosophy that raises should be linked strictly to the employee's performance and contribution to the success of the business.

If you give your employees unequal raises, be sure to document the reasons for the differences. How? As a part of the process of coaching and managing employees, most employers take some time every six months or every year to sit down with employees and discuss their performance. At the time of this performance appraisal, you can explain the employee's raise and the reason for the amount.

Another approach would be to give everyone small, cost-of-living raises, but then recognize superior performance with annual bonuses, based on criteria that are clear to everyone in advance.

MINIMUM WAGE AND OVERTIME LAWS

One of the most important parts of paying your workers is making sure you're in compliance with the many federal and state laws that regulate the paying of employees. The most important law to be aware of is the federal Fair Labor Standards Act (FLSA).

Today, almost all employees are covered by the federal wage and hours law by virtue of being involved in interstate commerce. It's a rare business that doesn't use the phone or the mail to communicate across state lines, or send or receive goods from out of state.

Exempt and Nonexempt Employees

Under the FLSA, all employees in your business must be classified as either exempt or nonexempt.

When an employee is classified as nonexempt, it means that the employee is entitled to a minimum wage, overtime pay at the rate of time and one-half the regular rate for all hours worked in excess of 40 hours per week, as well as other protections prescribed by the FLSA. As you can guess, exempt employees aren't covered by these rules.

If you want to treat an employee as exempt, you must pay him or her a salary. Employees paid by hourly wage are automatically considered nonexempt. However, you can have nonexempt employers paid by salary.

Which employees are considered "exempt?"

- **Executives** — employees who have discretionary powers and exercise managerial functions at least 50 percent of the time.

- **Administrative** — employees who assist an executive or administrative official in the performance of his or her duties or perform any of the following: (1) act in a staff or a functional capacity (such as a tax advisor), (2) perform special assignments, (3) perform office or nonmanual work directly related to management policies, or (4) customarily and regularly exercise discretion and independent judgment.

- **Professional** — employees in one of these categories: (1) learned professions with recognized status based on the acquisition of professional knowledge through a prolonged course of study, (2) artistic professions, or (3) teachers.

There are a few other minor exemptions for apprentices, workers with disabilities, newspaper carriers, and certain homeworkers.

Minimum Wage Requirements

The federal Fair Labor Standards Act requires, among other things, that all nonexempt employees be paid at least the federal minimum wage. As of September 1, 1997, the minimum wage is $5.15 per hour.

This rate must be paid to all nonexempt employees for each hour worked up to and including 40 hours in a calendar workweek. Any time beyond 40 hours must be paid as time and one-half overtime, which works out to a current overtime minimum of $7.73 per hour.

The minimum doesn't just apply to hourly workers. The law applies to all nonexempt workers, regardless of what method you use to pay them. Employees may be paid on an hourly, a salary, a monthly, a piecework, or any other basis as long as the minimum requirement of $5.15 per hour is satisfied.

Also, the minimum wage doesn't have to be paid in cash. For example, you can pay it in room and board. However, you can't be making a profit on the noncash payments. If the employee's use of the facility is primarily for your benefit, you can't count it as pay.

Who Must Be Paid Minimum Wage?

There are some types of workers who don't need to be paid minimum wage under the FLSA, but are still protected by other provisions such as overtime pay and child labor, most notably:

- outside sales staff

- certain agricultural employees

- tipped employees, in conjunction with the tip credit discussed below

- learners, apprentices, messengers, and workers with disabilities or students employed in retailing or farming who can be paid a subminimum wage of $4.25 per hour

State Minimum Wage Laws

Sometimes individual states set minimum wages at, above, or below the federal minimum wage. In some cases, a state's minimum wage will vary by the type of worker. If both state and federal minimum wage laws apply to you, you'll have to pay the higher of the two.

If your workers are not subject to federal minimum wage law because they're not involved in interstate commerce or they fall into some narrow exception to the FLSA, they must be paid the state minimum. The following states currently have minimum wage laws:

State	Minimum Wage
Alaska	$5.65 per hour
Arkansas	$5.15 per hour
California	$5.75 per hour by wage order
Colorado	$5.15 per hour
Connecticut	$6.15 per hour
Delaware	$6.15 per hour
DC	$6.15 per hour
Georgia	$3.25 per hour
Hawaii	$5.25 per hour
Idaho	$5.15 per hour
Illinois	$5.15 per hour
Indiana	$5.15 per hour; employers with at least two employees
Iowa	$5.15 per hour
Kansas	$2.65 per hour
Kentucky	$5.15 per hour
Maine	$5.15 per hour
Maryland	$5.15 per hour
Massachusetts	$6.00 per hour in 2000; $6.75 for 2001
Michigan	$5.15 per hour
Minnesota	$5.15 per hour for large firms (those with annual receipts of $500,000 or more) and $4.90 for small firms (those with annual receipts below $500,000)
Missouri	$5.15 per hour
Montana	$5.15 per hour, except that the minimum wage rate for businesses whose annual gross sales are $100,000 or less remains $4 per hour
Nebraska	$5.15 per hour
Nevada	$5.15 per hour
New Hampshire	$5.15 per hour
New Jersey	$5.05 per hour
New Mexico	$4.25 per hour
New York	$5.15 per hour. Other wage rates are in effect in specific industries.

North Carolina	$5.15 per hour
North Dakota	$5.15 per hour
Ohio	Employers in Ohio with $500,000 or more in gross annual sales must pay the current federal minimum wage rate ($5.15 per hour). Employers with less than $500,000 but at least $150,000 in gross annual sales must pay $3.35 per hour. Employers with less than $150,000 in gross annual sales must pay employees at least $2.80 per hour
Oklahoma	$5.15 per hour
Oregon	$6.50 per hour
Pennsylvania	$5.15 per hour
Puerto Rico	Different minimum wage rates are set for workers in different categories of agricultural work
Rhode Island	$5.65 per hour
South Dakota	$5.15 per hour
Texas	$3.35 per hour
Utah	$5.15 per hour
Vermont	$5.75 per hour
Virginia	$5.15 per hour
Washington	$6.50 per hour; subject to inflation adjustment after January 1, 2001
West Virginia	$5.15 per hour
Wisconsin	$5.15 per hour
Wyoming	$1.60 per hour

Counting Tips Toward Minimum Wage

If your employees normally receive over $30 per month in tips from customers, the federal law allows you, within limits, to count some of those tips toward your minimum wage obligations. The maximum tip credit is $2.13 per hour, which is 50 percent of the former minimum wage of $4.25. The credit cannot exceed the value of tips actually received by the employees.

There's one more catch: the federal minimum wage, minus the tip credit, may not be lower than the state minimum wage minus any tip credit permitted in your state. Many states provide for a lower tip credit than the federal one and, as usual with labor laws, when federal and state laws differ, the law that is more favorable to the employees is the one you must follow.

State laws. The following states have laws that also address tip credits (states that are not listed currently have no relevant law on the books).

State	Tip Credit
Alaska	Tips may not be counted towards the state minimum wage.
Arkansas	$2.58 per hour is allowed as a tip credit.
California	Tips may not be counted towards the state minimum wage.
Colorado	$3.02 per hour is allowed as a tip credit.
Connecticut	$1.41 per hour is allowed as a tip credit (23% of the state min. wage) for those in the hotel and restaurant industry, and $.35 per hour for those in other industries.
Delaware	Minimum wage is $2.23 per hour for tipped employees.
DC	$3.38 per hour is allowed as a tip credit (55% of the state min. wage).
Hawaii	$.20 per hour is allowed as a tip credit, provided the employee receives at least $.70 per hour in tips.
Idaho	$1.80 per hour is allowed as a tip credit (35% of the state min. wage).
Illinois	$2.06 per hour is allowed as a tip credit (40% of the state min. wage).
Indiana	$2.06 per hour is allowed as a tip credit (40% of the state min. wage) for employers with at least two employees.
Iowa	$2.06 per hour is allowed as a tip credit (40% of the state min. wage).
Kansas	$1.06 per hour is allowed as a tip credit (40% of the state min. wage).
Kentucky	$2.13 per hour is allowed as a tip credit (50% of the state min. wage).
Maine	$2.58 per hour is allowed as a tip credit (50% of the state min. wage).
Maryland	$2.77 per hour is allowed as a tip credit.
Massachusetts	$3.00 per hour is allowed as a tip credit (50% of the state min. wage).
Michigan	$2.50 per hour is allowed as a tip credit (the difference between $2.65 and the minimum wage).
Missouri	$2.58 per hour is allowed as a tip credit (50% of the state min. wage).
Montana	Tips may not be counted toward the state minimum wage.
Nebraska	Minimum wage is $2.13 per hour for tipped employees.
Nevada	Tips may not be counted toward the state minimum wage.
New Hampshire	$2.58 per hour is allowed as a tip credit (50% of the state min. wage).
New Jersey	$2.06 per hour is allowed as a tip credit (40% of the state min. wage); special rules for chambermaids.
New Mexico	Minimum wage is $2.125 per hour for tipped employees.
New York	For restaurant employees, $.95 per hour is allowed as a tip credit for employees receiving tips of $.95 to $1.35 per hour; $1.35 per hour is allowed as a credit for employees receiving tips over $1.35 per hour; other rules apply to workers outside the restaurant industry.

North Carolina	$3.02 per hour is allowed as a tip credit.
North Dakota	$1.70 per hour is allowed as a tip credit (33% of the state min. wage).
Ohio	$2.58 per hour is allowed as a tip credit (50% of the state min. wage).
Oklahoma	$2.58 per hour is allowed as a tip credit (50% of the state min. wage).
Oregon	Tips may not be counted toward the state minimum wage.
Pennsylvania	$2.32 per hour is allowed as a tip credit (45% of the state min. wage).
Rhode Island	Minimum wage for tipped employees is $2.89 per hour.
South Dakota	$3.02 per hour is allowed as a tip credit.
Texas	$1.68 per hour is allowed as a tip credit (50% of the state min. wage).
Utah	Minimum wage for tipped employees is $2.58 per hour (50% of the state min. wage).
Vermont	$2.70 per hour is allowed as a tip credit (47% of state min. wage).
Virginia	The minimum wage may be fully offset by tips.
West Virginia	$1.03 per hour is allowed as a tip credit.
Wisconsin	Minimum wage for tipped employees is $2.33 per hour for nonprobationary adults, $2.20 for probationary adults, $2.13 for nonprobationary minors, and $2.00 for probationary minors.
Wyoming	Minimum wage for tipped employees is $1.10 per hour.

Overtime Requirements

Federal law mandates that you pay your nonexempt employees one and one-half times their regular rate, for any hours worked in excess of 40 hours in a workweek. A "workweek" is defined by law as any seven, consecutive 24-hour periods that begins at any time on any day. For example, you could decide to start your employees' workweek at noon on Wednesday and end at 11:59 a.m. on the following Wednesday.

The overtime rules apply to all nonexempt employees. A common mistake employers make is to presume that the overtime rules don't apply to salaried employees. In fact, the rules apply to all salaried employees, unless they fall into one of the exempt categories (most commonly, executive, administrative, and professional employees).

State Overtime Pay Laws

As is the case with minimum wage, many states have laws pertaining to overtime. The vast majority of them follow the federal system; that is, time and one-half is required after 40 hours in a single week.

If your state's law is more generous to workers regarding overtime pay, you must follow the state law. The states with more generous overtime requirements are listed below.

State	Overtime Requirements
Alaska	Time and one-half for any hours over eight per day or 40 per week (applies to employers with four or more employees).
California	Time and one-half for any hours in excess of 40 per week or eight hours per day; double time for any hours in excess of 12 per day and in excess of eight on the seventh day of work. Some alternative schedules are permitted, depending on the industry.
Colorado	Time and one-half for any hours in excess of 12 per day or 40 per week.
Florida	Time and one-half for any hours in excess of 10 per day, unless a written contract provides otherwise.
Kentucky	Time and one-half for any hours in excess of 40 per week, and for the seventh day if an employee works for seven days in a workweek.
Nevada	Time and one-half for any hours in excess of eight per day or 40 per week, unless a four-day, ten-hours-per-day workweek has been arranged.
Puerto Rico	Double time must be paid for all hours in excess of 40 per week, unless the Board of Minimum Wages or individual or collective agreement provides otherwise. Double time is also required for hours in excess of eight per day, unless the position is covered by the FLSA (in which case time and one-half must be paid).
Rhode Island	Time and one-half for hours over 40 weekly or for work in a retail business on Sunday or holidays.

Equal Pay Requirements

In a nutshell, the Equal Pay Act (a part of the federal wage and hour laws) says that if you have a male employee and a female employee doing the same work, you must pay them equally *unless* the higher-paid employee has more experience, qualifications, seniority, or some other distinction besides gender.

If you are subject to the federal Fair Labor Standards Act, you are also subject to Equal Pay Act requirements. Moreover, executive, administrative, and professional employees and outside salespeople (who are not covered by minimum wage and overtime laws) do qualify for equal pay protection.

If you see a situation where there is clearly a problem with a female being paid less than a male for the same work, or vice versa, *it is illegal to reduce the pay of one gender to match the lower pay of the other.*

BENEFITS FOR YOUR WORKERS

While virtually every business has to give workers a paycheck, most benefits are optional. However, the law does require you to provide a few things that might be considered benefits. You must:

- Allow employees time off to vote, serve on a jury, or perform military service.

- Comply with all requirements of workers' compensation.

- Withhold FICA taxes from employees' paychecks and pay your own portion of the FICA taxes, thus providing minimum retirement and disability benefits.

- Pay state and federal unemployment taxes, thus providing benefits for unemployed workers.

- Contribute to state short-term disability programs in states where such programs exist (California, Hawaii, New Jersey, New York, Puerto Rico, and Rhode Island).

On the other hand, you are *not* required to provide:

- retirement plans

- health plans, except in Hawaii

- dental or vision plans

- life insurance plans

- paid vacations, holidays, or sick leaves

Remember, many benefits are tax-deductible to your business and tax-exempt for the recipients. As a result, your out-of-pocket cost will be much less than what employees would pay to buy the benefit on their own.

If you want to offer benefits in order to compete with other employers in your area, you need to know what you're up against. Find out what other employers are offering, by conducting an informal survey among your networking contacts, or by calling other businesses in your area and explaining that you're trying to get a feel for which benefits to offer.

Time-Off Benefits

Some types of time off are required by law. They include time off to vote, jury duty leave, military leave, and family leave (for employers with 50 or more employees).

In addition to these mandated time-off benefits, there are others that you might consider offering to your employees. These leaves can be paid or unpaid: holidays, vacations, sick leave, personal leave, funeral leave, and maternity/paternity leave.

Some time-off plans can be covered under a federal law known as ERISA, which has rigorous administrative requirements. You can generally avoid these if you make time-off plans more of a payroll practice than a separate plan.

Example

A determination of whether a vacation plan is an ERISA plan or not depends on how the program is structured (i.e., how employees are paid). If the vacation policy is an organized "plan" where a separate check would be issued for vacation time, it is an ERISA plan. However, if the vacation plan is just a payroll practice, and employees are paid out of the employer's general assets, it is not an ERISA plan.

Time Off To Vote

While there are no federal laws that require you to give employees time off to vote, 31 states have laws that require private employers to give employees time off to vote.

In most of these states, if the employee has sufficient time before or after work to vote (generally, two hours in which the polls are open) he or she need not be allowed time off from work. Otherwise, the employee must usually be given time off at the beginning or end of the work day so as to have at least two hours in which to vote.

States Requiring Time Off To Vote

*These states have laws that require employers to give time off for voting. The states listed in **bold** have laws stating that if the employee takes time off to vote, no deduction from pay is permitted.*

• ***Alaska***	• *Illinois*	• *Mississippi*
• ***Arizona***	• ***Iowa***	• ***Missouri***
• *Arkansas*	• ***Kansas***	• ***Nebraska***
• ***California***	• *Kentucky*	• ***Nevada***
• ***Colorado***	• ***Maryland***	• *New Mexico*
• *Georgia*	• *Massachusetts*	• ***New York***
• ***Hawaii***	• ***Minnesota***	• *North Dakota*

- *Ohio*
- *Oklahoma*
- Puerto Rico
- *South Dakota*

- *Tennessee*
- *Texas*
- *Utah*
- *Washington*

- *West Virginia*
- Wisconsin
- *Wyoming*

Jury Duty Leave

Under federal law, employees have the right to take leaves of absence to serve as jurors in federal courts.

As you might have guessed, the state laws are the ones that protect employees who serve on state and local juries. Every state except Montana has laws requiring employers to allow time for jury duty, but the laws are not exactly alike.

Most states prohibit an employer from discharging someone who takes leave to serve on a jury. Some prohibit other forms of reprisal or threats of reprisal. Some states specifically say that an employer does not have to pay for the lost time or that it may set off from wages any money received by the employee for juror service.

The following states require that employees be paid for at least some of the time they serve on a jury:

- Alabama
- Colorado
- Connecticut
- Delaware
- Georgia

- Louisiana
- Nebraska
- New York
- Tennessee

What about witness leaves? Jury duty is not the same as leave to appear as a witness in a court case. Generally, you can set your own policy in this area. Employers in Florida and Michigan, however, are required to provide employees with time off to serve as a witness.

Military Leave

All employers, regardless of size, must provide military leaves of absences to employees under federal law, and the law in most states.

You do not have to pay reservists during the period they are on active duty, although many employers pay reservists the difference between their regular salary and their military pay. However, you must reinstate the employee to his or her position upon completion of the active duty.

In addition to active duty leave, the law mandates that you grant annual leave to attend reserve or national guard encampment, maneuvers, drills, training, or any other duty of a short-term nature.

What about benefits? Any benefits or employment rights that you provide to employees who are on leave of absence for other reasons must be provided to employees who are on military leave.

Family and Medical Leave

Family leave is now mandated under the federal Family and Medical Leave Act. *Only employers with 50 or more employees are subject to this law.* Essentially, it requires that covered employers allow employees to take the equivalent of 12 weeks of unpaid leave each year due to a birth or adoption of a child, or to attend to the serious health condition of the employee or an immediate family member.

After the 12 weeks of unpaid leave, you must reinstate the employee in the same job or an equivalent one. Note that the leave does not have to be taken all at once; in some instances family leave can be taken one day at a time.

California, the District of Columbia, Louisiana, Maine, Massachusetts, Minnesota, New York, Oregon, South Carolina, Vermont, and Washington have family leave laws that place requirements on private employers with fewer than 50 employees. If you have 25 or more employees in Maine or Oregon, 21 or more in Minnesota, 20 or more in D.C., Louisiana, New York, or South Carolina, 10 or more in Vermont, six or more in Massachusetts, or one or more in Washington, consult your state labor department to find out the requirements. California requires employers with five or more employees to allow maternity leaves.

Sick Leave

Unpaid sick leave may be legally required if you are subject to either federal or state family and medical leave laws. However, the amount of *paid* sick leave you offer is up to you. Most businesses establish a limit on the number of days, which can:

- depend on the circumstances, at your discretion;

- be a fixed, predetermined amount, such as 10 days each calendar year; or

- be based upon the length of service of the employee.

In explaining your sick leave policy, be sure to cover these points:

- how the sick leave program coordinates with your short-term disability policy, if you have one

- what constitutes a sickness (i.e., is a doctor's note necessary)

- whether the policy extends to a child's or spouse's illness

- whom an employee should contact in the case of sickness

- whether employees can accrue and carry over unused sick days from one year to the next

Some employers designate a separate limit for personal leave, which is time off to cover personal or family emergencies or things like house closings, car breakdowns, or doctor appointments. If you don't allow for such time off, you may find employees "calling in sick" more frequently than you'd like.

Pregnancy/Parental Leave

If you have 15 or more employees, you are subject to a federal law that protects pregnant women, by providing that women affected by pregnancy, childbirth, or related medical conditions must be treated the same as other applicants and employees on the basis of their ability or inability to work. The law protects women against being fired, being refused a job, or being denied a promotion merely because they are pregnant. In addition, a pregnant woman usually may not be forced to go on leave as long as she is able to work.

Pregnant women are to be treated in the same manner as other persons with temporary disabilities for purposes of leave as well as participation in benefit plans and health and disability insurance. Further, if other employees who take disability leave are entitled to get their jobs back when they are able to work again, so are women who are unable to work because of pregnancy.

Pregnancy leave versus parental leave. Pregnancy leave is *medical* leave that is provided in connection with a pregnancy-related disability, either before or after the birth of a baby. Parental leave, on the other hand, is leave to care for a child and may be treated differently. If you allow new mothers to take time off beyond the six weeks or so required for medical disability after childbirth, you should allow new fathers to take an equivalent amount of time off, to avoid trouble with the federal or state antidiscrimination laws (or the FMLA, if you have 50 employees or more).

State laws. If an employee, male or female, is expecting a birth in the family, you should also check with your state labor department or your attorney to see if state laws might affect your policy.

Holidays

You aren't legally required to give your employees days off for federal or state holidays. However, most employers do allow time off on certain holidays, and many pay employees for at least some nonworking holidays. The average number of paid holidays for full-time employees is nine. Virtually all companies provide paid holidays for: New Year's Day, Memorial Day, Independence Day, Labor Day, Thanksgiving Day, and Christmas Day.

Many employers either allow employees to use vacation time for religious holidays, or take the holidays off without pay. The basic rule is that an employer's refusal to accommodate the religious needs of employees becomes religious discrimination if the employer could make such accommodation without undue hardship to the business.

Vacations

Although you are not legally required to offer paid vacation benefits to your employees, most full-time employees will expect to get at least two weeks.

In explaining your vacation scheduling policy to employees, you should specify how far in advance the request must be made. If vacations need to be coordinated so everyone isn't gone at the same time, those restrictions should be conveyed ahead of time.

Funeral Leave

There are no laws requiring you to provide employees with funeral leave, but most employers allow between two and four days per funeral for close family members. Employers that don't provide funeral leave generally allow employees to use some other form of paid leave, such as sick days or vacation.

Workers' Compensation

Every state has enacted workers' compensation laws to protect employees against loss of income and to pay medical payments they have due to a work-related injury, accident, illness, or disease.

Do the laws apply to you? In the vast majority of states, workers' compensation coverage is mandatory; in Texas and New Jersey, it is voluntary. In most states, all employers who have at least one employee are covered. The following chart shows the exceptions: those states that cover only employers above a certain size.

State	Workers' Compensation Coverage
Alabama	Employers with five or more employees.
Arkansas	Employers with three or more employees, except employers engaged in repair work (two or more), contractors who subcontract part of their work (one or more), and subcontractors (one or more).
Florida	Employers with four or more employees (one or more for construction).
Georgia	Employers with three or more employees.
Kansas	Employers whose payroll for the preceding year was less than $20,000 and who don't expect the current year's payroll to exceed $20,000 are excluded.
Michigan	Employers with three or more employees.
Mississippi	Employers with five or more employees.
Missouri	Employers with five or more employees; construction employers with one or more employees.
New Mexico	Employers with three or more employees (one or more for construction).
North Carolina	Employers with three or more employees.
Rhode Island	Employers with four or more employees.
South Carolina	Employers with four or more employees; employers with total annual payroll under $3,000 for the previous year are exempt.
Tennessee	Employers with five or more employees (one or more for employees that mine or produce coal).
Virginia	Employers with three or more employees.
Wisconsin	Employers with three or more employees, or that pay wages of $500 or more in a calendar quarter.

If participation is not mandatory, should you join the system anyway? If you join, your liability for on-the-job injuries is limited to the remedies available under the system; you can't be sued for everything you own. This saves both time (disputes are resolved quickly) and money (legal fees are much lower). Although you have to pay for coverage, the costs are predictable.

Benefits Provided by Workers' Compensation Laws

Here are some common elements shared by the state workers' compensation laws:

- Benefits are provided for accidental job-related injuries or illnesses.

- Benefits include wage-loss, medical, and death benefits. Wage-loss benefits usually cover about one-half to two-thirds of the employee's average weekly wage.

- Covered "employees" are defined by law, and generally don't include independent contractors.

- The worker gets paid regardless of whose "fault" caused the injury.

- Employees retain the right to sue third parties, if a third party's negligence helped cause the accident.

Paying for Workers' Compensation

To participate in workers' compensation, each state provides its own menu of choices, which generally include some or all of the following: a state insurance pool, individual insurance with private companies, or self-insurance by the employer itself.

Generally, small employers will find that the state insurance pool is the least expensive choice. Self-insurance is a route typically taken only by the largest employers.

What To Do When Accidents Happen

- ***Respond to the injured employee*** — *this includes providing assistance, getting the facts from the employee about the accident, and telling the employee that there is a system available that will take care of the injuries.*

- ***Give first aid or get medical attention*** — *this includes accompanying the employee to the medical provider.*

- ***Document the accident*** — *this includes writing down what happened, which should be done within 24 hours of the accident.*

- ***Follow up with the medical care provider*** *(although you should first get permission from the employee to contact the provider).*

- ***Follow up with the employee*** *to file an accident report with the insurance company or state agency within the time limit they require.*

You should, at least initially, treat every injury as legitimate, even if the circumstances surrounding the injury make you suspicious. Workers' comp. does not insulate you from lawsuits claiming that you failed to provide workers with benefits to which they are entitled.

Health Care Benefits

Unless you are an employer in Hawaii, you are not required by law to offer your employees health insurance benefits. However, health care benefits are usually the most important and popular benefits for employees.

If the insurance seems too expensive, remember that you can ask your employees to pay for part (or even all) of their own premiums, through payroll deductions.

Self-employed individuals can deduct 60 percent of health insurance premiums for themselves and their dependents as a business expense in 1999 through 2001 (rising to 70 percent in 2002 and 100 percent in 2003). However, you can deduct 100% of the costs for your employees and their dependents. If you hire your spouse, you can include yourself in the spouse's family coverage, which is a "back-door" way of deducting 100% of your own coverage.

If the business is incorporated and you work for it as an employee, all costs for your own insurance as well as those for your employees' insurance are deductible.

Warning

The potential for liability for selecting a health care provider that commits malpractice on an employee does exist. While this risk is small and should not be the driving reason behind a decision not to offer health insurance, you should be aware that several employers have been sued by their employees for what they contend was their employer's carelessness in selecting a provider.

Small employer reforms. In the last few years, most states have enacted laws that are designed to enable small employers to obtain health insurance more easily. The reforms may include laws that guarantee renewals; that limit the extent to which your group's health status can be used to set rates; that provide basic, low-option policies; and that require insurers to make coverage available to you regardless of your employees' health condition.

Recently, Congress extended some of these state reforms to the federal level. Beginning July 1, 1997, insurers that offer health plans in the small business market cannot exclude any small business from coverage. Thus, for example, an insurer cannot choose to drop your coverage because one of your employees develops a heart condition. To gain the protection of these rules, you must have at least two employees.

Deciding Whom To Cover

Generally, you can provide health insurance to all of your employees, or only to certain ones you select. For example, you could decide to cover only your managers, or only full-time workers, or only workers who've been with you for more than a year.

Once you have established your rules, you must apply them

consistently, to avoid civil rights discrimination charges.

You don't have to offer coverage to spouses or dependents of workers, but if you do, you should clearly define who is a dependent. If you decide to cover unmarried domestic partners, the partner's coverage will not be deductible for you, and will be taxable to the employee.

Should you have age limits? Generally, an employer that places age maximums on employees eligible for health coverage runs the risk of violating the age discrimination laws. Federal age protection covers businesses with 20 employees or more.

Health Plan Options

In a given geographic area, most health plans will cover the same types of medical services, in part because state laws regulate the categories of treatment and expenses that must be covered. The major differences among plans are in the existence and amount of the deductible (the annual amount that the insured must pay for medical expenses before the insurance plan pays), the amount or percentage of co-payments the insured must make, and the degree of choice among doctors and hospitals that the plan permits. And, of course, in the price of the premiums.

Health Maintenance Organizations (HMOs) are relatively lower in cost than traditional fee-for-service plans and offer broad health coverage, including preventive care. Employees insured under the HMO are required to choose a general practitioner from the HMO's list of doctors, who acts as a gatekeeper in determining which services the plan will cover and which specialists, if any, they may see.

Warning

If you have at least 25 employees, a federal law requires you to offer an HMO as one of your employees' health care options, provided that one exists in your area.

Preferred Provider Organizations (PPOs) are similar to HMOs, except that the insured employees can go outside the plan's network of doctors and hospitals for treatment and still be covered, albeit at a lower reimbursement level.

Fee-for-service plans, also known as indemnity plans, are more expensive, traditional insurance plans that give employees absolute freedom in choosing physicians and medical facilities. In return, insurance companies require patients to fulfill a yearly deductible (usually between $200 and $500 per person per year).

After the deductible has been paid, the insurance company will pay a specified percentage (e.g., 80%) of the fees.

Major medical plans are a special type of fee-for-service plan, designed to provide protection against long-term chronic or catastrophic illness or injury. These plans cover a broad area of health care services but typically require the insured to pay a high deductible before receiving any benefits.

Vision and dental care can sometimes be purchased in addition to basic medical care, or they can be purchased as a separate policy from a separate provider.

Medical savings accounts (MSAs) are a new variation of Flexible Spending Accounts (see the discussion of these below). Both MSAs and FSAs are similar to Individual Retirement Accounts in the sense that each employee can make tax-free contributions to an account through payroll withholding, and then withdraw funds as needed to pay for medical expenses. In an MSA, money remaining in the account can accumulate to be used in later years or to be saved until retirement. MSAs must be combined with a high-deductible health insurance plan (often referred to as a "catastrophic health plan," which is a variety of major medical plan as discussed above).

What To Ask Your Health Plan Provider

In order to best evaluate the plans that you are considering offering to employees, you should ask the companies to provide you with the following information:

- *the premium schedule*

- *the benefits schedule*

- *a list of participating physicians, clinics, and hospitals that are located near your employees*

- *an explanation of the quality control measures they use to screen for quality medical providers*

- *in your chosen geographic area, an adequate number of licensed primary care givers and an adequate number of licensed specialists*

- *statistics on patient satisfaction*

- *a list of other employers in the area that contract with them*

- *a copy of a sample agreement they would ask you to sign*

Purchasing Alliances

Small businesses have a particularly hard time finding good, reasonably-priced insurance coverage. Often, insurance companies are not eager to insure small businesses because the risk pool is small and they tend not to make big profits on them. When small businesses band together into larger groups, however, they have a larger risk pool, which makes them more attractive to insurance companies.

Some states and communities have Health Purchasing Alliances. These are local, private non-profit groups that get small businesses together and offer them health care benefits at competitive prices. To find out if your state has health purchasing alliances and how to contact them, check your phone directory in the state government listings or check with your chamber of commerce.

COBRA Continuation Benefits

COBRA is a federal law that applies to employers with 20 or more employees who have a company health plan. These employers must offer covered individuals who resign, are fired, or would otherwise lose their health benefit protection the option of continuing their health care plan coverage at their own expense. Covered individuals include not only your employees, but spouses and dependents who were covered under the employee's insurance.

The following are the events that can trigger COBRA coverage:

- an employee's voluntary or involuntary termination of employment, unless it is for gross misconduct

- an employee's reduction in hours (e.g., from full time to part time)

- a covered spouse's divorce or legal separation from an employee (the spouse and any dependents would be entitled to coverage, whether or not the employee still works for you)

- an employee's death (in that case, the surviving spouse or dependents would be entitled to continuation coverage)

- an employee's entitlement to Medicare

- a covered dependent's change in status (for example, reaching an age that no longer qualifies the dependent for coverage under the parent's health plan)

- active military duty when you don't maintain health coverage

- your business's bankruptcy

Coverage continues for up to 18 months in the case of termination of employment or reduction in hours, or 36 months for other qualifying events. The employee must pay the costs of the coverage at your group rates, and you can charge an extra 2% to compensate you for the administrative hassles.

State law. Every state except Alaska, Alabama, Delaware, and the District of Columbia has laws concerning continuation of benefits. Some of these laws cover all employers in the state, so you might be subject to a state law even if you are exempt from federal law. To find out more, contact your state labor agency or your attorney.

Health Insurance Portability Act

As of July 1, 1997, group health plans may exclude coverage of preexisting health conditions for no more than 12 months after an employee enrolls, or for no more than 18 months if the employee declined coverage at the first opportunity to join the employer's plan. If the employee was previously covered by a group health plan, HMO, COBRA coverage, private insurance, or governmental health plan, that coverage counts toward the preexisting condition period unless the employee had a break in coverage of more than 63 days. This federal law applies to all group health plans that cover at least two employees.

To promote this health insurance "portability," a certificate of coverage must be provided to an employee whenever a covered employee or dependent ceases to be covered by your health plan (including COBRA benefits). Your health plan provider should be able to supply these certificates of coverage whenever they're needed.

Flexible Spending Accounts

FSAs, also called flexible spending arrangements, allow employers and employees to use pretax dollars to pay for health care expenses that aren't otherwise covered by insurance, or to pay for dependent care such as day care.

In an FSA, employees agree to payroll deductions that put pretax dollars into an account, and then use the funds during the year for reimbursement of certain types of expenses. The employee may set up an account for health care expenses and/or an account for dependent care expenses, and up to $5,000 per year can be put into each account. These amounts are not subject to Social Security, Medicare, or federal income tax, or state income tax in many jurisdictions. However, if the employee doesn't use up the entire account during the year, any leftover amounts are forfeited.

These plans are usually very cheap for an employer to maintain, since all contributions are made by employees, and the money the employer saves on its own FICA taxes will usually pay for the cost of administering the plan.

Disability Benefits

Disability benefits are payments that guarantee income when an employee can't work because of sickness (physical or mental) or injury.

They are often divided into two categories: short-term disability benefits (for up to six months), and long-term disability.

Workers' compensation can be thought of as a state-mandated disability program, and Social Security provides long-term coverage for the totally disabled after a six-month waiting period. Some states run programs providing short-term disability benefits (California, Hawaii, New Jersey, New York, Puerto Rico, and Rhode Island) that are funded through payroll taxes.

To cover the gaps in these programs, you can purchase private disability insurance policies for yourself and/or your employees.

Short-term disability policies are designed to provide income to disabled employees after a waiting period of one to seven days. Government statistics show that these benefits typically replace about 50 percent to 67 percent of an employee's income. Typically, after six months, benefits terminate and the individual's long-term benefits or Social Security would kick in.

Long-term disability typically provides 50 percent to 60 percent of pay to disabled employees. In most plans, benefits are paid for the duration of the disability up to the age of 65. There is usually a maximum dollar amount per week or month.

Life Insurance Benefits

Most employers offer group-term life insurance as an employee benefit, although other types can be offered. Term insurance is life insurance that is in effect for a certain period of time only.

The value of up to $50,000 in group-term life insurance is tax-exempt for each employee, if you have at least 10 full-time employees, or if you provide coverage to all full-time employees and (a) there is a uniform method for computing the amount of each employee's coverage, and (b) no physical exams are required to obtain coverage.

There are other types of life insurance that you can offer, including:

- **Group accidental death and dismemberment** pays benefits to the employee's beneficiary if death occurs due to an accident or if the employee loses use of portions of the body (loss of a limb, hand or foot, or an eye, for example).

- **Business travel accident insurance** covers the death of the employee while traveling on business. If your employees don't travel much, this may not be worth your money.

- **Split-dollar life insurance** for which the cost of the insurance is paid by both the employer and employee and has a substantial investment element to it. When the employee dies, the premiums paid by the employer are returned to it. It is most frequently used for key employees only.

For more information on life insurance, see the discussion in *Chapter 30: Building Wealth Outside the Business.*

Retirement Benefits

Retirement benefits are attractive to employees because they allow them to save for their future in a relatively pain-free way and enjoy some tax advantages while they're at it. These plans are most popular with older, more highly compensated employees. Most importantly, however, offering a qualified retirement plan allows you to take advantage of the plan yourself.

If you decide that you want to offer a retirement plan, you are *definitely* going to need some professional advice and guidance. But before you call your accountant and attorney, check out our discussion of plan options in *Chapter 30: Building Wealth Outside the Business.*

Administering Employee Benefits

The great temptation as a small business owner will be to handle the administration of your compensation package yourself. Many a small business owner has said, "I just have two [or whatever the number] employees; how hard can it be?" Resist the temptation, if at all possible. In today's market, you should be able to find an able administrator for a fair price, so that you can concentrate more of your time on what you know best.

Work Smart

Although you have the option of switching administrators every year, switching can be costly and disruptive; therefore, take great care in making your choice, and assume that your relationship will be continuing.

Chapter 20

Managing
Your Employees

Anyone who has ever had even one employee can tell you that the secret to a productive workforce (and therefore a successful business) is an elusive thing known as good morale. "Morale" refers to the way that your employees feel about working for you and your business. It's important because it directly affects your bottom line.

Good morale doesn't just mean that your employees are happy. It also means that they have a positive attitude towards each other, and towards being responsible, productive members of your team.

In a perfect world, your employees would think exactly the way that you do. They would come in and leave when you expect them to, they would dress the way you expect them to, and they wouldn't do anything that would necessitate formal rules and discipline. But no two people think alike, and everyone has a different perception of what the work environment should be. You need to think about setting some basic ground rules, to be sure that your employees understand what is expected of them.

And, of course, if you have any workplace rules or policies, sooner or later some of them will be broken, and you may have to enforce those rules with some form of discipline. If set up correctly, discipline systems can become a positive force for helping employees to improve their performance, as well as their job satisfaction.

MORALE AND THE BOTTOM LINE

It's easy to see how an employee who sells a lot of your product helps your business's financial bottom line, whereas an employee who misses important deadlines hurts your company's profitability. But what about the employees who fall somewhere in between? An employee who is becoming increasingly dissatisfied can cost your business money through low productivity, decreasing loyalty, high absenteeism, and, ultimately, high turnover.

What Keeps Morale High?

In a recent study, employees were asked to rank 10 items, in order of importance, that they wanted from their jobs. Their employers were then asked to guess how they thought their employees would rank the same 10 items. The results were surprising:

Employees' Rank	Item	Employer's Rank
1	Interesting work	5
2	Appreciation and recognition	8
3	Feeling "in on things"	10
4	Job security	2
5	Good wages	1
6	Promotion/growth	3
7	Good working conditions	4
8	Personal loyalty	6
9	Tactful discipline	7
10	Sympathetic help for problems	9

(Source: Niebrugge, Vicki, *Declining Employee Morale: Defining the Causes and Finding the Cure*, NOVA Group, July 1992.)

Notice that employees ranked "interesting work" as what they want most in their jobs, although their employers thought that the employees would rank "good wages" as the most important.

This is good news for you, since working for a small business tends to mean employees have to wear a lot of hats and have more interesting jobs.

Pay tends to become very important only when the employee feels his or her pay is below standard for what similar workers earn elsewhere. If your pay is in line with industry averages, chances are that your employees' job satisfaction hinges more on the "soft issues" than on the fact that they may earn a few dollars more or less than their peers.

Improving Morale and Motivation

If you suspect that you may have a problem with low morale, you need to determine which aspects of your workplace are creating the dissatisfaction with the job and then remedy them.

Even if you don't have a morale problem, you may want to jump-start your workforce into higher levels of productivity. There are several good ways to increase morale and motivation without spending a lot of money.

Building Employees' Involvement

Every employer's dream is to have employees who care as deeply for the success of the business as they would for their own company. Here are some steps to building commitment and involvement:

- **Share your vision and the mission of the business.** You undoubtedly have many goals for the business. Employees need to know exactly what they should be striving for.

- **Give some power to employees.** If you want employees to care, give them some responsibility and some decision-making latitude. Let them see that their decisions have impact.

- **Encourage risk-taking.** Let employees experiment a bit and try to find new ways to help the business reach its goals. Don't create a culture where employees are afraid to try anything new because if they fail they will be punished.

- **Build employees' self esteem** by occasionally sending them to professional development classes, trade shows, industry conventions, or other "outside" business events.

- **Plan social and athletic activities.** They allow people to interact with each other on a level that can build stronger professional bonds.

Warning

Be sure to protect yourself from workers' compensation liability by making the event completely voluntary, and during non-work hours. If you have questions about whether a particular event will expose your business to liability, consult an attorney.

Recognizing/Rewarding Employees

Workers are usually not averse to putting out an extra effort when the business needs help in overcoming a problem or meeting a production deadline. But if the extra effort goes unnoticed, employees will wonder why they bothered.

Some of the more common reasons for recognition and reward are:

- meeting sales or other productivity goals

- excellent customer service

- outstanding effort and achievement on a specific project

- length of service (usually landmark anniversaries like one, five, 10, and 20 years of service)

- retirement

- safety (more common in manufacturing businesses, this includes recognition for achieving a certain number of days without an on-the-job injury)

- attendance (six months or a year without an absence)

Typical rewards given in conjunction with employee recognition are certificates, plaques, trophies, pens or desk accessories, watches or clocks, tickets to sporting or entertainment events, cash, savings bonds, and vacation trips.

Don't give awards out every day or else they will lose their meaning. Be especially careful not to give them to everyone, but only to those people whose work really stands out.

Inexpensive Ways To Recognize Employees

Here are some other inexpensive forms of recognition suggested by Rosalind Jeffries and Kathryn Wall, professional human resources consultants:

- ***Write personal notes to employees*** *— jot down a message to one of your employees, recognizing him or her for better performance on the job, or write a thank-you note to an employee for putting in extra time in the workplace. Use your personal stationery.*

- ***Give courtesy time off*** *— grant employees an afternoon off, or even a day or two of leave for special, personal events in their lives.*

- ***Give credit when credit is due*** *— remember to give credit to those who have introduced great ideas and completed special projects.*

- ***Put up a bulletin board*** — *construct a bulletin board at your place of business to recognize employees through letters, memos, pictures, thank-you cards, and other methods.*

- ***Have a "Friday surprise"*** — *surprise your staff with donuts, candy, or some other treat on a Friday, recognizing them for working hard or just hanging in there.*

- ***Get a traveling trophy*** — *establish a trophy that goes each month to the employee exhibiting the best overall performance in the business.*

RULES FOR YOUR WORKERS

If workplace rules are carefully selected, clearly related to the business, and fairly enforced, they can help you to better manage your workplace and your workers.

Moreover, some rules are required by law, and some, while not required, are definitely a good idea to establish. Having certain work rules and policies in place may be the best way to protect your business from problems such as wrongful discharge claims and discrimination charges.

If you have a very small number of employees, you may want to avoid having any work rules other than those required by law. Having *no* work rules about a given activity will give you more freedom to handle each situation based on the individual circumstances. The circumstances of each situation will probably be sufficiently different so that discriminatory treatment or wrongful discharge will not be an issue.

At any rate, if you have work rules you must enforce them consistently. The worst possible position to be in is to have rules, but not follow them yourself.

Some Work Rules Are Required

While the federal and state governments have not handed down a list of all the work rules that you must have, there are laws that specifically require certain types of rules, and laws that implicitly require you to establish rules in your workplace to ensure that your employees comply with applicable laws.

For example, some states require employers to have a specific policy against smoking or regulating where employees can smoke. Under OSHA, you may need to have safety rules to avoid citations.

Anti-Harassment Policies

If you have 15 or more employees, you are subject to federal antidiscrimination laws, which means you have a legal obligation to provide a work environment that is free from intimidation, insult, or ridicule based on race, color, religion, gender, or national origin. Many states have similar laws that apply to smaller employers, sometimes those with as few as one employee. Often, the best way to combat harassment (and avoid liability for it) is to have a specific, written policy against it that is distributed to all your employees.

As an employer, you may be held liable for any harassment that affects employees in the workplace, including harassment by customers, suppliers, and others who regularly do business with you.

What Is Unlawful Harassment?

Harassment is verbal or physical conduct that denigrates or shows hostility or aversion toward an individual because of that person's (or that person's relatives', friends', or associates') race, skin color, religion, gender, national origin, age, or disability, and that:

- *has the purpose or effect of creating an intimidating, hostile, or offensive work environment*

- *has the purpose or effect of unreasonably interfering with the individual's work performance*

- *otherwise adversely affects the individual's employment opportunities*

Most courts use a "reasonable person" standard in deciding whether conduct is harassment; that is, the issue is not whether the particular individual found the conduct hostile or intimidating, but whether a reasonable person (and not an overly sensitive, or overly thick-skinned person) would have done so.

What is sexual harassment? Unwelcome sexual advances, requests for sexual favors, and other verbal or physical conduct of a sexual nature constitute sexual harassment, if one of the following is true:

- A person feels that submission to the conduct is necessary in order to get or keep a job.

- A person feels that employment decisions such as raises, promotions, and demotions depend on whether he or she submits to or rejects the conduct.

- The conduct interferes with a person's work performance or creates an intimidating, hostile, or offensive working environment.

Preventing and handling harassment. The best way to reduce your liability is to have policies and procedures in place that show that you did everything you could to prevent harassment from occurring. Having a policy against harassment will also help you deal more effectively with any complaints you get from employees.

In addition to federal laws prohibiting discrimination and harassment, some states have similar (and sometimes more far-reaching) laws.

State Laws on Sexual Harassment

The following states have laws regarding sexual harassment that apply to all private employers, even those with only one employee:

- Alabama
- California
- Colorado
- Delaware
- Hawaii
- Idaho
- Illinois
- Maine
- Minnesota
- New Hampshire
- New Jersey
- North Dakota
- Pennsylvania
- Vermont
- Washington
- West Virginia
- Wisconsin

In addition, Connecticut's law applies to employers with three or more employees, Massachusetts' law applies to employers with six or more, and Alaska's law applies to employers with 15 or more.

Smoking in the Workplace

In handling the issue of smoking in the workplace, take the following steps:

1. Determine if your state's laws require you to restrict smoking at work or have a smoking policy. Presently, only Arizona has no specific laws on smoking in the workplace. Check your state's law with your attorney or state department of labor.

2. Determine if you can refuse to hire or retain employees who smoke (see chart on state civil rights laws at page 266).

3. If you are required to or want to have a policy limiting smoking in the workplace, determine if you will allow smoking areas (and decide where the areas will be), or limit whether, when, and where customers can smoke.

4. Write up your policy, and communicate or post it if required. Also, post no-smoking signs where appropriate.

Drugs and Alcohol in the Workplace

You may want to consider having a written policy about drugs and alcohol in the workplace and you may be required to have one in certain instances. There are two types of policies you can have:

- One that indicates that you will not tolerate drug and alcohol abuse in the workplace, but that does not provide for drug testing. This type of policy allows you to discipline workers for possession or use of alcohol or drugs in the workplace, or for coming to work "under the influence."

- One that does provide for drug testing. In this case, you may also be required to distribute a written policy regarding when, how, and under which circumstances testing takes place.

Transportation workers. Department of Transportation regulations require that many employers engaged in commercial transportation industries must have workplace drug abuse programs. Be sure to consult your attorney to determine your obligations.

Government contractors. If you are a federal government contractor or grantee, you must comply with the Drug Free Workplace Act. Your business is covered by this law if:

- You have at least one contract with the federal government worth $25,000 or more. Subcontractors and subgrantees are not covered by the Act.

- You receive a grant from the federal government.

Warning

If you have 15 or more employees, your business may be subject to the Americans with Disabilities Act, in which case other factors may come into play in the treatment of employees with medical conditions including drug or alcohol abuse. If you have questions about such a circumstance in your business, consult your attorney about your specific situation.

Optional Work Rules To Consider

Instead of having a lengthy, involved set of work rules, we suggest you create a simple list of rules and guidelines to make it clear to employees what kind of behavior you expect. We recommend that you keep the rules as general as possible, to give yourself as much flexibility as possible in enforcing them. You can create a simple one- or two-page handout for employees, covering such things as:

- safety rules that must be observed

- absence and tardiness policy (how to report, and the number of permitted sick days and personal days off)

- how to record time worked (for example, using a time clock or time sheet)

- lunch period and break rules

- overtime policy

- telephone rules

- prohibition on use or possession of alcohol, illicit drugs, or firearms on company property

- no-smoking policy

- dress code or personal appearance rules

- no selling or soliciting on work time

- rules covering use or damage to employer's property

- rules about keeping employer's and customers' sensitive information confidential

Be sure to begin your list of rules with a statement like the following:

"It would be impractical to list all activities that are considered to be illegal or contrary to good business practices and good employee-employer relations. This is intended only as a guideline."

In general, it's not necessary to say that things like stealing, insubordination, or competing with your business are prohibited. Employees are expected to know these things, although you can create a written rule if you wish.

You may also want to explain the consequences and discipline an employee may expect for breaking the rules. However, once again we recommend that you build some flexibility into your system by including a general statement that "any employee found engaging in these behaviors will be subject to disciplinary actions including reprimand, warning, layoff, or dismissal."

AVOIDING SERIOUS WORKPLACE PROBLEMS

There are a few workplace problems that, while not exactly common, can cause serious problems for your business if and when they do arise. Here are a few tips for avoiding workplace violence, dealing with theft by employees, and preserving the confidentiality of important business information.

Violence in the Workplace

To curtail violence among employees in your business, take the following steps:

- Review your recruiting and hiring procedures — institute criminal background checks and carefully check all references and former employers.

- Check external and internal security. Use external security to prohibit uncontrolled access by outsiders throughout the company.

- Identify those members of your staff (such as yourself) who may be likely targets, and establish procedures to control access to them.

- Take every known threat seriously. Follow up and investigate.

- Prohibit the possession of all weapons, either inside the workplace or in an employee's vehicle on company property.

- Make sure all employees know how to reach your local police, ambulance, and security company if you have one.

- Attempt to develop a workplace environment that fosters trust among employees and management.

- If you need to fire an employee, do so with sensitivity, in a way that preserves the employee's dignity.

- Establish exit interview procedures that collect company keys, identification, etc., and alert you to any potential problems.

Warning Signs of a Violent Employee

In many cases, there are early warning signs of a potentially violent employee that are not communicated to the people who could take action or that are not taken seriously:

- *depressed or paranoid behavior*

- *recent acquisition of a weapon*

- *talking about or posting a clipping of a violent incident in another workplace*

Theft by Employees

Most general work rules contain a statement prohibiting theft, but some employers choose to emphasize "zero tolerance" in order to prevent stealing by employees.

Warning Signs of Theft

Detecting theft can be difficult, especially if the thief is good at what he or she does. Here are some things to watch for.

Look for unusual occurrences in the workplace such as:

- *discrepancies in cash amounts*

- *missing merchandise or supplies*

- *vehicles parked close to exits, i.e., an employee's vehicle parked in a loading area*

- *unlocked exits*

Watch the employee's behavior for:

- *unusual working hours*

- *poor work performance*

- *unjustified complaints about employment*

- *defensiveness when reporting on work*

- *an unexplained close relationship with, or unjustified favoritism by, a supplier or customer*

- *a personal lifestyle that doesn't match salary*

If you suspect an employee of theft, first contact your legal counsel so that your rights are protected. Your lawyer may suggest that you ask the employee to explain or to take a polygraph test, and help you to decide whether to press criminal charges, seek restitution, discipline the employee, or fire the employee.

Here's a list of things you should definitely *not* do:

- **Do not detain or restrain an employee.** False imprisonment is against the law, and charges can be brought against you if you force an employee to remain somewhere (e.g., your office) unwillingly. Depending on the situation and the employee you're dealing with, there may also be an element of personal danger involved in trying to detain someone.

- **Do not accuse or defame the employee.** Publicizing the fact that a person was fired because he stole six plants and some artwork from the office may not be worth the expense that a possible defamation action may cost you.

- **Do not threaten to prosecute if you are not sure that you are going to bring charges.** Keep in mind that bringing charges against someone is a money- and time-consuming process, too.

Protecting Confidential Information

If your business has spent a lot of time and effort developing its customer lists, highly specialized operating procedures, or some revolutionary technology or product and you want to protect your secrets from possible competitors, you may need some kind of policy to address the matter.

How To Protect Confidential Information

Here are some basic steps for protecting your business's information. Use only those that you feel are necessary to achieve the degree of security with which you are comfortable.

- *Define as much as possible the type of information that you are trying to protect.*

- *Explain to employees the need to protect certain types of information. Educate them on the kind of situations in which they might unwittingly reveal confidential information.*

- *Explain the penalties for violating the company's policy.*

- *Make employees sign a confidentiality policy and/or a noncompete agreement when they are hired.*

- *Remind employees that work product belongs to the business, not to individual employees.*

- *Set up procedures for identifying and safeguarding company proprietary information (for example, establish passwords for computers, or keep certain files locked).*

- *Be prepared to prosecute the theft of secrets.*

A noncompete agreement is either a separate agreement or a clause in an employment contract that prohibits an employee from working in a related business in your area for a certain length of time. The idea is to prevent an employee from using your business's confidential information against you.

Most courts will insist that a noncompete agreement be reasonably limited in geographic scope and duration, or they won't enforce it.

To improve the chances that your noncompete clause or agreement will be enforceable in your state, have your agreement drafted by your attorney.

ENFORCING THE RULES

In most small businesses, most enforcement of rules is done rather casually. When you're working closely with someone on a daily basis, it's usually best to talk to them about any behavior that is inappropriate, without waiting until the problem gets so bad that you need to issue a formal warning. Sometimes employees are unaware of what they've been doing and what you expect of them, and a few words will be enough to set them on the right track.

Sadly, open and frequent communication doesn't always do the trick. In fact, if you have more than one or two workers, it's almost certain that at some point you will have to discipline an employee for something, but don't wait until then to set up a program. Employees need to know the consequences of bad behavior or poor performance before it happens.

Progressive Discipline Systems

"Progressive discipline" is a system where the severity of the penalty increases each time an employee breaks the rules. Typically the progression is from oral warnings to written warnings to suspension and, finally, to termination.

Usually, after a specified time period passes without another infraction, the worker gets a "clean slate." Later infractions will start the process again with an oral warning.

Some cases of misconduct are so severe that you may skip the first one, two, or even three steps. For example, assaults or fighting, stealing, intoxication on the job, gross insubordination, destruction of company property, etc., may all justify immediate action. But *don't fire the worker on the spot!* Sometimes situations are not as they appear. Give yourself some time to investigate and to be sure of what really happened and who was responsible.

For very small businesses, progressive discipline may be too time-consuming to use, especially if discipline problems are rare. Or, you may decide to use it only for the most common rule infractions, such as unexcused absences or tardiness.

In creating your progressive discipline policy, follow these guidelines:

- Tailor the progressive discipline system to your business.

- Specify the types of conduct that are not subject to progressive discipline (usually these will be serious behaviors that warrant immediate termination).

- Decide what your progressive discipline steps are.

- Decide how you will maintain documentation (i.e., memos about oral warnings, written warnings, etc.), and how long the documents will remain in an employee's file.

Performance Review Systems

While progressive discipline is designed to address the problem of employees who break work rules, it is not very effective when dealing with an employee who doesn't violate any rules, but is incompetent or is not performing work to an acceptable level.

For example, you may have a worker who can't seem to get much done or who keeps making mistakes that cost you a lot of money. Assuming that any new-hire probation period has passed, you can resolve this problem by establishing periodic performance reviews.

The easiest way to do this is to take some time every year or so to meet with each employee and evaluate his or her work. During the meeting you should go over your expectations for the job the employee holds, and discuss how he or she is meeting these goals. If the employee is not meeting expectations, you should make clear exactly what must be done to correct the performance, and give a time limit for improvement. If the employee needs further instruction or job training, explain how this can be achieved. Finally, write a memo for the employee's file describing your conversation, and have the employee sign and date it.

If sufficient improvement does not occur after a few negative reviews, at least you'll have proof that you tried to be fair. Only you can decide how many chances to improve you'll allow before dismissing the person, but you should consider factors such as the employee's length of service, past good reviews, and the seriousness of the employee's mistakes.

Work Smart

You should be aware that performance reviews can be a two-edged sword. A fired worker can use good appraisals as proof that he or she was not fired for incompetence, but for some reason such as racial, age, or gender discrimination. One of the worst positions you can be in is to fire an employee for poor performance, but have five years of appraisals that rate the employee as a good worker.

Handling Employees' Complaints

Some common strategies for handling complaints about the behavior of workers are an open door policy, or periodic employee meetings.

With an open door policy, you make it known to employees that when they have a problem or complaint, they are free to come to you with it. This is a good approach if you have a relatively small number of employees and a reasonably happy workforce.

If your employees work as a team or if work requires periodic meetings anyway, you may want to allot some time during your meeting for complaints or problems that employees can share. This approach allows you to address an issue only once instead of individually.

Tips on Dealing with Complaints

- *Make sure that you understand the problem. Allow the employee to talk without interruption, and then ask questions until you have a clear understanding of the facts.*

- *Ask the employee what he or she would like to see in the way of a resolution. If the employee wants another employee fired over a minor problem, there may be more to the employee's anger than meets the eye.*

- *Establish a record by taking notes. This will also assure the employee that you are taking the matter seriously. You may want to have the employee write down the complaint, as well.*

- *Don't make a decision until you have obtained all the facts. If you must talk to others, explain that to the employee. Also explain that you cannot act on a complaint until you have the other party's side of the story. It's better to postpone a decision than to make one that you would regret or reverse later.*

- *Check to see if any of the business's other policies (if there are any) address the problem. Have there been other similar cases? How were they handled in the past?*

- *Advise the employee of the decision as soon as possible.*

- *If the employee's complaint is without merit, explain it to the employee in a pleasant, low-key manner. If the complaint is sound, thank the employee for calling it to your attention so that you can resolve it.*

- *Follow through with corrective action as soon as possible. Delay may result in other problems.*

- *Check back with the employee after taking action in order to determine if the issue has been completely resolved to his or her satisfaction.*

Conducting an Investigation

If you witness some improper behavior or if one of your employees or customers complains of inappropriate behavior on the part of one of your employees, you'll need to check it out.

- Thank the person who brought the problem to your attention (you want to encourage people to speak up and be open about these matters with you).

- Ask them, in private, to describe exactly what they witnessed. Ask for specifics. Get details. Do not assume anything.

- Identify and interview all possible witnesses.

- Review every relevant file and document.

- Visit the place where the incident occurred, if necessary.

- Ask open-ended questions that don't require witnesses to confirm or deny your stated or implicit conclusions.

- Keep confidences and conduct the investigation in private.

- Maintain your objectivity.

- Take good notes for documentation purposes. Ask witnesses to give you a written statement, if the situation warrants one.

- Be sure to follow up with the complaining person when the situation has been addressed (don't divulge anything about the disciplinary action — you must protect the confidentiality of the disciplined employee, too).

Advanced Investigation Methods

When a normal investigation, including interviews and statements from employees and other individuals, does not seem to be giving you the information you want, you may consider some alternative information-gathering methods.

Searches. Whether a workplace search is legal or not depends in part on the reasonableness of the employee's expectation of privacy and the reasonableness of the employer's actions. If you are in doubt about whether you should do a search, consult an attorney.

If you do conduct a search of employee's desks, lockers, or other "personal space," there are a few things to do beforehand:

- Issue a broad policy statement saying that you will conduct unannounced and unapparent surveillance or searches.

- Have all employees acknowledge your policy, preferably with a signed statement.

- When you do conduct surveillance or searches, do so only when you have an important business purpose.

Workplace surveillance. Workplace surveillance might include the installation of cameras in your office, production facility, or showroom floor. Regardless of what you are monitoring, surveillance should not extend to the restroom or lounge areas of the workplace. Once an employee leaves the workplace, surveillance should end.

Telephone monitoring. It is best to monitor only those telephone lines that, *with the employee's knowledge,* are dedicated exclusively to business use. Monitoring should stop as soon as any particular call has been identified as personal in nature.

Electronic mail monitoring. Your right to monitor employee's E-mail is somewhat controversial. If you think you may need to monitor it, be sure that you let your employees know that anything on business computers, including E-mail, is considered the property of the company.

Polygraph testing. Generally, you cannot use polygraph testing to screen prospective employees or current employees. There are exceptions permitting polygraph testing of current employees under the following circumstances:

- if there are national defense or security reasons

- if the employees have direct access to controlled substances in the course of employment

- if the employees are security guards

- if there is an ongoing theft investigation or other similar situations

There are numerous guidelines to follow under the federal Employee Polygraph Protection Act. Consult your attorney before you order a test.

Dealing with Problem Employees

After you've investigated a problem or complaint, you may find that some action is necessary.

Coaching the employee is the preferable course of action for a minor offense, a first-time, nonserious offense, or a work performance problem. A coaching session might include the following steps:

- Express the performance standards for the job and review past performance of the employee. Explain why it is important to the business for the employee to perform well.

- Describe the areas of performance that the employee must improve. Describe what good performance looks like, providing concrete examples of good work, if possible.

- Discuss possible solutions. Have the employee develop steps to solve the problem to create a sense of ownership in the solution. Suspend the session if the employee needs more time to develop a plan. If the employee cannot develop a plan, develop one for the employee.

- Agree to a written action plan containing specific goals and timetables for meeting those goals.

- Have the employee orally commit to the action plan and provide the employee with a copy. Retain another copy as documentation of the meeting.

- Follow up on the goals stated in the action plan. Offer ideas for improvement, and praise any improvement that occurs.

Coaching to improve poor performance is often the first step of the progressive discipline process. If the employee does not improve, you may be required to take more severe discipline steps, such as a formal oral or written warning, or even a suspension. You can use the following steps as a guide to imposing a penalty for breaking a rule:

- Inform the employee that he or she has engaged in specific conduct that is unacceptable. Refer to the rule or policy.

- Discuss the penalty you are imposing and the negative consequences that will occur if the employee fails to change unacceptable behavior.

- Develop an action plan that you and the employee agree on to change the unacceptable behavior.

- Document the disciplinary process.

Documenting Disciplinary Actions

Whether you are coaching an employee for a performance problem or disciplining an employee for improper conduct, you must document your reasons for discipline, any fact-finding that you do, and the actions that you take. These records can help you to defend yourself in case a lawsuit is filed as a result of your actions.

Here's an example of a form you can use to document disciplinary actions.

Discipline Documentation Form

Employee Information

Name of Employee:_____

Employee's Job Title: _____

Incident Information

Date/Time of Incident:_____

Location of Incident:_____

Description of Incident:_____

_____

_____

_____

Witnesses to Incident:_____

Was this incident in violation of a company policy?   Yes   No

If yes, specify which policy and how the incident violated it. _____

_____

_____

Action Taken

What action will be taken against the employee?_____

_____

_____

Has the impropriety of the employee's actions been explained to the employee?   Yes   No

Did the employee offer any explanation for the conduct? If so, what was it? _____

_____

_____

Employee's signature:_____Date:_____

Employer's signature: _____Date:_____

Other documentation. You can also consider having witnesses (if applicable) provide you with a written statement. Witnesses can be fellow workers, customers, or bystanders. Getting as much information from as many different perspectives as possible can help you make the best decision about disciplinary action. Documenting that information can help you defend that action.

Get the employee's signature. If the employee disagrees with the action, allow the employee to record his or her disagreement on the form.

If the employee refuses to sign the document, you at least have proof that the employee refused to participate in the process should the employee later challenge your actions. Write a notation on the document that the employee refused to sign.

Chapter **21**

Firing and Termination

As careful as you may be to select the best employees available and to manage them well, it's likely that, at some point, you'll have to fire somebody. Making this difficult job worse are the facts that there is a growing body of law that limits your right to fire workers, and that more and more workers seem to be filing (and winning) lawsuits against their former employers.

Fortunately, there are a number of steps you can take to limit your risks in this area. In this chapter, we'll explain how you can minimize problems by "firing right."

LEGAL RESTRICTIONS ON FIRING

In all states other than Montana, working relationships are governed by the "employment-at-will" doctrine. "Employment-at-will" means that there's a presumption that the worker is employed for an indefinite period, not a fixed term.

Traditionally, both the employer and the employee have had the ability to end an at-will relationship at any time and for any reason. However, at least from the employer's perspective, the unlimited freedom to fire at-will employees at any time for good cause, bad cause, or no cause at all has been eroded in recent years by the legal system.

Firing Restrictions in Written Laws

What's one of the easiest ways to find yourself defending a wrongful discharge lawsuit? Fire an employee in a way that violates a fair employment law. Numerous federal, state, and even local laws prohibit the firing of an employee for discriminatory or retaliatory reasons. For more information on these laws, see Chapter 18.

Warning

Many fair employment laws provide exemptions for employers having some minimum number of employees. However, merely because you qualify for a law's exemption does not mean that you're free to fire those employees whom the law was designed to protect without any risk of being sued. *Courts can, effectively, extend the law to you under the "public policy" theory. They may rule that the fact that a law protecting a certain class of employees was adopted indicates that there is a public policy in favor of that protection.*

Implied Employment Contracts

If you and an employee enter into a formal agreement that defines the terms of the employment relationship, you have an "express" employment contract.

In contrast, an "implied" employment contract is not an agreement that you knowingly enter. Rather, an implied employment contract arises when a court finds that you effectively made some promise that was broken when the employee was fired. In other words, the court "implies" that there was a contract, even though you may not have intended it to exist.

Written statements are particularly troublesome, so you should review job application forms, employee handbooks, and any other documents that you may distribute to your employees. Look for any statement that may restrict your right to fire your employees and decide if you really want to live with that restriction. If not, delete the statement.

Example

Examples of statements that may be found to constitute an implied contract:

"Upon completing a six-month probationary period, an employee can expect to be employed as long as his or her work is performed satisfactorily."

"An employee will be dismissed following a third warning that the employee has failed to meet performance standards or has violated company policy."

Your spoken words can also get you into trouble. Although you need to watch your words at all times, you need to be especially careful during job interviews and performance reviews when statements about an employee's future with your business tend to come up.

Bad Faith Limitations on Firing

Let's assume an employer fires an employee who is about to close a sale that will entitle her to a substantial commission. Assume also that the firing violates no federal or state statute, public policy, or provision of an express or implied employment contract. Can the fired employee successfully sue for wrongful discharge?

Courts in a number of states (Alaska, Arizona, California, Connecticut, Delaware, Idaho, Kansas, Massachusetts, Nevada, Utah, and Wyoming) have ruled that employers are generally obligated to deal fairly and in good faith with their employees.

So far, however, the courts that have acknowledged a bad faith limitation on firings have done so where the discharge deprived employees of compensation or benefits that had already been earned.

When Is It Improper Not To Fire?

Not only can employers be sued for improperly firing employees, they also can be sued for failing to fire employees. This problem arises when an employer becomes aware or should have become aware that an employee may cause harm to others, yet doesn't take any action to prevent the employee from causing harm.

If the employee should later injure another employee, a customer, or other person, the injured party may sue the employer for being negligent in retaining the dangerous employee. Clearly, you need to screen people carefully before you hire them to find out if they have a past history of violence or erratic behavior. You also have a continuing obligation to be aware of your employee's activities, to be sure they don't become dangerous on your watch.

Example

A laundromat employee with a known history of drug use, extreme violence, and sexual offenses assaulted a female customer. The employer was liable for negligent retention because it was reasonable for the employer to know that a customer using the laundromat at night might be in danger in the presence of an employee with such a history.

Investigate thoroughly any complaints of employee misconduct. In some situations, you may be able to effectively deal with the problem through training or by changing the employee's responsibilities. In others, however, your safest recourse may be to fire the employee.

This is especially true with respect to employees who threaten or harass others.

USING PROPER TERMINATION PROCEDURES

There are a number of steps you need to take before you fire somebody for breaking a work rule or any other type of misconduct, or for simply performing poorly on the job. These steps include documenting the problem, using fair rules and procedures, and investigating the "last straw" incident thoroughly.

The safest way to fire someone, from a legal standpoint, is to be sure that you have a valid, nondiscriminatory business reason for the action, and that you have enough documentation to prove it. Your documentation must be created in the normal course of business, *before* you fire the worker.

Warning

Don't get caught trying to reconstruct documentation (such as warnings or poor performance reviews) after the fact, when you should have been creating them all along. Also, the documentation process should not be used to "build a case" against one worker when other workers in similar situations did not have their actions documented. Selective documentation may be proof that a person was the victim of discrimination.

Before an Economic Layoff

When economic reasons demand that you eliminate an employee's job, either temporarily or permanently, few courts will question your judgment. But if you decide to lay off some but not all of your workers, you must be sure that your *selection process* does not discriminate on the basis of age, sex, or race, or violate some other public policy.

In most small businesses, if it becomes necessary to lay anyone off, the decision will be based on the desire to keep the business going. Obviously, those whose jobs are most essential to the business will be kept, and those whose jobs are least essential (or whose tasks can be taken over by a remaining worker or the owner) will be let go. In some cases, workers who are family members or close friends of the owner will be kept, while "outsiders" will be let go. Neither of these two strategies is likely to cause legal problems provided that your business is small enough to escape coverage by the civil rights laws.

Laying people off in order of seniority (that is, keeping the people with the greatest length of service) is most likely to be seen as fair by your employees. It's also the easiest to defend in court. Generally, if you use this method, you won't have to provide any other evidence as to why certain workers were chosen for layoff.

Given the choice, however, most employers would prefer to keep their best workers and lay off those who are less productive, regardless of seniority. If you have done regular performance reviews you can eliminate the positions of those employees whose performance has been documented as least satisfactory. If there is no documentation, you cannot eliminate that person's position for purely merit reasons without facing possible liability.

Also, if you are choosing between two or more equally qualified candidates for layoff, you should be prepared to show that the "downsized" workers reflect the demographic mix (race, gender, and age) of your workforce as much as possible.

What If You Fire Someone on the Spot?

First of all, we recommend that you make a personal commitment that you will *never* fire an employee on the spot.

Employees who are fired in the heat of anger or frustration are the most likely to sue you or to cause other trouble for you and your business. If you feel that you must take immediate action, tell the worker that he or she is suspended, effective immediately, while you investigate the incident (or just cool down).

If you do fire someone impetuously, go through the worker's file to see if you have enough documentation of previous violations or poor performance reviews to justify your action.

If you have little or no documentation of any previous problems, the safest course of action would be to call the worker, say that you acted too quickly, and offer to reinstate him or her. If the worker refuses, you have just transformed the firing into a voluntary quit, so your possible liability has decreased dramatically.

If you don't want to take the worker back, you have a choice. You can sit tight and hope the whole thing blows over, or you can try to work out a deal with your ex-employee: you can agree to provide some severance benefits to the worker, in exchange for a signed release form that waives his or her right to sue you.

Releases and Severance Agreements

To avoid the threat of legal actions against you, you can negotiate a severance agreement with the employee. As part of the agreement, the worker will sign a release stating that he or she gives up some or all rights to sue you.

Although employee releases have many uses, they are most often used when you lack proper documentation to fire, but you want to safely cut off an employment relationship.

To be effective, the release must be a knowing and voluntary waiver, in writing, that is signed by the employee.

Like all contracts, in order to be valid, a waiver must be supported by "adequate consideration." That means you must give the worker something of value in exchange for the waiver beyond what you are required to do by law.

Courts tend to like to see some dollars changing hands, so you might consider offering a lump-sum payment of at least two weeks' pay. However, you can also offer terms like an agreement not to contest payment of unemployment benefits, or an agreement that you will provide a satisfactory job reference if requested by any prospective employers. These things take little or nothing from your bank account, but can be very valuable to the worker.

Work Smart

Here are a few tips to increase the chances that your release will be "iron-clad" if challenged in court:

- *Allow the employee time to think about signing it. The more time the employee has, the more likely that a court will not believe that the employee was forced to sign the release.*

- *Encourage the employee to review the document with an attorney of his or her choice before signing it.*

- *Allow the employee a period of several days to change his or her mind after the release is signed.*

- *Allow the employee to negotiate the terms and conditions of the release (for example, let him or her substitute different benefits for the ones you offered). That way, a court will be more likely to believe that the document was signed willingly.*

If the federal Age Discrimination in Employment Act applies to you (generally, if you have 20 or more employees during 20 or more weeks in the year) and if the worker is more than 40 years old, there are special rules that apply to the release. Be sure to ask your lawyer about these requirements if you find yourself in this situation.

Following is a sample of a release form to be used when an employee leaves your company.

General Release for Employment Termination

Notice: Various state and federal laws prohibit employment discrimination based on age, sex, race, color, national origin, religion, handicap, or veteran status. These laws are enforced through the Equal Employment Opportunity Commission, Department of Labor, and state human rights agencies. If you feel that your election of [Your Business]'s severance package was coerced and is discriminatory, you are encouraged to speak with [designated person] at your earliest convenience. You may also want to discuss the release below with an attorney.

In any event, you should thoroughly review and understand the effect of the release before acting on it. Therefore, please take this release home and consider it for at least [pick a number — we recommend at least 21] days before you decide to sign it. If you do sign this release, you will have seven days after signing to reconsider your decision and to rescind your acceptance of the offer if you so desire. [Note: the preceding sentence is required only in the case of workers over 40.]

This release, unless signed by both parties, will expire as of [pick a date that coincides with the number of "consideration days" you chose in paragraph two, above].

General Release

As consideration for the following: [list here the severance pay, extended benefits, or other valuable items you are agreeing to provide] offered to me by [Your Business], I release and discharge [Your Business], its successors, subsidiaries, employees, officers, and directors (hereinafter referred to as "the Company") for all claims, liabilities, demands, and causes of action known or unknown, fixed or contingent, which I may have or claim to have against the Company as a result of this termination and do hereby agree not to file a lawsuit to assert such claims.

This includes but is not limited to claims arising under the Age Discrimination in Employment Act or other federal, state, or local laws prohibiting employment discrimination or claims growing out of any legal restrictions on the Company's right to terminate its employees.

This release does not have any effect on any claim I may have against the Company unrelated to this termination.

I have carefully read and fully understand all of the provisions of this agreement and release, which sets forth the entire agreement between me and the Company, and I acknowledge that I have not relied on any representation or statement, written or oral, not set forth in this document.

Signed:_____   Date:_____

(employee)

Signed:_____   Date:_____

(for the Company)

CONDUCTING A TERMINATION MEETING

We can't say it strongly enough: when firing a worker, you should make every possible attempt to maintain the employee's dignity. Everything you do in a termination meeting should be designed to minimize, as much as possible, the natural resentment the employee is bound to feel towards you and your business.

We say that not so much out of concern for the worker who is being discharged, but for your own self-protection. Most lawsuits in this area are filed because of the employee's feelings, not because the facts of the case are particularly strong. If you can soften the blow to the person's ego, or at least keep from making it worse, your odds of being sued go down dramatically.

Finally, there have been times when fired employees become so distraught that they threaten to harm (or actually do harm) their former boss, coworkers, or the business. Treating workers as humanely as possible will minimize the chance that this might happen to you.

Setting Up the Termination Meeting

Any firing or layoff should be done face-to-face, never by letter or over the phone. In most cases the immediate supervisor of the worker should be the one who handles the meeting, because he or she is usually most familiar with the reasons for the discharge. Also, the supervisor will usually be most familiar with the worker's personality and most able to handle him or her in the face of bad news.

Besides the supervisor and the worker who's being fired, there are situations where you may want to have a third party attend the meeting (i.e., if trouble is expected or if an objective third person is needed). If the person being terminated requests a witness, it's probably best that you allow this, so that the worker doesn't feel that he or she is being railroaded out the door unfairly. But do explain that the person is there as an observer only, not to act as a representative or argue on behalf of the worker.

Where and When To Conduct the Meeting

You'll want to conduct the meeting out of sight and earshot of any other employees, in a quiet place where you won't be interrupted. Try not to alert other employees as to what is taking place.

Privacy may be difficult to find in a small business and especially if you work out of your home, so consider holding the meeting in a nearby restaurant. Holding the meeting in a quiet public place has other advantages: it may be easier to avoid emotional outbursts on anyone's part, and it will be easy for you to end the meeting by getting up and walking away (after picking up the tab, of course).

Avoid conducting the meeting on a Friday or the day before a holiday or vacation. An employee who is let go on a Friday has two days to brood about his or her treatment by the company and to look for ways to retaliate. On the other hand, discharging a person early in the week provides him or her with an opportunity to focus on the future and begin looking for a new job right away.

For similar reasons, the discharge should be conducted early in the day. People are fresher, more rested and better equipped to deal with adversity and stress earlier in the day.

What To Do at a Termination Meeting

The actual termination meeting should last 10 to 15 minutes and have the sole purpose of providing a simple and concise statement of the decision to terminate the employment relationship.

Prepare what you will say ahead of time. It's a good idea to write some notes out, or have a checklist in front of you so that you don't get sidetracked and forget any important points.

Give an adequate reason for the discharge. Many workers who sue their ex-employers do so because, at heart, what they really want is a full explanation of why they were let go, and a chance to give their side of the story.

Seek out the employee's explanation or interpretation of events. If the employee feels that he or she was forced out because of discrimination, harassment, or some other allegedly offensive or illegal conduct on your part, you'll want to know about it now so that you can alert your attorney.

Make it clear that the decision is final. If you take the position that the decision has already been made, all alternatives have been considered, and any other managers or owners are in agreement, and that you are merely giving this information to the worker, you'll find it easier to keep your cool and keep control of the situation.

Briefly run through the benefits. Briefly cover the vacation pay, separation pay, continuation of health insurance or life insurance benefits, etc., that you are offering. If you are attempting to get a release from the employee, now's the time to present it. It's a good idea to have the employee's final paycheck ready so that he or she has something positive to carry away from the meeting.

Explain your job reference policy. If it is your policy to provide only job title, dates of employment, and salary history, now is the time to say so. In some states you may be required to provide a service letter on request (see "Providing Employment References" below). You may be willing to provide a satisfactory job reference, if the employee is willing to sign a release form.

Collect what's yours from the employee. You'll need to collect any keys, beepers, company car, company credit cards, important files, work in progress, or property belonging to a customer that the employee has in his or her possession. Make it clear that the payment of any severance pay depends on cooperation in this area.

Handling Voluntary Resignations

You can't, of course, stop people from quitting on you. But you can, if you want:

- **Request advance notice** — ask employees who resign to give you some warning ahead of time.

- **Request an exit interview** — ask the employee to fill out a form or participate in an exit interview.

Of course, you can't force a departing employee to follow your procedures. However, you can suggest that if he or she does, that will allow you to give a good job reference and tell any prospective employers that the worker was responsible and cooperative.

Handling Prompted Resignations

A "prompted resignation" is a resignation that appears to be voluntary on the surface. However, the idea or motivation for the employee to resign came from somebody else, like the person's boss.

In general, it's better for you if the employee resigns. An employee who wants a job reference that says he or she resigned, rather than a reference that shows he or she was fired, is less likely to sue you. However, it's always possible that the worker could change his or her mind and story sometime in the future, so be sure you document the situation carefully.

In some cases, workers resign because they believe they are being forced out, harassed, or treated unfairly for unlawful reasons. It's important to uncover these situations in advance, so that you can begin to prepare a defense if a lawsuit is ultimately filed. For that reason, it's advisable that you conduct an exit interview and/or have the worker fill out an exit questionnaire whenever someone leaves your employ.

On the next page is a sample exit interview questionnaire.

Employee Exit Interview Form

TO: _____

FROM: _____

I would appreciate it if you would take a few minutes to respond to the questions below. All answers will be held in strict confidence. Thank you.

How long were you employed? _____

Job classification? _____

Why are you leaving? _____
_____
_____
_____

Would you describe your working relationship (with respect to both your particular job and your relationship with fellow workers) as pleasant or unpleasant?_____
_____
_____
_____

Do you feel that your particular job was important and significant in the overall operation of the business? Why or why not? _____
_____
_____

Are there any particular practices or working conditions that either led to your decision to resign or that you feel are detrimental to a satisfactory working relationship? If so, have you any suggestions on how to eliminate them?_____
_____
_____
_____

Are there any particular practices or working conditions that you feel are particularly beneficial to an effective working relationship and that should be maintained?_____
_____
_____
_____

Would you care to make any other comments?_____
_____
_____

Signed: _____   Date: _____

PAYING TERMINATED EMPLOYEES

When employment terminates, there are certain things you'll have to take care of, including issuing the employee's last paycheck. If possible, it's best to give the check to the employee on the last day of employment. Some state laws require that you get the last paycheck out within a certain number of days, or even by the end of the next business day.

Benefits for Terminated Workers

Under federal and state laws, employers have certain legal obligations to the employees they fire with respect to continuing health coverage (see page 309), unemployment insurance benefits, and vested retirement benefits. Apart from those benefits, the law generally does not require employers to provide severance payments or other benefits to the employees they fire. However, you may agree to provide such payments or benefits as a matter of company policy or pursuant to a negotiated separation agreement with a fired employee.

Fired employees remain eligible to receive any pension or profit-sharing benefits with respect to which they have vested under the terms of the plan.

Warning

Federal law prevents an employer from firing an employee solely to prevent the employee from qualifying to receive benefits under most pension, benefit, and deferred compensation plans.

Employers must notify each fired employee of the employee's possible eligibility for unemployment insurance benefits. An employer who fails to provide this notice runs the risk of being sued if the employee is eligible but fails to timely file a claim. In most states, an employer can avoid this obligation by posting state-supplied information about unemployment benefits at a place where employees are likely to see the information.

DEFENDING UNEMPLOYMENT CLAIMS

There are two main reasons why you should try to prevent an improper unemployment benefits claim from being paid.

1. You'll want to keep your tax rates as low as possible. Your state unemployment tax rate is directly affected by the number of your ex-employees who collected unemployment after leaving your business.

2. A disgruntled worker's first contact with the legal system is usually in the unemployment setting. If you win in this arena, you're more likely to win in any later suit for wrongful termination, where the stakes may be much higher. On the other hand, if you lose in the unemployment matter, you may decide that the facts are not in your favor and that you should settle with the worker rather than going to trial in the other lawsuit.

How the Unemployment System Works

The benefits paid to jobless workers are financed through federal and state payroll taxes paid by employers. If you fire or lay off workers only when absolutely necessary, use the proper procedures to do it, and routinely contest unemployment benefit claims when you think the worker is ineligible, you can lower your state unemployment tax rate. In some states, you can lower your rate to zero, and pay no unemployment taxes at all! If you don't pay attention to these things, you may find your taxes rising to 10 percent of payroll or more.

Unemployment Benefits Eligibility

To be eligible for unemployment benefits, a person must have at least some minimum amount of work experience within the last one and one-half years before filing for benefits.

Your local unemployment office should be able to tell you what the minimum is in your state. You should think about setting up a probationary period for new hires that is less than the minimum time that would qualify a worker for benefits.

Work Smart

In most states, time spent and money earned in self-employment does not count toward these minimums. If you decide to pack up your business, you probably won't be able to get unemployment benefits.

There are a few other eligibility requirements. If you suspect your ex-employee doesn't meet them, consider contesting the benefits.

- The worker must be truly unemployed (i.e., not self-employed or holding down a lucrative part-time job).

- In most areas the unemployment office also helps jobless workers find a new position, and the worker must cooperate with the office.

- The worker must be ready, willing, and able to work.

Disqualification Factors

Those who are eligible for benefits because they've worked and earned the minimum amount required in their state, and because they are available to work, can still be disqualified from receiving benefits depending on how and why they lost their jobs. Generally, unemployment benefits are designed for people who are laid off because the employer doesn't have enough work for them, or who lose their jobs because of something the employer did wrong.

Disqualification Factors for Unemployment Benefits

A worker will be disqualified for unemployment benefits if:

- *The worker turned down a "suitable" job offer during the period of unemployment.*

- *The worker was fired for misconduct (poor performance is not considered misconduct).*

- *The worker left the job voluntarily, without a good cause connected to the job.*

- *The worker is unemployed because of a strike or labor dispute.*

- *The worker is receiving workers' compensation payments, social security payments, a private pension, or severance pay.*

- *The worker has lied on the benefit claim or has omitted some important information, in order to get or increase benefits.*

When To Defend Unemployment Claims

There's no point in wasting your time and possibly running up legal bills by contesting the payment of benefits to a worker who clearly deserves them. So, if you lay someone off for economic reasons, or if you fired someone because you want to hire your brother instead, don't bother to object when your ex-employee makes a claim.

On the other hand, if you have to fire someone for stealing or someone quits to start their own business, you can and should make an effort to prevent your tax rate from rising as a result.

What do you do if it's a gray area, and you're not sure whether the worker deserves benefits or not? Go ahead and contest the claim as discussed below, up to the point where you'd need to hire a lawyer. At that point, if the worker has won, you may want to reevaluate whether the issue is worth pursuing. Your lawyer should be able to tell you whether your chances of winning are good, or slim to none.

When not to contest a claim. There may be times when it's not in your interest to prevent your worker from collecting benefits, even if you would probably win if you tried.

The most common situation is where you want to get rid of someone but don't have a good (or a legal) reason for doing it, or you suspect the worker is going to sue you. You may be able to "buy out" the worker by offering a severance package, which may include your promise not to contest unemployment benefits.

How To Defend Unemployment Claims

When one of your former employees files for benefits, you'll get an official report form in the mail from the state unemployment agency. Fill it out and return it within the deadline stated on the form! These deadlines are rarely extended, even if you have a good excuse. If you don't respond, or respond too late, the worker will automatically get benefits in most states.

Work Smart

If you are away from work for an extended time, be sure you have authorized someone responsible to check your mail — if no coworker is available, a friend, family member, or even someone from your lawyer's office may agree to perform this service for you. The person should be told to open up any official-looking letters from the IRS, from the state unemployment agency or any other government office, or from any law office.

Typically, the report will ask how long the employee worked for you, what his or her earnings were, whether the worker quit voluntarily or was dismissed, and what the facts surrounding the termination were. Don't give just a one-word explanation — but don't write a whole novel either! A few sentences should do it.

Example

For a discharge for excessive absences, you might say, "John was absent from work without notice six times within two months. He received oral warnings after the first two absences, and written warnings after the second two. After the fifth absence he was warned in writing that another such absence would lead to being fired. On Feb. 21 he failed to return to work following a scheduled vacation and was dismissed."

If you later learn of facts that would disqualify the claimant for benefits (for example, he or she turned down a job offer or went on a long vacation without looking for work), report these facts to the state unemployment agency.

Go to the Hearing

You should attend any hearings, formal or informal, before the state unemployment insurance officials. This is the only effective way to present your side and to respond to any false or incomplete statements your ex-employee might make. The "burden of proof" is on the employer — that means it's up to you to prove your statements, by testifying or presenting documents. The supervisor who actually witnessed the misconduct or other action that led to the termination should be present to testify.

It's a good idea to have an attorney represent you at any hearing, especially the first time you are involved in an unemployment case. Attorney representation becomes a virtual necessity if you lose at the hearing level and decide to appeal to the court.

If You Lose, File an Appeal

If the employee is found eligible for benefits despite your objections, follow up with an appeal to the administrative agency, and (if you lose again) to the courts — unless, of course, your lawyer tells you this would be fruitless in your particular case.

Even though a successful unemployment claim may raise your tax rates, don't let the fear of a rate increase keep you from firing an employee who is truly dragging your business down. One bad apple can destroy the morale of an entire office.

PROVIDING EMPLOYMENT REFERENCES

If you've had employees who left your business, you can expect prospective employers to contact you at some point for information about them. Currently, six states have laws that *require* a private employer to provide some information about the employee's work history, upon the employee's request. The states are Indiana, Kansas, Minnesota, Missouri, Montana, and Nevada.

Before you or anyone else in your business responds to an employment reference request, you must realize that certain types of statements about former employees may form the basis for lawsuits against you. Your primary risk is that the former employees may claim that your statements are false and damaging to their reputations and sue you for defamation.

Warning

There is one situation when you may have a legal obligation to provide information about a former employee to a prospective employer.

Assume that you know that a former employee has a history of criminal violence or extremely aggressive behavior. Another employer approaches you for a reference in connection with a job that would have your former employee working closely with members of the public. Must you disclose what you know about the employee's past conduct?

Your risk in remaining silent is that you could be sued for negligently failing to disclose the information if the former employee were to subsequently harm someone while on the job. On the other hand, you could be sued for defamation if you do disclose the information and it turns out not to be true. Faced with this type of situation, you should consult an attorney to determine what, if anything, you may be obligated to disclose.

Employment References and Defamation

The claim that former employees are most likely to assert is that the reference you gave was false and damaging to their reputations and, therefore, defamatory.

Because employment references play an important role in hiring decisions, *the law usually protects an employer who in good faith discloses information that the employer believes is true to a prospective employer* or other person who has a legitimate interest in receiving the information. This protection may be lost, however, if the information is not limited in scope to the inquiry being made, is disclosed at an improper time, or is disclosed in an improper manner.

Guidelines for Giving Employment References

- ***Be truthful*** — *if your statements are true, they are not defamatory. Give objective facts or opinions and conclusions that you can support with objective facts, rather than mere allegations, speculation, or gossip.*

- ***Be clear and unambiguous*** — *keep in mind that statements that are technically true may still be defamatory if they are incomplete or misleading.*

- ***Stick to job-related facts*** — *do not provide any information that is irrelevant to the employee's performance or behavior in the workplace. Comments about an employee's personal life are especially hazardous, because even if the comments are true, they may raise invasion of privacy issues.*

- ***Be selective in choosing your audience*** — *a statement that is not defamatory when made to a prospective employer may be defamatory if it is made to friends, spouses, employees, or others who have no business reason to know the information.*

- ***Limit telephone references*** —*at a minimum you should arrange to provide the information in a return call. This will give you an opportunity to verify who the caller is.*

- ***Get signed releases or consents*** — *your best protection against defamation and other claims that may arise from giving employment references is to get the former employee to consent to your release of information.*

Using Job Reference Releases

Your best protection against reference-related lawsuits is to get the employee's permission to disclose information in advance. You can save yourself a lot of potential future headaches if you make it a practice to discuss with an employee who is leaving your business, either voluntarily or involuntarily, what you are willing to say in response to employment reference inquiries. You should then document the employee's consent by having the employee sign a written release authorizing your disclosure.

To ensure that any release you obtain will stand up in court, you want to avoid any signs that you forced the former employee to sign the release. Don't try to rush the employee into signing the document. A signed release will serve its purpose as long as you get it back before you provide the reference.

You should also consider adopting a policy of providing detailed references for former employees who have signed written releases, and restricted references of only basic employment data for former employees who have not signed releases. This type of flexible policy will help show that the employee had a real choice in deciding whether or not to sign the release.

A sample release form that you can use follows.

Employment Reference Release

I acknowledge that I have been informed that it is [Your Business's] general policy to disclose in response to a prospective employer's request only the following information about current or former employees: (1) the dates of employment, (2) descriptions of the jobs performed, and (3) salary or wage rates.

By signing this release, I am voluntarily requesting that [Your Business] depart from this general policy in responding to reference requests from any prospective employer that may be considering me for employment. I authorize [Your Business] to disclose to such prospective employers any employment-related information that [Your Business], in its sole discretion and judgment, may determine is appropriate to disclose, including any personal comments, evaluations, or assessments that [Your Business] may have about my performance or behavior as an employee.

In exchange for [Your Business's] agreement to depart from its general policy and to disclose additional employment-related information pursuant to my request, I agree to release and discharge [Your Business] and [Your Business's] successors, employees, officers, and directors for all claims, liabilities, and causes of action, know or unknown, fixed or contingent, that arise from or that are in any manner connected to [Your Business's] disclosure of employment-related information to prospective employers. This release includes, but is not limited to, claims of defamation, libel, slander, negligence, or interference with contract or profession.

I acknowledge that I have carefully read and fully understand the provisions of this release. I further acknowledge that I was given the opportunity to consult with an attorney or any other individual of my choosing before signing this release and that I have decided to sign this release voluntarily and without coercion or duress by any person.

This release sets forth the entire agreement between [Your Business] and me, and I acknowledge that I have not relied upon any representation or statement, written or oral, not set forth in this document.

Signed: _____ Date: _____

       (Employee)

Part VII

Managing Your Business Finances

If you want to succeed in business, you need to know about financial management. No matter how skilled you are at creating a product, providing a service, or marketing your wares, the money you earn will slip between your fingers if you don't know how to efficiently collect it, keep track of it, save it, and spend or invest it wisely.

Poor financial management is one of the leading reasons that businesses fail. In many cases, failure could have been avoided if the owners had applied sound financial principles to all their dealings and decisions. Financial management is not something that you can leave to your banker, financial planner, or accountant — you need to understand the basic principles yourself and use them on a daily basis, even if you plan to leave the more complicated work to hired professionals.

In this section, we'll outline the basic concepts of financial management as they apply to you, starting with the simplest, everyday bookkeeping tasks and moving on to more sophisticated concepts:

Chapter 22: Your Basic Bookkeeping, explains the basics of the accounting system, including how to record daily transactions, keep track of your cash, and work with your accountant.

Chapter 23: Credit and Collections, discusses the pros and cons of accepting credit cards or offering trade credit, and tells you how you can more quickly and effectively collect the money your customers owe you.

Chapter 24: Managing Your Cash Flow, shows how to monitor and manage your cash flow to reduce the lag between cash outflows and inflows, and includes a few tips on investing the surplus cash you'll soon have on hand!

Chapter 25: Analyzing Your Financial Position, delves into some of the more sophisticated ways of examining your financial statements to identify trends, spot problems before they become too large, and compare your business to others in your industry.

Chapter **22**

Your Basic Bookkeeping

As a small business owner, you probably rely on an outside accountant to do your taxes and prepare financial statements. However, it's too expensive to pay an accountant to do routine bookkeeping chores. Someone in your organization must take on the responsibility of keeping an accurate set of financial records. Fortunately, you may find this task easier than you thought, especially if you use your computer.

In the following sections, we'll discuss the importance of good records, how to work with your accountant, the basics of how the accounting system works, how to record daily transactions, closing the books, preparing financial statements, and tax accounting.

THE IMPORTANCE OF GOOD RECORDS

If you are going to run a successful business, accurate and timely financial information is a must. The following are some of the reasons you need a good financial recordkeeping system:

- **Monitoring the success or failure of your business** — it's hard to know how your business is doing without a clear financial picture. Are sales increasing? Are expenditures increasing faster than sales? Do some expenditures appear to be out of control?

- **Providing the information you need to make decisions** — evaluating the financial consequences should be a part of every business decision you make.

- **Budgeting** — you must have solid financial information to prepare a meaningful budget, which will help you stay on track by forecasting cash needs and expenditures.

- **Obtaining bank financing** — a banker will usually want to see your financial statements for the most current and prior years, as well as your projected statements showing the impact of the requested loan. A banker may even want to look over your bookkeeping procedures to verify whether you run your business in a sound, professional manner.

- **Obtaining other sources of capital** — if you need capital and are thinking of taking in an outside investor, you will need to produce a lot of financial information. The information may be produced by your outside accountant, but it is based on your day-to-day recordkeeping.

- **Preparing your income tax return** — with good records, preparing an accurate tax return will be easier and you're more likely to be able to do it on time. If your accountant prepares your income tax return, poor records will almost certainly result in your paying higher accounting fees.

WORKING WITH YOUR ACCOUNTANT

In most cases, with a little study and help from computer software tools, you should be able to manage your most basic financial records without the help of an accountant. This includes the daily recording of transactions, and maintenance of a general ledger and cash records.

You may need an accountant to help with less routine tasks, such as closing the books at the end of the accounting period, preparing financial statements, completing income tax returns, or helping you prepare a budget. Depending on the size of your business, you may want to have your accountant close the books every month, particularly if you need to submit monthly sales tax to the state.

You may also decide to have your accountant set up your books when you first open your business. If you've been in business for a while, your accountant could give your bookkeeping procedures and records a one-time or periodic checkup.

Selecting an Accountant

If you don't already have an accountant, you should shop around for one just as you would for any other service provider. Talk with your peers in the business community about their accountant. Interview several candidates. Ask yourself the following:

- Does he or she specialize in small businesses of my size? Some firms specialize in and look for large clients.

- Does he or she specialize in income taxes?

- Has he or she received positive recommendations from my peers in the business community?

- Did the accountant explain the fee structure to me? Am I comfortable with it?

- Does he or she adequately understand my business and its unique problems?

- Am I comfortable using this person as a business advisor?

Many small business owners choose a CPA as their accountant, because it assures them a high level of professional competence. Certified Public Accountants have attained their title by passing a rigorous examination covering accounting, business law, auditing, and taxes. A CPA is required to have a college degree or a high level of work experience, and must meet an annual continuing education requirement. A CPA must also abide by a code of professional ethics as administered by a state board of accountancy.

Non-CPA professionals may not have as broad an education as a CPA, but a given individual might have the perfect accounting and tax expertise for your business.

Work Smart

Don't wait for an upcoming deadline to begin looking for an accountant. Try to do it well in advance of your need for his or her services. The worst time to shop for an accountant is during the "busy season" (January through April). Most accountants don't have time for new-customer interviews during that time of year.

Getting Records Ready for Your Accountant

You can save yourself some cash by doing as much of your own bookkeeping as possible. Your accountant does not want you to drop a shoe box full of receipts and records in his or her office. Such a strategy will cost you a lot of money in accounting fees; you don't want to pay your accountant for routine clerical work.

You should be able to keep track of the day-to-day transactions, and have a preliminary general ledger ready for your accountant. If you keep good records, your accountant will produce more accurate financial statements and tax returns, and will do it faster and cheaper.

With the proliferation of personal computers and software, there are many programs on the market to help you automate your accounting procedures. Some are more sophisticated than others.

You may even be able to find a program that was designed specifically for your industry, which can be a major time saver.

Be sure to choose a program that is compatible with the system your accountant uses. If you do, you may be able to keep most of your records on your computer, and simply hand your accountant a diskette whenever he or she needs your records.

THE ACCOUNTING SYSTEM

At the most basic level, accounting is the method in which financial information is gathered, processed, and summarized into financial statements and reports.

1. Every accounting entry is based on a business transaction, which is usually represented by a business document, such as a check or a sales invoice.

2. A journal is where the transactions are recorded, in chronological order. The typical journals used to record the day-to-day transactions are a sales and cash receipts journal and a cash disbursements journal. A general journal is used to record special entries at the end of an accounting period.

3. While a journal records transactions as they happen, a ledger groups transactions according to their type, based on the accounts they affect. For example, in the ledger, all your inventory purchases would be recorded in one place, your payroll expenses in another, etc. Essentially, every transaction will be reflected in two places: a journal and a ledger. At the end of the month you can compare the totals in each and make sure that they match, which functions as a check on your work.

4. A trial balance is prepared at the end of an accounting period by adding up all the account balances in your general ledger. The sum of the debit balances should equal the sum of the credit balances; if not, you must track down the errors.

5. Finally, financial statements are prepared from the information in your trial balance.

Accounting Basics

If you understand the definition and goals of an accounting system, you are ready to learn the following definitions and concepts:

Assets: things of value held by the business. Examples of assets are cash, accounts receivable, inventory, equipment, and real estate.

Liabilities: what your business owes creditors. Examples are accounts payable, payroll taxes payable, and loans payable.

Equity: the net worth of your company. Also called owner's equity or, for corporations, paid-in capital. Equity comes from investment in the business by the owners, plus accumulated net profits of the business that have not been paid out to the owners. It essentially represents amounts owed by the business to the owner.

The accounting equation: assets = liabilities + owner's equity. The financial statement called the balance sheet is based on this equation.

Balance sheet: also called a statement of financial position, a balance sheet is a financial "snapshot" of your business at a given date in time. It lists your assets, your liabilities, and the difference between the two, which is your equity or net worth. The balance sheet is a real-life example of the accounting equation, because it shows that assets = liabilities + owner's equity.

Once you master the above accounting terms and concepts, you are ready to learn about the following day-to-day accounting terms.

Debits: an increase in assets or a decrease in liabilities or equity is called a debit. For this reason, you will sometimes see debits entered on the left-hand side (the asset side of the accounting equation) of a two-column journal or ledger.

Credits: an increase in liabilities or equity or a decrease in assets is called a credit. For this reason, you will sometimes see credits entered on the right-hand side (the liability and equity side of the accounting equation) of a two-column journal or ledger.

Work Smart

In bookkeeping texts, examples, and ledgers, you may see the words "Debit" and "Credit" abbreviated. Dr. stands for Debit; Cr. stands for Credit. Getting the debits and credits straight is, for many people, the most difficult part of learning accounting. Luckily, many bookkeeping software packages will automatically classify your entries for you.

Double-entry accounting: In double-entry accounting, every transaction has two journal entries: a debit and a credit. The debits must always equal the credits, which prevents some common bookkeeping errors and makes those that do occur easier to find. Double-entry accounting is the basis of a true accounting system, and is the system we describe in this chapter.

Example

You provide consulting services for $1,500, on credit, to one of your regular customers, Betty Fry. When you write up the invoice, you would make the following bookkeeping entry in your sales journal:

	Debit	Credit
Accounts receivable (Fry)	1,500	
Consulting revenue		1,500

These entries show that your accounts receivable (an asset account) has increased by $1,500, and your consulting revenue (an income account) has also increased by $1,500.

Upon receipt of the invoice, your customer sends you a check for $1,500 in payment of her account. When you receive the check, make the following entry in your cash receipts journal:

	Debit	Credit
Cash	1,500	
Accounts receivable (Fry)		1,500

These entries show that your cash (an asset account) has increased by $1,500, and your accounts receivable account has decreased by $1,500.

Single-entry accounting: rather than dealing with debits and credits, some very small businesses just record one side of the transaction. This is a single-entry accounting system. In the above example, you would simply record the revenue amount of $1,500 in your sales journal. However, you would also want to make a separate entry in your accounts receivable ledger, so that you keep track of all customers that owe you money.

Work Smart

We recommend a double-entry accounting system, because it will result in more accurate financial records. If you use a computer, the good news is that many accounting software programs will allow you to make a single entry for each transaction, and the software will make the second entry for you. The double-entry system is still there, but it exists mostly "behind the scenes."

Cash vs. Accrual Accounting

There are two basic accounting methods available to most small businesses: cash or accrual.

If you use the cash method, you record income only when you receive cash from your customers. You record an expense only when you write the check to the vendor. Most individuals use the cash method for their personal finances, because it's simpler and less time-consuming. However, this method can distort your income and expenses, especially if you extend credit to your customers, if you buy on credit from your suppliers, or you keep an inventory of the products you sell.

With the accrual method, you record income when a sale occurs, regardless of when you get paid. You record an expense when you receive goods or services, even though you may not pay for them until later.

The accrual method gives you a more accurate picture of your financial situation than the cash method. Income earned in one period is accurately matched against the expenses that correspond to that period, so you get a better picture of your net profits for each period.

However, with the accrual method, you will typically record more transactions. For example, if you make a sale on credit as in the example above, you would record the transaction at the time of the sale. Then, when the customer pays the bill, you will record the cash received as another transaction. With the cash method, you record only one transaction, when the customer pays the bill.

Another issue to be considered is the accounting method you use for tax purposes. It's much easier to use the same method for your internal reporting that you use for tax purposes. The IRS allows most small businesses to use the cash method, but if you maintain an inventory, you'll be required to use the accrual method, at least for sales and purchases of inventory for resale.

Work Smart

We recommend the accrual method for all businesses, even if the IRS permits the cash method, because accrual gives you a clearer picture of the financial status of your business. If you are using a computer program, there really isn't much extra effort involved.

DAILY RECORDING OF TRANSACTIONS

In order to take control of your financial recordkeeping, you must accurately record all your day-to-day sales, purchases, and other transactions. Specifically, you need to record:

- sales and revenue transactions

- cash transactions (remember, cash flows in and out of the business)

- accounts receivable, if you extend credit to your customers

- accounts payable, if you purchase from your suppliers on credit

- summaries of transactions in your general ledger

Sales and Revenue Transactions

At the most basic level, you need to know how much money is coming into your business each day, week, month, and year. When you think about it, there are two basic things you need to keep track of: the actual dollars that come in (cash receipts), which you will deposit in the bank at the end of each day, and your sales. Sales can include both cash and credit transactions; moreover, your sales records should show the customer name and the items sold in each transaction, so you can keep track of your inventory and become aware of whom you are selling to.

Daily sales are recorded in a "sales journal." To simplify your bookkeeping, we recommend that you keep a combined sales and cash receipts journal, in which you can record all your sales (cash and credit), and all cash receipts, including collection of accounts receivable, in one place.

Entries in your sales and cash receipts journal are based on the sales invoices, and/or daily cash register totals you use in your business every day.

Sales invoices. If your business is of a type where invoices are used, the invoice should show, at a minimum, the date of the sale, products or services sold, price or rate, and a payment due date. If you use a computer software program to perform your accounting, it probably has a pre-designed sales invoice that you can use.

Prepare three copies of every invoice, and give one copy to the customer. The other two copies are for your records. File one copy alphabetically by customer name, to keep track of what each customer has bought and how much he or she still owes you. The other copy would be filed by invoice number. Include canceled or voided invoices when filing by number, so that you can account for all of them. The information from each invoice will become an entry in the sales journal as shown in the example that follows.

If you are going to be recording sales and cash receipts manually in a journal, visit an office supply store. They will have many different kinds for you to choose from. Look at the different column headings, and choose the one that has headings that meets the needs of your business. If you will be using computer software, your program will probably have some type of sales and cash receipts journal, but may allow you to customize it based on your type of business.

Case Study — Using the Sales and Cash Receipts Journal

Assume that your business is a retail sales outlet that extends credit to some customers. Here is an example of a few entries in a combined sales and cash receipts journal. The following transactions occurred:

- *On February 2, you sold, on credit, $476 worth of goods to Sandra Shaw. Sales tax on that amount is $24. Since Shaw owes you a total of $500 (476 + 24), your accounts receivable have increased by that amount.*

- *Also on February 2, Tamara Dwight paid you her account balance of $1,359.*

- *On February 5, several customers bought merchandise for cash. Total cash sales were $682. On those sales, $34 of sales tax was collected, adding up to a total of $716 of cash receipts from your customers.*

- *On February 6, Sandra Shaw paid her balance of $500.*

SALES AND CASH RECEIPTS JOURNAL FOR: FEBRUARY 2000							
Date	Descrip.	Invoice Number	Cash Dr.	Accounts Receivable Dr.	Cr.	Sales Cr.	Sales Tax Payable Cr.
2	S. Shaw: sale on account	10034		500		476	24
2	T. Dwight: received on account		1,359		1,359		
5	Daily Cash Sales		716			682	34
6	S. Shaw: received on account		500		500		
	Totals		2,575	500	1,859	1,158	58

Upon completion of this journal page, you should foot (that is, add up the amounts in) all five amount columns. Make sure the sum of the debits equals the sum of the credits. In this case, total debits: 2,575 + 500 = 3,075. Total credits: 1,859 + 1,158 + 58 = 3,075.

If the sum of the debit columns doesn't equal the sum of the credit columns, you have a problem that you should investigate right away. You may have recorded one of the amounts in the wrong column, charged a customer the wrong amount, or simply computed the totals incorrectly.

Cash register totals. If your business uses a cash register, daily sales can be totaled on the register. Most new cash registers should be able to separately record cash sales and charge sales, and keep track of sales tax. Some should also be able to record cash received on customers' charge accounts. At the end of the business day, record your cash register totals in the sales journal.

Case Study — Posting Cash Register Receipts to the Sales Journal

Kurt totals the cash registers of his automotive supply store at the end of the day. The totals show cash receipts of $1,640, cash and charge sales of $1,325 and $450, respectively (for total sales of $1,775 which includes sales tax of $75), and $315 received for payment on customer charge accounts. Kurt will make the following entry in his combined sales and cash receipts journal:

	Debit	Credit
Cash	1,640	
Accounts receivable	450	
Sales		1,700
Accounts receivable		315
Sales tax payable		75

Cash sheets and sales registers. If you don't use a cash register, you could record your sales on a paper sales register, which is simply a record of each sale for the day. You would record your cash receipts on a daily cash sheet, discussed below.

At the end of each day, you would total the cash sheet and sales register, and enter the totals in the sales and cash receipts journal.

Cash Transactions

A typical small business has a variety of different types of cash transactions, which should be recorded in a number of different places: the sales and cash receipts journal (discussed above), the daily cash sheet, the bank reconciliation, a cash disbursements journal and, if you like, a petty cash fund.

Daily Cash Sheets

A cash sheet is a reconciliation of cash received and cash paid out during a single day. If you don't have more than a few transactions each day, you probably won't need one. If, however, a lot of your business is transacted in cash, such as in a retail store, you should prepare a cash sheet like the one that follows at the end of each day.

Daily Cash Sheet   **Date:** _____

Beginning Cash on Hand   _____

Plus:

    Total Daily Sales (cash, checks, and charges)   _____

    Collections on Accounts Receivable   _____

    Other Cash Receipts   _____

Subtotal   _____

Less:

    Charge Account Sales (included in Total Daily Sales above)   _____

Total Cash to Account For   _____

Cash Paid Out:

    Cash Refunds   _____

    Cash Returns   _____

    Deposited to Bank   _____

    Owner's Draw   _____

    Misc. Cash Expenses   _____

                                                        _____

                                                        _____

                                                        _____

                                                        _____

Total Cash Paid Out   _____

Cash on Hand Should Be   _____

Cash on Hand -- Actual Count   _____

Cash Over (Short)   =====

It's good business practice to deposit all cash receipts in your bank account daily. Your daily cash receipts should generally be the same amount as your daily bank deposit. If they are not the same, you'll need to investigate and find out why.

An important reason to do a cash sheet is to alert you to any shortage or surplus of cash for the day. A shortage could be the result of theft, or it could simply result from your failure to record a special transaction, such as an expense you paid in cash.

Bank Reconciliation

When you receive your bank statement every month, you should prepare a bank reconciliation, which is a document that balances your business checkbook.

The cash balance in your books will never match the balance shown on the bank statement because of the delay in checks and deposits clearing the bank, automatic bank charges and credits you haven't recorded, and errors you may have made in your books. After preparing the bank reconciliation, you can be comfortable that the account balance shown on your books is up-to-date.

How To Prepare a Bank Reconciliation

1. ***Prepare a list of deposits in transit.*** *Compare the deposits listed on your bank statement with the bank deposits shown in your cash receipts journal. On your bank reconciliation, list any deposits that have not yet cleared the bank statement. Also, take a look at the bank reconciliation you prepared last month. Did all of last month's deposits in transit clear on this month's bank statement? If not, find out what happened to them.*

2. ***Prepare a list of outstanding checks.*** *In your cash disbursements journal, mark each check that cleared the bank statement this month. On your bank reconciliation, list all the checks from the cash disbursements journal that did not clear. Also, take a look at the bank reconciliation you prepared last month. Are there any checks that were outstanding last month that still have not cleared the bank? If so, be sure they are on your list of outstanding checks this month.*

3. ***Record any bank charges or credits.*** *Your statement probably shows bank fees and charges that you have not recorded in your books. If so, record them now just as you would have if you had written a check for that amount. By the same token, if there are any credits made to your account by the bank, those should be recorded as well. Post the entries to your general ledger (see the discussion of ledgers below).*

4. ***Compute the cash balance per your books.*** *Foot the general ledger cash account to arrive at your ending cash balance.*

5. ***Enter bank balance on the reconciliation.*** *At the top of the bank reconciliation, enter the ending balance from the bank statement.*

6. **Total the deposits in transit.** Add up the deposits in transit, and enter the total on the reconciliation. Add the total deposits in transit to the bank balance to arrive at a subtotal.

7. **Total the outstanding checks.** Add up the outstanding checks, and enter the total on the reconciliation.

8. **Compute book balance per the reconciliation.** Subtract the total outstanding checks from the subtotal in step 6 above. The result should equal the balance shown in your general ledger.

Here's an example of what your bank reconciliation should look like:

Alpha Company
Bank Reconciliation
March 31, 2000

Balance per bank statement		$4,672.98
Deposits in Transit:		
Date	Amount	
3/30	$500.25	
3/31	1,890.33	2,390.58
	Subtotal	7,063.56
Outstanding Checks		
Check Number	Amount	
1656	22.50	
1693	150.00	
1696	32.00	
1697	1,902.00	
1698	1,105.80	3,212.84
Balance per books:		3,950.72

In this example, if the general ledger cash account does not show a balance of $3,950.72, you will need to track down the cause.

Cash Disbursements Journal

A cash disbursements journal is where you record all the transactions in which you paid out cash or checks. It can also be called a purchases journal or an expense journal.

If you will be recording expenses manually in a journal, visit an office supply store. Look at the column headings of the journals, and choose one that best meets the needs of your business. If you are using computer software, your program will have some type of disbursements journal, but may allow you to customize it based on your business needs.

What about credit card purchases? If you use the accrual basis of accounting, as we recommend, you'll record expenses in the journal at the time you purchase goods or services, even if you purchase on credit. If you use the cash method, you record the payment when you pay the credit card company, but you'll have to record the various items shown on your credit card statement separately.

Case Study — Using the Cash Disbursements Journal

You own a variety store. You purchase from your main supplier, on account, items totaling $7,800. Most of the purchase is inventory for resale, but also included are $100 of office supplies. Make the following entry in your purchases journal:

	Debit	Credit
Purchases	7,700	
Office supplies expense	100	
Accounts payable		7,800

Next month, after receiving a statement from your supplier, you write a check to settle your account. Make the following entry in your purchases journal:

	Debit	Credit
Accounts payable	7,800	
Cash		7,800

Assume that your business is a retail store that sells merchandise for resale. Here is an example of a few entries in a purchases journal. The following transactions occurred (note: all dollar amounts have been rounded off to the nearest dollar):

* *On February 2, you paid your electric bill of $177.*

* *Also on February 2, you bought merchandise inventory on account from Ash Wholesale at a cost of $9,500.*

* *On February 5, you spent $82 at Atkins Service Station to fill up your delivery vehicles with gas. You charge it all to the account you maintain with Atkins.*

* *On February 8, you write a check for $9,500 in payment of the bill you receive from Ash.*

* *On February 10, you write a check for $82 to Atkins Service Station to settle your account.*

PURCHASES JOURNAL FOR: FEBRUARY 2000								
		Cash		Accounts	Payable	Purchases	Delivery Expense	Util. Exp.
Date	Descrip.	Dr.	Cr.	Dr.	Cr.	Dr.	Dr.	Dr.
2	Edison Util.-electricity		177					177
2	Ash Whlsle-inventory				9,500	9,500		
5	Atkins Serv. Station-gas				82		82	
8	Ash Whlsle-on account		9,500	9,500				
10	Atkins Serv.-on account		82	82				
Totals		0	9,759	9,582	9,582	9,500	82	177

Upon completion of this journal page, you should foot all seven amount columns. Since you are using a double-entry accounting system, you can see if all entries were recorded correctly. Check to see if the sum of the debits equals the sum of the credits. Total debits: 0 + 9,582 + 9500 + 82 + 177 = 19,341. Total credits: 9,759 + 9,582 = 19,341.

Petty Cash Fund

Set up a petty cash fund if you need cash on hand to pay miscellaneous small expenses of your business. If your business uses a cash register, you probably don't need a petty cash fund, as long as you carefully record all expenses you pay out of the cash register.

How To Use a Petty Cash Fund

A petty cash fund is set up and used as follows:

1. *Start a petty cash fund by writing a check to "Petty Cash." Cash the check.*

2. *Physically place the money in a petty cash drawer or petty cash box.*

3. *As you pay for expenses out of petty cash, keep an itemized list of each expenditure.*

4. *When the cash is almost depleted, add up the expenses on your itemized list.*

5. *Write another check to "Petty Cash" for the total of the expenses. That check should replenish the fund back to the initial balance.*

Accounts Receivable

Accounts receivable are unpaid customer invoices, and any other money owed to you by your customers. The sum of all your customer accounts receivable is listed as a current asset on your balance sheet. Accounts receivable is abbreviated as A/R.

When a customer purchases something, you'll first record the sale in the sales and cash receipts journal, as discussed above. This journal will have accounts receivable debit and credit columns. Sales on credit (and by this we mean credit *you* extend to customers, not sales using bank or other credit cards that are treated like cash sales) and payments on a customer's credit account are entered in these two columns.

Then, each day, the credit sales recorded in the sales and cash receipts journal is posted to the appropriate customer's accounts in the accounts receivable ledger. This allows you to know not only the total amount owed to you by all credit customers, but also the total amount owed by *each* customer.

Entries made in the sales and cash receipts journal are also totaled at the end of the month, and the results are posted to the accounts receivable account in your general ledger. This account is called your accounts receivable "control account," which means that after all your posting is completed, the total amount of customer balances in the accounts receivable ledger will be the same as the balance in the control account in the general ledger. If they aren't the same, you can tell that you made an error somewhere along the line.

If you use a computer program, posting to the accounts receivable ledgers will occur automatically.

Accounts Receivable Ledger

If you use a manual system, keep all your accounts receivable ledger accounts in one binder. To save paperwork, we recommend that copies of each customer's account in the A/R ledger also serve as the statements you mail to your customers each month, as shown on the next page. If you are going to mail them out as statements, begin a new ledger sheet every month. The monthly ledger sheet should start with a balance forward, which is the ending balance from the previous month.

[Your Business Name]   [Date]

[Your Address]

[Your Phone]

Statement of Account

[Customer's Name]

[Customer's Address]

Date	Description	Charges	Credits	Account Balance
	Previous Balance			$0.00
		$0.00		
		$0.00		
		$0.00		
		$0.00		
		$0.00		

Ending Balance: [Statement Date]   **$0.00**

Balance Due: [Due Date]

What To Include in Customers' Statements of Account

For most businesses, statements should be sent once a month to all customers with an account balance. The statement should show the following:

- *a beginning balance (the previous month's ending balance)*

- *all invoices charged during the month*

- *payments on account during the month*

- *any debit memos or credit memos. A credit memo would be required, for example, when a customer who bought merchandise on account returned some merchandise, or overpaid the account. A debit memo is used to bill a customer again; for example, when a customer has made a payment on account by check, but the check bounced.*

- *an ending balance and a due date*

Accounts Payable

Accounts payable are the unpaid bills of the business, the money you owe to your suppliers and other creditors. The total amount you owe is listed as a current liability on your balance sheet. You will often see accounts payable abbreviated as A/P.

If you use the accrual method of accounting, as we recommend, you will record your expenses in the cash disbursements journal (discussed above) at the time you purchased the goods or services, even if you buy on credit.

Your credit purchases from the cash disbursements journal are, at the end of each day, posted to the accounts payable ledger, which is the place to record what you owe to each vendor.

At the end of the month, your credit purchases and payments on account that have been recorded in the cash disbursements journal are totaled and posted to an accounts payable account in the general ledger, which acts as your control account. You can compare the figures in your control account to the total balances in your accounts payable ledgers, to be sure they are the same. You can use your A/P ledgers to check the bills you get from your suppliers.

General Ledger

The general ledger is a permanent summary of all your supporting journals, such as the sales and cash receipts journal and the cash disbursements journal. Your financial statements are built from the general ledger.

For each account in your sales and cash receipts journal and in your cash disbursements journal, there is a general ledger account. For example, cash, accounts receivable, accounts payable, sales, purchases, telephone expense, and owner's equity are all examples of general ledger accounts. There are also separate general ledger accounts for miscellaneous or rarely encountered items that don't have their own columns in the journals, but are entered in a "miscellaneous" column in the general ledger.

When all journal entries are posted, you can arrive at the ending balance for each account. Then the amounts in the total columns for your journals become entries in the general ledger. The sum of all general ledger debit balances should always equal the sum of all general ledger credit balances.

CLOSING THE BOOKS

When you reach the end of an accounting period, you need to "close the books." At a minimum, you will close your books annually, because you have to file an income tax return every year, and you should prepare annual financial statements as well.

Most businesses, however, close their books at the end of each month. Sending out customer statements, paying your suppliers, reconciling your bank statement, and submitting sales tax reports to the state are probably some of the tasks you need to do every month. You may find it easier to do these if you close your books.

Unless your business is very small and has few transactions each month, it's likely that you'll want to have your accountant close your books for you. We describe the basic procedure here just to give you a feel for what you're paying your accountant to do.

How to Close Your Books

After you finish entering the day-to-day transactions in your journals, you are ready to "close the books" for the period.

1. **Post entries to the general ledger.** *Transfer the account totals from your journals (sales and cash receipts journal and cash disbursements journal) to your general ledger accounts.*

2. **Total the general ledger accounts.** *By footing the general ledger accounts, you will arrive at a preliminary ending balance for each account.*

3. **Prepare a preliminary trial balance.** *Add all of the general ledger account ending balances together. Total debits should equal total credits. This will help assure you that your accounts balance prior to making adjusting entries.*

4. ***Prepare adjusting journal entries.*** *Certain end-of-period adjustments must be made before you can close your books. Adjusting entries are required to account for items that don't get recorded in your daily transactions, such as accrual of depreciation, accrual of real estate taxes, etc. In a traditional accounting system, adjusting entries are made in a general journal.*

5. ***Foot the general ledger accounts again.*** *This will give you the adjusted balance of each general ledger account.*

6. ***Prepare an adjusted trial balance.*** *Prepare another trial balance, using the adjusted balances of each general ledger account. Again, total debits must equal total credits.*

7. ***Prepare financial statements.*** *After tracking down and correcting any trial balance errors, you (or your accountant) are ready to prepare a balance sheet and income statement.*

8. ***Prepare closing entries.*** *Get your general ledger ready for the next accounting period by clearing out the revenue and expense accounts and transferring the net income or loss to owner's equity. This is done by preparing journal entries that are called closing entries in a general journal.*

9. ***Prepare a post-closing trial balance.*** *After you make closing entries, all revenue and expense accounts will have a zero balance. Prepare one more trial balance. Since all revenue and expense accounts have been closed out to zero, this trial balance will only contain balance sheet accounts. Remember that the total debit balance must equal the total credit balance. This will help ensure that all general ledger account balances are correct as of the beginning of the new accounting period.*

PREPARING FINANCIAL STATEMENTS

One of the major purposes for closing your books at the end of each accounting period is to allow you to prepare financial statements that give you a picture of your business's financial status. The financial statements prepared for most small businesses are:

- a balance sheet

- an income statement

Usually these are prepared by an accountant. But with the help of computer software, you may be able to prepare your own financial statements. If you need to prepare financial statements for third parties, such as a banker, sometimes the third party may request that the financial statements be prepared by a professional accountant or certified public accountant.

The Balance Sheet

Also called a statement of financial position, a balance sheet is a financial "snapshot" of your business at a given date in time. It lists your assets, your liabilities, and the difference between the two, which is your owner's equity, or net worth. The accounting equation (assets = liabilities + owner's equity) is the basis for the balance sheet.

The following is an example of a balance sheet for a sole proprietorship. (Note that financial statements normally do not show cents. All amounts should be rounded to the nearest dollar.)

Beta Sales Company
Balance Sheet
December 31, 2000

Assets			Liabilities and Capital		
Current Assets:			Current Liabilities:		
Cash	$12,300		Accounts payable	$ 8,900	
Accounts receiv.	22,900		Wages payable	11,525	
Inventory	32,090		Total Current Liabil.		$20,425
Prepaid insurance	2,500		Long-term Liabilities:		
Total Current Assts.		$69,790	Bank loan payable	17,500	
Fixed Assets:			Total long-term Liab.		17,500
Equipment	100,200		Total Liabilities		37,925
Less: accum. deprec.	(78,321)				
	----------		Capital:		
Total Fixed Assets		21,879	Tom Beta, Capital		53,744
		---------			---------
Total Assets		$91,669	Total Liabilities and Capital		$91,669

For more detailed information on balance sheets and other financial statements, see our discussion in Chapter 25.

Income Statement

Also called a profit and loss statement, or a "P&L," an income statement lists your income, expenses, and net income (or loss). The net income (or loss) is equal to your income minus your expenses. Your business's tax return will use a variation of the income statement to determine your potentially taxable income.

Beta Sales Company
Income Statement
For the Year Ended December 31, 2000

Sales		$462,452
Cost of Goods Sold:		
Beginning inventory	$ 27,335	
Add: Purchases	235,689	
	263,024	
Less: Ending inventory	32,090	
Cost of Goods Sold		230,934
Gross Profit		231,518
Expenses:		
Advertising	1,850	
Depreciation	13,250	
Insurance	5,400	
Payroll taxes	8,200	
Rent	9,600	
Repairs and maintenance	13,984	
Utilities	17,801	
Wages	98,852	
Total Expenses		168,937
Net Income		$ 62,581

ACCOUNTING FOR TAX PURPOSES

One of the most important uses of your financial records is to help you comply with federal and state tax laws and prepare tax returns. A good bookkeeping system will help make dealing with Uncle Sam relatively painless.

You don't always have to use the same accounting rules for tax purposes as you do for financial reporting. However, we highly recommend that you *do* use the same rules for both purposes, to avoid complicating your life with two sets of financial records.

For more information on your federal tax obligations, see Chapter 26.

Chapter 23

Credit and Collections

A lot of small business owners avoid developing a credit and collections policy until they have no other choice. As their customer base builds, and more and more customers want to pay by credit, they realize that they need to open up a credit card account or offer credit terms. Or they ignore those few customers who don't pay their bills, until the few grow into many, and suddenly they realize that they need to spend time collecting overdue accounts.

The problem with this approach is that you'll end up spending a lot more of your time fixing the trouble than it would have taken to set up a good credit policy beforehand.

The purpose of this chapter then, is to walk you through the process of setting up a credit policy, and explain some techniques for collecting debts if (or, more likely, when) the need arises.

UNDERSTANDING YOUR CREDIT OPTIONS

Some small businesses don't take anything other than cash. If you have a storefront and sell inexpensive items (like a newsstand or a fast food outlet), you can expect people to pay cash. But if other businesses like yours take credit cards or extend payment terms, you'll probably have to follow suit. Most businesses have to accept some type of credit, at least personal checks.

Your guiding principle should be to get as much of your payments up front and in cash as possible. Extend credit only if you must, or if you have a strong competitive reason for wanting to offer more generous terms to your customers.

The three major types of credit accepted by small businesses are credit cards, checks, and credit terms. Of these three, credit cards are the least risky, but will cost you between 2.5% to 5.5% of your sales.

Accepting Personal Checks

Checks are usually considered to be cash rather than credit, but they do involve risk on your part. If the check bounces, you — not the bank — will be the one left holding the bag. When you receive a check from a customer, you should take the following precautions:

- Make sure that the check is signed and dated, that the amount is properly filled out in both places, and that the payee line is either filled in or left blank for you to fill in.

- If you don't know the person giving you the check, ask for a driver's license, a phone number, and a credit card. Take down the driver's license number; you might need it (and the phone number) if you have to track the customer down later. The credit card is just to satisfy yourself that the customer was able to establish credit somewhere. Don't write the credit card number down on the back of the check — that's illegal.

- Look for hints that something may be out of order. Is the customer's address pre-printed on the check? Does the address on the check match the address on the driver's license?

- If the check is for an unusually large amount, call the customer's bank to verify that sufficient funds are in the account.

- Don't take multiparty checks. You may also decide not to take out-of-state checks.

In some cities there are check guarantee services that, for a small fee per check, will guarantee that the check will be paid.

Accepting Credit Cards

From the business owner's standpoint, the advantage to accepting credit cards is that your bank account will be credited with the amount of the sale by the end of the business day. The credit card company bears the hassles of billing and collecting from customers, and the risk that the customer will pay late, or not at all.

If you want to accept credit cards, the first step is to open a credit card merchant account with a bank. If you have an established business reputation or a long-standing relationship with your banker, you probably won't have any trouble opening up an account.

If, however, you're just starting out, you have a mail order business, or you work out of your home, you may have some trouble. The reason is that banks and credit card companies are scared to death of fraud, and they've become much more cautious in recent years about opening up new accounts. In fact, some larger banks won't even deal with you unless you have a storefront.

If you operate a home or mail order business, your best bet may be to start with a medium- or small-sized bank. If possible, find out from other home or mail order businesses where they have their merchant account.

What Banks Want from You

When you go to your lender to open up a credit card account, you'll need to make a full financial disclosure in much the same way that you would if you were asking for a loan. (Or even more so: we know of one small business owner who was asked to submit to an FBI check before being granted a merchant account!)

The likelihood of obtaining a merchant account from a bank will depend upon the following factors:

- **Your type of business** — certain types of businesses are considered higher credit risks than others.

- **The length of time in business** — if you don't have an established track record, you'll have more difficulty.

- **Your general creditworthiness** — banks will want to know whether you've ever declared bankruptcy or if you have any judgments or liens against you.

- **Your previous merchant account status** — banks will want to know if you've ever had a merchant account before because it's a good indication of your creditworthiness.

Save Time

If your bank won't let you open up a merchant account, consider using an Independent Service Organization. You can contract with the ISO to open a merchant account, and the ISO will contract with the bank. The ISO, in effect, bears the risk of doing business with you.

Please be careful here. Although there are more than 1,400 ISOs in the U.S., they are not regulated. Make sure that you understand all the extra charges before you enter into an agreement. Sometimes you can be grossly overcharged for the equipment that the ISO provides you, and there may be other hidden charges.

How Credit Card Transactions Work

The typical credit card transaction begins when your customer hands you the credit card. You will either manually imprint the card onto a triplicate paper draft, if you still use the older technology, or you'll swipe the card through an electronic terminal, if you use the newer technology.

If the transaction is handled over the telephone or through the mails, the customer will give you the credit card number, and you'll either fill out a paper draft or key in the number at your terminal.

The next step is to obtain authorization for the sale from the credit card company. If you're using the older technology, you'll have to call a special number to obtain an authorization code (typically, this is only required with sales over a certain amount, such as $50). If you're using the newer technology, the authorization code will be obtained automatically. Once you have the authority, you must have the customer sign the receipt, unless it's a phone sale.

Then you'll send the credit card sales receipts to the bank so that you can get paid. If you use the older technology, you'll have to take the receipts to your bank. If you use the newer technology, you can send the receipts electronically. This process is usually done at the end of the day and is referred to as settling your accounts.

Your bank will authorize the charge and notify the credit card company (or some company acting on its behalf) of the charge. The credit card company (or the company acting on its behalf) will collect the money from the bank that issued the card, and send it to your bank. Once your bank has the money, it will put it in your account, minus a processing fee, which is split between your bank and the credit card company.

Meanwhile, the credit card company bills your customer. When your customer pays the bill, the credit card company sends the money to the bank that issued the card, minus a processing fee. . . and everyone lives happily ever after.

The Equipment You'll Need

The older credit card technology is still useful if you make sales in places without access to a phone line, such as at a neighborhood art fair. You can pick up a card imprinter for about $25.

The scanner terminal, on the other hand, is much more expensive. A four-year lease may run as high as $50-$70 a month. You can purchase the equipment, but before you do, find out what your bank will charge you to connect your own equipment to their system. The extra costs may make renting less expensive than buying.

You may also need a receipt printer, although many cash registers are able to print receipts.

Shopping for the Best Rates

Shopping for the best merchant account rate is like shopping for anything else: you want the best value at the lowest price. Don't make the mistake of assuming that you'll get the same rate at every bank. Generally, lower-risk businesses will qualify for better rates.

Discount rate. The discount rate is the sum that's deducted and paid to the credit card company and the issuing bank. It usually ranges from 2.5 percent to 5.5 percent of your credit sales, depending upon the volume of your sales and the typical transaction size. The discount rate is comprised of the transaction charges, the interchange rate, and the transmission costs.

Transaction charge. The transaction charge is essentially the profit that the processing network makes. It's usually included in the discount rate, but it may be charged separately. This is really the only element of the discount rate that you can negotiate.

Interchange rate. The interchange rate is the cost of processing the charge through the Visa or MasterCard network. The current interchange rate for swiped transactions is 1.30 percent for MasterCard and 1.35 percent for Visa. Federal regulations require an additional charge of about 0.30 percent per transaction to the cost of non-swiped transactions.

Transmission costs. The cost of transmitting the sale information through the processing network is expressed as a cost per ticket, and runs about 18 cents to 23 cents per transaction.

Chargebacks on Credit Cards

If you get too many chargebacks (that is, amounts that the credit card company was unable to collect that are charged back against your account), you can lose your merchant credit card account.

Here's are some of the most common reasons for chargebacks:

- unauthorized use of credit card

- no signature on the receipt

- processing error (e.g., the same charge was processed twice)

- expired credit card

- customer disputes the charges (e.g., wrong items delivered)

Procedural chargebacks. The first four items in the list above are examples of procedural chargebacks. You can reduce the frequency of these chargebacks by developing a routine that you (and your sales staff, if any) will always follow. For example, take the credit card from the customer, check the expiration date, run it through the electronic terminal, make sure the signature on the receipt matches the signature on the card, etc.

Phone orders, of course, pose a problem. For phone orders, you should get the caller's home and work phone numbers, in addition to the information you would need to fill the order, such as name and address.

Customer-initiated chargebacks. Customer-initiated chargebacks occur when customers attempt to cancel the transaction for some reason, usually because the goods were damaged or because they claim the charges were excessive. A chargeback differs from a simple return of your merchandise because the customer has complained not to you, but to the credit card company. If the customer complains directly to you, you can repay the customer without affecting your chargeback rate.

Work Smart

A good way to combat customer-initiated chargebacks is to have a generous return policy. You'll just have to weigh the benefits of a lower chargeback rate against the chances that some customers may abuse your lenient policy.

Violations of Credit Card Policy

The surest way to lose your merchant account forever is to get caught doing something that violates credit card company policy. There are two things in particular that you should avoid at all costs.

Misrepresentation. When you're filling out your merchant account application, don't fudge on the numbers in order to improve your chances of getting the account. Don't misrepresent the nature of your business or the extent of your business experience. If you're caught, you may never get another chance to open an account.

Suppose you fill out your application honestly but business conditions change so that the information is now inaccurate. Do you have a duty to inform the bank? It depends on what has changed. If you said that you wouldn't be taking any credit card sales over the phone, but now you want to, you probably should tell the bank. On the other hand, if your annual sales drop slightly, you probably don't need to tell the bank. The dividing line for determining whether to tell the bank is whether you believe the information alters the credit risk the bank is taking. If you're in doubt, tell the bank.

Factoring. In this context, factoring is the process of running the charges of another business through your merchant account to generate profits. Don't do it. If one customer initiates a chargeback, you can lose your merchant account forever.

Offering Credit Terms

Professionals such as doctors, consultants, and accountants, and small businesses that sell goods and services to other businesses, usually offer credit terms to their customers. In most cases, the terms (payment due in 30 days, due in 60 days, etc.) are determined by industry customs. Such terms are commonly called trade credit and have important implications for your cash flow.

To Whom Should You Offer Credit?

The only foolproof way to avoid bad debts is not to offer *any* credit. Since that isn't practical for most businesses, you'll have to do the next best thing, which is to take all reasonable precautions to protect yourself and to ensure you're not extending credit to the wrong person or business.

Essentially, you want to gather enough credit information on your customers to give you a good idea whether they are a good credit risk. Also, the information you'll want to gather will depend on your business. For example, if you operate a mail order business, you may need to take extra steps to make sure the credit card is legitimate, because you can't see your customer at the time of sale.

Credit Information on Individuals

If you offer credit terms to an individual, you can get a credit report that will give you information about his or her credit history from any of the credit reporting firms, such as Experian or Equifax. Look in the Yellow Pages under "Credit Bureaus," or some similar listing.

Obviously, it's not worthwhile to do a credit check for a small sales amount. It generally costs around $15 to do the check, once you've set up an arrangement with the credit reporting agency.

Before you can get a credit report, you must have permission from the customer. The permission can be oral. There are, however, two situations where you don't need permission from the customer: if you already offer open account terms to the customer or if the customer owes you money.

Warning

If you run a credit check on an individual, and the report turns up nothing, warning sirens the size of Montana should be going off in your head. A report that turns up no credit activity at all is commonly a sign of what is referred to in the industry as a "credit criminal."

Credit Information on Businesses

Credit information is generally easier to obtain for businesses than for individuals because businesses often have more publicly available information than do individuals.

The amount of information you collect should be in proportion to the amount of credit you intend to extend. If the credit limit you're offering is relatively low (say, $500), and the company has a good credit reputation as far as you know, you may not want to spend your time gathering more credit information. If, on the other hand, you intend to offer a high credit limit to a company that you don't know well, you may want to collect as much information as possible.

Just as there are credit bureaus that collect information about individuals, there are business credit agencies that collect information about businesses. The best-known is Dun & Bradstreet, which will provide you with an extensive report on a business for about $75. If you think you'll need many such reports, you can set up a contract with them that will allow you to obtain reports for about $35.

Work Smart

If you wish, you can voluntarily list your business with Dun & Bradstreet, so that other businesses can find out more about your credit history and may be more willing to extend credit to you.

Financial statements. Financial statements (which are included in the D&B reports) will tell you some important information about the company.

The balance sheet is probably the most useful of the documents. It will show you both the cash the company has on hand and the amount of money it owes to other businesses. That will give you a general idea of its present ability to pay its debts.

A good way to gauge a business's creditworthiness is to compare two sets of numbers. The first set is the ratio of the company's current assets to its current liabilities, called the current ratio. If the current liabilities are greater than the current assets (in other words, the ratio is less than 1:1), the company is probably not a good credit risk. Anything over 2:1 is a sign that the company is probably a good risk. A ratio between 2:1 and 1:1 is an iffier proposition, and you should probably seek more information.

The second set of numbers to compare is the company's total equity to its total debt, known as the debt to equity ratio. If the total debt is more than the total equity (the ratio is less than 1:1), be careful.

Credit references. Businesses can also give you credit references. But let's realize up front that credit references are, for the most part, worthless. Almost inevitably, you'll only get references that will say good things about the business in question.

A possible alternative is to find out on your own who else they do business with, and ask those companies about them. If you have salespeople, they are often a good source of information about who else the company does business with.

Work Smart

If you get a call for a credit reference on someone else, be careful what you say. Don't give any opinions. Tell them only the amount the customer owes you, the current amount due, and the amount that is 30 days, 60 days, or 90 days past due. In short, give them only what they could get if they saw a statement you sent to the customer.

How Much Credit To Offer?

Extending a line of credit to your business customers means that you'll have two more decisions to make: how much of a credit line to extend ($200? $500? $1,000?) and which repayment terms to impose on them (30 days? 60 days? Interest on the unpaid amount?).

There aren't any hard-and-fast guidelines for determining how much credit to extend to your customers. But here are a few suggestions that might help you with your decision.

Guidelines for Setting Credit Limits for Customers

- *Start small, particularly if your credit checking reveals that the company may be having financial problems. Depending upon what you're selling, you might start with a $100 credit line with payment to be made within 10 days. Make your customers earn higher credit limits and better terms.*

- *Don't assume that everyone is entitled to the same level of credit. If you're leery of a particular customer, keep the credit level low until he or she proves to be creditworthy.*

- *Don't presume that larger companies are necessarily better at paying their bills than smaller companies. The bureaucracy at most large companies can make debt collecting an extremely time-consuming process. Of course, if you want the large company's business badly enough, you may have to give in to their payment cycle. A large company is generally not going to change its payment cycle just for you.*

- *Don't hesitate to reduce a customer's line of credit or shorten the terms if that customer begins to be late with its payments. If you reduce the terms, however, you must inform the company before its next purchase. You cannot inform it of a change in your policy after it's already purchased your goods or services.*

- *Your credit policy should be coordinated with your business needs, particularly with your cash flow needs.*

IMPROVING YOUR COLLECTION CYCLE

Collecting overdue accounts is, for many small business owners, the most unpleasant task of all, for two main reasons: because keeping track of which accounts are overdue can be very difficult, and because most people don't enjoy pressing others for money.

Tracking Past-Due Accounts

The best place to start improving your collection cycle is to get organized. If you have a lot of customers buying on credit throughout the month, each with different terms, keeping track can be extraordinarily difficult. However, there are a number of software programs on the market that can greatly simplify this task.

Accounts receivable are part of your assets. Of course, in reality they are valuable only if you're able to collect them. And if you're going to be able to collect them, you'll have to develop a system for keeping track.

Accounts Receivable Aging Reports

An accounts receivable aging report is really just a fancy name for a piece of paper (or, if you prefer, a computer screen) that tells you exactly which accounts are past due, and by how much.

There a couple of ways you can go about generating an aging report. Far and away the easiest and most effective way is to buy some basic accounting software that will be able to generate such a report. If you don't use a computer you can produce an accounts receivable aging report the way it's been done for many, many years: by hand. This should be done every month. For an example of what the report should look like, see page 399.

When To Get Help

The next question is, *who* is going to collect your overdue accounts? Are you going to do it yourself? Will you use a collection agency? Will you use a lawyer?

Generally, doing the collecting yourself is the least expensive of the three choices, while having a lawyer do it is the most expensive. But don't forget to consider the value of your time to the business. Also, while doing it yourself is usually the least expensive approach, it's also usually the least *effective* approach. Hiring a lawyer to do it is usually both the most expensive and the most effective approach.

A good way to tackle the problem is to decide ahead of time how past-due accounts will be handled. One approach is to base your decision on the amount of the past-due account, and the length of time it's been overdue.

Sample Collection Policy

- *All debts will be collected by you for 30 days after they're past due.*

- *After 30 days, all past-due accounts greater than $1,000 will be turned over to your lawyer. You will continue to collect all other debts.*

- *After 60 days, all past-due accounts of between $500 and $1,000 will be turned over to a collection agency or to a lawyer.*

- *After 90 days, all past-due accounts under $500 will be turned over to a collection agency.*

Hiring Lawyers and Debt Collectors

Lawyers and debt collectors usually get paid by taking a percentage of what they collect. The rate is usually 33 percent, but can range from as low as 15 percent to as high as 50 percent.

In addition, if you have your lawyer file suit on your behalf, you'll usually have to pay the court costs (about $50-$100) up front, although you can recover those costs from the debtor if your suit is successful.

Following are a few guidelines for hiring a lawyer or debt collection agency.

- Don't turn over a past-due account for collection until you're sure that it's "uncollectable" by you. You're throwing money away if you turn over a past-due account that you could have collected with a single phone call.

- It's not cost-effective to have a lawyer collect your small debts, and most lawyers won't agree to do it anyway. What constitutes a "small debt" will depend upon the lawyer.

- Collection agencies usually will handle smaller debts, but only if you give them volume. They're probably not going to be interested in collecting two $25 debts, but they may be interested if you have 100 of them.

- If you want to use a collection agency first and then a lawyer when you reach the point of filing suit, make sure that you discuss with the agency how the files will be transferred to the lawyer. In fact, if you don't already have a lawyer, you may want to consider getting a referral from the collection agency. If the lawyer and the collection agency have worked together in the past, the transition shouldn't be difficult.

- If you turn over your accounts to a lawyer, carefully spell out your fee arrangement.

Save Money

 Be extremely wary of paying a lawyer by the hour to collect your debts. In fact, don't do it unless you have a specific task you want the lawyer to perform (for example, write two letters). Otherwise, you could end up paying out more than you collect.

What To Do When a Debt Is Uncollectable

Here are some guidelines you can use for determining when a past-due account should be turned over to a lawyer:

- If the customer tells you he or she has no intention of paying the debt and you can't do anything about the "why" (for example, the customer won't give you a reason why), you've reached the point where you need to turn the account over.

- If the customer gives the impression of wanting to work with you, but never seems to come across with any money, the best way to approach it is to place a deadline on collecting.

- If the customer declares bankruptcy, you have to stop your collection efforts. You should at this point discuss your options with a lawyer.

Skip-Tracing

Skip-tracing is the process of tracking down someone who owes you money. When an individual skips out, he or she generally moves away to another city, to another state, or to another country. When a corporation skips out, it generally ceases to exist.

You should consider running a skip-trace as soon as you see any sign that the debtor may have disappeared, such as your mail being returned or the debtor's phone being disconnected.

To find a professional skip-tracer, look in the Yellow Pages under "skip tracing" or "private investigators." It'll cost you at least $30 per skip-trace, so don't skip-trace an account unless the dollar value is high enough above that figure to justify the trouble.

Bankruptcy

A debtor may hide from you, he may stonewall you, he may run from you, but he can never escape the fact that he owes you money — unless he declares bankruptcy. The laws give the federal bankruptcy courts the right to wipe away your customer's debt to you in one stroke of the pen.

There are a few things, however, you should know about bankruptcy, before one of your customers threatens you with it to get you to stop your collection efforts.

To begin with, there are really two types of bankruptcy. The first is called straight, or Chapter 7, bankruptcy, in which the debtor is seeking to have all or most of his debts wiped clean. The debtor in straight bankruptcy is allowed to keep a few of his or her assets, such as a house and some belongings.

The second type is called reorganization or Chapter 11 bankruptcy (or Chapter 13, for individuals who want to reorganize). In this case, the debtor is attempting to work with all the creditors to formulate a repayment plan, and to continue in business while the debts are being repaid. Your chances of collecting from the debtor are better in Chapter 11 or Chapter 13 than in Chapter 7.

The second thing you need to know is that once you discover that your customer has filed for bankruptcy, you must stop all your collection efforts. At this point, you should contact your lawyer. Any payments you've received within the last 90 days of the bankruptcy may have to be returned to the bankruptcy estate.

The third thing you need to know is that the best protection you can have against someone going into bankruptcy is to have collateral for your debt (i.e., some piece of property that can legally be seized or foreclosed upon if the debt is not paid). If you have collateral, you are considered to be a secured creditor, and will be paid before unsecured creditors. Statistics indicate that the average secured creditor receives about 77 cents on the dollar, while the average unsecured creditor receives *only about 2 cents*.

Streamlining Your Collection Tactics

Conventional wisdom holds that you start your debt collecting with a letter gently reminding the customer that the account is past due. That letter is followed up with still more letters, each one becoming a little more threatening than the previous one. After the sixth or seventh letter, you've threatened them with collection agencies, lawyers, and lawsuits. Sometimes it works, but most often it doesn't.

Most people know how the game is played. They know that if they receive the gentle reminder, they still have a few letters to go before they have to get serious about paying the debt.

Save Time

If you want to start with a letter, consider paying an attorney to write it for you. You can probably get one to write it for you for no more than $50-$75. The attorney's letterhead serves to show the debtor that you are serious.

If letters are the least effective method, then personal visits are the most effective. Telephone calls fall somewhere in between.

The actual combination of approaches that you will take — letter/phone call/visit, lawyer/collection agent/yourself, etc. — will probably vary from customer to customer and will depend upon factors such as the location of your customers, your relationship to each one, and your cash flow needs.

Following are some sample collection letters that you can use if you want to try the conventional approach. The first one is a very gentle reminder, while the second and third provide escalating levels of gravity.

First Letter

Re: [Account balance]

[Account number]

Dear [debtor]:

Here's a reminder that your account of $_____ was overdue as of _____, _____. Please play this account promptly. If you have already put the check in the mail, we apologize for the inconvenience and thank you for your payment.

Sincerely,

Second Letter

Re: [account balance]

[account number]

Dear [debtor]:

This is the second reminder that you owe us $_____.

Please pay this account promptly. We would like to continue doing business with you, but we need your cooperation and payment to do so. Thank you for your prompt attention to this matter.

Sincerely,

Third Letter

Re: [account balance]

   [account number]

Dear [debtor]:

This is your final reminder that your account of $_____ is past due. It has been past due since _____,_____. If payment is not received by _____,_____, we will have no alternative but to turn your account over to a [lawyer or collection agency] for collection. Thank you for your prompt attention to this matter.

Sincerely,

Here are some tips that may help you to improve your technique.

Collection Tips

- When you contact customers, don't hand them an excuse ("Did you receive your bill?"). It's better to ask them, "When was payment made?" If they tell you it hasn't been made, ask them if they intend to pay it today. If they say "no," ask them when they have scheduled it to be paid. Get a commitment from them.

- If they haven't scheduled it, ask them if they intend to pay the bill. If they say "no," ask them why. Once you have the reason, hang up or walk away. If you continue the call or visit at this point, you may be crossing over into harassment. At this point, it's time to turn to a collection agency or lawyer.

- If you ask your customers if they intend to pay their bill, and they say "yes," you should continue the discussion. Ask them why they haven't paid it. They'll give you either a reason or an excuse. In either case, get a firm commitment from them for when they can pay you.

- If they give you a reason ("The goods you delivered to me were damaged"), try to remedy the condition, if it's within your control.

- If they refuse to give you a commitment ("I'll put you on the list to get paid"), you'll have to review your options. In some cases, you can force a commitment by taking away their credit on future purchases. In other cases, your only options are to turn it over to an attorney, turn it over to a collection agency, or bring suit yourself in small claims court.

- *If you deal with large companies, you need to get in tune with how they pay their bills. Find out from them what is the last day for getting an invoice approved to get into this week's (or bi-week's or month's, depending upon how they pay their bills) check run. When you need to collect from them, call a couple of days before that date to make sure that they have all the documentation from you that they need.*

- *If you have a problem with payment from a large company, talk to the person who is responsible for buying your goods or services (perhaps in the purchasing department). Don't allow yourself to be sent to accounts payable. Your best leverage is to threaten to withhold your goods if payment is not made. While the purchaser may respond to that threat, the accounts payable person almost surely will not.*

- *If you do business with the government, consider taking a government-sponsored seminar on how to get paid. They're offered quarterly in all major cities.*

Bringing a Collection Suit

If you reach the point that you need to take some action on a past-due account, you can file suit yourself in small claims court.

Each state has a small claims court or its equivalent. Depending on the state, the most you can recover in any suit brought in small claims court is about $5,000 or $10,000 (plus the court costs you have to pay when you file your suit). You do not have to be a lawyer to file a suit in small claims court. In fact, the system is set up to help nonlawyers who want to use it.

To get started, go to your local state courthouse, and tell the clerk that you want to file a small claims complaint. The clerk will help you fill it out. You'll pay court costs of about $40-$75.

The sheriff will serve a copy of the complaint on the customer, who will have a certain period of time to respond (usually about two weeks). If the customer does not respond within the allowed time period, you can go back to the courthouse and get a default judgment against the customer. The clerk will help you. The judge will ask you to swear to the truth of the statements in your complaint, and then will sign an order giving you a judgment in the amount you requested. When you go to get your judgment, you should bring any signed sales receipts or other proof of the debt with you.

Once you have your default judgment, you should have it recorded. Ask the clerk for help. Essentially, this will involve taking a certified copy of your judgment to the property records clerk, who, for a small fee, will place your judgment on the official record.

If, on the other hand, your customer files an answer within the allowed time period, the clerk will set a court date. You should bring whatever written documentation you have with you. Generally, the judge will ask each of you to tell your side of the story in your own words. You'll both be given the chance to ask each other questions. Since it's usually your word against the customer's, the written documentation is particularly important.

However the judge rules, the losing party can appeal. You'll generally need an attorney to help in the appeals process.

Avoiding the Legal Pitfalls of Collections Work

If you're going to extend credit and to do some of your own debt collecting, you'll need to be aware of the basic guidelines for what you can and cannot do. Here's an overview of the legal rules you'll have to obey.

Disclosure of interest rates and terms. Federal law requires you to disclose your annual percentage rate or finance charge, if you sell on credit *to an individual* any personal, household, or agricultural goods. The law does not apply to commercial transactions.

Debt collection practices. The federal Fair Debt Collection Practices Act prohibits what are called abusive, deceptive, and unfair debt collection practices. They do not apply to you if you are collecting on your own behalf, but they do apply to your lawyer or collection agency. Here are the highlights:

- You can't contact an individual debtor before 8 a.m. or after 9 p.m., unless you have the debtor's permission.

- If you know the debtor is represented by an attorney, you can't contact the debtor directly, without permission. Instead, you must contact the attorney.

- You can't contact the debtor at his or her place of employment, if you know or have reason to know that the employer prohibits such communication.

- You can't contact the debtor's family members or employer.

- If the debtor notifies you in writing that he or she will not pay the debt or wants you to stop contacting him or her, you can't make contact again except in a few limited situations, most notably to inform the debtor that you're filing suit.

- You can't threaten your customer with violence or other criminal conduct, or use obscene or profane language.

Chapter 24

Managing Your Cash Flow

If you fail to satisfy a customer and lose that customer's business, you can always work harder to please the next customer. But if you fail to have enough cash to pay your suppliers, creditors, or your employees, *you're out of business!* No doubt about it, proper management of your cash flow is a very important step in making your business successful.

In this chapter we'll explain how cash moves in and through your business, show you how to examine the health of your cash flow, introduce the cash flow budget, and give you tips on how to improve your business's cash flow.

UNDERSTANDING HOW CASH FLOW WORKS

Simply stated, cash flow is the movement of money in and out of your business.

If you were able to do business in a perfect world, you'd probably like to have a cash inflow (a cash sale) occur every time you experience a cash outflow (pay an expense). But you know all too well that business takes place in the real world, and things just don't happen like that.

Instead, cash outflows and inflows occur at different times, and never actually occur together. More often than not, cash inflows lag behind your cash outflows, leaving your business short of money. Think of this money shortage as your cash flow gap.

Profit vs. Cash Flow

If a retail business is able to buy a retail item for $1,000 and sell it for $2,000, then it has made a $1,000 profit. But what if the buyer is slow to pay his or her bill, and six months pass before the bill is paid? Using accrual accounting, the retail business still shows a profit, but what about the bills it has to pay during those six months? It will not have the cash to pay them, despite the profit earned on the sale.

As you can see, profit and cash flow are two entirely different concepts. The concept of profit is somewhat narrow, and looks only at income and expenses at a certain point in time. Cash flow, on the other hand, is more dynamic. It is concerned with the movement of money in and out of a business. More importantly, it is concerned with the time at which the movement of the money takes place. You might even say the concept of cash flow is more in line with reality! If you use the accrual accounting method, it is helpful to know how to convert your accrual profit to your cash flow profit.

Converting Accrual Profit to Cash Flow

If you keep your books on the accrual method of accounting as we recommend, you'll have to make some adjustments to determine your actual cash flow. These adjustments are necessary because certain expenses are taken into account to determine your accrual net profit, even though these expenses do not currently require a cash outlay. To convert your accrual profit to your cash flow profit, you need a balance sheet for the beginning and end of the period under examination.

As a general rule, you can convert your accrual net profit using the following formula:

> *Net Profit*
> *+ Depreciation*
> *− Increases (or + Decreases) in Accounts Receivable*
> *− Increases (or + Decreases) in Inventories*
> *+ Increases (or − Decreases) in Accounts Payable*
> *− Decreases (or + Increases) in Notes Payable (Bank Loans)*
> *= **Net Cash Flow***

For an illustration of how this works, see the case study below.

Case Study — Profit vs. Cash Flow

The following example looks at the adjustments necessary to convert the accrual profits of Bug Busters Exterminating Service to its cash flow for its year ending December 31, 2000.

To convert its accrual profit to its cash flow profit, Bug Busters will need balance sheets from the beginning and end of the period it wishes to examine. In this case, Bug Busters will examine the period starting on January 1, 2000, and ending on December 31, 2000. Below is the comparative balance sheet provided by Bug Busters' accountant for December 31, 1999, and December 31, 2000:

Bug Busters Exterminating Service
Comparative Balance Sheets

	12/31/99	12/31/00
Cash	$17,845	$4,375
Accounts Receivable	12,185	27,371
Inventory	6,034	9,133
Property and Equipment	83,239	83,239
Less: Accumulated Depreciation	(44,826)	(48,989)
Total Assets	$74,477	$75,129
Accounts Payable	$6,977	$7,630
Notes Payable (Bank Loans)	27,500	12,000
Total Liabilities	$34,477	$19,630
Stockholder's Equity	$40,000	$55,499
Total Liabilities and Equity	$74,477	$75,129

The conversion process also requires an income statement for the end of the period under examination.

Bug Busters Exterminating Service
Income Statement
December 31, 2000

Sales	$267,189
Less: Cost of Goods Sold	132,122
Gross Profit	$135,067
Less: Operating Expenses	(115,405)
Less: Depreciation	(4,163)
Net Profit	$15,499

Using the formula from the discussion above, Bug Busters can adjust its accrual net profit to determine its cash flow for the year:

Adjustment Description		Amount
Net Profit — December 31, 2000		$15,499
Add:	Depreciation	4,163
Subtract:	Increase in Accounts Receivable between 12/31/99 and 12/31/00	(15,186)
Subtract:	Increase in Inventory between 12/31/99 and 12/31/00	(3,099)
Add:	Increase in Accounts Payable between 12/31/99 and 12/31/00	653
Subtract:	Decrease in Notes Payable between 12/31/99 and 12/31/00	(15,500)

Net Cash Flow for the year ended December 31, 2000		($13,470)
		=======

The income statement prepared using the accrual method of accounting reports a profit of $15,499 for the year. However, in terms of a cash flow, Bug Busters had a negative cash flow of $13,470 for the same year. In other words, Bug Busters spent $13,470 more than it collected during the year.

ANALYZING YOUR CASH FLOW

To properly manage your business's cash flow, you must first analyze the components that affect the timing of your cash inflows and cash outflows. A good analysis of these components will point out problem areas that lead to cash flow gaps for your business.

Some of the more important components to examine are your amount and volume of accounts receivable and payable, the discounts you offer, and your inventory.

Accounts Receivable and Cash Flow

Accounts receivable represent sales that have not yet been collected as cash. In the worst case scenario, unpaid accounts receivable will leave your business without the necessary cash to pay its own bills. More commonly, late-paying or slow-paying customers will create chronic cash shortages. The following pages discuss two analysis tools that can be used to examine the effect that your accounts receivable have on cash flow.

Measuring Your Average Collection Period

The average collection period measures the average length of time it takes to convert your sales into cash. A *longer average collection period requires a higher investment in accounts receivable. A higher investment in accounts receivable means less cash is available to cover cash outflows, such as paying bills.*

Here's how to calculate the average collection period:

$$\textbf{\textit{Average collection period}} = \frac{\textit{Current Accounts Receivable Balance}}{\textit{Average Daily Sales}}$$

The average daily sales volume is computed as follows:

$$\textbf{\textit{Average daily sales}} = \frac{\textit{Annual Sales}}{360}$$

Using the Average Collection Period

The average collection period can be used to determine the effect of different collection periods on your business's cash flow. This is best illustrated by the chart that follows.

For example, assume that your average sales amount per day is $300, and that your average collection period is 40 days. If you were able to reduce your average collection period from 40 days to 30 days, you could reduce the investment in accounts receivable from $12,000 to $9,000, and generate an additional $3,000 in cash flow!

Average Collection Period	Sales per Day				
	$200	**$300**	**$400**	**$500**	**$600**
	Investment in Accounts Receivable				
30	$6,000	$9,000	$12,000	$15,000	$18,000
40	8,000	12,000	16,000	20,000	24,000
50	10,000	15,000	20,000	25,000	30,000
60	12,000	18,000	24,000	30,000	36,000

Accounts Receivable Aging Schedule

The accounts receivable aging schedule is a listing of the customers making up your total accounts receivable balance. Most businesses prepare an accounts receivable aging schedule at the end of each month, so they can identify potential cash flow problems.

The following is a sample accounts receivable aging schedule:

Accounts Receivable Aging Report Roth Office Supply October 31, 2000					
Customer Name	**Total Accts. Rec.**	**Current**	**1-30 Days Past Due**	**31-60 Days Past Due**	**Over 60 Days Past Due**
Quick Computer Supply	$1,600	$300	$500	$500	$300
Kitchens by Voels	2,800	2,800	—	—	—
Jansa's Sport Stores	1,000	1,000	—	—	—
Bradley Farms, Inc.	1,600	—	1,600	—	—
TrueBrew Unlimited	2,000	1,100	500	400	—
Enneking Enterprises	400	—	400	—	—
Hove & Sanborn LLC	600	600	—	—	—
J. Siegel, CPA	1,200	1,200	—	—	—
Total	$11,200	$7,000	$3,000	$900	$300

Save Time

If you're using one of the many available accounting software packages for billing and accounts receivable processing, check it first to see if it prepares the aging schedule automatically. Most accounting software packages will prepare an accounts receivable aging schedule at the touch of a button!

Offering Trade Discounts

Some businesses allow customers to take a trade discount off the original sales price if the customer pays within a specified period of time.

The amount of the trade discount is typically 1 percent or 2 percent if the customer pays within 10 days. Full payment is normally due within 30 days if the customer doesn't take advantage of the trade discount.

The main advantage of offering trade discounts is that it shortens the average collection period. The primary disadvantage of offering trade discounts is the cost to your bottom line profit associated with the lost revenues. The cost of trade discounts must be weighed against the improved cash flow expected.

Case Study — Cost of Trade Discounts

Quick Computer Supply has been experiencing a steady buildup in accounts receivable over the last six months. Quick has decided to look at the possibility of offering a trade discount to its customers if their payments are received 10 days after shipment. The company's current credit terms call for full payment within 30 days of shipment. Sarah Quick, founder and CEO, has provided the following information:

- *Sales have been averaging about $25,000 per month.*

- *Ms. Quick estimates that about 50 percent of the company's customers will take advantage of a 1-percent discount. She expects 75 percent of the company's customers will take advantage of a 2-percent discount. For analysis purposes, she assumes all customers not taking advantage of the trade discounts will pay within 30 days.*

- *The company's annual carrying costs for its investment in accounts receivable is 11 percent.*

The following analysis shows the effect on the company's bottom line for each of the options.

(A) Credit Terms	(B) % of Customers Taking Discounts	(C) Average Accts. Rec. (Note 1)	(D) 11% Annual Carrying Costs (C x 11%)	(E) Cost of Trade Discounts (Note 2)	(F) Effect on the Bottom Line (D + E)
no discount	N/A	$25,000	$2,750	—	($2,750)
1/10 Net 30	50%	16,666	1,833	1,500	(3,333)
2/10 Net 30	75%	8,333	917	4,500	(5,417)

Note 1: Average accounts receivable is computed as a weighted average of the accounts receivable for the month.

Note 2: Cost of the trade discount is computed as follows: ((percent of customers taking discount x monthly sales) x discount percentage) x 12

Ms. Quick sees that offering no discounts has the smallest impact on the bottom line, reducing the company's profits by $2,750. Offering a 2-percent discount is the most costly, reducing the company's bottom line by $5,417.

From the cash flow perspective, a lower average investment in accounts receivable means a quicker inflow of cash for the company. Offering the 2-percent discount significantly reduces the company's average investment in accounts receivable. This option would have the most favorable impact on cash flow problems.

Ms. Quick determined that offering a 1-percent discount strikes a comfortable balance between the two perspectives. Offering a 1-percent discount reduces the company's bottom line by only $3,333 — a small sacrifice for an increase in the company's cash flow. At the same time, this option increases the company's cash flow by $8,333.

Inventory and Cash Flow

Much like accounts receivable, inventory represents an investment of your business's cash — cash that cannot be used for other purposes. Typically, a business purchases inventory and either pays for it at the time of the purchase, or within 30 days. Depending on the nature of your business, it may be days or weeks before the inventory is resold; or used in the manufacturing of a final product, and then sold.

The next few pages discuss average inventory investment period and turnover analysis, tools that can be used to help manage inventory.

Average Inventory Investment Period

The average inventory investment period measures the amount of time it takes to convert a dollar of cash outflow, used to purchase inventory, to a dollar of sales or accounts receivable from the sale of the inventory. *A longer average inventory investment period requires a higher investment in inventory. A higher investment in inventory means less cash is available for other cash outflows, such as paying bills.*

The average inventory investment period is calculated as follows:

$$\textbf{\textit{Average inventory investment period}} = \frac{\textit{Current Inventory Balance}}{\textit{Average Daily Cost of Goods Sold}}$$

Remember, the average daily cost of goods sold is computed like this:

$$\textbf{\textit{Average daily cost of goods sold}} = \frac{\textit{Annual Cost of Goods Sold}}{360}$$

Using Average Inventory Investment

The average inventory investment period can be used to determine the effect of different inventory investment periods on your business's cash flow. This is best illustrated by the chart that follows.

Cost of Goods Sold per Day					
Avg. Inventory Invest. Per. (days)	$200	$300	$400	$500	$600
	Investment in Inventory				
70	$14,000	$21,000	$28,000	$35,000	$42,000
80	16,000	24,000	32,000	40,000	48,000
90	18,000	27,000	36,000	45,000	54,000
100	20,000	30,000	40,000	50,000	60,000
110	22,000	33,000	44,000	55,000	66,000

For example, assume that your cost of goods sold per day is $300, and that your average inventory investment period is 100 days. If you were able to reduce your average investment period from 100 days to 70 days, you can reduce the investment in inventory from $30,000 to $21,000, generating an additional $9,000 in your cash flow!

Turnover Analysis

There are some limitations to the information provided by the average inventory investment period calculation. Because it is an average, it assumes that all products are the same, each selling at the same rate, and each costing the same amount.

Turnover analysis goes beyond the average assumptions made by the average inventory investment period. It does this by requiring you to look at each product or line individually.

Using Turnover Analysis

Performing turnover analysis requires you to look at each individual inventory item or product line for the following information:

- the number of items currently held in inventory

- the number of items sold during the measurement period (expressed in days, generally 30 to 60 days)

- the number of items held in relation to the measurement period

Once the information is compiled for each inventory item, you can then determine if the level for each item is excessive, too low, or just right.

Case Study — Turnover Analysis

Jeff Hammer, owner of Handy Hardware, has noticed a significant buildup in the inventory of the home repair and improvement section of the store. Sales in this department have remained steady, but the average inventory investment period has increased over the last three months. Jeff's goal is to stock the number of inventory items necessary for about 30 days of sales.

Jeff has decided to perform a turnover analysis on the home repair and improvement inventory items. He has just completed his mid-year physical inventory count so the number of items held in inventory is already available. The number of a particular item sold was compiled using information gathered at the time a customer checks out. The following is an excerpt from his turnover analysis schedule:

Handy Hardware Inventory Turnover Analysis June 30, 2000				
Description	**Number in Stock**	**Number Sold in Last 30 Days**	**Days Sales in Inventory**	**Jeff's Action**
Paint (gals)	392	121	97	Reduce level
Paint Brushes/Rollers	66	54	37	Just right
Paint Remover (gals)	10	15	20	Increase level
Paint Thinner (gals)	130	44	89	Reduce level
Sandpaper sheets	922	192	144	Reduce level

Based on the information from Jeff's turnover analysis, he has determined that his inventory level in three of the five items listed above is too high, and his inventory in paint remover is too low.

Accounts Payable and Cash Flow

Accounts payable are amounts you owe to your suppliers that are payable sometime within the near future — "near" meaning 30 to 90 days. They represent eventual outflows of cash, which you will ordinarily want to delay as long as possible.

Average Payable Period

The average payable period measures the average amount of time you use each dollar of your trade credit. *A longer average payable period allows you to maximize your trade credit. Maximizing your trade credit means that you are delaying your cash outflows and taking full advantage of each dollar in your own cash flow.*

The average payable period is calculated as follows:

$$\textbf{Average payable period} = \frac{\textit{Accounts Payable Balance}}{\textit{Average Daily Purchases on Account}}$$

The average daily purchases on account is computed this way:

$$\textbf{Average daily purchases on account} = \frac{\textit{Annual Purchases on Account}}{360}$$

Using the Average Payable Period

The average payable period can be used to see the benefits of the basic rule regarding cash outflows — *pay your bills on time, but never pay your bills before they are due.* The following chart illustrates the benefits of this basic rule.

Average Daily POA*	Increments in the Average Payable Period (Days)			
	1	3	5	10
	Amount of Delayed Cash Outflow			
$100	$100	$300	$500	$1,000
$300	300	900	1,500	3,000
$500	500	1,500	2,500	5,000
$800	800	2,400	4,000	8,000
$1,000	1,000	3,000	5,000	10,000

*POA = purchases on account

For example, assume that your average daily purchases on account is $300 a day, and that your average payable period is 20 days. If you were able to extend your average payable period from 20 days to 30 days, you could add 10 days to your average collection period and defer $3,000 in cash outflows. This represents $3,000 of interest-free financing that you can use for reducing debt, or making other necessary purchases.

Accounts Payable Aging Schedule

Using an accounts payable aging schedule can help you determine how well you are (or aren't) paying your accounts payable. If the schedule indicates that you have some bills that are past due, you may be relying a little too heavily on your trade credit.

An accounts payable aging report looks very much like an accounts receivable aging schedule. However, instead of showing the amounts your customers owe you, the payables aging schedule is used for listing the amounts you owe your various suppliers. Most businesses should prepare this schedule at the end of each month.

The following is a sample accounts payable aging schedule:

Accounts Payable Aging Schedule **Fortmann's Hawkeye Haven** **December 31, 2000**					
Supplier's Name	*Total Accts. Payable*	*Current*	*1-30 Days Past Due*	*31-60 Days Past Due*	*Over 60 Days Past Due*
Hove Advertising	$1,600	$1,600	—	—	—
Citizen Press Daily	2,800	2,600	200	—	—
Jansa Distributing	1,000	600	100	300	—
Bradley's Bookkeeping	600	300	300	—	—
TrueBrew Unlimited	2,000	1,100	500	400	—
Enneking Insurance Co.	400	400	—	—	—
Roth Office Supply	600	600	—	—	—
Handy Hardware	350	350	—	—	—
Total	$9,350	$7,550	$1,100	$700	—

Looking at the schedule allows you to spot problems in the management of payables early enough to protect your business from any major trade credit problems. For example, if Jansa Distributing was an important supplier for Fortmann's, then the past due amounts listed for Jansa Distributing should be paid in order to protect the trade credit established with this supplier.

CREATING A CASH FLOW BUDGET

A cash flow budget is a projection of your business's cash inflows and outflows on a month-to-month basis. Because of the uncertainty involved in the cash flow budget, trying to project too far into the future may prove to be less than worthwhile.

A six-month cash flow budget minimizes the amount of uncertainty involved in the budget. It also predicts future events early enough for you to take corrective action. However, if you're applying for a loan, you may need to create a cash flow budget that extends for several years into the future, as part of the application process.

Preparing a cash flow budget involves four steps:

1. preparing a sales forecast, generally based on last year's sales figures

2. projecting your anticipated cash inflows

3. projecting your anticipated cash outflows

4. putting the projections together to come up with your cash flow bottom line

For a sample of a completed cash flow budget, see the financial statements at the end of the sample business plan in Chapter 6.

Work Smart

The cash flow budget is an excellent tool to help you determine when or when not to make major purchases. If your cash flow budget shows that additional funds may be available at a certain point, this should provide you with the opportunity to make advance purchase decisions. Planning ahead may allow you to take advantage of lower prices, discounts, or better financing options. Likewise, if your cash flow budget shows that your cash supply might be a little tight, it's probably not a good idea to make a major purchase, or take on an additional monthly loan payment.

Projecting Cash Inflows

If your business only accepts cash sales, then your projected cash receipts will equal the amount of sales predicted in the sales forecast.

If you extend credit to your customers, you must take into account the collection of accounts receivable and the timing effect that collection has on the projection of your cash receipts. Applying your accounts receivable collection pattern from the past to your sales forecast is the best way to predict the timing of your future cash receipts.

Case Study — Projecting Cash Receipts

Linn Vernon is starting a business as a financial planning consultant. Linn will receive 10 percent down when a consulting agreement is signed. The customer will be billed for the remainder after the job is completed. Linn's credit terms are Net 30 (the full amount due within 30 days). Relying on her accountant's past experience with accounts receivable collections, she assumes the following:

*   *70 percent of the accounts receivable are collected in the month following the completion of the consultation*

*   *20 percent of the receivables are collected in the second month following the consultation*

- *10 percent of the receivables are collected in the third month following the consultation*

Using her accounts receivable collection pattern and her sales forecast, Linn can now complete her cash receipts projection for the first six months of 2000.

Vernon Consulting Service
Cash Receipts Projection

	Jan. 2000	Feb. 2000	Mar. 2000	Apr. 2000	May 2000	June 2000
Forecasted Sales	$30,000	$35,000	$40,000	$50,000	$40,000	$30,000
10% down	3,000	3,500	4,000	5,000	4,000	3,000
70% 1st month		18,900	22,050	25,200	31,500	25,200
20% 2nd month			5,400	6,300	7,200	9,000
10% 3rd month				2,700	3,150	3,600
Total receipts	$3,000	$22,400	$31,450	$39,200	$45,850	$40,800

Projecting Cash Outflows

Your accounts payable aging schedule may help you determine your cash outflows for certain expenses in the near future — 30 to 60 days.

Another approach is to look at your most recent income statement, and estimate whether the expenses shown will increase, decrease, or remain constant.

Putting the Projections Together

The final step in preparing a cash flow budget is putting together your projected cash inflows and outflows to come up with your cash flow bottom line. In its basic form, the completed cash flow budget combines the following information on a month-by-month basis:

Beginning Cash Balance
+ *Projected Cash Inflows*
− *Projected Cash Outflows*
= **Your Cash Flow Bottom Line (the ending cash balance)**

The ending cash balance for the first month becomes the second month's beginning cash balance. The second month's cash flow bottom line is determined by combining the beginning cash balance with the second month's anticipated cash inflows and cash outflows. The ending cash balance for the second month then becomes the third month's beginning cash balance. This process continues until the last month of the cash flow budget is completed.

IMPROVING YOUR CASH FLOW

Improving your cash flow means three things:

- accelerating your cash inflows — the flow of money into your business

- delaying your cash outflows — the flow of money out of your business

- minimizing expenses — the amounts you pay for operational costs of your business

Accelerating Cash Inflows

The cash conversion period measures the amount of time it takes to turn the sale of your product or service into cash available for cash outflows. Here's is an illustration of the typical conversion period:

Cash Conversion Period

```
┌─────────────────────────┐
│   The Purchase Decision  │
│       and Ordering       │
└─────────────────────────┘
             ⇓
┌─────────────────────────┐
│    The Credit Decision   │
└─────────────────────────┘
             ⇓
┌─────────────────────────┐
│    Order Fulfillment,    │
│  Shipping, and Handling  │
└─────────────────────────┘
             ⇓
┌─────────────────────────┐
│    Billing the Customer  │
└─────────────────────────┘
             ⇓
┌─────────────────────────┐
│   The Average Accounts   │
│   Receivable Collection  │
│          Period          │
└─────────────────────────┘
             ⇓
┌─────────────────────────┐
│    Payment and Deposit   │
└─────────────────────────┘
```

Completing each event takes a certain number of days. To shorten the conversion period, take a look at each event, and see if you can reduce the time necessary to complete it.

Purchase Decision and Ordering

Allowing your customers to make their purchase decisions, and communicate their decisions to you as quickly as possible, is an important step for shortening the cash conversion period event.

Let your customers know what you're selling. Your customers' purchasing decisions will take longer if they're not sure of exactly what you're selling, or what it will cost them. Price lists, catalogs, displays, and proposals or quotations are just a few ways you can quickly and accurately communicate what your business can provide.

Make it easy for your customers to place an order. Making the task of ordering your goods or services quick and convenient by bypassing the postal service is another way to accelerate your customer's purchase decision. Accepting orders over the phone, via fax, or using a computer and modem are just a few ways you can make your customer's ordering task quicker and easier.

Credit Decisions

Depending on your credit policy, the time involved in deciding whether to extend credit to a customer can add a significant number of days to your cash conversion period.

With existing customers or clients, it is best to anticipate a raise in their credit limit whenever possible, before they place their next order.

The credit decision for new customers or clients can be more difficult and time consuming, if you want to check their credit references, obtain credit reports, and check with their banks. Starting your credit decision making processes when first meeting with new customers or clients is one way to reduce the amount of time it takes.

Fulfillment, Shipping, and Handling

Unnecessary delays in the shipping and handling of your products or services can add a significant number of days to your cash conversion period, not to mention the negative impact this can have on your customer relationships.

Most important is the ability to quickly fulfill your customers' orders with your products or services. For a retail business, or any business that sells products, this means that you need to control your inventory. For a service-related business, this means you must be able to provide the services requested by your customers when they need them.

Billing the Customer

You've probably figured out by now that most customers don't pay without first receiving some form of invoice for the goods or services you sold them. If possible, try to prepare invoices immediately after you've delivered your goods or services to each customer. *Don't* wait until the end of the month to prepare invoices — this could add as many as 30 extra days to your cash conversion period!

The invoices should include the dates they were prepared. These dates are important because they serve as the starting date for your credit terms. Customers generally have 20 to 30 days from the date of the invoice to pay the amount listed as due.

Improving Your Average Collection Period

For most businesses, the time it takes to collect on a customer's account is generally the step requiring the most amount of time in the cash conversion period. For more information on improving your collection efforts, see *Chapter 23: Credit and Collections.*

Payment and Deposit

Receiving the payment and depositing it in your bank account is the final event in the cash conversion period. Typically, a customer waits until the payment due date before dropping the check in the mail. There is nothing wrong with this — your customer is just taking advantage of a good cash flow management technique.

For your business, on the other hand, using the postal service to receive your customers' checks can add one to three days (possibly more) to your cash conversion period.

Post office boxes. Some of the delay in the postal service is the result of having your mail delivered directly to your place of business. This type of delivery entails extra sorting so that your mail gets into the hands of the correct mail carrier, not to mention the time it takes the carrier to actually deliver it to your address. Using a post office box can reduce this delay by one to three days.

Lockbox banking. Using lockbox banking is a cash flow improvement technique in which you have your customers' payments delivered to a special post office box instead of your business address. Your bank's couriers have a key to the post office box, and they remove its contents and deliver your customers' payments to your bank. Your bank opens the payments and then processes the payments for deposit directly into your bank account.

Depending on the nature of your business, the contents of your lockbox can be removed and processed once a day, or more often if required. A basic rule is that your lockboxes should be set up nearest to your customers to reduce the amount of time between when they mail their payments and when the cash is deposited into your bank account.

Delaying Cash Outflows

The key to improving your cash flow with regard to cash outflows is to delay all outflows of cash as long as you possibly can, without actually making late payments.

Using Trade Credit

Your suppliers are extending you trade credit whenever they allow you to purchase their goods or services without making you pay for them at the time of purchase. In essence, trade credit is actually a short-term loan with interest-free financing.

Most of your suppliers will determine in advance the maximum amount of trade credit they are willing to extend to you, based on their estimate of your creditworthiness, and your capacity to pay for your purchases.

If you're a new customer to the supplier, you may have to fill out a credit application, give some credit references, and provide other financial information about your business. If you're an existing customer of the supplier, the supplier's credit decision is based primarily on your past payment history, so it's important to maintain a dependable and consistent payment history with your suppliers.

Work Smart

If you find it necessary to pay one or more of your suppliers later than they allow, call them to let them know in advance, before they pick your name off their list of overdue accounts. When notified in advance, you'll find that most suppliers are willing to extend their credit terms and carry an account past its due date.

Taking Trade Discounts

Some suppliers may allow you a trade discount off the total amount of their invoice if you pay within a specified period of time. Trade discounts are generally listed on an invoice in the following format: "1/10, Net 30" or 2/10, Net 30." 1/10 or 2/10 indicates that a 1-percent or 2-percent discount is being offered if the payment is made within 10 days of the invoice's date. "Net 30" indicates that the full amount of the invoice (without the discount) is due in 30 days.

Trade discounts are the only exception to the basic rule of delaying cash outflows — always pay your bills on time, but never before they are due. In most cases you are better off to pay the bill early and take advantage of the trade discount.

Save Money

As a rule, you should always take advantage of trade discounts of 1 percent or more if your suppliers require full payment within 30 days. If your suppliers offer payment terms extending beyond 30 days, it may be more advantageous to skip the trade discount and delay payment until the full amount is due.

Negotiating Payment Terms

If you're like most other business owners, you probably assume that your suppliers' payment terms are non-negotiable. However, that may not always be the case. Your suppliers' willingness to agree to better credit terms may be based on your past and present business relationship with them, or the possibility of securing a large order or your continued business. This is one of those situations where it can't hurt to ask.

Deferring Expenses

To a limited extent, your business may be able to delay cash outflows by deferring the payment of certain expenses. Payroll is one example of an expense that you may be able to defer. If your business pays its employees once a week, you may want to consider switching to paying your employees once every two weeks instead. Likewise, if your business writes payroll checks once every two weeks, you might switch to a monthly payroll cycle, if permitted in your state.

Sales commissions or sales bonuses are two other expenses that may provide you with some deferral possibilities. Be sure to review your business for any other expenses that can be reasonably deferred.

Minimizing Expenses

Of course, the best way to improve your cash flow, and in particular to improve your accounts payable situation, is to minimize your business's operational expenses and to make sure that you make the most efficient use of every dollar you spend. Exactly how you can do this depends on the type of business you have, but you should constantly be on the lookout for ways to save money while maintaining or even improving your product or your service.

FILLING CASH FLOW GAPS

Any business, large or small, may experience a cash flow gap from time to time — it doesn't necessarily mean the business is in financial trouble. Cash flow gaps are often filled by external financing sources. Revolving lines of credit, bank loans, and trade credit are just a few of the external financing options available for your business. For more information, see *Part III: Getting Financing for Your Business.*

WHAT TO DO WITH A CASH SURPLUS

Managing and improving your cash flow should result in a cash surplus for your business; that is, cash that exceeds the cash required for day-to-day operations. How you handle your cash surplus is just as important as the management of money into and out of your cash flow cycle.

Paying Down Debt

Paying down any debt you may have is generally the first option considered when deciding what to do with a cash surplus. And rightfully so, because a short-term investment of your cash surplus is not likely to yield a return equal to or greater than the rate of interest on any of your debt. It doesn't make any sense to invest a cash surplus at 3 percent when you can pay down a bank loan that is charging interest at 9 percent. However, the decision to automatically pay down debt may not be correct in all cases.

Example

You may feel that interest rates are relatively low at this time and that you expect them to rise in the near future. Therefore, instead of using your cash surplus to pay off a two-year loan at 8.5 percent, it may be beneficial to invest the surplus temporarily, and avoid a much higher interest rate on a bank loan one year from now.

Investing the Cash Surplus

When investing a cash surplus, it's only natural to seek the highest rate of return for your investment. Four factors must be considered when making your investment decisions: risk, liquidity, maturity, and yield.

The investment of your cash surplus should never be speculative — that is, high risk. As in most businesses, your surplus may only be temporary. Any permanent losses resulting from a high risk investment could be devastating, even to the point of making you unable to continue your business.

If the amount and duration of your cash surplus are uncertain, then you should consider only those investments that offer a high level of liquidity. Preparing a cash flow budget should help you determine the amount and the duration of your cash surplus.

Once you've determined your acceptable level of risk, maturity, and liquidity, the type of investment and the yield of the investment are pretty much determined for you, or at least you've narrowed your options.

Warning

We suggest you consult with a professional before making any investments. Professionals who specialize in helping their customers make wise investment decisions can help you determine the best possible investment opportunities for you and your business. Many banks offer cash management services to their customers as part of their banking services. Contact your bank for more information.

Checking Accounts with Interest

Interest-bearing checking accounts are the simplest method of investing a cash surplus. These accounts are generally required to maintain a minimum balance at all times. The bank or financial institution might also place limits on the number of transactions that can occur during one month in the account. Transactions over the maximum number of transactions will be subject to additional transaction fees.

Money Market Funds

Money market funds are pooled funds investing in various money market investments — including treasury bills and notes, CDs, and commercial paper. Money market funds minimize your risk by diversifying your investments and offer a favorable yield. Funds can be withdrawn immediately or on one-day notice. Money market fund accounts are available at banks, but they can also be established through stockbrokers or directly with mutual fund companies.

Sweep Accounts

Sweep accounts were designed with small businesses in mind since most small business owners do not have the time or the large cash surpluses necessary to take advantage of more profitable investments.

By combining a regular checking account and a money market fund, sweep accounts eliminate the need for you to estimate bank balances and move funds from your checking to an investment account when necessary.

With a sweep account, you are required to maintain a certain balance in the account. The bank then "sweeps" the account and removes any funds that exceed your required balance. The bank automatically invests the excess funds in a money market account selected by you. When your account drops below its required balance, the bank automatically "sweeps" back enough money to your account to bring it up to its minimum balance.

Chapter 25

Analyzing Your Financial Position

After you've gotten the basics of financial recordkeeping down pat, and you have a good handle on your company's cash flow and other day-to-day issues, you may want to take a longer and deeper look at the financial state of your company. In some cases, you may need to undertake a fairly detailed financial analysis because you are looking for additional capital in the form of loans or investors.

Over the years, accountants and financial professionals have developed a number of systematic ways of arranging and comparing the financial facts about your business, so that they can be used to make sound decisions about future actions. In the following section, we'll discuss some of the most commonly used tools for financial analysis, including financial statements, business ratios, and cost/volume/profit analysis.

UNDERSTANDING FINANCIAL STATEMENTS

If you want a clear understanding of how your business is doing financially, and you want to be able to predict and plan for the future, a fairly thorough understanding of your financial statements is essential. A sound understanding of financial statements will help you:

- Identify unfavorable trends and tendencies in your business's operations (for example, the unhealthy buildup of inventory or accounts receivable) before the situation becomes critical.

- Monitor your cash flow requirements on a timely basis, and identify financing needs early.

- Monitor important indicators of financial health (for example, liquidity ratios, efficiency ratios, profitability ratios, and solvency ratios).

- Monitor periodic increases and decreases in wealth (specifically, owners' or stockholders' equity).

- Monitor your performance against your financial plan, if you have developed one.

There are four basic kinds of financial statements that can help you determine the present condition of your business:

1. The income statement, also referred to as a "profit and loss statement," or "P&L," tells you or your investors:

   — the income the business has earned during the accounting period

   — the costs or expenses that were incurred by the business during the period

   — the difference between the income and expenses for the period, which is your net profit (or loss).

2. The balance sheet is a statement of a company's relative wealth or financial position at a given point in time. It shows assets, liabilities, and owners' equity.

3. The position statement, also known as the "statement of changes in financial position" or "sources and uses of cash," helps to explain how a company acquired its money and how it was spent.

4. The statement of changes in owners' equity is used to bridge the gap between the amount of owners' equity at the beginning of the period and the amount of their equity at the end of the period.

Work Smart

 Keep in mind that your financial statements are only a starting point for analysis. Individual numbers aren't good or bad in themselves — you may have to dig for the reason behind any numbers that seem out of whack.

For instance, if your statements show that your accounts receivable have trended significantly downward over the last few years, it could mean that you're collecting the accounts more aggressively (which is good), or it could mean that you're writing off accounts as uncollectable too soon (which is bad). The key is to use your statements to spot trends and anomalies, and then follow these up with further investigation.

Income Statements

The income statement shows you a summary of the flow of transactions your business has had over the entire accounting period. In other words, the income statement shows you what happened during the period between balance sheets.

Frequently, three years' worth of income-statement data are presented, so that you can make comparisons and identify trends. The format of a typical income statement is presented below.

Smith Manufacturing Company
Income Statement
Years Ended December 31, 200Z, 200Y, and 200X

	200Z	200Y	200X
Sales	$X	$X	$X
(Sales returns and allowances)	(X)	(X)	(X)
Net sales	$X	$X	$X
Cost of goods sold:			
Beginning inventory	X	X	X
Cost of goods purchased	X	X	X
(Ending inventory)	(X)	(X)	(X)
Cost of goods sold	X	X	X
Gross profit	$X	$X	$X
Expenses:			
Selling expense	($X)	($X)	($X)
General and administrative expense	(X)	(X)	(X)
Total operating expenses	($X)	($X)	($X)
Income from operations	$X	$X	$X
Interest expense	(X)	(X)	(X)
Pretax income	X	X	X
Income taxes	(X)	(X)	(X)
Net income	($X)	($X)	($X)

Using the income statement. An in-depth knowledge of accounting is not necessary for you to make good use of the income statement data. For example, you can use your income statement to determine sales trends. Are sales going up or down, or are they holding steady? If they're going up, are they going up at the rate you want or expect? If you sell goods, you can use the income statement to monitor quality control. If your sales returns and allowances are rising, it may indicate that you have a problem with product quality.

Gross profit margin should be closely monitored to make sure that your business is operating at the same profitability levels as it grows. To find this margin, divide your gross profit (sales minus cost of goods sold) by your sales for each of the years covered by the income statement. If the percentage is going down, it may indicate that you need to try to raise prices, or look for opportunities to lower costs.

General and administrative expenses should also be closely watched. Increases in this area may mean that the company is getting too bureaucratic and is in line for some cost-cutting measures, or that equipment maintenance is too expensive and new equipment should be considered.

Balance Sheets

The balance sheet is a statement of your company's relative wealth or financial position *at a given point in time*. It gives you a fairly clear picture of the business at that moment, but does not reveal how the business arrived there or where it's going next. That's one reason why the balance sheet is not the whole story — you must also look at the information from each of the other financial statements (and at historical information as well) to get the most benefit from the data.

The balance sheet consists of three categories of items: assets, liabilities, and stockholders' or owners' equity.

Assets. Assets are generally divided into current assets and fixed (long-term) assets. They are usually presented in order of liquidity, with current assets (cash and those that will be converted to cash within one year) appearing first:

Cash	$X
Short-term investments and marketable securities	$X
Accounts and notes receivable	$X
Inventories	$X
Prepaid expenses	$X
Other current assets	$X

Fixed assets (those that won't be converted to cash within one year) usually are presented after current assets and look like this:

Land	$X
Buildings	$X
Machinery and equipment	$X
Capitalized leases	$X
(Less accumulated depreciation and amortization)	$X
Deferred charges	$X
Other fixed assets	$X

Liabilities. Liabilities are normally presented in order of their claim on the company's assets (i.e., liabilities due within one year are presented before liabilities due several years from now).

The liability section of the balance sheet might look something like this:

Current liabilities:

Accounts payable..$X

Notes payable..$X

Income taxes currently payable..$X

Current portion of long-term debt..$X

Other current liabilities..$X

   Total current liabilities ....$X

Long-term liabilities:

Long-term debt..$X

Capital lease obligations ....$X

Deferred income taxes...$X

Other long-term liabilities...$X

   Total long-term liabilities...$X

Equity. For sole proprietorships, equity is usually a one-line entry that represents the difference between the business's assets and liabilities.

For corporations, stockholders' equity (or owner's equity or net worth) is presented properly when each class of ownership is presented with all its relevant information (for example, number of shares authorized, shares issued, shares outstanding, and par value). If retained earnings are restricted or appropriated, this also should be shown. Stockholders' equity for an incorporated business normally would take this form:

Stockholders' equity:

Preferred stock, $20 par value (authorized 1,000 shares; issued and outstanding 500 shares) ....$X

Common stock, $15 par value (authorized 10,000 shares; issued and outstanding 5,000 shares) ....$X

Additional paid-in capital, common stock ....$X

Retained earnings..$X

Improving Your Balance Sheet

Although steps can be taken just prior to the balance sheet date (generally, year end) to improve it, you should be aware of how your actions and decisions throughout the year affect the "balance sheet appearance" of your company that may be presented to outsiders.

Often, the individual balance sheet items can be improved to give a better-looking overall picture. For instance, cash balances often can be improved simply by retaining most of the cash collected on receivables until after the balance sheet date, rather than promptly spending the money.

Whatever your business, you may want to hold off on writing off receivables as uncollectable bad debts, or writing down marketable securities to reflect a decline in value (assuming the delays are justifiable).

Sometimes year-end planning to reduce taxes may be in conflict with year-end planning to improve financial statements. This is because higher income looks good on your financial statements, but can cause you to pay more income tax. In such a case, you may have to choose between paying higher taxes to make your company's financial statements look better, or foregoing improved statements to reduce taxes. Depending on the business and its needs, lower tax payments are not always your best choice.

Work Smart

The fact that a business owner can take steps to improve the balance sheet's appearance illustrates one of the shortcomings of the statement. To the extent that it can be manipulated, it becomes less reliable as an indication of a business's true financial condition.

If you are ever in the position of considering whether to buy or invest in another business, be sure to look beyond the balance sheet!

Statement of Changes in Position

The statement of changes in financial position, often called the "sources and uses of cash statement," provides data that are not explicitly present in the balance sheet or the income statement.

This statement helps to explain how your company acquired its money and how it was spent. This statement can also help to identify financing needs, to identify cash drains, and to identify holes in the cash budgeting process.

Use the statement as a tool to analyze cash inflows and outflows. Also, use it as a starting point to forecast future cash flows and financing requirements.

An example of the format of a cash-focused statement of changes in financial position follows.

Jones Tool Company
Statement of Changes in Financial Position
for the Years Ended December 31, 200Z, 200Y, and 200X

	200Z	200Y	2009X
Sources of cash:			
Net income	$X	$X	$X
Add back non-cash deductions from net income:			
Depreciation	X	X	X
Deferred taxes	X	X	X
Cash provided by operations	$X	$X	$X
Issuance of stock	X	X	X
Sale of fixed assets	X	X	X
Total sources of cash	$X	$X	$X
Uses of cash:			
Purchases of equipment	($X)	($X)	($X)
Purchase of company debt	(X)	(X)	(X)
Total uses of cash	$X	$X	$X
Net increase in cash	$X	$X	$X
Cash, beginning of year	X	X	X
Cash, end of year	$X	$X	$X

The statement of changes in financial position should also include a supplement detailing the net changes in working capital. Specifically, this would include increases (or decreases) in accounts receivable, inventory, and accounts payable.

Statement of Changes in Equity

This type of financial statement is used to bridge the gap between the amount of equity the owners have in the business at the beginning of the accounting period and the amount of their equity at the end of the period.

There are several variations or types of statements that can be used to summarize the changes of the rights of owners (e.g., statement of retained earnings, statement of changes in net worth, statement of shareholders' equity, etc.). The type your business uses will depend on the nature of your business, and your accountant's preference.

Here's an example of a Statement of Changes in Equity for a partnership:

	Geoff	Marty
Marty & Geoff's Entrepreneurial Adventureland and Camp		
Statement of Owners' Equity		
For the Year Ended Dec. 31, 20___		
	Geoff	*Marty*
Partners' equity	$ 7,000	$ 9,000
Add: canoe rental income (net)	20,000	20,000
	$27,000	$29,000
Deduct: tents & water flume repair	19,000	18,000
Partners' equity Dec. 31	$ 8,000	$11,000
Notes: Partnership agreement limits withdrawals to:		
Geoff	$5,000 per year	
Marty	$7,000 per year	

Statements of shareholders' equity. A corporate owners' (stockholders') equity statement shows the paid-in capital invested in the business in exchange for stock, as of the beginning of the accounting period. It also shows how the income shown on the income statement was paid out as dividends, or plowed back into the business as retained earnings.

What To Do with Your Financials

The real value of the statements comes after their creation, when you analyze them to see how your business is doing in numerous areas. You must have a sense of what the numbers mean in order to interpret and analyze these financial records. Raw data in isolation does not make sense — it is in relation to *what* that counts.

Checklist of Issues to Consider After Financials Are Prepared

❑ *Develop common size financial statements to compare present performance with past performance and the condition of your business with that of other similar businesses.*

❑ *Develop the key business ratios for the business to compare present performance with past performance and the condition of your business with that of other similar businesses.*

❑ *Consider the impact on the performance picture of inflation and different accounting practices and procedures.*

❑ *Project income and construct a cash flow budget to assess production requirements and financing needs.*

❑ *Determine whether you're achieving a fair return on investment (capital) at a level of risk acceptable to you.*

❑ *Maintain working capital at sufficient levels to support operations.*

❑ *Maintain a proper balance between current assets and fixed assets.*

❑ *Establish and maintain a proper level of capitalization with the best mix of short-term and long-term debt financing, and equity financing.*

❑ *Examine your fixed and variable costs and relate them to profits.*

❑ *Evaluate and project how markets, products, competition, and sales are affecting and will affect your profits.*

❑ *Establish the contribution margin for your business and for your various product or service lines.*

❑ *Establish a break-even point for the business as a first step in determining how changes in sales will affect costs and profits.*

❑ *Review the degree of operating leverage in the business and its effects on operating profit and return on equity.*

❑ *Consider whether growth in sales and profits will increase the need for financing.*

Common-Size Financial Statements

An easy way to spot trends in your balance sheet and income statement data from a number of years, or to compare your information with that of another company or industry group, is to use "common-size" financial statements.

To create common-size statements, you simply take the information from your regular statements, and express it as percentages rather than as absolute dollars. This makes it much easier to pinpoint differences from year to year, and to compare your data with that of one or more companies that may be considerably larger or smaller than yours. Moreover, if you get industry data from a commercial service, the data will almost always be expressed in the common-size format.

Warning

When comparing data from several companies using common size statements, keep in mind that different accounting practices among companies exist, so the data many not be precisely comparable to yours.

Here's an example of an income statement that shows both absolute dollar values for four years, and also common-size percentages for the same four years.

Note that all items on the common-size part of the statement are expressed in terms of a percentage of sales.

To arrive at the common-size percentage for an item, we simply divided the dollar value of that item by the dollar value of sales for the period.

Dollars, in Thousands					Common-Size Percentage			
1	2	3	4	Years	1	2	3	4
$525	$595	$630	$724	Sales	100	100	100	100
158	190	208	217	Selling Exp.	30	32	33	30
79	95	95	101	Gross Margin	15	16	15	14
31	31	32	32	Gen. & Admin.	6	5	5	4
$48	$64	$81	$84	Operating Inc.	9	11	13	12
6	6	6	8	Interest	1	1	1	1
$42	$58	$75	$76	Pretax Income	8	10	12	10
14	20	26	26	Fed. Inc. Tax	3	3	4	4
$28	$38	$49	$50	Net Income	5	6	8	7

Next, we'll present an example of a balance sheet that shows both absolute dollar values for four years, and common-size percentages for the same four years.

Notice that items normally appearing on the asset side of the balance sheet are presented as a percentage of total assets. Items normally on the liabilities and equity side of the sheet are presented as a percentage of total liabilities and equity.

Dollars, in Thousands					Common-Size Percentage			
1	2	3	4	Years	1	2	3	4
$50	$40	$45	$70	Cash	6	4	5	7
230	250	175	225	Accts. Rec.	26	27	19	22
175	180	195	185	Inventory	20	19	21	18
10	15	10	310	Other Current Assets	1	2	1	1
$465	$485	$425	$490	Total Current Assets	53	52	46	48
400	425	500	515	Plant & Equip.	45	46	54	51
15	20	5	10	Other Non-Current Assets	2	2	1	1
$880	$930	$930	$1015	Total Assets	100	100	100	100
200	225	220	210	Accts. Pay.	23	24	24	21
50	45	20	80	Bank Debt	6	5	2	8
$250	$270	$240	$290	Total Current Liabs.	28	29	26	29
150	100	60	250	Long-term Debt	17	11	6	25
$400	$370	$300	$540	Total Liabs.	45	43	32	53
480	560	630	475	Owner's Equity	54	52	68	47
$880	$930	$930	$1015	Total Liabs. & Equity	100	100	100	100

BUSINESS RATIOS

In order to assess how your business is doing, you'll need more than single numbers extracted from the financial statements. Each number has to be viewed in the context of the whole picture.

Example

Your income statement may show a net profit of $100,000. But is this good? If this profit is earned on sales of $500,000, it may be very good; but if sales of $2,000,000 are required to produce the net profit of $100,000, the picture changes drastically.

When you routinely calculate and record a group of ratios at the end of every accounting period, you can assess the performance of your business over time, and compare your business to others in the same industry or to others of a similar size. By doing so, you won't be alone — banks routinely use business ratios to evaluate a business that's applying for a loan, and some creditors use them to determine whether to extend credit to you.

A number of sources, including many trade or business associations and organizations, provide data for comparison purposes; they are also available from commercial services like Dun & Bradstreet. Your accountant may be a good source of information on how your business compares to similar ones in your particular locale.

While there are dozens of financial ratios that you can look at, we'll concentrate on those that are most commonly considered to have the most value for making small business decisions. The ratios fall into four categories: liquidity, efficiency, profitability, and solvency.

Liquidity Ratios

Liquidity ratios are probably the most commonly used of all the business ratios. Your creditors may be particularly interested in these, because they show the ability of your business to quickly generate the cash needed to pay your bills. This information should also be highly interesting to you, since the inability to meet your short-term debts would be a problem that deserves your immediate attention.

Liquidity ratios are sometimes called working capital ratios, because that, in essence, is what they measure. The two most commonly used are the current ratio and the quick ratio.

Liquidity ratios are commonly examined by banks when they are evaluating a loan application. Once you get the loan, your lender may also require that you continue to maintain a certain minimum ratio, as part of the loan agreement. For that reason, steps to improve your liquidity ratios are sometimes necessary.

Current Ratio

The current ratio is a way of looking at your working capital and measuring your short-term solvency. The ratio is in the format x:y, where x is the amount of all current assets and y is the amount of all current liabilities.

Generally, your current ratio shows the ability of your business to generate cash to meet its short-term obligations. A decline in this ratio can be attributable to an increase in short-term debt, a decrease in current assets, or a combination of both. Regardless of the reasons, a decline in this ratio means a reduced ability to generate cash.

Merely paying off some current liabilities can improve this ratio.

Example

For example, if your business's current assets total $60,000 (including $30,000 cash) and your current liabilities total $30,000, the current ratio is 2:1.

Using half your cash to pay off half the current debt just prior to the balance sheet date improves this ratio to 3:1 ($45,000 current assets to $15,000 current liabilities).

Quick Ratio

The quick ratio, also known as the *acid test*, serves a function that is quite similar to that of the current ratio. The difference between the two is that the quick ratio subtracts inventory from current assets and compares the resulting figure (also called the quick current assets) to current liabilities.

Why? Inventory can be turned to cash only through sales, so the quick ratio gives you a better picture of your ability to meet your short-term obligations, regardless of your sales levels. Over time, a stable current ratio with a declining quick ratio may indicate that you've built up too much inventory.

Example

If your quick current assets are $90,000 and your current liabilities are $30,000, your acid test ratio would be 3:1 (90,000:30,000).

How to improve your quick ratio. Since this ratio is quite similar to the current ratio, but excludes inventory from current assets, it can be improved through many of the same actions that would improve the current ratio. Converting inventory to cash or accounts receivable also improves this ratio.

Work Smart

In general, a quick or acid-test ratio of at least 1:1 is good.

That signals that your quick current assets can cover your current liabilities.

Efficiency Ratios

As a business owner/manager, you're concerned with making the best use of your assets and being a low-cost (or at least reasonable-cost) producer in your industry. You can determine how efficiently your business uses its assets, and where there's room for improvement, by looking at ratios for inventory analysis, ratios for accounts receivable analysis, fixed asset turnover, and total asset turnover.

Ratios for Inventory Analysis

Inventory is the amount of merchandise, parts, supplies, or other goods your business keeps on hand to meet the demands of your customers. Depending on the nature of your business (i.e., retail, wholesale, service, manufacturing), the efficiency of your inventory management may have a significant impact on your cash flow and, ultimately, your business's success or failure.

The following inventory analysis tools can be used to help manage your investment in inventory: average inventory investment period, and inventory turnover analysis. For a discussion of how to compute and use these tools, see page 402.

Ratios for Receivables Analysis

Accounts receivable represent sales for which payment has not yet been collected. If your business normally extends credit to its customers, the payment of accounts receivable is likely to be your single most important source of cash inflows.

The average collection period can be used to help determine the effect your business's accounts receivables are having on your cash flow. For a discussion of how to compute and use them, see page 398.

Fixed Asset Turnover

Fixed asset turnover is the ratio of sales (on your income statement) to the value of your fixed assets (on your balance sheet). It indicates how well your business is using its fixed assets to generate sales.

Generally speaking, the higher the ratio, the better, because a high ratio indicates your business has less money tied up in fixed assets for each dollar of sales revenue. A declining ratio may indicate that you've over-invested in plant, equipment, or other fixed assets.

Total Asset Turnover

The ratio of total sales (on your income statement) to total assets (on your balance sheet) indicates how well you're using all your business assets, rather than just inventories or fixed assets, to generate revenue.

A high asset turnover ratio means a higher return on assets, which can compensate for a low profit margin. In computing the ratio, you might compute total assets by averaging the total assets at the beginning and end of the accounting period.

Profitability Ratios

You can use another set of ratios to assess the profitability of your business and changes in its profit performance. These ratios are probably the most important indicators of your business's financial success. Investors (including yourself, as the owner) will be interested in these ratios insofar as they demonstrate the performance and growth potential of the business.

There are five key profitability ratios: gross profit margin ratio, operating profit percentage, net profit margin or net profit percentage, return on assets, and return on equity.

Gross Profit Margin Ratio

Your gross profit margin can be calculated with the following formula, using figures taken from your income statement:

$$\frac{Gross\ Profit}{Sales}$$

Recall that gross profit is the amount of sales dollars remaining after the cost of goods sold has been deducted.

If your gross profit margin is declining over time, it may mean that your inventory management needs to be improved, or that your selling prices are not rising as fast as the costs of the goods you sell. If you are a manufacturer, it may mean that your costs of production are rising faster than your prices, and adjustments on either side (or both) are necessary.

Operating Profit Percentage

The operating profit percentage can be calculated using the following formula, with figures taken from your income statement:

$$\frac{Operating\ Income}{Sales}$$

This ratio is designed to give you an accurate idea of how much money you're making on your primary business operations. It shows the percentage of each sales dollar remaining after all normal costs of operations. By looking at this ratio over time, you can get a fix on whether your overall costs are trending up or down.

Net Profit Margin

Your net profit margin shows you the bottom line: how much of each sales dollar is ultimately available for you, the owner, to draw out of the business or to receive as dividends. It's probably the figure you are most accustomed to looking at. This ratio takes into account all your expenses, including income taxes and interest.

You should have some idea of the range within which you expect your profit margin to be, which will be determined in large part by industry standards. If you fail to meet your target, it could mean that you've set an unrealistic goal, or it could mean that you're doing something wrong. (However, the ratio itself will not point to *what* you may be doing wrong. Looking at your gross margin or operating margin is a better way to get a fix on the problem.)

Even if you meet your goal, you should always keep an eye on your profit margin. If it should decline, for example, it may indicate that you need to take a look at whether your costs are getting too high.

Return on Assets

Return on assets is the ratio of net income to total assets. It is basically a measure of how well your business is using its assets to produce more income. It can be viewed as a combination of two other ratios, net profit margin (ratio of net income to sales) and asset turnover (ratio of sales to total assets):

$$\frac{Net\ Income}{Sales} \times \frac{Sales}{Total\ Assets} = \frac{Net\ Income}{Total\ Assets}$$

A high return on assets can be attributable to a high profit margin, a rapid turnover of assets, or a combination of both.

Return on Equity

The return on equity ratio can be calculated as follows:

$$\frac{Net\ Income}{Owner's\ Equity}$$

The ratio of net income (from the income statement) to net worth or stockholders' equity (from the balance sheet) shows you what you've earned on your investment in the business during the accounting period. Bankers often refer to this ratio as ROI — return on investment.

You can compare your business's return on equity to what you might have earned in the stock market (or even a simple bank account) during the same period. Over time, your business should be generating at least the same return that you could earn in more passive investments like stocks, bonds, and bank CDs. Otherwise, why are you spending your time, trouble, and capital on it?

A high return on equity may be a result of a high return on assets, extensive use of debt financing, or a combination of the two.

In analyzing both return on equity and return on assets, don't forget to consider the effects of inflation on the book value of the assets. While your financial statements show all assets at their book value (i.e., original cost minus depreciation), the replacement value of many older assets may be substantially higher than their book value. A business with older assets, generally, should show higher return percentages than a business using newer assets.

Work Smart

If you're assessing return on equity for a corporation, keep in mind that net income reflects your expenses for any salary paid to yourself or other owner-employees. Since many shareholder-employees of closely held corporations — for tax purposes — draw the highest salaries possible, return actually may be higher than indicated by this ratio.

Solvency Ratios

The final group of ratios are designed to help you measure the degree of financial risk that your business faces. "Financial risk," in this context, means the extent to which you have debt obligations that must be met, regardless of your cash flow. By looking at these ratios, you can assess your level of debt and decide whether it is appropriate for your company.

Commonly used solvency ratios are: debt to equity, debt to assets, coverage of fixed charges, and interest coverage.

Debt to Equity

The debt to equity ratio can be computed with the following formula, using figures from your balance sheet:

$$\frac{Total\ Debt}{Owners'\ (or\ Stockholder's)\ Equity}$$

The ratio of debt to owners' equity or net worth indicates the degree of financial leverage that you're using to enhance your return. A rising debt to equity ratio may signal that further increases in debt should be restrained.

Improving this ratio involves either paying off debt or increasing the amount of earnings retained in the business until after the balance sheet date.

Debt to Assets

This ratio measures the percentage of a business's assets that are financed with debt, and can be calculated using the following formula:

$$\frac{Total\ Debt}{Total\ Assets}$$

This ratio measures the percentage of assets financed by creditors, compared to the percentage that have been financed by the business owners. Historically, a debt-to-asset ratio of no more than 50 percent has been considered prudent. A higher ratio indicates a possible overuse of leverage, and it may indicate potential problems meeting the debt payments.

Improving this ratio means taking steps to either increase the value of your assets, or to pay off debt. For example, you might explore whether inventory or other assets can be given a higher value. If you go the route of paying off debt, you'll also improve your current ratio and debt-to-equity ratio.

Coverage of Fixed Charges

Coverage of fixed charges is also sometimes called "times fixed charges earned."

It can be computed by taking your net income, *before* taxes and fixed charges (fixed charges are debt repayment, long-term leases, preferred stock dividends, etc.), and dividing by the amount of fixed charges. The resulting number shows your ability to meet your fixed obligations of all types — the higher the number, the better.

Obviously, an inability to meet any fixed obligation of the business threatens your business's well-being. Many working capital loan agreements will specify that you must maintain this ratio at a specified level, so that the lender has some assurance that you'll continue to be able to make your payments.

Interest Coverage

Interest coverage is also sometimes known as the "times interest earned ratio." It is very similar to the "times fixed charges earned" ratio but focuses more narrowly on the interest portion of your debt payments.

To calculate this ratio, you can use the following formula:

$$\frac{Operating\ Income}{Interest\ expense}$$

By comparing the ratio of operating income to interest expense, you measure how many times your interest obligations are covered by earnings from operations. The higher the ratio, the bigger your cushion and the more able the business is to meet interest payments. If this ratio is declining over time, it's a clear indication that your financial risk is increasing.

COST/VOLUME/PROFIT ANALYSIS

Do you know what your most profitable products or services are, so that you (or your salespeople) can really push those? Do you know what will happen if your sales volume drops? How far can it drop before you really start to eat red ink? If you lower your prices in order to sell more, how much more will you have to sell?

Cost/volume/profit analysis can help you answer these, and many more, questions about your business operations. CVP analysis, as it is sometimes known, is a way of examining the relationship between your fixed and variable costs, your volume (in terms of units or in terms of dollars), and your profits.

There are three main tools offered by CVP analysis:

- **breakeven analysis,** which tells you the sales volume you need to break even, under different price or cost scenarios

- **contribution margin analysis,** which compares the profitability of different products, lines, or services you offer

- **operating leverage** examines the degree to which your business uses fixed costs, which magnifies your profits as sales increase, but also magnifies your losses as sales drop.

Fixed and Variable Costs

Virtually all of your business's costs will fall, more or less neatly, into one of two categories:

- "Variable costs," which increase directly in proportion to the level of sales in dollars or units sold. Some examples would be cost of goods sold, sales commissions, shipping charges, delivery charges, costs of direct materials or supplies, wages of part-time or temporary employees, and sales or production bonuses.

- "Fixed costs," which remain the same regardless of your level of sales. Some typical examples would be rent, interest on debt, insurance, plant and equipment expenses, business licenses, and salary of permanent full-time workers.

Your accountant can help you determine which of your costs are fixed and which are variable.

Combination costs. Some costs are a combination of fixed and variable: a certain minimum level will be incurred regardless of your sales levels, but the costs rise as your volume increases. As an analogy, think about your phone bill: you probably pay an access or line charge that is the same each month, and you probably also pay a charge based on the volume of calls you make. Strictly speaking, these costs should be separated into their fixed and variable components, but that may be more trouble than it's worth for a small business.

Save Time

To simplify things, just decide which type of cost (fixed or variable) is the most important for the particular item, and then classify the whole item according to the more important characteristic. For example, in a telemarketing business, if your phone call volume charges are normally greater than your line access charges, you'd classify the entire bill as variable.

If you add up all your variable costs for the accounting period, and divide by the number of units sold, you will arrive at the cost per unit. This cost should remain constant, regardless of how few or how many units you sell. For a service business, you may be able to divide your variable costs by the number of jobs performed (if the jobs are similar) or by the hours spent on all jobs.

Contribution Margins

Your company's contribution margin is simply the percentage of each sales dollar that remains after the variable costs are subtracted. When you know the contribution margin, you can make better decisions about whether to add or subtract a product line, about how to price your product or service, and about how to structure any sales commissions or bonuses.

How is your contribution margin computed? It's done by using a special type of income statement that has been reformatted to group together your business's fixed and variable costs.

Here's an example of a contribution format income statement:

Beta Sales Company		
Contribution Format Income Statement		
For Year Ended December 31, 200X		
Sales	$462,452	
Less Variable Costs:		
Cost of Goods Sold	230,934	
Sales Commissions	58,852	
Delivery Charges	13,984	
Total Variable Costs	$303,770	
Contribution Margin	$158,682	34%
Less: Fixed Costs:		
Advertising	1,850	
Depreciation	13,250	
Insurance	5,400	
Payroll Taxes	8,200	
Rent	9,600	
Utilities	17,801	
Wages	40,000	
Total Fixed Costs	$96,101	
Net Operating Income	$62,581	

You can tell at a glance that the Beta Company's contribution margin for the year was 34 percent. This means that, for every dollar of sales, after the costs that were directly related to the sales were subtracted, 34 cents remained to contribute towards paying for the fixed costs and for profit.

Contribution format income statements can be drawn up with data from more than one year's income statements, if you're interested in tracking your contribution margins over time. Perhaps even more usefully, they can be drawn up for each product line or service you offer. On the next page is an example, showing a breakdown of Beta's three main product lines.

Although we've only shown the top half of the contribution format income statement, it's immediately apparent that Product Line C is Beta's must profitable one, even though Beta gets more sales revenue from Line B.

	Line A	Line B	Line C
Sales	$120,400	$202,050	$140,002
Less Variable Costs:			
Cost of Goods Sold	70,030	100,900	60,004
Sales Commissions	18,802	40,050	0
Delivery Charges	900	8,084	5,000
Total Variable Costs	$ 89,732	$149,034	$ 65,004
Contribution Margin	30,668 (25%)	53,016 (26%)	74,998 (54%)

Moreover, the statement indicates that perhaps prices for line A and line B products are too low. This is information that can't be gleaned from the regular income statements that your accountant routinely draws up each period.

Breakeven Analysis

A second tool for management decisionmaking that has grown out of cost/volume/profit analysis is breakeven analysis.

Once you know what your variable costs are, as well as your overall fixed costs for the business, you can determine your breakeven point: the volume of sales needed to at least cover all your costs. You can also compute the new breakeven point that you'd need to meet if you decided to increase your fixed costs (for example, if you undertook a major expansion project or bought some new office equipment).

Your breakeven point can be determined by using the following formulas:

1. Sales price per unit — variable costs per unit = contribution margin per unit.

2. Contribution margin per unit ÷ sales price per unit = contribution margin ratio.

3. Breakeven sales volume = fixed costs ÷ contribution margin ratio.

Case Study — Breakeven Point

Assume that the financial statements for Lillian's Bakery reveal that the bakery's fixed costs are $49,000, and its variable costs per unit of production (loaf of raisin coffee cake) are $.30.

Further assume that its sales revenue is $1.00 per loaf. From this information, it can be determined that, after the $.30 per loaf variable costs are covered, each loaf sold can contribute $.70 toward covering fixed costs.

Dividing fixed costs by the contribution to those costs per unit of sales tells Lillian's Bakery at what level of sales it will break even. In this case: $49,000/$.70 = 70,000 loaves.

As sales exceed 70,000 loaves, Lillian's Bakery earns a profit. Sales of less than 70,000 loaves produce a loss.

Lillian's Bakery can see that a 10,000 loaf increase in sales over the break-even point to 80,000 loaves will produce a $7,000 profit, and a 30,000 loaf increase to 100,000 will produce a $21,000 profit. On the other hand, a decline in sales of 10,000 loaves from breakeven to 60,000 loaves will produce a loss of $7,000, and a 30,000 decrease from the 70,000 breakeven point produces a $21,000 loss.

Operating Leverage

In the example above, a 25 percent increase in sales from 80,000 loaves to 100,000 loaves would produce an increase in profits from $7,000 to $21,000. Similarly, a small drop in sales below breakeven would produce a substantial increase in loss. How is this explained? There is obviously more involved than simply the breakeven point.

The concept of operating leverage explains why the mix of fixed and variable costs can have a large effect on your profit levels, as your sales volume increases and decreases.

The extent to which a business uses fixed costs (compared to variable costs) in its operations is referred to as "operating leverage." The greater the use of operating leverage, the larger the increase in profits as sales rise and the larger the increase in loss as sales fall.

Work Smart

The employment of a high level of fixed assets (with fixed costs) at high volume increases the profit potential of a business. At low sales volume, however, losses multiply; and difficulty in meeting your fixed costs, such as payments for plant and equipment, may ensue. For most small businesses, limiting downside risk is more important than increasing potential profits, so it's wise to keep your fixed costs low wherever possible.

Part **VIII**

Controlling Your Taxes

One of the biggest challenges you'll face in running your business is staying on top of the numerous tax obligations to federal, state, and local tax agencies. A tax headache is only one mistake away, be it a missed payment or filing deadline, an improperly claimed deduction, or incomplete records. And you can safely assume that a tax auditor presenting an assessment of additional taxes, penalties, and interest will not look kindly on an "I didn't know I was required to do that" claim. The old legal saying that "ignorance of the law is no excuse" is perhaps most often applied in tax settings.

Although retaining a good accountant or other tax professional may be invaluable in avoiding tax troubles, possessing a working knowledge of your general tax obligations is also essential. After all, even if you delegate your tax obligations to someone else, you'll be the one paying the penalties if those obligations aren't met.

What's more, the greater your familiarity with the workings of deductions and other tax breaks, the better you can plan your business activities to take advantage of them. If you follow the rules, Uncle Sam will subsidize your car, home office, business travel and entertainment, continuing education, and many benefits like health insurance and retirement savings plans.

To help you along, in this Part we'll discuss each of the major types of taxes that may apply to you and your business.

Chapter 26: Federal Income Tax Obligations, explains the basics of tax planning, how the structure of your business affects your taxes, and tax payment and return due dates. It focuses heavily on the ins and outs of business deductions, which require you to follow a lot of complicated rules but also provide many opportunities to save money.

Chapter 27: Your State Tax Obligations, explains how sales taxes work and to which businesses they apply. It also includes a chart that provides tax rates on individual and corporate income, sales, and franchise taxes in each of the states.

Chapter 28: Doing the Payroll, discusses how to set up your payroll system and comply with federal FICA and FUTA taxes, state unemployment tax, and federal and state income tax withholding. It also includes a discussion of payroll taxes that apply to a business owner who's actively involved in running the company.

Chapter 26

Federal Income Tax Obligations

If you're like most small business owners, you pay an accountant or other professional advisor to handle your income taxes. So, why should you spend your time reading about this subject? One good reason is that you'll better understand the various tax choices that your tax pro may lay out for you.

Also, with a little knowledge on selected topics, you'll be able to identify potential tax advantages — and tax traps — in time to do something about them. Wouldn't it be nice *not* to hear your tax pro say, "I could have saved you a lot of money if you had told me sooner that you were thinking about . . ."

Our underlying goal for this chapter is to call your attention to those income tax provisions that will most affect your small business. The major issues include the basic rules of tax planning, choosing the operating structure of your business (sole proprietorship, partnership, corporation, LLC), tax elections, business deductions, tax credits, and payment obligations.

THE BASICS OF TAX PLANNING

Tax planning is a process of looking at various tax options in order to determine when, whether, and how to conduct your business and personal transactions, so that taxes are eliminated or reduced.

As an individual taxpayer, and as a business owner, you will often have several different options as to how you want to complete a certain taxable transaction. The courts strongly back your right to choose the course of action that will result in the lowest *legal* tax.

In other words, *tax avoidance* is entirely proper.

However, tax *evasion* — the reduction of tax through deceit, subterfuge, or concealment — is not. IRS examiners will be on the lookout for the following four situations, among others, as pointing to possible fraud:

- a failure to report substantial amounts of income, such as a shareholder's failure to report dividends, or a store-owner's skimming cash from the register without including it in the daily business receipts

- a claim for fictitious or improper deductions on a return, such as a sales representative's substantial overstatement of travel expenses

- accounting irregularities, such as a business's failure to keep adequate records, or a discrepancy between amounts reported on a corporation's return and amounts reported on its financial statements

- allocation of income to a related taxpayer who is in a lower tax bracket, such as where a corporation makes distributions to the controlling shareholder's children

A business owner may *not* reduce his or her income taxes by labeling a transaction as something it is not. Thus, if payments by a corporation to its stockholders are in fact dividends, calling them "interest" or otherwise attempting to disguise the payments as interest will not entitle the corporation to an interest deduction. It is the substance, not the form, of the transaction that determines its taxability.

How a tax plan works. There are countless tax planning strategies available to a small business owner. But regardless of how simple or how complex a tax strategy is, it will be based on structuring the transaction to accomplish one or more of these often overlapping goals:

- reducing the amount of income that is subject to tax

- subjecting taxable income to the lowest possible tax rate

- reducing the amount of the tax itself by claiming tax credits

- controlling both the time that the tax liability will arise and the time when it must be paid

In order to plan effectively, you'll need to estimate your personal and business income for the next few years. This is necessary because many tax planning strategies will save tax dollars at one income level, but will create a larger tax bill at other income levels. You will want to avoid having the "right" tax plan made "wrong" by erroneous income projections. Of course, you also need to estimate your sales volume, revenue, expenses, etc. for many other business purposes.

Reducing Income Subject to Tax

There are several ways to reduce income that is subject to tax, including the following:

- Take advantage of all available deductions, both business and personal. But before you rush to do this, remember that claiming some kinds of deductions may have a tax impact in later years. (An example of this is the recapture of depreciation tax breaks upon the sale of a business property.)

- Structure transactions in a way that any income will be tax-exempt (such as investments in tax-exempt municipal bonds), or tax advantaged (such as capital gains).

- Accelerate expenses into the current year and postpone receipt of income into the next tax year. This will be easier to do if you are on the cash method, rather than the accrual method, of accounting. If you successfully do this, you might also accomplish two other tax planning strategies: delaying the due date for taxes, and lowering your tax rate (assuming that you would be in a lower tax rate next year). You should consider the contrary strategy if you think that you'll be in a higher tax bracket next year (for instance, if you expect your business to generate more income, or if one of your dependents will no longer be claimed on your return). In that case, accelerate income into this year, and postpone expenses until the next.

Reducing Your Tax Rate

Although you can't actually lower your federal income tax rate, you can take actions that will have a similar result. These include:

- Shift income from a high tax rate taxpayer (such as yourself) to a lower rate taxpayer (such as your child). The tax law limits the usefulness of this strategy for shifting *unearned* income to children under age 14, but some tax-saving opportunities still exist.

- Choose the correct form of business organization (such as sole proprietorship, partnership, or corporation). If your business income is under $75,000 and you're not in a personal service business such as medicine, law, architecture, engineering, accounting, the arts, or consulting, you may be able to save tax dollars by incorporating. Otherwise, the sole proprietorship or pass-through entities (partnerships, LLCs, S-corporations) offer more tax benefits.

- Structure a transaction so that the money you receive is classified as capital gains. Long-term capital gains earned by noncorporate taxpayers are subject to a maximum tax rate of 20 percent, compared with the maximum rate of 39.6 percent that applies to other taxable income.

Delaying the Date Your Tax Is Due

Although your former grade school teachers may not want to hear it, putting something off can sometimes be a good idea. It's usually worthwhile to delay for as long as possible the date on which you have to pay your tax liability.

What you gain is the use of the tax money for a longer period of time. The advantage may be as little as passbook earnings on the money, or as much as the growth resulting from a needed investment of money or equipment into your business.

With rare and very narrow exceptions, you don't have the option of directly delaying payment of your income tax. You may be able to get an extension of time to pay tax if you can demonstrate to the IRS's satisfaction that you could not pay the tax on time without undue hardship. However, even with this extension you will owe interest on the unpaid taxes, beginning on the original due date.

So how do you delay paying the taxman? You have to do so indirectly, by taking actions that delay when particular income items must be reported on your return.

For small business owners, a common way to do this is to postpone receipt of income until the next year, and accelerate payment of expenses into your current tax year. (This will be easier to do if you use the cash method of accounting.) This will have the effect of delaying the due date for some of your tax liability to the next quarter, or even the next tax year.

Another way to defer the day of reckoning is to plow as much money as you can into qualified, tax-free retirement plans. The business will get a tax deduction for the amount contributed, but you won't have to pay income tax on it until you start taking money out of the plan when you retire. Meanwhile, any income earned on the plan's investments will build up, tax-free. You have a great deal of control over the way the plan is set up, and there's sure to be a plan that fits into your business goals and retirement objectives.

Postponing Income, Accelerating Deductions

As a general rule of thumb, you should *always* try to minimize your taxes in the present year, even if doing so means you may have to pay slightly more tax in the future.

After all, no one knows what the future holds. The tax laws are constantly changing, and there's a good chance that whatever you think you'll owe in the future will be different by the time you get there. Furthermore, economic changes or personal plans can change, and your business may look entirely different even one year down the road. In the worst-case scenario, you could die unexpectedly, and in some cases you can avoid tax altogether if you die before paying it.

In broad terms, you can minimize taxes in the current year by postponing the receipt of income so that more of it will be taxed next year, and by accelerating deductions into the current year.

A few more specific ideas for doing this are listed below.

Year-End Tax Saving Strategies

- **Delay collections** — *delay year-end billings until late enough in the year that payments won't come in until the following year.*

- **Dividends** — *if you operate your business as a C corporation, arrange for any dividends to be paid after the end of the year.*

- **Capital gains** — *if you are planning to sell assets that have appreciated in value, delay the sale until next year if you can do so without reducing the price significantly.*

- **Accelerate payments** — *where possible, prepay deductible business expenses, including rent, interest, taxes, insurance, etc.*

- **Large purchases** — *close the purchase of depreciable personal property or real estate within the current year.*

- **Accelerate operating expenses** — *if possible, accelerate the purchase of equipment or supplies or the making of repairs.*

- **Depreciation** — *elect an accelerated method of depreciation.*

But what if you use the accrual method? Although these strategies are usually more difficult to accomplish using the accrual method, this does not mean that they're impossible.

- If you want to delay taxation of an item of income, make sure that all events fixing the liability for payment are *not* met by year's end. A good way of doing this for goods that you sell would be to delay shipment until the next year.

- If you want to accelerate a deductible expense into the current year, make sure that all events fixing the liability and amount of payment have been completed by year's end. If you are purchasing goods, services, or the use of a property, make sure that you have a valid contract covering all necessary terms, and that the goods, services, or properties are delivered, performed, or used by year's end.

Accelerating income, postponing deductions. In certain limited circumstances, you may want to do the reverse of the usual strategy, and recognize more income this year, while postponing deductions to next year. A good example of this would be when Congress raises the tax rates, and you know you'll be in a higher tax bracket next year. If you simply reverse our suggestions in the box above, you'll find that you can accomplish your goals.

Alternative Minimum Tax: Impact on Planning

Because in the past some taxpayers—particularly wealthy taxpayers— were so successful in their efforts to legally minimize their tax bills, Uncle Sam came up with another way to tax them: the alternative minimum tax (AMT). The AMT provides a formula for computing tax that ignores certain preferential tax treatments that taxpayers (both corporations and individuals) are otherwise entitled to under the tax law. Thus, these taxpayers are required to compute their income tax liability twice; once under the regular method and once again under the AMT method. If the AMT liability is higher than the regular tax bill, the taxpayer will have to pay the difference.

Will you be subject to AMT? Unless you are a true tax aficionado, we *strongly recommend* that you consult your tax advisor for the answer to this question. Our discussion here is intended to alert you to the fact that the AMT exists, and that it is something that you and your tax advisor must consider as you begin the tax planning process. More and more taxpayers are subject to the AMT each year, because although your income is likely to rise with inflation, the amounts at which AMT applies do not change.

For individuals, the taxpayer's AMT exemption is determined by filing status and amount of alternative minimum taxable income (AMTI). AMTI is basically your taxable income, with your personal exemptions and many of your deductions added back in.

If your AMTI exceeds the amount shown in the second column for your filing status, you must reduce your exemption amount by 25% of the excess (e.g., if you are married filing jointly and your AMTI is $200,000, you must reduce your exemption by 25% of $50,000, or

$12,500. Thus, your exemption would be $32,500). As you can see, the exemption amounts are wiped out at the higher income levels.

Filing Status	AMT Exemption	AMTI
Single or head of household	$33,750	$112,500
Married filing jointly or surviving spouses	45,000	150,000
Married filing separately	22,500	75,000

A noncorporate taxpayer who is taxed under the AMT may be subject to two rates: a 26 percent rate applies to the first $175,000 of alternative minimum taxable income that exceeds the exemption amount, and a 28 percent rate applies to alternative minimum taxable income above this $175,000 amount.

SELECTING YOUR FORM OF BUSINESS

One of the most important decisions that you will have to make in connection with starting a business is the legal form in which you'll operate. And, as time passes and your business grows, you may decide to change the form to conform to changing business goals.

You have a number of choices: a sole proprietorship, a partnership, a corporation (including an S corporation), a limited liability company, or a limited liability partnership (LLP). In this chapter, we'll focus on the income tax consequences that flow from each of these choices. For non-tax issues relating to choice of business form, see Chapter 4.

Sole Proprietorships

A sole proprietorship is not a taxable entity. All income and expenses generated by it are reflected on Schedule C, which is part of the business owner's individual tax return. This means that there is no separate tax rate schedule that applies to a sole proprietorship; whatever rate the business owner is taxed at will determine the amount of tax paid on the earnings of the sole proprietorship.

If your business has only one owner, the IRS will presume that it's a sole proprietorship unless you incorporate under state law.

The main advantage of a sole proprietorship is simplicity. Because there is only one owner, the accounting rules that apply are simple. Also, there are no tax effects to keep track of if the business owner transfers money or property into or out of the business.

Sole proprietors are generally required to pay self-employment taxes on all net business income and to make estimated tax payments.

A sole proprietor who sells the business is treated as if he or she sold each asset of the business, and gain or loss on each item must be computed. Intangible assets such as patents, copyrights, and business goodwill are also considered business assets, and separate gain or loss is computed on them.

Partnerships

Although a partnership is not a taxable entity, it is required to file a tax return that reports its income and loss, and reports each partner's share of income and loss. Each partner is taxed on his or her share of partnership income or loss (which is known as "distributive share"), even if it was not actually distributed, and even if the partnership agreement requires that the money be retained in the business as partnership capital.

Partnerships are generally the most flexible form of business for tax purposes, since the income and losses distributed to each of the partners can vary (i.e., one partner can receive 40% of any profits but 60% of any losses) as long as a business purpose other than tax avoidance can be shown for the split. In the early years of most businesses, the company generates losses rather than profits, and the partnership form allows the partners to use these losses to offset other income they may have from investments or another job. (However, a partner may not deduct losses that exceed his or her amount of investment in the business.)

Although the individual partners (not their partnership) are the ones paying the income tax, most of the choices affecting how income is computed are made by the partnership itself, rather than the individual partners on their own returns. These choices include elections of general methods of accounting, methods of depreciation, and accounting for specific items such as organization and business startup expenses and installment sales. Partners are required to treat partnership items in the same way on their individual tax returns as they were treated on the partnership return.

For businesses with more than one owner, the partnership is the "default form" of business; that is, the IRS will presume that your business should be taxed as a partnership unless you have incorporated under state law, or you elect to be taxed as a corporation by filing IRS Form 8832.

Comparison with Corporations

Because the taxation of partnership income is determined by the tax bracket that applies to each individual partner, a comparison of tax rates that apply to corporations and to individuals can tell you which form of business would save taxes at a particular income level.

Comparison of corporate and individual tax rates. The following chart compares the tax rates for 2000 for corporations and married individuals filing jointly, at various income levels.

Taxable Income	Corporation	Married/Joint	Single
$0 — 26,250	15%	15%	15%
26,250 — 43,850	15%	15%	28%
43,850 — 50,000	15%	28%	28%
50,000 — 63,550	25%	28%	28%
63,550 — 75,000	25%	28%	31%
75,000 — 100,000	34%	28%	31%
100,000 — 105,950	39%	28%	31%
105,950 — 132,600	39%	31%	31%
132,600 — 161,450	39%	31%	36%
161,450 — 288,350	39%	36%	36%
288,350 — 335,000	39%	39.6%	39.6%
335,000 — 10,000,000	34%	39.6%	39.6%
10,000,000 — 15,000,000	35%	39.6%	39.6%
15,000,000 — 18,333,333	38%	39.6%	39.6%
Over 18,333,333	35%	39.6%	39.6%

Note: personal service corporations (those whose employees spend at least 95% of their time in the field of health, law, engineering, architecture, accounting, actuarial science, performing arts, or consulting) are taxed at a flat rate of 35% of net profits.

At the lower income levels (non-personal-service businesses with taxable incomes up to $75,000), corporations have the advantage, but this advantage shifts the other way for income between $75,000 and $288,350. But this rate comparison is only part of the tax picture to consider: distributions (money taken out) from a partnership to its partners are taxed only once, while distributions made by a corporation to its shareholders are taxable dividends and are essentially taxed twice.

Corporations

Under the rules of the federal income tax, there are two kinds of corporations: "regular" or C corporations, and a special variety, the S corporation.

Regular C Corporations

In a C corporation, business income is taxed at the corporate level, using the corporate income tax rates shown in the table, above.

After the corporate tax is paid on the business income, any distributions made to stockholders are taxed again at the individuals' rates, as dividends. Because of these two levels of tax, a regular corporation may be a less desirable form of business than the other types of business entities (sole proprietorships, partnerships, limited liability companies, or S corporations). This may be true even though regular corporations are taxed at lower tax rates on their first $75,000 in income, when compared to the other business forms.

Salaries may offset corporate tax. In comparing the tax advantages of operating a business as a partnership or sole proprietorship rather than as a corporation, it should be remembered that not all of the corporate profits will be subject to double taxation. The operators of the corporation may withdraw reasonable salaries, which are deductible by the corporation. These salaries are therefore free from income tax at the corporate level (though the recipients will have to pay income and FICA tax on them). In some cases, the entire net profits may be paid out as salaries to the owners and other employees, so that no corporate tax is due.

Warning

 If your corporation is profitable but does not pay any dividends for an extended period of time, the IRS is likely to conclude that some of the salaries paid to owners are really disguised dividends. The IRS can disallow some or all of the salary deductions, resulting in a large tax bill plus interest and penalties. If you have a corporation, your best bet is to make sure that salaries are not significantly higher than industry standards, and to pay out at least some dividends each year.

Accumulated earnings tax. Because a corporation is a taxable entity that is separate from its stockholders, its profits are not, as in the case of unincorporated businesses and S corporations, automatically taxed to the owners when they are earned. The profits are taxed only if and when they are distributed to the stockholders as dividends. However, a corporation may not safely accumulate earnings indefinitely. If the accumulations are higher than the reasonable needs of the business, an accumulated earnings tax of 39.6% will apply in addition to the regular corporate tax. Virtually any corporation can accumulate up to $150,000 in retained earnings without becoming subject to this tax.

Transactions between corporation and owners. Transactions between a closely held corporation and its stockholder-owners will be closely looked at by IRS agents. If corporate property is diverted to the stockholders, they will be considered to have received what is called a "constructive" or "preferential" dividend.

This tax treatment is *highly* unfavorable, since this dividend will be taxable to the owners, and will not be deductible to the corporation.

The most common type of preferential dividend received by stockholders involves the payment of personal expenses on behalf of stockholders. Typically, the corporation claims deductions for these expenses as business expenses on its income tax return, but where the expenses are clearly personal expenses, the corporation will be denied a deduction and the officer-stockholder is deemed to have received a taxable dividend.

Stockholders are also considered to have received constructive dividends when: (1) corporate property is sold to a stockholder at less than its fair market value, (2) employee-stockholders are given unreasonably high compensation, (3) the corporation pays excess rents to shareholders for property leased by the corporation, and (4) the corporation loans the shareholder funds and there is no intention to repay the loan.

Corporate Alternative Minimum Tax. Like individuals, corporations can become subject to an alternative minimum tax of 20%, if they have gained the benefit of "too many" tax preference items. Corporations with less than $5 million in annual gross receipts are exempt from the AMT. If your corporate income is higher than that, your tax professional's help will almost certainly be needed in deciding whether you owe AMT, and if so, how much.

S Corporations

An S corporation is a creature of the federal tax laws. For all other purposes, it's treated as a regular corporation. Thus, to form an S corporation you first have to incorporate under state law.

Then, you must file a special IRS form electing to be taxed similarly to a partnership. This election preserves the corporation's limited liability under state law, but avoids taxation at the corporate level.

As a result, the annual income or losses of the S corporation are passed through to shareholders in much the same manner as a partnership passes through such items to partners.

One exception is the rule that all profits, losses, and other items that pass through must be allocated according to each shareholder's proportionate shares of stock; thus, if you own 50% of the stock, you must receive 50% of the losses, profits, credits, etc. This is not the case with a partnership, where one partner can receive different percentages of different tax items if the partnership agreement so specifies.

S Corporation Requirements

To obtain S corporation status under the federal income tax law, all of the following requirements must be met:

- *The corporation must be a domestic corporation (a corporation organized under the laws of the United States, a state, or territory).*

- *All shareholders must agree to the election.*

- *The corporation may not have more than one class of stock (voting and nonvoting shares are not considered to be two separate classes, however).*

- *The corporation may not have more than 75 shareholders .*

- *The corporation may not have any shareholder that is a nonresident alien or nonhuman entity (such as other corporations or partnerships), unless the shareholder is an estate or trust that is authorized to be an S corporation shareholder under the tax law, or unless the shareholder is on the list of certain exempt organizations, such as qualified pension, profit-sharing, and stock bonus plans, that are be allowed to be shareholders.*

Limited Liability Companies

The limited liability company (LLC) is a hybrid of a corporation and a limited partnership that is created under state law. Although this is a relatively new business form, all states have now enacted legislation providing for limited liability companies.

Formerly, the IRS had treated limited liability companies as partnerships (that is, income will "pass through" and be taxed to LLC members at their individual rates) rather than as corporations, provided that the business did not possess more than two of four characteristics of corporations: centralized management, continuity of life, free transferability of interests, and limited liability.

Under regulations that went into effect at the start of 1997, newly formed LLCs can obtain partnership tax treatment even if they have all four corporate characteristics; in fact, a multiple-owner LLC will be presumed to have partnership treatment unless it elects to be treated as a corporation. Single-owner LLCs are treated as sole proprietorships.

Although limited liability companies are taxed as partnerships for federal tax purposes, the same may not be true for state tax purposes. You'll need to check your state law (see Chapter 27).

For growing businesses, LLCs enjoy other advantages over an S corporation that may prove valuable to you. These include the fact that, unlike an S corporation, an LLC can: (1) have investors that are corporations (either regular or S corporations), partnerships, trusts or nonresident aliens; and (2) can have more than 75 investors.

Limited Liability Partnerships

Just like an LLC, the LLP permits limited liability for partners and partnership tax treatment. This form of organization is relatively new, but is recognized in almost every state, although a handful only allow it for certain professional services such as doctors or attorneys.

An LLP is formed by a simple registration that indicates the partnership elects to be treated as an LLP. All aspects of general partnership law, except as to partner's personal liability for business liabilities, governs the entity. If a partnership can qualify as an LLP, there are virtually no disadvantages to electing this status. The relatively minimal filing fee should be viewed as an inexpensive insurance premium.

TAX YEAR AND ACCOUNTING METHODS

There are certain tax-related choices that are likely to have a long-term effect on how you determine your business income, and possibly even how you run your business. Once made, these choices are more or less permanent, since you may not be able to change them without the IRS's permission, which may be difficult to get.

The most commonly encountered decisions you'll need to make are your tax year, your accounting method, and for businesses that have inventory, your inventory valuation method.

Choice of Tax Year

Your tax year may be either a calendar year, or a fiscal year (a 12-month year that ends on the last day of any month other than December). It is on the basis of your tax year that your taxable income will be computed.

Since a sole proprietorship does not exist apart from its owner (at least in the eyes of the IRS), a sole proprietorship must use the same tax year as the owner. Most sole proprietors use the calendar year as their tax year, since they must continue to use the same tax year that the owner used in his or her initial individual tax return (and since most of us began filing early in life, we used the calendar year for our first tax return). If you want to switch to a fiscal year, you'll need permission from the IRS.

A partnership or LLC must generally use the same tax year as the majority of its owners. An S corporation or a personal service corporation (a C corporation in which employees spend 95% of their time providing services in the field of health, law, engineering, architecture, accounting, actuarial science, performing arts, or consulting) must generally use a calendar year. Exceptions to these general rules may be made if you can establish to the satisfaction of the IRS that you have a business purpose for using a different tax year, and in most cases, a seasonal business would be able to show a valid business purpose.

A new corporation. If you have started a new business, it may initially have large expenses or losses. Because of this, if operations are begun during the year (rather than on January 1), it may be helpful to choose a fiscal year that extends beyond the end of the first calendar year so that as much income as possible will be offset by the opening expenses and losses.

Accounting Methods

There are two basic accounting methods available to most small businesses: cash or accrual. For a discussion of the differences between the two, see Chapter 22. Some business owners can use special accounting methods under the tax law. These include farmers, builders and contractors, and business owners receiving income under long-term contracts.

C corporations with average annual cash receipts over $5 million that are not personal service corporations generally *must* use the accrual method. Furthermore, any type of business that has an inventory must also use the accrual method, at least for sales and for merchandise purchases.

If your business has many complex transactions during the year you will usually find the accrual method more desirable, because expenses are customarily deducted in the same year that the income to which they relate is reported. Because of this, income tends to be leveled out, thus avoiding income "peaks" that are subject to higher tax rates.

For other business owners, the accrual method does not necessarily reduce taxes, and may create many unnecessary accounting headaches when compared with the cash method.

On the other hand, most accountants feel that the accrual method is the only one that accurately reflects the true financial state of your business.

Inventory Valuation Methods

If your business maintains an inventory, the amount of your business's income and when it will be taxed will be affected by your choice of inventory valuation method.

Although there are many ways of valuing inventories, most small sellers and manufacturers value inventories under one of these methods: (1) cost, or (2) lower of cost or market. The second method, in effect, permits you to reduce gross income to reflect shrinkage in the value of inventories.

Case Study — Inventory Valuation

In 2000, John Newsome purchased merchandise for $50,000 and sold half of the goods for $60,000. On December 31, 2000, his inventory was valued at $25,000 (under the cost method) and $15,000 (under the market method). In 2001, he sells the remaining goods for $50,000. If he had used the lower of cost or market method, his income would have been $10,000 less in 2000 and $10,000 more in 2001 than if he had used the cost method. (This is illustrated in the computations, below.)

	Cost	Cost or Market
2000		
Sales	$60,000	$60,000
Cost of sales (purchases, less ending inventory	25,000	35,000
Gross income	$35,000	$25,000
2001		
Sales	$50,000	$50,000
Cost of sales (beginning inventory)	25,000	15,000
Gross income		
	$25,000	$35,000

In this example, the selling price of the goods in 2001 is $10,000 less than in 2000, the same amount by which the market value of the goods sold in 1999 fell below cost on December 31, 2000. But suppose that the selling prices do not drop in relation to the market values. Then, the lower of cost or market method may produce a higher total tax over a two-year period than would the cost method because of an imbalance of income and the graduated tax rates. This would be especially true if the business owner knows that there is a tax increase scheduled for the next year.

If you are just starting your business and do not use the LIFO cost method discussed below, you may select either the cost or the lower-of-cost-or-market method of accounting. *You must use the same method to value your entire inventory, and you may not change to another method without the IRS's consent.*

Identification of inventory items. Besides deciding how you will value your inventory — at cost, or at the lower of cost or market — you must also decide how you will identify which items were sold, and which are still in inventory. The most basic way of doing this is called the "specific identification method," which requires you to match each item sold with the price that you actually paid for it.

The specific identification method is easy to understand, but may be totally impractical for your business. If your business has a large and quick-moving inventory, you soon would be doing little else than tracking inventory.

Example

The "We're Widgets World Wide" ("4W") company buys and sells thousands of Widgets each year. Because 4W must depend on several suppliers for Widgets, and frequently must outbid other Widget wholesalers for the right to buy them, the price that 4W must pay usually varies daily. Listed below are just four of the thousands of Widgets that came into 4W's inventory in 2000:

Widget 2301, bought 1/1/00, $49.00; sold 12/1/00

Widget 3904, bought 6/1/00, $49.50; sold 9/1/00

Widget 5039, bought 6/30/00, $50.45; sold 7/14/00

Widget 7932, bought 7/1/00, $50.20; sold 12/15/00

Although modern computer-based inventory control systems could allow you to track each item, the IRS doesn't require this. Instead, you can usually choose one of two identification methods. These systems make broad *assumptions* about which inventory items were sold and which remain in inventory, without reference to the particular inventory items that were actually bought and sold. These two methods are known as the "first-in, first-out" (FIFO) and the "last-in, first out" (LIFO) methods.

The FIFO method assumes that sales are made from the items that have been longest in the inventory. This conforms to the usual business practice of trying to sell the older items first, before they become obsolete, spoiled, or out of fashion. This is also the method the IRS prefers.

One consequence of using FIFO is that, in a period of rising prices, gross income may be increased by the increase in the cost of the inventoriable items. You may avoid such an artificial increase in income by electing to use the LIFO method. LIFO works in reverse in a period of declining prices, when the decrease in the cost of the inventoriable items does not result in a corresponding reduction of income. The IRS does not favor LIFO and, if you want to use it, you must file IRS Form 970 and follow some very complex tax rules. There is also a "simplified" dollar-value LIFO method available to small businesses (those with average receipts of $5 million or less for the last three tax years). For more information, see your tax advisor.

CAPITAL ASSETS AND DEPRECIATION

Think about any property used in your business (other than land), and you'll have to face the fact that sooner or later it will break, wear out, be used up, become obsolete, or will otherwise lose its value to your business. Depreciation, or cost recovery, is an allowance provided under the tax laws to account for this economic harm that regularly befalls businesses.

Depreciation is really an accounting concept that has been adopted by the tax laws. One of the goals of financial accounting is to accurately measure a business's gross and net income during a given period of time, usually a year. If a business were allowed to reduce one year's gross income by an expense deduction for the total cost of an item that would be used by the business for a number of years, the result would be an understatement of net income in the year the asset was purchased, and an overstatement of net income during the following years.

Instead, under the depreciation rules, each year you can deduct a specified part of the cost of each business asset having a limited life.

Case Study — Depreciation

Ian Turner needs to purchase a large machine, at a cost of $50,000, to be used in his table leg manufacturing company. For simplicity's sake, let's assume that the machine would be Ian's only item of expense or depreciation, and that it will have a useful life of four years, after which it will have no commercial or salvage value. If the entire cost was deducted in the year of purchase and Ian's business grosses $50,000 in income each year, his net income would be as follows:

Year 1	0	($50,000 income - $50,000 deduction)
Year 2	$50,000	($50,000 income - 0 deduction)
Year 3	$50,000	($50,000 income - 0 deduction)
Year 4	$50,000	($50,000 income - 0 deduction)

In order to more accurately determine the net income of a business on a year-by-year basis, financial accounting has long required that when an asset has a useful life of more than one year, its cost must be allocated (that is, depreciated) over the number of years that the asset will be used. So, in this example, Ian Turner's company will have yearly net income of $37,500 in each of the four years ($50,000 income - $12,500 deduction).

What Can Be Depreciated?

In general, property is depreciable if it meets all of the following requirements:

1. It is used in a trade or business (which will be the focus of our discussion here) or held for the production of income.

2. It has a determinable life that is longer than one year.

3. It wears out, decays, gets used up, becomes obsolete, or loses value from natural causes.

Examples of depreciable property are cars, machines, buildings, patents, and copyrights. Land is probably the most commonly encountered property that is *not* depreciable. Thus, when a business operator purchases a business building and the land upon which the building is situated, the cost of the land must be subtracted from the total cost of the property before the depreciation expense for the building can be determined.

Depreciation is not allowed on personal assets, such as a residence used by you and your family, or an automobile used for pleasure purposes only. If an asset is used partly for personal purposes and partly for business, only the portion of the asset used for business purposes is depreciable.

Equipment Expensing Election

As we said above, you normally can't take a current business deduction for the entire cost of a "capital asset" in the year you purchase it. However, there is an exception to this rule.

A special tax provision allows small businesses the option of claiming a current deduction for the entire cost of such business assets, up to a certain limit. For 1999, the maximum amount that could be expensed during the year was $19,000, and this limit is scheduled to increase in later years.

Year	Expensing Limit
1999	19,000
2000	20,000
2001 and 2002	24,000
2003 and later	25,000

If the cost of qualified property placed in service during the year is more than $200,000, the ceiling is reduced by the amount of such excess. This limit is intended to keep the expensing election targeted toward small businesses.

In 2000, Bobscarts, Inc., a company that manufactures electric golf carts, purchases for $205,000 a machine to be used in its business. Bobscarts would be able to expense $15,000 of the cost of the machine ($20,000 - [$205,000 - $200,000]).

What qualifies for the election? To qualify for this expensing election, the property that you purchase must be tangible personal property that you actively use in your business, for which a depreciation deduction would be allowed, and newly purchased property rather than property you previously owned but recently converted to business use.

Tangible personal property is property, other than real estate, that can be seen or touched, such as a typewriter, chair, or desk. This is to be contrasted with *intangible personal property*, such as stocks, bonds, copyrights, and trademarks.

Intangible property that must be amortized rather than depreciated (such as business goodwill or covenants not to compete, which must be amortized over 15 years) is also ineligible for the election.

If you fully qualify for the expensing deduction, you can get a significant, up-front reduction in the cost of a needed piece of business equipment. For example, for 2000, if you are a sole proprietor in the 28 percent tax bracket, the net cost of buying an $18,500 piece of machinery is reduced to $14,400.

Timing the purchase. You'll get the same expense deduction for the year, regardless of the month in which you started using the piece of equipment.

Business income limitation. The total cost of property that may be expensed for any tax year cannot exceed the total amount of your taxable income that is derived from the active conduct of any trade or business, including any salary or wages from jobs you may have.

Costs that are disallowed because of this limit can be carried forward to the next year, so the fact that this income limitation rule knocks out a portion of your expensing deduction does not mean that it is permanently lost.

Recapture of tax benefits. If, in any later year after the one in which you claimed the expensing election, you either sell or stop using the property predominately in your business, you may have to give back part of the tax benefits that you previously claimed.

Cars. Generally, for cars and certain other business vehicles, the amount that may be expensed under this election is limited to $3,060 for vehicles placed in service in 1999 (this amount rises periodically due to inflation). For more information on recovering the cost of cars, see page 497.

Depreciation Methods

In some situations, the tax laws give you more than one depreciation choice. The most common situation is where you need to decide whether to claim the expensing election for up to $20,000 of new business property as discussed above, or to recover the cost of the property over a longer period of time through depreciation.

Taking the fastest depreciation deduction possible will often make sense, for several reasons:

- It gives you the use of more money now, as opposed to having it only in the future.

- Taking a faster deduction is better if you think that at some point in the future your tax rates will be reduced.

For most business assets placed in service after 1986, if you don't claim the business expensing election, the IRS requires you to depreciate the asset using a method called "MACRS," which stands for Modified Accelerated Cost Recovery System. This method categorizes all business assets into classes and specifies the time period over which you can write off assets in each class, as follows:

Class of Property	Items Included
3-year property	Tractor units, racehorses over two years old, and horses over 12 years old when placed in service.
5-year property	Automobiles, taxis, buses, trucks, computers and peripheral equipment, office machinery (faxes, copiers, calculators etc.), and any property used in research and experimentation. Also includes breeding and dairy cattle.
7-year property	Office furniture and fixtures, and any property that has not been designated as belonging to another class.

10-year property	Vessels, barges, tugs, similar water transportation equipment, single-purpose agricultural or horticultural structures, and trees or vines bearing fruit or nuts.
15-year property	Depreciable improvements to land such as shrubbery, fences, roads, and bridges.
20-year property	Farm buildings that are not agricultural or horticultural structures.
27.5-year property	Residential rental property.
39-year property	Nonresidential real estate, including home offices. (Note: the value of land may not be depreciated.)

Some assets are not eligible for MACRS depreciation, including intangible assets such as patents, trademarks, and business goodwill. Generally these must be amortized evenly over a 15-year period, beginning in the month of acquisition. Off-the-shelf computer software must be amortized over 36 months.

Once you know the classification of the asset you need to depreciate, you use a special table provided by the IRS to determine the percentage of the item's cost that can be deducted each year. MACRS provides for a slightly larger write-off in the earlier years of the cost recovery period.

Example

The following chart shows the depreciation amounts under MACRS for a computer system purchased in 2000 for $10,000:

Year	Basis	Percentage	Deduction
2000	$10,000	20.00%	$2,000
2001	10,000	32.00%	3,200
2002	10,000	19.20%	1,920
2003	10,000	11.52%	1,152
2004	10,000	11.52%	1,152
2005	10,000	5.76%	576

In most cases, small business owners should opt to take the expensing election to the greatest extent possible, but there are some situations where you may want to postpone your deductions to later years when your income will be higher, and you may be in a higher tax bracket. Thus, you may opt to use MACRS depreciation instead.

There is also an alternative MACRS system under which depreciation is deducted under the straight-line method (i.e., the same depreciation deduction must be taken each year) over generally longer periods than under regular MACRS.

Listed Property

Certain types of business property are called "listed property" and are subject to additional restrictions. Listed property includes cars, cellular phones, and equipment that's normally used for entertainment or recreation such as photographic, audio, communication, and video recording equipment.

Generally, your business usage of listed property must exceed 50 percent in order for you to take the special expensing election or to depreciate the property under MACRS. If your business use drops below 51 percent in any year after the first year you use the property in your business, you may have to pay back some of the excess depreciation you claimed.

And, as you might guess, you'll have to keep records showing that your business usage was at least 51 percent of total usage of the property. You should keep a log showing each time the property was used, for how long, and for what purpose. For cars, your mileage records will suffice.

Depreciable Basis

The starting point to determine how much depreciation you can claim on a business asset is usually its purchase price, plus the cost of any additions or improvements, and minus any casualty losses. This is called "basis." If you take property you already own and convert it to business use, the basis is the lesser of the basis as described above, or the fair market value at the time of the conversion.

Thus, if you buy a piece of machinery for $1,000, this is the total amount that you normally will be allowed to claim as depreciation over the life of the asset. In each year, you multiply the $1,000 cost by the applicable depreciation percentage from the IRS table to determine the dollar amount of your depreciation deduction.

Things aren't always so simple. What if, for a single purchase price, you purchase an asset that is only partly depreciable? You must allocate the purchase price between the depreciable part and the nondepreciable part.

Raymond Anthony buys a property for use in his auto repair business. On the lot is a building that was formerly used as a gas station. Considering the size and location of the property, and the size and repair of the building, a fair allocation of the $100,000 that Ray paid for the property is $70,000 for the building and $30,000 for the land.

In this example, the $70,000 paid for the building could be recovered through depreciation, while the $30,000 paid for the land could not. But wouldn't it be better from a tax perspective, to allocate as much as possible to the building (say, $90,000)? Absolutely, but you can expect the IRS to attack your allocation if it doesn't reflect economic reality. If an IRS auditor raises objections, you may wish to bring in a real estate appraiser to support the allocation. In any case, the allocation should be made a part of the sales contract with which you acquired the property, and you should be prepared to prove that the allocation was a part of good faith negotiations with the seller.

Allocation is also necessary if you use an asset partly for business, and partly for personal use. For example, if you have a desk at home that you use 50% of the time for business, you can only depreciate 50% of the cost of the desk.

When To Place Property in Service

Buying a depreciable piece of property is not enough: in order to receive the deduction for the property, you must "place it in service" (put it to productive use in the business).

The date on which you place the property in service determines how much of a full year's deduction you will get for the first year. For most types of depreciable property, no matter what month of the year you begin to use the property, you must treat it as if you started using it in the middle of the year. Thus, you will get one-half of the first year's depreciation, regardless of when you placed the property in service.

If Uncle Sam is going to give you a half year's tax break for a purchase made *any time in the year*, what's to keep you from purchasing a business asset and placing it in use in the final days of December? Doing this would allow you to get the half year's depreciation, while avoiding any actual cash outlay until late in the year. Unfortunately, the IRS is well aware of this strategy, and rules are in place that will limit its use. If, during the last calendar quarter, you place in service more than 40% of the total basis of all property placed in service for the year, you'll have to use somewhat less favorable depreciation tables.

Nonresidential real property (a classification that includes home offices) does not follow the rules discussed above. Instead, it must be depreciated using a mid-month convention; that is, you're treated as placing the property in service at the middle of the month in which you actually began using it. There are special depreciation tables for real estate, showing the different percentages that would apply depending on the month the property was placed in service.

Purchasing vs. Leasing

Depreciation generally may be claimed by the owner of a capital asset, although a business owner who leases property may be entitled to depreciation if the owner is able to show that the lease is, in actuality, a sale of the property.

If you lease property under a "true" lease — that is, not under an arrangement that approximates a sale — you won't be able to deduct depreciation, but you will generally be able to deduct the entire lease payment as a business expense.

Which alternative (depreciation vs. lease payment deduction) is better from a tax perspective depends on your particular situation. The question of whether you should lease or purchase an asset that you need in your business should not be totally dependent on the tax questions involved. For more information, see the discussion of leasing your equipment in Chapter 16.

Recapture of Depreciation Deductions

If you sell, trade in, or otherwise dispose of depreciable property at a gain, you will lose the tax benefit of some or all of the depreciation that you claimed (or were entitled to claim, if by chance you didn't actually claim it).

If the property you sell is subject to the MACRS depreciation system (which means property placed in service after 1986), all gain from the sale of business personal property is "recaptured," meaning that it is taxed as ordinary income rather than capital gains, to the extent of previously allowed depreciation deductions. Depreciation claimed on nonresidential real property (which includes home offices) is subject to recapture at a special rate of 25 percent, for sales after May 7, 1997. Prior to that date, there was generally no recapture of MACRS depreciation on real property.

Timing the sale. All things being equal, it's probably best to be hit with recapture liabilities in years in which your business has suffered an operating loss (which can be used to offset the recapture amount), rather than in profit years, when the recapture liability will increase your taxable income, and possibly put you into a higher tax bracket.

But don't let the tail wag the dog. Strategies aimed at the timing or minimization of depreciation recaptures may be worthwhile, but there are many other important issues to consider when disposing of a business asset, such as finding a buyer at the right price, finding replacement property at the right price, etc.

BUSINESS EXPENSE DEDUCTIONS

Although there are other types of tax planning opportunities available under the tax law, the business deduction rules are often the best place to look for tax savings.

In this section we'll give you the basic rules about deductions so that you'll be able to spot likely deductions in time to take advantage of them.

Business Deduction Basics — What the IRS Looks For

When you claim a business deduction, the IRS may raise questions about several technical tax rules with you and your tax advisor. In plain English, here's what the IRS agent may be looking for:

1. *The agent will ask you to show that the expense was in fact paid. This is where the recordkeeping routines come into play. If you have kept good records, proving your deductions won't be a problem. Remember, on most tax matters, the IRS can require you to prove that your deduction is correct, or lose it.*

2. *The IRS agent may ask you to show that the expense was related to your business, and that it was "ordinary and necessary" to your business activity. The IRS is keenly aware that the business deduction rules can tempt taxpayers to write off things that are really nondeductible personal expenses.*

3. *The IRS may investigate whether you claimed the deduction in the correct tax return year. The agent here is looking for two possible problems: did you claim a valid deduction in the wrong return year, or did you claim a current deduction for something that can only be deducted over several years (such as depreciation)?*

Allocation between business and personal expenses. Expenses for property used for both business and personal purposes must be allocated between personal and business use. The allocation must be made on a reasonable and consistent basis. The method of allocation depends on the nature of the expense.

What if deductions exceed income? If your business's deductions are greater than its income for the year, it has sustained a loss. You could mitigate this situation somewhat if you could fully deduct these losses from other income that you have (or your spouse has, if you file joint returns) during the year. Unfortunately, there are tax rules that may block this result, depending on how the IRS classifies your business activity. If it sees it as a "trade or business," you could benefit from a net operating loss deduction. This deduction is not available, however, if the IRS views your activity as a hobby.

Save Money

 Getting a tax deduction may be nice, but only if the deductible expense is a wise one.

Particularly if you are in the startup phase of your business, the money you have to spend is limited. You don't want to fall into the trap of the business owner who justifies buying a gold-plated white elephant by saying, "So what if I really don't need it, it's deductible!"

Recordkeeping and Substantiation

All taxpayers are required to keep accurate, permanent books and records so as to be able to determine the various types of income, gains, losses, costs, expenses, and other amounts that affect their income tax liability for the year. These records must be retained for as long as they may be relevant for any tax purpose.

Deduction rules. In order to claim any deduction, a business owner, like any taxpayer, must be able to prove that the expenses were in fact paid or incurred. A receipt or a canceled check is the best way to prove this.

In many cases, if you don't have records of a particular business expense but it's obvious that you must have incurred it, in an audit situation the IRS will estimate the amount of your expense and allow you to deduct it. An example would be a retailer who has no records of inventory purchases — the IRS will come up with a reasonable estimate of what the purchases should have been.

Certain expenses, which the IRS has found to be particularly susceptible to cheating, are subject to special documentation (*substantiation*) rules. The following expenses must generally be proven by adequate records or other evidence corroborating the taxpayer's own statements; if you have no records, the deduction will be completely disallowed:

- expenses for travel away from home

- meals and entertainment expenses

- business gifts

- expenses for the following types of property: cars and other means of transportation, property of a kind that is generally used for entertainment or recreation, and cellular telephones or telecommunications equipment

For these types of expenses, you must keep receipts for any expense over $75, and for all lodging expenses whatever the amount. You must also substantiate each individual expense as to: (1) amount, (2) time and place, and (3) business purpose. For entertainment and gift expenses, you must also note the business relationship of the person being entertained or receiving the gift. These things can be noted on the back of the receipt, or recorded in a formal expense log.

Save Money

There is no requirement that you keep a contemporaneous log of your business deductions. However, the closer in time to the expenditure or use that you record the expense (and provide necessary documentary evidence), the more valuable it will be to prove the deduction. Also, if you get into the habit of systematically recording your expenses and all the necessary supporting facts and records, you may discover that you had been forgetting to claim perfectly legitimate deductions.

Did the Expense Pertain to a Business Activity?

In order for business deductions to be allowed, you must have a "trade or business," that is, an activity that is carried on for a livelihood or for profit. A *profit motive* must be present (though you may in fact have experienced a loss) and some type of economic activity must be conducted. This profit motive separates a business from a hobby, which is an activity engaged in purely for self-satisfaction that may generate some income incidentally.

"Profit" for purposes of the business activity rules means real economic profit, independent of any tax savings.

To be deductible, business expenses must be incurred in carrying on an *existing* trade or business. Costs associated with starting up a business are considered capital expenditures, which are not fully deductible as current expenses.

How To Demonstrate a Profit Motive

Listed below are nine factors that the IRS looks at to decide whether an activity is a business run for profit, or as a hobby. A "yes" answer supports a finding of a profit motive, although no one factor settles the matter.

- **How the business is run** — does the owner keep complete and accurate business records and books? Has the owner changed business operations to increase profits?

- **Expertise** — does the owner have the necessary expertise to run the business? If not, does he or she seek (and follow) expert advice?

- **Time and effort** — does the owner spend the time and effort needed for the business's success?

- **Appreciation** — is it likely that business assets will appreciate in value, so that there will be some profit on gains from the sale even if there's no profit in current operations?

- **Success with other activities** — has the owner engaged in similar (or dissimilar) activities in the past and converted them from unprofitable to profitable enterprises?

- **History of income or loss** — were the business losses incurred because the business was still in a startup phase, or because of unforeseen circumstances?

- **Amount of occasional profit** — are any occasional profits significant when compared to the size of the owner's investment in the activity, and the losses suffered in other years? (An occasional small profit for an activity generating large losses, or in which the owner has a large investment, will not establish a for-profit objective.)

- **Financial status of owner** — is the business activity the only source of the owner's income?

- **Personal pleasure or recreation** — is the type of business one that is not usually considered to have elements of personal pleasure or recreation?

Save Money

How you can go about showing that your activity is operated for profit will depend, in large part, on whether you expect it to profit over either the short run or long run.

- ***Profit possible over short term*** — *by planning when to receive income and when to purchase items that generate deductions, try to maximize income (and minimize deductions) in at least three years (the "profit" years), and maximize deductions (and minimize income) in the remaining two years (the "loss" years). This may allow you to qualify for the presumption of profit motive discussed below.*

- **Profit possible only over long term** — *if it appears that the business will not be profitable for some years, you won't be able to come within the presumption of profit motive. You'll have to rely on qualifying under the IRS's nine point inquiry to establish profit motive.*

- **No possibility of profit** — *face it, what you have here is a hobby. With a hobby, losses can only be taken against income generated by the hobby, not against any other income that you make. You can try to argue that you qualify under the IRS's nine-point inquiry, but in all likelihood you'll fail. If you want to continue this activity, you may as well either resign yourself to the limitation on hobby losses, or figure out a way to conduct the activity in a way that generates profits.*

Presumption That Activity Is for Profit

An activity is presumed not to be a hobby if it is profitable in three out of five consecutive years. (A narrow exception to this rule applies to horse breeding activities, where profitability must be shown in two out of seven consecutive years.)

If your business qualifies for this presumption, it means that the IRS (not you) would have the burden of proving that your business is a hobby, if the issue comes up in an audit.

Hobby Loss Rules

As discussed above, if you are in business with the "objective of making a profit," you can generally claim all your business deductions. If your deductions exceed your income for the year, you can claim a loss for the year, up to the amount of your income from other activities. Remaining losses can be carried over into other years. Your ability to deduct these losses will be limited, however, if the IRS considers your "business" to be a hobby.

Losses incurred by individuals, partnerships, and S corporations in connection with a hobby are generally deductible *only to the extent of the income produced by the hobby.* Some expenses that would be deductible whether or not they are incurred in connection with a hobby, such as taxes, interest, and casualty losses, are deductible even if they exceed hobby income. These expenses do reduce the amount of the hobby income against which other hobby expenses can be offset.

Although the IRS is not limited in the kind of businesses that it can attack as hobbies, businesses that look like traditional hobbies (such as "gentleman farming" and craft businesses run from the home) may well face a greater chance of IRS scrutiny than other businesses.

Expenses Appropriate to Business

A deduction for an expense paid in connection with your business will be allowed only if the expense is "ordinary and necessary" for the operation of the business. The IRS is rather flexible in this regard: it defines "ordinary" as an expense that is common and accepted in a field of business, and defines "necessary" as an expense that is helpful and appropriate to your business. An expense does not have to be indispensable to be a necessary expense.

You can expect that almost any common business expense for your type of business will pass muster without serious question. Rather, IRS agents use this test to make sure that the expense is actually spent, and (1) furthers the business (instead of personal or family needs), (2) is not also being deducted elsewhere on the return (such as in the cost of goods sold computation), and (3) is a current, rather than capital, expense.

Common Deductible Business Expenses

- advertising
- bad debts from sales or services
- car and truck expenses
- commissions and fees
- cost of goods sold
- depreciation
- employee benefit programs
- insurance
- interest
- legal and professional services

- meals and entertainment
- office expenses
- pension and profit-sharing plans
- rent or lease expense
- repairs and maintenance
- supplies
- travel expenses, including lodging
- utilities
- wages for employees

Common Nondeductible Expenses

- bar or professional examination fees
- capital expenditures (not fully deductible in the year placed in service, but yearly depreciation deductions are allowed to recover the cost over a specified time period)
- country or social club dues
- commuting expenses

- estate tax (even if largely due to the ownership of a business interest)

- expenses, including interest, paid to generate tax-exempt income

- federal income tax

- fines and penalties incurred for violations of law, such as child labor violations, federal income tax penalties, and traffic tickets

- gift tax

- gifts to individuals that are valued at more than $25

- hobby losses

- inheritance tax

- interest on indebtedness incurred by a business taxpayer to purchase life insurance coverage in excess of $50,000 on the life of any its officers, employees, or other person having a financial interest in the taxpayer's trade or business

- interest on indebtedness incurred to purchase single premium life insurance contracts, or any life insurance contract under a plan of financing the purchase by withdrawing some or all of the yearly buildup in policy cash values

- job hunting expenses (new trade or business)

- life insurance premiums, if the business, or the business owner, is a direct or indirect beneficiary

- lobbying expenses (appearances before legislative bodies and expenses to influence voters)

- partnership organizational expenses, unless amortization election is made

- personal, living, or family expenses — however, certain interest, taxes, bad debts, medical expenses, theft or casualty losses, or charitable contributions may be deductible in whole or in part as an itemized deduction. Child or disabled dependent care costs are allowed as a credit.

- political contributions, including tickets to political dinners

- tax penalty payments

- transfer taxes on business property

Net Operating Losses

What happens if you add up all your allowable business expenses, try to subtract them from your income, and find out that you're "in the red" for the year?

The net operating loss deduction allows you to offset one year's losses against another year's income. This deduction is an exception to the general income tax rule that your taxable income is determined on the basis of your current year's events.

If you have a net loss from the operation of a trade or business, and you have insufficient other income in the current year to offset the loss, a net operating loss may be carried back two years and used to offset the income of those previous years, to the earliest year first. Any unused portion of such loss may then be carried forward for up to 20 years. If the entire loss isn't used up in this way, no further net operating loss carryover is permitted. If you like, you can elect to forego the carryback period, instead choosing to deduct the net operating loss over the next 20 years.

Save Money

 Because carrying back a net operating loss to a prior tax year can result in a quick tax refund, it's usually the best course of action. If you forego this opportunity, be sure you have a reasonable prospect of sufficient income in future years against which the net operating loss can be offset.

COMMON DEDUCTION PROBLEMS

Now we're ready to get into the special rules that apply in commonly encountered business situations:

- distinguishing nondeductible capital expenditures from currently deductible business expenses

- how to handle the "startup" expenses you incur in getting a new business up and running

- qualifying your travel, meal, and entertainment expenses for business deductions

- deducting the cost of business gifts for your clients and customers

- determining which employee benefits are deductible

- deducting owner compensation

- deducting costs of running your business out of your home

- deducting car and truck expenses

Nondeductible Capital Expenditures

One of the principles underlying the tax rules for deductions is that your income for the year should be offset only by those expenses that contributed to earning that income. If you purchase an asset that will be used in the business for more than a year, you generally have to depreciate it rather than deduct it currently (see the discussion of cost recovery for capital assets, above).

What if the expense is not a new asset, but instead a permanent improvement to an existing asset you already own? For example, what if you do substantial remodeling to your business facility? You add the expense to your total investment in the asset (which is also known as your tax basis). For depreciation purposes, the improvements are usually treated like a separate depreciable asset that has a depreciation period of the same length as that of the original asset.

You will eventually recover all of the expense through (1) a reduced amount of taxable gain or an increased amount of taxable loss on your sale or other disposition of the property, or (2) increased annual depreciation deductions.

Usually, the trickiest issue is deciding whether an expense is a repair that is deductible currently, or an improvement or replacement that must be capitalized. Expenses that add to the value or useful life of an item of property are considered capital expenditures. In contrast, an expense that keeps an asset in ordinary efficient operating condition and that does not add to its value or appreciably prolong its useful life generally is a deductible repair expense.

Drawing the line isn't easy. However, over time, the IRS and the courts have classified some categories of items as capital expenditures. Below, we provide a listing of these capital expenditures as a guide.

Illustrative Capital Expenditures

- *abstract of title costs*

- *appraisal costs paid in obtaining possession of premises*

- *author's publishing costs*

- *boiler patching and welding costs*

- *burglar alarm installation charges*

- *business facility improvement costs (for example, waterproofing; replacing a roof; planning, designing, and constructing an addition; remodeling costs)*

- *cable replacement costs upon sudden failure*

- *copyright development costs*

- *credit card membership fees*

- *display cases, remodeling costs*

- *drainage costs*

- *electric wiring costs (new wiring, replacement, and rearrangement)*

- *electrical system replacement costs*

- *Federal Communications Commission (FCC) license preparation fees*

- *fire escapes, costs of cutting exits to, and cost of new*

- *flood protection costs (such as costs of raising floors, or rearranging bins)*

- *insulation costs*

- *irrigation system costs*

- *merger negotiation costs*

- *moving costs (changing location and moving equipment)*

- *mutual fund setup costs incurred by investment advisors*

- *package design costs*

- *performance bond premiums*

- *Security Exchange and Commission (SEC) statement preparation cost*

- *settlement costs for threatened lawsuit*

- *well drilling costs*

- *zoning change costs that increase the value of property beyond the tax year*

Remember that the same item that was a deductible expense to one taxpayer might be a capital expenditure to another, if the two taxpayers use an the item in different ways in their businesses.

Business Startup Expenditures

Investigating the potential for a new business and getting it started can be an expensive proposition. However, but for a special rule, you generally can't claim these expenses as business deductions because you incur them prior to the time that you're actually in business.

Fortunately, there is a way around this dilemma: if your startup expenditures actually result in an up-and-running business, you can amortize the costs (that is, deduct them evenly) over a period of at least 60 months. So, you can eventually deduct both the cost of investigating the creation of the business and the costs of actually creating it. However, only those costs that would be deductible if they were incurred by an existing trade or business are eligible for the election.

Investigation expenses that can be deducted over the 60-month period include those relating to business conditions generally, and those relating to a specific business, such as market or product research to determine the feasibility of starting a certain type of business. The costs of checking out the various factors involved in site selection would also be an amortizable investigation expense.

Amortizable costs of creating a business include advertising, wages and salaries, professional and consultant fees, and necessary travel before the business actually begins.

What costs don't qualify? Although they are frequently incurred before a new business goes into operation, the following costs don't qualify for 60-month amortization:

- Startup expenditures for interest, taxes, and research and experimental costs that are otherwise allowed as deductions do not qualify for amortization. These costs may be deducted when incurred.

- The costs of organizing a partnership or a corporation are not considered startup costs, but they may be eligible for separate amortization.

- The costs attributable to the acquisition of a specific property that is subject to depreciation or cost recovery do not qualify for amortization. Generally, they would be added to the basis of the property and capitalized.

If you never start the business. Costs incurred to decide whether to go into business aren't deductible. Costs of trying unsuccessfully to buy or start a specific business are a capital loss.

Save Money

It's usually best to claim the 60-month amortization deduction as early as possible if there is any doubt about when business begins. If the IRS determines that your business began in a year before the election to amortize startup costs is made, the right to deduct these costs is lost.

Expenses Paid to Incorporate

If you decide to do business as a corporation, you can have your corporation elect to deduct its organization expenditures over a period of at least 60 months. If this election is not made, the expenditures must be capitalized and will not be recovered until the corporation is liquidated.

If the corporation makes this election, the expenditures incurred before the end of its first tax year (whether or not paid in that year) may be allowed as a deduction to be taken ratably over the period elected.

Examples of expenditures that can be deducted include:

- fees paid to the state of incorporation

- legal and accounting fees to obtain the corporate charter

- legal fees for drafting the charter, by-laws, minutes of organizational meetings, and the terms of original stock certificates

- expenses of temporary directors

Examples of nondeductible expenditures include costs of issuing shares of stock, such as commissions, professional fees, and printing costs.

Expenses Paid to Organize a Partnership

If you decide to conduct your business as a partnership, neither the partnership itself nor you as one of the partners will normally be able to deduct the expenses you paid out to organize the partnership. However, your partnership can elect to treat these organizational costs as deferred expenses that can be amortized (deducted ratably) over a period of at least 60 months, starting with the month the partnership begins business.

If you decide that your partnership should not make this election, the organizational costs must be capitalized as a part of the tax basis of your partnership interest. One way you will benefit from this increased basis would be when the partnership is dissolved. At such a dissolution, the amounts paid for the organizational expenses will reduce the amount of your gain on the partnership interest, or increase the amount of your loss.

Examples of organizational costs that can be amortized include:

- legal and accounting fees for services related to the organization of the partnership, such as negotiation and preparation of the partnership agreement

- filing fees

Examples of costs that can't be amortized include:

- expenses for acquiring assets for a partnership, or for transferring assets to it

- expenses connected with the admission or removal of partners (other than at the time the partnership is first organized)

- expenses relating to a contract involving the operation of the partnership business

- expenses incurred to promote the sale of partnership interests

Travel, Meal, and Entertainment Expenses

One of the most fertile areas for tax savings is in the area of meals, entertainment, and travel expenses. However, this area is also one of the most confusing! When is the cost of a trip or a meal deductible as a business expense? Where can you take a client out and be able to deduct the cost? How about meetings and conventions — particularly in other cities? What you consider business-related as opposed to what the IRS considers business-related may surprise you.

What Does the IRS Consider "Business Travel"?

What requirements do your travel expenses need to meet in order to be deductible? The IRS is basically looking for the following:

- The travel expenses must be incurred in connection with an existing business.

- The expenses must be incurred away from home.

Business purpose. You can deduct travel expenses only if they are ordinary and necessary expenses that you incur in connection with the pursuit of an existing business.

You can't deduct travel expenses to the extent that they are lavish or extravagant — the expenses must be reasonable considering the facts and circumstances.

What about travel that has a combined business and personal aspect? Here's where it gets a bit more complicated. The IRS is on the lookout for taxpayers who might try to classify a nondeductible personal trip as a deductible business one. If you travel to a destination and, while you're there, you engage in both personal and business activities, you can deduct your traveling expenses to and from the destination only if the trip is *primarily* related to your business. If the trip is primarily personal in nature you can't deduct any of your traveling expenses. This is true even if you engage in some business activities while you are there. (You can, however, deduct expenses you incur while you're at your destination if they qualify as business deductions.)

The primary purpose of a trip is based on the facts and circumstances of each case. An important factor is the amount of time spent on personal activities during the trip as compared to the amount of time spent on activities directly relating to business. Travel expenses outside the U.S. may be further limited if part of your trip is for personal purposes.

Away from home. You may only deduct travel expenses incurred when you are "away from home." For this purpose, you are traveling away from home if you meet the following two conditions:

- **The travel is away from the general area or vicinity of your "tax home."** Generally, your principal place of business establishes your tax home. The tax home encompasses the entire general area or vicinity of your principal place of business. If you conduct your business in more than one place, you should consider the total time you ordinarily spend working in each place, the degree of your business activity in each place, and the relative amount of your income from each place to determine your "principal" place of business. When you are temporarily (a year or less) working away from your main place of business, your tax home doesn't change.

- **You can't reasonably be expected to complete the round trip without obtaining sleep or rest.** This doesn't necessarily mean you have to spend the entire night; in some cases, needing to take a nap in a hotel is sufficient.

Spouses and dependents. For the travel expenses of a spouse (or dependent, or any other individual for that matter) to be deductible, the spouse (or other individual) must also be an employee traveling for business reasons.

Conventions, seminars, meetings, and the like. You can deduct your travel expenses when you attend a convention if you can show that attending the convention benefits your business. You can satisfy the business relationship test by showing that your business duties and responsibilities tie into the program or agenda of the convention.

The rules become even stricter when the convention is held outside North America or on a cruise ship. Basically, the IRS doesn't want people deducting their vacations. However, they recognize that at least some of these trips are for bona fide business purposes. Here's what you need to know:

- **Conventions held outside North America** — the convention must be directly related to your business and it must be as reasonable to hold the convention outside the North American area as in it. You must also satisfy the requirements for deducting business travel expenses outside the U.S.

- **Conventions held on cruise ships** — the following requirements must be met:

  - The convention must be directly related to the active conduct of your business.

  - The cruise ship must be a vessel registered in the U.S., and all of the cruise ship's ports of call must be located in the U.S. (or its possessions).

  - You must attach to your income tax return a written statement signed by you that includes the total days of the trip (excluding the days you spent traveling to and from the ship's port), the number of hours each day that you devoted to scheduled business activities, and a program of the scheduled business activities of the meeting.

  - You must attach to your income tax return a written statement signed by an officer of the organization or group sponsoring the convention that includes a schedule of the business activities of each day of the convention, and the number of hours you attended the scheduled business activities.

If you meet the requirements, you can deduct up to $2,000 annually of the expense of attending a seminar or convention on a cruise ship.

Foreign Travel

If you travel outside the U.S. purely for business purposes, all your travel expenses of getting to and from your business destination are deductible.

However, if you spend part of your time in a foreign country engaging in personal activities, you may have to allocate your travel expenses in proportion to the number of days you spent on nonbusiness activities during your trip, unless you meet one of the following conditions:

- You were outside the U.S. for a week or less, combining business and personal activities (a week is seven consecutive days — not counting the day you leave the U.S., but counting the day you return to the U.S.).

- You were outside the U.S. for more than a week, but you spent less than 25 percent of the total time you were in a foreign country on personal activities (counting both the day your trip began and the day it ended).

- You can establish that a personal vacation was not a major consideration in taking the trip.

If you don't meet at least one of these conditions and you spent 25 percent or more of your time on personal activities, you'll have to allocate the expenses of getting to and from your destination between your business and personal activities, to determine your deductible amount. You must allocate your expenses *even if* your trip was primarily for business reasons. Remember, if your trip was primarily for vacation purposes, the entire cost of the trip is a nondeductible personal expense. You would be able to deduct only the expenses that you incurred on the trip that were directly related to your business (if any).

Which Travel Expenses Are Deductible?

Generally, deductible travel expenses are the ordinary and necessary expenses that you incur while you're away from home in pursuit of your trade or business. In order to claim travel expenses as deductions, you must keep adequate records and be able to substantiate the expenses.

The following is a list of expenses you may be able to deduct depending on the facts and circumstances.

Deductible Travel Expenses

- *air, rail, and bus fares; car rental fees*

- *expenses of operating and maintaining a vehicle, including the cost of gas, oil, lubrication, washing, repairs, parts, tires, supplies, parking fees, and tolls*

- *hotel expenses*

- *baggage charges and transportation costs for sample and display materials and sample room costs*

- *cleaning and laundry expenses*

- *expenses of operating and maintaining housetrailers*

- *taxi fares or other costs of transportation between the airport or station and a hotel, from one customer to another, or from one place of business to another; and tips incidental to the foregoing expenses*

- *computer rental fees*

- *telephone or fax expenses*

- *public stenographer fees*

- *tips (on all eligible expenses)*

- *50% of the cost of meals you eat alone, only if your business trip is overnight or long enough to require that you stop for sleep or rest*

- *50% of the cost of meals with clients, customers, etc. are deductible under the usual rules for meals and entertainment expenses*

Standard meal allowance. If the cost of your meals while you're traveling qualify for deduction, you have an alternative to deducting 50% of the actual cost of the meals: you can deduct a standard amount for your daily meals and incidental expenses (costs for laundry, cleaning, and tips).

In 1999, the standard meal allowance is $30 a day for most areas in the U.S. Some locations in the U.S. are considered high-cost areas and qualify for higher rates of $34, $38, $42, or $46 per day. These rates are periodically adjusted for inflation and are available in IRS Publication 1452 or on the Internet at http://www.policyworks.gov.

You can deduct 50% of the amount that applies to your area each day you are traveling, though partial days must be pro-rated.

For travel in areas outside the continental U.S., you must use federal per diem rates that are published monthly by the government. The foreign per diem rates can be purchased from the Government Printing Office and are also available on the Internet from the State Department (http://www.state.gov).

Save Money

The advantage to using the standard meal allowance is that you don't have to keep records of actual meal expenses (you still have to keep records to prove the time, place, and business purpose of your travel). A disadvantage is that the standard meal allowances are not very generous — chances are that your actual expenses will be higher.

Meal and Entertainment Expenses

As a small business owner, you may find yourself in the position of having to entertain clients or customers. You'll be glad to know that the IRS allows you to deduct 50 percent of your qualifying business entertainment expenses.

Generally, you can deduct ordinary and necessary expenses to entertain a customer or client (including your own meal) if the expenses meet at least one of the following two tests:

- the directly-related-to test

- the associated-with test

Directly-related-to test. If the entertainment that you are claiming a deduction for takes place in a clear business setting (for example, you provide a hospitality room at a convention) directly for the furtherance of your business, the expense automatically satisfies the directly-related-to test. If you can't meet the clear business setting requirement, the expense must meet *all* of the following requirements:

- You must have more than a general expectation of deriving some income or other specific business benefit (other than the goodwill of the person entertained) from the meal or entertainment. However, you don't need to show that any income or other business benefit actually resulted from each deducted expenditure.

- During the meal or entertainment, you actively engaged in business discussions.

- The main purpose of the combined business and entertainment is the active conduct of business.

What kind of expenses are generally *not* considered directly related? In situations where there are substantial or noisy distractions, such as meetings or discussions at night clubs, theaters, or sporting events; meetings or discussions at social gatherings, such as cocktail parties;

and situations in which you meet with a group that includes persons other than business associates; for example, cocktail lounges, country clubs, golf or athletic clubs or vacation resorts, there's a presumption that the entertainment is not directly related to the business.

Associated-with test. Meals and entertainment expenses may also be deductible if they meet the following two requirements:

- The expenses are associated with the active conduct of your business.

- The meal or entertainment directly precedes or follows a substantial and bona fide business discussion.

   — Entertainment that occurs on the same day as the substantial business discussion meets the "directly precedes or follows" requirement. If the entertainment and the business discussion don't occur on the same day, the facts and circumstances of each case are considered. The relevant facts are the place, date, and duration of the business discussion, whether you and your business associate are from out of town (and the dates of arrival and departure), and the reasons the entertainment didn't take place on the same day of the business discussion.

   — Whether a business discussion (such as a meeting, negotiation, transaction, etc.) is substantial and bona fide depends on the facts and circumstances of each case. You do have to establish that you actively engaged in the business discussion (not the entertainment) for the purpose of obtaining income or some other type of specific business benefit. You would have to show that the principal character of the combined entertainment and business activity was the active conduct of business to demonstrate that the business discussion was substantial in relation to the entertainment. However, you *don't* have to show that more time was devoted to business than entertainment.

Spouses. Can you deduct the cost of entertainment for your spouse or a customer or client's spouse? You can deduct these costs only if you had a clear business purpose, rather than a personal or social purpose, for providing the entertainment. For example, you would be able to deduct otherwise permissible entertainment expenses of an out-of-town client's husband when it is impracticable to entertain the client without him.

What kind of expenses? Generally, if you meet one of the two tests above, expenses for any activity that provides entertainment, amusement, or recreation will be allowed.

For example, entertaining guests at nightclubs; at social, athletic, and sporting clubs; at theaters; at sporting events; or on hunting, fishing, vacation and similar types of trips constitutes entertainment. Meeting personal, living, or family needs of individuals (for example, providing meals, a hotel suite, or a car to business customers or their families) can be an entertainment expense as well. A meal expense includes the cost of food, beverages, taxes, and tips for the meal.

It's important to note that the type of business you run can determine whether an activity is entertainment. For example, if you're a theater critic who is paid for your reviews, and you attend a theatrical performance in your professional capacity, this is not a deductible entertainment expense. Instead, it's a cost of doing business and you can deduct the entire cost, not just 50% of it.

Business Gifts

The IRS will let you deduct business gifts of $25 or less per recipient during your tax year. This means that any number of your employees, co-owners, or business partners may give a client business gifts. However, the deduction will be limited to $25 per recipient.

It also means that if you give a client a $50 dollar watch as a gift, you can only get a $25 deduction.

In addition, if you and your spouse both give gifts, you're both going to be treated as one taxpayer. Consequently, the deduction both you and your spouse, together, will be able to claim is $25 per donee. This is true even if you have separate businesses, are separately employed, or whether each of you has an independent connection with the gift recipient.

The $25 limit for business gifts includes indirect gifts.

Example

Let's say you give your client's live-in relative, Aunt Mabel, a single ticket for a basketball game. Now, at the time you gave her the ticket, you probably had a pretty good idea that she would ultimately give the ticket to your client who is an avid basketball fan. So, will the IRS will classify this as an indirect gift to your client? You can bet on it.

The $25 limit for business gifts doesn't include incidental costs such as packaging, insurance, and mailing costs or the cost of engraving jewelry.

Items excepted from the gift limitations. The following items are not counted towards the $25 limit for business gifts and their cost is deductible without limitation:

- items that cost $4 or less, have your name clearly and permanently imprinted on them, and are one of a number of identical items you widely distribute

- signs, display racks, or other promotional material to be used on the business premises of the recipient

Entertainment gifts. What happens if you give tickets to a play or sporting event to a customer or client? Is this expense a gift or entertainment? The general rule is that any item that could be considered either a gift or an entertainment expense must be considered an entertainment expense.

However, under certain circumstances, you may have the choice of determining whether an item is either a gift or entertainment expense. For example, if you give a client tickets to go see a play or sporting event, you may treat the tickets as either a gift or entertainment expense if you don't go with the client to the play or sporting event. If you go with the client, you *must* treat the cost of the tickets as an entertainment expense—you have no option.

Save Money

Taking into account the $25 limit for gifts and the 50 percent limitation on entertainment expenses, it's generally advantageous to treat an expense as entertainment when it is over $50.

For example, let's say you gave a client ballet tickets that cost $140. If you deduct them as a gift expense, your deduction is limited to $25. If you deduct them as an entertainment expense, your deduction is 50 percent of $140, or $70. Conversely, if you gave a client tickets to a movie premiere that cost $30, you would get a bigger deduction by claiming a gift expense ($25 as opposed to $15 for an entertainment expense).

Gifts to employees are covered under different rules. See the discussion of such gifts in *Chapter 28: Doing the Payroll.*

Fringe Benefits

If you have employees, chances are you're providing them with some fringe benefits, whether or not you're aware of it. When you give your employees discounts on the services you sell or the products you produce, or if you give them paid vacation time, you are providing a fringe benefit—a form of compensation for their services.

Generally speaking, you get an income tax deduction for all your compensation payments to employees, but you must pay FICA taxes on these payments unless they are specifically excluded from FICA coverage. For more information, see the discussion of employee benefits on page 548, or consult your tax advisor.

Deducting Owner's Compensation

If you're doing business as a corporation, you should be aware that your corporation can take a deduction for compensation it pays to you, its owner-employee. But be forewarned: payments made to an employee who is also the owner of the employer company are subject to very close scrutiny by the IRS.

If anything looks questionable, your compensation could very well be attacked as unreasonable. Your compensation could then be recharacterized as a disguised corporate dividend and your compensation deduction denied. Not only that, you'll have to pay corporate income tax on the recharacterized dividend.

However, your compensation may not be recharacterized as a disguised dividend if you can establish that your personal efforts, highly specialized experience or technical ability allowed your corporation to receive *extraordinary* revenues. If this doesn't sound easy to prove, that's because it's not! The courts have traditionally been swamped with these types of claims.

Usually, these issues arise in an audit situation where a corporation hasn't paid any dividends or has only paid nominal dividends during its existence, and has, at the same time, paid unusually large salaries to employee-owners.

Does your corporation *have* to issue dividends to escape this kind of challenge to a deduction for compensation? Not necessarily. You may be able to present legitimate business reasons for not paying dividends, such as the need to conserve capital for expansion. Or, perhaps it may have been more prudent to reinvest the earnings of your business if it's relatively new.

Another factor that increases the likelihood of disallowance is a close relationship between salaries and stockholdings. If an employee's salary closely tracks his or her stockholdings, as opposed to the amount of work he or she put in, it's strong evidence that the salary is in fact a disguised dividend payment.

Warning

In a corporation, you may also want to avoid paying out year-end bonuses determined after the corporate profits for the year are calculated. These types of bonuses may arouse suspicion that, rather than being compensation for services, they're actually a distribution of profits. This rule does not hold true for sole proprietors, partnerships, or LLCs, however.

The Home Office Deduction

If you use a part of your home for business, perhaps to perform paperwork; to store records, inventory, or product samples; or even to meet customers, you may be able to claim a tax deduction for some of your expenses of maintaining the home. That can include a portion of your mortgage interest or rent, property taxes, homeowner's insurance, utilities, and home repairs.

Not one deduction, but many. In reality, when we speak of the "home office deduction," we're talking about a whole series of deductions. These smaller deductions are totaled up to get an overall deduction amount. The common denominator among these deductions is that they relate to a portion of your home that is used exclusively for business purposes.

Claiming the deduction involves two questions. Whenever you're considering a home office deduction, you must answer two questions. The first is, given the nature of your business, are you qualified to claim the home office deduction? The second is, assuming that you are so qualified, what expenses can you claim as part of that deduction?

Warning

Historically, the home office deduction has been subject to quite a bit of abuse. Consequently, the IRS has developed strict requirements about who is eligible for it. Don't let this dissuade you from taking the deduction if you're entitled to it. Do let it motivate you to keep good records.

Qualifying for the Home Office Deduction

Everyone who wishes to claim the home office deduction must use a portion of their home exclusively and regularly for business. You don't necessarily have to use the space as an office; it could be a showroom or storage area.

"Regular use" means that you must use it more than just occasionally.

"Exclusive use" means that the business part of the home may not be used for any personal, family, or investment activities, or for any other business activities that don't meet the home office requirements. There is an exception to the "exclusive use" requirement if your home is the only fixed location of a retail or wholesale business.

In that case, you can deduct expenses that pertain to the use of part of your home for the storage of inventory or product samples. There is also an exception to this requirement available in some cases for those who operate a child care business in their home.

Example

Patrick Daley's home is the sole, fixed place of his business selling personal computers at retail. He regularly uses half of his basement for inventory storage, although he also uses that part of the basement for personal purposes when it's not full of inventory. The expenses allocated to the storage space are deductible even though he does not use that part of the basement exclusively for business.

Other requirements. In addition to the exclusive and regular use tests, you must meet *one* of the following requirements:

- the part of the home must be your principal place of business

- you must use it as a place to personally meet clients or customers in the normal course of your business (telephone calls don't count)

- if it is a separate structure that is not attached to your house or residence, it merely has to be used in your trade or business

An important change. As of 1999, the "principal place of business" definition is significantly easier to meet.

The law has been changed to state that the home office will qualify as the principal place of business if: (a) the office is used by the taxpayer to conduct administrative or management activities of a trade or business, and (b) there is no other fixed location where the taxpayer conducts substantial administrative or management activities of the trade or business.

Example

Joe Ditto operates his photocopier service and repair business out of his home. His only office is a room in his house used solely for business purposes. Although Joe never meets with customers in his home office, he spends about 12 hours per week working there, scheduling service calls, and writing up orders and other reports. He spends an average of 30 hours per week on service calls at his customers' businesses at various locations in the metropolitan area.

As of 1999, Joe's home does qualify for the home office deduction, even though the essence of his business requires him to service and repair photocopiers at the customers' places of business, and he spends less time in his home office than he does at the customers' offices.

This means that the fact that you may conduct management activities in a non-fixed location, such as a car or hotel room, will not cause you to lose the deduction. Similarly, the fact that you conduct some management activities in another fixed location of the business will not cause you to lose the deduction, as long as those activities are not "substantial."

Keep in mind that even if you don't meet these strict requirements, you can still deduct expenses that are directly related to your business. For example, office supplies, postage, and insurance payments for business would be deductible, and you can depreciate the cost of computers, fax machines, or office furniture used at home. You can't deduct the costs of basic telephone service on the first line, but you can deduct any extra charges for business calls, or a second line.

Which Home Office Expenses Are Deductible?

If you meet the tests described above, you'll be allowed to deduct the portion of your mortgage interest or rent, real estate taxes, insurance, utilities, repairs, disposal, security system expense, and depreciation that pertains to the business portion of your home. First, though, you must figure out what the business portion is.

Ordinarily, you would divide the area of floor space in the business portion of the home by the total floor space, to arrive at a business percentage. You could also divide the number of rooms you use for business by the total rooms in the home, if the rooms are all approximately the same size.

Example

If Rick Shearson has a 3,000 square foot home and a 120 square foot office, he would calculate 120 ÷ 3,000 = .04. Thus, 4 percent of the home is used for business.

Then you multiply the expenses that pertain to the whole house (real estate taxes, mortgage interest, and depreciation if you own; rent if you're a tenant; insurance, utilities, security system etc.) by the business percentage to get the deductible amount.

Example

Donna Baxter is a sales representative who qualifies for the home office deduction. She has an electric bill of $400 for lighting, cooking, laundry, and television. Only the lighting is used for business. She figures that $250 of the bill is for lighting alone. Because she uses 10 percent of the house for business, 10 percent of the lighting bill or $25 is deductible.

Repairs that pertain to the whole house, such as furnace or roof repairs, are multiplied by the business percentage to get your deduction. Repairs that pertain only to the business portion of the home, such as painting or plastering your office, are fully deductible, while repairs that pertain only to personal rooms aren't deductible at all.

Depreciation. If you own the home, you cannot deduct any part of the price you paid for the home, the principal payments you make on the mortgage, or the fair rental value of the home. Instead, you can recover the cost of the business percentage of the home through depreciation. See the discussion of depreciation on page 459, above.

Limits on the deduction. With most business expenses, if you have more expenses than you have income, your business can show a loss that may be deductible against any other regular income you have (such as interest, dividends, or income from another job or business). This may even be true if the loss is a "paper loss" resulting from depreciation. However, it's not true of the home office deduction.

You can only take this to the extent you have any profits left after deducting all your other allowable business expenses. In other words, you can't use the home office deduction to create a loss that would offset other income. If your expenses exceeded your income, you apply the limit in this way: from your gross income, you first subtract the home office portion of your mortgage interest, real estate taxes, and casualty losses. (These expenses would be allowed as itemized deductions even if you didn't use the home for business.)

Then you subtract any other direct costs of your business, such as car expenses, travel expenses, meals and entertainment, etc. Finally, if you have any profit left, you can subtract the rest of your home office expenses such as insurance, utilities, repairs, and depreciation, but only up to the amount of your income.

If you can't claim your entire home office deduction because of the limitation, the IRS will let you carry it over and deduct it in a future year in which your expenses don't exceed your income.

Taxes and Vehicles

Before you purchase a vehicle, becoming familiar with a few key tax matters may help save your business money. There are two federal excise taxes that may be a hidden cost that could influence your choice of a vehicle.

First, there's the "gas guzzler tax" imposed on makers of new cars that fail to meet federal fuel economy standards, which becomes part of the retail price. Before computing the depreciation deduction for a car, you must subtract any gas guzzler tax from the purchase price.

Secondly, there's a luxury tax imposed on new cars that sell for more than a specified amount. For 1999, the tax is 6 percent, imposed on any part of the vehicle's sales price that exceeds $36,000. For 2000, the tax rate is reduced to 5 percent of the price that exceeds $38,000. The tax is scheduled to drop by 1 percent a year until it expires in 2003.

Save Money

The luxury car tax does not apply to trucks, vans, and sport-utility vehicles that weigh over 6,000 pounds. This includes certain Chevy Suburbans and Range Rovers. If you bought a qualifying sport-utility vehicle that cost $50,000 in 2000, this special rule would save you $600 ($50,000 - $38,000 x 5%). In addition, if you use this type of vehicle for your business, it also escapes the annual depreciation dollar caps and the annual lease income inclusion rules discussed below.

Business Use of a Car

If a vehicle is used exclusively for business purposes, you may generally deduct the full cost of operating the vehicle. If, like most people, you use your vehicle partly for business and partly for personal purposes, you must allocate your expenses between your business, commuting, and personal use of the car, and deduct only the business portion.

This means that you must keep mileage records for your car that show your driving patterns over the year. At a minimum, you should keep a notebook in the car and jot down your starting and stopping mileage for each deductible business trip. You should also make some notation of the reason for each trip.

Despite the fact that you may use all your driving time to make cell phone calls to prospects or to plan out your next business expansion project, the IRS will not allow you to deduct commuting costs or personal driving costs. Most people instinctively know what trips are considered "personal," but it's not always clear what the IRS calls "commuting" and what it recognizes as deductible business travel.

As a rule, vehicle expenses incurred commuting between your home and your main or regular place of business are non-deductible expenses.

However, costs incurred in traveling between business locations, including your regular place of business, are deductible. Typical travel expenses that are deductible include expenses for:

- travel from your regular place of business to a customer, client, supplier, etc.

- travel from one job to another

- travel from one customer or client to another

- travel from your office or business location in order to perform business tasks, such as delivery and pickup of supplies and inventory, making bank deposits, etc.

If your home qualifies for the home office deduction, it's considered your regular place of business. Consequently, any time you go from home to a business location, you can deduct the costs!

If you have a regular place of business, whether it's your home or some outside facility, the cost of traveling between your home and a temporary work site is deductible, regardless of the distance traveled. A temporary work site is where you perform services on an irregular or short-term basis. The term "short-term" generally means a matter of days or weeks.

Example

Bobby Burnett is a self-employed accountant and his home qualifies as his principal place of business. Burnett may deduct the round-trip business-related transportation expenses incurred in traveling between his home office and clients' places of business.

Also, if you do *not* have a regular place of business (for instance, you spend most of your time at various customers' locations) and you travel *outside of the metropolitan area* in which you work to a temporary work site, you are allowed a deduction for your travel costs.

No deduction is available for the cost of commuting to a permanent job location, or one that's expected to last for a year or indefinitely. This is so even though neither public transportation nor housing is available near the job site.

Hauling tools or equipment. If you incur expenses for transporting required tools, equipment, or materials above the ordinary, nondeductible expenses of commuting, you may deduct the additional expenses (such as the cost of renting a trailer that is towed by a car).

However, you can deduct only the portion of the cost that is higher than the cost of commuting by that *same* mode of transportation *without* the work implements. The fact that you would have used a less expensive mode of transportation were it not for the tools is immaterial.

Example

Robert Jensen takes the train from his home to his workplace each work day. His daily round-trip train ticket costs $10.00. Once every two months he must bring drafting tools and display charts to his workplace for a presentation. When he transports these tools and materials he uses his car instead of taking the train. Driving to his workplace costs him $20.00 in gas, tolls, and parking fees. Jensen cannot deduct the extra $10.00 it costs him when he drives to his workplace.

Methods for Determining Vehicle Expenses

If you own a vehicle that you are using for your business, you may determine deductible vehicle expenses under one of the following:

- the actual cost method

- the standard mileage rate (SMR) method

With either method, you have to keep track of your business mileage as described above.

If you use the actual cost method, you must keep records of the actual amount of your vehicle costs during the year, and then multiply the total by the percentage of total car mileage that was driven for business purposes.

Deductible Vehicle Expenses

The cost of operating a vehicle includes these expenses:

• *gas and oil*	• *tires and supplies*
• *cleaning and waxing*	• *parking and garage rental*
• *repairs and maintenance*	• *tolls*
• *insurance*	• *auto club memberships*
• *interest on a vehicle loan*	• *personal property taxes*
• *routine maintenance*	• *depreciation, if you own*
• *lease payments, if you rent*	• *license fees, if based on car's value*

The cost of the vehicle itself is not a deductible expense, nor is the cost of replacements, modifications, or extensive repairs that prolong the useful life of the vehicle or increase its value. Such costs are capitalized, which means they are added to your basis in the vehicle. The capitalized costs are recovered through depreciation deductions.

Example

Judy Swan, who owns a temporary employment business, drove a total of 10,120 miles in 2000. Of that total, 5,042 miles were driven for business purposes. Therefore, her business percentage is 50%. She can deduct 50% of her actual expenses for the vehicle.

If you use the standard mileage rate method, you calculate the costs of your vehicle by multiplying the number of business miles traveled by the business standard mileage rate. This rate is adjusted annually; the rate is 32.5 cents per mile for 2000. The standard mileage rate is designed to take into account the depreciation, gas, and other common operating costs. It does not include parking fees, tolls, interest on a car loan, or personal property taxes, and if you're self-employed you can write off these additional business expenses on your Schedule C.

Example

If Judy Swan, from our example above, is eligible to claim the standard mileage rate, she can deduct 5,042 x $.315 = $1,588, plus any parking or tolls she paid on business trips, and 50% of her car loan interest payments.

If you want to use the standard mileage rate, you must use it in the first year that you use that particular car for business (and thus you can't claim the expensing election). You don't have to use the SMR every year thereafter, as long as you used it in the very first year.

The standard mileage rate method may not be used to compute the deductible expenses for:

- vehicles used for hire, such as taxis

- two or more vehicles simultaneously, as in fleet-type operations

As of 1998, the SMR method may be used for leased vehicles as long as you use this method for the entire term of the lease.

Work Smart

Let's assume you've just purchased a new car, and you have a choice of these two methods. What are the advantages of one over the other?

Using the actual expense method usually results in a greater deduction than using the standard mileage rate method. However, the cost and time burden for the associated substantiation and recordkeeping required by the actual cost method must be taken into account. It's really your call as to what method will reap a better overall financial reward for your business.

Recovering the Cost of Your Vehicle

If you are using the actual cost method of deducting car expenses, you can recover the purchase price of the vehicle through depreciation deductions or, if you wish, through expensing part of the cost in the first year using the expensing election.

While you can expense up to $19,000 in business equipment for 1999, and up to $20,000 in 2000, there is a special, much lower limit for cars. If you purchased a new car in 1999, you can write off in the current year no more than $3,060 (this limit is adjusted periodically to reflect inflation). The deduction must be reduced if you used the car only partly for business; for example, if your mileage records show that you used the car 60% for business and 40% for personal purposes, you can use only 60% of the maximum expensing deduction, or $1,836. Furthermore, if you elect to expense the maximum amount allowed under the expensing election, no other first-year depreciation is allowed for that particular automobile.

For later years, or if you did not elect the special expensing election in the first year, you are generally required to use the modified accelerated cost recovery system (MACRS) to compute your depreciation deduction. Under MACRS, vehicles are generally depreciated over a five-year recovery period. The IRS provides tables showing the percentage of the vehicle's tax basis that can be deducted each year under MACRS.

However, the IRS has also set "luxury car limits" on the dollar amount of depreciation that can be claimed each year. If these limits prevent you from writing off your car within the MACRS recovery period, you can keep claiming a depreciation deduction each year until you finally recover the cost of the car.

For Cars Placed in Service		Depreciation Allowable in—			
After	Before	Year 1	Year 2	Year 3	Year 4 etc.
12/31/88	1/1/91	2,660	4,200	2,550	1,475
12/31/90	1/1/92	2,660	4,300	2,550	1,575
12/31/91	1/1/93	2,760	4,400	2,650	1,575
12/31/92	1/1/94	2,860	4,600	2,750	1,675
12/31/93	1/1/95	2,960	4,700	2,850	1,675
12/31/94	1/1/97	3,060	4,900	2,950	1,775
12/31/96	1/1/98	3,160	5,000	3,050	1,775
12/31/97	1/1/99	3,160	5,000	2,950	1,775
12/31/98	1/1/00	3,060	5,000	2,950	1,775

The maximum annual amounts are based on 100 percent use of a vehicle for business. The amounts must be multiplied by your business-use percentage, if the business use of a vehicle is less than 100 percent.

Warning

If business use of your vehicle drops to 50 percent or less in a subsequent year, you must switch to the straight-line method of depreciation (i.e., 10% in year one, 20% in years two through five, and 10% in year six). However, the yearly caps placed on depreciation deductions for luxury cars still apply.

Standard mileage rate users. For years in which you use the standard mileage rate, you won't have to worry about depreciation, since it's already figured into the cents-per-mile allowance. For 1999, the SMR is 32.5 cents for the first quarter, 31 cents for the last three quarters, and the depreciation component is 12 cents. For 2000, the SMR is 32.5 cents and the depreciation component is 14 cents. If you switch to the actual cost method or if you later sell your car, you'll have to subtract the depreciation component of the SMR deductions claimed over the years from the basis of the car. Once you switch to the actual cost method, you will have to depreciate the car using the straight line method.

Leasing Vehicles

If you elect to lease a vehicle, you may use the actual method for claiming vehicle expenses or the standard mileage rate.

You can generally deduct the lease payments as one of your actual auto expenses. However, if your business use of the vehicle is less than 100 percent, the rental deduction is scaled down proportionately. For example, if you use a leased car 75 percent for business, you can deduct only 75 percent of the lease payments.

Moreover, if a vehicle with a fair market value in excess of about $15,500 is leased, there is a limitation on the amount you can deduct (these limits are adjusted each year for inflation). These rules were enacted to prevent individuals from avoiding luxury car limits that apply to purchased vehicles. Basically, lease deductions for vehicles having an initial fair market value over the annual limit are reduced. The amount is listed on a price-based table issued yearly by the IRS.

Work Smart

The rules governing the use of leased vehicles in business are a bit complex. We suggest you consult with an accountant or tax professional if you have questions on this subject.

If Employees Use Your Vehicles

There are two things you need to understand about how employees' use of your vehicles affects your overall tax picture. The first is that all business use of your vehicles by employees must be substantiated. The second is that if you allow employees to use your vehicles for personal reasons, you must make arrangements to treat the value of this use as a taxable fringe benefit.

Substantiation. For purposes of substantiating the business use of vehicles provided to employees, you may rely on records maintained by the employees, as long as you keep a copy of them.

The business use substantiation rules do not apply to vehicles that, by their nature, are not likely to be used for more than a minimal amount of personal use. Examples include a delivery truck with seating only for the driver, or a specialized repair truck.

Vehicles as fringe benefits. When you provide a vehicle to an employee for the employee's personal and business use, you must include the *value* of that personal use in the employee's wages for income and employment tax purposes.

An allocation between the two types of use is required to be made on the basis of the number of miles driven. The portion allocable to the employee's personal and commuting use is generally taxable to the employee as a fringe benefit. The portion allocable to business use is generally considered a working condition fringe benefit and is excludable from the employee's income.

The amount included in an employee's wages for income and employment tax purposes due to personal use is determined by the fair market value of the vehicle's availability. Generally, this value is the cost that would be paid to lease the same or comparable vehicle from a third party in your geographic area, but the IRS has developed a number of alternative methods of valuation. Consult your tax advisor for more details.

If Employees Use Their Vehicles

If you have employees, they may be using vehicles that they own for your business needs. You may choose to reflect this in their wages, or you may choose to reimburse them for their expenses.

Reimbursements made under an "accountable plan" are excluded from the employee's gross income, and are tax-deductible to you.

If they are made under a nonaccountable plan, you must include the reimbursements in taxable wages on the employee's Form W-2 and the employee must generally claim a miscellaneous itemized deduction if he or she wants to get any tax benefits for the allowable business expenses. Your business will still get an income tax deduction for these payments, but you'll have to pay payroll taxes (the employer's portion of FICA, FUTA, and state unemployment tax) on them.

What is an accountable plan? It's a reimbursement arrangement that meets all of the following requirements:

- The reimbursements must be for expenses that are paid or incurred by an employee in the course of performing services for you.

- The employee must be required to substantiate the elements of amount, time, use, and business purpose of the reimbursed expenses to you. In order to do this, the employee should submit an account book, diary, log, statement of expense, trip sheet, or similar record, supporting each of these elements, that is recorded at or near the time of the expenditure. The records should include any supporting documentary evidence, such as receipts. An employee who receives a mileage allowance is considered to have substantiated the amount of the expenses if the employee substantiates the time, place (or use), and business purpose of the travel.

- The employee must be required to return to you any excess of reimbursements over substantiated expenses within a reasonable period of time. A mileage allowance in excess of the standard mileage rate that is reasonably calculated not to exceed the employee's actual or anticipated expenses is treated as meeting this return requirement even if the employee does not have to return the excess of the allowance over the standard mileage rate. However, the employee must be required to return any portion of the allowance that relates to unsubstantiated miles of travel.

CLAIMING TAX CREDITS

Besides taking care to claim all your available deductions, you can minimize your income tax bill by claiming all the tax credits available to you.

When they're available, tax credits are generally better for you than deductions would be, because credits are subtracted directly from your tax bill. On the other hand, deductions are subtracted from the *income* on which your tax bill is based.

So, a dollar's worth of tax credit reduces your tax bill by a dollar, but a dollar's worth of deductions lowers your tax bill by 36 cents if you're in the 36-percent bracket, by 28 cents if you're in the 28-percent bracket, etc. In cases where you have a choice between claiming a credit or a deduction for a particular expense, you're generally better off claiming the credit.

As wonderful as tax credits can be, with the IRS (as you've probably figured out by now) there's almost always a catch. In this case, the catch is that tax credits are only available for certain very specific situations. Many of them apply only to certain industries (like restaurants and bars, or energy producers). And credits come with a set of very complicated rules, which you (or, more likely, your tax pro) must follow in order to claim them.

Before 1986, federal income tax credits were available for many of the investments a small business might typically make. Now, however, most credits are very narrowly targeted to encourage you to take certain actions that lawmakers have deemed desirable (generally, to benefit disadvantaged/low-income individuals or the environment). There are also a few credits designed to prevent double taxation, and a few designed to encourage certain types of investments that are considered socially beneficial.

The forms and procedures used to calculate and claim business tax credits are quite complicated. In fact, we recommend that you leave the technical details to your tax pro. However, we do provide an outline of the basic rules for the most commonly used credits.

Credits for Certain Taxes

You might not believe it, but sometimes the IRS does have a heart: it occasionally gives certain people a break for taxes that might be considered unfair. There are four major types of business tax credits that give a "rebate" for certain kinds of taxes.

Credit for FICA tax on tips. Under current law, employees who get $20 or more in tips in a single month must report their tips to their employers. If you have tipped employees, you have to pay Social Security and Medicare (FICA) taxes to the tune of 7.65 percent on tips that are reported to you, even though you don't have any control over the amounts. The purpose of the rule is to make sure that tipped employees are adequately covered by Social Security pension, disability, and survivors' benefits. However, the rule was seen to place a particularly heavy burden on the restaurant industry.

So, if your business is one that provides food or beverages for customers to consume on or off the premises, and if your waiters, waitresses, or delivery personnel are customarily tipped by your patrons, you're entitled to a tax credit for any FICA taxes you pay on the tips.

Note that there's an exception to this general credit rule. If you pay your employees below the minimum wage, with the expectation that tips will bring them up to the minimum, you can't claim the credit for FICA on the portion of the tips that is used to bring them up to the minimum wage.

No double-dipping is allowed. If you are eligible for and decide to claim this credit, you can't deduct the FICA taxes on which the credit is claimed. However, because tax credits are generally worth more than deductions, this is not usually a problem.

Gasoline tax credit. You can claim a credit for any federal excise taxes you pay on gasoline and special fuels (like undyed diesel, heating oil, Liquefied Petroleum Gas, and compressed natural gas), when you use the fuel for certain purposes: for farming; for nonhighway purposes of your trade or business; for intercity, local, or school buses; or for export or foreign trade. You can't claim this credit for any personal (nonbusiness) use, so forget about claiming it for your snowmobile or pleasure boat! The credit is *refundable*, meaning that the IRS will pay it to you even if you have no tax liability for the year.

Foreign tax credit. You can claim a credit for foreign income taxes, or taxes imposed by possessions of the U.S., that you paid or accrued during the tax year. For example, you might have become liable for foreign taxes on profits from overseas operations or investments. You can elect to deduct these taxes instead of taking the credit, if you prefer, although claiming the credit will generally save you more money.

Credit for prior years' AMT. If you paid alternative minimum tax in a prior year, you may be eligible for a credit for a portion of it against your regular tax liability for the current year, and for subsequent years as well. However, the prior AMT credit can't be used to reduce your tax bill below a certain level, namely, your tentative minimum tax for the current year plus any other nonrefundable tax credits for the current year. If you have paid AMT in prior years and think you might be eligible for this credit, see your tax advisor. The AMT rules are a morass of confusion, and interpretation of them is best left to professionals.

Credits Benefiting Disadvantaged Groups

The tax law has historically been used to encourage certain activities that the government deems desirable, but that people might not otherwise undertake on their own because the economic rewards are perceived as insufficient. This group of tax credits is a good example of that type of policy.

Disabled access credit. Under the Americans with Disabilities Act of 1990 (ADA), businesses that are open to the public ("public accommodations," in legal language) must accommodate or help persons with disabilities seeking to use their services. They must also remove physical barriers to the disabled, if removal is "readily achievable" (the regulations say that moving tables in a restaurant is "readily achievable," but widening a doorway is not). What's more, any renovations or new construction must include provisions for accessibility by the disabled, in accordance with certain very technical specifications.

Small businesses that are faced with making changes to obey the ADA have been given a "carrot," in the form of a tax credit, to encourage them to comply with the law. For any year, the tax laws allow you to claim a credit for 50 percent of your eligible access expenditures that exceed $250 but don't exceed $10,250. So, you can't claim more than $5,000 in any one year. The "eligible access expenditures" include not only expenses for removal of physical barriers (in renovations, but not new construction), but also expenses for deaf interpreters, readers for the blind, equipment or devices to make services available to the deaf, blind, or other disabled persons, or similar expenses.

Save Money

If you anticipate that your disabled accommodation expenses will exceed $10,250, try to spread them over more than one year in order to take maximum advantage of the tax credit.

This tax credit is available only to small businesses—that is, those having: (1) gross receipts of $1 million or less, or (2) no more than 30 full-time employees.

Work opportunity tax credit. This credit was designed to provide an incentive to hire persons from certain disadvantaged groups that have a particularly high unemployment rate (including urban youths, government assistance recipients, ex-convicts, disadvantaged Vietnam vets, and vocational rehabilitation referrals). The credit was created in 1996 to replace the expired targeted jobs credit.

The work opportunity tax credit is available for a limited time—it applies to the wages of employees who begin work after October 1, 1996, and before January 1, 2002. Until October 1, 1997, the credit was for 35 percent of up to $6,000 of each worker's first-year wages, for a maximum credit of $2,100. For summer youth employees, the maximum credit is 35 percent of up to $3,000 of wages paid during a 90-day period, for a maximum credit of $1,050. From October 1, 1997 until January 1, 2002, the credit has been increased to 40 percent for work of 400 or more hours, and dropped to 25 percent for work between 120 and 400 hours.

Welfare-to-work credit. For employers who hire qualified long-term family assistance (AFDC or its successor) recipients, there is a credit of 35 percent of up to $10,000 in wages in the first year and 50 percent of up to $10,000 in the second year, for a two-year maximum of $8,500 per employee. The credit applies to employees hired after January 1, 1998 and before January 1, 2002.

Empowerment zone employment credit. If your business is located in a federal "empowerment zone," and you hire workers who also live and work within the zone, you can get a tax credit for 20 percent of the first $15,000 of wages paid to each of your workers. The workers can be full-time or part-time, so long as a substantial part of their work is done within the zone and as part of your trade or business. You can't count wages paid to employees who worked for less than 90 days (unless the worker became disabled or was fired for misconduct), employees who are closely related to you, employees who own 5 percent or more of the business, or employees at golf courses, country clubs, massage parlors, hot tub facilities, suntan facilities, racetrack or gambling facilities, or liquor stores.

Where are these zones? They are certain designated parts of Atlanta; Baltimore; Boston; Chicago; Cincinnati; Columbus, OH; Detroit; El Paso, TX; Gary/East Chicago; Huntington, WV/Ironton, OH; Knoxville, TN; Miami; Minneapolis; New Haven, CT; New York; Norfolk/Portsmouth, VA; Philadelphia; Santa Ana, CA; St. Louis/East St. Louis; Washington, D.C.; Riverside County, CA; Crisp and Dooly Counties in Georgia; Alexander, Johnson, and Pulaski Counties in Illinois; Clinton, Jackson, and Wayne Counties in Kentucky; Bolivar, Sunflower, Leflore, Washington, Humphreys, and Holmes Counties in Mississippi; Cumberland County, New Jersey; Griggs and Steele County in North Dakota; Pine Ridge Indian Reservation in South Dakota; Starr, Cameron, Hidalgo, and Willacy Counties in Texas. Beginning in 2000, portions of Cleveland and Los Angeles are eligible. If you live in one of these cities or areas, contact your city or county government to find out the exact boundaries of the empowerment zones.

Indian employment credit. If your business is located on an Indian reservation, and you have employees who live on or near the reservation, you may be eligible for a special tax credit. You can claim a credit for 20 percent of your wages or health insurance costs for the year (up to $20,000 per employee) that exceed the total of comparable costs you had in 1993. However, the employee must be an enrolled member, or the spouse of an enrolled member, of an Indian tribe.

Credit for contributions to community development corporations. The government wants to encourage you to make gifts or long-term loans to certain organizations that provide employment and business opportunities to low-income individuals. If you made such a gift before June 30, 1999, you can claim a tax credit for 5 percent of the amount you contributed, for each of 10 tax years beginning with the year you make the contribution. Eventually, you'll get tax credits for 50 percent of the contribution.

If the contribution is a gift, you could also take a charitable contribution deduction for the full amount, in the year you make it. If the contribution was a loan, the loan term must be at least 10 years. The CDC must be one of 20 organizations selected by the Secretary of HUD.

Credits Benefiting the Environment

Currently, the largest group of tax credits are those designed to encourage energy conservation or other actions that benefit the environment. However, most of these credits are very narrowly targeted, so the number of people eligible for them is actually quite small. The credits available are: the alternative fuels credit, the credit for qualified electric vehicles, the reforestation credit, the energy credit, the alcohol fuel credit, the enhanced oil recovery credit, and the renewable resources electricity production credit.

Credits for Certain Investments

A small number of tax credits remain for investments that are not necessarily targeted towards the disadvantaged or the environment. In some cases, investments that take advantage of one of these credits can become, in effect, a tax shelter for cash-rich small businesses. These include the real estate rehabilitation credit, the research and development credit, and the orphan drug credit. Consult your tax advisor for more details.

TAX RETURNS AND PAYMENT OBLIGATIONS

As a small business owner, it's important for you to be aware of what your tax payment obligations are and when they are due. Even if you use a tax advisor or accountant to keep track of your taxes, you should know what is required from you and when.

This information is crucial so you can plan ahead if you need to make regular and estimated tax payments. There's no sinking feeling like the one you have when you thought you had a cash surplus on your books and then suddenly have to make a payment to the IRS that depletes your entire balance. Worse yet is the scenario where the funds have been spent elsewhere because you didn't realize a tax payment was due.

Your filing and payment obligations and due dates will generally be based on the legal form in which you operate your business and on whether your business uses a calendar year or a fiscal year.

In addition, please note that if a due date that is set by law falls on a Saturday, Sunday, or legal holiday, it is delayed until the next day that isn't a Saturday, Sunday, or legal holiday. However, a statewide legal holiday delays a due date only if the IRS office where you are required to file your returns is located in that state.

Due Dates for Sole Proprietors

If you are a sole proprietor, you must file Schedule C (or Schedule C-EZ if you qualify), *Profit or Loss From Business*, with your Form 1040, *U.S. Individual Income Tax Return*, on an annual basis to report your business income and deductions. Sole proprietors are also required to file Schedule SE, *Self-Employment Tax*, with their Form 1040 as well. For calendar year taxpayers, the filing and payment of tax due date for these returns and schedules is April 15.

If you want an automatic four-month extension to file these returns, you can file Form 4868, *Application For Automatic Extension of Time To File U.S. Individual Income Tax Return*, by April 15. However, you must pay any tax you estimate will be due by April 15 or you may be subject to interest and penalties on overdue taxes. Your returns would then be due on August 15.

Warning

Remember, the automatic extension applies only to the filing of your return, not to the payment of any tax that may be due.

If you decide that you want an additional two-month extension to file your returns, you must file Form 2688, *Application for Additional Extension of Time to File U.S. Individual Income Tax Return*, by August 15. This additional two-month extension is not automatic — you must give the IRS a reason as to why you need the additional time. If the IRS grants you this extension, your return must be filed by October 15.

If you are a sole proprietor who uses a fiscal year rather than a calendar year, you must file your individual income tax return (including all the applicable schedules) no later than the 15th day of the fourth month after the end of your tax year. Additional four-month and two-month extensions are available under the rules described above.

Due Dates for Partnerships and LLCs

If you operate your business as a partnership (or as an LLC, since most LLCs are taxed as partnerships under federal law) the business must file Form 1065, *U.S. Partnership Return of Income*, on an annual basis to report income and deductions. Each partner or LLC member must receive a copy of Schedule K-1 (part of Form 1065), *Partner's Share of Income, Credits, Deductions, etc.*, or a substitute K-1. For partnerships with a calendar year, the due date for the annual return and Schedule K-1 is April 15.

A partnership may apply for an automatic three-month extension to file its annual return by filing Form 8736, *Application for Automatic Extension of Time to File U.S. Return for a Partnership*, by April 15. The return would then be due on July 15. If the partnership needs more time to file, it can file Form 8800, *Application for Additional Extension of Time to File U.S. Return for a Partnership*, by July 15, to apply for an additional three-month extension. This extension is not automatic. If the IRS grants the partnership this additional time to file, the return will be due on October 15.

If your partnership uses a fiscal year rather than a calendar year, the annual partnership return (including all the applicable schedules), must be filed no later than the 15th day of the fourth month after the end of the partnership's tax year. Two additional three-month extensions are available under the rules described above.

Due Dates for C Corporations

If you operate your business as a C corporation, the corporation must file Form 1120, *U.S. Corporation Income Tax Return* (or if it qualifies, Form 1120-A, *U.S. Corporation Short-Form Income Tax Return*), on an annual basis, to report income and deductions. For corporations with a calendar tax year, the due date for the annual return is March 15.

The corporation may apply for an automatic six-month extension to file its annual return by filing Form 7004, *Application for Automatic Extension of Time to File Corporation Income Tax Return*, by March 15. The return would then be due on September 15. If your corporation is filing for the six-month extension, it must deposit (at an authorized financial institution or a Federal Reserve Bank), any remaining taxed owed for the year by the March 15 due date. A corporation can use a Federal Tax Deposit (FTD) Coupon (IRS Form 8109) or it can deposit the amount due electronically. If a corporation doesn't make a payment of the tax owed by the due date, it may be subject to interest and penalties on overdue taxes.

If your corporation uses a fiscal year rather than a calendar year, the annual corporate return must be filed by the 15th day of the third month after the end of the corporation's tax year. A fiscal year corporation is entitled to the same automatic six-month extension to file its return to which a calendar year corporation is entitled. The due date for the filing of the extension is the original due date of the return

— the 15th day of the third month after the end of the corporation's tax year. The actual corporate return would then be due by the 15th day of the sixth month after the original return due date.

Due Dates for S Corporations

If you operate your business as an S corporation, the S corporation must file Form 1120S, *U.S. Income Tax Return for an S Corporation*, on an annual basis to report income and deductions. Each shareholder must receive a copy of Schedule K-1 (part of Form 1120S), *Shareholder's Share of Income, Credits, Deductions, etc.*, or a substitute K-1. For S corporations with a calendar tax year, the due date for the annual return and the Schedule K-1 is March 15.

The rules for extensions and fiscal-year S corporations are the same as for regular C corporations.

If you are currently a C corporation but want your business to be treated as an S corporation, you must make an election by filing Form 2553, *Election by a Small Business Corporation*. For S corporations using a calendar tax year, this election must be filed by March 15. For S corporations using a fiscal tax year, the election must be filed by the 15th day of the third month of the first tax year to which the choice will apply or at any time during the preceding tax year.

Warning

If the election to be treated as an S corporation is filed late, S corporation treatment will begin with the next calendar or fiscal year.

Estimated Tax Payments

If you are a small business owner, chances are good that you will have to make estimated tax payments. The IRS wants to get most of its money ahead of time, rather than all at once on April 15. If you don't pay enough of your federal income taxes through payroll withholding, you'll pay a penalty to the IRS.

Quarterly estimated tax payments are used to pay tax on income that is not subject to payroll withholding. The payments include income taxes, as well as self-employment taxes (the Social Security and Medicare taxes paid by self-employed people). Your estimated tax payments should be calculated so that they add up to the least of these three amounts:

1. The amount of tax you expect to owe for the year, minus $1,000;

2. 90 percent of the amount you expect to owe for this year; or

3. 100 percent of the tax you owed last year. However, if your adjusted gross income last year was over $150,000 ($75,000 for marrieds filing separately), you must substitute "108.6 percent of the tax you owed last year" for payments in 2000, "110 percent of the tax you owed last year" for payments in 2001, 112 percent for payments in 2002, and 110 percent for payments in 2003 or later.

The total amount of estimated tax due for the year is normally divided into four equal payments, due on April 15, June 15, and September 15 of the current year and January 15 of the following year. There is a special rule in the tax law that excuses you from making the last quarter's estimated tax payment if you file your annual tax return and pay any tax due by January 31.

If your business is of the type that doesn't receive income evenly throughout the year (for example, you sell surfboards year-round in the Northeast), you may want to use the annualized income installment method to compute your estimated tax payments for each period. Under this method your required estimated tax payment for one or more periods may be less than the amount figured using the regular installment method. However, the computations needed to use this method are complex, and you'll probably need the assistance of a tax professional or accountant to determine the payment amounts.

Corporations are generally required to make installment payments equal to 25 percent of the required annual estimated tax.

Fiscal year businesses. If you operate your business on a fiscal year, your estimated tax payment due dates are:

- the 15th day of the fourth month of your fiscal year

- the 15th day of the sixth month of your fiscal year

- the 15th day of the ninth month of your fiscal year

- the 15th day of the first month after the end of your fiscal year

For corporations that use a fiscal tax year, the due dates are the same for the first three periods of the fiscal year. However, the last estimated tax payment is due on the 15th day of the twelfth month of the corporation's fiscal year.

Tax Penalties

What happens if you don't file returns or pay taxes that you owe by their due date? Generally, the IRS will hit you with interest and penalties. The IRS will charge you interest on taxes not paid by their due date, even if you've gotten an extension of time to file your tax return.

If you pay your taxes late, the penalty is usually 0.5 percent of the unpaid amount for each month or part of a month the tax is not paid. The penalty can't be more than 25 percent of the unpaid amount and applies to any unpaid tax on the return. Please note, this penalty is *in addition to* the interest charged for late payments. The interest rates fluctuate each quarter, but currently run about 8 percent.

If you don't file your tax return by its due date (including extensions), the penalty is usually 5 percent of the amount due for each month or part of a month your return is late, unless you have a reasonable explanation. If you think you have a reasonable explanation, attach it to your return. It's possible that you won't be charged with the penalty. In any case, the penalty usually can't be more than 25 percent of the tax due. If your return is more than 60 days late, the minimum penalty will be $100 or the amount of any tax you owe, whichever is smaller.

Interest is also charged on the penalties imposed for failure to file a return itself, as well as other penalties imposed for negligence, fraud, etc. This interest is charged on the penalty from the due date of the return, including extensions.

What happens if you underpay your estimated tax? You may have to pay a penalty in the form of interest on the underpayment for the period when the underpayment occurred. As a matter of fact, if you didn't pay enough tax by the due date of *each* of the payment periods, you may owe a penalty even if you are ultimately due a refund from the IRS when you file your income tax return.

You can request a waiver of the penalty if the underpayment was caused by a casualty, disaster, or some other unusual circumstance that would make its imposition unfair. Generally, corporations are subject to the same rules as individuals.

Chapter 27

Your State Tax Obligations

While keeping abreast of your federal obligations may seem daunting enough, we don't want you to forget about your state tax obligations. All sorts of requirements are imposed on businesses on a state level and complying with them is crucial to your business.

Unless you happen to live and do business exclusively in one of the five states that do not impose general sales taxes (Alaska, Delaware, Montana, New Hampshire, and Oregon), you've probably had some exposure to state and local sales taxes.

To help ensure that you don't pay any more sales taxes than you're absolutely required to pay and that you don't receive an unexpected visit from an assessment-waving sales tax auditor, we'll explain how sales taxes apply, what transactions are taxable, and how sellers must collect taxes.

Following our general discussion of sales taxes, we provide a chart showing the basic elements and rates of sales, personal and corporate income, and franchise tax laws in each of the states.

SALES TAXES

While visiting a local furniture store, you spot a $500 desk that's just perfect for your home office. You whip out your checkbook, write a check for $500, and the desk is yours. Or is it? As you're probably already aware from your everyday shopping experiences, you can't always purchase an item priced at $500 by paying just $500. In most states you're likely to pay anywhere from $520 to $550, with the added amount representing state and local sales taxes.

But what exactly is a "sales" tax? And how, if at all, does your being a small business owner affect the way you deal with such taxes?

Among the states, there are several different types of sales tax systems. The biggest difference is whether the seller or the purchaser is the main taxpayer. In some states, the tax is imposed on sellers, who then have the *option* of passing the tax along to their purchasers. In other states, the tax is imposed on the purchaser, with the seller being *responsible* for collecting the tax and remitting it to the state. And then there are other states where the liability for the tax is *shared* by sellers and purchasers. However, these different systems do share a few common elements:

- **Taxable event** — the triggering event for imposing the tax is the consummation of a retail sale. Initially, the states were content to limit their taxes to retail sales of tangible personal property. However, in recent years most states have expanded the scope of their sales taxes to encompass leasing transactions and at least some services.

- **Presumption of taxability** — each retail sale is presumed to be taxable. Unless a recognized exemption applies and, in most cases, the purchaser affirmatively establishes his or her right to claim the exemption, the sales tax must be paid.

- **Taxable amount** — sales taxes are computed on some measure of gross receipts of the seller. In other words, the tax generally applies to the full amount a seller receives from a purchaser as opposed to the net profit the seller realizes on the sale.

- **Use taxes** — a state's sales tax applies only to retail sales that are consummated within the state. This creates a big loophole, from a taxing state's perspective, in that purchasers can avoid the state's sales tax by making their purchases in other states. To close this loophole, each state having a sales tax also has a complementary "use" tax that applies to the storage or other use of tangible personal property or taxable services in the state.

Types of Sales Taxes

When we use the term "sales taxes" in a generic sense, we're referring to the taxes that states impose on retail sales. However, there are actually different types of sales taxes. In fact, in many states there are actually several distinct taxes that together comprise the state's sales taxes. For example, in Arizona, there are distinct sales taxes on such businesses as retailers, restaurant operators, contractors, and rental companies.

Let's identify the three general types of sales taxes:

- **Seller or vendor privilege taxes** — these taxes are imposed on retailers for the privilege of making retail sales in the state. Retailers usually have the option of absorbing the tax (that is, paying the tax out of their own pockets) or passing it along to their purchasers.

- **Consumer excise taxes** — these taxes are imposed on the persons who make retail purchases in the state. In the states that impose this type of tax, sellers serve purely as agents who must collect the tax on the state's behalf. Because the tax is primarily the purchaser's responsibility, sellers don't have the option of absorbing the tax and usually must separately state the tax on the receipts or invoices they provide their purchasers.

- **Retail transaction taxes** — these taxes are imposed on the retail sale transaction itself, with the primary liability for paying the tax falling upon both the sellers and the purchasers. Sellers are responsible for collecting and paying the tax, and purchasers are responsible for paying the tax that the sellers must collect and pay. In essence, this type of sales tax is a hybrid of the other two types. Operationally, however, it's closer to a consumer excise tax because sellers are not given the option to absorb the tax.

As a practical matter, the real distinction is between privilege taxes on the one hand and consumer excise and retail transaction taxes on the other. For example, in privilege tax states, holding a "we'll pay the sales tax" sale may be a good way to draw customers away from competitors and to your business. We've identified only seven states that impose this type of privilege sales tax: Arizona, California, Hawaii, Michigan, New Mexico, South Carolina, and South Dakota.

Taxable Transactions

One of the common elements of the different types of sales taxes is that the taxable event is a retail sale. In each of the states that impose a general sales tax, the main target of the tax are retail sales of tangible personal property. "Tangible personal property" refers to items that may be seen, weighed, measured, felt, or touched or that are in any other manner perceptible to the senses. By this definition, sales of real property and of intangibles (such as cash, stocks, and bonds) are not subject to sales tax.

However, in recent years many states have broadened the scope of their sales taxes to encompass at least some services.

What are "retail sales"? Each state has its own technical definition for what it considers to be a "retail sale." The usual method of operation is to define the term as broadly as possible and then state that all such sales of tangible personal property are presumed to be taxable unless a specific exemption from tax applies. In essence, the result is that any sale and, for that matter, most leases of tangible personal property to the ultimate user or consumer are potentially taxable retail sales.

The notion that a sales tax arises only on sales to the ultimate user or consumer fosters two of the principal exemptions. One is the *resale exemption*, which applies to sales to persons who will resell the purchased property, either in the same or in an altered form. The other is a *manufacturing exemption* for raw materials that become an ingredient or component part of property that is being manufactured, processed, assembled, or refined for future sale.

As a general rule, the method of payment has no effect on whether a sale is subject to sales tax. Credit sales, installment sales, lay-away sales, conditional sales, and sales involving trade-ins or other exchanges of property are no less taxable than are sales for cash.

Sales Taxes on Services

Traditionally, sales taxes have been limited in application to retail sales of tangible personal property. However, given the fiscal straits that most states encountered a few years back, many states have started looking to the services industries for additional sources of sales tax revenues.

In taxing services, the states have pretty much followed a piecemeal approach. Currently, only Hawaii, New Mexico, and South Dakota generally impose their sales taxes on all services, subject to specified exceptions. The other states specify which services are taxable, with the services that are not so specified remaining exempt.

Combining services and property. Even if a service is generally exempt from sales tax, it may end up being taxable if it is provided in a taxable sale of tangible personal property. For example, otherwise nontaxable delivery or assembly charges generally will be taxable if they are included in the sales price of the property. To avoid this problem, the nontaxable service charges must be separately stated. In general, the ability to avoid taxation of separately stated charges for labor or services applies only with respect to labor or services that are provided *after* a sale is completed (for example, installation of carpeting in your office).

Charges for services provided prior to the purchaser's taking title to the property (for example, the labor involved in manufacturing the carpeting) usually must be included in the amount subject to tax, even if those charges are separately stated from the taxable sales price.

In contrast, merely because tangible personal property is transferred in connection with an otherwise nontaxable service transaction does not necessarily make the entire transaction taxable.

In fact, in most states, if the property element of the sale is "incidental" (for example, it represents less than 10 percent of the total sale), then that element is ignored and the sale is treated entirely as a nontaxable service. If the property element is not incidental, then the sale should be treated as two distinct sales transactions, one involving the property and the other involving the services. To maintain that distinction and to avoid having the entire transaction taxed, the charges for each of the transactions must be separately stated.

Materials used in rendering services. As a general rule, service providers are considered to be the final consumers of the materials and supplies they use in performing their services. Accordingly, sales of such materials and supplies to the service providers (for example, cotton swabs used by your doctor in performing a medical test for a patient) generally are taxable to them.

Leases and Rentals

Because states generally impose their sales taxes on retail sales of tangible personal property, you may be thinking that you can reduce your sales taxes by leasing property instead of purchasing it. If so, think again. With the exception of Illinois and Maine, all the states that impose general sales taxes have closed this potential loophole by defining "retail sales" to include leases or by separately taxing rental charges at the same rate as ordinary sales transactions.

In some cases, a lease is used to effectively finance the lessee's purchase of the leased property. In financing leases, sales tax must be paid at the beginning of the lease rather than as the rental payments are made.

Common Exemptions from Sales Tax

In every state that imposes a sales tax, you generally must collect or pay sales tax with respect to each sale unless you can show that the sale was exempt from tax or that the purchaser supplied you with a direct payment certificate.

Types of exemptions. Each state offers its own unique set of exemptions from its sales tax. In general, exemptions are provided on the basis of the type of property being sold, the identity of the purchaser, or the use to which the property will be put. However, every state allows two distinct exemptions that do not fit neatly within these categories: an exemption for sales for resale and an administrative exemption for occasional sales.

- **Property-based exemptions** — every state recognizes that there are certain commodities that individuals must purchase to subsist. Accordingly, most states offer product-specific exemptions (or lower rates) for items such as food, clothing, prescription medicines, and medical (prosthetic) devices.

- **Purchaser-based exemptions** — under federal law, states are prohibited from taxing sales that are made to the federal government or its various agencies. Similar exemptions exist in each state, with the exception of California, for sales to the state and its agencies and to cities, counties, and other local jurisdictions in the state. Also common are exemptions for sales to nonprofit charitable, religious, and educational organizations.

- **Use-based exemptions** — the exemptions that fall into this category are those that are provided to support certain industries (such as agriculture, manufacturing, or industrial processing) or to encourage certain activities for the public good (such as industrial development or expansion or pollution control). For example, many farming states offer exemptions for sales of products or equipment that are used to produce food for human or animal consumption. Similarly, most states offer exemptions for sales of materials or supplies that are used in manufacturing a product for sale.

Exemption certificates. Except with respect to property-based exemptions, entitlement to which is obvious by looking at the property itself, a seller cannot refrain from collecting or paying tax on a sale unless the seller believes in good faith that the sale is exempt. Generally, the purchaser must provide the seller with a written certificate of exemption.

Resale Exemption

Perhaps the most common sales tax exemption flows from the fact that sales taxes are assessed on retail sales, which essentially are sales to the ultimate user or consumer of the item being sold. In other words, the tax applies only to the final sale of the property.

Accordingly, a sale to a purchaser who intends to resell the purchased item prior to making any significant use of it is an exempt sale for resale. In general, the exemption continues as long as you don't use an item for reasons other than display or demonstration purposes.

Let's assume you operate an art gallery. Among the items you sell are lithographic prints that you purchase from a commercial printer. The printer's sales of the prints to you would be exempt because you plan to sell them to your customers. However, if you took a couple of the prints to hang in your home office, you would be liable for use tax for those prints.

As is the case with most other exemptions, purchasers claiming the resale exemption must furnish their sellers with written proof that they are entitled to the exemption. This proof is usually provided in the form of a resale certificate.

Occasional Sale Exemption

To avoid requiring every person who happened to sell a piece of tangible personal property during the year to collect or pay sales tax, most states offer an exemption from sales tax for occasional, casual, or isolated sales. In most cases, eligibility for the exemption is based on the seller not having more than a specified number or dollar amount of sales during the year. Colorado, Oklahoma, and Wyoming are the only states that do not provide specific exemptions for occasional sales.

Direct Payment Permits

Many states authorize purchasers to apply for a direct payment permit. Purchasers holding such permits do not pay any sales tax to their sellers. Rather, the permit holders assume the full responsibility for determining which of their purchases are taxable and which are exempt, and remit any tax that may be due directly to the state. Upon receiving a valid direct payment certificate, a seller is relieved of all responsibility for collecting tax from the permit holder.

Computing the Sales Tax

Regardless of the type of sales tax with which you're dealing, the amount of tax that is owed on each taxable sale comes down to applying the applicable *tax rate* to the *total sales price*.

The tax computation is complicated by the fact that not all states have a single sales tax rate. Rather, many states have both a general rate and one or more special rates that apply to specific types of sales. And in many states, local jurisdictions impose their own sales taxes. The general sales tax rate that applies in each state imposing such a tax is shown in a chart that appears at the end of this chapter.

Items To Consider When Computing the Sales Price

The following are some of the items that may affect the tax base:

- **Cash or trade discounts** — *as a general rule, discounts that are known and taken at the time of sale are excluded from the tax base. However, the states are split as to whether a discount that is taken after the sale, such as a prompt payment discount, may reduce the tax base.*

- **Coupons and rebates** — *manufacturer coupons that are used to reduce the amount of cash a purchaser tenders generally will not reduce the tax base, because the retail seller can return the redeemed coupons to the manufacturer for credits. A similar rule applies with respect to manufacturer rebates. A purchaser's redemption of coupons that the retail seller issued generally are treated the same as cash discounts.*

- **Trade-ins** — *most states allow the tax base to be reduced by the value of any property that is taken in trade for the item that is sold. Other states allow the exclusion only with respect to trade-ins of specified vehicles and similar items, while some states don't allow any exclusion for trade-ins.*

- **Transportation charges** — *generally, separately stated charges for transportation that occurs after the sale are excluded from the tax base. However, in some states, transportation charges are taxable if property is sold f.o.b. (freight on board) destination, but not if the property is sold f.o.b. origin (and the charges are separately stated).*

- **Post-sale labor and service costs** — *although most states specify that "labor and service" costs are included in the tax base, if the costs are incurred after the sale is completed and are separately stated, they generally may be excluded. Of course, the key issue here is determining when a sale is "completed." For example, if you sell a satellite dish that can't be used until you install and configure it, your charges for such services will likely be included as part of the sale even if they are separately stated.*

- **Returns** — *most states allow a deduction from the tax base when merchandise is returned. However, the deduction may be limited if the full purchase price is not refunded or credited to the customer (due to a restocking charge, for example).*

- **Bad debts** — *most states allow bad debts to reduce the tax base for the reporting period that the debt is deducted for income tax purposes. Other states allow a credit equal to the tax that was paid in connection with the sale to which the debt related.*

Use Taxes

As a general rule, a state's taxing power reaches only to its borders. What this means is that a state cannot impose its sales tax on retail sales that are consummated in other states.

This restriction created the concern that purchasers could avoid paying a state's sales tax by making their purchases outside the state. To close this perceived loophole, each state that has a sales tax also has a complementary "use" tax. The use tax applies to the "use, storage, or other consumption" within the state of tangible personal property, the purchase of which would have been subject to the sales tax had the transaction occurred within the state.

Example

Let's assume you operate a commercial photography studio in California. You regularly go to Oregon to purchase all the cameras you use in your business. California can't impose its sales tax on your camera purchases, because those purchases were made outside the state. However, California can subject the cameras to its use tax once you bring them into the state.

The following are the key elements of use taxes:

- **Complementary tax** — a state's use tax is designed to be no broader in scope than its sales tax. For the most part, exemptions are the same for both of the taxes. Similarly, the basis for computing the use tax is generally the "selling price" of the property, just as it is for purposes of computing the sales tax. Finally, a state's use tax rates are identical to its sales tax rates.

- **Self-assessment** — perhaps the biggest difference between a state's sales tax and its use tax is the manner in which the taxes are paid. For the most part, sales taxes must be paid or collected by the seller. In contrast, the responsibility for reporting and paying use taxes generally falls on the purchaser. This is commonly the case because the triggering event for the tax — the taxable "use" of the property in the state — occurs after the sale is completed and because the state may not have the power to force the out-of-state seller to collect its use tax.

- **Credits** — every state other than Nevada allows purchasers a use tax credit for sales taxes paid to another state with respect to the same property. In our example, you would be able to offset your California use tax liability on the cameras by any Oregon sales tax you paid on the purchase.

- **Other taxable uses** — in some situations, a use tax liability may arise with respect to property that was not purchased in another state.

Perhaps the two most common of these situations arises when (1) you purchase an item free from sales tax by claiming an exemption, but then use the item in a manner that is inconsistent with that exemption or (2) you withdraw from your inventory an item that you produced for sale.

Example

 Let's assume you operate a computer store where you sell computers that you personally construct and peripherals such as printers that you purchase from others under the resale exemption.

If you were to start using for business or personal purposes one of the printers that you purchased tax-free, you would be liable for use tax with respect to that printer. This is an example of the first situation.

If you were to start using in your business or for personal purposes one of the computers you built, this would also subject you to use tax in many states. This is an example of the second situation.

Sales Tax Concerns of Sellers

When it comes to dealing with sales taxes, the biggest problems seem to be reserved for sellers, who generally are responsible for seeing that the taxes are timely paid to the state. So, if your business makes taxable retail sales of property or services, you need to be prepared to handle the following obligations.

Where Must You Register?

If you plan to make sales that are subject to sales tax in a state, you must register to collect the tax by applying for a sales permit for each separate place of business you maintain in the state. Depending on the state, such a document may be referred to as a "permit," "license," or "certificate of registration."

In some states, it's a criminal offense to operate without the requisite permit, so you should get a permit before you make your first sale. Once you receive the permit, you must display it at your place of business.

Although the cost of sales permits is generally nominal, you may be required to furnish a deposit or a surety bond as part of the registration process. Many states require new sellers to post such deposits or bonds to secure the timely payment of their taxes.

Use tax registration. In recent years, most states have stepped up their attempts to require out-of-state retailers such as mail-order sellers and telemarketers to register for the purpose of collecting their use taxes. What you need to know is that a state can't compel you to register or to collect its use tax unless you have established a physical presence within the state.

What types of actions will create a physical presence? Here are some possibilities:

- You maintain an office, store, or other business facility in the state.

- You or your employees enter the state to take orders, perform services, or otherwise do business on your behalf.

- Real property that you own or lease is located in the state.

- Personal property that you own or lease is stored or used in the state on a more than occasional basis.

We do know that if you truly limit your contacts with a state to communicating with customers in the state by mail or common carriers such as Federal Express, you won't be obligated to collect the state's use tax. Presumably, a similar standard will apply with respect to telemarketers and to retailers who sell over computer networks and the Internet (so-called "cybersellers"), although this area of the law is not yet settled.

Collecting the Tax

Unless you're doing business solely in one of the nine states where sellers can elect to pay the sales tax themselves instead of collecting it from their purchasers, you're going to be obligated to collect sales tax on your taxable sales. In other words, you're generally going to have to compute the tax owed on each sale you make.

Arizona, California, Hawaii, Michigan, New Mexico, South Carolina, and South Dakota are the states where sellers have the option of absorbing the tax.

Determining the amount to collect. If you make regular sales, it may be well worth the expense to set up a computer or a cash register that is programmed to determine the tax amount whenever you input or ring up a sale, and that generates a detailed receipt that separately states the tax on the sale.

Virtually every state requires sellers to separately state the collected tax on the invoices or receipts they provide their purchasers. Requiring that the tax be separately stated basically forecloses later arguments by sellers or purchasers that an unbilled tax was included in the purchase price.

The alternative is to do the computation manually or on a calculator. Most states do provide useful tables of bracket schedules that show how much tax should be collected on a given sale at a given tax rate.

Collection discounts. About half the states allow sellers to claim a fee as compensation for their time and expenses in collecting the sales tax on the state's behalf. The fee is set at a fixed percentage (0.5% — 5%) of the collected tax, but is generally subject to a ceiling amount.

Absorption of tax. Consumers will generally go to great lengths to avoid or reduce the sales taxes they pay. As proof of this phenomena, you need only go to a shopping mall parking lot in a state that's adjacent to a state with higher sales taxes. Based on the number of out-of-state license plates, it's clear that people will take a longer drive to reduce their shopping bill. Accordingly, if you're in one of those states where sellers can elect to pay the sales tax themselves, you may be tempted to exercise this option in hopes of drumming up business. For example, you may decide to use your ability to absorb the tax as a negotiating point with selected purchasers. Or you may go whole hog and hold an "I'll pay your sales tax" sale. But is this really a good idea?

Well, in either case, don't lose sight of the obvious fact that absorbing sales taxes will involve significant costs. Depending on the sales tax rate in your area, you could be adding to your operating costs an amount equal to more than 10 percent of the sales price of each item you sell. Therefore, if you're already operating at a minimal profit margin, you'll want to analyze whether the increased costs will be offset by the additional revenues.

Remitting the Tax

After you've collected sales tax from your purchasers, the obvious next step is reporting and paying the tax to the appropriate authorities. Most states generally require you to file a tax return and remit the sales and use taxes you have collected on a monthly basis; for example, on the 10th day of the month following the taxable month. However, many states have special rules that may require you to file and pay on a more frequent or less frequent basis, depending on the amount of your tax liability.

Claiming refunds. If you remit more tax than you actually owe, either because of a clerical error or because of a misinterpretation of the law, a state will generally refund the excess payment. However, if the overpaid tax was collected from a purchaser, most states will require proof that you reimbursed the purchaser for the overpaid tax as a prerequisite to providing the refund.

Recordkeeping. As is the case when you file any tax return, you must maintain an accurate set of books and records that substantiates the sales tax liability you reported on the return, in case you are selected for an audit by the state tax authorities. The records generally must include such items as receipts, invoices, cash register tapes, working papers, and exemption certificates provided by purchasers. Each state specifies a length of time for which the records must be maintained.

STATE TAX CHART

The following chart is designed to alert you to the presence of the most important types of tax in your state, and the tax rates that are currently imposed for each type of tax.

Corporate income tax. The corporate income tax column shows taxes based totally or partly on corporate income. Rates for states that impose similar taxes on S corporations or unincorporated businesses are also noted.

Franchise taxes. This column shows taxes imposed by states for the privilege of doing business in the state as a corporation, based on some measure other than income. The rates shown are those for domestic corporations (i.e., those organized in the state); other taxes or fees may be imposed on out-of-state businesses that do business within a particular state. Note that most states also impose an annual flat fee on each domestic corporation, which is not included in the rates shown.

Personal income taxes. This column shows the range of tax rates imposed on individual income. It does not include the local income taxes imposed by cities in some states. For information on withholding state and local income taxes, see Chapter 28.

Sales tax. The rate shown in this column is the statewide general rate and does not include city, county or other tax rates, or tax rates for special industries or particular classifications of products or services.

State	Corporate Income Tax	Franchise Tax	Personal Income Tax	Sales Tax
AL	5%	$10 per $1,000 capital stock, min. $50	2% to 5%	4%
AK	1% to 9.4%; LLCs taxed as corporations	None	None	None
AZ	7.968% for 2000; $50 min.	None	2.87% to 5.04% for 1999	5%
AR	1% to 6.5%	0.27% outstanding capital stock; $50 min.	1% to 7%	4.625%
CA	8.84%; 1.6% for S corps.; $800 min. for all corps.	8.84%; $800 min. 1.6% for S corps in 2000	1% to 9.3% for 1999	6%
CO	4.75%	None	4.75%	3%
CT	7.5% for 2000; S corps. taxed as corporations	None	3% to 4.5%	6%
DE	8.7%	Max: $90 on 10,000 shares + $50 for each additional 10,000 shares	2.6% to 6.4% for 1999	None
DC	9.5% tax on all corporations and unincorporated businesses; $100 min.	None	6% to 9.5%	5.75%
FL	5.5%; LLCs taxed as corporations	None	None	6%
GA	6%	ranges from $10 on paid-in capital not exceeding $10,000; to $5,000 on paid-in capital over $22 million	1% to 6%	4%
HI	4.4% to 6.4%	None	1.6% to 8.75%	4%
ID	8%; $20 min.	None	2% to 8.2%, plus $10	5%
IL	4.8%; additional 2.5% personal property replacement tax on C corps; additional 1.5% personal property replacement tax on S corps, partnerships, LLCs	0.1% of corporate paid-in capital; $25 min.	3%	6.25%

State	Corporate Income Tax	Franchise Tax	Personal Income Tax	Sales Tax
IN	3.4%	None	3.4%	5%
IA	6% to 12%	None	0.36% to 8.98% for 1999	5%
KS	4% + surtax of 3.35% of taxable income in excess of $50,000	$1 per $1,000 of shareholder's equity	3.5% to 6.45%	4.9%
KY	4% to 8.25%	$2.10 per $1,000 of capital	2% to 6%	6%
LA	4% to 8%; S corps. taxed as corporations	$3.00 per $1,000 of capital stock, surplus, undivided profits, and borrowed capital	2% to 6%	4%
ME	3.5% to 8.93%	None	2% to 8.5%	5.5%
MD	7%	None	2% to 4.85% for 2000; 2% to 4.75% for 2001	5%
MA	Excise tax equal to the sum of $2.60 per $1,000 of qualified taxable tangible property or qualified taxable net worth, + 9.5% of taxable net income; min. $456	None	5.95%	5%
MI	2.2% for 1999; 2.1% for 2000; business tax applies to all corporations, individuals, estates, trusts, and partnerships with business activity in state	None	4.4%	6%
MN	9.8%, plus min. tax up to $5,000 based on property, payrolls, sales & receipts, and type of corp. or partnership	None	5.5% to 8%	6.5%
MS	3% to 5%	$2.50 per $1,000 of value of capital, min. $25	3% to 5%	7%
MO	6.25%	0.05% of par value of outstanding shares and surplus if in excess of $200,000	1.5% to 6%	4.225%

State	Corporate Income Tax	Franchise Tax	Personal Income Tax	Sales Tax
MT	6.75%; $50 min.	None	2 % to 11%	None
NE	5.58% to 7.81%	From $13 for $10,000 or less of domestic paid-up capital stock, to $11,995 for over $100 million	2.62% to 6.99%	5%
NV	None	None	None	6.5%
NH	8% on all business organizations with gross income over $50,000	0.25% of enterprise value for every business enterprise with gross receipts over $100,000 or value over $50,000	No general tax, but 5% tax on interest and dividends	None
NJ	7.5% to 9%; $200 min. S corps: 0.05% to 2%	None	1.4% to 6.37%	6%
NM	4.8% to 7.6%	None	1.7% to 8.2%	5%
NY	8% to 9%; min. based on gross payroll; S corps. pay a special franchise tax and surcharge	None	4% to 6.85%	4%
NC	6.9% for 2000	$1.50 per $1,000 issued and outstanding capital stock, surplus, and undivided profits allocable to state, min. $35	6% to 7.75%	4%
ND	3% to 10.5%	None	2.67% to 12%	5%
OH	5.1% to 8.5%, or .004 times the value of stock; min. $50	None	0.716% to 7.228%	5%
OK	6%	$1.25 per $1,000 of capital used, invested, or employed in OK, min. $10	0.5% to 7%	4.5%
OR	6.6%; $10 min.	None	5% to 9%	None
PA	9.99%; S corps. and LLCs must make a state election to escape tax	Greater of $200 or .10.99 mills x each dollar of taxable stock value	2.8%	6%

State	Corporate Income Tax	Franchise Tax	Personal Income Tax	Sales Tax
RI	9%; $250 min.	$2.50 for each $10,000 of authorized stock, min. $250; S corps. taxed as corporations	26% for 2000; 25.5% for 2001; 25% for 2002 of federal income tax liability	7%
SC	5%	$15 + 1 mill per $1 paid to capital stock and surplus, min. $25	2.5% to 7%	4% + 1% for persons under age 85
SD	None	None	None	4%
TN	6%; S corps. taxed as corporations	$.25 per $100 of outstanding capital stock, surplus, and undivided profits, min. $10	6% of stock dividends or interest on bonds, notes, and mortgages	6%
TX	None	Sum of 0.25% per year of net taxable capital and 4.5% of net taxable earned surplus; S corps and LLCs taxed as corporations	None	6.25%
UT	5%; $100 min.	None	2.3% to 7%	4.875%
VT	7% to 9.75%; $250 min.	None	25% of federal income tax liability	5%
VA	6%	None	2% to 5.75%	3.5%
WA	None	None	None	6.5%
WV	9%	Greater of $50 or .70% of value of corporate capital	4.77% to 6.77%	6%
WI	7.9%; surcharge may apply	None	4.9% to 6.93%	5%
WY	None	$25 to $200 on property under $1 million, plus $200 on each additional $1 million portion of corporate property and assets	None	4%

Chapter 28

Doing the Payroll

If you have employees, you'll have to pay them. And that means setting up a payroll system.

Doing the payroll is much more complicated than just writing out a check to each employee every week or two. Numerous federal and state laws come into play, and dictate how you must calculate the employees' pay and any overtime required, make any necessary deductions from paychecks, and get the pay into the workers' hands.

A large part of doing payroll correctly is being aware of and complying with the payroll tax laws. Not only must you calculate the taxes correctly, you must deduct some tax from employees' paychecks, pay some yourself, and deposit them with the government's bankers within tight deadlines.

Remember that you have the option of using an outside payroll service, or even your accountant, to handle these administrative tasks for you. An outside service will relieve most of the burden from your shoulders — for a price. You'll still need to become aware of the major tax and legal issues that apply, however, since ultimately you are responsible for seeing that the task is done correctly.

If you don't use an outside payroll service, we strongly suggest that you purchase some basic bookkeeping software that includes payroll and that can be used to calculate and even print out the actual checks each pay period. You'll find it infinitely quicker and more accurate than doing the payroll by hand.

SETTING UP YOUR PAYROLL SYSTEM

Here are the steps in setting up a successful payroll program:

1. Get a federal Employer Identification Number (EIN).

2.   Get state and (where necessary) local account/identification numbers.

3.   Determine whether each of your workers is an independent contractor or an employee. For employees, classify each worker as exempt or nonexempt (see the discussion in Chapter 19.

4.   Get Social Security numbers from all workers.

5.   Obtain a Form W-4 from each employee.

6.   Establish a pay period.

Once you've done these things, you can begin paying employees by determining the hours they've worked, determining what their regular rate of pay is, taking tax and other deductions from their checks, and getting the money to employees.

Federal Employer Identification Numbers

Every employer must apply for and obtain a federal Employer Identification Number from the Internal Revenue Service. You can do so by completing IRS Form SS-4. You must file this form if you have not obtained an EIN before and you pay wages to one or more employees.

An EIN is a nine-digit number that takes the form: 12-3456789. If you become the owner of an existing business, do *not* use the EIN of the former owner. There's one exception to this rule: if you become the owner of a business by purchasing stock, use the business's EIN.

State Identification Numbers

In addition to the federal EIN, you may also need to get identification numbers or account numbers from the various state and local taxing jurisdictions to which you will be reporting, depositing, and paying taxes. In many states, the federal EIN is also used for state income tax reporting purposes.

Call your state department of revenue to find out how to get a number. In most cases, you will then receive forms or coupon books to use when making required deposits of payroll taxes.

Which Workers Are on Your Payroll?

As part of the initial setup of your payroll, you'll need to determine which of your workers are "employees" who must receive a paycheck, and, perhaps more importantly, whose paychecks are subject to payroll taxes.

Each federal and state law imposing a payroll tax has its own definition of the classes of taxable workers. However, as a practical matter, the basic governing standard is whether an individual who performs services for you meets the definition of "employee" under the common-law rules. Under the common-law rules, your workers are employees if you have the right to direct and control not only the results of the work, but also the details of when, where, and how their work is done.

The important issue here is whether you have the *right* to control your workers' activities. Even if you grant your workers considerable discretion in determining how they do their work, as long as you retain the legal right to control their activities, the workers are common-law employees. The fact that your worker may have signed an agreement that he or she will be treated as an independent contractor does not hold water with the IRS.

Warning

You take on a significant risk whenever you improperly treat an employee as an independent contractor or as an employee with respect to whom you have no payroll tax obligations. The risk is that the IRS and your state tax authorities will hit you with penalties that at a minimum make you personally liable for paying, with interest, both the taxes you should have paid and the taxes you should have withheld.

Generally, if you make a mistake in the other direction and treat someone as an employee when he or she is really an independent contractor, the IRS rarely imposes penalties.

Just how much control on your part is enough to cause a worker to be classified as an employee rather than an independent contractor is by no means clearly defined. Rather, each case really turns on an analysis of its own particular set of facts.

The IRS has identified the 20 factors that its auditors use as guidelines in resolving the employee-or-contractor issue. As you work through the list, keep in mind that the factors don't necessarily hold equal weight. The importance of each factor will vary depending on the type of work being done and the circumstances of your own particular case. Because this is a highly subjective analysis, your goal should be to honestly assess how great a risk you'll be taking if you plan to treat a worker as an independent contractor.

The IRS's 20-Factor Test

1. ***Instructions*** *— workers who must comply with your instructions as to when, where, and how they work are more likely employees than independent contractors.*

---

2. ***Training*** — the more training your workers receive, the more likely it is that they're employees. The underlying concept here is that independent contractors are supposed to know how to do their work and, thus, shouldn't require training from the purchasers of their services.

3. ***Integration*** — the more important that your workers' services are to your business's success or continuation, the more likely it is that they're employees.

4. ***Services rendered personally*** — workers who must personally perform the services for which you're paying are more likely employees. In contrast, independent contractors usually have the right to substitute their workers' services for their own in fulfilling their contracts.

5. ***Hiring assistants*** — workers who are not in charge of hiring, supervising, and paying their own assistants are more likely employees.

6. ***Continuing relationship*** — workers who perform work for you for significant periods of time or at recurring intervals are more likely employees.

7. ***Set hours of work*** — workers for whom you establish set hours of work are more likely employees. In contrast, independent contractors generally can set their own work hours.

8. ***Full time required*** — workers whom you require to work or be available full time are likely employees. In contrast, independent contractors generally can work whenever and for whomever they choose.

9. ***Work done on premises*** — workers who work at your premises or at a place you designate are more likely employees. In contrast, independent contractors usually have their own place of business where they can do their work for you.

10. ***Order or sequence set*** — workers for whom you set the order or sequence in which they perform their services are more likely employees.

11. ***Reports*** — workers whom you require to submit regular reports are more likely to be employees.

12. ***Payment method*** — workers whom you pay by the hour, week, or month are more likely employees. In contrast, independent contractors are usually paid by the job.

13. ***Expenses*** — workers whose business and travel expenses you pay are more likely employees. Independent contractors are usually expected to cover their own overhead expenses.

14. ***Investment*** — the greater your workers' investment in the facilities and equipment they use in performing their services, the more likely it is that they're independent contractors.

15. **Tools and materials** — *workers whose tools, materials, and other equipment you furnish are more likely employees.*

16. **Profit or loss** — *the greater the risk that your workers can either make a profit or suffer a loss in rendering their services, the more likely it is that they're independent contractors.*

17. **Works for more than one person at a time** — *the more businesses for which your workers perform services at the same time, the more likely it is that they're independent contractors.*

18. **Services available to general public** — *workers who hold their services out to the general public (for example, through business cards, advertisements, and other promotional items) are more likely independent contractors.*

19. **Right to fire** — *workers whom you can fire at any time are more likely employees. In contrast, your right to terminate an independent contractor is generally limited by specific contractual terms.*

20. **Right to quit** — *workers who can quit at any time without incurring any liability to you are more likely employees. In contrast, independent contractors generally can't walk away in the middle of a project without running the risk of being held financially accountable for their failure to complete the project.*

Safe Haven Rule for Independent Contractors

The federal tax law provides a safe haven rule that minimizes your uncertainty when it comes to the proper treatment of workers as employees or independent contractors.

This rule provides that an individual who has consistently *not* been treated as a common-law employee for all periods after 1977 will not be reclassified as an employee if the employer has filed all required federal tax returns (including 1099-MISCs) consistent with independent contractor treatment, and if you had a reasonable basis for not treating the individual as an employee.

What's a "reasonable basis" for not treating someone as an employee? There are three factors you may use:

- judicial precedent, published rulings, technical advice you received, or a letter ruling you received from the IRS

- a past audit by the IRS in which there was no assessment attributable to the tax treatment, for employment purposes, of workers holding positions substantially similar to the position held by the worker in question

- long-standing recognized practice of a significant segment of the industry in which the individual works (i.e., many similar workers in your industry are treated as independent contractors)

Recent legislation in this area has clarified and added to the requirements for qualifying for the safe haven. Here we highlight the most important changes (which generally apply for 1997 and forward):

- Employers can't rely on an audit beginning in 1997 or thereafter, unless it includes an examination for employment tax purposes of whether the worker involved or any worker holding a substantially similar position should be treated as an employee. (Employers can still rely on prior audits that began before 1997, even if they weren't related to employment tax matters.)

- To prove that a "significant segment" of your industry treats such workers as independent contractors, it's not necessary to prove that more than 25 percent of your industry follows this treatment (though if less than 10 percent of the industry follows it, it's unlikely to be considered a "significant segment").

- An industry practice need not have continued for more than 10 years for it to be considered long-standing based on the particular facts and circumstances.

An employer who treats certain workers as employees, and others with very similar positions as independent contractors, will more than likely be denied relief under the safe haven rule. Also, if you have treated someone as an employee anytime after 1977 and try to convert him or her to an independent contractor, you are not eligible for the safe haven.

Finally, what happens if your workers don't satisfy the requirements of the safe haven rule? They can still qualify as independent contractors under the IRS's 20-factor test, discussed above.

Requesting an Advance Ruling

We suggest that you talk to your tax professional before you take the position that any of your workers are independent contractors.

In close cases, you'd be well advised to take the added step of requesting an IRS determination as to a worker's proper classification. If the IRS is going to disagree with your classification, you can save a lot in tax penalties, interest, and legal costs if you find that out now as opposed to several years down the road.

You request an advance ruling by filing Form SS-8, *Determination of Employee Work Status for Purposes of Federal Employment Taxes and Income Tax Withholding.*

Work Smart

Never submit an advance ruling request without first having it reviewed by your tax professional. You want to be sure that each favorable factor is highlighted. At the same time, you need to be sure that no material facts are omitted or presented in a misleading fashion. An experienced tax pro can help ensure that each statement in the request reflects your case in its best light. This is important because you're asking the IRS to make a very subjective decision.

Statutory Employees

For workers in certain occupations, you will be required to withhold and pay certain payroll taxes even if those workers are not your common-law employees. These so-called "statutory employees" are:

- **Agent-drivers and commission drivers** who deliver specified products — individuals who (1) operate their own trucks or the trucks of the persons for whom they perform services, (2) serve customers designated by their principals and customers they solicit on their own initiative, (3) make wholesale or retail sales, and (4) are paid commissions on their sales or earn the difference between what they charge their customers and what they pay their principals for the products or services they sell. Such drivers are "statutory employees" if they distribute beverages (other than milk) or meat, vegetable, fruit, or bakery products or if they pick up and deliver laundry or dry cleaning.

- **Traveling or city salespersons** (other than agent-drivers or commission drivers) who work full time on your behalf and remit orders from certain customers — if they send you orders from customers who are retailers, wholesalers, contractors, or operators of hotels, restaurants, or other businesses whose primary function is the furnishing of food or lodging. The orders must be for items that your customers will resell or will use as supplies in their business operations.

- **Homeworkers** — individuals who perform work for you, generally on a contract or piecework basis and usually in their own homes or in the homes of others.

- **Full-time life insurance salespersons** who work primarily for one insurance company.

When you use statutory employees, you are not required to withhold income taxes from their compensation. However, you must withhold and pay FICA (social security and Medicare) taxes and, in the case of drivers and salespersons, federal (FUTA) and state unemployment taxes, if all of the following conditions exist:

- The service contract, whether written or oral, contemplates that the worker will personally perform substantially all of the work.

- The worker's investment in equipment and property, other than transportation equipment, is insubstantial.

- The worker performs services for you on a continuing (that is, regular or frequently recurring) basis.

- With respect to homeworkers, you've paid the workers at least $100 in cash wages during the year.

Warning

Just to clarify, the "statutory employee" designation becomes relevant only if a worker is not a common-law employee. All the normal payroll tax obligations apply if a statutory employee is in fact a common-law employee.

Family Members

There is no specific exception from income tax withholding for wages you pay to family members. So, if family members are common-law employees of your business, you'll generally have to withhold income taxes from the wages you pay them.

However, assuming you don't run your business through a corporation or partnership, you will be relieved from some FICA taxes, federal unemployment (FUTA) taxes, and state unemployment taxes in the following cases:

- **Spouse and parents** — you don't have to pay FUTA taxes with respect to a spouse or parent who works as an employee of your business. However, you do have to withhold and pay FICA taxes for those relatives.

- **Children** — for a child who works as an employee of your business, you don't have to withhold or pay FICA taxes until the child reaches 18, or pay FUTA taxes until the child reaches age 21.

Salespersons

For the most part, salespersons are treated the same as any other workers for payroll tax purposes. Thus, you'll generally have to withhold and pay payroll taxes if your salespersons are your employees. And, except for certain traveling or city salespersons who are "statutory employees" as discussed above, you won't have any payroll tax obligations with respect to salespersons who are independent contractors.

However, there are two types of salespersons for whom you may be relieved of all federal and most state payroll taxes even if they are properly classified as being your employees: real estate agents and direct sellers. Direct sellers are persons who sell or solicit the sale of consumer products at a place of business, such as a home, that is not a permanent retail establishment. The sales can be to the ultimate consumer or to a buyer who purchases the products for resale and on a buy-sell basis, deposit-commission basis, or similar basis.

This payroll tax relief is available only if both of the following are true:

- Substantially all the compensation you pay these salespersons is directly related to sales or other output (e.g., commission-based pay), as opposed to the number of hours they work.

- The salespersons perform their services under written contracts specifying that they will not be treated as employees for payroll tax purposes.

Putting Yourself on the Payroll

Even if you don't hire anyone else to help you run your business, you're always going to have at least one "employee," and that would be yourself. So, what kind of payroll tax obligations do you have with respect to yourself?

If you run your business through a corporation, you're likely to have all the same obligations you would have if you actually hired another employee. This is because corporations are treated as distinct legal entities from their founders and shareholders. If you do work for the corporation, you'll generally be treated as its employee, even if you are the sole shareholder.

But what if you don't incorporate? For starters, although you won't have to go through the formalities of withholding income taxes and payroll taxes from the income you draw from your business, you may have to make regular estimated tax payments, based on your quarterly net profits from the business.

Furthermore, if you earn at least $400 a year from your business, you'll have to pay "self-employment" taxes. In essence, self-employment taxes are FICA taxes that are imposed on those who are in business for themselves.

Like the FICA taxes, the self-employment taxes consist of a Social Security tax and a Medicare tax. For 2000, the total rate is 15.3 percent, with a Social Security rate of 12.4 percent and a Medicare rate of 2.9 percent, the same rates you would get by adding the employer and employee portions of the FICA taxes together. The self-employment taxes are imposed on your "net self-employment income," which is basically your business income reduced by your business deductions. The Social Security tax applies only to your first $76,200 of net business earnings in 2000 (this amount is adjusted for inflation each year). You report the tax on your annual income tax return, and you must include it in the amount you owe for estimated income tax payment purposes.

Employees' Social Security Numbers

In order to make your payroll program work, you must have the Social Security number of each employee you pay. You'll also need the Social Security numbers (or employer identification numbers, if applicable) of independent contractors, so that you can report payments of over $600 per year on Form 1099-MISC.

Form W-4

You need to get a signed Form W-4 from each employee, not only because the employee's Social Security number will be included on the form, but also to know how many allowances an employee is claiming for purposes of federal and state income tax withholding.

You should give all new employees a Form W-4 to complete as soon as they come in for their first day of work, if not before. A good time to take care of this and other necessary paperwork is during employee orientation. Employees should also complete a new W-4 if they get married or divorced, have a baby, gain or lose another dependent, or want to change their withholding amounts for any other reason.

If you don't have a valid W-4 on file for an employee, you must treat the employee as being single with no exemptions for withholding purposes.

Permissible exemptions. On their W-4, your employees can claim withholding exemptions for themselves, their spouses, and each individual they claim as a dependent on their tax return. In addition, any employees who expect to claim large amounts of itemized deductions on their return may be entitled to additional withholding exemptions.

Employees don't have to claim each exemption to which they're entitled, if they want to have more income tax withheld from their wages. Furthermore, employees can request on their W-4 that you withhold additional dollar amounts from their wages. As long as these additional withholding amounts do not exceed the employees' wages, you must comply with the requests.

No-tax-liability exemptions. An employee who anticipates having no federal income tax liability for the year may claim a complete exemption from withholding on Form W-4. This exemption fully relieves you from any obligation to withhold federal income taxes (but not FICA taxes) from the employee's wages. To qualify for the exemption, the employee (1) must have had no tax liability for the prior year, (2) cannot be claimed as a dependent on another person's tax return, and (3) cannot have any nonwage income such as interest or dividends, unless the employee expects to have a total income of less than $600. The exemption from withholding lasts only to February 15 of the following year, unless the employee files a new W-4 that renews the exemption claim.

What to do with the W-4s. In most cases, you don't have to send the W-4 forms to the IRS; you just have to keep them on file in case the IRS asks to see them. However, you must send the IRS copies of any W-4 on which an employee claims more than 10 withholding exemptions, or on which an employee earning more than $200 a week claims complete exemption from withholding. Also, if you learn that an employee has improperly claimed exemptions, you must inform the employee that the W-4 is invalid, request a new W-4, and send the invalid W-4 to the IRS.

State exemption certificates. Most states have their own exemption certificate form that for state withholding purposes serves the equivalent function of the federal Form W-4.

Establishing a Pay Period

A payroll period is the interval at which you pay your employees. It can be defined as the period of service for which a payment of wages is ordinarily made to an employee.

The length of the payroll period is important, mainly because it determines the method for withholding federal income tax. The payroll period also triggers the date and timing of payments that you owe the government because of payroll taxes you collected.

While there are no federal laws that require you to pay employees at regular intervals, most state laws mandate that every employer must pay all wages due to its employees on regular paydays designated in advance by the employer. The majority of states specify that employees must be paid at least twice a month, though a significant number allow exempt employees to be paid once a month.

Many states specify the length of the holdover period that is permitted; for example, they may require that employees be paid for a particular pay period within 10 days of the end of the pay period, thus allowing you 10 days to collect your attendance and time records and calculate each employee's paycheck. Check with your state department of labor for the specific rule in your state.

The general rule under the federal wage and hours law is that overtime compensation earned in a particular workweek must be paid on the regular payday for the period in which such workweek ends. If, for some reason, you're unable to determine the correct amount of overtime pay until after the regular pay period ends, you're required to pay the employee as soon after the regular pay period as is practicable.

CALCULATING AN EMPLOYEE'S HOURS WORKED

For employees who are paid by the hour, obviously, it's important to know how many hours each employee worked in each pay period, in order to draw up the paychecks. But there's another important reason: federal minimum wage and overtime laws revolve around how many hours an employee works in a workweek. (Note that these issues don't apply to exempt workers, since by definition they must be paid a fixed salary regardless of the actual hours worked each week.)

For purposes of the minimum wage, the "hours worked" will be the number you divide into your employee's pay to determine the hourly wage, to make sure that it meets or exceeds the federal minimum wage. For purposes of overtime, the "hours worked" will be the number you use to determine whether an employee worked more than 40 hours in the week, and if so, how much overtime pay you owe.

In calculating how many hours an employee has worked in a workweek, you must take into consideration the following factors:

- what counts as compensable time and what doesn't

- how to handle meal and break times

- how to keep track of an employee's hours

- when you may give employees "comp time"

- when you may deduct pay for tardy employees

What Counts as Compensable Work?

Generally, the federal law says that a nonexempt employee must be paid for all time for which *both* of the following are true:

- The employee is required to be on duty, on the employer's premises, *or* at a prescribed workplace.

- The employee performs work for the employer.

There are a lot of rules to remember about what counts as hours worked and what doesn't:

- **Orientation or training** — once the decision is made to hire an employee, any time spent on activities that you require, such as filling out additional forms, is considered part of working time, and the employee must be paid for that time. This is true even if you send them to a class before or after the work day or on a nonwork day. Compensation is not required for training that is truly voluntary.

- **Employees' absences** — absences due to illness, holidays, vacation, time off to vote, or similar causes can be ignored for minimum wage and overtime purposes, even if the employee is paid for the absences. Whether you have to pay an employee for that time depends upon the policies and rules you've set up (and, in some cases, the state where you live).

- **Meals and breaks** — generally, you have to include as working time, and to pay employees for, breaks or rest periods that last for 20 minutes or less. See our separate discussion of meals and breaks below.

- **Working at home** — if the employee does work at home, but you know nothing about it, you don't have to pay the employee for that work. If you have reason to believe the employee is working at home, you have to pay the employee for that work.

- **Unauthorized overtime** — if an employee works overtime that you didn't authorize, you will still have to pay the employee for that time, if you knew or had reason to know that the employee was performing the work. You might want to consider having a policy to discipline employees who work unauthorized overtime to keep it from happening.

- **Multiple jobs** — if you own more than one business and an employee works for more than one of your businesses, you have to total all of his or her time to figure out the hours worked for minimum wage and overtime purposes.

- **Travel time** — ordinarily, time spent traveling during normal working hours must be compensated. Time spent commuting and time spent traveling from home to a train station or airport do not have to be compensated.

- **On-call time** — depending upon the circumstances, you may have to pay an employee for time on call. If a nonexempt employee has to sit by the phone and be available to come in to work immediately, you have to pay that employee. But, generally, if the employee is free to do whatever the employee wants to do, you don't have to pay that employee. This is true even though you require the employee to carry a pager.

- **Incidental activities** — some activities, such as changing clothes or washing up after work, or waiting in line to punch out, do not have to be compensated. However, time spent setting up a machine or passing out supplies before work must be compensated.

Handling Meal and Break Times

Generally, for nonexempt employees, you have to pay employees for breaks or rest periods that last up to 20 minutes. If the break lasts more than 20 minutes and the employees are free to pursue independent activities, you don't have to pay them for it.

Meals that last at least 30 minutes do not have to be included in computing work time under the FLSA, as long as the employee is completely relieved of all duties and is free to leave the work post.

Federal law does not require breaks at all, but some state laws do.

State Laws on Meal and Break Periods

The following states currently have laws on the books that require private employers to provide meal or rest periods for adults. If you employ workers in any of these states, follow up with your state department of labor to find out what the rules are. Many other states require meal and break periods for minors only; if you employ minors, check with the state.

- *California*
- *Colorado*

- *Massachusetts*
- *Minnesota*

- *Oregon*
- *Pennsylvania*

- Connecticut
- Delaware
- Illinois
- Kentucky
- Maine
- Maryland
- Nebraska
- Nevada
- New Hampshire
- New Mexico
- New York
- North Dakota
- Puerto Rico
- Rhode Island
- Tennessee
- Utah
- Washington
- West Virginia

Keeping Track of an Employee's Hours

Federal wage and hour laws do not require you to have a time clock. Whether you decide to have one or not, you should have a reliable system in place for keeping track of your nonexempt employees' hours worked.

Many companies use sign-in sheets that employees must complete when they come in, when they leave for lunch, when they return from lunch, and when they leave work for the day. They also request that the employee total the number of hours worked per day.

While you may rely on your employees to keep their time, it's up to you to make sure that what they put on that sheet is correct. If an employee totals his or her hours wrong and you don't catch the error, with the result that the employee appears to be underpaid, a government auditor will hold you responsible, not the employee.

Determine how you will treat fractional parts of an hour. Generally, you are required to determine precisely the compensable time your employees have worked, including fractional parts of an hour. However, if you round off your time (for example, to the nearest tenth of an hour), the practice is acceptable if it is shown that over a period of time, the rounding results in the employees' getting paid for all the time they actually work.

Giving "Comp" Time

Giving "comp" time refers to the practice of giving compensatory time off to nonexempt employees who work extra hours instead of paying them time and a half. Under federal law, the practice is illegal.

However, it's perfectly legal to give comp time to your exempt employees (generally, executive, administrative, and professional employees are exempt).

Deducting Pay for Tardy Employees

Federal wage and hour laws don't prevent you from making deductions from a *nonexempt* employee's pay for tardiness or for failure to punch a time clock (if you have one).

However, by definition, exempt workers are paid by salary, which means that they get the same amount of pay per week regardless of how many hours they work in a week. Deducting pay from an exempt employee for absences of less than one day is illegal. You can, however, "dock" an exempt employee's pay for an absence of a whole day.

CALCULATING EMPLOYEES' REGULAR RATES

To compute the paycheck for a nonexempt employee, you must first determine how many hours the employee has worked during the pay period, as discussed above.

Once you've done that, if your employees are paid by the hour, you know how much to pay: the employee's hourly rate multiplied by the number of hours up to 40 per week, plus 1 ½ times the hourly rate for the number of hours over 40.

If your employees are paid on some other basis (i.e., salary or a piece rate) but are still entitled to overtime because they worked more than 40 hours and are nonexempt, you will have to figure out what their "regular rate" is.

Warning

Unless you pay your workers on an hourly rate basis, calculating the regular rate is complicated and time-consuming, and must be recalculated for each employee, each week. We recommend that you avoid this problem by paying all your nonexempt employees on an hourly wage basis. Otherwise, consult your accountant or payroll service for details on computing the regular rate.

What is the "regular rate?" Technically speaking, the regular rate is the employee's total weekly compensation for employment, less certain exclusions required by law, divided by the total weekly hours worked for which such compensation was paid.

The regular rate is computed *before* any kind of payroll deduction is made. Regardless of how you pay employees — hourly, by piece, monthly — the rate must not fall below the minimum wage rate of $5.15 per hour.

PAYROLL TAXES

Take a moment to think back to the day you received your first real paycheck. If you're like many of us, you may recall experiencing some shock upon noticing that the check amount was not quite what you'd expected. A quick glance at the accompanying pay stub showed that your employer had reduced your pay with a number of deductions, the most significant of which were probably for federal and state taxes.

Once you assume the role of an employer, you too will be required to withhold taxes from your employees' pay and to deposit the withheld amounts with the appropriate tax agencies. Furthermore, as an employer, you'll be personally liable for paying certain taxes on the amounts you pay your workers.

Together, those taxes that you're required to withhold and those that you're directly required to pay comprise your payroll taxes. Specifically, by hiring employees, you take on the following payroll tax obligations:

- to withhold federal, state, and local income taxes

- to withhold an employee's share of Social Security and Medicare taxes (which together are called FICA taxes), and to pay an equal amount as the employer's share

- to pay federal and state unemployment taxes

- to pay and/or withhold state disability insurance taxes, if required in your state

- to pay all these taxes on time and to file any required returns or reports

On the next few pages we'll discuss payroll taxes, beginning with the types of compensation that are subject to these taxes, and moving on to the various rates and computation methods for each tax. Finally, we'll discuss the tax returns and payment methods that you need to be aware of.

What Compensation Is Taxable?

Once you've identified the workers for whom you have payroll tax obligations, you need to determine what portion of the compensation you pay those workers is actually taxable.

This is not always as simple as you might think, especially when you consider employee benefits.

The federal and state payroll tax laws generally define taxable "wages" to encompass virtually every payment to an employee for services rendered.

The label you give a payment (salary, fee, bonus, commission, etc.) is unimportant in determining whether it constitutes wages. Nor does it matter that a payment is designed to supplement an employee's basic salary or that it is not made in cash. Also immaterial is the basis (hours worked, percentage of profits, etc.) upon which the payment is made.

Rather, whenever you transfer something of value to an employee as compensation for the employee's services, you've potentially made a taxable wage payment. The bottom line is that you should assume that all compensation you provide your employees constitutes taxable wages, unless you're aware that the law specifically exempts a given payment from taxation.

Taxable Wage Caps

While the types of payments to employees that are taxable is basically the same for each type of payroll tax, the dollar amount of each employee's wages that is subject to each of the taxes will differ.

Specifically, wage caps apply to the Social Security tax (for 2000, only the first $76,200 each employee makes is taxable), to federal unemployment taxes (only the first $7,000 per employee), to state unemployment taxes (the amount varies depending on the state), and to state disability insurance taxes (again, the amount varies).

Tips

Cash tips that your employees receive from your customers may constitute taxable wages for payroll tax purposes. In contrast, noncash tips from customers, such as a bottle of wine or theater tickets, are never considered wages.

"Tips" are payments that customers make without compulsion. If the amounts are dictated by your own policy, the so-called tips may in fact be service charges.

Example

Let's assume you operate a restaurant and do not permit direct tipping. However, on each check you include a "mandatory gratuity," which you distribute among your employees. Such a mandatory charge is not a "tip." And, in all cases, it constitutes taxable wages upon its distribution to the employees.

What are your obligations? An employee's cash tips are not taxable wages unless they amount to $20 or more in a calendar month and the employee reports them to you by the 10th of the month following the month in which they were received. Once the $20 threshold has been reached, however, all cash tips are wages, including the initial $20.

You are responsible for withholding income taxes and FICA taxes and paying FICA and FUTA on reported tips, even though you had no control over the amount of the tips.

However, you must withhold only to the extent that you have sufficient employee funds (e.g., the non-tip wages you would otherwise pay the employee) under your control. If insufficient funds are available, your obligation to withhold the uncollected portion ends. In contrast, any outstanding *income tax* collections should be withheld from your next payment of wages to the employee.

You may be eligible for an income tax credit against the FICA tax you paid on tips. See the discussion on tax credits in Chapter 26.

Employee reporting. You are not responsible for verifying the accuracy of the amount of tip income your employees report to you. If the IRS later finds out that your employees failed to report tips of $20 or more per month to you, you can be held liable only for the employer's portion of FICA and this liability does not arise until the IRS sends you a notice and demand.

Large food and beverage establishments. Employers that are "large food and beverage establishments" are subject to special tip reporting and allocation rules. The IRS says a large food or beverage establishment is any trade or business that:

- is a food or beverage operation where tipping is customary; and

- normally employed more than 10 employees on a typical business day during the preceding calendar year

If you meet the definition, you have some extra obligations with regard to tips: you must allocate additional tips to employees if they report tips of less than 8 percent of your gross receipts for a payroll period.

If you feel that 8 percent is too high and doesn't accurately reflect the tips your employees are actually getting, you can petition the IRS District Director to lower the percentage. If convinced, the District Director can lower the percentage to as low as 2 percent.

Large establishment reporting requirements. If you operate a large food or beverage establishment, you will also have to file Form 8027, Employer's Annual Information Return of Tip Income and Allocated Tips, with the IRS every calendar year for each large food or beverage establishment in which you have employees. You must also provide specific information to your employees regarding their tips as part of their Form W-2, Wage and Tax Statement.

Warning

 Filing these forms and making the tip allocations can get pretty complicated, particularly if you have more than one establishment. We suggest you consult with an accountant or tax advisor when filing these forms.

Fringe Benefits

The value of all fringe benefits *not specifically excluded* by the tax laws are considered taxable wages for payroll tax purposes, and you may have to withhold and pay the taxes on the basis of the fringe benefits' fair market value.

However, the law does include a rather lengthy list of fringe benefits that you can provide your employees without incurring any FICA or FUTA tax obligations. For the most part these fringe benefits are also excluded from an employee's income for income tax purposes.

The following benefits are excluded from taxable wages:

- health plan payments, including both insurance premiums and payments from health plans for medical expenses

- long-term care insurance premiums and payments

- any sick pay or disability payments made later than six months after the employee last worked for you

- payments made on account of retirement for disability or death, including wages earned before the employee died but paid to a survivor

- employer's contributions to a qualified pension or retirement plan, including profit sharing, SEP, or SIMPLE plans (employees' elective contributions to retirement plans, such as contributions to 401(k) or SIMPLE plans, are subject to FICA and FUTA taxes but *not* income tax withholding)

- group term life insurance premiums on policies of up to $50,000 per employee

- worker's compensation premiums and benefits

- up to $5,250 in non-graduate-school education assistance, regardless of whether the education is job-related, for courses beginning before June 1, 2000

- meals and lodging furnished for the employer's convenience to employees and their dependents

- dependent-care assistance, up to $5,000 per employee

- services that your business provides to an employee at no additional cost to yourself and that you offer for sale to your customers; generally speaking these are "excess capacity" services like free standby air travel for airline employees, free hotel rooms for hotel employees, etc.

- certain employee discounts on the services or products you sell (the discount on services may be up to 20%; the discount on products may be as high as your gross profit percentage)

- property or services that you provide to an employee and for which the employee would have been entitled to a tax deduction had the employee paid you for the property or services (for example, company car used for business purposes; business travel, meals, and entertainment expenses; safety equipment; job training; education expenses to improve or maintain skills needed on the job but not to qualify for a new business or trade)

- benefits that have minimal value, such as occasional parties, occasional supper money or taxi fares when an employee works late, coffee and donuts, occasional tickets to entertainment or sporting events, use of company telephone or copy machines for personal purposes, etc.

- reimbursements for qualified moving expenses

- certain van pooling services, transit passes, and parking privileges

Business Expenses

If you pay advances or reimbursements to employees for business expenses they incur on your behalf, the payments will generally be considered taxable wages for payroll tax purposes unless the advances and reimbursements are made under an "accountable plan."

Furthermore, amounts provided under accountable plans in excess of substantiated expenses are also taxable wages, unless the employee returns the excess to you within a reasonable period of time.

An accountable plan is one that has all of the following characteristics:

1. It provides for advances or reimbursements for *deductible* business expenses that employees incur in connection with their performance of services for their employer.

2. It requires employees to substantiate the expenses within a reasonable time, usually by providing receipts or a detailed expense report.

3. It requires employees to return any advances or reimbursements in excess of substantiated expenses within a reasonable period of time.

Holiday or Vacation Pay

If you've extended your employees the benefit of paid holidays or vacation time, the amounts you pay them while they are on vacation are considered taxable wages, notwithstanding that the payments are for periods when the employees are absent from work.

The same rule applies to any payments you make to employees who do not take their vacations and instead receive additional pay for the time they could have taken off.

Jury Duty Pay

In general, amounts you pay your employees while they are serving on jury duty are considered taxable wages for payroll tax purposes, notwithstanding that the payments may be for periods when the employees are absent from work. However, the taxable amount will differ depending on how you treat your employees' jury duty pay:

- If you reduce your employees' regular wages by their jury duty pay, your payroll tax obligations apply to the reduced wage amount.

- If you pay your employees their regular wage, but require them to assign their jury pay to you, your payroll tax obligations apply to the regular wage amount as reduced by the assigned jury duty pay.

- If you pay your employees their regular wage and allow them to keep their jury duty pay, your payroll tax obligations apply to only the regular wage amount.

Noncash Wages

Virtually anything of value that you transfer to your employees as compensation for services constitutes taxable wages, unless the law specifically excludes the payment.

Payments made in the form of food or lodging are generally taxable to the employees, unless they are made in that form for the convenience of the employer, and: (a) in the case of meals, they are made on the business premises, and (b) in the case of lodging, the employee is required to accept lodging on the business premises as a condition of employment.

One of the first problems you'll encounter when you choose to compensate employee with food, lodging, equipment, or other noncash items is determining how much you paid. Generally speaking, for noncash payments, the amount of taxable wages is the fair market value of the benefits or property at the time of payment.

Most state unemployment agencies have regulations stating the minimum values that can be used for room and/or board, for state unemployment tax purposes. Consult your state department of labor for more details.

Perhaps the biggest problem with paying an employee noncash wages is that you must see to it that the income taxes and FICA taxes that you're required to withhold with respect to the payments are available for collection. If you also pay the employee some cash wages, you can withhold all the required taxes from the cash remuneration. If the cash wages you pay are insufficient to cover all of the withholding taxes, you must try to get the necessary funds from the employee. Unfortunately, this is frequently easier said than done.

Save Money

If you are going to pay noncash wages to your employees, especially if it's at their request, get a written commitment from them that they'll turn over to you any funds necessary to meet a tax withholding shortfall. Keep in mind that if you use your own funds to make up the shortfall, you've effectively paid additional wages to the employees and will thus incur additional payroll tax liabilities.

Gifts

Because the IRS does not believe that employers can act with a detached and disinterested generosity towards their employees, most gifts that you give to your employees are presumed to be a form of compensation.

Accordingly, unless you can show that a gift is connected with an event that's totally unrelated to your business (for example, an employee's wedding), gifts to your employees are considered taxable wages for payroll tax purposes.

During the holiday season, the IRS does allow you to show a little generosity towards your employees without incurring additional payroll tax liabilities. Christmas gifts are not considered taxable wages if the gifts are items of property having nominal value (for example, a turkey or a ham). This exception does not apply to small gifts of cash.

Awards and Prizes

Employee prizes and awards also are generally considered taxable wages, on the theory that you present them in return for an employee's performance or services. However, there are two limited circumstances under which you may be relieved from payroll tax obligations on noncash awards:

- An item of property that is valued at no more than $400 will not be considered taxable wages if it is given to an employee as a length-of-service or safety-achievement award.

- When you give a noncash award to a retail commission salesperson to whom you ordinarily pay only cash commissions, you can elect not to withhold federal income taxes with respect to the award. However, you will remain responsible for FICA taxes, unemployment taxes, and possibly state income taxes on the award.

Advances

In general, payments you make to your employees for services they'll perform or complete in the future are considered taxable wages for payroll tax purposes.

Example

Let's assume you employ Jim as a salesperson and pay him on a monthly commission basis. Each week you advance Jim $200 against his later-earned commissions. If the advances exceed Jim's commissions for the month, you carry the excess as an account due from future commissions. However, Jim has no obligation to repay that account if he should quit while his account has an outstanding balance. Under these facts, the advances are taxable wages.

Advances are not taxable wages if the employees are legally obligated to repay the advanced amounts. In our example, if you required Jim to sign a note or agreement that obligated him to repay the advanced amounts upon your demand or upon specified events (for example, his termination), the advances would likely be considered nontaxable loans rather than taxable wages.

Payments for Casual Labor

Occasionally, you may pay workers to do work that does not promote or advance your business. For example, during a slow period you may pay an employee to do some work around your home. Or you may pay one of your computer technicians to set up your personal home computer.

Unless certain dollar thresholds are met, your payments for such "casual labor" will not constitute taxable wages for payroll tax purposes. Furthermore, in no event will noncash payments for casual labor be taxable (on the other hand, you can't deduct your payments for personal services as a business expense).

Income and unemployment taxes. You're not required to withhold federal and most state income taxes or to pay federal (FUTA) and state unemployment taxes with respect to your cash payments to an employee for casual labor unless

- the cash payment is $50 or more in a calendar quarter, and

- the employee was engaged in casual labor for some portion of 24 different days during that quarter or during the preceding calendar quarter.

FICA taxes. You're not required to withhold or pay FICA taxes with respect to your cash payments to an employee for casual labor unless the payments amount to $100 or more during the calendar year.

Income Tax Withholding

Whenever you pay wages or other compensation to an employee, you can assume that the IRS will expect you to collect a portion of the employee's federal income tax on the payment by withholding the taxes from the employee's paycheck. Depending on where you do business, you may also have an obligation to withhold state and local income taxes.

Once you've determined the amount of each employee's paycheck that is subject to withholding, calculating the dollar amount to withhold is fairly straightforward.

Although the law provides specific rules for calculating that amount, the IRS and your state tax agencies have reduced the rules to simple tax tables that you can use in most cases. The tables show you how much you have to withhold on a payment, given the employee's marital status, your payroll period, and the number of withholding exemptions the employee claims on the W-4 form.

You can get the federal tax tables by calling 1-800-TAX-FORM and asking for Circular E and the supplement to Circular E, both of which are free publications that are updated annually.

State and Local Income Taxes

If you do business in a state that imposes a personal income tax, you can add the withholding of the state tax to your list of payroll tax responsibilities.

Only nine states don't impose a personal income tax: Alaska, Florida, Nevada, New Hampshire, South Dakota, Tennessee, Texas, Washington, and Wyoming. Every other state has a personal income tax, and requires employers to withhold the tax from employees' wages (for more information on state income tax rates, see the chart at the end of Chapter 27).

Most states allow employers to use methods that are similar to those used for federal tax purposes in determining their state income tax withholding amounts. With the exception of Arizona and North Dakota, where the state withholding amount is a fixed percentage of the federal withholding amount, and Pennsylvania, where the state withholding amount is a fixed percentage of an employee's gross wages, all of the states provide wage-bracket tables as one of the alternatives for computing state withholding amounts.

Multistate employment. If you only do business in one state and all of your employees are residents of that state, your state withholding obligations will be quite similar to your federal withholding obligations. However, complexities can arise once your operations expand beyond the borders of a single state.

Example

Let's assume you have a California office where you employ five California residents. You also have a second office in Oregon, where you employ two Oregon residents. Your employees never leave their state of residence to work in the other, out-of-state office. Under these facts, you'd withhold California income taxes from the wages of your five California employees and Oregon income taxes from the wages of your two Oregon employees. In other words, you'd have separate withholding obligations in each state.

More difficult situations arise when you send your employees to other states to perform services or employ residents of other states at a single in-state site. In these situations, we recommend that you seek the advice of your accountant or other tax professional.

Local taxes. In a few states there are cities, counties, and other local governmental units that impose their own income tax. However, if you happen to do business in one of these localities, you may very well have an additional income tax withholding obligation. Apart from local income taxes, you may also find yourself paying local taxes measured by your total payroll (payroll expense taxes) or withholding local occupational fees from your employees' wages.

The following states impose responsibility for local payroll taxes on employers:

State	Localities and Types of Tax
California	Los Angeles (employers' payroll expense tax); San Francisco (employers' payroll expense tax).
Colorado	Aurora (employees' occupational privilege tax); Denver (employees' occupational privilege tax); Greenwood Village (employees' occupational privilege tax).
Delaware	Wilmington (employees' earned income tax; employers' business licensing tax).
Illinois	Chicago (employers' expense tax on employers having at least 50 employees).
Indiana	Most counties impose one or more local income taxes that must be withheld from employees' wages.
Kentucky	Numerous cities and counties impose an occupational license fee that must be withheld from employees' wages.
Michigan	Numerous cities impose a uniform city income tax that must be withheld from employees' wages.
Missouri	Kansas City (employees' earnings tax); St. Louis (employers' payroll expense tax and employees' earnings tax).
Nevada	Entire state (employer's expense tax based on average number of employees)
New Jersey	Newark (employer's payroll tax).
New York	New York City (employees' income tax); Yonkers (employees' income tax).
Ohio	Numerous cities impose local income taxes that must be withheld from employees' wages.

Oregon	Lane County Mass Transit District (employers' excise tax); Tri-County Metropolitan Transportation District (employers' excise tax).
Pennsylvania	Numerous cities and boroughs impose local income taxes that must be withheld from employees' wages.

Social Security and Medicare Taxes (FICA)

The Federal Insurance Contributions Act (FICA) is a federal law that requires you to withhold two separate taxes from the wages you pay your employees: a Social Security tax and a Medicare tax.

Each of the FICA taxes is imposed at a single flat rate. For 2000 (as was the case for 1999), the Social Security tax rate on employees is 6.2 percent and the Medicare tax rate is 1.45 percent. To compute the tax to be withheld, you merely multiply an employee's gross wage payment by the applicable tax rate.

The law also requires you as the employer to pay an equal amount of these taxes on each employee's behalf.

Example

Let's assume you have one employee, to whom you pay gross wages of $500 every two weeks. You must withhold from each paycheck $31.00 in Social Security taxes ($500 x 6.2%) and $7.25 in Medicare taxes ($500 x. 1.45%). You will also owe equal amounts as the employer's portion of the taxes. In other words, each $500 wage payment will create a combined FICA tax liability of $76.50.

The Social Security tax is subject to a wage ceiling, which is adjusted annually for inflation. For 2000, your obligation to withhold and to pay the Social Security tax for an employee ends once you've paid that employee total wages of $76,200. However, there is no ceiling on the Medicare tax. You must continue to withhold and to pay the Medicare tax regardless of how much you pay an employee.

Advance Payment of the Earned Income Credit

Most employees whose family income is less than $30,580 in 1999 and who support a dependent child are eligible for the earned income credit (EIC) against their federal taxes. The IRS permits this credit to be paid in advance, over the course of the year rather than through a tax refund at the end of the year.

How does this affect you? You, the employer, must pay the employee a portion of the credit amount in each of his or her paychecks. The IRS "reimburses" you for the amount of advance EIC you pay, by allowing you to deduct it from the employment taxes you would otherwise have to send to the IRS.

You must make these payments if the employee so requests by giving you a completed IRS Form W-5, *Earned Income Credit Advance Payment Certificate*. The employee must fill out a new W-5 each year in order to get the advance payments. Also, you must notify the employees that the advance credit is available. The easiest way to do this is by giving the employee the official IRS W-2 form, which includes a notice about advance EIC payments on the back of Copy C.

Directions for figuring out the amount of an employee's EIC that must be added back to the paycheck are included in IRS Publication 15, *Employer's Tax Guide*, which also contains a more detailed explanation of the EIC.

Unemployment Taxes

The unemployment benefit system is a combined federal-state program, and as an employer you'll generally have to pay both federal and state unemployment taxes based on your payroll.

Federal Unemployment Taxes (FUTA)

You must pay the FUTA tax on your total payroll if during the current or the preceding calendar year you meet either of the following tests:

- You pay wages totaling at least $1,500 to your employees in any calendar quarter, or

- You have at least one employee on any given day in each of 20 different calendar weeks (the 20 weeks need not be consecutive and the "one employee" need not be the same individual).

Once you meet either of the tests, you become liable for the FUTA tax for the entire calendar year and for the next calendar year as well. For example, if you first met the 1-in-20 test in December 1998, you would have been responsible for the tax with respect to the wages you paid during the entire 1998 calendar year as opposed to just the wages you paid after you met the test. You would also continue to be liable for the FUTA tax on any employees during the 1999 calendar year, even if you fail to meet both the wages-paid test and the 1-in-20 test during that year.

Computing the tax. The FUTA tax is imposed at a single flat rate on the first $7,000 of wages that you pay each employee. Once an employee's wages for the calendar year exceed $7,000, you have no further FUTA liability for that employee for the year. Unlike the FICA tax, the FUTA tax is entirely paid by employers and may not be withheld from the employees' wages.

For 2000 (as was the case for 1999), the FUTA tax rate is 6.2 percent. However, you can generally claim credits against your gross FUTA tax for a portion of the state unemployment taxes you pay. By claiming these credits, you can effectively reduce the FUTA tax rate to 0.8 percent.

State Unemployment Taxes

Each state operates its own unemployment compensation program that is funded largely by taxes on employers. Only two states, Alaska and Pennsylvania, also assess unemployment taxes on employees.

Most states follow the federal rules for determining whether an employer must pay unemployment taxes. In the remaining states, broader tests for taxability are applied, and you may have to pay state unemployment taxes even though you're not obligated to pay the federal tax.

Computing the tax. Calculating what you owe in state unemployment taxes is simply a matter of multiplying the wages you pay each of your employees by your state unemployment tax rate. However, every state limits the tax you must pay with respect to any one employee by specifying a maximum wage amount to which the tax applies. Once an employee's wages for the calendar year exceed that maximum amount, your state tax liability with respect to that employee ends.

Unemployment tax rates are assigned to each employer individually. Every state uses an experience-rating system of some kind to determine each employer's applicable tax rate for the year. Although these systems vary in how they're actually administered, they share the goal of assigning lower tax rates to employers whose workers suffer the least involuntary unemployment and higher rates to employers whose workers suffered the most involuntary unemployment.

However, if you're new to the system because you've only recently hired your first employees, you'll pay tax at a fixed rate until you've contributed to the state's unemployment compensation program for a specified period of time (generally one to three years, depending on the state) and established "experience" with your employees and unemployment.

For more information on the taxable wage base and tax rates that apply in your state, contact your state unemployment agency.

Disability Insurance Taxes

If you happen to run your business in one of the handful of states where state-mandated short-term disability insurance programs are operated for the benefit of workers in the state, you can add to your payroll tax obligations a duty to withhold and/or pay taxes that fund the state's program.

The states with disability insurance programs are California, Hawaii, New Jersey, New York, Puerto Rico, and Rhode Island. In California, Hawaii, and Rhode Island, the programs are funded entirely through a payroll tax on employees. In New Jersey, New York, and Puerto Rico, employers also pay a small payroll tax. In every state but New York, the program is run by the same agency that handles unemployment insurance, and the two forms of tax are paid together; in New York, the Worker's Compensation Board handles the tax.

Payroll Tax Filing and Payment Deadlines

So you've identified the workers for whom you have payroll tax obligations, determined their taxable wages, and computed how much you owe for each of the different payroll taxes. What next?

Well, your main task is to see that your taxes are paid and reported in a timely fashion to the appropriate tax agencies. For federal payroll taxes, this usually means depositing the taxes with an authorized financial institution on at least a monthly basis, and filing quarterly or annual returns.

For most state payroll taxes, you usually send your payment with an accompanying return on a quarterly basis, directly to the agency that administers the particular tax.

However, your payroll tax obligations do not end with the filing of your tax returns. You also have reporting obligations to your employees and, in some cases, to your independent contractors. Furthermore, you must maintain for a specified period all records pertaining to the payroll taxes and wages you paid.

Federal Tax Deposits and Returns

For federal payroll tax purposes, paying the taxes you owe is usually done at a different time and place than filing the tax returns. That is, you deposit your taxes at a bank on a periodic basis (usually monthly) and you file your tax returns with the IRS on a quarterly or annual basis.

Withheld income taxes and FICA taxes. You generally pay these federal payroll taxes by depositing them with a bank or other financial institution that is authorized to accept federal tax deposits, or with the Federal Reserve Bank or branch serving your locality. In most cases, you should use Form 8109, *Federal Tax Deposit Coupon*, to make the deposit (a supply of coupons will be sent to you when you apply for your Employer Identification Number).

Electronic Federal Tax Payments System (EFTPS). Instead of using deposit coupons when depositing federal payroll taxes with an authorized financial institution, larger employers are required to use electronic transfers of funds to pay their taxes. Over the past few years, the threshold amount triggering this requirement has been around $50,000, and severe penalties for failure to comply with this method of deposit were legislated...but never enforced.

Under revised requirements proposed for 2000, if your total annual deposits of all federal income taxes (corporate income, FUTA, FICA, withholding, excise, etc.) exceed $200,000, you will have to use EFTPS in the second succeeding calendar year. That is, if your 1999 deposits were at least $200,000, you'll be required to use EFTPS starting in January 2001.

EFTPS is easy-to-use, secure and accurate. It saves taxpayers time and money, and you may (and really should) use this method even if you fall below the mandated threshold. To enroll, call 1-800-555-4477.

For withheld income taxes and Social Security taxes, you must deposit the taxes on a monthly basis (larger employers must deposit them semiweekly, or in some cases on the next banking day after payday). Towards the end of each year, the IRS informs you of which method you should use during the upcoming calendar year. However, if your total taxes for a quarter will be less than $500, you can simply send in the tax money with your quarterly return.

Whenever you deposit less than you're required, you run the risk of being hit with a penalty on the underpaid amount. However, as long as any shortfall does not exceed the greater of $100 or 2 percent of the amount due, no underpayment penalty will be assessed.

You must file Form 941, *Employer's Quarterly Federal Tax Return*, to report the federal income taxes you withheld, the FICA taxes you withheld and paid, and any advance EIC payments you made during a calendar quarter. The deadline for filing the return is the last day of the first month after a quarter ends. However, if you've been timely with each of your deposits during the quarter, you're entitled to an automatic 10-day extension. No other extensions are permitted for filing Form 941.

FUTA taxes. You must usually deposit any FUTA taxes you owe on a quarterly basis. However, if your quarterly FUTA tax liability is $100 or less, you don't have to deposit it. Rather, you may carry it forward and add it to your FUTA liability for the next quarter. Whenever the unpaid FUTA adds up to more than $100 by the end of the quarter, you must deposit the tax by the last day of the month following the quarter. If you never reach the $100 limit, you simply remit the tax with your annual FUTA tax return.

For FUTA taxes, you must file an annual return on Form 940, Employer's Annual Federal Unemployment Tax Return. A shorter and simpler form (Form 940-EZ) is also available if you meet certain conditions. The deadline for filing the return for each year is January 31 of the following year. However, if you've been timely with each of your FUTA tax deposits during the year, you're entitled to an automatic 10-day extension. The IRS may allow you a further extension of up to 90 days upon your written request.

Nonbanking days. If the date that you're required to make a federal tax deposit falls on a weekend or bank holiday, you have until the close of the next banking day to make a timely deposit.

Meeting deposit deadlines. In general, the timeliness of a deposit is determined by the date it's received. However, a mailed deposit received after the due date will be considered timely if you can establish that it was mailed at least two days before the due date.

Warning

Most financial institutions have a specific daily cut-off time for recording deposits. Any deposits received after that time won't be recorded until the following day. So, if you're planning to make deposits in person, be sure to arrive before the cut-off time.

Also, if you're planning to make your deposits using checks drawn on a bank that is different from the one where you're making your deposits, confirm whether the depository bank will consider the check an immediate payment of your tax deposits.

State Payments and Returns

Every state that has a personal income tax has its own forms and procedures for depositing payroll taxes. In most cases, when you file for a state employer's identification number, you'll also be sent information about the filing requirements in your state. For more information, you can contact your state department of revenue.

W-2 Forms for Employees

In addition to your obligation to file payroll tax returns with your taxing authorities, you have a reporting obligation to your employees. In essence, you must tell the employees how much you paid them in taxable compensation and how much you withheld from their wages for federal and state income taxes and FICA taxes.

For federal tax purposes, you make the report by providing each employee who worked for you during the year with a Form W-2, Wage and Tax Statement. The W-2s must be distributed by January 31 of the year following the calendar year covered by the form. However, employees who resigned or were laid off during the course of the year may request that you provide their W-2s earlier. If for any reason you're unable to distribute a W-2 to an employee, you should retain the undeliverable form as part of your records.

By the end of February, you must file copies of each of your employees' W-2s with the Social Security Administration (SSA). When you send the forms you should also file Form W-3, *Transmittal of Wage and Tax Statements*, which summarizes all the information on your W-2s.

State reporting. All states that have an income tax also require you to report your withholding of state income taxes on the employee's federal form W-2, and to send a copy (or a similar form) to the state tax authority.

Information returns for independent contractors. You don't provide W-2s to your independent contractors, because you don't have to withhold or pay payroll taxes with respect to them. However, you are required to fill out an information return (Form 1099-MISC) for any independent contractor to whom you've paid at least $600 as compensation for services. Copies of the return must be provided to the contractors by January 31, and to the IRS by February 28.

Payroll Tax Penalties

In the area of payroll taxes, many of the potential tax penalties are the same ones you'll find when you're dealing with other types of federal taxes. For example, there are both criminal and civil penalties for failing to timely file payroll tax returns or to timely deposit taxes you owe.

However, there are a couple of penalties of which you should be particularly mindful as you deal with your payroll tax obligations:

- **100-percent penalty.** The biggest risk you face in administering your payroll tax obligations is that you (not just your business) can be held personally liable for all income and FICA taxes that you willfully either fail to withhold from your employees' wages or fail to pay to the IRS and your state tax agencies. Even if you avoid the 100-percent penalty because your conduct wasn't "willful," you could face smaller penalties if your failure to withhold was due to your misclassification of an employee as an independent contractor.

- **Form W-2.** If you fail to prepare Form W-2 for your employees, or if you willfully furnish incorrect ones, you will be subject to a $50 penalty for each statement that should have been sent or that was incorrectly prepared.

MAKING OTHER DEDUCTIONS FROM PAY

Aside from payroll taxes, you may wish or be required to make other types of deductions from employees' pay. What seems simple on the surface — deducting money from an employee's paycheck — can be extremely complicated. Several federal laws apply and, potentially, many state laws may apply as well.

Deductions can be broken into three types:

- Deductions required by law — examples are payroll taxes and wage garnishments.

- Deductions for the employer's convenience — examples are those made to cover docking (for things such as spillage, breakage, or cash register shortages), or uniforms.

- Deductions that are done as a favor for employees — examples are benefit premiums or charitable contributions.

Garnishments

A garnishment is a court order letting you know that a legal claim has been made against an employee's wages. The order generally will have arisen from a legal proceeding filed by someone to whom your employee owes money.

The most common reason for garnishment is that the worker owes child support payments to a divorced spouse; in some states everyone who is paying child support will automatically have their paycheck garnished.

But other creditors may obtain garnishments against your employee as well. In effect, you, as the employer, will be responsible for collecting the money from the employee's pay and getting it to the court for payment of the debt.

In many cases, your involvement will begin with receipt of what is usually called a notice of garnishment.

Here's how the situation usually unfolds: a creditor wants to collect a debt from your employee. The creditor finds out that the employee may be working for you and sends you a notice of garnishment telling you of the debt and asking you to confirm that the employee works for you.

What should you do if you get a garnishment order? First and foremost, contact an attorney right away! Writs of garnishment are serious business. In some states, you have only a certain amount of time to respond (sometimes a matter of days) and if you do not honor the writ and begin withholding, you can be held responsible for the entire debt of the employee!

How much can be garnished? You can deduct garnishments from wages without violating the minimum wage rules.

However, the amount that can be garnished is limited to no more than the lower of either 25 percent of your employee's disposable earnings (earnings after legally required deductions like payroll taxes), or the amount by which disposable earnings exceed 30 times the current minimum hourly wage set by the FLSA (currently, that amount is $154.50).

You cannot terminate employees because their wages were garnished.

State laws. State laws on garnishment are detailed and complex, and may afford more protection for employees than the federal rules. When you talk to your attorney, be sure to ask how the following points are handled under your state's laws:

- how much can be garnished

- how multiple garnishments are treated

- what fees you, as an employer, can charge to the employee for garnishments

Docked Pay

When people talk about docking pay, sometimes they mean reducing an employee's pay for time not worked and sometimes they mean reducing it to recoup expenses due to breakage, spillage, cash register shortage, and the like. Technically, reducing an employee's pay for hours not worked is not "docking."

Why is the distinction important? Although the federal law does not prevent you from docking your employee's pay, it does require that any such deduction not reduce pay below the minimum wage. So if you're docking for things like spillage or shortages, you might have to carry over some of the amount to the next pay period, to avoid breaking the minimum wage law.

When you reduce an employee's pay for time not worked, the minimum wage issue doesn't come into question.

Example

Suppose you have an employee who is paid $5.50 per hour and thus makes $220.00 in a typical 40-hour workweek. You cannot dock that employee more than $14 in a typical week because that would drop his pay below the minimum wage level ($5.15 x 40 = $206).

On the other hand, suppose the employee shows up late and leaves early on a couple of days so that he only works 32 hours in the week. Even though you pay him only $176 for that week ($5.50 x 32), you have not violated federal law because you're not "docking" him for time worked.

Deductions for Uniforms

If the cost of purchasing, renting, or maintaining a required uniform would reduce an employee's wage below the minimum hourly rate in any workweek, you must reimburse the employee to the extent of the deficiency.

Example

Don makes $5.00 per hour and works 40 hours per week. He is required to buy and wear a uniform for his job. The uniform costs $35.00. Since Don makes $200.00 per week, after buying the uniform, Don's weekly pay is reduced to $165.00. That reduces Don's regular hourly rate (pay divided by hours) to $4.13, which falls below the minimum wage.

Instead, the employer should spread the cost of the uniform out over four weeks. The employer could deduct $10.00 a week for three weeks and $5.00 in the fourth week. That way, Don's pay will never drop below the minimum wage of $4.75 per hour, or $190.00 for a 40-hour workweek.

Deductions for Benefit Premiums

If you offer benefits for which employees must share in the cost, you should deduct the amounts of premiums for those benefit plans to make sure that premiums are paid appropriately. For tax-exempt benefits, deductions should be made before you calculate the payroll taxes.

Minimum wage implications. Where the deductions for pension or health plans cut into statutory minimum wage and overtime pay requirements, you can deduct them only if the employee voluntarily agrees and you don't get any profit or benefit from the transaction.

Generally, if you enroll in any kind of employee benefit plan, the insurance carrier or benefit provider will provide you with the necessary forms to enroll employees in the plan and get their permission for payroll deductions.

GETTING THE MONEY TO EMPLOYEES

Whether your employees are paid by check or cash, or participate in a direct deposit program, you should provide them with a statement that details their gross wages, what deductions have been made, and what their net pay is. In fact, many states require that a statement showing gross pay and deductions must be provided to employees when they are paid.

Rules to Follow When Distributing Pay

To be on the safe side, there are a couple of rules that you should follow when you are distributing pay:

- *Deliver pay to each employee personally and discreetly.*

- *Encourage employees not to leave checks or money in an unsecured area.*

- *Do not leave one employee's pay with another employee (unless it's a supervisor) to be delivered.*

- *Do not allow relatives of the employee to pick up an employee's pay unless you have express permission from the employee (preferably in writing).*

Direct Deposit of Payroll

Direct deposit of payroll is a method of paying employees where an employee's pay is electronically "delivered" to the employee's account in an indicated bank on or before each payday.

The employee receives a stub listing the gross amount of pay, any withholding or deductions, and the net amount of the check.

Automatic deposit of employees' wages directly into their bank accounts can streamline payroll operations, increase productivity, and *save money for your business.*

A direct deposit transaction can cost as little as four or five cents to process, versus 30 to 50 cents for a check. In a direct deposit program, employee pay is deposited right into the employees' personal accounts, eliminating costly steps in the payroll process, including the need to stop payment on and reissue lost or stolen checks. Direct deposit means fewer check processing charges and reconcilement maintenance fees from the employer's financial institution.

RECORDKEEPING REQUIREMENTS

If you have employees, several federal and state laws require you to keep and preserve certain employees' records relating to payroll.

For federal tax purposes, you must retain any records needed to substantiate your tax returns for at least four years after the due date or the date the tax return is filed, whichever is later. The types of information you should retain include:

- the name, address, and Social Security number of each employee

- the total amount and date of each payment of compensation

- the period of service covered by each payment of compensation

- the portion of each payment of compensation that constituted taxable wages

- copies of each employee's withholding exemption certificate (Form W-4)

- dates and amounts of tax deposits you made

- copies of returns you filed

- copies of any undeliverable W-2 Forms

Your records must be available at all times for IRS inspections.

Similar laws apply to payroll tax records in the states. Currently, the longest period that any state requires records to be kept is eight years (in Minnesota).

For federal minimum wage and overtime law purposes, you must keep more extensive records on the employees' wages, hours, terms and conditions of employment, sex, and occupation. Most of these records must be kept for three years, so we recommend that you keep them all for at least three years. State laws have similar requirements.

Even if your employees are exempt from the federal (and state) minimum wage and overtime law, you'll need to keep records to prove that fact.

Recordkeeping form or media. The law does not specify what form your records should take. Whatever method you use is sufficient if the records establish the information or data required by law. You may choose to keep the records on paper, on microfiche, on microfilm, or on your computer.

Warning

If you keep records on microfiche or microfilm, you must have the equipment available to read them, should Wage and Hour Division auditors drop in.

If you keep your records on your computer, make sure you have a backup on a disk.

Part IX

Building Your Personal Wealth

As a small business owner, your personal finances are closely tied to how successfully you manage your business finances. But even if business is booming and your company is incredibly well managed (of course!), this does not mean that your personal financial picture will always be so rosy.

One of the most often-repeated mantras of financial planners is "diversify, diversify, diversify." This is something that far too many small business owners neglect to do. It's very easy to become so personally identified with your business, and so caught up in its day-to-day problems and concerns, that most of your profits are ploughed directly back into the company, and virtually all of your family's future is riding on its success.

In the early years, this may be a necessity, but as your business matures, you need to begin to pull money out, and build up your personal wealth *outside* the business. At the very least, you need to set aside some funds for retirement, and make sure that you have adequate health, life, and disability insurance protection.

Chapter 29: Creating Your Wealth-Building Plan shows you how to get started by taking inventory of your current assets, budget, and other arrangements; setting and quantifying goals; and developing a plan to get "from here to there."

Chapter 30: Building Wealth Outside the Business helps you to examine the elements of your plan, including compensation and benefits, retirement planning, and life, disability, and long-term care insurance.

Chapter 29

Creating Your
Wealth-Building Plan

The 1990s have challenged middle-class America's traditional optimism about the country's continued economic progress. Many small business owners, as well as the employees of large and small businesses find themselves questioning, as never before, whether their current standard of living is secure, whether their retirement hopes are attainable, and whether their children will even be able to match, much less exceed, their current financial status. Several factors have contributed to this feeling of economic unease, including:

- lower earnings on passbook saving accounts and certificates of deposit, long the staple of middle-class saving

- the slow growth — and in some areas of the country, the actual decline — in the value of residential real estate, undercutting what has been the middle-class's premier safe and tax-advantaged leveraged investment

- foreign competition with U.S. businesses, threatening the livelihood of employees, and the very existence of the affected businesses

- questions about the long-term existence of the Social Security system, at least in its present form and benefit levels

Additionally, before starting your small business, you may have had painful experiences with some or all of these personal-wealth-draining situations:

- stagnant wages (sometimes accompanied by a longer workday) that didn't keep up with inflation

- corporate downsizing, reductions in workforce, and forced early retirements

- reductions and terminations of company health and retirement plans

What can you do? Because you're reading this, chances are good that you have taken the first step (or at least are thinking about taking it) that may enable you to rise above these stresses on your personal financial wealth: starting your own business. U.S. government statistics show that about two-thirds of the country's economic growth in the last decade has occurred as a result of small businesses. A successful small business can often be the best source of financial independence.

But operating your business is not enough. You need to step back and look at the whole of your family's financial picture, and think about your long-term goals for the future as well.

In this chapter, we'll guide you through five steps to allow you to create your own individualized financial plan:

1. **Identifying what you have now** — the first step in any financial plan is taking stock of your wealth, income and expenses, and existing planning documents.

2. **Deciding what you want** — next, you have to set your goals and quantify them in terms of dollar amounts, and the time you have to achieve them.

3. **Determining how to get there** — you need to figure out what you must do to achieve your goals, or readjust them so they become attainable.

4. **Implementing the plan** — this may be the most important step for you to take. Many plan, fewer implement.

5. **Monitoring the plan** — even a good plan can sour with age. You need to keep your plan up to date by making sure your investments perform as expected, and by adjusting your plan for changed circumstances.

What if you need help? Most successful business owners turn to professionals for advice. So, we offer a few words about using professionals to refine and maintain your plan.

WHAT DO YOU HAVE NOW?

A journey of a thousand miles may begin with one step, but chances are that you won't know what direction to walk in unless you first know where you're starting from. In much the same way, creating a wealth-building plan should start with a look at what assets you now have.

So, how do you answer the question: "What do you have now?" We suggest that you follow our three-step process:

1. Create an organized inventory of your assets and liabilities.

2. Build a current family budget of income and expenses.

3. Identify and organize the documents and arrangements that will affect the creation of a plan to build personal wealth and pass it along to your heirs.

Taking Inventory of Your Assets

Your financial planning asset inventory should list the major assets that you have, their value, and what income (if any) they generate. You don't need to list your personal effects, clothing, or furniture, unless you have some valuable collections, art, jewelry, or antiques that you are holding as an investment.

You'll also need to consider the other side of the coin — your liabilities including your mortgage, car loan, credit card balances, and any other consumer loans.

Since you probably already are drawing up regular balance sheets for your business, we suggest that you don't include assets and liabilities that pertain to your business here. The purpose of this exercise is to see how much you're worth without the business.

Here is an example of a portion of a simplified asset inventory:

(1)	(2)	(3)	(4)	(5)	(6)
Asset	Date acquired/ Price per unit	Market value now (per unit)	Units bought	Total value (col. (3) x (4))	Yearly income
Personal effects	various	various	—	$15,000	none
Twin Lakes Power 9% 40-yr bonds	1-3-79/$925	$1,260	5	$6300	$450
Econo-Eat common stock	4-24-95/$24	$13	100	$1,300	$10
Coin collection	about $750 over several years	$2,600	—	$2,600	none
Life insurance: $100,000 whole life	12-28-83/$900/yr premium	—	1	$5,000 (cash value)	none

Listing your liabilities. Your list of liabilities should include a brief description of each liability, including: to whom the debt is owed, when you incurred it, the interest rate, the monthly payment, the date you expect to have it paid off, and any security pledged on the debt.

After you have completed the inventory, you can subtract your liabilities from your assets to determine your net worth.

Of course, your true net worth would also include the value of your business. Since the valuation of a small business can be extremely complicated, we'll leave it out for now. *Part X: Getting Out of Your Business* contains an extensive discussion of valuation techniques.

Personal Budgeting

A personal budget is a tool to help you to reach your personal financial goals. It's an organized way to compare income and expenditures over a relatively short time frame (a week, month, or sometimes a year). It should allow you to forecast your income and expenses, monitor your progress, and make changes as needed to achieve your goals.

The idea of a personal budget means different things to different people. Some people might think of a budget as merely living within one's means. That is, if you haven't completely run out of money by the end of the month, you have stayed within your budget. While we are all for simplicity, such a "budget" is really no budget at all, because it doesn't give you any information about where your money went, and it doesn't provide the structure and discipline conducive to making changes where necessary.

Whatever the form your personal budget takes, it should give you a detailed picture of how money comes to you, and how you spend it, within the reporting period you choose. We recommend that you choose a reporting period that gives the most accurate picture of your financial cash inflow and outflow.

Save Money

While many financial advisors recommend a monthly budget, we think a weekly or bi-weekly budget can help you save more money. If you budget bi-weekly and plan to pay half of each month's bills in each budget period, you'll wind up with some extra money at the end of the year. The reason is that there are 26 bi-weekly periods in the year, but only 12 months (and, for example, only 12 mortgage payments that you need to make).

Income Budgeting

Many people figure that if they closely watch and diligently control the expenditure side of the budget, the income side will take care of itself. This may be OK for individuals whose only income is derived from fixed salaries. However, if your income varies from month to month — like that of most small business owners — you will also want to track income received as part of the process.

As a worst case example, you obviously wouldn't want to be in the situation of thinking you are bringing in $5,000 a month (and making spending decisions on this belief), only to find out several months later that your income has been averaging $4,000 a month.

What income do you include? If the business pays you a formal salary (this is generally required for C corporations), you should use your monthly net income — that is, income after taxes and payroll deductions. If you're operating as a sole proprietorship, partnership, S corporation, or LLC, you may be taking an owner's draw without making any payroll deductions.

In that case, look at your draw over the past year, and take an average figure. You can adjust this upwards or downwards, depending on your expectations for this year's performance. Don't forget to adjust your net income figure by the amount of the taxes you'll need to pay on that income. You can determine this by looking at last year's income tax return, if you were in business last year; otherwise, check with your accountant.

Also include any investment income from stocks, bonds, checking accounts, rental properties, royalties, etc.

Budgeting for Expenses

Budgeting for expenditures may be broken down into several steps:

1. **Forecast your major expenditures.** The best way to do this is to look at your checkbook register and credit card statements for the last six months or so, and see how much you spent each month in various categories of expenses such as savings, housing, utilities, phone, car payments, gas and transportation, insurance, clothing, gifts, entertainment, and whatever other categories make sense for your life.

2. **Don't forget to account for out-of-pocket cash expenses** that will arise during the month (or other budget period you choose). If you don't know precisely how much you spend this way, you can start by penciling in an estimated figure. Then, keep track of your actual cash expenditures for a month. You may be surprised at where your money goes.

3. **Track your expenses each month.** Compare your actual expenses for each category with what you budgeted for that category.

4. **Make adjustments.** For categories where the budgeted amounts don't match your actual expenditures, you'll need to make adjustments.

When it turns out that you have paid more for a category of expenses than what you had budgeted, you may want to consider one or more of the following:

- Decrease amounts budgeted for other items, either in the current or future budgets.

- Increase income, either in the current or future budgets.

- Do nothing, and let the change to the "bottom line" for the current budget (the amount of decreased cash or increased deficit) be carried over to the next budget. This assumes that eventually you will spend less in this category than you had budgeted, so you can "catch up."

If you are dealing with the situation where a budgeted item was either acquired for less than the budgeted amount, or the expenditure was not made at all, you may want to:

- Increase amounts budgeted for other items, either in the current or future budgets.

- Do nothing, and let the change to the "bottom line" for the current budget (the amount of increased cash or decreased deficit) be carried over to the next budget.

Work Smart

If it turns out that you're spending less than your income, congratulations! You're among a very select group of Americans. We usually recommend that you try to save at least half of the excess cash, for other times when you might have more expenses than you forecasted.

Budgeting Tools

Many people like to create a budget on paper. It's easy to use, can be used by either spouse, and can be carried around in your briefcase if you desire. For a sample personal/family budget form, see page 33.

On the other hand, an electronic budget is easy to use, saves time, and provides more useful information than a budget done in paper. You can always print out the budget if you want paper records.

The biggest advantage of an electronic budget is that it can provide "what if" projections, such as "can I double up on my Visa payment this month, without running into trouble next month?" Besides this, an electronic budget can save time by doing the math for you, and saving repetitive monthly expense entries.

Included among the business tools at the *CCH Business Owner's Toolkit,* our Internet website (http://www.toolkit.cch.com), is an interactive personal budget form that you can easily download and customize. We've formatted the worksheet and put in most of the income and expense categories for you. All you have to do is put in your numbers and print it.

There are also a number of good, inexpensive software packages on the market that can fill the bill, and can also keep track of your checking account and facilitate electronic banking. Check out the shelves of your local electronics, computer, or bookstore to see the latest versions.

Current Arrangements and Documents

While you may want to write on a clean slate when constructing your plan for building wealth, you should consider the effect that existing legal documents and arrangements may have on your plans.

Some of these arrangements may be readily changeable, such as most wills and trusts. Others, such as contracts and marriage dissolution agreements, may be difficult or impossible to amend. Still others can be changed if you're willing to pay some kind of penalty or fee, such as variable annuities, or mortgages that can be refinanced.

Your first task is to locate and organize any documents and other evidence of your legal obligations and relationships. Once you have done this, you'll need to make sure that you account for these arrangements wherever they would be relevant to your wealth-building plans.

Existing Contracts and Arrangements

Here is a list of some of the items you should take a look at:

- **Marriage dissolution agreements** — *alimony, property settlements, pre-nuptial agreements, and child-support agreements fall within this category. Whether you receive such payments, or are the one required to make them, they will have to be factored into financial and estate plans.*

- **Business organization documents and materials** — *how you have organized your business from a legal standpoint (sole proprietorship, partnership, limited liability company, or corporation) will impact on your exposure to legal liability, how your business is taxed, and several issues relating to constructing a financial and estate plan.*

- **Business transfer/continuation agreements and plans** — *any documents pertaining to your plans and agreements aimed at continuing or disposing of your business (including insurance policies to implement such plans) should be located. Unless you have made reasonably detailed plans to continue your business at your death or disability, and also have a workable plan to fund them — whether by insurance or an accumulated side fund — as a practical matter it is extremely unlikely that your business will survive as a going concern.*

- **Contracts** — *contracts (including those that may require a continuing monetary outlay by you, and those that may provide you with an income source) can be expected to affect your current personal cash-flow situation. If the contracts are large, and of long duration, they may also have to be factored into your plans for passing on your wealth to your chosen heirs.*

- **Wills and trusts** — *having these documents available will be necessary when you begin work on putting together a plan to dispose of your wealth to your chosen heirs at your death.*

- **Joint ownership property** — *property that is held as a joint tenancy or as a tenancy in common. Knowing which of these forms of joint ownership applies to each piece of property you own is important for planning your estate.*

- **History of making large gifts** — *if you have made any gifts of money or property worth more than $10,000 to individuals, or have made large charitable gifts, you'll want to collect records of these gifts (including any federal gift tax returns you filed). This information will be needed by you — or your advisors — to create your estate plan.*

WHAT ARE YOUR GOALS?

We've all heard the adage: "Be careful what you wish for, you may get it." A more realistic statement about attaining financial security might be: "Be careful what you wish for and *how you plan to get it*, or you won't." This may sound pessimistic, but it's really not. You *can* succeed in reaching your goals for building wealth for your lifetime use and passing it along to your heirs. But, in order to do it, you'll need to do things a bit differently than most people, who rarely create workable personal financial plans or, if they do, don't follow through long enough to see the benefit in them.

Envisioning the Goal

For most of us, one of the first steps in goal setting is finding a concrete goal or goals that motivate us emotionally. How about that powder blue '59 Caddy convertible, the retirement on Maui, the ability to cut back the hours you work, or the satisfaction you would gain from setting up and funding your own charitable foundation? Spend a day or two making up a list of the things you've always wanted, and prioritizing them. You'll probably find that you have some short-term goals, and some long-term goals.

Once you have come up with the goals that will push you on to action, don't let the dream die. Do enough research on your goal so that you know it "inside and out." Imagine at least once a day how it would be to have your goal, and how your life would be improved by having it. If the goal can be represented by a picture (such as the '59 Caddy), keep one or more pictures of it where you're bound to notice it.

Making Your Goals Measurable

In order to make your goal measurable, we suggest two steps: reducing your goals to a monetary amount and setting a deadline to reach the goal.

Case Study — Measuring Your Goals

Nathan Chicago, who owns and operates a newsstand, has been dutifully saving $500 each month. He has a detailed picture in his mind's eye of what would be the ultimate retirement property: a small cottage overlooking a white sand beach on an island in the Caribbean.

Although Nathan's vivid imagination may be enough to encourage him to continue saving the $500 per month, this will not necessarily ensure that he will reach his retirement goal. Without knowing how much such a property would cost, Nathan runs the risk that he won't have enough saved at his retirement to buy such a property. After a lifetime of saving for the goal, this would be a devastating disappointment. But his disappointment probably could be avoided if he had known from the beginning that he would have to increase his monthly saving, or channel the savings into higher yielding investments.

But even if Nathan knows what his "dream property" would cost, he still has a problem: he hasn't set a target date to attain the goal. Setting a deadline will tell you how long it will take you to save for the goal, and tell you at any point in time whether you are on track for meeting the goal.

Now let's assume that Nathan is saving $500 each month for his retirement goal. He has so far saved $12,000 (which he has invested in CDs paying 4½-percent interest). He finds out that his ideal retirement property now costs about $100,000 (with local real estate agents telling him that it's likely to appreciate in value at about 5 percent per year), and he wants to retire in 20 years.

To figure if he is on track to meet his goal, let's compare the price he'll have to pay for a similar property in 20 years with how much money he will have accumulated by this time:

Cost of property:		$ 265,300
Projected savings:		
Growth of $12,000 at 4.5 percent for 20 years:	28,944	
Growth of $500 per month at 4.5 percent for 20 years:	188,228	217,172
		(48,128)

Nathan has a problem: he will be $48,128 short! He has a couple of obvious choices to remedy this situation: (1) he could increase his monthly savings (an increase of $148/mo. would do it), or (2) he could move some or all of his savings into higher yield investments. If he increases his yield from 4.5 percent to 6.25 percent, his present savings of $500 per month would be sufficient.

PLANNING TO REACH YOUR GOALS

If you have a financial calculator, you can closely estimate how much attaining your goal will cost and whether you will reach it based on a particular saving and investment plan, by following the steps outlined below (if you're not familiar with these very useful business tools, your accountant or financial planner can help you with the computations):

First, estimate the cost of the goal at the date you plan to attain it. Take the current cost of the goal and adjust it for inflation up through the time you will reach the goal.

Example

After investigation, you believe that the cost of your goal (which is currently $50,000) will go up about 4.5 percent per year for the next 25 years. Assuming you want to reach the goal at the end of year 25, you must accumulate $150,270.

Second, take the amount of your current savings on hand, if any, that you will earmark for the goal. Compute how much these savings will grow between now and the date on which you want to reach your goal. (The process of doing this is identical to that of figuring how much a particular item will increase in cost over time, except that instead of an estimated inflation rate, you'll use an estimated growth rate that should exceed inflation.)

Third, determine how much you will periodically save to reach your goal, and how much this investment will increase over time based on the estimated yield over the life of the investment. Unless you will accumulate these savings in a tax-free form (such as municipal bonds or an insurance policy), you should make this computation based on after-tax yields.

Fourth, add the amount of your projected investments as of the date you wish to attain the goal (amounts determined under the second and third steps, above) and compare this amount to the amount of your projected future cost of the goal.

If the amount of your projected investments is greater than the amount of your projected cost of the goal, you'll know your saving and investment plan should work out to allow you to attain your goal, provided that the various assumptions you made in the course of setting up your plan are correct, and do not change for the worse over the course of time.

If the amount of the projected cost of your goal exceeds what your saving and investment plan will generate, you'll need to consider making changes necessary to reach your goal.

Making Necessary Changes

If the amount of your projected investments is less than the amount of your projected cost of the goal, something must be done or it's unlikely that you will be able to achieve the goal. If this is the case, you can make one or more of the following adjustments to bring your plan back on track:

- Save more money toward the goal.

- Look for investments with higher yields.

- Give yourself a longer period of time to attain the goal.

- Reduce the cost of your goal.

Implementing the Plan

You have now taken the important steps of identifying what you have now, setting goals, and planning how to reach your goals. But as important as each of these steps is, none of them is as vital as that of carrying the plan forward and making it work.

The importance of not waiting is illustrated by this example:

Case Study — The Importance of Putting Your Plan into Action

John Morris, a 28-year-old business owner, has gone through all the steps suggested in this chapter. Based on his investigations, John is seriously considering making a yearly investment of $2,000 in an IRA-qualified mutual fund that invests primarily in small, growth company stocks. He learns that although he won't be able to get a tax deduction for his contributions because he's over the applicable income limitations, the income that accrues in the account will not be taxed until he begins to withdraw it at retirement.

Based on the track record of a particular growth company mutual fund over its entire lifetime, John asks the broker to project what an annual $2,000 IRA contribution would grow to by age 65, assuming an annual yield of 12 percent. If John will begin contributing this year on his 29th birthday, the broker's projections show the following:

Age	Projected Account Balance on Birthday (not guaranteed!)
30	$ 4,240
35	16,230
40	41,309
45	85,507
50	163,397
55	300,679
60	542,604
64	863,357
65	968,959

John will have something approaching one million dollars ($968,959) at retirement by contributing $2,000 each year beginning at age 29. But if he waits just one year later to begin his investment plan, and still retires at 65, he will have $863,357, which is $105,602 less!

Monitoring the Plan

Nothing lasts forever, and certainly not a personal financial plan.

A lot of things can happen in life that may make it necessary for you to change one or more parts of your plan. When you are confronted with such a change in circumstances, the first rule is: don't panic! It's quite likely that some, if not most, of your plan will still be O.K. Nevertheless, you'll need to carefully review it to see if it still represents what you want, what you need, and how to get there.

Remember, as bad as living with an outdated plan is, *dying* with an outdated plan may be worse, since your family may no longer be able to correct the problem.

Some changes will have a direct and immediate monetary effect on your financial plan. Such changes include:

- The cost of your goal increases or decreases.

- Your ability to make the required savings to reach your goal increases or decreases.

- The yield (interest, dividends, and capital gains) on your savings or investment increases or decreases.

- You need (or want) to change the time for attaining your goal.

In addition, there are changes that affect your financial plan less directly. These indirect changes may be just as important, but you may be less likely to think about their connection to the financial planning that you have done.

- **Tax law changes** — if, for example, the tax rates go up, you may well have to count on increased savings or increased yields to make up for the additional money lost to the tax collector.

- **Business climate changes** — significant changes in how the U.S. economy is functioning quite likely will affect your plan. A general rise in interest rates, for instance, can be expected to drive down the value of your fixed interest rate investments, making it necessary for you to increase your savings or increase your investment yield (something that should be less difficult because of the climbing interest rates).

- **Personal family changes** — this category is probably hardest to get a handle on, since any number of changes to your family situation may greatly impact on your financial plan. No list can contain all of the things you should watch for, but the following list includes some of the most common factors:

  — new children (by birth, adoption, or by marriage), new grandchildren, nieces, or nephews

  — changes to marital status: divorce, separation, remarriage

  — health problems suffered by you or your family members

  — job or business changes that affect your current income

  — sudden wealth (such as by inheritance), and sudden financial reverses (such as from a legal judgment)

— your disability or death (or the disability or death of family members or business partners or associates)

— changed educational plans for your children or grandchildren

What If You Need Help?

Most small business owners simply don't have the time to spend creating a detailed financial plan, let alone monitoring the investment choices needed to keep the plan on track.

Thus, it will be imperative to get help from professionals: your lawyer, accountant, stock brokers, bankers, insurance agents. In order to make sure that all these professionals are working together towards the same goal, many people find it helpful to consult a fee-based financial planner who can keep your "big picture" in mind and who will call in specialists as needed. We suggest you go to a *fee-based* planner because these people are not working on commission and thus are less likely to suggest that you purchase expensive financial products that you don't need.

You can seek help on a particular part of the plan, or a particular question, or ask for a full-fledged financial plan to be created for you.

Warning

Before you commit to working with a particular financial planner, and especially before you agree to hand over any money to be actively managed for you, we strongly recommend that you request a number of references to other clients that the financial planner has worked for. Preferably, they should be other small business owners. Ideally, you want a planner who has at least five years of successful experience.

Chapter 30

Building Wealth Outside the Business

If you are like many small business owners — particularly those just starting out — you have virtually all of your personal assets invested in your business. Perhaps you've even taken a second mortgage on your house to gain needed capital. This may be necessary and advisable now, but as your business develops, it will become prudent to branch out into other investments as well.

A diversified investment portfolio embodies that old saw that warns you against "putting all your eggs in one basket." By having several different kinds of investments, such as stocks, bonds, real estate, and precious metals, you greatly reduce the chance that a particular economic or legal change will devastate your financial security.

In the previous chapter, we dealt with the important topic of following a step-by-step process for identifying and reaching your goals. Here, we focus on the major areas that you'll have to consider when you start to actually construct your plan: compensating yourself as a business owner, as the starting point for pulling money out of your business; building a retirement fund, which is generally the parking place for outside investments; and insuring your life and income. (For a discussion of health insurance, see Chapter 19.)

COMPENSATING YOURSELF

How to get money out of your business . . . the entrepreneur's eternal quest! Since you're in business for yourself, you can pay yourself what you always knew you were worth or you can elect to plow most of your cash back into growing your business.

You may also partake of the tax advantages inherent in paying family members who are in lower brackets, or granting yourself and your employees company benefits such as a nice retirement plan or a company car.

Chances are you'll eventually do a little of each. Often it comes down to a decision as to what's more urgent, your needs or the needs of the business. You need to pay your mortgage and feed your kids, but the business may need to meet debt/equity ratios to pacify your bankers. How much personal luxury are you willing to forego or defer to achieve stability in your business?

There are an amazingly large number of legal, and even tax-advantaged, ways to take money out of your business. The form they take often depends on whether your business is incorporated or not. Generally, corporations can provide better tax-advantaged fringe benefits to the owners, because owners are treated as employees. However, you'll have to balance that advantage with the fact that corporate profits are taxed twice.

On the next few pages, we'll outline the most commonly used ways to get money out of your business in a form that's most useful to you.

Your Salary or Owner's Draw

The level of compensation you draw from your business will undoubtedly vary widely from time to time due to the ebb and flow of your personal and business needs. At least initially, don't plan on taking more out of the business than will cover your bare-bones needs for food, clothing, and shelter. Better yet, try to keep an alternate source of income going to support yourself and your family until you can be sure that your business is financially viable. It's much more common for new business owners to underestimate their business's hunger for cash, than to overestimate it.

Once your business is in the black, you can begin pulling some money out as compensation for all the hours of hard work you've contributed. If your business is structured as a sole proprietorship, you will pay yourself directly out of the profits through an "owner's draw." It's best to take your draw at regular intervals such as weekly or monthly, so that you can arrange to have adequate cash flow from the business to cover it.

If your business is organized as another type of "flow through" entity (such as a partnership, LLC, or S corporation), your cash compensation level will be dictated more by the cash-flow characteristics of the operation than by tax law imperatives.

Since you will pay individual income and payroll taxes on your portion of the profits of any non-corporate business whether you draw a formal salary or not, it's a distinction without much difference. In an S corporation, you'll pay income taxes on your share of the profits, but payroll taxes only on your salary

Of course, employees having no ownership interest are paid wages or a salary, regardless of the structure of the business.

Salary from a C corporation. The term "salary" is very important to owners of C corporations. While corporate profits are taxed twice, the corporation gets a business deduction for your salary.

Thus, a key determination in setting your salary is the difference between the corporation's and your personal tax rate. For a comparison of these rates, see the table on page 451.

If your corporation's highest tax bracket is lower than your highest personal bracket, the tax benefit derived from the company's deduction of your compensation will be less than the tax you personally must pay on it as income. Conversely, if your corporate bracket is higher than what you think your personal tax rate will be for a certain year, you might consider increasing your compensation.

With a C corporation, it's usually a good idea to keep your compensation as regular and level as possible to avoid waving any red flags at the IRS. The major problem to avoid is having the IRS recharacterize some of your salary as disguised dividends, which are not deductible to the company. This becomes a danger if your salary grows beyond what is considered reasonable for your position.

Work Smart

The criteria for judging "reasonable compensation," as determined by years of IRS examination and litigation, include:

- *the nature and size of the business claiming the deduction*

- *the nature and scope of the work you do for the business*

- *any special qualifications you may have*

- *the availability of others to perform the same duties*

- *general economic conditions*

- *compensation compared to business income and profits*

- *compensation relative to dividends*

- *compensation relative to other employees*

- *compensation relative to stock ownership if the business is a corporation with more than one shareholder*

- *your compensation history for past services*

Personal service corporations. You should also be aware that for personal service corporations (PSCs), all profits are taxed at a flat rate of 35 percent. PSCs are defined as corporations performing services in the fields of health, law, engineering, architecture, accounting, actuarial science, the performing arts, or consulting, where substantially all of the stock is held by employees, retired employees, or their estates. PSCs can generally pay out all or most of the corporation's profits as salary, since arguably all the company's profits are the result of the efforts of its owners.

Corporate Dividends

Dividends sound nice. You buy a stock, it pays dividends, and you're a happy investor. In fact, if you own a C corporation and it owns some GM or Disney or IBM, a whopping 70 percent of the dividends your company receives from those great investments are *excluded* from taxation (as long as your company owns less than 50 percent of GM, Disney, or IBM, that is).

But for a privately held company, dividends are usually an expensive pain in the neck. When your closely held company pays dividends to you and your fellow shareholders, you must pay income tax on them but your company does not enjoy a deduction for them. But that's double taxation, you say! And you're right, it is!

On the other hand, your salary is subject to FICA taxes, whereas dividends are not. So, if your corporation's tax rate is 15 percent, it's worth it to pay at least some dividends in lieu of salary. An amount paid as dividends may be taxed twice (at the corporate tax rate, and then again at the individual tax rate) but your salary is essentially taxed twice also (at the combined FICA tax rate of 15.30 percent and again at the individual tax rate.) The minute your company makes more than $50,000 it gets into the 25 percent corporate bracket and payroll taxes look cheap by comparison.

Then there's the rule that if you don't pay your profits out, your company could get socked with an accumulated earnings tax. A C corporation can usually retain up to $250,000 without adverse consequences, but a personal service corporation can only retain $150,000.

Both types of entities may be permitted to retain amounts in excess of these limits if it can be demonstrated that the additional working capital meets the reasonable needs of the business; for example, if you need to retain cash to buy a new plant.

There is a happy medium to be struck in your dividend policy. If your firm is profitable, it's usually wise to declare a modest but regular dividend. Think of it as insurance against future audits.

Delayed Compensation

In the early stages of your business, you may be investing in the business first and planning to pay yourself later on.

In this instance, it's okay to minimize salary and document your undercompensation for that particular year by noting in your corporate minute books the complete details of why you took less pay than you earned. Also note that you elected to defer or delay payment until such time as the company can afford to disburse what it owes you. This will help defray contentions of excess compensation in later years.

There is almost never a problem with this method as long as you document the process as you go along. Startup is a cash-critical phase and even the IRS understands that. And this technique will help you in the event that you decide to take in another shareholder down the road. The debt of the company to you for services already rendered will be duly recorded and will not be in doubt.

Bonuses

In a C corporation, paying yourself a large, last-minute bonus at the end of a good year is not a habit you want to get into. A large end-of-year bonus will frequently be attacked by the IRS as a disguised dividend. Bonuses in a C corporation should be performance-based, with parameters established and documented in writing *in advance*.

On the other hand, if your business is organized as a sole proprietorship, partnership, LLC, or S corporation, it's not a bad idea to take a small owner's draw during the year, and then pay yourself a year-end bonus after you know how profitable your operation was that year. Regardless of what the payments are called, all the profits will be taxable to the owners, so the IRS has little concern about the timing of bonuses for these types of businesses.

Loans

What are loans doing in this list? Loans aren't compensation, are they? Well, the answer to that is that they often get reclassified as compensation (or, worse yet, as dividends) by the IRS, so you may as well think of them in that context. Then you'll be motivated to avoid the pitfalls that cause this reclassification.

The temptation for a small business owner to use his company as a bank is a mighty one, and one to be mightily resisted. The owner of a closely held corporation is able to borrow from the company on favorable terms and repay when convenient, two considerations usually absent with outside lenders. Going the other way, an owner can also make loans *to* the company and earn a self-determined rate of interest. And the potential for the abuse of these powers is what inspires the IRS to increased vigilance in this area.

Loans, in order to elude reclassification, must be documented in writing, have a set repayment schedule, and carry an interest rate that can be considered consistent with the going rates charged by third parties. Otherwise, the IRS will generally treat the parties as having paid and received interest at the market rate on loans over $10,000. This means you'll pay tax on an amount of interest you never even received!

Basic Fringe Benefits

The value of so-called fringe benefits can enhance your total compensation enormously. Many have the advantage of being deductible to your business but not taxable to you.

The whole laundry list of fundamental fringe benefits — medical, dental, disability and group life coverage, dependent care and education assistance, business travel expense reimbursement, director liability insurance, employee discounts, spousal death benefits, group legal coverage, low-interest loans, company cars, professional association dues and subscriptions (and maybe even use of the company gym) is all very nice — but the *real* wealth-building benefits to small business owners come in two forms: retirement plans (see page 592) and life insurance (see page 610).

Warning

While C corporations can fully deduct the cost of medical insurance for owners as well as employees, there is a limitation on medical benefits provided to partners, proprietors, and S corporation shareholders who own more than 2 percent of the stock. These costs are deductible by the business but must be reported as income to the owners. On the owner's tax return, only 60 percent of the insurance premium is deductible in 1999-2001. (For 2002, 70 percent is deductible. This percentage is scheduled to rise in later years.) If your spouse is an employee of your business, however, group insurance premiums will be deductible for the spouse and for you as well, because you'll be the spouse of an employee who qualifies for coverage.

Expenses Paid by the Business

Legitimate deductible expenses permitted for travel, meals, entertaining clients, automobile expenses and the like, if properly claimed and documented, give an owner many advantages not enjoyed by regular employees. Considerable benefit can be gained through the use of deductions for company cars and expense accounts, as long as they are supported by extensive documentation that substantiates their legitimate business purpose.

But often the business owner is tempted to go too far, and gets into difficulty. In some cases the founder, failing to differentiate between himself and his business, plunders the business assets at will. After all, it's his business, so it's his money and he can spend it on himself if he likes, right? He's worked hard to build the business up and now he's going to reap the tax-free rewards. Forget compensation on which taxes must be paid, he thinks. He'll just pay his expenses directly out of the company. Or, if he's in a cash-heavy business, skim some off the top and not run it through the books.

But an owner who uses his business to finance his personal living expenses or extravagant indulgences can expect frequent and costly visits from Uncle Sam's minions at the IRS.

Warning

IRS agents can look at many sources of information, not just the books of the company, for proof of a business owner's spending habits. The type of car you drive, the value of your residence, your travel patterns, and general spending habits are all grist for the IRS mill. If your "official" salary and other distributions from your business would not appear to support your lifestyle, you're a sitting duck for severe penalties.

Rental Income

One widely used method for building personal wealth is for you to retain any real estate used in your business in your own name rather than the business's name.

Then, you lease the property to your company. This gives you income that can be increased in later years as the business prospers. At the same time it gives your company a deduction. More importantly, down the road, when the property has appreciated significantly, that appreciation will not be double-taxed as it would if your corporation owned it.

Warning

The IRS expressly forbids this method, however, if you are using a home office. If you want to lease part of your own home to yourself, don't try to deduct the rent on your tax return.

Real estate is also a good vehicle for family income shifting when the time comes, since the property can be given away to the younger generation even if the business is eventually sold to a third party.

Family Payroll

Another way of getting money out of your business at a minimum tax cost is to employ family members and put them on the payroll.

For example, if your kids help in your business, you can pay them and they'll undoubtedly be in a lower tax bracket than you are. Then they can save their earnings to pay for college. But they must actually perform legitimate jobs for your firm, and jobs that they are qualified to do. If not, you run the risk of having their pay reclassified as "gifts," which are not deductible to the business.

The most common way to utilize young children in your business is for them to provide cleaning services, or routine copying, filing, and typing. These are jobs that even a 10-year-old is clearly capable of performing, and jobs that you'd arguably have to pay someone to do if your child were not available.

Putting your spouse on the payroll won't give you any tax savings if you file a joint return, but it will permit you to include the spouse in the retirement plan of the business, which would be a big tax benefit of a different sort.

RETIREMENT PLANNING

Many small business people think they can rely on the value of their business when they sell it at retirement and fail to see the importance of a retirement plan. This is a big mistake for two reasons. First, there is no guarantee your business will be worth anything, much less what you expect, when the time to hang up your spikes arrives. A willing and able buyer may not be waiting breathlessly on your doorstep.

Secondly, as tax-favored, wealth-building vehicles, retirement plans are hard to beat. Contributions to a qualified plan are deductible to the business, but not taxed to the individual until distributed at retirement. And income earned on the plan assets accumulates on a tax-deferred basis as well. Hence, profits can be taken out of your business and not taxed to you until you receive them at retirement, at which time most folks are in a lower tax bracket.

It's almost foolish to pass up these tax-favored methods of reaping the benefits of the miracle of compound interest. At the same time, your retirement funds can be invested in a wide variety of assets, providing much-needed diversification and sheltering you against the possibility that your business may suffer an unexpected reversal down the road.

Estimating Your Retirement Needs

The first step in retirement planning is to determine what you will need and want during retirement and what amount of income will sustain that lifestyle. One method is to prepare a detailed proposed budget of your living expenses during retirement. This is a good strategy for those who are fairly close to retirement, and who can therefore make fairly accurate budget assumptions.

An easier way to plan for retirement, particularly for those who are under 55 or so, is to state your retirement income objective as a certain percentage of your preretirement income. Many retirees live on anything from 60 percent to 80 percent of their preretirement income. It's usually better to plan at the high end of the range to allow yourself flexibility should your investments not work out as you hoped.

For example, suppose you are a 45-year-old, single male who intends to retire at age 65. You estimate your annual retirement needs at 80 percent of your preretirement income of $60,000. You also estimate that your Social Security benefits will amount to 20 percent of your current salary.

A quick computation would result in the following:

Retirement Needs Computation	
Current annual salary	$ 60,000
% of current salary to be replaced	x 80%
Annual retirement income target	$ 48,000
Minus: employer-provided pension benefits	(21,000)
Minus: Social Security benefits (assume 20% of salary)	(12,000)
Required annual income from savings and investment funds (in today's dollars).	$ 15,000
Life expectancy — years of retirement as shown in insurance tables	x 15 years
Required target savings and investment fund needed at retirement (in today's dollars)	$ 225,000

Required target savings and investment fund needed at retirement (in today's dollars)	$ 225,000
Minus: Current savings and investments:	
Individual Retirement Account	(20,000)
401(k) Plan	(50,000)
Savings account	(5,000)
Other investments	(25,000)
Required additions to savings and investment fund	$ 125,000
Years to retirement (retirement age - current age)	÷ 20 years
Annual savings required to reach savings and investment fund target	$ 6,250

Notice that this calculation is based on current dollars. For ease of computation, we've assumed that the positive investment return on the funds saved and the negative effect of taxes and inflation on the savings are approximately equal. This would generally be the case if you invested all your money in balanced mutual funds.

If, in fact, your retirement goal is at least 4 years in the future, you should consider higher-risk investments that have a greater potential for yields that significantly beat the inflation rate over the long-term.

Estimating What You Currently Have

The second phase of retirement planning is to estimate the resources you currently have that will provide income to you during your retirement years. You may have heard about the so-called "three-legged stool." What this means is that most people will fund their retirement primarily through three main sources.

- **Social Security,** which will pay you a percentage of your annual income based on how much you made over your lifetime. On the average, Social Security benefits amount to about 40 percent of preretirement income, but those at the higher end of the pay scale may receive a much lower percentage.

- **A company pension** which, depending on your work history, may be generally equal to anywhere between 50 percent to 70 percent of your preretirement salary. Small business owners should seriously consider setting up a pension plan to take advantage of the important tax breaks available.

- **Personal savings and investments** which will provide as much or as little as you saved during your working years.

Social Security

The role Social Security will play in your retirement plan depends on your opinions about the system's continued viability and on what action the government takes between now and the time you retire. For younger people, it may be best not to count on receiving any benefits at all, and then perhaps be pleasantly surprised if any are available when you retire!

Currently there are four distinct types of benefits provided, all financed by payroll taxes:

- **Retirement benefits,** which you can elect to receive at any time after age 62, are based on the number of years that you have worked and the amount of money you have earned. Your spouse and, in some cases, your children may also be eligible for benefits based on your earnings records. Coverage has also been extended to ex-spouses if the marriage lasted at least 10 years and the ex-spouse has not remarried.

- **Survivor's benefits** are a form of life insurance, providing annuity payments to your spouse and dependent children after your death.

- **Disability insurance** ensures you a monthly income if you are unable to work because of an illness or disability, regardless of age.

- **Medicare** provides both hospital insurance (Part A) and voluntary medical insurance (Part B) for men and women over age 65 and disabled younger people.

How Much Will Your Benefits Be?

Your Social Security benefit will be based on the Social Security Administration's record of your earnings during your 35 highest-paid years. You can get a copy of this record at any time. And you should definitely do so! The record is called the "Earnings and Benefit Estimate Statement" and can be requested by contacting the SSA via the Internet at http://www.ssa.gov or calling their toll-free number at 1-800-772-1213.

The SSA will also calculate your estimated retirement benefit, based on the assumption that your earnings will remain relatively constant for the rest of your career. This information is free; of course, it's not guaranteed to be accurate since your earnings might not remain constant and, more importantly, the laws regarding calculation of benefits can change at any time.

When Can You Collect Benefits?

At the earliest, Social Security retirement benefits can begin at age 62 at a reduced level. Normal retirement with full benefits begins at 65, 66, or 67 depending on the year you were born; or you can wait until age 70 and get higher benefits.

Early retirement. If you take early retirement, your monthly benefit is reduced depending on the number of months between your early retirement and your normal retirement. The following table can be used to calculate how early retirement will affect your monthly benefit.

How Early Retirement Will Reduce Monthly Benefits					
Months Early	**% of Full Benefits**	**Months Early**	**% of Full Benefits**	**Months Early**	**% of Full Benefits**
2	98.9	22	87.8	42*	77.5
4	97.8	24	86.7	44*	76.7
6	96.7	26	85.6	46*	75.8
8	95.6	28	84.4	48*	75.0
10	94.4	30	83.3	50*	74.4
12	93.3	32	82.2	52*	73.3
14	92.2	34	81.1	54*	72.5
16	91.1	36*	80.0	56*	71.7
18	90.0	38*	79.2	58*	70.8
20	88.9	40*	78.3	60*	70.0
*These percentages apply as full retirement age rises to 67.					

Although each monthly check is smaller, you will probably get more of them, so retiring early may result in greater total benefits.

Normal (full) retirement. You can receive full benefits by waiting until you attain normal or full retirement age. Full retirement age is rising in stages to age 67 for people born between 1938 and 1960.

Age at Which Full Benefits Are Available			
Year of Birth	**Full Retirement Age**	**Year of Birth**	**Full Retirement Age**
pre-1938	65	1955	66+2 months
1938	65+2 months	1956	66+4 months
1939	65+4 months	1957	66+6 months
1940	65+6 months	1958	66+8 months
1941	65+8 months	1959	66+10 months
1942	65+10 months	1960 or later	67
1943-1954	66		

Late retirement. Uncle Sam gives you an added incentive to stay in the work force by giving you a bonus for each year you delay collecting benefits. Up to 1990, the bonus for delaying benefits meant a 3.5 percent increase for each year delayed. But this percentage is being raised in steps up to 8 percent.

Late Retirement Bonus			
Year You Were Born	**Annual % Increase in Benefits**	**Year You Were Born**	**Annual % Increase in Benefits**
1917-1924	3.0%	1935-1936	6.0%
1925-1926	3.5	1937-1938	6.5
1927-1928	4.0	1939-1940	7.0
1929-1930	4.5	1941-1942	7.5
1931-1932	5.0	1943 or later	8.0
1933-1934	5.5		

Working while receiving benefits. If you begin receiving benefits and continue to work, your benefits may be reduced. If you were age 65-69, your benefits would be reduced by one-third of the amount of any earnings over $17,000 for 2000, $25,000 for 2001 and $30,000 for 2002.

Under the current law, if you think you'll earn more than the limit for your age group, it's usually best to delay starting Social Security benefits. The combination of losing 33 to 50 cents on the dollar in benefits, plus having to pay normal FICA and income taxes on your earnings, can mean that you'll pay an effective tax rate of 75 percent or more. Although, this may change, as efforts by lawmakers to modify or repeal this earnings limit are gaining momentum.

Company Pension Plans

Company pension plan benefits may be the second source of your retirement income. You may be getting benefits from a plan you participated in before starting your business, or you may establish one as an employer, to cover yourself as well as your employees. There are two categories of pension plans: qualified plans and nonqualified plans.

- **Qualified plans** meet the requirements of the Employee Retirement Income Security Act of 1974 (ERISA) and the Internal Revenue Code and qualify for four significant tax benefits.

  — The income generated by the plan assets are not subject to income tax.

— An employer is entitled to a current tax deduction for contributions to the plan.

— The plan participants (you and your employees) do not have to pay income tax on the amounts contributed on their behalf until the year the funds are distributed to them by the employer.

— Under the right circumstances, beneficiaries of qualified plan distributions are afforded special tax treatment.

- **Nonqualified plans** are those not meeting the ERISA guidelines and the requirement of the Internal Revenue Code. They cannot avail themselves of the preferential tax treatment.

Because the tax benefits are so valuable, most employers make use of qualified plans if at all possible. Nonqualified plans are used more rarely, when the goal is to provide deferred compensation exclusively for one or more executives or key employees.

Save Money

If a business owner has employees but is unable to afford retirement contributions for all of them, as would be required under a qualified retirement plan, one solution is for the owner to (a) contribute to an IRA, and (b) individually purchase a tax-advantaged insurance product such as a variable annuity. The business will not get any tax deductions for payments into these vehicles, but the owner may be able to deduct IRA contributions, depending on income level. Investments in both the IRA and the annuity will build up, tax-free, and the owner will have a retirement fund outside the value of the business.

Requirements for a Qualified Plan

To satisfy the general requirements, a qualified plan must be permanent, meaning it cannot have a planned, definite expiration date. Although the employer may reserve the right to change or terminate the plan or to discontinue operations, abandoning the plan for other than business necessity within a few years is evidence that the plan was not a bona fide program from its inception.

The plan must be a definite written program that is communicated to all employees. All plan assets must be held in trust by one or more trustees. The plan must be for the exclusive benefit of the employees and their beneficiaries. There can be no reversion of the trust's assets to the employer, other than forfeitures. Funding can be provided from employer's or employees' contributions, or both.

Participation/coverage rules. To meet the minimum standards, at least a certain percentage of the non-highly-compensated employees must be covered by the plan and a certain number of those covered employees must actually be in the plan. There are limits on the plan's ability to discriminate in favor of employees who are officers, shareholders, or highly compensated, by making larger contributions on their behalf or providing them with better benefits. The plan may condition eligibility on age and service, but generally cannot postpone participation beyond the date the employee attains the age of 21 and the date on which the employee completes one year of service.

Vesting rules. Qualified plans must allow participants to "vest," or acquire a nonforfeitable right to the money being set aside for them, within a fairly short period.

There are two permitted vesting methods: five-year cliff vesting in which the participant become fully vested after five years of service (with zero vesting for the first four years), and seven-year gradual vesting in which the participant becomes increasingly vested (usually 20 percent per year) after three years of service. Although the employer can have vesting rules more lenient than these, the rules cannot be more restrictive. An employee must become fully vested no later than the normal retirement age specified in the plan. The plan must also provide rules on how breaks in service affect vesting rights.

Required communications. Each year the employer must furnish a document called a Summary Plan Description, written in plain English understandable to the average plan participant, detailing the amount of pension benefits, requirements for receiving those payments, and any conditions that might prevent someone from receiving them.

Qualified pension plans can be divided into two broad categories: defined benefit plans, and defined contribution plans. There are also some hybrid plans that combine features of both types of plans.

Defined Benefit Plans

A defined-benefit plan is one set up to provide a predetermined retirement benefit to owners and employees, or their beneficiaries. The retirement benefit is expressed either in terms of a certain dollar amount per month, or a specific percentage of the worker's compensation at the end of his or her career.

The amounts an employer must contribute each year to a defined benefit plan are very complex to determine, and require the work of an actuary. The assets of the plan are held in a pool, rather than in individual accounts for each employee, and as a result, the employees have no voice in investment decisions. Once established, the employer must continue to fund the plan, even if the company has no profits. Since the employer makes a specific promise to pay a certain sum in the future, it is the employer who assumes the risk of fluctuations in the value of the investment pool.

The maximum annual retirement benefit you can receive from a defined-benefit plan is the lesser of a stated amount adjusted for inflation (in 2000 it is $135,000), or 100 percent of the participant's average compensation for the three highest consecutive years.

Defined Contribution Plans

In recent years, defined contribution plans have become much more popular than defined benefit plans. The primary reasons are that they are much easier (and thus, cheaper) to administer, and they don't require the employer to guarantee a certain level of benefits to retired workers. Instead, the employer, participant, or both contribute a set dollar amount or percentage of compensation for each worker every year, and these contributions are invested. When the worker retires, he or she gets whatever value the investment account may have at the time.

The government sets a limit on how much can be contributed in each employee's name each year, no matter how many different plans he or she participates in. The total amount that can be contributed in your name is the lesser of $30,000 or 25 percent of your annual earnings.

Defined-contribution plans come in several flavors:

- **Profit-sharing plans** — profit-sharing plans are now the most popular type of pension plan, especially for small businesses. They offer the greatest flexibility in contributions and are simple to administer. With this type of plan, each year the employer has the discretion of contributing nothing to the plan, or making contributions based on a predetermined formula that may take into account company profits for the year. The ceiling on total contributions for the year is 15 percent of the compensation of all plan participants.

- **Money-purchase plans** — in the money-purchase plans, the employer is obligated to contribute to each employee's account every year even if the company didn't make a profit. The contributions are determined by a formula, usually a specific percentage of each employee's compensation and must be made annually.

Target Benefit Plans

A target benefit plan is a plan in which you, as the employer, establish a target benefit for your employees and make contributions on that basis, but where each employee's actual pension is based on the amount in the employee's individual account. The employer does not guarantee that the target will be reached. In a sense, target benefit plans combine elements of both defined benefit and defined contribution plans and are known as "hybrid plans."

Case Study — Target Benefit Plans

Here's some general information about the Smith-Jones Corporation's employees and owners:

Smith-Jones Corporation Census			
Names of Employees	**Age**	**Years of Service**	**Annual Compensation**
Owner Smith	50	25	$60,000
Owner Jones	49	25	60,000
Joe Employee	30	5	35,000
Jim Employee	27	4	30,000
June Employee	26	3	27,000

To illustrate the owners' advantage in having a target benefit plan, let's see how a straight profit-sharing plan, with 15 percent of compensation contributed for each participant, would serve its owners.

Profit-Sharing Proposal		
Names of Employees	**Contribution Amount**	**Percentage of Plan's Total Contribution**
Owner Smith	$9,000	28.3
Owner Jones	9,000	28.3
Joe Employee	5,250	16.5
Jim Employee	4,500	14.1
June Employee	4,050	12.7

Now let's assume that the company establishes a target benefit plan that weighs age and service in determining the amounts of contributions for each employee.

Target Benefit Plan		
Name of Employee	Contribution Amount	Percentage of Plan's Total Contribution
Owner Smith	$13,000	40.8
Owner Jones	13,000	39.3
Joe Employee	2,700	8.5
Jim Employee	2,200	6.9
June Employee	1,400	4.4

A much greater portion of the total contribution is shifted to the business owners in a target benefit plan that considers owners' higher ages and longer service.

Keogh Plans

Keogh plans are the most flexible type of qualified pension plans for the self-employed.

You are eligible to establish a Keogh plan if you own a business or part of a business that is not incorporated. In other words, you must be operating as a sole proprietorship, a partnership, or a limited liability company (LLC). Note, however, that you must actually perform personal services for the business; mere passive investment is not enough.

Keogh plans can take the form of defined contribution, defined benefit, or hybrid plans. They also permit the largest contributions, if you're interested in socking away a lot of your company's profits in a tax-free retirement account.

It is not necessary to have any employees to establish a Keogh, but if there are employees, they must be allowed to participate in the plan.

Also, you do not have to be self-employed on a full-time basis to become eligible to open a Keogh plan. An individual who has another job during the day, but decides to supplement his or her income by turning his or her weekend hobby into a business, is eligible to open a Keogh plan based on the net earnings derived from the part-time self-employment.

Contributions to a Keogh plan. There are limits on how much can be contributed to a Keogh plan each year. Contributions on behalf of any owner or employee to a Keogh defined benefit plan for 1998 are limited to the amount needed to eventually produce an annual pension payment of the lesser of (1) $130,000 or (2) 100 percent of the employee's average compensation for his or her three highest-paid years. A Keogh defined contribution plan contribution for 1998 is limited to the lesser of $30,000 or 25 percent of the participant's earned income for the year. If you make contributions that are higher than the limits, you are considered to have made a nondeductible contribution which may also be subject to a 10 percent excise tax penalty.

Prohibited transactions. There are certain transactions that are prohibited if made between the plan and a "disqualified person": the employer, a plan fiduciary, a partner owning more than 10 percent of the partnership, highly compensated employees, or family members related to any of these. An excise tax penalty of 100 percent is charged on prohibited transactions. It is the disqualified person taking part in the transaction who must pay the tax, not the company or the Keogh plan. One type of prohibited transaction is any loan from the plan to the self-employed individual.

Setting up a Keogh plan. To qualify, the Keogh plan must be in writing and must be communicated to the employees. The plan's provisions must be stated in the plan. Most Keogh plans follow a standard form (a master or prototype plan) approved by the Internal Revenue Service. You can sign up for a standard plan at the bank, mutual fund, or investment house that you select to manage your Keogh plan investments. If you prefer, you can set up an individually designed plan to meet specific needs, but you will usually need the help of a pension professional in doing so.

401(k) Plans

A 401(k) is a special type of defined contribution retirement plan that allows participants to have part of their pre-tax pay deducted from their paycheck and put into an investment account that will be held tax-free until such time as the money is actually used (generally at retirement).

From your point of view as an employer, the advantage of a 401(k) is that the plan is funded mainly through voluntary contributions by each employee — rather than contributions out of the employer's pocket.

In some cases, the employer agrees to match each dollar that the employee contributes to the 401(k) plan with a contribution to the account. While some large employers match employee contributions dollar for dollar, most match at the rate of 50 cents on the dollar. Matching contributions are a cost that you cannot control once the matching formula is set because you cannot control how much each employee will contribute (though you can set an upper limit of a certain percentage of an employee's compensation, such as 5 or 10 percent).

The main disadvantage to a 401(k) plan is that the participants' voluntary contributions are limited. For 1999, the maximum amount for each individual was $10,000 (this amount periodically increases to reflect inflation). Also, 401(k)s are subject to nondiscrimination rules that make it difficult for a business owner to contribute a lot of money to his or her own retirement account.

Borrowing issues. Because funds in a 401(k) plan are subject to stringent restrictions on withdrawal, employees may be reluctant to tie up their money for a long period of time. Some plans allow employees to borrow against a portion of their own account, at low interest rates. Allowing employees to borrow from the plan may encourage employee participation, especially among low-paid employees. Of course, it means extra administrative time and cost.

Simplified Employee Pensions (SEPs)

A simplified employee pension, or SEP, is the simplest, most efficient, and least expensive way for a small business to establish a qualified retirement plan for its owners and any employees. While not as flexible as Keogh plans, they are far easier to set up. They are also more flexible than SIMPLE plans, because you don't have to make contributions every year (for example, if your business didn't meet its profit targets or you simply don't want to contribute).

What is a SEP? SEPs are essentially individual retirement accounts (or IRAs). If you use this plan, an account must be set up for each employee who is over 21, who has worked for you in at least three out of the last five years, and has received at least $400 from you in the current year. You then make contributions directly into the participant's accounts.

Save Time

In the interest of administrative simplicity, we advise you to have all employees set up IRAs with the same institution; for example, the bank that handles your business checking account. Once the contributions have been made, the individual employees can roll them over into other IRAs of their own choosing.

How much will you contribute? Generally, your SEP contributions must be made in an amount that is the same percentage of total compensation for every employee. Note that this requirement does not require you to use the same percentage every year (or even to contribute every year).

As a practical matter, you'll want to wait until you know how much money you have available for SEP contributions (usually after the books are closed at the end of the year) before determining the percentage. After you have determined the percentage and made the contributions, you must give written notice to each participant detailing your contributions to their SEPs, by the later of January 31 of the year following the year for which a contribution is made, or 30 days after the contribution is made.

The maximum contribution you can make to a SEP in a given year is the lower of 15 percent of an employee's pay or $30,000.

As the owner, the limits for your own contributions are slightly lower. You will have to reduce the contribution rate called for in your plan by using the Self-Employed Person's Rate Table found in IRS Publication 560 (you can get a free copy by calling 1-800-TAX-FORM). Under the Rate Table, if, for example, you chose to contribute the maximum 15 percent for each employee, your own contribution is limited to 13.0435 percent of your compensation.

SARSEPs

First of all, you should know that SARSEPs are a type of pension plan that can no longer be set up after 1996. Those who already have such plans can continue to contribute to them, but no new SARSEPs can be established.

SARSEPs are a special form of SEPs that act like 401(k) plans in the sense that employees who participate in the SARSEP can elect to have salary-reduction contributions made to the SEP, just as they can in a 401(k) plan. Essentially, the employees are funding their own retirement.

The amount that can be deferred in a SARSEP is the lesser of 15 percent of compensation or $10,000 (in 1999; this amount is adjusted periodically for inflation). To participate, an employee must be at least 21, must have worked for you in at least three of the preceding five years, and must have received at least $400.

SIMPLE Plans

Beginning in 1997, employers with no more than 100 employees could set up a new kind of retirement plan: the savings incentive match plan for employees (SIMPLE). SIMPLE plans are easy to administer, but they have much lower annual contribution limits than other types of retirement plans. SIMPLE plans avoid the nondis-crimination requirements of other retirement plans by requiring that each employee be treated exactly the same — there is no possibility for weighting the contributions more heavily in favor of the business owner or key employees.

Basic Rules for SIMPLE Plans

- *A SIMPLE must be the only retirement plan you offer.*

- *The funding mechanism can be either an IRA for each participating employee, or a 401(k) plan. Existing 401(k) plans can be converted to SIMPLE plans.*

- *The employee may contribute up to $6,000 annually.*

- *The employer must either (a) match each participating employee's contribution dollar for dollar, up to 3 percent of the employee's pay, or (b) make an across-the-board 2 percent contribution for all employees regardless of whether they participate in the plan. The maximum contribution total for any employee (including yourself) would be $12,000 per year.*

- *Employees vest immediately in all contributions made by themselves or the employer to their account.*

- *Eligible employees are those who received at least $5,000 in compensation during any two preceding years and who are reasonably expected to receive $5,000 in compensation during the year in question.*

- *There are no reporting requirements imposed on the employer except for a single report to the government when the plan is created (employers do have to notify employees as to account balances, investment performance, etc.).*

- *Any distribution to an employee during the first two years after the plan is created is subject to a 25 percent excise tax. After two years, distributions to anyone under age 59 1/2 are subject to a 10 percent excise tax.*

- *Upon separation from employment, distributions may be rolled over tax-free to an IRA or to another SIMPLE plan.*

If you're interested in setting up a SIMPLE plan, contact anyone who offers IRAs or 401(k) plans, such as banks, insurance companies, or investment houses.

Nonqualified Plans

In some cases, you may want to provide supplementary compensation for key executives or employees, and you may want to defer payment into the future. For example, you may want to induce a particularly valuable employee to remain with you for a certain number of years. In that case, you could offer the employee a deferred compensation plan that would pay the employee additional compensation upon the completion of a certain number of years of service to you.

In other cases, you may want to defer compensation for yourself, or for yourself and your partners, to avoid paying taxes on it this year.

You cannot achieve these goals through a traditional retirement plan (assuming you want the tax advantages) because qualified plans require you to provide benefits that are uniform and that don't discriminate too much in favor of key executives. The best arrangement, then, for accomplishing your goals may be through a nonqualified plan.

By "nonqualified," we mean simply that the plan is not subject to certain federal pension law provisions, such as the ones on nondiscrimination, eligibility, funding, and vesting. As a result, it doesn't get as many tax breaks as regular pension plans do.

Too good to be true? The main downside to these plans is that although the covered employee doesn't recognize plan contributions as taxable income until he or she receives the benefits some years down the road, your business is not entitled to a deduction for the deferred compensation until that same point in time.

The world of nonqualified plans has a colorful language all its own. There are:

- **Top-hat plans** — a top-hat plan is an unfunded plan maintained primarily to provide deferred compensation to a select group of management or highly compensated employees. Special reporting and disclosure rules apply.

- **Rabbi trusts** — a rabbi trust is a nonqualified deferred compensation arrangement in which amounts are transferred to an irrevocable trust to be held for the benefit of executive employees. The funds in the trust can still be reached by creditors of the company; for example, in a bankruptcy.

- **Golden handcuffs** — a golden handcuff is an agreement between companies and their key executives under which the executives are paid supplemental retirement benefits if they meet certain conditions, such as if they remain with the company until a certain age. Golden handcuffs are designed to encourage long-term employment relationships.

Behind the interesting language, however, are all the familiar (and complex) pension concepts. If you're interested in a nonqualified plan, speak to your attorney.

Individual Retirement Accounts (IRAs)

Individual Retirement Accounts (IRAs) function as *personal* tax-qualified retirement savings plans.

Anyone who works, whether as an employee or self-employed, can set aside up to $2,000 per year in an IRA, and the earnings on these investments grow, tax-deferred, until the eventual date of distribution. Moreover, certain individuals are permitted to deduct all or part of their contributions set aside in the IRA.

IRAs are easy to set up at any bank, mutual fund, brokerage house, or other financial institution, which will act as trustee or custodian. An individual cannot be his or her own trustee, but some financial institutions will allow you to direct the investment of your IRA funds.

Amount. The most that an individual can contribute in any year to an IRA is the smaller of $2,000 or an amount equal to the compensation includible in income for the year. The same limit applies even if the individual has more than one IRA. The contribution must be from compensation, meaning wages, salaries, commissions, and other sources of earned income. It does not include deferred compensation, retirement payments, or portfolio income such as interest or dividends.

Under certain conditions, nonworking spouses can contribute up to $2,000 to an IRA. Separate accounts must be used for each spouse. The couple must file a joint tax return to claim the deduction, and the combined compensation of both spouses must be at least equal to the amount contributed to both spouses' IRAs.

Deductibility of the contribution. Everyone is eligible to establish an IRA, but whether the contributions into the IRA will receive special tax treatment depends on circumstances. If neither the individual nor spouse is covered under another retirement plan, they may take full advantage of the tax deduction for the amount contributed. If the individual is covered under another retirement plan, the amount of the contribution eligible for deduction is determined by the filing status and adjusted gross income (AGI) as shown on the Form 1040 Income Tax Return. The following table applies in 1999; phaseout ranges will increase in future years.

Figuring Your Maximum IRA Deduction		
If you file a single return and AGI is up to:	*If you file a joint return and AGI is up to:*	*Maximum deduction is lesser of 100% of AGI or:*
$31,000	$51,000	$2,000
$32,000	$52,000	$1,800
$33,000	$53,000	$1,600
$34,000	$54,000	$1,400
$35,000	$55,000	$1,200

If you file a single return and AGI is up to:	If you file a joint return and AGI is up to:	Maximum deduction is lesser of 100% of AGI or:
$36,000	$56,000	$ 1,000
$37,000	$57,000	$ 800
$38,000	$58,000	$ 600
$39,000	$59,000	$ 400
$40,000	$60,000	$ 200
$41,000	$61,000	$ 0

If your spouse is covered by a plan but you are not, you may make deductible contributions if your AGI is $150,000 or less. The deduction is phased out gradually for those with AGI between $150,000 and $160,000.

Even if the contribution is nondeductible, you can still make it. Just be sure that you make any nondeductible contributions to separate IRA accounts — don't mix deductible and nondeductible contributions in the same account. The earnings on nondeductible contributions will still accumulate on a tax-deferred basis.

Roth IRAs. Beginning in 1998, some taxpayers can set up an IRA that is backloaded: that is, the contributions are not deductible, but the withdrawals from the account, including all the buildup in value over the years, are tax-free as long as certain conditions are met. The withdrawals must be made five years or more after the account was opened, and after you attain age 59 ½ or have become disabled. Joint filers with income under $150,000 can make full contributions to Roth IRAs; those with income between $150,000 and $160,000 can make partial contributions. For singles, the phase-out range is between $95,000 and $110,000.

You may be able to convert a "regular" IRA to a Roth IRA, if your adjusted gross income is under $100,000 (single or joint).

Transfers and rollovers. The shifting of funds from one trustee/custodian directly to another trustee/custodian of the same type of plan is called a transfer. A transfer is tax-free and there are no waiting periods between transfers.

Generally, a rollover is a tax-free distribution to you of assets from one retirement plan that you then place in a different retirement plan. Under certain circumstances, you may either roll over assets withdrawn from one IRA into another, or roll over a distribution from a qualified retirement plan into an IRA. If the distribution is made directly to you, the payer must withhold 20 percent of it for taxes. You can avoid withholding by having the payer transfer the funds directly to the trustee/custodian of your IRA.

You must complete the rollover within 60 days of your receipt of the funds, or it will be treated as a taxable distribution; either way you must report it on your tax return.

Withdrawals/distributions from an IRA. There are numerous rules limiting the withdrawal and use of your IRA assets. Violation of the rules generally results in additional taxes. Generally, you cannot withdraw assets from your IRA until you reach the age of 59 1/2. However, there are special rules that allow you to take distributions from an IRA if the amounts are used to pay medical expenses in excess of 7.5 percent of adjusted gross income or if the distributions are used by certain unemployed, formerly unemployed, or self-employed individuals to pay health insurance premiums. Beginning in 1998, you can take a penalty-free withdrawal from any type of IRA to purchase your first home.

For IRAs that are not Roth IRAs, you can also take penalty-free withdrawals before age 59½ to pay certain education expenses for yourself or your dependents, or if you set up a schedule to take "substantially equal" periodic payments for the rest of your life.

You must begin withdrawing the balance from any IRA that is not a Roth IRA by April 1st of the year following the year in which you reach age 70 1/2 or the year in which you retire. Such a withdrawal, net of the portion representing return of any nondeductible contributions, is includible in your ordinary income.

LIFE INSURANCE

If properly fitted to your needs and purchased at a competitive price, life insurance offers important advantages, including: income replacement for your survivors, investment/forced savings for you, reduced income and transfer tax liability, a ready source of cash when it's likely to be needed most, and funding of small business buy/sell agreements.

Term or Cash Value Policies

Life insurance policies can be divided into two main categories, term insurance and cash value insurance.

Term insurance. Term insurance provides a death benefit only — you die within the specified term, the insurance company pays; you don't die within the term, they don't pay. Such a policy has no investment (cash value) component. Although it's called "term" insurance because the coverage runs for a specified term (such as a year), many modern term policies may be renewed at the option of the insured for as long as he or she is willing to pay the premiums.

The simplest form of term must be renewed annually, for a premium price that increases each year. There are also term policies that provide for a premium that won't increase for five, ten, 15, or even 20 years, after which the premium will jump up sharply.

Cash value insurance. There sometimes appears to be a nearly unlimited number of types of cash value policies. While they all have important differences, they all boil down to this: they provide a death benefit (term protection) and they provide for a savings feature.

Cash value insurance is more expensive than term (particularly at younger ages), but typically provides insurance throughout the policyholder's lifetime at a level premium. A policyholder normally can receive the benefit of these cash values during his or her lifetime in one of two ways: (1) by taking a loan against them, or (2) by cashing in the policy (the policy will no longer be in force, but the policyholder will receive the cash surrender value).

The investment return on cash value policies has typically been rather low, particularly for the first five to 10 years after purchase. Some modern cash value policies give policyholders the right to choose from several mutual-fund-like investment options for the cash-value portion of the premiums. Although these policies offer the possibility of higher returns within the policy, they require the policyholder to make the decisions about policy investments.

Cash value policies allow the owner to borrow up to a specific percent of the cash value, frequently 95 percent, at fixed or variable rates that are often lower than those charged by commercial lenders.

Comparison of Life Insurance Policies

Life insurance policies are complicated things. They use terms and provisions that are nothing more than legalistic mumbo-jumbo to most of us. Added to this is the fact that there seem to be countless types and varieties of these policies.

The most common forms of cash value and specialized policies are the following:

Whole (ordinary) life. Whole life provides a guaranteed death benefit and guaranteed cash value throughout life. The premiums stay the same and are payable to age 95 or 100. Low-interest loans against the cash value may be available. Some policies are "participating" and may provide a cash value build-up beyond the guaranteed level.

Universal life. The policy is made up of a term component and a cash-value component split into two distinct accounts. The owner controls the premium amount (within limits) and can raise or lower the face amount and the amount going into the investment account.

Variable life. Like universal life, the policy is split into two accounts: term and investment component. The owner can direct the latter into several mutual fund-like investment choices. Premiums are fixed; face value is guaranteed but cash value depends on performance of the investments chosen.

Universal variable life. Like universal life, the owner controls the amount of premium; like variable life, the owner directs the investment of premiums into several investment choices. Premiums, face amount, and cash value can increase or decrease.

Joint first-to-die policies. Various types of cash value policies (whole, variable, or universal life) can be used to insure two persons, but pay out proceeds only on the first death. These are less expensive than buying a separate policy on each person. They may be used to fund a business buy/sell agreement.

Joint second-to-die policies. Similar to a first-to-die policy, but pays out only on the second death. They may be used to pay estate tax liability of a surviving spouse.

Split-dollar life insurance policies. With these policies, the premiums for the life insurance policy on an employee are split between the insured employee and his or her employer. In the most traditional form of split-dollar, the employer pays the portion of the premium that relates to the yearly build-up in the cash value, while the employee pays the portion that relates to the term (pure insurance) protection.

Split-dollar insurance is an important benefit for the employee and, ultimately, it costs the employer nothing: the premium costs paid by the employer are recouped by sharing the death benefit with the insured's beneficiary or by the employee's purchase of the employer's premium costs (and hence the policy) at retirement. The employer may select for participation anyone it chooses. Thus, it's a good way to cover yourself and any co-owners or key employees.

If the employer pays the employee's part of the premiums and calls it a bonus to the employee, the cost can be deducted by the business, but it will be taxable compensation for the employee.

Life Insurance in Your Business

Business owners may have some special questions to consider when it comes to planning their insurance coverage:

- Is your business currently profitable?

- Do you intend that family members would continue to operate the business if you died?

- Do you need to set up a contingency fund for your business, to pay estate taxes when you die (thus saving your heirs from having to sell the business in order to pay estate taxes), or to fund a buy-sell agreement among your heirs or co-owners?

Is Your Business Profitable?

If your business is making money, you should ask yourself how your spouse, family, or dependents will be economically damaged if you are not there to run the business. Unless one or more of these people can step in to run the business at your death, you should think about whether the income from your business needs to be replaced.

Example

John Stead's business (writing handicapping information for horse racing publications) generates yearly profits of $45,000, the only source of his family's income. Because no one in his family has the specialized skills to run the business, he does not intend that it will be operated after his death, and the business has no value after his death. He figures that if he is not alive, his family expenses will be decreased by $10,000 per year. He will need to replace $35,000 of yearly income.

After you have figured the amount of income that needs to be replaced, you need to estimate how much investment return your survivors can obtain on the insurance funds. If, for instance, you estimate that your heirs must replace $20,000 of income at your death, and can make 5 percent on their money, they will need $400,000 from insurance or other sources to do this.

It may sound cruel, but at least from an economic point of view, if your business is not profitable it's a liability, not an asset. Generally speaking, you should insure assets (such as a magic machine that makes money) rather than liabilities (a machine that eats money).

Will Your Survivors Run the Business?

If you plan that your surviving spouse, family, or others will continue to operate your business after your death, the question then becomes whether they can pick up where you left off without a period of lessened profits.

Profits may stay level. The best situation is where there will be no let-up in profits. If you are at this point, you have probably involved your family in all aspects of business operation already. If this is the case, you have no particular increased need for life insurance because of your business itself. However, you may wish to purchase life insurance to provide a ready fund to pay any estate taxes that will be due, so that your heirs don't have to sell off needed business assets to pay Uncle Sam.

Profits may drop off for a time. It certainly would not be unusual if the family members who continue to run your business could not do so as profitably as you could — at least, not right away. No matter how talented or industrious they are, if they have not been intimately involved in the day-to-day running of the business, they probably will not be able to do everything as well as you did. This is particularly true with businesses that require specialized knowledge or training, and businesses that depend on long-standing personal relationships with clients, customers, or suppliers.

If you think that it will take your family members or heirs a few months, or a few years, to get the business back to where it's making the same profits that it did for you, life insurance can be used to bridge the period of diminished profits.

DISABILITY INSURANCE

Throughout much of a business operator's life, the chances that he or she will become disabled are greater than the likelihood of death. However, many more people have life insurance policies than have disability policies.

Unlike a life insurance policy, which is primarily designed to provide a lump-sum payment in the event of death, a disability policy provides income to an individual who becomes disabled because of an accident or illness. There are many kinds of disability policies, which differ on how liberally or restrictively they define disability, how much periodic income they pay, how long you have to wait (called the "elimination period") for payments to begin, and how long payments will go on.

How you should plan to meet the threat of disability depends on how you answer the following question: if you become disabled (whether permanently or not), could family members or others keep the business running (even at reduced profits) until you return?

If the Answer Is Yes

If you believe that your business can be continued by others after your disability, chances are that the business does not require your constant personal supervision or specialized skills or knowledge that only you possess. However, it's unlikely that whoever runs it for you in the interim will be able to turn the same profit you did. Income from a disability policy could help make up the difference for you.

Because you foresee the business continuing during your disability, you might consider disability overhead insurance. Upon the owner's disability, such a policy pays out a portion of the business's fixed (overhead) expenses. In this way, the business may have a better chance to survive a period of decreased profits until the owner returns.

If the Answer Is No

If you believe that your business can't be operated by family members or others while you are disabled, it's probably true that your business depends on your constant supervision, or specialized skills or knowledge that only you have. Because this is true, there's no need for disability overhead insurance. But the fact that you don't expect your business to survive the period of your disability means that you probably have a greater need for disability insurance than if the business continued.

Disability Policy Provisions

If you are considering the purchase of a disability policy, you should note that such policies may differ in several important ways:

When do the benefits start? *Do benefits begin at the onset of disability or is there a waiting period? Common elimination periods include 30, 90, or 180 days. A lengthy waiting period means cheaper premiums, but gives no protection for short-term disability.*

How is disability defined? *Many older policies pay no benefits if the disability permits some type of gainful employment. Newer policies may grade benefits with the level of job function permitted by the disability.*

Is there a monetary limitation on payments? *State law may impose such a limit. No matter what the owner earns or how the policy is phrased, an insurance company may not pay out more than the maximum permitted by law. For example, a business owner who earns $150,000 per year has a policy that promises to pay 80 percent of the pre-disability salary in the event of permanent and total disability. If state law sets a $100,000 limit on such payments, that is all that will be paid to the owner, even though it appears that the policy will pay $120,000 ($150,000 x 80 percent).*

In such instances, the owner has "overpaid" premiums, since he or she did not receive the full amount contracted for under the policy. If you move to a new state, check with a local agent to see whether your existing policy will conflict with your new state's laws.

Will multiple policies generate multiple benefits? *State law may also affect whether benefits are cumulative. If they are, there's no use in carrying multiple policies. For instance, an owner has three separate disability policies, each one providing a benefit of $100,000. If state law requires that benefits be cumulative and if there is a $100,000 limit, each insurer will contribute 1/3 of the $100,000. Thus, even though the owner paid for three separate $100,000 policies, he or she actually gets the benefits as if only one of these policies was purchased.*

LONG-TERM CARE INSURANCE

Long-term health care contracts are relatively new arrangements designed to provide insurance that will meet your health care needs, particularly your nursing home needs, should you become chronically ill or disabled after reaching a specified age, such as 50.

As is apparent from their name, long-term care policies greatly expand the time period over which benefits will be paid out, when compared to standard accident and health policies. Another advantage is that, unlike Medicare coverage, long-term care contracts will cover the cost of custodial care, as well as skilled nursing care. These two advantages often make long-term care contracts a preferred way of pre-funding nursing home care for the elderly, particularly for higher-income people who know that they won't qualify for Medicaid.

If certain specified requirements are met, long-term care insurance contracts issued after December 31, 1996, will generally receive the same income tax treatment as accident and health policies. That means that amounts received under a long-term care insurance contract are tax-exempt as amounts received for personal injuries and sickness. This exclusion is capped at $175 per day on *per diem* contracts (this amount will be adjusted for inflation after 1997).

It also means that company-paid premiums for long-term care can be excludable from income tax for an employee, and are tax-deductible for the employer. However, the owner can only deduct 60% of the premiums for his or her own policy, as with any health care policy.

Part **X**

Getting Out Of Your Business

If you've been at all successful in your business, you've most likely put tremendous amounts of time, energy, and plain old hard work into it. It's probably one of your proudest achievements.

However, at some point you're going to have to think about a subject that may seem completely foreign to you: what's the best way to untangle yourself from the company that you've spent so much time putting together?

You may already be thinking in this direction for a number of reasons, some good, some bad. Perhaps you're looking forward to retiring in a more agreeable climate, you've gotten a purchase offer you want to consider, or your business has done so well that you want to pass it on to your children. Perhaps you hope to "die in the saddle," but you want the business to continue beyond your lifetime, and you don't want the IRS to confiscate your hard-earned gains through estate taxes.

On the other hand, perhaps your business isn't doing as well as you hoped, or it's doing well but you're getting tired of all the time and energy it requires. Other reasons for getting out might include the death of a partner or co-owner, divorce, your realization that the competition is winning out, pressure from family members or employees who think you ought to retire, or your own health.

Don't wait until one of these events hits you over the head — start thinking about your exit strategy now, even if it might be a long time before you actually need to get out. That way, you'll have plenty of time to consult with professionals and put your plan in place, and you can optimize your chances of getting the most financial and personal satisfaction from the results.

Chapter 31: Selling Your Business, guides you through one of the most important transactions you'll ever undertake, from timing your decision to putting a price tag on the business, finding a buyer, structuring the deal, and completing the sale.

Chapter 32: Planning for Succession, presents the special issues facing entrepreneurs who'd like to see their business successfully transferred to the next generation.

Chapter 31

Selling Your Business

Whatever your reasons for wanting to divest yourself of your company, selling your business will be one of the most important things you'll ever do. Unlike virtually every other business decision you've made over the years, *you'll only do this once.*

You'll come out way ahead, both financially and personally, if you make an effort to understand the steps in selling, formulate your plan carefully with the help of your professional advisors, and, when the time comes, take the time to negotiate a price and terms that satisfy your reasons for getting out of the business.

Even if you think you're many years away from selling out, you should consider what your heirs or successors would have to do if you died unexpectedly. If you don't have a workable exit strategy in place, you (or your heirs) may have no choice but to liquidate the business and sell off the assets piecemeal, getting *nothing* for the goodwill you've built up over the course of the years.

In this chapter we'll discuss the major issues you need to think about when it's time to sell your business, including how to time your decision and choose experts to help, how to set a price, how to find a buyer, what your options are as to terms, how to finance the deal, and what the typical steps are in closing the sale.

INITIAL ISSUES IN SELLING OUT

In a perfect world, you'd sell your business when the national economy was humming along towards a peak in the business cycle, when your industry was "hot" among investors, and when your particular business was having a banner year.

However, your decision to sell out will probably have much more to do with your personal circumstances than with what's happening on

Wall Street. The point we're making is that, everything else being equal, you should aim to sell when things are good, rather than not-so-good or downright ugly.

Regardless of the state of the economy or your industry, there are a number of things you can do to shape up your business to make it more attractive to purchasers (see the discussion on page 627). However, this process is likely to take a year or more.

Start planning early. On average, once your business is on the market, it will take another year to find a buyer and complete the deal. If you are planning to sell to family members or key employees, many of the more creative tax-planning methods can take three to five years to put into place.

Work Smart

It's best not to try to sell right before your major leases or other key contracts expire. When prospective purchasers look at your business, they'll want to be able to predict what they'll need to spend for rent, labor, materials, supplies, and all the other major items. They won't want to have to renegotiate key contracts right off the bat, or take the chance that a lease may not be renewable at all. If you must sell right before a contract is scheduled to expire, we suggest that you try to renegotiate it early, so that you'll get a favorable rate (or at least a predictable one) locked in for your purchaser.

Assembling Your Expert Team

Even if you've been a determined do-it-yourselfer from day one, selling your business is not a job you should attempt to do alone. Even for a relatively small business, there's a myriad of federal, state, and local regulations and tax issues to consider, not to mention one or more extremely important contracts to negotiate.

The process of selling can take a lot of time. The more involved you get with it, the less time you'll have to spend actually running the business, at the very time when you need your business to run most successfully. You'll be much better off leaving some of the work to experts who've crafted dozens of deals.

At a minimum, you'll need to involve your lawyer and accountant. You may also need a business broker, business appraiser/valuation expert, and a tax expert.

Accountant's Role

If you've used an accountant regularly to prepare your tax returns and draw up financial statements, he or she will be in a good position to know whether your business would be attractive to a potential buyer, and can give you some ideas on how to make it more attractive.

Your accountant will also be essential in drawing up the historical and projected financial statements and other data required to place a proper value on your business, and in gathering and organizing financial data requested by the buyer during the due diligence phase of negotiations.

It's very important that your accountant and your lawyer work well together. If they don't communicate frequently, they may end up duplicating some of each other's work, which means you may have to pay twice.

Lawyer's Role

Many small business owners have established a relationship with a business lawyer over the years, and as a matter of course decide to have this lawyer handle the sale. If your business is a small one or your attorney is very experienced in all aspects of transition plans, this may very well be a wise course of action.

You may also decide to use an attorney who specializes in mergers and acquisitions and who actually enjoys putting a deal together. Most larger law firms have M & A specialists on staff, though these experts don't come cheap. However, when you're talking about a once-in-a-lifetime deal, it's well worth it to get the best legal advice that you can afford. If your deal will be too small to interest a high-profile attorney, he or she might be able to recommend an associate who would be interested.

Retainer agreements. Ordinarily, your lawyer will expect you to sign a retainer agreement and to pay some substantial portion of the fees upfront. It's to your advantage to sign such an agreement, since it will lay out the scope of the services the attorney will provide, and put the fee arrangement in writing.

Whom does the attorney represent? Theoretically, all parties to the transaction (i.e., each individual partner or shareholder and each individual purchaser, plus the business entity itself if incorporated) should have a separate lawyer. This can get very expensive if there are a number of shareholders, so many attorneys will agree to represent more than one party if proper waivers are signed.

Warning

We don't advise that you go so far as to have only one attorney representing both the buyer and the seller.

That situation presents a real conflict of interest, rather than just a potential difference, and few attorneys would agree to such representation anyway. Any time there is a real conflict of interest, the parties in conflict should retain separate counsel (for example, if some shareholders want to sell but others do not).

Broker's Role

If you don't already have a buyer lined up, it's likely that you can benefit greatly from the increased exposure to a large pool of potential buyers that a business broker can provide. Perhaps even more importantly, a broker can guide you through the process of selling based on experience gained from many similar transactions.

A broker can contact likely purchasers (including competitors, suppliers, major customers, and investors known to the broker) directly and tell them the key facts about your business, without "naming names" until the contact has shown definite interest. The broker can also screen interested parties for financial ability, so you won't waste time talking to unqualified buyers.

As a general rule of thumb, business brokers are interested in listing companies valued at several hundred thousand dollars or more. If your business is worth more than one million dollars, you may want to hire a mergers and acquisitions intermediary — a more sophisticated type of agent who functions as a consultant for both buyers and sellers and whose organization may even have in-house valuation specialists and financing available.

Because brokers are compensated by a commission based on a percentage of the sales price, very small businesses may find it hard to locate an agent willing to take on their listing. Instead, they'll have to try to locate a prospective buyer on their own, or sell off their assets as best they can.

Work Smart

As when hiring any professional, it's a good idea to ask the broker about recent sales he or she has handled, and for the names of satisfied clients you can contact. Make sure you follow up on these references. The main advantage to using a broker is experience, and you want to be sure your broker has some.

Fees and listing agreements. You'll be expected to sign a listing agreement, which will lay out the fee schedule. Usually, brokers' fees are contingent, meaning that they are paid only if and when the business is sold. Brokers' fees may range as high as 10 to 12 percent of the sales price for a smaller business.

In some cases, the fee will be split between your agent and an agent hired by the buyer, or you may be able to convince the buyer to pay some or all of your broker's fees.

Work Smart

One clause you should attempt to have written into the listing agreement is that the fee will be paid at the time you receive the purchase price, not at the time the deal is closed. That way, if you wind up financing a good portion of the price over a number of years, you'll pay the agent only as you actually get the money.

Your listing agreement will be for a specified period of time — if a buyer is located within that period, the agent will be entitled to the fee. Anything under three months won't give the agent enough time to effectively market your business. We suggest you initially list for no longer than six months so you can be sure your agent will get moving quickly — you can always extend the listing later.

Confidentiality. In the course of representing you, your broker may learn all sorts of confidential information about you and your business — information that could be damaging if it gets into the wrong hands. For that reason, the two of you should sign a confidentiality agreement stating that all information about your business is deemed valuable and confidential, and that the broker can disclose it only to qualified buyers for the purpose of evaluating the acquisition decision. This agreement should be included in your listing agreement, and should be examined by your attorney before you sign.

Appraiser's Role

If you are a small service company with few assets, or have only common assets like cars, real estate, and office equipment, your regular accountant's assessment of your book value may be adequate. You may also choose to rely on your business broker's assessment.

However, in many cases, it's worth the time and money to hire an experienced business appraiser. The value of your business depends on a very large number of interrelated factors. When buyers question your price during the negotiation process, it helps to be able to point to the precise reasons why your asking price is justified.

Tax Expert's Role

It is absolutely essential that at least one of the members of your team be an expert in dealing with the tax aspects of business sales and acquisitions. This person may be your accountant, your lawyer, or even your mergers and acquisitions consultant. You may also decide to hire a specialist solely for this purpose, most likely a lawyer associated with or recommended by the lawyer who is handling your sale.

Ethical Issues in Selling Out

Selling a business is a high-stakes transaction, especially for your buyer. Your potential exposure to a lawsuit can be huge, if the buyer spends a lot of money and foregoes other opportunities to buy a business that is not what it appears to be, or if you have partners or shareholders who feel they are not getting what they deserve.

Disclosure Obligations

If there's one overriding principle to observe, in the realm of dealing with potential buyers, it's that you must be truthful and complete in the information you share about your business. It's fine to be optimistic and present the positive side of things. However, you also need to be careful that your buyer knows about any potential problems in your business.

Fraud. The primary legal reason for full disclosure is that you can be sued for fraud if you make material misrepresentations of fact about your business. Anything that, if known to the buyer, would cause a change in the price paid for the business is "material."

Misrepresentation doesn't just mean affirmative lying — it can also mean remaining silent when you should speak up. The fact that the buyer didn't ask you if your customers were likely to cancel their contracts next year doesn't mean that you can't be sued for not mentioning it. Have your lawyer review any written material you pass on to buyers, to be sure that it is accurate and covers all the ground that it should.

Securities fraud. If you're contemplating a transaction that involves a sale or exchange of stock, you'll need to get expert legal assistance on a variety of issues, including specific disclosure obligations under federal and state securities laws.

Fraudulent conveyance. Basically, this legal concept means that if you and the buyer set up a deal in such a way that you should have known that the transferred company would fail (leaving business creditors high and dry), you may be forced to pay back the purchase price. For example, if your predictions about the company's future growth are far too optimistic, and lead the buyer to take on more debt than the company can support, the company may go bankrupt. The bankruptcy judge can require you to pay back the purchase price and essentially "undo" the sale.

Your potential liability for fraudulent conveyance lasts for up to six years after the sale.

Responsibilities to Co-Owners

Partners have the most demanding duties to each other, and under state laws are required to act with the utmost good faith toward each other and to the partnership. In the context of the sale of the business, this means that no partner can seek to benefit himself by the sale, to the detriment of the other partners. If he does, the other partners can sue to obtain their fair share of the benefits, whatever those might be.

Depending on your state law, shareholders of close corporations may be treated as having essentially the same duties to each other as partners do.

Officers and directors of corporations also are considered to have a fiduciary duty to the shareholders. They must act in good faith, in a manner reasonably believed to be in the best interests of the corporation.

Many small businesses have buy-sell agreements in place that specify what happens if one of the owners dies, becomes incapacitated, or wants to get out of the company. The agreement may state that the corporation will redeem (buy back) shares using a specified valuation formula, or that other owners have a right of first refusal to purchase your interest. If your company has ever set up such agreements, your lawyer needs to look them over and determine their effect before you try to sell.

VALUATION OF SMALL BUSINESSES

The value of a typical small business should be greater than the total values of its hard assets. For a buyer, the key is that an ongoing business has everything necessary — equipment, location, and inventory if applicable, not to mention experienced employees, suppliers, business processes, and a customer list — all in place, in the right amounts for successful operation of the business.

But how do you put a price on this intangible value, which is frequently referred to as goodwill or going-concern value? Moreover, how do you determine the true market value of the hard assets used in your business? The answer is that you make a business appraiser a key player on your selling team.

Business appraisers have established a number of ways to quantify the value of key aspects of your business, and roll them up into an overall figure. As part of the process they will write up a valuation report, which explains in detail how they arrived at their final value. This document adds credibility to your asking price, because the buyer will be able to see exactly how you arrived at your final figure.

On the other hand, remember that value is in the mind of the beholder. A professional valuation can tell you the price that an average buyer might pay for your business. However, when it comes to negotiating with an *actual* buyer, the appraisal is just a starting point.

Warning

 If you do have a professional appraisal prepared for your business, but then decide not to sell, it's a good idea not to keep the appraisal document with the rest of your business documents.

In the event of your death, you won't necessarily want your executor to be tied down by the numbers shown in the appraisal, for estate tax purposes. After all, the appraisal purports to show market value, but if no sale occurred it's hard to know whether that assessment was reasonable. Moreover, any number of things can happen in intervening years to make the appraisal obsolete, but the IRS has been known to dig up old appraisals and assert that they show the true value of the business (after adjustments for inflation, etc.)

You'll often come out better by having your executor do a completely new appraisal for the purpose of computing estate taxes, if and when the time comes.

Some brokers prefer not to set a listing price at all. Instead, they'll hold a controlled auction where a number of potential buyers are contacted and given key information about your business, and bids are solicited. This can be a way to achieve a fairly quick sale at a competitive price, provided the market for your type of business is fairly strong.

Key Factors for Buyers

The essential thing that most buyers will be interested in is earnings and cash flow. They'll want to know that your business will provide a stream of dollars that's predictable, and high. Some buyers prefer to look specifically at historical cash-flow statements, while others will focus on your income statement to examine earnings before interest and taxes (EBIT). Still others will place the most weight on earnings before interest, taxes, and depreciation (EBITD). You'll need to prove the size and constancy of your positive cash flow, preferably with audited financials going back at least three years.

A very important aspect of your cash flow and earnings is their ability to be replicated in future years, *without your presence*. If your professional expertise or salesmanship is the main reason the business makes money, you will have a hard time convincing the buyer that the cash stream will continue in future years.

You will also be expected to provide projected financial statements that show how the business might be expected to perform after the sale. You may also want to emphasize your future plans: new products in development, promising new distribution methods, and other items that should contribute to income growth in the future.

Warning

Don't make your predictions about the future too rosy — they may come back to haunt you in the form of a lawsuit for fraudulent conveyance if they don't pan out. For example, some advisors say that you should predict that your business will match, not surpass, current growth in your industry.

Secondary factors. Most buyers will look at the verifiable assets of the business: the real estate, equipment, patents or trademarks, and even such things as inventory, customer lists, and contractual relationships you've established. These items are the buyer's "insurance" — things that can be sold or used elsewhere if the earnings stream dries up.

Buyers will examine your key financial ratios to see how your business compares to the industry average, to other acquisitions they may be considering, and to the criteria for purchases they have set up for themselves. A key consideration is that your business have a clean balance sheet with low debt. The buyer may have to increase the debt burden in order to make the acquisition, and won't want total debt to be too heavy for the business to support.

Some buyers will be interested in knowing that you have an experienced manager or team of employees in place to take over when you leave. They'll want to know that you have groomed your successors, and that the successors will stick around. Other buyers will be looking for a business to actively manage, and will want to avoid long employment contracts with existing managers.

Add Value Before the Sale

There are any number of things that you can do to improve your business's appeal to buyers before the sale. The main problem is that a lot of these things take time.

Improve your income. One way to clean up your income statement is to have your accountant recast your financials to reflect the way the company should look with new owners. However, some buyers (particularly larger corporations) will judge you only by your true, audited financials. To hook these buyers you have to clean up the *business itself*, not just the statements.

Basically, this means doing whatever it takes to increase your EBIT. This may mean something as simple as increasing your advertising expenditures, hiring another salesperson on a commission basis, or dropping some of the perks the business provides to you or your family members. You may also want to have your accountant capitalize certain items that might otherwise have been expensed, and review your depreciation and inventory reporting methods. Ideally, you'd start working on this three years before the sale, since most buyers will want to see three years of financials.

Improve your assets. Certainly, you'll want to sell off or dispose of any unproductive assets or unsalable inventory. The buyer won't want to pay you for them, and they will only make you look like a poor manager. The business may own certain assets that are primarily there for your personal use (the most common example is a company car) but that you want to retain after the sale; now's the time for you to "buy" the asset from the business, perhaps at the current book value.

Another move you may want to make is to replace any machinery that's nearing the end of its useful life, and do any necessary repairs and upgrades. The average buyer wants to purchase a turnkey operation, meaning that all they have to do is walk in, turn on the lights, and the business will operate with no immediate need for further investment on their part.

Clean up potential liabilities. You should make an effort to clear up any pending or potential legal problems, such as product liability claims, employee lawsuits, IRS audits, insurance disputes, etc. The very existence of lawsuits or other problems may raise red flags in potential buyers' minds or even turn them completely off.

One concern that buyers increasingly have is whether there might be any lurking environmental problems on your property. If real estate will be part of the sale of your business, you should make every effort to see that there are no leaking underground storage tanks, asbestos, lead paint, hidden hazardous waste, or other nasty surprises around the property. If it's reasonable to conclude that problems are unlikely, an environmental transaction screen conducted at your attorney's direction may be all that's necessary.

However, to be safe from future claims, you'll generally have to obtain a satisfactory Phase I environmental audit by an environmental consultant. The Phase I report will document the clean condition of your property at the time of sale.

Simply not telling the buyer about existing problems is *not* an option; in fact, a number of states require you to sign a disclosure form that reveals any and all problems you know about.

Recast Financial Statements

If you're like most small business owners, you've operated your business in a way that's calculated to minimize taxes. You may have given yourself and family members as many perks and benefits as possible, kept your children on the payroll, plowed a lot of profits back into capital improvements, etc. These and other tactics are designed to keep your profits (and your taxes) low, perhaps artificially so.

Now, however, you want to make your company look as profitable as possible, by having your accountant recast your past income statements to reflect what would have happened if you:

- removed your salary and perks, and those of family members you don't expect to remain with the company

- removed any investment or other nonoperating expenses or income, or any expenses or income that would not be expected to recur or continue after the sale

- removed interest payments on any business loans, since you'll be removing such liabilities from the balance sheet.

Furthermore, your accountant can adjust your past balance sheets to:

- Remove any assets that will not be sold with the company.

- Remove any obsolete or slow-moving inventory. Value the remaining inventory at current replacement cost.

- Value your remaining balance-sheet assets at current fair market value.

- Write off any accounts receivable that are uncollectable.

- Write off any loans the company made to you.

- Remove other debt that will not be assumed by the buyer.

Warning

Whatever you do in the way of recasting your financials, make sure that any changes to your historical statements are carefully documented on the face of the statements, so that the buyer knows you aren't trying to cover anything up.

Business Valuation Formulas

Hopefully, you'll take our advice and hire an expert business appraiser to help you set an asking price. The process can be very complex and time-consuming, and takes quite a lot of experience to do well. There are a number of valuation methods that business appraisers have at their disposal, and even choosing the correct method (or more likely, the correct combination of methods) to use in a given situation can be considered more of an art than a science.

Asset-Based Valuation

Two commonly used business valuation methods look primarily at the value of your hard assets.

Book value is the number shown as "owner's equity" on your balance sheet. This is not a very useful number, since the balance sheet reflects historical costs and depreciation of assets rather than their current market value. However, if you adjust the book value in the process of recasting your financials, the current adjusted book value can be used as a "bare minimum" price for your business.

Liquidation value is the amount that would be left over if you had to sell your business quickly, without taking the time to get the full market value, and then used the proceeds to pay off all debts. There's little point in going through all the trouble of negotiating a sale of your business if you end up selling for liquidation value — it would be easier to simply go out of business, and save yourself the time, broker's commission, attorney's fees, and other costs involved in selling a going concern.

Historical Earnings Valuation

Most small companies are valued using one or more of the following methods, which take into account the company's historical earning power. Historical earnings methods allow an appropriate value for the goodwill of your business over and above the market value of the assets, *if that's justified by your earnings*. Accordingly, the starting point for all these methods is the recast historical financials discussed above.

Debt-paying ability. This is probably the method most commonly used by small business purchasers, because few buyers are able to purchase a business without taking out a loan. Consequently, they want to be sure that the business will generate enough cash to pay the loan off within a short time, usually four to five years. The price must be set at a point that makes this possible.

Simply put, to determine the company's debt-paying ability, you'd need to start with the historical free cash flow; this is usually defined as the company's net after-tax earnings (with a reasonable owner's salary figured in) minus capital improvements and working capital increases, but with depreciation added back in.   Interest on any existing loans is usually ignored, so that you start with a picture of the company as if it were debt-free.

Multiply the annual free cash flow by the number of years the acquisition loan will run.   From this figure, subtract the down payment. The remainder is the amount available to make interest and principal payments on the loan, and to provide the new owner with some return on investment.

Example

If your free cash flow was $80,000 a year and it's reasonable to expect the loan to be repaid in four years, 4 x $80,000 = $320,000.

If the down payment were $80,000, then no more than $240,000 (or $60,000 per year) would be available to make interest and principal payments on the loan, and to provide the owner with some return on the investment ($320,000 - $80,000 = $240,000. $240,000/4 = $60,000).

If the owner expected a 20 percent return on this $80,000 down payment, that would translate to $16,000 per year, further reducing the amount available to make debt payments to $44,000 ($60,000 - $16,000 = $44,000).

An annual payment of $44,000 could support a four-year loan of approximately $130,685 at 10 percent interest, or $145,000 at 8 percent interest. Add the loan amounts to the downpayment, and you arrive at a total purchase price of $210,685 at 10 percent, or $225,000 at 8 percent. If the lender is willing to finance the deal for a longer term or a lower rate, a higher price would be possible.

Capitalization of earnings or cash flow. This commonly used method involves first determining the historical annual earnings of the company, such as EBIT. The chosen figure is divided by a capitalization rate (cap rate) that represents the return the buyer requires on the investment in light of the market rate for other investments of comparable risk.   For example, if the EBIT was $100,000 and the buyer required a return of 25 percent, the capitalization of earnings method would yield a price of $100,000/.25 or $400,000.

Gross income multipliers/capitalization of gross income. Where expenses in a particular industry are highly predictable, or where the buyer intends to cut expenses drastically after the sale (for example, where the buyer is already in a similar business and can centralize administrative functions), it may be reasonable to value the business based on some multiple of gross revenues. For example, some service businesses can be valued at four times their gross monthly income.

Assets and Earnings Valuation

The excess earnings method of valuing a small business takes both assets and historical earnings into consideration, and is the method prescribed by the IRS for estate and gift tax situations when there's no other more appropriate method. It can also be used in appraising a business that's being put up for sale.

To use this method, you must first recast your historical financials as discussed above. For the income statement, the IRS prefers to see figures that represent a five-year average. For the balance sheet, use the most recent month's sheet, recast to reflect current market value.

From your recast financials you can determine your historical annual earnings figure (generally, EBIT). From this you'll subtract the portion of earnings that's attributable to your assets alone. Anything left over is the "excess earnings" — the portion that's attributable to the going-concern value of the business.

The excess earnings can be divided by a cap rate to arrive at their value. In today's market the cap rate will generally be somewhere around 20 to 25 percent, or enough to recover the investment in four to five years.

Example

Let's say that your recast balance sheet shows a net current asset value of $80,000, and a net long-term asset value of $200,000. So, the minimum or base price for your business should be $280,000 — the market value of your assets.

Now let's assume that your historical annual earnings figure is $150,000. How much of this earnings figure is attributable to the assets? You might calculate that under current market conditions the return on current assets should be $80,000 x 7.5% or $6,000, and your return on long-term assets should be $200,000 x 9.4% or $18,800. Thus, your total earnings attributable to your assets is $6,000 + $18,800 or $24,800. Subtracting this "asset return" figure from your total earnings, you arrive at an excess earnings amount of $125,200 ($150,000 - $24,800 = $125,200).

Using a cap rate of 20 percent, the value of your excess earnings is $626,000. Add to this the current market value of your assets, and you arrive at a total price of $906,000 for the business ($626,000 + $280,000 = $906,000).

Market-Based Valuation

Several business valuation methods are based primarily on the market price for similar businesses at a given point in time.

The comparable sales method attempts to locate similar businesses that have recently sold in your area, and uses those comparable sales figures to set a price for your business, adjusting appropriately for differences.

Rules of thumb/industry averages are frequently used by business brokers, based on their experience and on published standards for their industry. For example, your broker may tell you that lately your type of business has been selling for about four times the gross monthly revenues. However, a rule of thumb does not take into account any of the factors that make your business unique, and using one can result in setting a price for your business that's much too high or too low. Nevertheless, small businesses are often sold at a price based on rule of thumb, simply because it's a relatively fast, cheap method to use, and because it will result in a price that seems reasonable to buyers who have been looking around at a lot of similar businesses.

Future Earnings Valuation

Theoretically, anyone purchasing a small business is interested only in the business's future. Therefore, a valuation based on the company's expected earnings, discounted back to arrive at their net present value (NPV), should come the closest to answering the question of how much the business is really worth today.

However, in practice, valuations based on future performance of the company are the most difficult to do because they require the appraiser to make numerous estimates and projections about what's around the bend.

Nevertheless, if you think that your most likely buyer is a larger company, it may be worth while to have your appraiser use one of these methods, because they can result in setting the highest reasonable price for your business.

The first step is to look at your recast financial statements. Working from these, your appraiser will create projected statements that extend for five or more years into the future. Each year's free cash flow will be determined (some appraisers prefer to look at EBIT).

Once you have done this, the projected free cash flow from each year is discounted back to the present (using a financial calculator) to arrive at the NPV of each year's cash flow. These NPVs are added up to get the NPV of the company's earnings for the near future.

The next step is to determine the residual value that the company will have after the five (or more) years of your projected statements. One of the easier methods is to take the estimated cash flow from the last year you've forecasted, and divide this number by the discount rate to arrive at the residual value.

Finally, the NPV of cash flow from each of the projection years, plus the NPV of the company's residual value after these years, is added up to arrive at the present value of the business.

Case Study — Calculating a Company's Future Earnings Value

Let's say that after doing your best to look into the future and forecast the next five years' cash flow, you arrive at the figures in column two. Assuming a 20 percent discount rate, you come up with the following figures:

Year	Free Cash Flow	NPV at 20% discount	
1	$ 80,000	$ 68,383	
2	85,000	62,175	
3	92,000	57,580	
4	99,000	53,075	
5	108,000	49,563	
		$290,776	= present value of five-year cash flow
residual value* of business at five years:	$540,000	223,174	
		$513,950	= total present value of company

*Note: the residual value was computed by taking the fifth year's projected value and dividing by the discount rate: $108,000/.20 = $540,000.

Partial Interests in Business

If only part of the company is being sold, or given away as part of a succession plan, minority interests are valued at a discount from their pro rata price. A minority owner is not likely to have much influence on the way the company is run. He or she can't control the board of directors, control the payment of dividends, or even prevent himself from being fired as an employee.

The IRS recognizes this and will allow a minority discount (typically, 20 to 40 percent) on the price of the stock. The discount allows you to give away part of the company while minimizing gift taxes, or to sell part of it while minimizing capital gains taxes and allowing the purchaser to buy into the business at a reasonable cost.

Majority interest premiums. Majority interests, when sold or given away, are typically valued at more than their pro rata share of the company's value. For example, a majority interest of 75 percent of the stock might actually be worth 90 percent of the total value of the company.

Work Smart

If you're planning to pass your business on to the next generation of your family, carving out minority interests and giving or selling them to your successors can be a good way to reduce your estate or capital gains taxes.

FINDING A BUYER

Buyers who are unrelated to you and who may be unearthed by your business broker can usually be divided into two groups: financial buyers and strategic buyers. A third group of potential buyers is composed of people you already know well: your family, managers, or employees.

Financial Buyers

Financial buyers are primarily interested in your company's cash flow. They are typically individuals or companies with money to invest, and are willing to look at many different types of businesses or industries. In some cases they are former executives of larger corporations who want to buy themselves a job by finding a company to actively manage. Or they may be holding companies that are simply looking for good returns on their investments, and that would like your current management to stay in place.

Financial buyers will scrutinize your financial statements and your assets very closely. Most are looking for a solid, well-managed company that won't need a great deal of immediate change, but there are some investors who specialize in turnaround situations and will be willing to look at companies that are not currently profitable.

Strategic Buyers

Strategic buyers are those who are interested in your company's fit into their own long-range business plans. They may be one of your competitors, or a similar company from another region that wants to expand into your area. However, another possibility is a company in a related business, whose management can see that your company has strengths from which they can benefit — for example, you may already produce a product that they want to sell, or you may have distribution channels that they want to exploit. Sometimes these types of buyers — who are in related, but not completely parallel businesses — are referred to as "synergistic buyers."

Whether synergistic or competitive, strategic buyers are generally the ones who will pay you the most for your company. The better the fit, the more they will want your business and the greater the premium they will pay.

Warning

 You must be careful in speaking with competitors or people your business currently deals with directly as suppliers, vendors, or customers. Although they may be legitimately interested in buying your business, if the deal falls through, you don't want them to have gained enough information to ruin you.

It's best to let your agent deal with all potential buyers initially, revealing only enough to whet their appetite. If negotiations progress, you'll want to have them sign confidentiality agreements to protect your legal rights, but don't rely solely on the paper — you need to keep your sensitive information under lock and key until the final sales contract is signed.

Company Insiders

A third group of potential buyers for your company is your family, friends, and key employees. These people know your business from the inside, and may already have a personal stake in seeing that it survives and prospers. They may be more willing to buy your company than an outside financial buyer would, because their inside knowledge lowers their risk.

The main problem with insiders is that they frequently lack cash. You may have to finance a large part of the transaction yourself, or arrange third-party financing through a leveraged buy-out. The flip-side of this is that if you know the parties well, you may be more willing to recover part of the sales price via an earnout provision, a consulting arrangement, or even a non-qualified pension plan.

How Can You Reach Buyers?

So, now that you have a sense of who your potential buyers might be, how do you go about reaching them, assuming that you're not going to be selling to people you've already identified like your children or manager.

You could start by sending out feelers to your friends, associates, and network of business contacts to see whether they or anyone they know might be interested in buying your business.

However, we don't recommend this. If your employees, customers, and suppliers find out that the business is up for sale, you could have big trouble on your hands. Key employees might start jumping ship, and other employees might stop putting forth much effort if they see you as a lame-duck boss. Many people assume that when a company goes on the block, the reason is that it's on shaky financial ground, so you may find that credit is not being extended to you or people don't want to sign long-term contracts. Avoid all these problems. Keep your divestiture plans to yourself and your team of advisors.

Let your business broker or mergers and acquisitions intermediary look for potential buyers for you. They should have a long list of contacts, including brokers in other areas of the country, to sift through in search of the perfect match. They may also advertise your business in local and national publications, trade journals, etc. under their name, not yours. Your broker should be able to approach potential buyers confidentially, keeping your name out of the discussion, until some positive interest is shown.

Prepare a Selling Memorandum

One of the best tools to promote the sale of your business is essentially a business plan in reverse. It should present all the important information about your company, products, industry, and market in an easy-to-grasp format that presents your company in a very positive light.

You'll need to start with an executive summary that briefly lays out your key selling points, and tells the buyer why you want to sell.

You'll also need sections that describe the facts about your company's history, structure, and operations; the asking price and basic terms you want; your industry, market, and products; your employees and assets; historical and projected financial statements; and anything else that will explain who you are and why your business is such a strong opportunity. Keep in mind who your audience is, and don't divulge any information that you wouldn't want your competitors to see. On the other hand, remember that a lot of your financial information is publicly available anyway, so there's no need to be paranoid.

Your selling memorandum is essentially a marketing piece, and it's likely that your business broker will want to have a hand in creating it. In addition, you should run it past your lawyer and accountant (in fact, it's likely that your accountant will provide the financial information you include).

STRUCTURING THE BUSINESS SALE

Terms drive price, and you should arrive at a general agreement with the buyer about the major terms before you start talking dollars. You may even include a short list of your absolute requirements as part of your selling memorandum, so that buyers who can't meet your minimum terms won't use up your precious time.

Some of the terms you should be considering are:

- What, exactly, are you selling? Which assets will go with the company, and which (if any) are you going to keep? Are your key contracts transferable to a buyer? If your business is incorporated, will you sell stock or assets?

- How much of the purchase price do you need to receive at closing? Will you consider an installment sale? An earnout?

- To what extent will you remain involved in the company, after the sale?

- How will tax considerations affect your net proceeds from the sale?

Once you've got a feel for what terms the buyer will accept and what you can live with, you can begin to negotiate the price.

Some business advisors say that you should let your broker or intermediary do all your negotiating for you — that you should not talk directly with the buyer until almost everything has been settled. Other advisors say, you are the best representative of your company and of your own expectations from the sale, and buyers will respond better to direct contact with you.

Just make sure the buyer understands that *anything you agree on is subject to your attorney's later review and approval.*

What, Exactly, Is for Sale?

Although it may seem obvious, you should give some thought to exactly which of your assets will be sold with the company.

There may be some valuable assets in the business that you want to keep, such as real estate or equipment that you want to lease to the buyer (or someone else). You may also be the owner of valuable patents, trademarks, or copyrights that you want to retain and license back to the buyer. If you retain some of the assets, the purchase price will be lower, thus making the business more affordable to a larger group of people.

Picking and choosing among the assets to be sold is easier if you aren't incorporated. In a sole proprietorship, you'll simply retain the assets you don't want to sell — you won't be taxed on any profits unless and until you eventually decide to sell them. Partnerships and LLCs can keep the unwanted assets and distribute them in kind to partners or members upon liquidation, although the individual partners may have to pay some tax upon what is technically a dissolution of their business.

In a corporation, it becomes even more complicated and you may have to purchase the asset at fair market value, with the corporation paying tax on any capital gains inherent on the asset, if you want to remove the asset from the business.

Key Contracts

Ideally, your most important contracts, including leases and contracts with customers and suppliers, should be assumable by the buyer. That way, you can get out from under the contract, and the buyer will have the resources needed to conduct business. If your business is organized as a corporation, selling stock, rather than assets, can solve the assumption problem since most contracts were probably made with the corporation rather than you personally. This is one reason some buyers may agree to or even prefer a stock sale.

The assignment of existing loans on the business can be a problem, if you had made personal guarantees to the lender. If you can't get the bank to release you from further liability on the loan, you'll need to make sure that the cash paid at the time of purchase is sufficient to pay off such loans.

Will You Sell Assets or Stock?

If your business is incorporated, you have a very important decision to make: will you sell the assets of the business, or the stock? In most cases, selling stock is better for you, but selling assets is better for the buyer.

If you agree to the buyer's demands for an asset sale, you should insist on a higher price because of the significantly higher taxes and liability risks you'll face.

With a C corporation, tax aspects are the main reason for the seller's preference for selling stock. Simply put, if you sell the stock, you'll pay capital gains tax on the sale, based on your tax basis in the stock (i.e., what you paid into the corporation in exchange for the stock). In contrast, if you sell the assets, you are essentially taxed twice: first, upon selling assets to the buyer, the corporation will pay capital gains tax on the value of the assets over their existing basis to the corporation. Second, when the corporation is liquidated, you'll personally pay capital gains tax on the excess of the net proceeds of the sale, over your existing basis in the stock. With an S corporation, you can usually avoid this double tax.

However, for either type of corporation, with a stock sale any unknown liabilities the company may have are transferred to the new owner. With an asset sale, the liabilities would remain with the seller. Some examples might be future product liability claims, contract claims, lawsuits by employees, pension or benefit plan liabilities, etc. stemming from the seller's ownership of the company.

Now, with careful legal drafting, these general rules can be altered in the sales contract. Because third parties won't be bound by the terms of the contract, the contract can also include escrow arrangements or indemnification clauses that will remove some of the buyer's risks, by stating that the seller's money will be used to pay for claims. However, if the drafting is not perfect and anything is left out, the general rules will kick in.

Payment Terms

Aside from terms relating to what you are selling with the business, terms relating to payment are the most important, and need to be generally agreed upon before the letter of intent is signed.

Some of the payment terms that you may want to consider are the down payment, earnouts, escrow arrangements, and stock as payment.

Down Payment

If you're going to help the buyer finance the deal, as more than half of small business sellers do, you'll need to decide the minimum down payment you will accept. You'll definitely want to be able to cover your tax bill, so you need to have an estimate of what that will be. You will also need to net enough cash after taxes to pay off any business loans that the buyer is not assuming.

Finally, don't forget to include other transaction costs that must be paid at the time of the closing, such as broker's commissions, appraisal fees, attorney and accountant fees, etc.

Most commercial lenders will require a down payment of at least 25 to 30 percent, to be sure that the buyer isn't going to walk away if the going gets tough. This is a good requirement for you to adopt.

Earnouts

An earnout is a contractual arrangement in which the purchase price is stated in terms of a minimum, but you (the seller) will be entitled to more money if the business reaches certain financial goals in the future. These goals should be stated in terms of percentages of gross sales or revenues, rather than net sales, because expenses are easy to manipulate and thus net sales are too easily distorted.

Example

A simplified example of an earnout provision would be one stating that the seller is entitled to 1 percent of all gross sales between 1 and 2 million dollars, and 2 percent of all sales over 2 million, payable annually for the first three years after the sale.

If you do use an earnout, it's important to state in the contract exactly who will be reviewing the books and verifying the business's performance. From the seller's perspective, you should be more likely to agree to an earnout if you'll maintain an employment or consulting relationship with the buyer. That way, you'll be able to keep an eye on things to make sure the buyer is taking all steps necessary to reach the goals, is not making unrecorded sales for cash, keeping two sets of books, etc.

Escrows and Indemnification Clauses

If it seems likely that there are significant unknown liabilities associated with your business, the buyer may be willing to assume them if some part of the purchase price is placed in escrow (that is, it's placed in the hands of a neutral third party such as a bank, to be released to either party upon the happening of certain events). If problems surface within a specified time period, the buyer will get some or all of the money back; if nothing goes wrong, the money will be released to you at the end of the escrow period.

Another possible solution is simply to write an indemnification clause into the contract; for example, if the buyer becomes subject to a lawsuit by a customer, employee, supplier, etc., the seller agrees to pay for the buyer's costs of defending the suit and also to pay any damages.

As the seller, you'd typically prefer an indemnification clause over an escrow, but the buyer may be concerned that you won't be around if problems arise. The buyer would much rather have some of your cash available, if the terms of the escrow agreement are met.

Stock as Payment

If one corporation sells out to another, it's often possible to structure the deal as a tax-free reorganization. This means that essentially no capital gains tax is due at the time of the sale, because each party is merely exchanging one type of security for another. The big catch is that you must agree to accept stock in the other company as virtually the only consideration for the sale. This is risky, but aside from structuring the deal as an installment sale, a reorganization is really the only way to push the capital gains tax on the sale into the future.

Your After-Sale Role

It's a rare buyer who won't want you to show him or her the ropes, by remaining involved with the business for a while after the sale. Often the deal won't fly unless you agree to this. At a minimum, the buyer wants to be sure that the business is indeed a going concern. But beyond that, buyers realize that most of the real business knowledge has never been written down, and when you leave, it will go with you unless the new owner takes steps to learn it from you.

After-sale involvement can take a number of different forms. The most common are employment contracts, consulting arrangements, and noncompete agreements.

Employment Contracts

Employment contracts are frequently used in family businesses as part of a succession plan. Where the older-generation founder really does intend to stick around for a while, and the younger-generation new owner can deal with any ego problems and make good use of the founder's advice, experience, and skills, such arrangements can make good economic sense.

Just be careful that you are really functioning as an employee, to satisfy the IRS. If you do too little for your pay, the payments won't be deductible; if you continue to do everything you used to do as owner, the entire sales or succession transaction can be treated as a sham by the IRS, bringing you an endless number of tax problems.

Consulting Contracts

When the buyer of a business is an unrelated third party, consulting agreements are more frequently used than employment agreements.

Usually the buyer will agree to make specified payments at certain intervals of time, and the seller agrees to be available for consultation for a specified number of hours per month. The seller still gets the payments even if no services are required.

Work Smart

One disadvantage to these agreements is that you may need to make yourself available for consultation, even if your plan was to retire to a yacht off of Tahiti. A possible solution is to set up your own consulting company and have it sign the agreement, so that you can substitute other consultants if you become too busy, ill, or simply don't want to continue.

Payments made under consulting agreements can serve a dual purpose of compensating you for your wisdom and also making a portion of the cash you get (which might otherwise be part of the purchase price) deductible to the buyer. The IRS is well aware of the potential for abuse in this situation, so make sure that the agreement is in writing and that any payments under consulting arrangements are within the range of fair market value, given your experience, contacts, knowledge of the business, etc.

Noncompete Agreements

One of the last things that a buyer wants to happen is for you to sell your company, and then turn around and start another one just up the street, taking most of your customers with you. For that reason, buyers will want you to sign a noncompete agreement as part of the deal.

The agreement will state that in exchange for a specified payment, you promise not to go into a similar type of business, within a certain geographic area, for a given period of time. Sometimes the agreement will specify that you promise not to use certain confidential trade secrets, business processes, customer lists, etc. that you are transferring to the buyer. Noncompetes are used in about 80 percent of business sales.

Warning

Most sellers think of signing a noncompete agreement as a "no-brainer." They are retiring, and weren't planning to go into a similar business anyway, so why not take money for doing nothing? However, you should know that there's a sizable number of business owners who find, a couple of years down the road, that they got out of their business too early and they miss it. When they decide they want to go back into business, a noncompete agreement can stand in their way.

Tax Aspects of Selling Out

If you're not careful, you can wind up with less than half of the sale price of your business in your pocket, after all the income taxes are paid! However, with skillful planning it's possible to minimize or defer at least some of these taxes.

The basic issue is that with any sale of a capital asset, including business property or your entire business, you have to pay income tax on your capital gains. Ordinarily the gains are taxed in the year of the sale. If your business is a sole proprietorship, a partnership, or an LLC, the gains must be computed separately for each and every asset in the sale (you can lump some of the smaller items together, however, in categories such as office machines, furniture, production equipment etc.).

Long-term capital gains on property held for more than 18 months are taxed at a maximum rate of 20 percent. Property held for more than 12 but no more than 18 months is called "mid-term gain" and is taxed at a maximum of 28 percent. Certain assets (like inventory, accounts receivable, and property held for less than a year) are not eligible for capital gain treatment; any gains on such property are treated as ordinary income and taxed at your normal rate, which can be as high as 39.6 percent.

The IRS requires that you and the buyer must agree as to what portion of the purchase price applies to each individual asset, and to intangible assets such as goodwill. The allocation will determine the amount of capital or ordinary income tax you must pay on the sale (except in the case of corporations, which have the option of structuring the sale as a stock sale).

That's the basic story. But things are never that simple with the IRS. There are a number of qualifications to the rules, and issues that present planning opportunities for sellers (and buyers) of businesses.

- **Installment sales:** if you defer receipt of the purchase price to later years with an installment sale, you may be able to postpone paying tax on your gains until you receive them.

- **Double taxation of corporations:** for businesses organized as corporations, the structure of the deal as an asset or stock sale can have very different tax results.

- **Tax-free reorganizations:** where one corporation is buying another by exchanging stock, you may be able to structure the sale as a tax-free merger.

Installment Sales — Now and Then

Now: When the Tax Relief Extension Act was signed in December 1999, the installment sales method of accounting for accrual method taxpayers was repealed. As a result, when a small business is sold to a buyer making payments over a period of time, the seller must report and pay capital gains tax on the entire purchase price, even though the seller hasn't received all the money from the buyer.

Small business groups have cited the tax change as decreasing the value of many closely held small businesses, most of which are sold using the installment sales method. It is estimated that the new tax treatment could reduce the sale price of such businesses by 5 to 20 percent or more. With this in mind, as of this printing, lawmakers are considering ways to provide relief for small businesses suffering under this new requirement.

Then: Previously, if you were willing to finance the sale of your business by taking back a mortgage or note for part of the purchase price, you might have been able to report some of your capital gains on the installment method, allowing you to defer some of the tax due on the sale until you get paid in future years. The installment method was used when you received at least one payment for your business after the year of the sale; it could not be used if the sale resulted in a loss.

The bad news is that payments for many (or even most) of the assets of your business were not eligible for installment sale treatment. If your business was incorporated and you were selling the stock of the corporation, as opposed to the assets, you could have used the installment method to report the sale of the stock, provided that it's was not traded on a public exchange. However, unincorporated businesses and those corporations who sell assets could only use the installment sale method for some of the assets sold with the business.

Generally, anything on which gains must be treated as ordinary income were not eligible for installment sale treatment. That included payments for inventory, accounts receivable, and property that had been used for one year or less. It also included payment for any personal property to the extent of any depreciation that must be recaptured, based on deductions you claimed over the years. And, it included any depreciation that must be recaptured on real estate. For all these items, you paid tax on any gains in the year of the sale, even if you hadn't yet received payments for the items. Looking at it another way, in most cases only gain on assets that have appreciated in value beyond their original purchase price were eligible for installment sale treatment.

Negotiating the Price

Whenever you negotiate price, it's almost always best to let the other party make the first offer. However, as a practical matter, you will often have to make the first price move because you will have to give a ball-park asking price to your business broker.

If your buyer knows that your asking price is based on a formal appraisal using recognized valuation formulas, he or she may take your asking price more seriously, and make an offer that is fairly close (e.g., within 20 percent or so) to it. However, don't be shocked if you get low-ball offers at around 50 percent of your asking price, or even less. You should always respond to each offer on its own merits, and don't allow yourself to feel insulted or angry at an offer that you think is far too low.

On the other hand, if the buyer names a price that's *more* than you anticipated, don't automatically accept the first offer. Buyers will expect you to bargain hard on this issue. If you give in too soon, they will think something is wrong. An exception to this rule applies to large corporate buyers — they sometimes bid on a lot of small companies, and if you don't bite, they'll simply move on to the next likely prospect.

Our general advice is that you try not to get too hung up on any particular price. If you feel that the buyer won't budge, you can go back and change some of the terms you've tentatively agreed on, to make them more favorable to you. Your broker or attorney may have some creative ways of bridging a price gap between you and the buyer.

You can also decide to keep some of the business assets yourself, and lease them back to the buyer (or anyone else) to reduce the business's price. The point is, there are almost infinite possibilities, if you are willing to be flexible.

Warning

 Include an expiration date in any firm offers or counteroffers. Under contract law, when someone makes a firm offer they can theoretically be forced to complete the deal at that price (though if they are smart they will hold back some contingencies, such as "this offer is contingent on my attorney's approval of the purchase contract").

FINANCING THE BUSINESS SALE

Early on in the negotiation process, you'll need to determine where the buyer is going to get the money to purchase your business.

Of course the most obvious source of financing is you. Seller financing is involved in up to 90 percent of small business sales and more than half of mid-size sales, and if you're not willing to finance at least some of the price, you may not be able to sell your company.

If the buyer is planning to obtain outside funding, the bank or other lender should confirm to you that the buyer is qualified and that the lender is willing to come up with the money, before negotiations go too far.

Seller Financing

If you allow the buyer to pay you off slowly over time, you'll retain many of the risks that come from continued ownership of the business while giving up control of its management. In most cases, the buyer's ability to make the payments will depend on the future success of the business, yet your buyer may know little about your company, your customers, or even your industry. If the buyer runs aground and stops making payments, your only real recourse may be to foreclose on the note and repossess the business, but that means you'll have to find another buyer and start all over again.

On the upside, carrying back a note for some or all of the purchase price can provide a tax break for you if you qualify for installment sale treatment.

Mechanics of seller financing. The simplest way to provide seller financing is to have the buyer make a down payment, with you carrying back a note or mortgage for the rest of the purchase price. The business itself, and/or the significant business assets, provides the primary collateral for the note. A lien on the property is filed with the secretary of state's office, so the world knows that it exists.

This type of deal can be very flexible — you can adjust the payment schedule, interest rate, loan period, or any other terms to reflect your needs and the buyer's financial situation. Most seller financing will be for a relatively short term (say, five to seven years), and at the end of the loan term there will a large portion of principal remaining. The buyer will have to obtain outside financing to pay off the balance of the loan in a balloon payment.

Protecting Your Interests

If you agree to finance part of the deal, you should try to get the buyer to provide more security for the loan, besides the business itself, by doing some or all of the following:

- *Thoroughly check out the buyer's background, including credit record, management experience, personal assets, and character.*

- *Require the buyer to put up a personal residence as additional collateral (assuming there is significant equity in the home).*

- *Require the seller to personally guarantee the loan, just as a commercial lender would.*

- *Require the buyer to take out a life insurance policy with yourself as beneficiary, so that the loan will be paid off if the buyer meets an untimely demise.*

- *If the buyer will be actively working in the business, consider getting disability insurance on the buyer, if not prohibitively expensive.*

- *Restrict the new owner's sale of assets, acquisitions, and expansions until the note is paid off.*

- *Have the buyer send you quarterly financial statements so you can keep tabs on the business.*

Outside Lenders/LBOs

When an outside lender such as a bank or investment firm finances the purchase of a business, the transaction is frequently called a leveraged buy-out or LBO.

LBO financing is usually a package that combines several types of loans, as well as equity. The components may come from different sources. The package itself may be put together by a bank, a commercial finance company, a venture capital firm, or a mergers and acquisitions intermediary that has access to capital markets.

Some typical components of the package might be 15 to 25 percent equity (stock held by the buyer); 10 to 50 percent subordinated debt (akin to a second mortgage); and 40 to 70 percent senior debt (akin to a first mortgage, and collateralized with assets such as real estate or even receivables).

As you can guess, the complexity of the structure and the players involved make a typical LBO an unlikely prospect for the average small business. However, if *you* are willing to act as the subordinate debtholder, the LBO model can work for even a very small business. The determining factor would be whether the business has sufficient assets and cash flow to interest one or more institutional lenders in making the senior loan(s).

Work Smart

If your buyer wants to do an LBO, recognize that it will require a lot of work on your part to make it happen. These deals are neither simple nor easy, and they take time to put together. Not only will you need to cooperate with the lender, you may even need to help sell the lender on the deal. However, the result can be significantly less risk to you than if you had financed the entire purchase yourself.

STEPS TO COMPLETING THE SALE

Once you've located a buyer for your company and come to an agreement as to the major terms and price, you are ready to move into the process of actually closing the deal. The major steps involved in the sale of a business are outlined below.

Letter of Intent

After you reach a general agreement with the buyer as to the price and terms of the sale, the buyer usually drafts and signs a non-binding letter of intent.

This document lays out the general terms of the deal, and, if signed by the seller, it indicates that both parties intend to move forward in completing the transaction.

Generally, the buyer will also make a monetary deposit on the purchase price. However, the letter is usually nonbinding in the sense that at any point, negotiations can be broken off by either party, and the buyer's deposit will be returned.

Once signed and accepted by the seller, the letter should give the buyer permission to contact your lawyer, accountant, banker, etc., to find out more about your operation. In the meantime, your respective lawyers can begin to hash out the contractual language of the purchase agreement.

Do you need a letter? The letter of intent stage can be skipped if you know your purchaser well (for example, the buyer is your child or a key employee), or if the deal is a very small one and it looks as if you can move directly on to negotiating the purchase agreement. However, even if you and your buyer decide to dispense with the formal letter, we would still recommend that you have the buyer sign a confidentiality agreement before moving on to the next step.

Due Diligence

Usually, after a buyer signs a letter of intent and the seller accepts it, the buyer will have a specified period of time in which to conduct a due diligence investigation of the seller and the company. During this period, your buyer should have access to your financial and other records, facilities, employees, etc., to investigate before finalizing the deal.

The buyer will want to see copies of all leases, contracts, and loan agreements in addition to copious financial records and statements. He or she will want to see any management reports you use, such as sales reports, inventory records, detailed lists of assets, facility maintenance records, aged receivables and payables reports, employee organization charts, payroll and benefits records, customer records, and marketing materials. The buyer will want to know about any pending litigation, tax audits, or insurance disputes.

A wise buyer will also want to take a look at your facilities, and spend some time "in the trenches" with you and/or your employees as you go about your business. We suggest that you accommodate this request, even if it will cause some disruption of your normal operations. Buyers will be most suspicious if they think you are hiding something. They tend to be more concerned about what they don't know, than they are concerned about minor or even major problems that might turn up in an investigation.

You should also do some serious investigating of your own. You'll want to find out the buyer's credit record, management experience, reputation, and the plans he or she has for your company's future operation. This is particularly true if you plan to continue an employment or consulting arrangement with the buyer after the sale, or if some part of the purchase price will be paid into the future though a financing arrangement, or an earnout.

Business Purchase Agreements

The purchase agreement for your business is one of the most important legal documents you'll ever sign. You don't want to have problems collecting the money due you or to have legal problems haunting you into the future, and a carefully constructed purchase agreement can be your best insurance policy for preventing such catastrophes.

Customarily, the buyer's lawyer provides the initial draft of the purchase agreement for a business. However, we suggest that your lawyer should draft the sections that are most important to you: the clauses containing representations and warranties about the business. Ideally, you should try to avoid or limit the making of any warranties for which you can be held legally accountable. Make sure that you maintain ongoing liability insurance for any liabilities that will remain with you — for example, product liability insurance on products that were sold during your tenure as owner.

Once both parties have agreed on the language of the purchase agreement, it will be signed by both parties. The contract will state the date at which the final transfer of ownership and possession of the business will occur, and when the seller will get the money. With a signed purchase agreement in hand, the buyer can finalize any financing arrangements with outside lenders in anticipation of the closing.

State Laws on Business Sales

State laws can impose a variety of obligations on both the seller and buyer of a business.

Bulk sales acts. Many states have laws on their books requiring that when a business sells the "bulk" of its materials, supplies, merchandise, or other inventory outside the regular course of business, it must formally notify all of its creditors at least 10 days before the pending sale. Otherwise, the sale will be ineffective against those creditors, meaning that they can still repossess the goods from the new owner, in repayment of the debt. In some states the creditors will also have a lien on the proceeds of the sale. Even if your business doesn't have inventory, you may be covered by the law because a number of states have extended it to apply to certain service businesses, most commonly gas stations, restaurants, and bars.

The state laws generally allow the notification requirements to be waived if both parties agree, but then the buyer will want you to agree to indemnify him or her against any claims made by your creditors.

Another part of the bulk sales acts requires you to give the buyer a list of all your known creditors, their business addresses, and the total amounts owed to them. The list must also be filed with the appropriate state agency, so that creditors have access to it.

Recorded security interests. Before the buyer closes the deal, he or she will want to be sure there are no recorded liens or other security interests (known to lawyers as UCC-1 filings) against any of the assets. Therefore, the buyer's lawyer will order a search, much like a title search for real property, through the appropriate state, county, or other records. Once the deal goes through, you in turn will need to have your lawyer record any security interests you will have in the buyer's business or in particular assets such as his or her home or other property.

State tax certificates. In some states, you must obtain a certificate from the appropriate tax authorities showing that no sales and use or unemployment taxes are currently owed, and provide this to the buyer.

State sales or transfer taxes. In some states, the sale of a business or its assets can itself be subject to sales tax. Other states tax the sale of stock or other securities.

Directors' and shareholders' approval. For corporations, state laws and your own corporate charter may require that your board of directors must approve the transaction. In some situations the stockholders must also vote. A vote of the buyer's board of directors and stockholders may also be necessary. Where the deal is structured as a stock sale, however, shareholder approval is not usually required.

Minority shareholders' rights. If you have any shareholders who are not pleased about the deal, your state law may give them certain protections. In many states, minority shareholders have the right to an independent appraisal of the business, and have the right to be cashed out based on the appraisal at the time of the sale.

Closing the Business Sale

The "closing" is the point in time at which all necessary documents are signed by all the parties, apportionment of expenses up to the date of closing is done, money and keys are exchanged, and the buyer becomes the new owner of the business.

Sometimes the closing occurs on a particular day, when the parties meet with their respective lawyers to sign all the documents in each other's presence. In other situations, each party signs the necessary documents as they become available, and forwards them to an escrow agent over a period of days or weeks. When the agent has everything from both parties, he or she will release the funds to the seller and the deal is "closed."

After the closing, be sure to take a well-deserved vacation, and concentrate on putting the proceeds of the sale to work!

Chapter 32

Planning for Succession

When a small business is a key component of family wealth, the owner usually has a strong desire to perpetuate it in one form or another. But perpetuating the business through an orderly succession to family members or other insiders is the ultimate management challenge.

Any transition must preserve the continuity of leadership and it is most important that the *succession of ownership and management be perceived as a process rather than an event.* Much as some successors might hope otherwise, it's not a matter of deciding to retire at 4:00 p.m. next Tuesday at which time Junior will take the reins or your partner, Charlie, will become the boss, while you'll fade into oblivion (or more likely onto the 10th tee).

Succession is a process requiring planning, teamwork, and constant re-evaluation. So infrequently is it done successfully that barely 30 percent of family businesses survive into the second generation and fewer than 15 percent of them endure into the third. If the business of succession is not done by *process* (through planning), it will be done by *crisis* (a failure to plan), with perhaps disastrous results.

A typical succession plan has two elements, which should be considered separately:

- the transfer of power, whereby control over the business's operation is transferred to those best suited to exercising it

- the transfer of assets, whereby the wealth concentrated in the business is transferred to designated family members, who may be a different or larger group than the person or persons who will be assuming power.

TRANSFERRING POWER

The family business environment is, of course, affected by all the issues faced by any type of business. Technology, laws, competitors, economic trends, and unrelated (non-family) employees are among these influences.

In addition, the family business environment is influenced by anything that affects the family itself, such as the relative health of its members, their various interests and skill levels, their individual marital status, and the level of business participation of each individual.

Managing a transfer of power while balancing the internal and external environmental influences of the business is a juggling act at best. If the Illustrious Founder is somewhat less than willing to give up control and/or the Designated Successor is not well prepared to accept it, the transfer can be a challenge for even the most skilled psychiatric social worker.

Fortunately in this enlightened day and age, most family business people are professionals who manage their companies to compete effectively in our global marketplace. They don't have time to dwell on petty jealousies and family squabbles.

The major issues confronting a family business owner seeking to transfer power to successors are: selecting a successor, handling intergenerational conflict and different agendas, training the successor, and timing the transition.

Selecting a Successor

Most family businesses will have one member of the next generation who is more active, qualified, and interested in the business than his or her siblings. Frequently, the founder has already spent a great deal of time grooming the successor-apparent or the successor has soaked up much of the necessary knowledge on his or her own over the years. The challenges in this scenario come in the form of finding ways to assure equitable treatment for the non-participating family members, be they spouse or siblings.

If succession has not already been determined by interest, proximity, or birth order, a group effort in choosing and grooming an individual is one way to proceed. Key employees who are not family members can often be recruited for a transition team.

If your valued, long-time key employees can participate in the selection and initiation of a successor, the entire team will benefit over the long run. Involving key employees is a good way to retain them, and retaining them is essential for continuity and credibility in dealing with outside sources such as banks and suppliers.

If there is competition between your children for the position, a decision to divide the power between them is not likely to be successful. Ownership may be divided but management should be clearly delineated. Often ownership can be split into passive and active shares, giving the active successor the necessary control over the business but providing an equal economic benefit to the inactive shareholders. In some cases the business can be divided along functional lines, so that different family members can assume control over well-defined functions or business units.

Intergenerational Conflict

Conflict between the founder of a family business and his or her successor is a matter of degree. It's normal for some intergenerational conflict to exist.

Founding fathers are, more often than not, conflicted about their successor sons. (It's too soon to know yet if this syndrome will carry over to daughters.) On one level Dad wants his son to succeed and make him proud and rich, but on another level he may see the son as a threat to his manhood and dominance.

The son who accepts the challenge of this ambiguity should be a well trained manager — of himself as well as others. He'll then be able to manage around the unbusinesslike emotional upheavals that can frequently be generated in power struggles. A true understanding of the feelings and motivations of the founder will enable the successor to deal rationally and effectively with them. After all, the founder spent his or her entire life building the firm and sees it as an extension of his or her self, which is only natural — even if it *is* a difficult act to follow.

The other side of the coin is, of course, the underprepared, disinterested, or lazy successor-elect. Sometimes the founder is willing and eager to give the business to the offspring but the child would rather be a marine biologist. Or, the child is anxious to get his or her hands on the business in order to get a classy company car and play golf every day since he or she will now be the boss. Or perhaps the child is interested and willing but hopelessly unqualified for the task.

Between these extremes are the majority of family business successions. Able founders need to pass along a hard-earned creation to able successors who have worked hard to become prepared to take on the task. There will be the usual number of differences of opinion and approach commonly found between generations and between co-workers of the same generation. These can and will be worked out mutually over time to the benefit of the individuals, the family, and the business. Planning and communication are the tools these successful teams must use consistently.

The first issue to be discussed should be "can this business support all the family members who will be relying on it after the transition?" Then, ways of passing ownership without creating inequities among siblings, jeopardizing security, or triggering excessive tax liabilities must be addressed.

Warning

 Be careful not to let tax planning control your decisions. A tax lawyer can make compelling arguments for strategies that can minimize estate and gift taxes. A CPA can be very convincing when suggesting strategies for controlling income taxes. But no matter how talented and earnest your professional advisors are, their limited specialties should not dictate your choices for your business or your family.

There are indeed more important planning considerations than saving on taxes. Don't be bullied into compromising what's important to you and your family just to keep a few bucks away from the IRS. First determine the result you want, and then let the professionals find the most tax-efficient way to achieve that result.

The agendas of non-participating family members must also be taken into account. The founder's spouse, for example, may feel she's entitled to some say in the matter of appointing a successor, transferring power, and particularly in transferring assets.

Unresolved issues or misunderstandings in areas like this can cause severe problems down the road, particularly if the founder dies unexpectedly and is therefore not present to referee.

Training the Successor

Training, on the job and otherwise, is the critical ingredient that can put success into a family business succession plan. It can take many forms.

Setting a good example for your successor in all aspects of business and family life is essential. Formal education, not just in the specialty of the business but also in management and accounting, is immensely valuable. And actual experience at a job outside of the family business is certainly preferable.

Experience in all aspects of the family business operation, from sweeping the floor to driving the truck or counting the inventory, is necessary. Where the successor is active over a period of time in the business, he or she will not only become familiar with what it takes to run the firm, but will also have a chance to interact with employees, suppliers, and customers and gain their confidence and respect. A formal job description for each task assigned during the training mode will clarify everyone's expectations and enable useful periodic performance evaluation and feedback to the trainee.

Work Smart

Many universities operate centers for family business education and research. Among the most prominent are Baylor, Cornell, DePaul, Loyola of Chicago, Northeastern, UMass, USC, and Wharton. Contact the universities in your area to see what workshops they may have to offer.

There are also many regional conferences on family business topics offered during the year. For a calendar of upcoming events, check out the Family Firm Institute's Website at http://ffi.org *and Netmarquee's very comprehensive site at* http://nmq.com.

Transition Timing

Transition of the control of a family business can take place over a period of months or even years, depending on the needs and wishes of the family members and the business itself.

As the successor gains confidence and credibility in day-to-day operations and dealings with outsiders, the founder can back away into an advisory role. If the founder encounters difficulty in "letting go" of the business entirely, the successor must be prepared to be reassuring and supportive and ensure some type of ongoing role for the founder so that he or she feels included. If the successor resists, it may only cause the founder to become more rigid and the successor to become more frustrated.

A transition plan or timetable should be roughed out initially to assure continuity of management, and should be reevaluated periodically to see if goals are being achieved. The transfer of power can be seamless and subtle if good communications and careful planning are practiced by all parties to the transition.

TRANSFERRING ASSETS

You can't take it with you, or so they say. Well, if you can't take it along, at least you can decide who gets it and when.

Accomplishing this without horrendous tax consequences is a complicated challenge, but it can be done. Passing it along after you're gone is a minefield of tax traps, but there are ways your lawyer can navigate through it.

But when the "IT" is a business, the techniques of giving it away or passing it along become even more specialized and highly evolved.

A laundry list of some of the more commonly used strategies for minimizing taxation on a transfer of assets would look something like this: liquidity strategies, private annuities, GRATs, recapitalizations, and using a family office.

Valuation of the business, as discussed in the preceding chapter, is the foundation of all these methods. Wherever possible, periodic reevaluation should be made a part of any technique used.

The value of assets transferred either by gift or bequest is subject to a federal tax at graduated rates applied on a cumulative, unified basis. Federal transfer taxes can be reduced by the unified tax credit, which for 2000 is the equivalent of exempting $675,000 worth of assets. That is, during life or at your death you may transfer up to $675,000 worth of assets free of tax, but any property in excess of that is taxed at rates from 37 percent to 55 percent.

This exemption will rise in future years until it reaches $1 million in 2006. Beginning in 1998, there's an additional exemption for small, family-owned businesses that is equal to the difference between the exemption and $1.3 million. But if your business is too large or doesn't qualify for the exemption, you'll need to provide for liquidity so that taxes can be paid without depleting the business's working capital.

Liquidity Strategies

Strategies for acquiring the liquidity needed for the payment of estate taxes can be handled three ways:

Deferral. Estate taxes on the value of the business interest may be paid over a period of up to 14 years, if the business interest is more than 35 percent of your adjusted gross estate. The business may be in the form of a proprietorship, a partnership, or a corporation. Of course, the IRS will charge interest at a special low rate set by law. In effect, Uncle Sam becomes your banker.

Redemption. The redemption of closely held stock of a corporation is a planning technique that can allow your heirs to maintain control of the company and gain liquidity to pay taxes. Stock can be redeemed with capital gain treatment to the extent that the proceeds of the sale of the deceased's stock are used to pay administrative and funeral expenses.

This is an important distinction because without it, the redemption can be treated as a dividend and the entire proceeds (not just excess over basis) would be taxed as ordinary income. To qualify, the 35 percent of gross estate test must be met and the beneficiary must share liability for tax and debts of the estate. Moreover, the company must have accumulated enough cash to redeem the stock.

Combination of redemption with the 14-year deferral provision is a tricky tactic for which you will need to hire a very talented attorney.

Buy/sell agreements. Buy/sell agreements can provide liquidity when the purchaser has funded the purchase price with life insurance on the decedent's life. The other advantages of a buy/sell agreement include the fact that it's an organized plan for the disposition of the business interest. It can also establish a value, which is always a problem in the case of a closely held business.

The agreement can be between the business and its owner (a redemption plan) or among the various owners (a cross-purchase plan). Frequently, the agreement will be backed by life insurance policies on all the principals, so a ready supply of cash will be there when needed. In a partnership, a buy/sell agreement is like a pre-nuptial agreement between the partners. For corporations, it's an attempt to set future value on some rational basis that may well hold up during IRS scrutiny. The tax benefits of a buy/sell agreement depend largely on careful drafting, so a very good lawyer will be necessary if this strategy is used.

Private Annuities

Where a private annuity is used as a business succession tool, the owner sells (transfers) the business to a family member in exchange for a lifetime income.

The value of the business will not be included in the owner's gross estate for tax purposes, provided the value of the annuity equals the value of the exchanged business interest. If the founder dies early, the appreciation in value of the business after the transfer escapes tax. If the owner outlives his or her life expectancy, the annuity payments will exceed the value of the business.

A drawback of a private annuity is that the seller retains no secured interest in the business. A variation of a private annuity is known as a secured interest note or SCIN, a vehicle where the seller retains a secured interest via a note from a family member. The tax treatment is the same as for a private annuity. The danger here is, if any remaining payments on the note will be forgiven at the founder's death, then any gains from the forgiveness of debt will be taxed in the estate of the founder.

GRATS

Grantor retained annuity trusts (GRATS) are a complex method of transferring assets to the next generation with minimal gift or estate taxation. They are actually fixed annuities for a fixed number of years. Their complexity requires expert legal advice.

GRATS are a way to make gifts, and transfer the fair market value of assets, on a discounted basis since only part of the gift gets valued in the irrevocable trust. There are several other forms of trusts, such as charitable lead trusts, grantor retained income trusts (GRITS), and so forth that are permutations of this concept.

Recapitalizations

Recapitalization, or the issuance of two classes of corporate stock, is another method used to transfer ownership at minimal tax cost. Stock is generally divided into voting and non-voting categories which permits control to remain with one individual or group, usually the family members who are active in the business. The non-voting stock is used to provide equity to the inactive family members. There are stringent laws limiting recapitalizations and, again, expert legal advice is necessary.

The Family Office

Many times where an operating business has been transferred down to the next generation, sold outright, or recapitalized, the family finds it useful to set up a family office for the administration and management of their remaining collective assets.

Such an office can fill the gap left when the operating business was sold and is no longer there to provide the recordkeeping, tax planning, and general support the family members had become accustomed to enjoying over the years. An employee, perhaps a bookkeeper or business manager, is generally hired to run the office. Having an outside third party to administer things and a businesslike location in which to do it can achieve a level of professionalism impossible in a strictly family setting (i.e., Dad's home office in Boca), and the cost need not be high.

Glossary

Accountable plan: An accountable plan is a plan for reimbursing employee's business expenses that has the following three characteristics: (1) it provides for advances or reimbursements for deductible business expenses that employees incur in connection with their performance of services for their employer; (2) it requires employees to substantiate the expenses within a reasonable time; and (3) it requires employees to return advances or reimbursements in excess of substantiated expenses within a reasonable period of time.

Accounting equation: Assets = liabilities + owner's equity. The financial statement called the balance sheet is based on the "accounting equation." Note that assets are on the left-hand side of the equation, and liabilities and equities are on the right-hand side of the equation. Similarly, some balance sheets are presented so that assets are on the left, and liabilities and owner's equity are on the right.

Accounts payable: Accounts payable are the unpaid bills of your business, the money you owe to your suppliers and other vendors. Accounts payable are generally payable within 30 days after receiving a bill from the supplier or vendor. "A/P" is the standard abbreviation for accounts payable.

Accounts receivable: Accounts receivable are amounts due, other than from promissory notes, from customers or other debtors of the business. Credit sales increase accounts receivable; the debts become due upon billing or within a stated time period, usually up to 90 days from purchase.

Accrual-basis taxpayer: An accrual-basis taxpayer is one who reports income in the year in which it is earned, whether or not it has been received, and who claims deductions in the year the expense is incurred, whether or not it has been paid. For example, an accrual-basis taxpayer who did work for someone in 1998, but who wasn't paid for it until 1999, would report it as income in 1998.

Accrual method of accounting: The accrual method of accounting is one of two main accounting methods available to small businesses (the other is the cash method). The accrual method says that a transaction occurs when the sale occurs, not necessarily when you receive payment. You record an expense when you receive goods or services, even though you may not pay for them until later.

Adjusted basis: Adjusted basis is the basis of acquired property that has been adjusted for items such as depreciation, interest, carrying charges, etc.

Adjusting entries: Adjusting entries are special accounting entries that must be made when you close the books at the end of an accounting period. They are necessary to update your accounts for items that are not recorded in your daily transactions.

Age Discrimination in Employment Act (ADEA): The Age Discrimination in Employment Act applies to employers with 20 or more employees and is geared toward protecting individuals over the age of 40 against employment discrimination in job advertisements, job qualifications, hiring decisions, job applications, interviews, discipline, and termination. The ADEA does say, however, that it is not unlawful for you to observe the terms of a bona fide seniority system.

Aging report: An aging report is a list of customers' accounts receivable amounts and their due dates. It alerts you to slow-paying customers and helps you manage their outstanding bills.

Allowance for bad debts: Also called a reserve for bad debts, this is an estimate of uncollectable customer accounts. It is known as a "contra" account, because it is listed with the assets, but it will have a credit balance instead of a debit balance. For balance sheet purposes, it reduces accounts receivable.

Alternative minimum tax (AMT): The AMT is an alternative tax system that is intended to ensure that no taxpayer who has substantial income avoids tax liability by using exclusions, deductions, and credits. It is a separate and distinct, but parallel, system of taxation. Alternative minimum tax is based on taxable income recomputed to take into account adjustments and preferences.

Americans with Disabilities Act (ADA): The federal Americans with Disabilities Act applies only to employers with 15 or more employees. The ADA covers those who: have a physical or mental impairment that substantially limits one or more life activities, have a history of such impairment, or are regarded as having such an impairment. As an employer, you must make reasonable accommodations for all individuals covered by the law. The ADA also affects such areas of employment as pre-employment medical exams, pre-employment inquiries about physical ability, job descriptions, job qualifications, absenteeism, and worker safety.

Asset: Asset is the term used to describe everything of value held by your business. For accounting purposes, assets can be current (e.g., cash, accounts receivable, inventory and merchandise, prepaid rent, prepaid insurance) or fixed (things that aren't held for resale such as furniture and equipment). Assets are balance sheet accounts.

Bad debts: A bad debt is the account of a customer who purchased goods and services on credit but who did not pay the amount due.

Balance sheet: The balance sheet is a picture of your business at a given point in time, generally at the close of your business year. It lists the assets, liabilities, and the difference between the two, which is the net worth (also called owner's equity) of your business.

Basis: See the definition of "tax basis," below.

Bona fide meals: A bona fide meal is generally one that lasts at least 30 minutes.

Bona fide occupational qualifications: BFOQs are limited exceptions to federal Title VII antidiscrimination laws allowing a company to hire employees based on their religion, gender, or national origin where those factors are "reasonably necessary to the normal operation of that particular business or enterprise." The law does not permit religion-based, gender-based, or national origin-based differences in pay to those holding the same job.

Buy-out: A buy-out is a contractual arrangement in which at least one owner promises to sell his or her ownership interests to another owner upon the occurrence of a specified event, e.g., a set time period, death of one owner, etc. A buy-out arrangement can be mandatory or optional.

C corporation: A C corporation is the classic type of corporation, also known as a regular corporation. The business is an entity or "person" in its own right and has the right to buy property, hire employees, and sign contracts. The business is owned by its stockholders, but stockholders are not personally liable for the business's debts, torts, or other liabilities. Corporate profits are taxed at the entity level, by corporate income tax, and then taxed again at the individual level when paid out as dividends to shareholders.

Capital: Capital is money invested in the business by the owners; also called equity.

Capital expenditure: A capital expenditure is one that is made to acquire or improve assets with a useful life of more than one year.

Capital gain: A capital gain is a gain that results from the sale of a capital asset.

Capitalized cost: A capitalized cost is a business expense that is written off or deducted over a period of time, through depreciation or amortization.

Carrying cost: A carrying cost is the cost associated with a business's investment in assets. Depending on the asset, a carrying cost may include interest, taxes, insurance, and lost-opportunity costs for the same funds if invested elsewhere.

Cash: As a balance sheet item, cash includes funds deposited in checking accounts and cash equivalents such as U.S. treasury bills/notes, certificates of deposit, commercial paper, bankers' acceptances, and money market accounts.

Cash-basis taxpayer: A cash-basis taxpayer is one who reports income in the year in which it is actually or constructively received and who claims deductions in the year in which the expense is actually paid. For example, a cash-basis taxpayer who did work for someone in 1998, but who wasn't paid for it until 1999, would report it as income in 1998. Most individuals are cash-basis taxpayers.

Cash flow: Cash flow is a measure of inflow and outflow of cash from the business. Positive cash flow refers to more money coming into the business than is going out; negative cash flow refers to the converse situation.

Cash method of accounting: The cash method is one of two major accounting methods for determining when a transaction takes place. For a taxpayer using the cash method of accounting, income is recorded only when it is received, and expenses are recorded only in the year they are paid.

Cash value life insurance: Cash value life insurance provides a death benefit (term protection) and a savings feature. This insurance is more expensive than term (particularly at younger ages) but typically provides insurance throughout lifetime at a level premium. Among the types of cash value insurance policies are whole life, limited pay life, endowment, flexible life, universal life, variable life, universal variable life, and vanishing premium policies, just to mention a few.

Centralization of management: An organization has centralized management if any person (or any group of persons which does not include all of the members of the organization) has continuing exclusive authority to make the management decisions necessary to the conduct of the business for which the organization was formed.

Chargebacks: A chargeback is the process by which a credit card company credits a customer's account because of some error by the merchant (for example, the proper signature was not obtained) or complaint by the customer (for example, the goods were damaged).

Charged tips: A charged tip is a tip included on a charge receipt. A charge receipt includes credit card charges and charges under any other credit arrangement.

Class of stock: Ownership rights in a corporation, represented by stock, can vary and each grouping of different kinds of stock is referred to as a class of stock. For instance, one class of stock could be nonvoting with a preferential dividend right.

Close corporation: A close or privately owned corporation is one which has shares of stock that are not listed or traded on a public stock exchange, and for which there are no published price quotations. Most states have separate statutory provisions that allow close corporations to be created and maintained with less formality and expense that an ordinary C corporation. Close corporation statutes typically also limit the permissible number and type of shareholders, e.g., no more than 35 shareholders.

Closing the books: Closing refers to procedures that take place at the end of an accounting period. Adjusting entries are made, and then the income and expense accounts are "closed." The net profit that results from the closing of the income and expense accounts is transferred to an equity account such as retained earnings.

COD: COD, or cash on delivery, is a credit term which means that the net amount of the invoice is due upon delivery of the goods or services.

Collateral: Collateral is property subject to a security agreement. For example, your house is collateral for your mortgage loan. If you were to default on the loan, the mortgage holder could claim your house in repayment of the debt.

Continuity of life: An organization has continuity of life if the death, insanity, bankruptcy, retirement, resignation, or expulsion of any member will not cause a dissolution of the organization.

Co-ops: A co-op arrangement is one in which a business buys a product with, from, or through another vendor.

Corporation: A corporation is a separate entity under the law. It can sue and be sued, does not dissolve upon the death of the owners (shareholders), and is taxed as a separate taxpayer. As long as the corporation follows all state law rules, its stockholders have limited liability. This means that the most that they can generally lose is their investment in the stock. Limited liability is one of the four corporate characteristics, the others being continuity of life, centralized management, and free transferability of interests.

Cost of capital: Cost of capital is an interest rate that represents the after-tax opportunity cost of funds to a business. The rate is used in the cash flow analysis to reduce future costs to the present value amounts (that is, to determine how to invest today at that interest rate to have the necessary funds available when the future costs come due). Two possible measures of cost of capital are the interest rate for purchase financing and the rate of return on invested funds (with either rate being adjusted for taxes).

Cost of goods sold: Cost of goods sold is the total cost of all the goods sold to customers over a certain period of time. The cost of goods sold is subtracted from sales to determine the gross profit on an income statement.

Coverage of fixed charges ratio: The coverage of fixed charges ratio is a measure of cash flow from operations to total debt burden. The debt burden includes contract and lease payments that, by law, must be paid.

Credit: A credit is one of the amounts in a double-entry accounting system entry. At least one component of every accounting transaction (journal entry) is a credit amount. Credits increase liabilities and equity and decrease assets. As a result, credits are entered on the right-hand side (the liability and equity side of the accounting equation) of a two-column journal or ledger.

Credit memo: A credit memo is used to reduce a customer's account balance. A credit memo would be required, for example, when a customer who bought merchandise on account returned some merchandise or overpaid on an account.

Credit policy: A credit policy is the blueprint used by a business in making its decision to extend credit to a customer. The primary goal of a credit policy is to avoid extending credit to customers who are unable to pay their accounts.

Current asset: Generally, a current asset is cash or an item that will be converted into cash within a year. Some typical current assets are cash; inventories of raw materials; prepaid expenses such as rent, insurance, and interest; and receivables. The relationship between current assets and current liabilities tends to show the business's ability to pay off its debt during the normal course of operations.

Current liability: A current liability is a liability payable within one year. The relationship between current assets and current liabilities tends to show the business's ability to pay off its debt during the normal course of operations.

Current ratio: The current ratio measures whether a business has enough current assets to meet its current debts — with a margin of safety for possible losses such as inventory shrinkage or uncollectable accounts. The current ratio is computed from the balance sheet by dividing current assets by current liabilities. A generally popular rule of thumb for a "good" current ratio is 2 to 1, but whether a specific ratio is satisfactory depends on the nature of the business and the characteristics of its current assets and liabilities.

Debenture: A debenture is an unsecured long-term bond backed by the general credit of the issuer, but having no special lien on the issuer's property.

Debit: A debit is one of the amounts in an accounting entry. At least one component of every accounting transaction (journal entry) is a debit amount. Debits increase assets and decrease liabilities and equity. As a result, debits are entered on the left-hand side (the asset side of the accounting equation) of a two-column journal or ledger.

Debit memos: A debit memo is used to bill a customer again. A debit memo would be required, for example, when a customer has made a payment on his or her account by check, but the check bounced.

Debt-to-equity ratio: The debt-to-equity ratio is a measure of total debt to total assets (or total capital). The ratio indicates the percentage of the business's assets that have been financed by creditors and the percentage financed by owners. The ratio is used by lenders to assess a business's ability to carry additional debt. A very general rule of thumb is that a sound debt ratio should be at least 1:2.

Depreciation: Depreciation is an annual write-off of the cost of fixed assets, such as vehicles and equipment. For accounting purposes, depreciation is listed among the expenses on the income statement. For tax purposes, depreciation is a reasonable deduction for the exhaustion, wear and tear, and obsolescence of property used in a trade or business or held for the production of income. The tax laws provide specific rules to follow when calculating annual depreciation deductions for vehicles and other business assets.

Direct seller: A direct seller sells or solicits the sale of consumer products at a place of business, such as a home, that is not a permanent retail establishment. The sales can be to the ultimate consumer or to a buyer who purchases the products for resale.

Directly tipped employee: A directly tipped employee is any tipped employee who receives tips directly from customers, including employees who turn all tips over to a tip pool. Employees who receive both direct and indirect tips, such as a maitre d', are treated as directly tipped employees.

Discount: A discount is an incentive offered to a customer to pay the account in full before the due date. For example, if the customer has 60 days to pay the account, some merchants might offer a 2 percent discount for payment within 10 days. Such a discount would appear as "2/10, n/60" on the invoice.

Donee/donor of property: The donee is the one who receives the property; the donor is the one who transfers it.

Double-entry accounting: In double-entry accounting, every transaction has two journal entries: a debit and a credit. Debits must always equal credits. Double-entry accounting is the basis of a true accounting system.

Drawing account: A drawing account is a general ledger account used by some sole proprietorships and partnerships to keep track of the amounts drawn out of the business by an owner.

EBIT: Earnings before interest and taxes.

EBITD: Earnings before interest, taxes, and depreciation.

EEOC: The Equal Employment Opportunity Commission is the agency that enforces federal antidiscrimination laws.

Earnings: Earnings generally are equal to net income after all expenses, owner's compensation, depreciation, taxes, and interest but before any capital expenditures or principal payments on debt.

Electronic funds transfer system (EFTS): The electronic funds transfer system processes the electronic transfer of funds from one bank account to another.

Employee: A worker is an employee under the common-law rules if the person for whom he or she works has the right to direct and control the way the work is done, both as to the final results and as to the details of when, where, and how the work is to be done. The employer need not actually exercise the control; it is sufficient that he or she has the right to do so. Where the employer does not possess that right, the individual involved is an independent contractor, not an employee.

Enterprise: An enterprise is the related activities performed by any person or persons for a common business purpose and includes all such activities whether performed in one or more establishments or by one or more corporate or other organizational units including departments of an establishment operated through leasing arrangements. An enterprise does not include the related activities performed for such an enterprise by an independent contractor.

Environmental transaction screen: An environmental transaction screen is a systematic way of gathering basic information about a commercial real estate site to determine whether further inquiry is needed. The American Society for Testing and Materials has developed formal guidelines for transaction screens. If the screen shows a need for further inquiry, the next step would be to have a Phase I audit conducted by an environmental professional.

Equity: Equity is the interest or investment that the owners have in the business. The amount of owner's equity is equal to the value of the business's assets, minus the value of its liabilities. Equity is also referred to as net worth. Equity accounts are balance sheet accounts.

Estate tax: An estate tax (whether levied by the federal government, or by a state) is a death tax imposed on the right to transfer wealth at death. The federal estate tax generally applies to the amount of the estate that exceeds $625,000.

Expense: Expenses are what is paid as the cost of doing business, or where the money goes. Examples are advertising, payroll taxes, and wages.

Expense account: Expense accounts are general ledger accounts used to keep track of the costs of doing business.

Expensed costs: Expensed costs are business expenses that are written off or deducted in the year they are paid.

Fair market value: An item's fair market value is the amount for which that item could be sold to a willing purchaser. Generally, the best measure of fair market value is a professional appraisal.

Financial projection: A financial projection is a *prospective* financial statement based upon assumptions that have been made regarding how a business is going to perform. The numbers in projected financial statements are estimates that illustrate how finances may look if the assumptions are correct.

Financing lease: Accountants use the term "financing" (or "capital") lease to refer to leases whose objective is to provide financing to the lessee for the eventual purchase of the leased property or to permit the lessee to use the property for most of its useful life. The significance of this characterization is that the property subject to a financing lease must be reported as an asset, and the corresponding rent obligation reported as a liability, on the lessee's balance sheet.

Fixed assets: A fixed asset is an asset that will not be converted to cash within a year, such as land, plant, equipment, vehicles, and intangible property (e.g., copyrights, patents, trademarks). Inventory held for resale, therefore, is not a fixed asset.

Fixed charge: A fixed cost or charge includes such items as rent or depreciation on plant and equipment items, property taxes, and salaries of executive or management personnel (who cannot be laid off because they are needed even during slack periods). A fixed cost does not respond to changes in a business's activity. It is a bill incurred regardless of revenue and is at a fixed rate.

Fixed rate: A fixed-rate loan bears an interest rate that remains the same ("fixed") over the life of the loan.

Flexible spending account (FSA): A flexible spending account is a benefit plan that allows employees to pay for certain medical and dependent care expenses on a pre-tax basis. This type of benefit plan is particularly popular in two areas — medical care accounts and child care accounts — because employees can actually save money by setting aside a portion of their wages for necessary expenses, such as day care for their children, before taxes are taken out.

Floating interest rate: A floating interest rate is a rate that can change over the life of the loan. Generally, it tracks a publicly available index such as the federal cost-of-funds rate or rates on a specified type of U.S. Treasury security. Floating rate loans may come with a "cap" or maximum rate above which they may not float, and/or a "floor" or minimum rate below which they may not sink.

Footing: To foot is to total the amounts in a column, such as a column in a journal or a ledger.

Free transferability of interests: An organization is considered to have the characteristic of free transferability of interests if each of its members, or those members owning substantially all of the interests in the organization, have the power to substitute for themselves in the organization a person who is not otherwise a member, without the consent of the other members.

General ledger: A general ledger is the collection of all balance sheet, income, and expense accounts used to keep the accounting records of a business.

Gross income: Gross income is income from all sources, except for certain items (such as tax-exempt interest) specifically excluded by statutory law. Gross income is reduced by allowable deductions to determine taxable income.

Head tax: A head tax is a tax that is computed with reference to number of people (count the heads!). Within a business setting, head taxes usually take the form of taxes assessed against a business based on its number of employees. For example, a city may assess a tax of $2.00 per employee for each month he or she is employed by the business.

Home equity loan: A home equity loan is a commercial loan or a line of credit secured by a mortgage on a residence. Usually, the funds may be requested for any purpose. Interest on these loans (for loans up to $100,000) is tax deductible regardless of the use of the funds.

Homeworker: A homeworker is an individual who performs work for you, generally on a contract or piecework basis and usually in his or her own home or in the homes of others. For example, a person you hire to type your correspondence and to do other word processing jobs on a home computer would be a homeworker.

Income account: An income account is a general ledger account used to keep track of sources of income. Examples are merchandise sales, consulting revenue, and interest income.

Income statement: Also called a profit and loss statement or a "P&L." It lists your income, expenses, and net profit (or loss). The net profit (or loss) is equal to your income minus your expenses.

Independent contractor: Generally, an independent contractor is a worker not subject to the direction or control of someone he or she is performing services for. Independent contractors are treated as owners of their own businesses.

Interest expense: When you borrow money or buy something on credit, you will be charged "interest." This is a premium you must pay for the use of another's capital. Interest is generally expressed as a certain percentage of the principal, per year.

Inventory: Inventory is goods held for sale to customers. Inventory can be merchandise bought for resale, or it can be merchandise manufactured or processed by a business, in which the end product is sold to the customer.

Inventory turnover: Inventory turnover is a ratio used in manufacturing or retail business to show how quickly merchandise is moving. The ratio expresses the time frame between the acquisition of inventory and its sale. Inventory turnover is found by dividing cost of goods sold by average inventory.

Itemized deduction: An itemized deduction is a deduction that is subtracted from adjusted gross income and that reduces taxable income only if it exceeds an individual's applicable standard deduction and, in the case of miscellaneous itemized deductions, exceeds 2 percent of adjusted gross income. Common itemized deductions are medical expenses, state and local taxes, and charitable contributions. The amount of otherwise allowable itemized deductions is limited if an individual's adjusted gross income exceeds a threshold amount. Itemized deductions are also known as "below-the-line deductions." The line referred to in this phrase is the line showing adjusted gross income on IRS Form 1040.

Joint tenancy: If a property is held in joint tenancy, at the death of a joint tenant, the surviving joint tenant(s) acquire the ownership rights of the deceased joint tenant. State law rules often provide for specific words or phrases that must be used in a property title to create a joint tenancy, such as : ". . . to be held as joint tenants with right of survivorship." Many states provide for a special form of joint tenancy that is available only for property held jointly by spouses, called tenancy by the entirety.

Journal: A journal is a book or page where accounting entries are made. The chronological, day-to-day transactions of a business are recorded in sales, cash receipts, and cash disbursements journals. A general journal is used to enter end-of-period adjusting and closing entries and other special transactions not entered in the other journals. In a traditional, manual accounting system, each of these journals is a collection of multi-column spreadsheets usually contained in a hardcover binder.

Leverage: Leverage is the advantage gained from using borrowed money to acquire income or cash-producing property. A highly leveraged company has a high debt-to-equity ratio, meaning it has a relatively large amount of debt (borrowed funds) in relation to its equity (invested funds).

Liabilities: Liabilities are what a company owes. For accounting purposes, current liabilities are those that are due within a year, such as accounts payable, taxes, and wages. Fixed liabilities (or long-term liabilities) are those that are due in more than one year, such as notes payable that have a five-year maturity. Liabilities are balance sheet accounts.

Lien: A lien is an intangible property interest that secures a debt on personal or real property. If the debtor defaults, the property can be seized or sold.

Limited liability: An organization has the characteristic of limited liability if under local law there is no member who is personally liable for the organization's debts.

Limited liability company: A limited liability company (sometimes known as an "LLC") is a combination of the characteristics of a corporation and a partnership. Although it is treated as a partnership for purposes of the Internal Revenue Code, its owners (members) have limited liability. This means that the most that they can generally lose is their investment in the company.

Limited liability partnership: A limited liability partnership (LLP) has the limited liability of a corporation, but otherwise functions as a partnership. In states that permit LLPs, they are generally reserved for professional service businesses such as accountants, doctors, and lawyers.

Line of credit: Lines of credit are funds that a lender promises to make available on demand, up to a set maximum amount, for a borrower. The borrower can draw as much of the maximum amount as he or she needs at any given time. Typically, the lines must be "paid down" or brought to a zero balance at least once during a given time period, e.g., six months. Lines of credit can be revolving, straight, or fixed. A revolving line of credit allows for continual fluctuation in the amount being used at a given time; interest is assessed only on the amounts actually borrowed. A straight line is basically the same as a short-term loan with a single balloon payment due at the end of the term. A fixed line is typically a very short-term loan of a set amount of money, and the line is "paid down" out of specific cash proceeds.

Liquidity: Liquidity refers to how quickly you can turn other assets into cash, at a price that matches the value of the asset.

Long-term loan: In the context of business loans, a long-term loan is a loan that will be paid back over a period longer than a year. Long-term loans are normally secured, first, by the new asset(s) purchased, then by other unencumbered physical assets of the business or, failing that, from additional funds from shareholders or personal guarantees from the principals.

Luxury car: The term "luxury car" applies to any four-wheeled vehicle that is manufactured primarily for use on public streets, roads, and highways and that has an unloaded gross weight of 6,000 pounds or less, and has a price over $36,000 (in 1997 — this amount is subject to change each year). A light van or truck may, therefore, be considered a luxury car. The term does not include ambulances, hearses, or other vehicles, such as taxis, that are used primarily in the trade or business of transporting persons or property for compensation or hire.

Miscellaneous itemized deduction: A miscellaneous itemized deduction is deductible only to the extent that its total amount exceeds 2 percent of adjusted gross income (also known as the 2 percent floor). Common miscellaneous itemized deductions include unreimbursed business expenses of employees and expenses for obtaining tax advice.

Mortgage: A mortgage is a lien on land or some other property as security for the repayment of a loan.

Net 10 days: "Net 10 days" is a credit term which means that the net amount of the invoice is due 10 days after the invoice date. It is represented on invoices or sales tickets as n/10.

Net 30 days: "Net 30 days" is a credit term which means that the net amount of the invoice is due 30 days after the invoice date. It is represented on invoices or sales tickets as n/30.

Net income: Net income is equal to the income, minus the expenses, of a business. It's also called profit or net profit. Net income is the bottom line of the income statement (also called the profit and loss statement).

Net worth: Net worth is how much a company is worth and is computed by subtracting liabilities from assets.

Non-swiped transactions: A non-swiped transaction is one in which the sale is handled over the phone or through the mail. Because the buyer and seller are in different locations, the credit card cannot be "swiped" through the terminal.

Nonvoting shares: The holder of a nonvoting share of stock does not have the right to vote in corporate matters pertaining to election/removal of directors and fundamental changes in the corporation.

Open account: An open account, or open-end credit, is consumer credit extended by a creditor under a plan in which: the creditor reasonably contemplates repeated transactions; the creditor may impose a finance charge from time to time on an outstanding unpaid balance; and the amount of credit that may be extended to the customer during the term of the plan (up to any limit set by the creditor) is generally made available to the extent that any outstanding balance is repaid.

Operating cycle: The operating cycle can be defined as the system through which cash flows, from the purchase of inventory through the collection of accounts receivable.

Operating income: Operating income is the sales income remaining after cost of goods sold, selling expenses, and general and administrative expenses have been subtracted, but before interest expenses, taxes, and investment income or expenses were considered.

Owner's equity: Also called equity or capital, owner's equity is the net worth of a company. Equity comes from investment in the business by the owners, plus accumulated net profits of the business that have not been paid out to the owners. It essentially represents amounts owed to the owner(s). Equity accounts are balance sheet accounts.

Partnership: A partnership is an unincorporated business entered into for profit with two or more owners.

Personal service corporation: A personal service corporation is a service-oriented business that is operated in a corporate form. These corporations generally perform services in the fields of health, law, engineering, architecture, accounting, actuarial science, the performing arts, or consulting. Substantially all of the stock of a personal service corporation must be held by professional employees, retired employees, or their estates.

Phase I environmental audit: A Phase I environmental audit is generally one that meets criteria specified by the American Society for Testing and Materials. The audit must be performed by an environmental consultant, who will review a wide variety of available information about the site and the operations that have been conducted on it, and also perform a non-intrusive physical inspection of the site and the current operations. State law may define who is qualified to perform a Phase I audit, and may also define what needs to be done in the audit itself. If the results of the audit are unsatisfactory, the next step should be to conduct a Phase II audit.

Phase II environmental audit: Phase II environmental audits of real estate are performed if a Phase I audit shows the presence or likely presence of a hazardous substance or pesticide. No specific standards have been established for Phase II audits — the nature and extent of the audit will be determined by the specific facts related to the site.

Policy rider: A policy rider is an additional provision that the insured and the insurance company agree to add to a policy. Although the insurance company may allow some riders at no additional cost, it will charge additional premiums for a rider that will in any way expand policy coverage (such as adding a flood damage rider to a homeowner's policy).

Posting: To post is to summarize all journal entries and transfer them to the general ledger accounts. This is done at the end of an accounting period.

Preferred shares of stock: These shares of stock are a separate class from ordinary, common stock of the company. They are "preferred" in the sense that they have a priority right over ordinary shares as to any dividends declared by the company and/or a priority in liquidation proceeds if the corporation is dissolved.

Prepaid expense: A prepaid expense is an amount paid in advance to a vendor or creditor for goods or services. A prepaid expense is actually an asset of a business because the vendor or supplier owes the business goods or services that have already been paid for. An example would be the unexpired portion of an annual insurance premium.

Prepaid income: Also called unearned revenue, it represents money you have received in advance of providing a service to your customer. Prepaid income is actually a liability of your business because you still owe the service to the customer. An example would be an advance payment to you for some consulting services you will be performing in the future.

Prime rate: The prime rate is the interest rate that banks charge their best business customers for loans or lines of credit.

Private land use restriction: A private land use restriction is a restriction that a land owner places on the use of property by its owner. If all legal requirements have been met (for example, the restriction has been properly recorded and does not violate public policy), the restriction will bind the property owner, plus all later buyers of the property. Common examples of land use restrictions are covenants by deed not to use the property for business purposes and condominium restrictions forbidding certain property uses. Unlike the process of obtaining a variance from a zoning rule, a court proceeding may be required to lift a private land use restriction.

Profit and loss statement: Also called an income statement or "P&L." It lists your income, expenses, and net profit (or loss). The net profit (or loss) is equal to your income minus your expenses.

Pro forma P & L statement: A pro forma P & L statement is an estimated profit and loss statement for a future year.

Promissory note: A promissory note is a written agreement in which the maker promises to pay a creditor, or to the order of a creditor, the amount of a debt, usually with interest. Contract formalities should be followed to ensure the enforceability of the note. A promissory note may be a negotiable instrument if the requirements for such an instrument are present on the face of the note.

Proposal: A proposal or quotation is a document that describes exactly which services will be performed for a particular customer and at what cost to the customer.

Proprietorship: An unincorporated business with only one owner.

Protected groups: Protected groups, in terms of employment laws, are groups of people who are distinguished by special characteristics such as race, color, ethnicity, national origin, religion, gender, age (over 40), disability, or veteran status. These particular groups are protected under federal antidiscrimination law, which mandates that people in one of these protected groups cannot be discriminated against in any facet of employment, including hiring, promotion, training, discipline, pay, and termination. State laws may protect other groups, such as individuals in different age groups, people who are smokers, and individuals with a particular sexual orientation.

Public accommodation: A public accommodation, under the Americans with Disabilities Act, is virtually any business that sells, gives, or offers something to the public, and is required to make all reasonable accommodations for accessibility by disabled persons.

Public relations: Public relations includes any material, event, or media coverage with indirect or direct product information or endorsement. Examples include a restaurant review, press coverage of a new store opening, and press releases distributed to local media.

Publicly held companies: A publicly held company is a business organization, usually a corporation, in which ownership is held by the public at large and transfers of ownership are largely unrestricted. There is no minimum number or shareholders required to be considered a publicly held company, but these entities are often traded on the security exchanges, or at least have published price quotations. Corporations with more than $5 million of assets and at least one outstanding class of securities that is held by more than 500 shareholders of record are subject to special regulation under the Federal Securities Exchange Act of 1934. Among these rules is the requirement that the corporation register that class of shares with the SEC and make public disclosure of periodic financial information.

Qualitative research: Qualitative research is market research defined by small numbers of respondents. And this small number may show research results with significant statistical variation. Typical qualitative research involves one-on-one interviews or focus groups with 5-10 people who are buyers or potential buyers of a product.

Quantitative research: Quantitative research is distinguished from qualitative research primarily by larger numbers of sampled respondents and the type of questions asked. Generally, sample sizes of 100 are adequate for simple "yes/no" questions, with 95 percent reliability of being accurate for the entire market of buyers. To increase accuracy to 97 percent to 99 percent, sample sizes would have to increase to 400 or more, depending upon the subject matter.

Quick current assets: The value of a business's quick current assets is the sum of its cash, net receivables, and marketable securities.

Rate of return on investment: The rate of return on investment (profit divided by investments) is probably the most common measure of profitability for the small business owner. It is necessary to clearly specify which items from the financial statements are being used in determining "profit" and "investment." For example, "profit" might be considered to mean net operating profit, net profit before taxes, or net profit after taxes. "Investment" could mean total assets employed or equity alone.

Redeemable shares: These shares of stock in a corporation are sold with the understanding that they can be redeemed, or repurchased, by the corporation upon certain conditions or if the corporation simply wants to repurchase them.

Refinancing: Refinancing is obtaining a new loan to pay off an existing loan. Refinancing is often done to obtain a more favorable interest rate, to extend the duration of the loan, or to obtain additional funds.

Regular corporation: A regular corporation (which is also called a "C" corporation after the part of the Internal Revenue Code that imposes tax on it) is a taxable entity. Therefore, the corporation (rather than its shareholders) accounts for its income and expenses. C corporations are contrasted with S corporations, which are pass-through entities (their income and expenses are not recognized at the corporate level but are passed through to their shareholders, who must account for them on their individual tax returns).

Regularly used vehicles: A vehicle is considered "regularly used" in an employer's business if either at least 50 percent of its total mileage for the year is for the employer's business or it is generally used each workday in an employer-sponsored car pool to transport at least three employees to and from work.

Reserve for bad debts: Also called allowance for bad debts, the reserve for bad debts is an estimate of uncollectable customer accounts. It is known as a "contra" account because it is listed with the assets but will have a credit balance instead of a debit balance. For balance sheet purposes, it is a reduction of accounts receivable.

Retail business: A retail business is a business that sells a product to the ultimate consumer (sometimes called "the end user") of the product. Some common retail businesses include grocery stores, new and used car dealers, jewelry stores, and mail order companies that sell directly to consumers.

Retained earnings: The term "retained earnings" means the profits of the business that have not been paid to the owner or profits that have been "retained" in the business. Retained earnings are classified as an "equity" account that is presented on the balance sheet.

Revolving line of credit: A revolving line of credit is a line of credit that may be used repeatedly, up to a certain limit. It is also sometimes called "open-end credit."

S corporation: An S corporation is a corporation that has complied with certain federal tax laws and has elected to be taxed as a partnership, rather than as a corporation. S corporation status is preferred by some small businesses because the individual operators can apply business losses to their personal income, and the double taxation problem faced by C corporations is avoided. In addition, the corporate form provides for limited personal liability for the business's contracts and torts. Restrictions on the number and type of shareholders and shares in an S corporation limit the entity's universal appeal: no more than 75 shareholders; shareholders can be only individuals, estates, or certain trusts; no foreign or corporate shareholders; only one class of stock (although voting rights can differ).

Sales promotion: A sales promotion consists of any material or event that involves direct product purchase incentives. Examples include "buy one, get one free" promotions, coupons, etc.

Salvage value: Estimated salvage value is the estimated resale or trade-in value of a vehicle at the end of its useful life in a business.

Secondary market: A secondary market is a market where certain investments are bought and sold after their original issue (which took place in a primary market). The proceeds from a sale in a secondary market go to the investor, not to the company or entity that originally issued and sold the investment.

Service business: A service business provides services — rather than products — to its customers. Common service businesses include barbers and hairdressers, doctors, lawyers, accountants, lawn care and snow removal companies, and bus companies.

Short-term debt: A short-term debt is a loan for which the scheduled repayment and the anticipated use for the money is expected to be a year or less. Working capital lines of credit and short maturity commercial loans are considered short-term debt financing.

Sole proprietorship: A sole proprietorship is an unincorporated business with only one owner.

Statutory employee: The term "statutory employee" includes full-time life insurance salespersons, certain traveling salespersons, agent or commission drivers, and certain homeworkers.

Stock: Stock represents ownership rights in a corporation. A stockholder has certain rights that can vary according to the type of stock owned, although typical rights include the right to vote, inspect records, and institute direct or derivative lawsuits against the corporation.

Swiped transactions: A swiped transaction is one in which the sale is handled through an electronic credit card terminal. The terminal is the machine through which the credit card is "swiped" to record the card's information.

Tangible personal property: Tangible personal property is property, other than real estate, that can be seen or touched, such as a typewriter, chair, or desk. This is to be contrasted with *intangible personal property*, such as stocks, bonds, copyrights, and trademarks.

Tax basis: The tax basis of property is the starting point for computing gain or loss on a sale or exchange of that property, or for depreciation. To compute the basis of property that was purchased, start with its cost and adjust for depreciation already claimed (in the case of business property), improvements (in the case of real estate), withdrawals or reinvestment (in the case of securities, funds, accounts, insurance, or annuities), certain tax credits claimed on the property, casualty losses, etc. Special rules govern the basis of property transferred between corporations and their shareholders, partners and their partnership, etc.

Tax home: Generally, the principal place of business of a taxpayer establishes a tax home. The tax home encompasses the entire general area or vicinity of a principal place of business. If business is conducted in more than one place, the total time ordinarily spent working in each place, the degree of business activity in each place, and the relative amount of income from each place should be considered to determine the principal place of business. When temporarily (a year or less) as opposed to indefinitely working away from the main place of business, the tax home doesn't change.

Term life insurance: Term insurance provides a death benefit only — the insured dies, the insurer pays; the insured doesn't die, the insurer doesn't pay. The value of this type of policy is that it is cheap. The insured's premium dollar can buy much more insurance with term, rather than whole life, insurance. The downside is that it becomes more expensive as the insured ages.

Term loan: "Term" refers to the time for which money is required and the period over which the loan repayment is scheduled. Term loans differ from lines of credit in that term loans provide a single payout of a specified amount at the beginning of the term, whereas lines of credit allow the borrower to withdraw loan proceeds as needed, up to a specified amount. Term loans often carry lower interest rates than lines of credit because the term is fixed and the return to the lender is more predictable.

Time value of money: The time value of money is basically the concept that a dollar received today is worth more than a dollar received at some point in the future because the dollar received today can be invested to earn interest. Time value of money problems generally involve the relationship between a certain amount of money, a certain period of time, and a certain rate of compound interest.

Title VII: Title VII of the Civil Rights Act of 1964, also known as Equal Employment Opportunity (EEO) mandates, prohibits employers with 15 or more employees from discriminating against applicants and employees in all aspects of employment — including recruiting, hiring, pay, promotion, training, and termination — on the basis of race, color, national origin, religion, or gender. There are exceptions to Title VII that allow an employer to require that an applicant be a certain race, color, religion, or gender. These exceptions are known as bona fide occupational qualifications (BFOQs). BFOQs are rarely used because they are exceedingly difficult to justify. Areas most affected by Title VII include job advertisements, job qualifications, hiring decisions, job applications, interviews, discipline, and termination.

Trial balance: A trial balance is prepared at the end of an accounting period by adding up all the account balances in your general ledger. The debit balances should equal the credit balances.

Unearned revenue: Unearned revenue is money received in advance of providing a service to a customer. It's also called prepaid income. Unearned revenue is actually a liability because the business still owes the service to the customer. An example would be an advance payment for consulting services to be performed in the future.

Variance: A variance legally excuses a property holder from complying with the strict letter of a zoning rule that, if applied, would cause undue hardship to the property holder. This is to be contrasted with a legal action to overturn the zoning rule itself. Because the variance is granted by a local zoning body and does not involve a court fight to void the zoning rule itself, the process of obtaining it is often relatively quick and inexpensive.

W-2: Form W-2 is used to report payroll information to employees at the end of each year. The employer must furnish all persons employed during the year with a copy of their Form W-2 by January 31, and send copies to the Social Security Administration by February 28.

Wholesale business: A wholesale business buys products from a manufacturer or other producer and sells them to retail businesses that in turn sell the products to their customers, the ultimate consumers of the product. Wholesalers make their profit by buying large quantities at discount from producers, and repackaging them in small amounts ordered by their customers, which are generally retail businesses.

Withholding/withhold: For payroll tax purposes, withholding is the mechanism that taxing authorities use to compel employers to collect taxes owed by their employees on their wages and other compensation. Withholding essentially requires employees to pay their taxes on a "pay-as-you-go" basis. For example, the object of income tax withholding is to collect currently as wages are paid most of the income tax liability employees will report on their personal tax return from having received the wages. Although withheld taxes represent amounts owed by your employees, you effectively become personally liable for those taxes if you fail to properly withhold or deposit them.

Workday: A workday is any fixed period of 24 consecutive hours.

Working capital: Working capital is the excess of current assets (cash, accounts receivable, and inventory) over current liabilities (short- term loans and accounts payable). Working capital represents the funds available to pay for the business's current requirements (one year or less) and a margin of protection for a company's short-term creditors. Working capital is essential for a company to meet the continuous operational needs of doing business.

Workweek: A workweek is any fixed regularly recurring period of seven consecutive workdays.

Zoning: Zoning is the classification of real property by government that controls the usage of the property. For example, the restriction of real property to specific uses, such as residential use versus commercial or business use, is zoning.

Index

E

J

K

N

Profit-sharing plans · 600
Progressive discipline · 325
Promissory notes · 121
Promotions · 78, 174, 205, 207
Protected groups · 275
Prototypes · 191
Public
accommodations · 503
policy · 334
relations (P.R.) · 205, 212
service · 212
Puerto Rico · 248, 269, 286, 294, 300, 311, 543, 559
Purchase incentives · 207
Purchasing alliances · 309
Put options · 128

Q

Qualitative research · 180
Quantitative research · 181
Quarterly reviews · 86
Questionnaires
customer satisfaction · 183
exit · 342
market research · 181
Quick ratio · 149, 429

R

Rabbi trusts · 607
Rates
credit card accounts · 381
interest · *See* Interest rates
Ratios, business · 150, 427, 627
Real estate · 146, 591
agents · 220
depreciation · 463
tax treatment · 466
Recapitalizations · 660
Recast financials · *See* Financial statements
Receivables · *See* Accounts receivable

Recordkeeping
business use of property · 464
employees · 330, 336
financial · 355
mileage · 493
OSHA · 249
payroll · 567
taxes · 468
Recruiting · 255
Redemptions, stock · 658
Reference checks · 283
References
checking · 283
credit · 385
job · 279
Registration requirements, securities · 131
Regulation D · 131
Reimbursement of expenses · 500, 549
Releases
employment termination · 337
job reference · 350
Remodeling expenses · 475
Rental income · 591
Renting · *See* Leasing
Reorganizations · 642
Repairs · 475
Replacement value insurance · 240
Repositioned products · 187
Representations and warranties · 650
Resignations · 342
Restaurants · 241, 547
Resumes · 69, 279
Retailing · 36, 173, 202, 217, 365, 410, 512
Retirement age · 596
Retirement plans · 298, 548, 592
401(k) plans · 603
defined benefit · 599
defined contribution · 600
IRAs · 607
nonqualified · 598, 606
qualified · 597
SEPs · 604

T

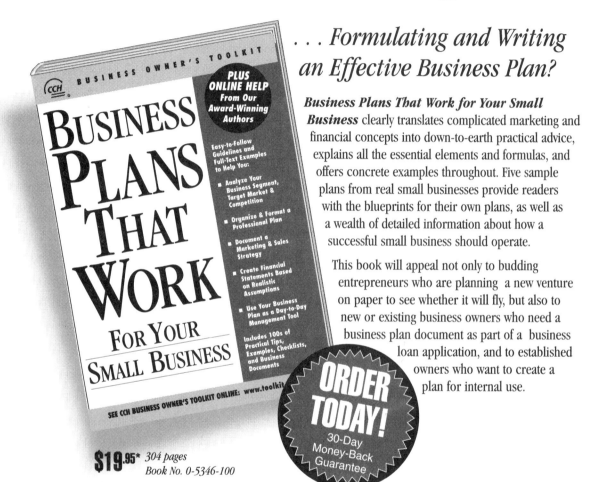

. . . *Generating Sales from New and Repeat Customers?*

Find & Keep Customers addresses the top priority for small business owners—creating loyal customers. This clear-language, no nonsense guide shows readers how to find a profitable niche; research and develop a realistic marketing plan; sell, price, communicate and compete in today's rapidly changing marketplace; and understand the advantagees and requirements of electronic commerce.

Simply put, the key to finding and keeping customers is solving customers' problems and getting them to see the benefits of your solutions. By using this book, you will learn how to target your time, money and energy toward those prospects who will offer you the highest chances for long-term success.

224 pages / Book No. 0-5180-100 **$16.⁹⁵***

. . . *Turning Your Small Business Dreams into Reality?*

Launching Your First Small Business provides readers with the information they need to successfully make the transition to self-employment, concisely detailing what factors to consider when assessing personal strengths and weaknesses, deciding on the type of business to open, considering the costs involved, choosing the form of business organization, and locating and staffing the operation.

By effectively organizing the dozens of activities that go into launching a new business, this book will help first-time entrepreneurs save time and money. More importantly, it increases the chance of success by informing new business owners of the various issues needing attention when starting a business from scratch.

$14.⁹⁵* *208 pages / Book No. 0-5345-100*

. . . *Securing the Necessary Financing for Your Business?*

Small Business Financing: How and Where To Get It thoroughly but simply discusses each source of debt and equity capital, whether public or private—from bookstrapping and IPOs to commercial loans and SBA-guaranteed programs, and everything in between. This book covers methods for determining the amount of capital needed, choosing an appropriate source and type of financing, selecting a business form, and planning successful applications or presentations.

Sample forms are integrated into the text to facilitate learning the details and the data-gathering skills needed for the financing process. A handy glossary is included to take the mystery out of dealing with bankers and other financial professionals.

224 pages / Book No. 0-5344-100 **$17.⁹⁵***

lus shipping, handling and applicable sales tax

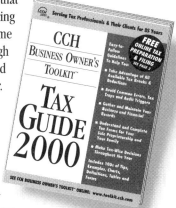